RESCUING BUSINESS

*The Making of Corporate Bankruptcy
Law in England and the United States*

D1647723

BRUCE G. CARRUTHERS & TERENCE C. HALLIDAY

CLARENDON PRESS · OXFORD
1998

Oxford University Press, Great Clarendon Street, Oxford OX2 6DP
Oxford New York
Athens Auckland Bangkok Bogota Bombay Buenos Aires
Calcutta Cape Town Dar es Salaam Delhi Florence Hong Kong
Karachi Kuala Lumpur Madras Madrid Melbourne Mexico
Nairobi Paris Singapore Taipei Tokyo Toronto Warsaw
and associated companies in
Berlin Ibadan

Oxford is a registered trade mark of Oxford University Pres

Published in the United States
by Oxford University Press Inc., New York

British Library Cataloguing in Publication Data
Data available

Library of Congress Cataloging in Publication Data
Carruthers, Bruce G
Rescuing business: the making of corporate bankruptcy law in England and
the United States / Bruce
G. Carruthers and Terence C. Halliday.
p.   cm.
Includes bibliographical references.
ISBN 0–1–826472–0
1. Bankruptcy–United States. 2. Business failures–Law and legislation–United States.
3. Bankruptcy–Great Britain. 4. Business failures–Law and legislation–Great Britain.
I. Halliday, Terence C. (Terence Charles) II. Title.
KF 1524.C345 1988
346.4107'8–dc21 97–47443

ISBN 0–19–826472–0

1 3 5 7 9 10 8 6 4 2

Typeset by Pure Tech India Ltd., Pondicherry
Printed in Great Britain
on acid-free paper by
Biddles Ltd., Guildford and King's Lynn

RESCUING BUSINESS

To Sam, Esther and Wendy
B.G.C.

To Holly
T.H.

Acknowledgements

Our study of bankruptcy reforms in England and the United States has been possible because a large number of participants, observers, scholars, and institutions committed extensive time and resources to our research.

We have obtained an extraordinary amount of cooperation from accountants, civil servants, lawyers, judges, politicians, and interest group leaders who reformed the bankruptcy law in either country. In England we thank Mary Arden, QC, G. A. Auger, Lord Benson, Gerald Bermingham, MP, Ian Bond, Lord Bruce of Donington, G. J. Carter, Nicholas Cave, I. D. Cheyne, Sir Kenneth Cork, L. T. Cramp, Michael Crystal, QC, Peter Farmery, Alfred Goldman, David Graham, QC, G. J. A. Harp, David Henry, Mark Homan, Andrew Hutchinson, Peter Karmel, Lord Lucas, Peter Lunn, Charles Maggs, Peter Millett, QC (now Lord Justice Millett), Nicholas Milner, D. L. Morgan, Steve Norris, MP, Ritchie Penny, Philip Pink, Professor Dan Prentice, David Saunders, S. J. Samwell, D. Schaffer, M. J. Sechiari, David Tench, Richard Thomas, Commander Trevor Traylor, Neville Trotter, MP, Edward Walker-Arnott, and Gerhard Weiss.

In the United States, we thank Donald Alexander, Representative Caldwell Butler, Scott Crampton, Murray Drabkin, Robert Fiedler, Samuel Gerdano, Sanford Harris, Charles Horsky, John Ingraham, Judge Joe Lee, Professor Frank Kennedy, Robert Kauffman, Professor Lawrence King, Kenneth Klee, Richard Levin, Harold Marsh, Robert Moses, Patrick Murphy, Alan Parker, David Stanley, George Treister, and Max Zimny.

Among the archives that gave us access to primary materials were the Insolvency Practitioners Association (London), the Public Record Office (Kew, London), the Washington and Lee Library for the papers of the Bankruptcy Commission, and the US Archives.

We thank Donald Harris, former Director of the Centre for Socio-legal Studies, Wolfson College, Oxford University, and other colleagues at the Centre, for ample hospitality over several years while we undertook our research in England.

The American Bar Foundation has generously funded this research. We thank William L. F. Felstiner and Bryant Garth, Directors of the

American Bar Foundation, and the ABF Board of Directors, for unflagging financial and collegial support over several years.

We have benefited a great deal from the comments of many scholars and lawyers who have read papers and chapters. We are most grateful to Benoit Bastard, Frank Dobbin, Neil Fligstein, David Graham, QC, Roy Goode, Mark Homan, Anthony Hopwood, Joe Lee, Richard Levin, Frank Kennedy, Bruce Markell, Peter Miller, Philip Pink, Alan Paterson, Walter Powell, Arthur Stinchcombe, John Sutton, and Sally Wheeler. Nevertheless, we maintain full responsibility for what benefit we have drawn from their insights and comments.

We express our appreciation to the following publishers for permission to incorporate previously published material in this book. Some sections of this book have appeared in prior publications: "Redistributing Property and Jurisdictional Rights across the Public–Private Frontier: Professions and Bankruptcy Reforms in Britain and the United States," *Droit et Société: Revue Internationale de Théorie du Droit et de Sociologie Juridique*, Vol. 23/24, August 1993, pp. 79–113 (sections of Chapter 8); "The Moral Regulation of Markets: Professions, Privatization and the English Insolvency Act 1986," *Accounting, Organizations and Society*, Vol. 21, No. 4, 1996, pp. 371–413 (sections of Chapter 9); "Making the Courts Safe for the Powerful: The Politics of Lawyers, Judges, and Bankers in the 1978 Rehabilitation of United States Bankruptcy Courts," in Terence C. Halliday and Lucien Karpik (eds.), *Lawyers and the Rise of Western Political Liberalism: Legal Professions and the Constitution of Modern Politics*, 1998, Oxford University Press (Chapter 10).

During the project we have had the good fortune to be supported by a team of talented research assistants: Jonathan Cohen, Tyler Colman, Chanung Park, and Peter Mason. We are particularly grateful to Scott Parrott, who has undertaken an enormous amount of creative research assistance for this project over several years. Among other things, Scott created all the tables and figures and is joint author of Chapter 4. His doctoral dissertation from the Department of Sociology, University of Chicago, examines the rhetorical structures of micro-political discourse in the Congressional subcommittees where U.S. bankruptcy law was negotiated. Throughout the entire project, Brenda Smith has provided superb secretarial and administrative support with good humour, patience, efficiency, and high quality.

Finally, we cannot express the measure of debt to our families, who have vicariously lived with bankruptcy law for as long as some of them can remember. Samuel Carruthers and Esther Espeland understand that bankruptcy consists of innumerable piles of paper permanently housed in their father's office (a belief not without merit), but nevertheless they, and Wendy Espeland, have provided crucial distractions and encouragement throughout. Holly Halliday, Tyler Colman, and Richard, Kimberly and Alastair Halliday have never ceased to support an enterprise that seemed mysterious at worst and distracting at best. It is to all of them that we dedicate this book.

Contents

Figures

Tables

Abbreviations

US Materials

The Bankruptcy Reform Act, Hearings on S. 235 and S. 236 before the Subcommittee on Improvements in Judicial Machinery of the Senate Judiciary Committee, 94th Cong., 1st Sess. (1975). Cited as *Bankruptcy Reform Act Hearings on S. 235 and S. 236.*

Bankruptcy Act Revision, Hearings on H.R. 31 and H.R. 32 before the Subcommittee on Civil and Constitutional Rights of the House Committee on the Judiciary, 94th Cong., 2nd Sess. (1976). Cited as *Bankruptcy Act Revision Hearings on H.R. 31 and H.R. 32.*

Bankruptcy Reform Act of 1978, Hearings on S. 2266 and H.R. 8200 before the Subcommittee on Improvements in Judicial Machinery of the Senate Committee on the Judiciary, 95th Cong., 1st Sess. (1978). Cited as *Senate Hearings on S. 2266 and H.R. 8200.*

Hearings on H.R. 8200 before the Subcommittee on Civil and Constitutional Rights of the House Committee on the Judiciary, 95th Cong., 1st Sess. (1977). Cited as *House Hearings on H.R. 8200.*

Minutes of the Commission on the Bankruptcy Laws of the United States. M. Caldwell Butler Papers. Washington and Lee University School of Law Library, Lexington, Virginia. Cited as *Minutes of the Bankruptcy Commission.*

Report of the Commission on the Bankruptcy Laws of the United States. 1973. Washington, DC: US Government Printing Office. Cited as *Report of the Bankruptcy Commission.*

United States Interviews. Cited as *US Interview year: number.*

UK Materials

Bankruptcy: A Consultative Document. 1980. Command Paper. No. 7967. London: Her Majesty's Stationery Office. Cited as the *Government Green Paper.*

Bankruptcy: Interim Report of the Insolvency Law Review Committee. HMSO. 1980. Command Paper 7968. Cited as *Interim Cork Report.*

A Revised Framework for Insolvency Law. 1984. Command Paper. No. 9175. London: Her Majesty's Stationery Office. Cited as the *Government White Paper*

House of Commons Parliamentary Debates. Insolvency Bill [Lords]. 1985. London: Her Majesty's Stationery Office. Cited as H.C., volume, date, columns.

House of Commons Parliamentary Debates. Standing Committee E. 1985. Insolvency Bill [Lords]. London: Her Majesty's Stationery Office. Cited as H.C., volume, St.Comm.E, date, columns.

House of Lords Parliamentary Debates. 1985. Insolvency Bill [Lords]. London: Her Majesty's Stationery Office. Cited as *H.L.*, volume, date, columns.

Minutes of the Insolvency Law Review Committee. 1977–1982. Chicago: American Bar Foundation. Cited as *Minutes of the Cork Committee.*

Papers, Insolvency Law Review Committee. Public Record Office. File BT 260. Kew, London. Cited as *Public Record Office.*

Insolvency Law and Practice. Report of the Insolvency Law Review Committee. 1982. Command Paper. No 8558. London: Her Majesty's Stationery Office. 8558. Cited as the *Cork Report.*

United Kingdom Interviews. Cited as *UK Interview year: number.*

Introduction

In the last twenty years corporate bankruptcy has been pushed out of the shadows of legal and corporate marginality into the spotlight of daily business news. Its financial and human repercussions are enormous. In many advanced economies, including Britain and the United States, corporate bankruptcy has variously emerged as a new strategic device for corporate managers, as a new frontier for highly expert lawyers and accountants, and as a matter of new urgency for governments and officials who want to encourage entrepreneurial risk-taking while they lower tariff barriers, but preserve jobs and protect home industries.

Bankruptcy is a defining characteristic of a market economy: it demarcates the limits of extending credit, confronting risk, entrepreneurial venture, and corporate self-determination; it engages all sectors of the economy; and it expresses fundamental conflicts at the heart of the capitalist political economy between labor and capital, owners and managers, debtors and creditors, and the state and the market.

Not only have major corporations in the United States become casualties (for example, W. T. Grant, Continental Airlines, Federated Stores, Macy's), but entire industries, such as steel, the airlines, retail clothing, high technology, communications, and savings and loans, have existed under a pall of financial failure. The number of concerns seeking shelter in Chapters 10 and 11 of the bankruptcy code rose from 1,435 in 1970 to 5,458 in 1980, then trebled to 17,465 by 1989, and reached a high of 24,029 in 1992 before falling back to 11,168 in 1995. The liabilities of failed companies skyrocketed from $1.89 trillion in 1970 to a high of $96.8 trillion in 1992 falling again in 1995 to $29.4 trillion.[1]

In Britain rates of insolvency have risen to historic highs, punctuated quite dramatically by company failures from Rolls Royce through the

---

[1] These statistics were taken from three sources: the *Statistical Abstracts of the United States* (1996) compiled by the US Department of Commerce, the *Judicial Business of the United States: Report of the Director* (1995) compiled by the Administrative Office of the US Courts, and *The Statistical History of the United States* (1976) compiled by the US Bureau of the Census.

Olympia and York failure (the developers of London's Docklands), and the collapse of the Maxwell communications empire. Company insolvencies numbered fewer than 4,000 in 1970, exceeded 14,000 by 1985 and reached over 20,000 in 1993, falling back to over 14,500 in 1995.[2] The scope and complexity of these failures are enormous. Olympia and York, for example, sank in 1991 under the weight of over $17 billion worth of debts. When the Bank of Credit and Commerce International (BCCI) also collapsed in 1991, it comprised 250 branch banks operating in 69 countries, with about $10 billion in total liabilities (Fletcher 1993). The list of creditors was staggering, and included 800,000 depositors scattered across the globe.[3]

The ripples of corporate bankruptcy reach out to the entire credit economy. As more companies seek shelter under bankruptcy law, United States corporate reorganization in or out of Chapter 11 has become a new form of business strategy. "Strategic bankruptcy" under Chapter 11 has been used to break labor contracts with a unionized workforce (by Continental Airlines), control mass tort damages (as Manville Corporation did over asbestos-related tort liabilities, and A. H. Robins in dealing with its Dalkon Shield liabilities), or frustrate corporate rivals (for example, Texaco's conflict with Pennzoil). Bankruptcy has become an arena for inter-corporate power and conflict.[4]

Corporate bankruptcy law may also affect day-to-day competition in whole industries. "Healthy" US companies allege that the profitability of major airlines has been depressed by the unfair advantage enjoyed by weak competitors who shelter in Chapter 11 bankruptcy for extended periods of time. And according to critics, company directors and managers have been given a perverse incentive by bankruptcy law to drag out the death throes of corporations that should have been liquidated promptly. By strengthening the hand of debtor-managers at the expense of creditors, the finance industry has been compelled to alter its lending practices in ways that restrict the extension of credit. Neither is the public purse exempt from the baleful effects of insolvency law. Because struggling debtor corporations frequently raid their pension funds for cash, which consequently are under-funded when companies declare bankruptcy, significant private costs have been off-loaded onto the

---

[2] The British statistics were taken from *Insolvency: General Annual Report for the Year* (1995) compiled by the Department of Trade and Industry.

[3] *The Economist*, 4 Jan. 1992.

[4] For some, these disparate applications have engendered considerable moral disquiet (see Payne and Hogg (1994); Salem and Martin (1994)).

government. Furthermore, failing firms do not pay their taxes, and so the tax authorities frequently join the list of unpaid creditors.[5]

Yet bankruptcy is not without its beneficiaries. Just as a deadly epidemic is lucrative for undertakers and morticians, the vast sums of money involved in the largest corporate bankruptcies have exerted a magnetic effect on the most sophisticated—and expensive—corporate lawyers and accountants. In the United States, the bankruptcy boom propelled bankruptcy lawyers from the periphery towards the center of the profession. In England, marginal company undertakers became transformed into respected corporate reorganizers. Bankruptcy and reorganization specialties in law and accounting, in both the United States and Britain, have become prestigious revenue-centers for law and accounting firms, so much so that in the United States there is increasing pressure to pare down the size of professional fees. During the 1980s, several of the largest accounting firms in Britain merged with small boutique insolvency firms, such as Cork Gully's assimilation by Coopers and Lybrand, just as numbers of large United States law firms absorbed smaller bankruptcy specialist firms simply in order to acquire their expertise in a quickly growing area.[6]

These developments on either side of the Atlantic were punctuated—some believe precipitated—by two massive pieces of legislation, which represented the most far-reaching bankruptcy reforms in Britain and the United States for close to a century. It seems not coincidental that many of the changes in the shape of corporate failure occurred in the wake of the 1978 Bankruptcy Code in the United States and the Insolvency Act 1986 in Britain. In the American case, for instance, passage of the 1978 code coincided with a dramatic upsurge in bankruptcy. In the ten years before the 1978 changes, annual failure rates among industrial and commercial firms averaged 36.5 per 10,000 firms. In the ten years after, the average rose to 87.1 per 10,000. Total liabilities increased at a comparable rate—from 1969 to 1978 the total annual liabilities for industrial and commercial firms averaged $2.54 billion while from 1979 to 1988 liabilities rose almost ten-fold to an average of $22.61 billion.[7]

The aftermath of the legislation has spawned more calls for remedial steps, especially in the United States, where the outcomes were the most

---

[5] On the case of the Pension Benefit Guaranty Corporation (PBGC), see Utgoff (1993).

[6] See "Boutique Firms Hold Their Own," *National Law Journal*, Mar. 7 1983.

[7] These figures are derived from United States Department of Commerce (1992: 22).

unpredictable and farthest reaching. Some United States bankers look admiringly at Britain, where major creditors have enormous power to categorically and swiftly reorganize insolvent companies with a minimum of expensive court intervention, where insolvency does not leave debtors in possession, where company directors are personally liable if they hesitate too long in protecting creditors' assets, and where "strategic bankruptcy" is effectively impossible.[8] Ironically, the British themselves looked back across the Atlantic for some inspiration, partly sharing American values of corporate reorganization, but consciously repudiating American ways of doing so. In the process, they have produced their own innovative methods of using bankruptcy law not only to reorganize companies, but to exercise some control over the everyday behavior of company directors.

A lively dispute among American legal academics contests the value and effect of Chapter 11: some denounce it as an inefficient and costly procedure (for example, Adler 1993, Bradley and Rosenzweig 1992) while others defend it as a sound measure given the imperfections of real world markets (LoPucki 1992, Warren 1993). In the wake of Continental Airlines and Wilson Foods, labor unions felt that Chapter 11 reorganizations were being unfairly used to attack workers and they clamored for revisions in the early 1980s. Hundreds of amendments have been proposed to the United States Bankruptcy Code, and indeed Congress modified the code in 1984 and again in 1994. Similarly, there is considerable question about the efficacy of the new provisions for English corporate rehabilitation: are they really preserving firms and saving jobs? Or do they work best only for large, or mid-sized corporations, and offer relatively little to small firms? Moreover, there is some considerable doubt whether provisions for regulation of directors have worked as anticipated, or that the regulatory role of insolvency practitioners has been particularly successful.

The bankruptcy reforms raise important pragmatic and theoretical issues. It has become clear from the aftermath of the reforms that bankruptcy is a much more controversial issue than most reformers expected. Many of the parliamentary debates took legislators by surprise: consequences of the legislation were unanticipated, and several of the interest groups that came late to the reforms, or not at all, came eventually to rue their political negligence.

---

[8] US Interview 91:02.

THEORETICAL ISSUES

Despite the far-reaching practical implications of such legal change, bankruptcy law opens up an almost virgin field of inquiry for socio-legal scholars and sociologists. Given the enormous impact bankruptcy reforms are alleged to have, little research has appraised what or who shaped the bankruptcy laws in either country. Empirical studies document the aftermath and apparent consequentiality of the reforms. In the United States the exemplary empirical research by sociologist and lawyers Sullivan, Warren, and Westbrook (1989) evaluates the functioning of consumer bankruptcy law under the new 1978 Bankruptcy Code. Several studies have been undertaken on the functioning of corporate bankruptcy law (see Glasberg (1989) on W. T. Grant, Chrysler, and Leasco) and its more dramatic effects on corporate strategic bankruptcy (see Delaney (1992) on Manville and asbestos, Continental Airlines and the unions, and Texaco and the Pennzoil lawsuit; and Sobel (1991) on the Dalkon Shield). In Britain, Sally Wheeler's (1991) study of retention of title provides a

fine analysis of trade creditors. However, insolvency politics and law-making have escaped scholarly attention almost entirely.

The general neglect of the origins of bankruptcy law reflects a more deep-seated socio-legal and sociological disinterest in the origins of statutory law. The same might be said for financial legislation in general. These deficits exact a substantial cost, not only in our understanding of major legal, economic, and social processes, but also in our intellectual understanding of legal change.

In this book we employ the case of bankruptcy law reforms to address three theoretical questions that lie at the intersection of law, organizations, and professions. First, comprehensive reviews of bankruptcy law, of the kind undertaken in Britain and the United States, present a rare but critical moment in which to comprehend the balance of power among organizations. Since Berle and Means (1932) posed the problem of competing interests between owners and managers, a massive body of scholarship has sought to map power relations between shareholders and managers, between corporations and their bankers, and between corporations and the state, among others. Scholars have studied these relations by focusing on such diverse topics as the dominance or financial hegemony of banks over firms, the effective autonomy of managers, and the reliance of corporations on resources that are controlled by external institutions.

We take a different view. We conceive of the balance of power in a corporate network as embedded in the nexus of contracts that constitute and surround the firm, as a function of a field of credit relationships that are governed by the distribution of property rights. Most, but not all, of these property rights are established through bargaining among the organizations in the credit network. All the property rights are established by law, whether directly through contracts, or indirectly through statutory provisions that impinge on corporate relationships.

Bankruptcy law provides an especially valuable site to account for the distribution of power among corporations for two reasons. On the one hand, at the moment of bankruptcy, every credit relationship, which is to say every financial relationship with other companies, banks, the state, consumers, suppliers, workers, and even communities, is *simultaneously* thrown into doubt. In principle, every player in the organizational network is at the bankruptcy table. All their interests are manifest, as each vies for a piece of a pie that will be too small to satisfy them all. On the other hand, who wins is directly contingent upon statutory priority or on the strength of their security—the legal instruments creditors have used to protect their interests. This conjunction between property rights, fixed by legal securities, and flows of credit, presents a quite distinct portrait of the distribution of power in the corporate field.

Secondly, if a corporate bankruptcy brings all creditors simultaneously into a bargaining situation, a comprehensive reappraisal of a nation's bankruptcy laws simultaneously places all these interests on the legislative table to decide what shall be the rules of the game that governs corporate death and resurrection. Since political "meta-bargaining" affects the interests of every major player in the market, and ultimately determines their relative power in all future corporate bankruptcy negotiations, it presents a tense arena for legal change—even more so given the rarity of bankruptcy reforms in this century.

The overwhelming bulk of research on law and society focuses on the complex and subtle ways in which law on the books—statutes, regulations—are interpreted, subverted, adapted, avoided, and redeployed in the process of implementation. Yet this is only half of law's encounter with corporations, markets, professionals, and the state. The other half completes what we term *the recursive loop*. It observes how law's operation in practice comes subsequently to be institutionalized in statutes. We will show how experiences in practice affect the deployment of political interests in legal reform, and we will demonstrate how professionals use their expertise to create, confirm, or adapt practice to a new institutionalization of laws and regulations. We reverse the classic treatment of law on the books in relation to law in action, and trace the complex interplay among political ideologies, private interests, and professional expertise that separated the real-world practices that precipitated legal reform, from the ensuing legal revisions (on the books).

Thirdly, just as commercial law, including bankruptcy law, is significantly shaped by the technical advice of the professionals who practice it, modern property rights are created and negotiated by professionals. However, scholarly research on professionals traditionally has stopped short of their creative role in shaping substantive statutory law. Theories of professions in the last twenty years have concentrated intensively on the mechanisms professionals employ to control markets for their own services. But they have generally failed to ask either how professionals shape wider financial, industrial, and labor markets, or how professionals' narrow self-interests in their own market projects cross over to structure market institutions, the state, and substantive law.

In this book we develop a theory of professionals' jurisdictional rights. We will argue that just as corporations and banks seek to create and secure property rights, so too professionals try to establish jurisdictional rights over areas of work and arenas of law reform. But property rights and jurisdictional rights are not two discrete spheres. The high stakes in bankruptcy law reforms created significant jurisdictional struggles that in turn had far-reaching substantive effects on the law itself, effects that far exceeded straightforward contests for exclusive provision of professional services. The location of the public–private frontier, the emphasis given corporate reorganization as a policy priority, the centrality of courts and judges in corporate rehabilitation, the control of company directors—all were affected in one degree or another by lawyers, accountants, judges, and magistrates who interposed their struggles for jurisdictional domination into the wider policy debates over the proper distribution of property rights among players in the credit network.

In short, the bankruptcy reforms in Britain and the United States provide a fertile site to explore how the reappraisal of property rights opened up a scramble for jurisdictional rights, which in turn shaped the redistribution of power in the organizational field—most especially at the point of corporate death. Together, a property rights perspective on the balance of power among corporations, the innovative engagement of professionals in the recursivity of law, and professionals' bids to establish jurisdictional rights offer new points of departure for the understanding of old problems in the theory of law, organizations, and professions.

These questions benefit from comparative research. The United States and the United Kingdom have a number of important similarities that might suggest similar bankruptcy laws and consonant cultures of credit. Furthermore, the organizational field—the cast of organizations and institutions surrounding corporations—is fundamentally similar in both countries. In the field of bankruptcy, however, there are striking differences between these countries both in the professional division of labor and in the principles of distributing property rights.

For instance, whereas accountants are the primary professionals of corporate insolvency in Britain, lawyers are the primary practitioners in the United States. Where judges and courts are the main forums for bankruptcy disputes in the United States, they are relatively unimportant in Britain. In American bankruptcy law, the property rights of creditors can be significantly compromised and attenuated in order to allow a debtor corporation to reorganize. In contrast, British insolvency law protects the rights of creditors in largely unmodified form. Whereas company directors in the United States remain in control of their bankrupt corporations, British directors lose control to a professional insolvency practitioner (usually an accountant). In the United States, bankruptcy law is narrowly concerned with economic reorganization or liquidation, whereas in Britain it also serves to further moral regulation of corporate governance.

By analyzing bankruptcy in a comparison of these two major industrial powers, we immediately problematize what either country, and its scholarly observers, take for granted—the contingent relationships between a market economy, the legal rules that govern it, and the professional division of labor. This book demonstrates that the divergent cultures of bankruptcy in Britain and the United States have resulted in distinctive models of corporate control and discernible differences in the financial balance of power. Differences in the structure of security permit the creditors of each country to configure their power relationships vis-à-vis debtor corporations in different ways.

This book follows the United States Bankruptcy Code from the establishment of the Bankruptcy Commission by Congress in 1970 through to the signature of President Carter in 1978. It is a period that coincides with economic stagnation in the world economy and an ebbing from the high water mark of government confidence that it could solve fundamental social and economic problems through adroit public policy and yet another executive agency. The bankruptcy reforms were not immune from the Watergate scandal, nor from the restructuring of American corporations and regulatory institutions. They reflected the aspirations of consumers and the frustrations of financial institutions. The Bankruptcy Code bears the stamp of fierce competition among judges that marked the beginning of the Commission and continued through to the moment the bill was signed into law at the White House. It embodies the aspirations of ethnic and religious groups excluded from the central institutions of their profession. And it carries the mark of weakened unions and assertive company managers.

On the other side of the Atlantic our account traverses the period from the creation of the Insolvency Review Committee in 1978 by a Labour Government through to its culmination in the far-reaching changes of the Insolvency Act, which obtained Royal Assent in 1985. Looming in the background were the near collapse of London's real property market, the reappraisals of nationalization as a panacea for industrial reorganization, and abuses of an unregulated market for bankruptcy services. Bracketed, on the one hand, by hard-hitting TV journalism and, on the other hand, by a resurgent conservative political ideology, the English insolvency legislation found itself embroiled in the fundamental reappraisals of state capabilities and market potentialities that accompanied the Thatcher revolution. Far from being an obscure technical exercise in statutory reform, the insolvency reforms were harnessed to a larger project of market reconstruction and business regulation that surprised even Mrs Thatcher's ministers in its ambition (Halliday and Carruthers 1996).

Since these reforms are so recent, they leave a rich residue of research materials. We employ three main sources of data for each country. First, the principal *primary documentary sources* include, for Britain, the archives and private papers of the Insolvency Law Review Committee; submissions to the Cork Committee; the archives of the Insolvency Practitioners' Association; committee and government reports; Parliamentary Debates; and some private papers. For the United States, we rely principally upon the minutes of the Commission on the Bankruptcy Laws of the United States; the Report of the Commission on the Bankruptcy Laws of the United States; and submissions and hearings from

1970–78 on bills leading to the Bankruptcy Reform Act of 1978. Secondly, we have been well-informed by more than fifty *interviews* with central actors in the reforms, including the chairmen of both reform commissions (Kenneth Cork in Britain, Harold Marsh in the United States), major politicians responsible for passage of the legislation (including Lords Benson, Bruce, and Lucas in Britain), key civil servants involved in formulating policy and drafting statutes, legislative aides to the principal Congressional committees, leaders of professional associations and lobbying organizations, and representatives of key interest groups. Thirdly, we have consulted a large number of *secondary documentary sources*, including newspapers, professional and trade journals, and periodicals.

Rescuing Business presents a theoretically-grounded interpretation of the two legislative episodes. In so doing, we endeavor to present a sociological view of law-making in the field of bankruptcy and to employ the case of bankruptcy reforms to develop theories of legal change, organizational power, and professions. This book does *not* purport to offer an exhaustive account of bankruptcy law, nor is it a conventional legislative history. Our concern is with antecedents, with the processes that produced legislative enactment, not with consequences, though the latter inevitably influence those aspects of the legislation on which we have chosen to focus. The distinctive character of the lens through which we view the Bankruptcy Code and the Insolvency Act can be seen from the structure of the volume.

Part One presents a theoretical framework and general context for the reforms. Chapters 1 and 2 argue that theories of organizational power, legal change, and professions may be juxtaposed to provide a distinctive perspective on bankruptcy reforms. Following our discussion of property and jurisdictional rights, we consider the relationships between bargaining and meta-bargaining in the shift from law in action to law on the books. Professions mediate these transitions; their powers of innovation enable, modify, and even subvert the substantive interests of all other actors in the credit network. Chapter 3 situates the political, economic, and legal changes within the framework of the global environment that shaped the national reform programs. Part Two analyzes meta-bargaining by powerful collective actors in the credit network over distributions of property rights. Part Three demonstrates how the politics of jurisdictional rights pervaded the legislation and came to shape the institutions in which bankruptcy administration subsequently has taken place.

Rescuing Business therefore makes the seemingly improbable case that a relatively technical and obscure area of law, traditionally avoided by most social sciences, offers fresh insights into hoary problems of power, professions, and legal change. However, not only social scientists may be surprised by the importance of changes in bankruptcy law. As one participant in the English legal reforms put it: "... this committee never realized, when it started, how interfering with the insolvency law goes right through the law of contract, right through half the law of this country, and how difficult it is not to upset things when trying to improve them."[9,10,11]

[9] Oral submission, 12 Nov. 1980, *Public Record Office*.

[10] It should be noted that the Insolvency Act 1985 remained in place for little more than a year. It was consolidated with some sections of the Companies Act 1985 into the Insolvency Act 1986, which received Royal Assent on 25 July 1986. Sections of the Insolvency Act 1985 that deal with the disqualification of directors were consolidated with related provisions in the Companies Act 1985 to form the Company Directors Disqualification Act 1986. Formally, this book treats the lawmaking that produced the Insolvency Act 1985. Since the Insolvency Act is known universally by practitioners and scholars as the Insolvency Act 1986, we often adopt that usage for convenience. However, it should be noted that technically our analysis deals only with the Insolvency Act 1985. See Sealy and Milman (1988: 1–4).

[11] Our analysis of insolvency law applies only to England and Wales, although we adopt England as a shorthand for both. Most of the insolvency legislation also applies to Scotland, although the Insolvency Act 1986 contains a number of specific provisions that distinguish between England and Scotland. It was the clear hope of the Cork Committee that a general homogenization of bankruptcy and insolvency law should occur so far as possible throughout the United Kingdom (Cork Report, pp. 429–33).

PART 1

The Balance of Power in the Corporate Credit Network

1 Meta-bargaining over Property Rights

To understand the revision of British and American bankruptcy law, we highlight two kinds of rights and two types of bargaining.[1] We distinguish between property rights and jurisdictional rights, on the one hand, and bargaining and meta-bargaining, on the other, and focus especially on how rights and bargaining interact in bankruptcy. We elaborate these distinctions below, but to start a simple definition will help. A legal right is a defensible claim or entitlement. Property rights pertain to things of value: land, machinery, company shares, patents, and the like. They specify who has the right to use an asset. Jurisdictional rights pertain to types of work. They designate who has the right to perform a job and how they acquire that right (through educational qualifications, experience, or state certification). Property and jurisdictional rights are commonly defined by the law. In the bankruptcy setting, these two sets of rights prove to be enormously important for the ways that the network of inter-organizational relationships is established and transformed. Property rights and jurisdictional rights are the substance of struggle and the foundation of control in the credit network.

Bargaining and meta-bargaining concern what people do with rights. In markets, for example, people exchange property rights. They bargain over price and the bundle of rights to be transferred from the seller to the buyer. The negotiation that occurs in automobile dealerships is a familiar instance of bargaining over property rights: the salesperson and customer negotiate a sale, and once consummated the property rights in the car shift to the buyer. This kind of bargaining presupposes a set of legal rules: the rules of contract, consumer law, and property. Bargaining occurs within a legal framework.

Bargaining can also occur about the legal framework itself. We term this meta-bargaining. People bargain about the rules rather than on their basis. Meta-bargaining about property involves the negotiation of the system of property rights rather than the exchange of specific property, and it occurs in the polity rather than in the market. Yet meta-bargaining

---

[1] British and American legal terminology differs somewhat: "corporate bankruptcy" in the United States is called "insolvency" in the UK, and "bankruptcy" in England refers to personal insolvency. We will use the term "bankruptcy" generically to cover American corporate bankruptcy and British corporate insolvency.

is highly consequential for bargaining. How people transact in the market depends on the rules of property (and contract, etc.), and these rules are set by meta-bargaining. Thus, meta-bargaining occurs at a different level than bargaining, and sets the context for the latter.

BANKRUPTCY AND PROPERTY

Property rights lie at the foundation of market society. Their importance derives from the ways they constitute and shape the economy. Property rights affect economic behavior by structuring incentives and disincentives (Libecap 1986). They determine who bears the risks and rewards of economic action. They also determine who controls economic assets, and so directly empower some but not others. Property rights affect economic growth, investment, and income distribution.

Market activity consists chiefly of the exploitation and exchange of property rights. A factory-owner uses the factory to produce goods for sale. Market exchange involves the exchange of property rights. In fact, the very possibility of legal exchange derives from property rights (in particular, the right of alienation).[2] To have a market, traders must be able to transfer ownership from one to the other.

Property rights pose fundamental distributional questions about who gets what. They frequently constitute a zero-sum situation wherein one person's exclusive claims come at the expense of others. For one to have, others must have not. Nevertheless, many economists who study property rights overlook such distributional issues and instead focus on efficiency. Early discussions (for example, Demsetz 1967, Alchian and Demsetz 1973) argued that more efficient property rights regimes would in the long run replace less efficient ones, and described the development of property in almost evolutionary terms. The shift from communal property to private property "internalized externalities" and made the economy more efficient. While efficiency is certainly relevant, we will here emphasize the distributional aspects of property and the conflicts that arise out of them (Knight 1992, North 1981). Distributional questions are frequently played out in political arenas, and so we must consider: "... the critical role played by competing interest groups, politicians, and bureaucrats in molding institutional development" (Libecap 1986: 234).

---

[2] By definition, inalienable rights cannot be bought and sold legally.

Under the ideal circumstances envisioned by classical liberal theory, owners exercise and exchange their property rights freely—they enjoy absolute property and freedom of contract. But circumstances often do not permit such total discretion. An owner's property rights may be modified, constrained and even terminated. For example, property rights get violated when property is stolen or used without the owner's consent. But there are legal ways to terminate property rights as well. One of the most important occurs within bankruptcy, for when a business is dissolved, its property rights get extinguished and the claims of others upon it are substantially modified. Bankruptcy is a "normal" catastrophe that legally transforms property rights.

Ownership is often considered a dichotomous trait. A person either owns a piece of property or does not, and all property has a clearcut owner. Furthermore, ownership is deemed an absolute and unconditional right. It is, according to Blackstone's classic definition of property in a capitalist society, that "sole and despotic dominion which one man claims and exercises over the external things of the world, in total exclusion of the right of any other individual in the universe" (Blackstone 1979 [1766]: 2). In fact, however, ownership is much more nuanced and complex, even in capitalist society.[3] It involves a bundle of distinct rights which may or may not belong to a single owner: different persons may have different rights over the same asset; the owner may be an organization or institution rather than a person; furthermore, rights may be contingent on the status, circumstances, or behavior of the owner. All these permutations of ownership make the classic questions of control and power in the credit network much more complex than conventional social science customarily recognizes.

BUNDLES OF PROPERTY AND JURISDICTIONAL RIGHTS

As varieties of rights, property rights and jurisdictional rights involve enforceable claims: they are both about the control a rights-holder has over something (a commodity or a work process). They diverge dramatically, however, in terms of what the rights are about.

---

[3] For a superb discussion of the continuing importance of fragmented, contingent, cross-cutting and overlapping communal property rights, see Gordon (1995).

Property Rights

Property rights concern objects of value (which may be tangible or intangible). The owner of a house, for example, has the right to use her house if and when she wants. The owner also has the right to prevent others from using the house, and she can permanently transfer all her rights to other persons, by selling the house or giving it away. She may also temporarily transfer a subset of those rights, by loaning or renting out her house. Thanks to property law, a court system, and the police, the owner's rights are enforceable. Should her property rights be violated, she can appeal to the law for protection or redress. In general, such rights are enforceable by a third party: an individual, group, or organization separate from the rights holder. Property rights encompass tangible things like cars and houses, but also intangible assets like company shares, patents, software designs, and trademarks.

In modern capitalist economies, the system of private property involves four separate rights over objects of value: usufruct, exclusivity, heritability, and alienability (in other property regimes, one finds different combinations of rights).[4]

Usufruct concerns an owner's right to use, control, exploit or otherwise enjoy the fruits of that which she owns. The meaning of usufruct varies from one type of property to another as they entail different usages. The owner of publicly-traded company stock typically has a claim on company dividends and the right to vote in company elections. She can enjoy the fruits of the financial and political characteristics of her property. In contrast, a car owner can exploit the physical attributes of her property: driving it to work, using the trunk to store her golf clubs, taking her children to swimming lessons, and so on.

With the right of *exclusivity* added to that of usufruct, the owner can not only enjoy her own property but also prevent others from using it. The owner controls access to the property and whatever benefits it can generate. Exclusivity marks the difference between private and communal property, and has been the focus of much work on property rights (Field 1989, Libecap 1986). Under the latter property regime, all members of a community enjoy usufructuary rights and cannot be excluded by others (for example, public parks are open to everyone). Shared or communal rights often led to the "tragedy of the commons"—over-

---

[4] See Christman (1994) for another way to categorize the bundle of property rights.

exploitation of communal property.[5] Private property means that owners can appropriate and monopolize all the benefits for themselves.

The last two rights, *heritability* and *alienability*, concern the ability of owners to pass their property on to others. Such transfers can occur either as a unilateral gift or as part of bilateral market exchange, and either while owners are alive or dead. Not all types of rights can be transferred to other persons. In modern capitalist democracies, for example, the right to vote in national elections is inalienable, that is, it cannot be bought, sold or otherwise transferred to other individuals. Only the voter can exercise his or her right. In contrast, most property rights are alienable, and thus can be traded in markets. But alienability isn't always absolute. In the contemporary United States, for example, the sale of guns, tobacco, and alcohol is heavily regulated, and property rights in these commodities are not freely alienable.

Traditionally, the right of heritability has been extremely important, for it has allowed property owners to determine who would receive their property after their death. With testamentary rights, wealthy property owners have typically favored their children and other family members over non-relatives, and so inheritance has played a major role in the inter-generational reproduction of economic inequality. Without testamentary freedom, other rules automatically determine the devolution of property, and the preferences of the deceased do not matter (consider, for example, the traditional common law rule of a "widow's third," whereby a surviving widow was automatically entitled to one-third of the real property ever owned by her deceased husband). Heritability clearly does not apply in the case of corporate ownership, for unlike real individuals, fictive individuals do not die (they can be liquidated and dissolved, but that is an entirely different matter).

Property rights concern the enforceable rights that an individual or corporation has to use, exploit, transmit, or bequeath an object. Such objects need not be tangible, for modern property law recognizes rights over ideas, designs, claims to income, and government benefits. In the historical transition from feudalism to capitalism, the prior system of usufructuary, cross-cutting, inalienable, communal and contingent property rights was substantially replaced by private property rights (see North 1981: 154–7; Weber 1981: 111; 1978: 378–80; MacPherson

---

[5] Communal property illustrates very nicely the economists' point about how property rights affect economic behavior (see Eggertsson 1990: 84–91). Switching from communal to private property rights reduced the incentive to over-exploit property.

1978: 10; Thompson 1976: 337, 341). The system of capitalist property originally developed at a time when owners were overwhelmingly living persons. Today, however, a vast amount of property is owned by organizations that are "fictive individuals" (for example, churches, pension plans, for-profit corporations, universities and governments). Property rights no longer structure relations only between individuals, but also among organizations. Much of the substance of inter-organizational relationships is woven out of property rights. And most bargaining over the saving or liquidation of businesses in bankruptcy turns on the strength and priorities of property rights.

Jurisdictional Rights

Property rights shape how people use, control, appropriate and transfer their claims over tangible things and intangible assets. They place decision-making power and control over economic assets in the hands of the owner. Jurisdictional rights, in contrast, pertain to an entirely different set of matters. Jurisdiction determines which people can govern or control an arena of work, how it is to be performed, and by whom. For example, doctors as a profession enjoy jurisdiction over most areas of medical work, just as lawyers monopolize legal work. In such instances, membership in the relevant profession (obtained through specialized training, accreditation, and licensure) is a necessary prerequisite to performing and regulating certain kinds of work.

Just as property rights govern who controls things of value, jurisdictional rights determine who controls valuable activities. The more valuable the activity, the more likely it is that others may try to intrude and "capture" it for themselves. Jurisdictional rights are frequently enforced by the same public institutions that protect property rights: the government, law, and police. Jurisdictional monopolies are state-enforced.

Like property, jurisdiction over work consists of a set of rights. Control over certain occupations or types of work can be extremely valuable, not only in terms of monetary compensation, but also prestige, autonomy, and working conditions. Like *usufructuary* rights over property, jurisdiction allows rights holders to control, regulate and perform valuable labor, and enjoy their fruits. Under a system of private property, property rights are held by individual owners. Jurisdictional rights, in contrast, are usually held collectively. A group of persons, rather than a single individual, lays claim over a category of work.

Jurisdictional rights are also usually *exclusive*: not only do professionals possess the right to perform work, but they can also exclude others from doing so (unless, of course, the others happen to be members of the appropriate profession). Professional monopolies reserve work for accredited professionals and preclude all others from performing it. Much of the struggle over jurisdiction between rival claimants focuses on their ability to prohibit each other from valuable types of work. It is precisely the right of exclusivity that structures much of the bankruptcy politics in both countries.

If property and jurisdiction seem quite similar with respect to usufruct and exclusivity, they differ sharply over rights of *heritability* and *alienability*. In general, property rights can be transferred among individual rights holders while jurisdictional rights cannot. The claims over a type of medical work that a surgeon enjoys cannot be given, sold or bequeathed to others. Jurisdictional claims are contingent on professional status— only a suitably trained and qualified surgeon can perform surgery, and thus surgeons cannot pass that right on to non-surgeons. Jurisdictional boundaries are not static, of course, but the movement of work from one jurisdiction to another is part of a larger political and cultural process (Abbott 1988). The inalienability of jurisdictional rights was not always the case, however. In old regime France, for example, venal offices entailed usufructuary rights and frequently involved jurisdiction over sets of activities (one might be the official beer-taster to the King). Such public offices could be bought, sold, and inherited, just like other forms of property. Venal offices were abolished at the time of the French Revolution and in general no longer exist.[6]

The transferability of property rights means that markets in property can arise. Conversely, the non-transferability of jurisdictional rights means that no market for them exists. Jurisdictional rights cannot be shifted in a market, and so are not subject to market bargaining. Their allocation usually occurs in the polity, and is therefore determined through political bargaining. The history of American medicine, for example, is partly a story in which doctors used their political clout and mobilized public opinion to obtain a state-mandated monopoly over medical work, at the expense of competing medical workers like homeopaths.

Professional jurisdiction has an important cultural component. As Abbott (1988) points out, jurisdiction gives to a group of professionals

---

[6] See Bien (1995), Swart (1949). In the professions, venality occurred widely in the English military and clergy (Reader 1966).

the right to dictate how certain "problems" are interpreted, diagnosed, and ameliorated. It grants to the professional the status of expert, and privileges the knowledge and expertise which she possesses. Thus, the right to monopolize work is not simply based on arbitrary laws, but grounded and justified in terms of professional knowledge. Some part of jurisdictional conflict between rivals consists of attempts by one profession to subsume its opponent's knowledge base under its own, and thus lay claim to a more fundamental expertise.

Property and jurisdictional rights possess some similarities, but differ in important respects. Both sets of rights entail enforceable and exclusive claims over value (either valuable things or valuable activities). Consequently, possession of these rights is desirable and open to contestation among competing claimants. But much of the movement and reallocation of property rights ordinarily occurs in markets, and results from decentralized economic bargaining among individual owners. Jurisdictional rights shift much less, and do so only through a centralized process of political bargaining, in which competing collective claimants try to establish jurisdictional monopolies using their access to the state. Property rights can also be redistributed politically, and thus their allocation occurs in two separate venues, the market and the polity. Since market institutions behave quite differently from political institutions, the allocation of property rights is distinctive from jurisdictional rights.

Bargaining in the marketplace is highly decentralized and privileges economic power: those with more economic resources and better organization can get what they want. Bargaining in the polity, or meta-bargaining, occurs in a much more centralized and structured institutional location (for example, in a legislature or executive branch agency), and privileges political resources, which are distributed differently than economic resources. Furthermore, tensions can arise between market bargaining and political meta-bargaining over property rights, a possibility largely foreclosed to jurisdictional rights since their allocations are determined mostly in one place, the polity. For property rights in the market, it is possible for economic actors to adjust to, or contract around, the allocations settled in the polity (Coase 1960). This may set off a dynamic in which political allocations are revised to take account of the market-based adjustments of property rights.

Although money is a useful resource in both politics and markets, economic strength does not automatically translate into political strength. In fact, some groups who enjoy a strong market position can for that very reason become politically vulnerable. For example, monopoly suppliers possess considerable economic leverage over their customers, and so can dictate higher prices. But squeezing customers in this fashion can also engender a political backlash that results in regulation and price controls to prevent such abuse. To voters and politicians, such market behavior appears "unfair," "exploitative," "illegitimate," and so invites political correction. Similarly, weakness in the market can be parlayed into political strength, if the weak, or their advocates, can make convincing appeals to norms of fairness or principles of equity.

Whatever their similarities and differences, it is important to recognize the interdependencies between property rights and jurisdictional rights. Perhaps the most significant concerns jurisdiction over the work of negotiating, allocating and adjusting property rights. Property rights are routinely shifted and transferred in markets. Sometimes, if a given "package" of property rights are no longer viable in the market (that is, the "nexus of contracts" which constitute a particular firm are unprofitable), they may also be transformed in a bankruptcy court. When the value of the property is high enough, the task of adjusting and transforming property rights can itself become a lucrative and desirable form of work. Inter-professional jurisdictional contests over such work therefore affect the work itself, because different professions use different knowledge systems and expertise to "define" and "interpret" the problem and process of insolvency in different ways, and locate the solution to the problem in different institutional sites. Hence, as a practical matter, these jurisdictional disputes can also influence property rights.

PROPERTY AND THE STATE

Formal property rights do not automatically maintain themselves, but are defined and enforced by the state. The reason is simple—coercion is ultimately necessary to protect valuable property and in the modern world the state provides coercive power (Weber 1978, North 1981). Those whose property rights are violated look to the police and courts for redress. The protection of property rights is one of the irreducible functions of the state, acknowledged even by those who wish to minimize government as much as possible.[7] For the same reason, those who want to change the system of property rights (as opposed to simply

---

[7] Adam Smith argued that one of the chief purposes of government was the protection of property and the provision of law (Smith 1976, II: 231–6).

shifting them around) must also look to the state. In a democracy, this means convincing politicians to rewrite property laws, or encouraging judges to clarify and reinterpret the law (Libecap 1989; Riker and Sened 1991).

Although property rights get applied and exchanged in the market, they are specified in the polity and legal system. The pursuit of economic self-interest can therefore occur in either site, and what one cannot accomplish in one, one can sometimes achieve in the other. For example, banks try to maximize their profits, and in the credit market this means minimizing loan-losses. Thus, banks will want to scrutinize borrowers carefully before lending any money. But banks can also pressure the government for legislation to bolster their profits. Regulation that minimizes competition from other financial institutions can certainly enhance bank profitability, and so can laws strengthening the claims that lenders have over borrowers. To pursue these strategies, banks testify before Congress, or make campaign contributions, or otherwise try to wield their political clout. Many groups pursue their economic interests in both the market and the political systems.

PROPERTY AND ORGANIZATIONS

Given the importance of organizations as property owners, the relevance of property rights to organizational relations seems obvious. Nevertheless, they are largely overlooked in the sociological literature on inter-organizational relations, power, and resource flows.[8] Resource dependency theory (Pfeffer and Salancik 1978), for example, shows how resource flows between organizations engender dependencies and power differences. An organization that gets all of a key resource from a single supplier, in the absence of alternatives, is highly dependent on that supplier and thereby the supplier gains power over the organization. Taken together, resource flows and their concomitant dependencies constitute an inter-organizational set of relations that determines who controls whom. But the central element in Pfeffer and Salancik's theory, a resource flow, is in fact a transfer of property rights.

Studies by Mintz and Schwartz (1985), Stearns (1990), and Glasberg (1989) have extended resource dependency theory to show how banks

---

[8] For some telling exceptions, see Campbell and Lindberg (1990), Stinchcombe (1983: 131–7), and Parsons and Smelser (1956: 106–7).

and other financial institutions gain power over non-financial corporations. Banks supply capital, a critical resource. Frequently, corporations have few alternative suppliers and so they become dependent on their banks (see Mintz and Schwartz (1985: 28); Mintz and Schwartz (1990: 203); Stearns (1990); Glasberg (1989: 3, 181); Kotz (1978: 20, 61)). The importance, volume, and pattern of capital flows produce power relations among debtors and creditors. For resource dependency theorists, property rights grant control over resources, and ownership is conceived in exclusive terms (consequently it is clear who is, or is not, the owner of an asset). But while property rights are mentioned, their treatment does little justice to the complexity of the phenomenon.[9]

It is not only organizational sociology that neglects property rights, however, for Yoram Barzel observes that in the economic theory of the firm: "The ownership of factors used by a firm . . . is seldom explored in the received analysis, even though the typical implicit ownership assumptions are not innocuous" (Barzel 1989: 45). Similarly, transaction-cost economics focuses on the distinction between markets and hierarchies (Williamson 1985). Whether or not a firm produces something internally is explained by transaction costs. But this simple dichotomy masks enormous contractual variability and the fact that "hierarchy" can be built into a market relationship, using property rights among other things (see Stinchcombe 1990: 194–239). By highlighting property rights, we can move beyond simple treatments of inter-organizational relationships and make better sense of how corporations manage their relations with one another.

To focus on property rights in organizational relationships has several advantages. Contractual agreements are the usual means through which bargains are struck and property rights exchanged and shared (Barzel 1989: 7). So much time and effort is spent in ordinary commerce negotiating, monitoring, enforcing, and disputing property rights that to ignore them is to overlook a substantial part of what business does. An examination of property rights takes account of a significant aspect of corporate life and illuminates the variety and legal meaning of contractual relations. This approach also gives salience to the distinctive and

---

[9] See, e.g., Stearns (1990: 179); Kotz (1978: 20); Glasberg (1989: 43); Palmer et al. (1986: 786, 792). There may be practical as well as theoretical reasons for the neglect. To take property rights seriously means paying attention to the details of financial contracts rather than simply the amount of capital that is being lent, or the fact of borrowing. Since financial contracts are private matters, the details are hard to study. The general aversion of social scientists to the technicalities of law may also be a factor.

problematic effects of bankruptcy. Bankruptcy rends apart the nexus of contracts at the heart of a firm. Many of the bankrupt firm's agreements are modified, nullified, or renegotiated. Bankruptcy is a contingency under which carefully negotiated commitments are reopened, and the bargaining among the interested parties begins anew. Much contracting occurs in light of the possibility of bankruptcy even when it is unlikely. Bankruptcy therefore is a key parameter of bargaining and meta-bargaining over property rights.

PROPERTY RIGHTS AND CORPORATE FINANCE

Debtor–creditor relationships form an important part of how socio-logists understand organizational power. Since organizational control depends on how corporations mobilize resources, what they can do with capital, the most general of resources, is crucial. In corporate finance, long-term and short-term capital resources are commonly distinguished. Long-term financing usually involves debt or equity, while short-term finance involves commercial paper and bank loans. Both methods for raising capital involve bundles of property rights.

Issuance of new stock is one way for corporations to raise money. In exchange for their capital, investors get ownership rights, a claim on residual income (as dividends), and the prospect of capital gains. Common stock usually includes the right to vote in company elections, and this gives the equity-holder a voice in company policy. Companies may issue different classes of stock with different voting and dividend rights (Lease, McConnell and Mikkelson 1983; Ang and Megginson 1989). Preferred stock gets priority in the payment of dividends, but seldom has full voting rights.

Using equity to raise money cedes some control to the supplier of capital since shareholders own the corporation and elect the company's directors (who select management). But as Berle and Means (1932) argued, corporate management can in practice be quite independent of owners. Many shareholders are passive investors, reluctant to exercise their control rights. The corporation acquires a resource over which it enjoys full property rights, subject to the variegated influence of share-holders. Since the corporation is not required to pay dividends, its financial obligations to shareholders are discretionary.

For various reasons, corporations sometimes prefer to issue debt rather than equity. Debt is of particular interest to organization theorists since it involves acquisition of a resource from an outside source (debt-holders are not proprietors of the firm), and thus raises the possibility of external control. Debt varies according to seniority (priority in the event of bankruptcy), maturity (the period over which debt is repaid), repayment provisions, and default risk. Yet it would be a mistake to suppose that debt holders, as compared to equity holders, have completely forgone control in order to get a more secure income stream. Through property rights, debt-holders can influence how the capital they supply to the borrower gets used.

Corporations and their lenders negotiate the property rights shared between debtors and debt-holders. Depending on these, the corporation will have to pay more or less for the money it borrows. One of the basic distinctions concerns security. When a debt is secured, the creditor possesses rights over property held by the debtor; a home mortgage, for instance, gives to the bank a property interest in the borrower's home. Or bonds may be secured by particular assets. If the debtor defaults, a secured creditor can seize the collateral as compensation. Collateralization of loans attenuates the property rights enjoyed by the debtor, and the property serving as collateral is said to be encumbered. A secured loan may mean lower interest payments for the debtor, but this is done at the price of ceding property rights to the lender.

Security is not the only way to fashion property rights between lenders and borrowers. Whether a corporation borrows from a financial institution or issues marketable securities (for example, bonds or debentures), loan contracts frequently restrict the debtor's behavior (Herman 1981: 126–8). Protective covenants constrain the debtor's rights of usufruct and alienation, and are a common feature of corporate finance (see Smith and Warner 1979, Thompson and Norgaard 1967: 31, and Lister 1985).[10]

Covenants are found in both term-loan contracts and bond indentures. The more detailed they are, the more they restrict the debtor. Bond holders and creditors do not have the voting rights of shareholders, but through the use of covenants they can shape property rights

---

[10] There are four general kinds: 1) production or investment covenants (which restrict the debtor's investments, assets, and merger activity); 2) dividend covenants (which restrain dividend payments); 3) financing covenants (which prohibit further borrowing under certain conditions, restrict debt-like obligations such as loan guarantees, or specify particular payoffs to bondholders (e.g., a sinking fund)), and 4) bonding covenants (which provide for audits, financial statements, accounting methods, insurance, and a periodic statement of compliance with covenants) (Smith and Warner 1979).

and so influence the actions of debtor corporations. The debtor acquires capital, but its dominion over that capital is neither sole nor despotic.

Corporations acquire capital through equity, debt, or retained earnings. Equity and debt become important when retained earnings cannot meet the needs of a corporation. Debt has been of particular interest to organization theorists since it provides the basis for external control over organizations. Yet, the ownership rights obtained over capital acquired using debt are neither simple nor absolute. The complexities are usually spelled out in laborious detail in a financial contract. Property rights are shared, restricted, and made contingent on any number of conditions.[11]

In the structure of organizational ties, forms of security in corporate debt are frequently overlooked, and the network of corporate relationships and resource flows may conceal radically different financial structures. Suppose a corporation has borrowed three equal sums from three creditors. In one case, credit is unsecured. In an second, credit is entirely secured so that the creditor has collateral in an asset of equivalent value to the sum lent. And in the third, credit is partially secured. If one considers only the volume of resource flows, then each of the creditors appears to have roughly similar power over the debtor (Pfeffer and Salancik 1978). But if one considers property rights and the extent of security, then relations of dependency, control, and priority vary dramatically in the three cases. Focusing on the magnitude and direction of resource flows is misleading because it overlooks the fact that the second creditor has more control than either the first or the third. The differences in control and ownership lie in the variations over strength of security devices.

Security devices originate from three sources. Statutory devices give certain creditors, such as the state, special privileges that ensure it is repaid ahead of other creditors. Judicial devices rely on the ruling of a judge, or on case law, to determine which creditors have stronger property rights than others. And contractual devices rely on private bargaining between banks and companies or other parties. All three are connected in various ways. Often it requires a court to uphold the force of a new security that may have been contracted between a trade supplier and customer, or bank and corporation. New statutes sometimes confirm and sometimes overturn property rights that have emerged in the courts.

---

[11] Ironically, financial property rights begin to look like pre-capitalist property rights: cross-cutting, usufructuary, contingent and of restricted alienability.

In general, lenders insist on stronger and more intrusive rights the larger and longer the loan, the bigger the risks, or the worse the debtors' financial condition (Ho and Singer 1982). Depending on the circumstances, creditors want collateral for their loans and will insist on numerous protective covenants, and equity holders will exercise their voting rights to have a stronger voice in company policy. Suppliers of capital will also demand a higher rate of return to compensate for the higher risk. In situations of real crisis, debt-holders may exchange their debt for equity to obtain direct and active control over company policy.

The probability of bankruptcy significantly affects the property rights negotiated between debtors and creditors. Large corporations in good financial health do not have to concede the same measure of property rights to creditors, and can borrow by issuing unsecured debt like commercial paper. Weaker companies, in contrast, must borrow at higher interest rates and concede to lenders various property rights through collateral and restrictive covenants. Many contractual complexities are motivated by the possibility of debtor default.

BANKRUPTCY AND PROPERTY RIGHTS

Bankruptcy is a defining feature of market economies and plays a central role in the process that drives less efficient firms out of the market. It is the unfortunate and unhoped-for possibility that overshadows all financial contracting. When it occurs, all kinds of property rights must be renegotiated. But even when firms remain solvent, those who negotiate property rights must take into account its possibility and so provide for "worst case scenarios." The significance of bankruptcy is completely out of proportion to its relative infrequency. In societies entirely dependent on credit, bankruptcy law has a pervasive influence.

As a rupture in the ordinary flow of business, bankruptcy provides a kind of natural experiment. By calling into doubt the very survival of a corporation, it permits all those with a stake in the firm to state explicitly and publicly the nature and magnitude of their interest. All those with property claims can register them with the bankruptcy court. Even those with no official claim on the failing firm may influence the proceedings, albeit extra-legally. Corporate failure involves more than shareholders and creditors. It affects employees' jobs, the economic viability of communities, the ability of suppliers and customers to conduct their business, the demand for professional services, and the competitive interests of the state. Bankruptcy upsets those commercial and employment relationships that are taken for granted, and lays bare *simultaneously* many of the power relations and economic interests that surround a firm. Since bankrupt firms cannot meet all their liabilities, there is a shortfall that must be distributed among claimants whose interests are consequently in conflict. One creditor's loss is another one's gain.

Bankruptcy is a complex legal and economic process, and involves a substantial amount of work. Claims must be registered and evaluated, assets need to be collected and valued, and conflicts must be resolved. The work may be routine in a straightforward liquidation, but in a large reorganization it will be protracted and technically demanding. Who is to perform such work? How are they to be compensated? The answers to these questions raise jurisdictional rights, the other major dimension of bankruptcy.

BANKRUPTCY AND JURISDICTIONAL RIGHTS

Property rights are not the only way a society regulates access to value. Jurisdictional rights function in a similar fashion. A jurisdictional right is a socially-sanctioned right to perform or control a particular kind of work. Modern jurisdictional rights are akin to special property rights which apply to work (exclusive rights of contingent usufruct, but not alienability or heritability). Both rights allow right-holders to exclude others. That is, whoever possesses jurisdiction can perform or oversee a type of work and exclude others. Many areas of work are subject to jurisdictional rights, but the one that concerns us here is bankruptcy work. Bankruptcy involves the suspension and modification of property rights and begins with recognition of the fact that claims on a debtor can no longer be satisfied. Assets are inadequate to meet liabilities and so there is a problem: somebody's property rights will be violated. The key bankruptcy question is who loses and how much: how will the shortfall be allocated among the competing claimants; how much will their property rights be attenuated? In a liquidation, bankruptcy law provides a way to determine total assets in an insolvent estate, to assess total claims on the estate, and to distribute the assets to the claimants. In a business reorganization, bankruptcy law provides an orderly way to stop the enforcement of rights by creditors, to renegotiate terms of credit, and to return the company to the market better able to compete successfully.

Jurisdictional and property rights intersect in bankruptcy because the determination, negotiation, allocation, modification and suspension of property rights, as a type of work, is subject to jurisdictional rights and conflicts. Administering and modifying property rights is an important and valuable job over which some group or profession can lay claim. For example, bankruptcy procedures in most countries involve the appointment of a public official or a private professional to administer and oversee the bankrupt estate. Who will qualify for appointment in either capacity? Who has authority to occupy this position of power and responsibility?

In the modern world, property rights concern the legal system, and negotiating and exchanging them often involves lawyers.[12] Modifying and suspending property rights occurs in bankruptcy court and therefore also involves lawyers and judges. But the role of lawyers and judges is a jurisdictional accomplishment, not a necessary result of the inherent qualities of bankruptcy. Such work could be performed by others in a different setting (as proposed by Stanley and Girth 1971). Trained civil servants, too, might easily process many of the routine business liquidations that occur each year and save valuable court time for more complex or controversial cases. How is it that lawyers and judges have established such an effective and lucrative claim over bankruptcy work? Were there other contenders and why did they lose out?

In bankruptcy, property rights and jurisdictional rights are not simply contiguous—they are interdependent and mutually influential. It is precisely the value of property rights that makes jurisdictional rights worth having. As a site for work, bankruptcy is now a lucrative territory. Furthermore, jurisdictional rights affect property rights because who performs work has implications for how the process of administering, adjusting, and reconciling property rights unfolds. If lawyers monopolize bankruptcy work, for example, bankruptcy proceedings will likely occur in judicial or quasi-judicial settings, and in an adversarial fashion. Such a process will probably make the resolution of creditors' property rights more expensive and time-consuming, but at least all parties can be confident their rights are protected by expert counsel. A less adversarial procedure, conducted by civil servants or private professionals, may be swifter and more decisive, although parties will have to forgo "their day in court."

---

[12] The importance of formal law and lawyers in everyday business should not be overestimated, however. See Macaulay (1963), Bernstein (1992).

BARGAINING AND META-BARGAINING

We use the term "bargaining" for the normal negotiation and transfer of property rights in the market. To "truck, barter and exchange" is to bargain for property rights. Such bargaining occurs within the parameters of a legal system that defines and protects property rights, and enforces contracts. Contractual rectitude is particularly important for financial contracts and debtor–creditor relations.[13] Even bargaining which does not directly use the law nevertheless occurs within its shadow (see Macaulay 1963, 1985; White 1982). Bargainers take the legal framework for granted and go about their business.

Deals get struck in the market, but they are also struck in politics. Rather than negotiate over specific property, periodically governments and interest groups reassess the whole system of property rights. They undertake meta-bargaining. Political issues typically include education, foreign policy, abortion and so on, but they can also involve more "technical" questions about commercial law and property rights. Although contract law rarely provokes the same level of contention as abortion or gun-control, it is highly consequential for the market. Meta-bargaining, that is, bargaining about the legal framework within which bargaining takes place, sets the economic terrain. If ordinary bargaining engages economic interests, then meta-bargaining does so on an even grander scale. Bargaining in the market is mundane and recurrent: everybody does it everyday. In contrast, meta-bargaining about the market framework tends to be extraordinary and irregular.[14] It affords the rare opportunity to make sweeping changes that will affect whole industries or sets of economic relations.

Labor law exemplifies the difference between bargaining and meta-bargaining. Every day, employers and employees negotiate the terms of employment, sometimes individually and sometimes collectively (when unions are involved). The terms of their bargains, and how they bargain, are framed by labor law. Not surprisingly, employers will seek their advantage when bargaining, but they can also pursue their interests

---

[13] Consequently, creditors are advised to make sure that formal contracts are complete and in order, and so debtor–creditor relations tend to be more formal–contractual than other commercial relations (see, e.g., Alexander and Downey 1988: 661; Grimmig 1986: 359, 360; Connor and Kent 1986: 615).

[14] How irregular the meta-bargaining will be varies greatly from field to field. Meta-bargaining about taxes occurs annually in most legislatures; meta-bargaining about bankruptcy may occur only once or twice a century.

through meta-bargaining—they can try to shape labor law to favor themselves. They can, for example, pressure governments for right-to-work laws that make it harder for unions to organize.

The importance of meta-bargaining about bankruptcy rules derives from the importance of bankruptcy. If bankruptcy had only a trivial effect on the disposition of property, there is no doubt but that few would care how and when bankruptcy law was revised. But in fact, the property stakes are very high under bankruptcy. And if bargaining *under* bankruptcy law is a relatively rare event, the opportunity for meta-bargaining *about* bankruptcy law is rarer still.

Examining statutory changes in light of their effects on property rights raises a basic question: who makes bankruptcy law? That in turn splinters into many other questions: who initiated the revisions? Who sought to influence the course of change, and in what direction? Who gained and who lost? How was meta-bargaining used to reshape property rights and jurisdictional rights? How did meta-bargaining over property and jurisdictional rights affect each other? Bankruptcy is a forum for renegotiating what was already negotiated, and provides an occasion to undo what was already done. When bankruptcy law is itself modified, an enormous opportunity exists for interested parties to lobby for rules that favor themselves over others.

In a perfect "Coasian" world of zero transaction costs, meta-bargaining would simply not matter (see Coase 1960). Market actors could costlessly adjust or adapt to the changes in rights and entitlements that political meta-bargaining generated. If property rights were substantially redistributed, then those affected would simply contract around the changes, with no net effect. In the real world, of course, transaction costs are not zero and it may be very difficult for affected parties to compensate in private bargaining for changes induced through meta-bargaining. Indeed, actors possess varying degrees of knowledge and sophistication. Some can make adjustments easier than others, although none will be able to compensate fully for the gains and losses caused by meta-bargaining.

The intersection of these two distinctions—property versus jurisdictional rights, and bargaining versus meta-bargaining—generates complex and consequential interactions. Much credit activity revolves around the negotiation and deployment of property rights. For example, to obtain a bank loan, a debtor must negotiate an amount, an interest rate, and terms of repayment. To a much lesser extent, jurisdictional rights may be bargained in the market, although more often they are simply applied or implemented. Professions constitute the paradigmatic case of jurisdictional rights-holders. A monopoly gives to the profession the right to undertake a particular type of work and to exclude others. Thus, in the late-nineteenth century American doctors were able to stop homeopaths from providing various medical services to the public, which simultaneously benefitted doctors and hurt homeopaths.

Jurisdictional rights and property rights are both specified and enforced by the legal system. In general, therefore, the revision of law provides an opportunity to remake both jurisdictional and property rights wholesale. This is where meta-bargaining occurs. As the economic historical Gary Libecap explains with respect to property:

Property rights institutions are determined through the political process, involving either negotiations among immediate group members or lobbying activities at higher levels of government. The political process of defining and enforcing property rights can be divisive because of the distributional implications of different property allocations... In political bargaining over institutional change, each of the parties attempts to maximize his or her private net gains. (Libecap 1989: 4–5)[15]

The stakes involved in meta-bargaining over property rights are considerable because it can produce significant shifts in wealth and power. Large-scale transformations of property systems often coincide with periods of dramatic social and political change. Consider, for example, how property rights changed during the Russian and Chinese Revolutions in the twentieth century, or during the French Revolution at the end of the eighteenth century.[16] Yet meta-bargaining does not occur only in revolutionary periods. During the enclosure movement in seventeenth and eighteenth century England, many collective and usufructuary rights over common land were extinguished and converted by Parliament into private property rights. In the United States during the nineteenth century, western timber companies and ranchers pressured the federal government to modify laws governing access to and use of federal land. But thanks to the political power of homesteaders, they were largely unable to obtain the changes they wanted (Libecap 1989, chapter 4).

Meta-bargaining for jurisdictional rights is similarly consequential. Lawyers, doctors, accountants and other professionals look to the state

---

[15] Libecap (1989: 11) fails to distinguish between bargaining and meta-bargaining, lumping both together under the rubric of "contracting." This oversight mars what is otherwise a very insightful analysis of the politics of property rights.

[16] On changes in property in revolutionary France, see Sewell (1980: ch. 6).

to enforce their jurisdictional claims (Abbott 1988: 62–3, 157–67). Their success at monopolizing work and enhancing occupational status is directly related to their political effectiveness, but also by how much their professional interests coincide with state interests. It is clear how advantageous a state-sanctioned occupational monopoly is to professions, but professions can be useful to states and governments in return (Halliday and Carruthers 1996).

Two sets of interests converge in meta-bargaining over property rights. First and most obvious are those whose property rights might be affected. Meta-bargaining over property rights is often highly conflictual, with clear-cut winners and losers. Second, and cross-cutting these propertied interests, are the jurisdictional stakes. Who will perform the work of crafting, exchanging, securing, modifying, or terminating property rights? Where is this work to occur? Jurisdictional conflict can also produce winners and losers, although the creation of new domains of work means that meta-bargaining can be non-zero-sum.[17] Furthermore, the two contests intermingle. Jurisdictional outcomes influence property outcomes. And settlements over property rights can have significant repercussions for the extent of work available for jurisdictional struggles. Substantive law, in other words, can be a by-product of jurisdictional contests, and jurisdictional domains will be shaped by the scope of property rights.

BANKRUPTCY LAW

Although ignored by most organizational sociologists,[18] bankruptcy law influences many organizational processes. Corporate bankruptcy or insolvency law provides the procedures and protections available to corporate debtors who want to dissolve, liquidate, or reorganize their assets and operations. Bankruptcy law also protects and empowers creditors—the lenders who may range from large financial institutions, to suppliers who provided goods on credit, to unpaid workers, and to consumers who prepaid for goods not yet received. Bankruptcy law determines what rights these parties have in the bargaining that occurs

---

[17] Non-zero-sum refers to those situations where the gains of one party do not necessarily entail losses for someone else.

[18] Two notable exceptions can be found in Delaney (1992) on strategic corporate bankruptcies, and the massive study of individual bankruptcies by Sullivan, Warren, and Westbrook (1989).

between creditors and an insolvent corporate debtor.[19] Each legal feature and procedure also provides a target of opportunity during meta-bargaining, a point where interests can be enhanced or undermined.

Bankruptcy law specifies the circumstances under which companies may seek protection from creditors. It indicates who—corporate directors, management, creditors, courts—can trigger legal interventions into corporate affairs. It also grants to directors or corporate managers various powers once bankruptcy law has been activated. The law allows some prior agreements, such as labor or commercial contracts, to be renegotiated or rejected. It ranks creditors for priority in the distribution of assets, and protects them from further losses incurred by the debtor. Furthermore, the law provides reorganization or rehabilitation opportunities to the debtor company, including terms for the repayment of debts or the reorganization of assets (Jackson 1986; Goode 1990).

The great divide in bankruptcy law falls between creditors and debtors. Creditors want to be sure that the money they lend will be repaid, that they will be paid for goods they provide on credit, and that prepayments—a form of credit—will result in delivery of the goods or service. In general, lenders prefer to have legal rights over the debtor's property and so increase the probability of repayment. In contrast, debtors want to maintain maximum control over the money they borrow or the goods they acquire. Consequently, lenders' and borrowers' interests clash. Creditors seek stronger forms of security, repossession of their goods, or repayment of their loans. Debtors try to hold off creditors and maintain maximum freedom to dispose of resources as they see fit. A great deal of bankruptcy law is committed to balancing these conflicting interests in situations of financial distress. And the complexity of the situation increases even further as many debtors are also creditors.

Creditors struggle with debtors, but creditors also struggle among themselves. Bankruptcy law governs conflicts among creditors who compete over insufficient assets. To forestall a destructive "race to the assets," bankruptcy law ranks creditors from the most senior, who are first to retrieve their assets, to the most junior, who will share whatever is left after other creditors have been satisfied. As a result, bankruptcy law

---

[19] For general introductions to bankruptcy law in the United States see Baird and Jackson (1990), Warren and Westbrook (1991), King and Cook (1985), Nickles and Epstein (1989), and Treister et al. (1988).

provides a framework for conflict resolution not only between creditors and debtors, but also among the creditors. By doing so, the dominant jurisprudence of bankruptcy law views it as a solution to the classic "common pool" and public goods problems (Jackson 1986; Goode 1990).

Bankruptcy law casts a long shadow. It is salient not only for financially distressed companies, but also for the risk calculations of lenders, for corporate managers who must assess the potential downside of their own decisions, and for creditors whose protections in bankruptcy law will affect the level, costs, and forms of credit they extend (White 1989). Moreover, the law of corporate reorganization and liquidation can influence the decisions of corporate managers about the organizational and legal structure of the firm—for example, whether to take multi-divisional or group forms—and the ways they protect their own autonomy and perquisites. Consequently, while bankruptcy law directly concerns only companies in financial difficulty, in fact it affects more generally all corporations in an "open credit economy" (White 1984).[20]

For our purposes, property rights within the corporate financial structure derive from two sets of legal rules—rights specification rules, contained in contract, corporate, and creditors' law; and rights modification rules, contained in bankruptcy law. The two interact since types and packages of property rights can be adapted or even invented to escape the effects of modification rules in bankruptcy law. And in reciprocal fashion, modification rules in bankruptcy law respond to the effects of security on the ranking of creditors in corporate insolvencies (Countryman 1971).

Rights Specification Rules

Forms of security are the building blocks that debtors and creditors use to build their financial relationships. They grant bundles of rights to a firm's lenders and investors, and restrict managerial control over corporate assets. Secured lenders include not only the banks and insurance companies which feature prominently in research on inter-corporate relations, but also suppliers, corporate bondholders, and the state.

Rights can be ceded on many kinds of property. Real estate, equipment, goods, inventory, stocks, bonds, cash, accounts receivable,

---

[20] *Report of the Bankruptcy Commission,* 1973.

copyrights, trademarks—all can secure a borrower's claim. Virtually any kind of tangible or intangible property can be secured or made subject to a "charge." Moreover, secured claims may be "fixed", and stake a claim to a particular building or piece of machinery, or "floating", and hover over all company assets as they change in the course of business. Forms of security take on an almost bewildering variety that is limited only by the imaginations of their creators—usually lawyers— and their users—corporate debtors and creditors. The most common include mortgages, liens, leases, conditional sales contracts, bonds and inventory loans (Ross, Westerfield, and Jaffe 1990).

Secured bonds provide a good example of the rights given by corporations to lenders.[21] In exchange for the bondholders' money, companies agree to pay interest, to repay the principal, and to abide by other terms or covenants. Such bonds, sometimes called mortgage bonds, may be secured against real estate or other property of the firm, and so if the firm defaults, the bondholders can seize the collateral. The property rights ceded to secured creditors are particularly important because debt covenants may restrict managerial autonomy. Companies may be required to maintain their property, to forgo additional debt, to promise not to grant other secured lenders higher priority, to agree to maintain certain financial ratios, and even to continue in the same line of business (Klein and Coffee 1990: 216–25).[22]

The rules that govern financial transactions also determine the order in which creditors can satisfy their claims if a firm defaults: creditors are ranked from the most senior to the most junior. As Table 1.1 demonstrates, secured creditors usually come first. Then sometimes follow administrative expenses that go to professionals for doing the work of liquidation or reorganization. The state frequently stands high in priority in order to recoup unpaid taxes. Workers and consumers also sometimes get a high priority. Then everyone else—the unsecured creditors—share equally with what is left—and often that is nothing at all. The great advantage of secured transactions is their seniority.

---

[21] The terminology of bonds is often confusing. In everyday speech, the term "bond" commonly includes secured and unsecured forms of corporate borrowing. Here, bonds refer to secured long-term debt (Klein and Coffee 1990). The definition of debentures also varies. In the United States they are unsecured corporate debt instruments; in Britain they are secured instruments (Brealey and Myers 1984).

[22] McDaniel (1986) argues that restrictive covenants are becoming less common and that they are ineffective in protecting bondholders. Yet his own data show that 82 of the Fortune 100 companies have negative pledge clauses, a type of restrictive covenant, in their bond indentures (p. 425). See also Smith and Warner (1979).

TABLE 1.1: **Ranking of Claims in Bankruptcy**

US

Pre-1978	Post-1978 Reform
* Secured Claims (e.g., liens)[a]	* Secured Claims

Priorities:	
1. Administrative Expenses: expenses for the preservation of the estate, creditor filing fees in involuntary bankruptcies, reasonable costs of recovering assets, one "reasonable" attorney's fee, cost of witness mileage, etc.	1. Administrative Expenses ("actual, necessary costs and expenses of preserving the estate, including wages, salaries (for professionals), or commissions for services rendered after the commencement of the case.")
2. Wages	2. For involuntary bankruptcies, claims arising in the ordinary course of business after the commencement of bankruptcy but before the appointment of trustee or order for relief
3. Third party: reasonable costs creditors incur in successfully challenging the confirmation of a bankruptcy plan	3. Wage claims (including sales commissions, vacation, severance, and sick leave pay)
4. Taxes	4. Claims for contributions to employee benefit plans
5. Statutory priorities for US laws and rent	5. Claims by consumers who have made a money deposit for property or services that were never provided
	6. Certain tax claims (e.g., income taxes, some property taxes, taxes withheld from employee paychecks)
Other Unsecured Claims	Other Unsecured Claims

UK

Pre-1986	Post-1986
* Secured Claims (e.g., liens)	* Secured Claims

Priorities:	
1. General rates dues within 12 months	1. Debts due to Inland Revenue (e.g., income tax)

2. PAYE deductions	2. Value added tax, car tax, and betting duty
3. Value added tax and car tax	3. Social security contributions
4. Betting duty	4. Contributions to occupational pensions schemes
5. Wages due within 4 months of insolvency	5. Wage and holiday remuneration to employees
6. Holiday remuneration to employees	6. Levies on coal and steel production
7. Social security contributions	
Unsecured Claims	Unsecured Claims

Sources: US: *Collier on Bankruptcy, 14th Edition.* 1978. New York: Matthew Bender. Epstein, David G. 1995. *Bankruptcy Law in a Nutshell.* St. Paul, MN: West. UK: *Insolvency Law and Practice: Report of the Review Committee.* 1982. Chair, Kenneth Cork. London: Her Majesty's Stationery Office. Sealy, L. S. and Milman, D. 1988. *Annotated Guide to the 1986 Insolvency Legislation.* Oxfordshire, England: CCH Editions Limited.

[a] Certain US tax liens under the pre-1978 bankruptcy law were paid only after some administrative expenses. Also, liens for wages and rent are paid according to their rank in the list of priorities.

Secured creditors almost always get to settle their claims before unsecured creditors and so despite the bother and expense, those who obtain security have an easier time recovering their money (Klein and Coffee 1990: 225–8).

The financial requirements of the firm embed it in a complex set of transactions and relationships whose legal provisions shape property rights and constrain managers and the disposition of the property they manage. Between the black of ownership and the white of non-ownership, there are many shades of contracted grey.

Rights Modification Rules

Financial relationships would be simple indeed if rights specification rules were all that defined the connection between debtors and creditors. But rights specification is not always the final move, for what we term "modification rules" establish when and how these property rights can be modified, abrogated, or suspended. When corporations descend into insolvency, the law of bankruptcy tests the strength and limits of property rights.

A first step in bankruptcy proceedings is to stop all claims made by creditors upon a firm and to sweep all a company's assets into a "pool," or estate. Stopping claims is variously referred to as a "freeze," a "moratorium," or a "stay." In a liquidation these assets will be allocated to creditors. In a reorganization, they will be used to try and rescue the business. But some creditors try to escape the pool by reclaiming their assets in full and not sharing them with other creditors. Secured transactions generally allow precisely this: a strongly secured creditor can seize that part of the debtor's property on which she has a claim and thus not share it with others. However, bankruptcy law complicates the general structure of security and may lead either to a delay in the seizure of property or to a redistribution of property rights.

Three types of modification rules illustrate how bankruptcy law can transform property rights. First, to stop creditors from gaining an unfair advantage in the scramble for assets just before bankruptcy, laws have "reachback" or voiding provisions which allow courts to undo transactions that occurred in the period immediately before bankruptcy.[23] In some cases, a sale or transfer of property rights can be retroactively annulled and the property returned to the estate. For instance, as a troubled company nears insolvency, an unsecured creditor may realize that she risks losing her money. To improve her situation, she may secure or strengthen the security of the loan and obtain a higher priority in the ranking of creditors—obviously at the expense of others. Under the United States Bankruptcy Code, this change in status can be voided, in certain circumstances, and the creditor's claim returned to its original unsecured status. Other securities will be invulnerable to attack by bankruptcy players (United States Bankruptcy Code, hereafter USBC, section 547; Treister et al., 1988: 137–91; Goode 1990: chapter 8).[24]

Secondly, bankruptcy law can impede the ability of secured creditors to realize their claims on the debtor. Some forms of security allow creditors to seize collateral assets immediately upon default. However, modification rules can alter rights that pertain outside bankruptcy. For instance, the "automatic stay" in Chapter 11 of the United States code,

---

[23] "Immediately" varies greatly from 30 days to 90 days to a year or more, depending on the creditor and the circumstances. The timing of the reachback is a "scarce good" subject to fierce contest in metabargaining. Voiding a prior change will usually drop a creditor well down the queue for allocation of moneys, and thus can be very expensive.

[24] The preference section on voiding powers of the trustee in the USBC is intended to ensure equality among creditors, and thus to forestall scrambling for unfair advantage in the weeks and months immediately preceding a bankruptcy filing. See Treister et al. (1988: 153).

or a "moratorium" in English insolvency law, permits courts to suspend or delay attempts by creditors to realize their claims or retrieve their collateral. Normal debt-collection procedures are halted. New forms of debt inside bankruptcy can be given a "super-priority" that induces lenders to provide new money to turn the business around, but that in turn lowers the priority ranking of other creditors.

Thirdly, some modification rules allow courts to over-ride the power of creditors to confirm or veto plans for corporate reorganization. While the value of claims and the kinds of security largely determine the relative influence of creditors in negotiations over corporate reorganization, courts can step in and usurp the power of higher ranked creditors in favor of creditors as a whole (Treister et al., 1988: chapter 9). In American parlance, this power is appropriately termed "cramdown," for the secured creditors can find a decision on a reorganization plan "crammed-down" over their objections.

In a near-continuous process of legal adaptation, lawyers representing debtors and creditors try to design financial contracts that establish a suitable set of property rights between the two parties, and which anticipate the kind of modifications those rights may suffer during bankruptcy. Control over the capital loaned from the creditor to the debtor is one consideration shaping the provisions of such contracts, but so is the potential for bankruptcy.

BANKRUPTCY AND INSOLVENCY REFORM

Bankruptcy reform in both the United States and Britain had the potential to upset well-entrenched jurisdictional and property rights. We analyze meta-bargaining over property and jurisdictional rights by examining the fortunes of eight groups whose rights and interests were potentially disturbed by legislative reforms: banks and secured lenders, consumers, trade suppliers, workers, corporate managers and directors, state agencies, utilities, and professionals. Each had distinctive patterns of property or jurisdictional interests. Some enjoyed superior property claims, which gave them the advantage in the pre-bankruptcy race for assets and in post-bankruptcy bargaining. Others started in a weaker position. By virtue of their diverging interests in bargaining, they also had different interests in meta-bargaining. For example, secured creditors, such as banks, sought always to maintain their advantages, while those with weaker claims wanted new rules that favored unsecured creditors.[25] Professionals frequently sought to protect or expand the occupational monopolies they enjoyed over the more rewarding aspects of bankruptcy work.

These eight groups differed in their ability to mobilize politically, and consequently some were better positioned for meta-bargaining than others. Political mobilization depended on several factors: the resources available for collective action; whether or not the groups were repeat players in the bankruptcy arena; their level of organization; and the quality of the professional expertise to which they had access. How groups meta-bargained depended on their property and jurisdictional interests in combination with their level of mobilization.

We analyze meta-bargaining over bankruptcy law against the backdrop of ordinary bargaining over property rights. The two levels of bargaining are linked because one set the context for the other (it is always easier to win a game if you can set the rules). The focus on property and jurisdictional rights makes salient the conflicting interests and distributional struggles that are the essence of bankruptcy, both as a legal procedure and a work site, and thus makes it easy to address questions of power and control. It also highlights the varied and ubiquitous contracting that governs credit relationships. The firm is a nexus of relations and interests, most but not all of which are contractually specified. Ordinarily, many such interests remain latent, but when a firm becomes bankrupt even latent interests come to the surface.

We shall demonstrate that meta-bargaining and bargaining are related in complex ways. Practices of bargaining under one set of laws may precipitate efforts to change the governing rules through meta-bargaining, which in turn create new patterns in everyday bargaining. But players with great strength at bargaining in the market may not exercise equivalent strength in meta-bargaining, or vice versa. The power of banks in the market sometimes becomes a liability in the polity, just as the weakness of consumers in the market can be translated into political strength in a legislature. Meta-bargaining has its own logic, and it may not reinforce patterns of rights' distributions in the market.

Similarly, property and jurisdictional rights in meta-bargaining can become so intertwined that negotiations about either one spill over to the other. Matters of public policy that would seem entirely to be resolved within the discourse of property rights nevertheless became

---

[25] Sauer's (1994) analysis of the 1898 Bankruptcy Act sees it as marking the triumph of financial and industrial capitalist interests over agrarian interests.

confounded with the impulses of professional groups for enhancement of their jurisdictional rights. And the scope of jurisdictional rights exercised by professionals inside or outside the state are intricately affected by the magnitude or scope of property rights over which bankruptcy professionals preside.

The arena for bankruptcy reforms, therefore, did not simply magnify the scale of disputes among actors habitually struggling with each other in the everyday world of credit and debt. These bankruptcy reforms provided a social laboratory for the working out of tensions among fundamental social processes. Bargaining and meta-bargaining over property and jurisdictional rights—these are the fundamental social processes that underlie the 1978 United States Bankruptcy Code and the English Insolvency Act 1986. They tell us much about the distribution of power among corporations in the credit network. They also tell us that saving businesses through bankruptcy law occurs in a frame whose making is as complex, and often as unpredictable, as corporate reorganizations in everyday Britain and the United States.

2 Professional Innovation and the Recursivity of Law

A property rights perspective offers a new way to comprehend the balance of power among corporations and their neighbors in the credit network. Meta-bargaining over property rights, or struggles among players in the political arena, are well exemplified in the field of bankruptcy law, because the stakes are high; statutes on corporate bankruptcy have far-reaching influence on power relationships among all organizations. However, meta-bargaining outcomes rest on two related processes: the dynamics of law-making itself, and the politics of those professions trying to control jurisdictional rights. In socio-legal studies, neither statutory law-making nor the politics of professions in law-making have been well treated. Yet theoretical initiatives on both law-making and professional innovation promise to expand our understanding of meta-bargaining over rights in general, and meta-bargaining over the law of corporate reorganization in particular.

Recent neo-institutional theory offers a promising start for an account of professional influence in legal change. Neo-institutionalism has stimulated a resurgence of sociological interest in the importance of law and professions for organizations of all sorts. While law has been taken for granted and professions considered generally irrelevant in many theories of corporate power, neo-institutional perspectives situate organizations in a context defined by law and the state.

The neo-institutionalist school in organizational sociology has developed a number of key insights. Neo-institutionalists recognize that organizations depend on external resources, and that, to survive, organizations must "fit" with their environment (what they sometimes term "organizational fields"). But they diverge sharply from classic sociological ideas about how such a "fit" emerges. In particular, neo-institutionalists argue that formal organizational structure frequently serves as a symbol or signal that helps to legitimize the organization in the eyes of key constituencies (Meyer and Rowan 1977; Scott and Meyer 1991). If an organization depends on an outside group for critical resources, it will try to placate them symbolically. In the creation of suitable appearances, organizational practices often become decoupled from formal structure. Neo-institutionalists have also remarked on the uniformity or isomorphism characteristic of organizational structure. Simply put, many organizations look the same. DiMaggio and Powell (1983) argue that professions and governments play a key role in diffusing models and paradigms, and ensuring conformity with them.

Yet neo-institutional theory itself needs to be advanced along an even broader front. We propose two extensions. The first elaborates the classic socio-legal account of "law in action" and its tension with "law on the books." Although this relationship lies at the heart of much law-and-society research, socio-legal studies have focused disproportionately on the move from law on the books to law in action.[1] This paradigm must be extended to account for the *recursive relationship* between law in action and law on the books, including the shift from practice to statute. Law in action and law on the books are mutually causal, which also implies that bargaining and meta-bargaining are mutually dependent (the former concerns law in action, the latter shapes law on the books).

The second extension addresses how professions affect legal change. Research on professions gives limited attention to the relationship between internal professional dynamics and professional innovations that are institutionalized in statutes. By focusing on this connection we can elaborate our recursive model and demonstrate how professionals not only, at some points, widen the gap between law on the books and law in action, but also, at others, try to narrow that gap through statutory reform.

Together, these perspectives on the innovative involvement of professionals in law-making will bring into sharper focus the dynamics of meta-bargaining over property and jurisdictional rights in bankruptcy law reform. We shall then be in a position to offer an analytical perspective on the politics surrounding the 1978 Bankruptcy Code and the Insolvency Act 1986. We consider, first, the opportunities and limitations of current institutional theory for a satisfactory account of change in statutory law. We then complement the institutional perspective with our concept of the recursivity of law, which depends heavily on the innovative agency of professionals.

---

[1] While much socio-legal scholarship has moved beyond this classic distinction, it has often done so for the wrong reasons and with unfortunate results. While it is clear there is much law that is *not* on "the books" and is not statutory law, nonetheless that is not a good reason for ignoring the constitution of law on the books itself as a socio-legal problem.

THE LEGAL CONSTITUTION OF ORGANIZATIONAL FIELDS

Neo-institutional research frequently posits a gap between law on the books (for example, labor law) and law in action (how employment relations really work)—a distinction that resonates strongly with socio-legal scholarship.[2] How implementation diverges from statutory intent, and the legal gaps and ambiguities that invite evasions or produce unintended consequences, are recurring themes. Law-and-society studies have much to say about regulatory, judicial, and "local" law-making, but much less about statutory reforms.[3] Statutory change and the role of professions as agents of reform remain the weak hand of socio-legal research. Neo-institutionalists follow the law-and-society movement by studying the *effects* of statutes, cases, or regulations, rather than explaining their causes. Most neo-institutional research focuses on organizational fields as prime movers in organizational change (Scott 1994).[4] How organizational fields are themselves constituted remains unclear (DiMaggio 1991).

Two bodies of work exemplify the strengths and possibilities of neo-institutionalism for the understanding of statutory law-making: Fligstein's study of American antitrust law, and research by Edelman, Sutton, Dobbin and their collaborators on organizations and Equal Employment Opportunity–Affirmative Action (EEO/AA) law.

In most neo-institutionalist arguments, legal statutes are exogenous. Edelman's (1990, 1992) point of departure, for example, is Title VII of the 1964 Civil Rights Act, but she focuses on its implementation and application. Moreover, statutory enactment is considered indeterminate, for the meaning of a statute remains ambiguous and open-ended. Law

---

[2] The "gap" paradigm in law and society has begun recently to attenuate as awareness has grown of legal pluralism and the multiplicity of formal and informal legal orders that stand in some tension with formal, state law. Moreover, in a reaction against the imperative, top-down cast of state law, several scholars have argued that law is constituted at the local level by actors who blend elements from multiple legal regimes into a legal order that bears the stamp of their own agency (Merry 1990). Nevertheless it remains true that state law overwhelmingly sets the parameters of legal ordering.

[3] Political science "staked out" statutory law-making before the emergence of law-and-society research. We are indebted to Jay Casper for the observation that whereas law and society has tended to take the law as given, and then traced its effects, political scientists have problematized law's existence, but have mostly ignored its implementation.

[4] DiMaggio and Powell define organizational fields as: "... those organizations that, in the aggregate, constitute a recognized area of institutional life: key suppliers, resource and product consumers, regulatory agencies, and other organizations that produce similar services or products." (DiMaggio and Powell 1991: 64–5).

on the books, as law-and-society scholars would call it, is inescapably equivocal. Consequently, the politics surrounding the passage of laws imply little about how law affects organizations. Edelman (1992) explains that EEO/AA statutes were ambiguous, procedural, and weakly enforced.[5] It was only through organizational interpretation and application that their legal meaning was constructed. Thus organizations are not simply targets of law, but its agents, effectively displacing "legislative intent" as the source of legal meaning.

Organizations are not the only relevant actors in the process of creating legal meaning, for personnel professionals also play a key role. (See Dobbin et al. 1988; Edelman, Abraham, and Erlanger 1992, and Sutton et al. 1994.) They often decide which due process procedures and internal labor market mechanisms are needed to "comply" with EEO/ AA law. Furthermore, their "solutions" diffuse through professional networks and organizations. The role organizations and professions play in constructing the meaning of law renders problematic any sharp distinction between legal compliance and non-compliance, for what constitutes compliance emerges only out of an ongoing interaction among organizations, professionals, and courts (Edelman et al. 1991, Dobbin et al. 1993).

The legal indeterminacy of ambiguous statutes is significant not only because it makes the process of statutory enactment less decisive in explaining changes in corporate behavior. Ambiguous laws also evoke symbolic responses precisely because it is unclear what "compliance" really means. Compliance must be signalled or represented inside corporations because it cannot simply be undertaken in direct response to unambiguous laws. Ambiguity does not mean that organizations can neglect EEO/AA issues, however, for as uncertain as the law may be, it still provides a mandate for fairness in employment (Edelman 1992).

Not all neo-institutionalists stress legal ambiguity. Fligstein (1990), for example, examines the effect of antitrust law on the strategy of large US corporations. At various points, Fligstein describes antitrust law as if its import were entirely clear: certain activities were prohibited while others were not. It was equally clear whether corporations complied or not.[6] Compliance was not the negotiated, interactive process posed by the

---

[5] Edelman and Suchman (1994) pose three different reasons for uncertain law: legal ignorance, legal pluralism, and legal ambiguity.

[6] For example: "The federal government and courts closed off the opportunity for firms to continue these unfair trade practices and restraints of trade by defining legal and illegal courses of action in markets..." (Fligstein 1990: 89).

other neo-institutionalists. Consequently, the corporate response to law was not simply ceremonial or decoupled: it was embodied in basic corporate strategy (termed "conceptions of control"). With passage of the Sherman Act, the Clayton Act, and the Celler–Kefauver Act, conceptions of control shifted correspondingly. Fligstein also attends to the causes of statutory change. Since antitrust statutes are not ambiguous, he argues, it is worthwhile studying their origins. His account of the Celler–Kefauver Antimerger Act of 1950, for example, discusses the influence of the judiciary, the Federal Trade Commission, the Antitrust Division of the Justice Department, and Congress. Party politics also feature in his account of how big business arrayed against populist, anti-business forces in Congress.

Fligstein's work has recently been criticized by other neo-institutionalists. In particular, Suchman and Edelman (1996) argue that Fligstein remains uninformed by legal realism or law-and-society perspectives. In Fligstein's argument, law acts as an exogenous cause of organizational change. Its rapid diffusion provokes organizational responses that are remarkably consistent. In this view:

the law (and by extension the state) represents a uniquely explicit, authoritative, and coercive exogenous constraint on organizational behavior. The legal environment depicted by institutional theory is largely an environment of "law on the books": Rules are clear, enforcement is firm, and legal effects are substantive. (Suchman and Edelman 1996: 905)

After Congress passed antitrust legislation, for instance, Fligstein's corporate America conformed with remarkable isomorphism, compliance, and alacrity—an image that does not accord with law-and-society studies of white collar crime, regulatory compliance on the environment, or civil rights legislation on housing, employment, or voting.

Whatever the neo-institutional position on legal uncertainty, the legislative process through which a bill becomes law is important enough to attract all kinds of attention from political actors. Were statutes no more than empty forms into which legal meaning was subsequently introduced through interpretation and implementation, it seems highly unlikely that interest groups would particularly care which statutes were passed or when. Yet this is not the case. Meta-bargaining over most statutory law is fiercely contested and highly consequential. Without knowing where laws come from, the connections between law and organizations cannot be fully understood. Not only must we discern the movement from law on the books to law in action, but also the reverse—how legal practice affects law on the books. The recursive quality of law warrants its own account.

Neo-institutionalists have re-introduced professions into the encounter between organizations and law. For DiMaggio and Powell (1983: 64), "bureaucratization and other forms of homogenization emerge ... out of the structuration of organizational fields. This process, in turn, is effected largely by the state and the professions." Following Larson (1977), among others, they assert that rationalization occurs through the standardization of education and the formalization of abstract professional knowledge, both sponsored by academic specialists. Professional associations adopt and diffuse concepts, theories, and models of professional behavior. High status professionals, in particular, influence the formulation, diffusion and acceptance of norms.

Professionals and the state exert a powerful influence over which organizations exist, what organizational processes are possible, and how organizations function: "They construct and legitimate organizational goals, standardize and distribute resources (tax laws, monetary policy, support for the banking system), and develop and maintain systems of bureaucratic control (personnel policy and labor law)" (Powell 1991: 188). All these functions reflect the power and status of modern professionalism. Together with the state, professions are cast as prime rationalizers of modern society.

Most commonly in neo-institutional writings, *professions mediate institutional innovation.* Thanks to the role of professionals as intermediaries, successful organizations get imitated. Professionals observe that there is sufficient identity between the imitated and imitator to make diffusion reasonable; they "isolate and define ... properties of the model;" and "theorize the particular elements to be copied" (Meyer 1994: 36). In other words, professionals mediate legal change to their clients or employers.

Many neo-institutional studies have an affinity with Abbott's (1988) jurisdictional model of professions. Legal change is implicated in professional projects for status and control over occupational territory. Edelman et al. (1992: 75), for instance, explain much of the personnel profession's predilection for enlarging legal threats to their firms as a ploy to secure itself in the corporate firmament: "Just as the personnel profession as a whole had greater influence when it can arguably offer protection against a threatening legal environment, individual personnel managers are likely to gain prestige and power in their organizations by emphasizing their ability to protect their employers from the uncertainty of the legal environment."

Despite its many virtues, the neo-institutional account of professions needs elaboration in several respects. First, neo-institutionalists commonly treat professionals as technicians who act as conduits between law on the books and its implementation in organizations. Professionals create isomorphism, acting as if there were no principled differences within professions over which organizational forms are most appropriate, how the law should be interpreted, and who should interpret it. Indeed, neo-institutional theory generally portrays an image of homogeneous professional communities bound together through socialization, associations, and networks (see Goode 1957; Parsons 1954, 1968).[7] This picture of professionalism betrays little conflict, segmentation, or struggle within professions over their membership, ideology, codes of ethics, forms of social organization, or rewards.[8]

Secondly, statutory changes frequently alter a field of work by opening up new domains and attracting competition, including insurgent occupations seeking full professional status (Parkin 1979; Murphy 1988). Other changes will precipitate border wars among established professions—between accountants and lawyers, doctors and health administrators, clergy and psychologists. Every one of these professions, as well as some segments within them, will try to frame the legal environment and favor their knowledge and expertise. To maintain control over a jurisdiction, professions must convince others that they offer the most authoritative interpretation of a problem. This will precipitate struggles over the cognitive construction of legal change—over whose meaning-system, and whose accompanying social organization, will control a setting. The implications for neo-institutional theory are

---

[7] For an exception, see Sutton and Dobbin (1996). It was precisely this image of professional community that was upended by the critical turn in professions' literature. Freidson (1970) demonstrated that the profession of medicine masked relations of dominance and subordination. Bucher and Strauss (1963) pointed to the conflictual repercussions of specialty segments within professions. Parry and Parry (1976) demonstrated how male doctors effectively pushed female midwives out of practice.

[8] There are few of the problems of social differentiation, mass–elite struggles, interspecialty conflicts, and collective mobilization that have been identified by Auerbach (1976), Heinz and Laumann (1982), Halliday (1987), Halpern (1992), and Dezalay (1992), among others.

rather severe because the greater the conflict within professions, the less likely it is that they can be unproblematic conduits to the isomorphic adoption of legal changes.

Thirdly, the muting of professional conflict and competition tends to minimize the creativity and innovation that acute observers of professions have begun to catalogue (Powell 1993). Research on bankruptcy, for instance, demonstrates the enormous creativity of lawyers and judges in such areas as the treatment of mass torts (Sobel 1991), and strategic bankruptcy (Delaney 1989). Dezalay goes so far as to argue that professionals use innovation as a strategy for upward mobility within a profession, or in competition with other professions (Dezalay 1992). The higher the stakes, the more intensive the innovation.

Fourthly, neo-institutional research has focused on the characteristics of firms, non-profit organizations, or government agencies. The individual organization, or a population of organizations, is the object of analysis. Organizational fields, however, cannot be understood without some account of the tissue that *connects* organizations—and this involves more than networks of professionals. Whether it be interlocking directorates, credit relationships, contracts, or other legal ties, organizations are bound together into networks and fields. Legal professionals play an important role in designing, negotiating, and crafting the relationships that conjoin organizations.

Some of these difficulties arise from a neo-institutionalist focus on personnel professionals (who are relevant to employment law). Compared to accountants and lawyers, these professionals have low status. In general, "heteronomous" professions have less autonomy in the workplace, less opportunity to form collegial communities, and less ability to engage in collective action (Larson 1977). Consequently, heteronomous professions are more likely to mediate the shift from law on the books to law in action, than to create new laws. By contrast, "autonomous" professions can mobilize and intervene in statutory revisions. Governments must accommodate the most powerful of them or risk compromising passage of a bill. It is difficult to restructure American medicine, for example, without the co-operation of the medical profession. The personnel profession is heteronomous—its jurisdictional claims are relatively insecure and it has few of the institutional trappings of a profession, including a codified body of knowledge, or professional schools. Thus the neo-institutional treatment of professions reflects its treatment of law. By highlighting civil rights law, current neo-institutional theory applies most convincingly to laws that share the ambiguity of the 1964 Civil Rights

Act. By focusing on personnel professionals, the theory has its greatest relevance to less institutionalized, less prestigious, or weaker professions. We expect an entirely different profile of political influence by lawyers and judges, accountants, and high status government officials.

PROFESSIONS IN THE RECURSIVE LOOP

The most important limitation of both neo-institutional theory and law and society research, is that *their accounts are non-recursive.* Legislatures create statutes, government departments issue regulations, courts hand down decisions. Law flows from the "books" into "action." This enormously fertile area of study nevertheless remains one-sided.

The logic of our argument is displayed in Figure 2.1, which presents the recursive relation between law and organizations, and the role that professions play. The discrepancy between top (law on the books) and bottom (law in action) is a staple of law-and-society research. The right side maps out how statutory law influences organizational practice in a manner mediated by professions. This has been the primary focus of neo-institutional research: how professions interpret and apply ambiguous laws that shape organizations. But this portrayal overlooks crucial jurisdictional questions about which professions mediate between law and organizations, and the effects of inter-and intra-professional conflict.

Law in action influences law on the books. This effect is also often

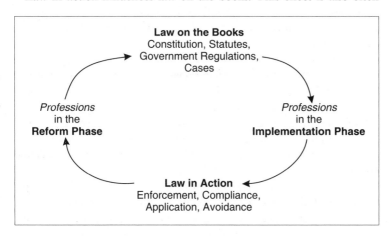

FIG. 2.1 **Law and Professions in the Recursive Loop**

mediated by professions, who because of their recognized expertise in interpreting and applying statutory law in the first place (that is, by virtue of their position on the right hand side), are frequently incorporated in statutory reform. If professionals are involved, we can anticipate dynamics that must be put under the microscope of empirical inquiry.

First, any theory of law-making that involves professionals must be alert to struggles *among* professions, or fractions of professions, for control of jurisdictions. Internal professional segmentation, by hierarchy, specialty, or any other number of potentially divisive attributes, can have major effects on the rules that structure organizational fields. Recursivity frequently occurs as a result of jurisdictional uncertainty, competition, and conflict. Law-making itself becomes an arena in which professions seek to bargain amongst themselves about relative control over work domains.

This model of professional conflict receives its fullest expression in Abbott's (1988) writings. Abbott posits a "system" of professions, each coveting the territory of its neighbors while defending its own. Knowledge is the primary medium of struggle: professions develop elaborate repertoires for deploying the knowledge bases of jurisdictional claims. Abbott's professions are driven by a territorial imperative that is not only settled in the market, but commonly involves the state and legislation.

Conflict occurs inter-professionally ("horizontally") and intra-professionally ("vertically"). Horizontal conflict results when adjacent professions contest jurisdiction. Vertical conflict occurs within professions as high status practitioners fend off the aspirations of low status practitioners (Bucher and Strauss 1963; Heinz and Laumann 1982; Halpern 1992). Conflicts over status and professional jurisdictions are a common subtext of statutory change, not only in laws directly relating to professions, but in substantive or procedural law. Yet overt conflict within and among professions does not always break out. Nor are professionals always eager to expand their domains, as we shall observe below (Karpik 1995). Thus an adequate theory of professional collective action must find those situations, and create a theory to account for the conditions in which the jurisdictional imperative occurs, and those in which it does not.

Secondly, professional creativity in legal implementation can decouple formal structure from organizational practice, or law on the books from law in action. Statutory reform begins for many reasons, but chief among them is the belief among reformers that law and practice diverge too much (and thus that professional creativity has been too successful): there may be unwanted practices which need to be foreclosed, or desirable practices which should receive legal sanction. Once begun, reform in any expert domain becomes vulnerable to the jurisdictional and status concerns of professionals.

Thirdly, in contrast to the neo-institutional focus on heteronomous professions, we will show that strong professions can not only divert law in action from law on the books, but they can mould the law which frames their own work and sets the rules for an organizational field. When professionals see an opportunity within statutory change, they can intervene in the process, deploying their own assets and jurisdictional powers. High status, high power professions have more assets to deploy and therefore will have a greater impact on law-making than low status, low power professions.

Occupational power therefore can translate into political power. Law-making provides one way to establish professional dominance, and will therefore be a forum for professional influence. Professional dominance also ensures that the mediation of legal environments is confined to particular professions, which in turn reinforces a relatively univocal interpretation of a given legal environment (Heimer 1995). Weak professional monopolies result in more fragmentary interventions in statutory reform, and the mediation of legal change or organizations will be less consistent.

Finally, while statutory reforms can stimulate professional conflict, the resulting legislation may not be a stable outcome. Contending professions may view the statutory outcome as an unsatisfactory resolution of their jurisdictional and status battles, and when they do, disputes over implementation will lead to conflicting applications, symbolic struggles, and eventually to further statutory measures. Uneasy truces engender a return to law on the books.

DIMENSIONS OF PROFESSIONAL ACTION IN THE RECURSIVE LOOP

Statutory reform engages many interests, including jurisdictional and property rights. However, to determine the interests of professionals remains a vexing task, and to show that certain actions followed from specific dispositions or motivations requires an even stronger burden of proof. Lawyers, for instance, can have at least three sets of potential interests. As *professionals*, in most models prevalent in the sociology of professions, lawyers will act rationally in their own self-interest, striving for enhanced status, power, or wealth. In the case of academic lawyers, for instance, there is great reward—intrinsic and extrinsic—from association with major new legislative innovations. As *advocates*, lawyers act on behalf of clients. In this representational role, lawyers in meta-bargaining would advance client interests, whether it be an industry association or some other collective actor.[9] As officers of the court, and as professionals with civic responsibilities, lawyers can also act in the *public interest*. If their commitment is to a more just legal system, or to a more efficient judicial system, then these ideals will shape their engagement in meta-bargaining.

Under some circumstances, these different sets of interests may coincide. A more efficacious means of saving business may also produce more work—more interesting and lucrative work—for lawyers, accountants, and insolvency practitioners. These interests may also conflict. A public interest in a more efficient administration of zero- or low-asset bankruptcies may take work away from professionals in ways either consistent with or in conflict with their client's interests. If a public good results from legal changes that also produce private goods, it becomes extremely difficult to disentangle self-interested from other-interested bases of action.

We do not therefore assume that the actions of professionals in the bankruptcy reforms can be simply attributed to one or another set of interests. We shall observe complex patterns of behavior where, sometimes, the satisfaction of private professional interests is a felicitous outcome of civic professional actions, while at other times, private professional advantage seems explicitly to drive substantive and administrative recommendations, and at other times yet again, public interests take priority over private advantage. Nevertheless, in all these cases, we affirm one central proposition: the recursive process of legal change, in bankruptcy as in many other areas of law, cannot be understood without a close analysis of professional innovation and intervention.

Whatever the dispositional theory of professional action, professional involvement varies along two principal dimensions: the scope of change and the form of intervention. These dimensions mark out how professionals affect the shift from law in action to law on the books.

---

[9] Of course, in serving their clients' interests, lawyers would be indirectly serving their own. But insofar as they meta-bargained, they would be representing someone else, not themselves.

The Scope of Change

Professional power and innovation in statutory reform can produce change at three levels: jurisdictional fields, organizational fields, and legal fields.

Change in *jurisdictional fields* occurs when statutory reforms reconfigure the professional and occupational division of labor. When one profession can simply exclude another without statutory intervention, jurisdictional reapportionment occurs within the market. More commonly, however, professions seek a legal mandate to secure a field of work as their exclusive domain, and so they meta-bargain. Many legislative initiatives by professionals have jurisdictional change as an outcome, if not always as a primary intent.

Change in *organizational fields* occurs when a new class of organizations is formed; when organizations are internally restructured in systematic ways; or when one class of organizations transforms into another (DiMaggio and Powell 1983; Halliday, Powell and Granfors 1993). In the case of bankruptcy law, we look less to changes within organizations than to *relational changes in the field as a whole*, particularly when law alters the balance of power among organizations. Since we consider organizational fields in terms of credit relations, we observe change when the claims of creditors such as banks or the state are modified in systematic ways.

Professional action may produce an even broader impact when it alters the basic principles that order a *legal field* (Bourdieu 1987). A legal field consists of a coherent body of law—cases, statutes, regulations, binding conventions—and the social relations that constitute and surround it. For our purposes, bankruptcy law constitutes such a field, for it consists of a distinct body of law that is served by professionals who systematically practice in specific institutions. Redefinition of that legal field occurs when a new doctrine radically alters its breadth, draws in new practitioners, forces change in the social arrangements of practice, and the like. The shift from punitive to rehabilitative doctrines of bankruptcy offers one example, as does the related move from company liquidation to corporate reorganization.

The Character of Intervention

The shift from law in action to law on the books also varies by the goal of statutory reform. For one type of professional intervention, the legislative process represents *statutory confirmation*. Professionals in everyday practice create new techniques and devices—academics and judges create rules of procedure. Professionals involved in reform may try to formalize these and institutionalize them in statutes. In this process, professionals confirm in statutes techniques already operating in practice.

For another set of changes, professionals engage in *statutory invention*. Here the statute itself institutes change which has been conceived in the expert, consultative process. Royal commissions, congressional subcommittees, departmental inquiries all permit professional experts to define problems and invent solutions (Kingdon 1984). They expect that new legal measures will alter practice so as to resolve the "problem." Innovation occupies a much more integral role in this second case.

The third set of changes are primarily reactive and take the form of *statutory sanction*. Statutes plug loopholes and prohibit existing abuses. In contrast to statutory invention, statutory sanctions act by negation, though even sanctions can involve inventiveness. Creating appropriate sanctions, after all, is a time-honored response by government in its ongoing contest with those who evade the law.

In combination, these two dimensions of scope and innovation form a matrix in which professionals complete the recursive loop (Table 2.1).

TABLE 2.1:   **Professional Innovation in the Constitution of Fields: Bankruptcy Law Reforms in the United States and England**

	Statutory Invention	Statutory Confirmation	Statutory Sanction
Legal Fields	1. Wrongful Trading (UK)	2. Cramdown (US) Floating Charge (UK)	3. Title Shopping (US)
Part II	*Chapter 6*	*Chapter 4*	*Chapters 4, 10*
Organizational Fields	4. State preferences (UK, US)	5. Retention of title (UK) Worker benefits (UK, US)	6. Utilities (UK, US)
Part II	*Chapter 5*	*Chapter 7*	*Chapter 5*
Jurisdictional Fields	7. Bankruptcy Courts (US)	8. Insolvency practitioners (UK)	9. Unqualifed practitioners (UK)
Part III	*Chapter 10*	*Chapters 8, 9*	*Chapter 9*

Bankruptcy reforms in the 1970s and 1980s shifted power in *organizational* fields by changing the rules under which market actors[10] played at the extreme as well as in the ordinary course of business activity. Professionals and professions occupied a strategic position to exert wholesale influence on the constitution of organizational fields. Table 2.1 summarizes a range of legal doctrines, devices, and organizations which exemplify the scope of professional innovation in the process of statutory change. Of course, not all of these emanated solely from professionals, although the professions were heavily invested in each. Table 2.1 also effectively summarizes the organization of this book. The reforms in legal and organizational fields are treated in Part 2, on the reconstitution of property rights among creditors and debtors. The reforms in jurisdictional fields, and their relationships to the administration of bankruptcy inside the government and within markets for professional services, are discussed in Part 3.

We shall argue that the 1978 Bankruptcy Code and the Insolvency Act of 1986 substantially altered the legal environment for organizations in markets. They institutionalized new forms of judicial administration, new professions, new sanctions, and new concepts of practice. They altered the balance of power among organizations by shifting discretion to debtors or weakening the influence of secured creditors. Legal reforms altered the property rights of debtors and creditors. They limited the rights of the state and sharply curtailed the de facto powers of utility companies.

Law must therefore be viewed as involving a dynamic tension between law on the books and law in action. Instead of treating law in action as a deviation from law on the books, we need to problematize law on the books as a response to law in action. The call for statutory change presupposes a problem with existing law, or reflects a goal that legislators believe can be achieved by new laws. Because there is delay in the courts, because jury awards appear excessive, because the health system doesn't adequately cover health needs, and because bankruptcy law seemed to hasten corporate liquidations, statutory and regulatory amendments are commonplace.

The constitution of organizational fields through law is a recursive process. Sociologists of law and organizations rightly focus on the

---

[10] By "actor," we denote entities, be they individuals, groups, or organizations, which act or behave in pursuit of goals. Thus, we speak of corporate actors, individual actors, bureaucratic actors, and so on.

distortions and unintended consequences that flow from print to practice. But professional groups are often Janus-faced—widening the gap between statute and action even as they find new ways to narrow it again. Sometimes these groups differ: professionals on the leading edge of practice open up new deviations from law on the books, while those in the academy and professional associations use their expertise to close the gap.

The recursive process rests heavily on professionals' capacity to construct the problems that eventually result in legal change. Legal and accounting professionals are strategically placed to formulate organizational problems because they are closely engaged in the practices from which problems derive. Because professionals are knowledge specialists, their expertise extends to the conceptualization and presentation of financial and legal information. Corporate balance sheets and accounting measures are symbolic expressions that project carefully cultivated images to investors (Carruthers and Espeland 1991). Lawyers, too, can make a persuasive case and craft "facts" to exemplify a point of view.

Resolution of the problems that professionals have helped construct frequently depends upon their own ingenuity. Professional creativity in the shift from law on the books to law in action is well documented. A measure of professional success is the facility of lawyers or accountants to circumvent new laws, or better yet, their ability to give laws an unexpected twist. This process of professional subversion is reflected in tax accountants' flair in using the letter of tax law against its spirit (Whelan and McBarnet 1990), or in the creativity of corporate lawyers who found that the bankruptcy code could be used as a weapon in labor negotiations (Delaney 1989). Professional creativity in the application of law, therefore, may be viewed as a primary stimulus to legal change, not because it advances the purposes of the law-makers, but because it exacerbates the separation between legislative purpose and everyday behavior.

If professional creativity drives a wedge between law on the books and law in action, professional innovation is also key to its solution. Like the mergers and acquisitions lawyers of the 1980s, who loaded corporations with debt and then restructured them as newly minted bankruptcy lawyers in the 1990s, professionals get to spread the disease and then preside over its cure. This view of professions and law-making is consistent with Stinchcombe's (1993) belief that studies of organizations, like those of law in action, have been unduly concerned with "variations from the mean," or deviations from formal structure. By focusing on informal and non-official patterns of behavior, organizational studies have taken for granted what makes informality possible—the formal structures that anchor the contours of action.

Legal ambiguity depends not only on the factors Edelman (1992) identifies, but derives from the recursivity of law. Professional creativity renders law on the books ambiguous. Those who exploit the equivocality of law, who use it in unanticipated ways, are agents of ambiguity who make it uncertain how practice will follow from law on the books. But professional creativity also figures on the other side of the loop, in the shift from law in action to law on the books. There, it can operate to clarify and extend law, to close loopholes and to sanction unexpected abuses. Recursivity means that law is not static, and its ambiguity fluctuates, subject to the effects of professional creativity on both sides of the recursive loop.

Bankruptcy reforms precipitated struggles over both property rights and jurisdictional rights. Jurisdictional struggles can have substantive effects on law and administration. Consequently, the redistribution of power among organizations occurs in two places. One concerns direct meta-bargaining among the primary actors with property rights interests—the creditors, debtors and other property owners concerned about corporate failure and reorganization. The other, less direct, location involves professions, whose contests for work and jurisdictional rights leave indelible prints on legal administration and the division of labor. Construction of law will frequently be a by-product of professional jurisdictional struggles. Thus the laws devised to treat financially distressed organizations reflected both interest group politics and the accommodations that professionals made to each other, their clients, and the state.

Professions are not, however, the only players in financial law reform, and often are not the most important. They face the power of the banking industry, the mobilization of unions, the interests of government and civil service departments, the complaints of consumers, not to mention corporate directors and business associations. Meta-bargaining over bankruptcy law therefore presents a vantage point to view political struggles among actors with very different sorts of resources and modes of political mobilization. The 1978 Bankruptcy Code and the Insolvency Act 1986 reveal not only the stratagems of professions, but also the limits of professional influence when confronted with the force of the Confederation of British Industry or the American Bankers Association, with the invisible maneuvering of the major London clearing banks or the alliances between powerful Senators and cabinet ministers, with the inside influence of the Department of Trade and Industry, or with the political imperatives of the Conservative party.

Meta-bargaining opens a Pandora's box of political interests. Our perspective takes seriously the "technicians" who operate inside legal institutions; we show how legal doctrine and devices take on a life of their own that constrains the range of policy options; and we shall indicate how legal innovation gives technical specialists a hand in law-making. Meta-bargaining opens up new opportunities for legal work and innovation that continues to alter the organizational balance of power.

3 The Structure of Influence in Bankruptcy Law-making

Political influence in law-making arrays along two dimensions. Law-making has a *temporal structure*: it unfolds along a time line. At first blush, this observation appears obvious to the point of triteness. Closer examination, however, reveals that how events unfold through time produces opportunities and introduces constraints that variously benefit those actors with the power to set and unset agendas. Time is a resource that can be manipulated by prolonging a reform cycle or speeding it up, by widening or narrowing agendas, by adding or subtracting stages, or by including or excluding participants at different moments.[1]

Law-making also has a *political* structure: it configures political actors in ways that broaden or narrow the range and profiles of interests brought to bear on issues in the political arena. The political structure emerges from negotiations among actors who seek access to the decision-making process, between actors that have conflicting or coinciding interests, among civil servants, government agencies, legislators, and private organizations, and between experts and generalists. The power to configure those political interests significantly determines both the form and content of the outcomes.

This chapter examines the interplay of temporal and political structures in the reform of bankruptcy law. We begin by sketching a general macro-economic context that itself framed the terms of debate and set the range of options available to English and American lawmakers. Holding this particular historical moment constant, we present some influential social science theories that seek to explain which actors have the highest probability of coming out ahead, and which political and economic struggles are most likely to dominate on the road to statutory enactment. With these economic and sociological contexts in place, we outline the main events and the primary actors who crafted the 1978 Bankruptcy Code and the Insolvency Act 1986. The chapter concludes with a theoretical stock-taking on theories and structures of influence.

---

[1] For an interpretation of the bankruptcy reforms as episodes of agenda-setting, see Carruthers and Halliday (1990). More generally, see Kingdon (1984).

The past two decades has been marked in many advanced industrialized countries by a conservative political shift, particularly in the US and Britain. The governments of Margaret Thatcher and Ronald Reagan clearly reflected a broader political movement towards the right. Although Reagan gets credit (or blame) for redirecting US policy to a more conservative direction, the shift began earlier. Deregulation, for example, started under the Ford administration and was pursued vigorously by Jimmy Carter (Derthick and Quirk 1985; Campagna 1995: 171–3). Carter was also willing to let unemployment rise in order to try to reduce inflation, and his fiscal and economic conservatism was one reason he so thoroughly alienated the other more liberal Democrats in Congress (Campagna 1995: 102, 174). Public policy has changed along with the political tides. In the main, this has meant greater concern for macro-economic problems like inflation and less about unemployment. It has also led to deregulation, privatization of nationalized industry or government functions, and retrenchment if not outright dismantling of the welfare state (Mishra 1990: 18, 23; Pierson 1994). Economically, the long post-World War II period of growth came to an end during the 1970s. Productivity growth, economic growth and incomes stagnated, unemployment rose, and inflation became a serious problem. Governments have had to enact public policy in a considerably less bountiful economic environment and in a political context where distributional struggles among interest groups are consequently sharper (Glyn 1995: 19–20; Glyn, Hughes, Lipietz and Singh 1990; Krugman 1990; Rowthorn and Glyn 1990: 239).

Ideologically, conservative governments celebrate the efficiency of the private sector and the dynamic quality of capitalism. Free markets, according to the conservative argument, will eventually lead to rising incomes for everyone (thanks to the "trickle down" effect). Furthermore, the argument goes, free markets are better able to respond to consumer demands than alternatives like planned economies or regulated markets (Hoover and Plant 1989: 55–7). Free market competition entails both winners and losers, however, and so the story of the invisible hand is not always optimistic. Competitive markets reward firms that are efficient, but they also punish those that are not. Bankruptcy is the downside of competitive markets, one of the necessary costs that market advocates tend to play down. Bankruptcy involves economic dislocation because productive assets must be redeployed, and unemployed workers have to search for new jobs. The dynamism of competitive markets nevertheless entails considerable uncertainty. People are happy to celebrate market efficiency so long as the company they work for can survive and they maintain their jobs.

The social costs of highly competitive markets are sufficient to induce many governments to try to buffer or protect their citizens from some of the more extreme consequences. In his analysis of welfare states in the twentieth century, Gosta Esping-Anderson uses the term "de-commod-ification" to refer to political attempts by government to protect the standard of living enjoyed by citizens from the vagaries of the market. Social programs like unemployment insurance, for example, protect workers from suffering the full consequences of the failure of their employer.[2] Such programs also protect elected politicians from the unhappiness of unemployed voters and the social unrest engendered by mass unemployment.[3] Agricultural price supports protect farmers from instability in commodity markets. More generally, Keynesian macro-economic policies attempted to smooth out the fluctuations of the economy as a whole.

By the 1970s it seemed in both Britain and the US that Keynesian demand management policies were increasingly ineffectual. To combat unemployment, it took an ever larger fiscal boost from the public sector, and by the late 1970s both countries had to live with stagflation: simultaneous high unemployment and high inflation. Both unemployment and inflation were worse in the two countries during the 1974–1980 period compared to 1948–1973. In addition, between 1974 and 1980, economic growth rates in the US and UK were 2.2 per cent and 0.93 per cent, respectively, compared to 3.86 per cent and 3.33 per cent for the 1948–1973 period (O'Shaughnessy 1994: 90). Clearly, growth had slowed down. The American position within the international economy diminished as the US share of worldwide exports declined substantially (Krieger 1986: 116). Meanwhile, Britain sank further into the ranks of the merely medium-sized industrial economies. Yet despite worsening economic performance, public spending on social services continued to rise in both countries.

---

[2] Esping-Anderson's (1990) debt to Karl Polanyi's analysis of market society is obvious. See Polanyi (1944: 43, 73, 77, 132).

[3] Esping-Anderson goes on to argue that there are important differences between countries in how they de-commodify (and how much) in order to reduce citizens' reliance on the market for their material well-being. He distinguishes between three different regimes, and clusters the US and Britain together in the "liberal welfare state" category (Esping-Anderson 1990: 26–7, 33).

Political conservatives in both countries argued that the growth in public spending was itself a major obstacle to improved economic performance (Hoover and Plant 1989: 16, 22). In addition, once governments got into the business of providing extensive social services, healthcare, jobs, and housing, it was very difficult for political parties in a competitive democracy to avoid a bidding war among themselves that further enlarged public spending. Such programs are often popular with voters. Thus, politicians were extremely vulnerable to interest group pressures, and so, according to the conservative diagnosis, the public sector suffered from an inherent tendency to grow. Such an argument was not implausible given how much public financial support for education, old-age pensions, welfare, and unemployment insurance had grown in the post-World War II period (Glyn et al. 1990: 60–1). The conservative remedy to economic malaise involved shrinking government.

A laissez-faire economic policy seeks to free market forces, to shrink the public sector through privatization, and to lighten the hand of government by means of deregulation. In general, such changes greatly enlarge the exposure of the economy to competitive market forces. Government regulation of an industry, for example, typically restricts entry of new competitors and often suppresses price competition between firms. Government ownership of an industry or corporation also shields firms from market competition. With privatization and deregulation, competition intensifies and the possibility of insolvency grows. Economic environments become harsher, more unstable, and less certain.

Such effects are clear from the example of the US airline industry. Before deregulation in the late 1970s, the airlines were protected from competition by the regulations and policies of the Civil Aeronautics Board (CAB). There was little price competition, and entry into the industry was rare. Consequently, the airlines enjoyed a stable environment and earned steady profits. After deregulation, the airline industry became much more competitive: ticket prices and firm profits dropped, new airlines appeared, and bankruptcy rates soared (Borenstein 1992: 45–73; Joskow and Noll 1994: 380–1, 394–403). The CAB itself was eventually abolished, leaving only the Federal Aviation Administration to regulate airline safety.

Both countries pursued deregulation as part of the conservative shift, but privatization was a particularly important issue in Britain. When Margaret Thatcher came to power in 1979, nationalized industries directly employed about 1.5 million workers and constituted a substantial proportion of the total British economy. Privatization simultaneously solved the fiscal, ideological and political problems that faced the Conservative government. Thatcher, like Reagan, wanted to cut personal taxes while increasing defense spending and at least holding the line on social spending. To do so would have required massive deficits, except that large-scale privatization could bring a lot of money into the Exchequer. Selling off publicly-owned industry generated a one-time windfall that helped subsidize popular tax cuts. Nationalized industry was long a favorite Labour policy, so to privatize would also sharply distinguish Thatcher's conservative policies from those of her predecessors. Privatization served as a convenient ideological marker.

Politically, privatization hurt the public sector unions, who were among Thatcher's bitterest enemies. Publicly-owned firms rarely went bankrupt because of soft budget constraints (if they lost money, the government invariably subsidized them rather than shut them down). Once in the private sector, however, they were subject to the discipline of the market, and management could better resist the wage demands of their unionized workforces. For all these reasons, Thatcher pursued privatization vigorously, and so between 1979 and 1993, roughly two-thirds of state-owned industries were sold off to the private sector. Not coincidentally, over the same period British unions lost members and economic power (Hoover and Plant 1989: 195–6; Riddell 1994: 30).

Given a choice between high interest rates and controlled public spending to reduce inflation, or lower interest rates and higher public spending to reduce unemployment, conservative governments in the recent era generally chose the first option. Their sympathies lie more with bankers (who dislike inflation) than with workers and unions (who oppose unemployment).[4] Margaret Thatcher's government, for example, was especially committed to controlling inflation and successfully brought down the inflation rate by about one half (Martin 1992: 128, 137). Unfortunately, reducing inflation came at the expense of unemployment, which roughly tripled between the late 1970s and the early 1980s. The conservatives blamed the unions and previous government policies for causing unemployment (Glynn and Booth 1996: 320–2). Nevertheless, the priorities were clear: "Under Thatcher inflation replaced unemployment as the central target of macroeconomic policy" (Hall 1992: 91).

---

[4] Not coincidently, in most advanced capitalist countries inflation and strike activity were higher in the 1970s than in the 1980s, while unemployment was higher in the 1980s than in the 1970s (Glyn 1995). See also Hall, P. (1992: 94, 100).

In the US, the 1946 Employment Act embodied a somewhat ambivalent commitment to Keynesian doctrines (Weir 1992: 27). The Kennedy Administration followed Keynesian arguments in its commitment to a "full employment budget," even if this meant tax cuts and a budget deficit. The passage of the Full Employment and Balanced Growth Act of 1978 (also known as the Humphrey–Hawkins bill) was the last explicit affirmation of such an approach, yet the Act was virtually ignored during the last two years of the Carter Administration as the federal government allowed unemployment to rise in the battle against inflation.[5] Thanks to pressure from business and financial interests, inflation displaced unemployment as the key macro-economic problem (Weir 1992: 130–62). Later on, supply side economics replaced Keynesianism as the preferred macro-economic doctrine. Furthermore, Reagan's antipathy towards unions shifted the balance between management and organized labor firmly towards the former, and monetary policy in the early Reagan years successfully brought down inflation. Like Britain, unemployment rose in the US from an average of 4.5 per cent in the 1965–1973 period to 8.4 per cent during 1980–1983 (Krieger 1986: 123, 161; Campagna 1995: 108–9; Glyn et al. 1990: 47).

Competitive markets have been the focus of the recent conservative shift, and bankruptcy is a distinguishing feature of competitive markets. Consider the costs of bankruptcy, and indirectly of unemployment. With generous unemployment insurance benefits, the government directly bears one of the main costs of bankruptcy: worker unemployment. Every laid-off worker is going to apply for unemployment insurance or some other form of public benefit. He or she no longer pays taxes and so increases government spending while decreasing revenues. With meager unemployment benefits, or a sparse social net (or what Esping-Anderson would term low-level de-commodification), more of the costs of unemployment are born directly by the fired or laid-off workers themselves. Hence, any reduction in publicly funded benefits to the unemployed is going to lower the fiscal cost of bankruptcy. Bankruptcy also involves a political cost in the sense that, as voters in a democracy, unemployed workers become unhappy with the economic status quo. They will punish politicians electorally. Nevertheless, conservative governments are less sensitive than centrist or leftist governments to the unemployed as a political constituency.

---

[5] This is further evidence of the economic conservatism of the Carter Administration.

In general, business failure that results in liquidation of a bankrupt company entails social, economic, political and fiscal costs. A rise in unemployment is perhaps the greatest social cost, while the increased demand for social services and the loss of tax revenues together create a fiscal cost. The economic costs, of course, derive from the losses suffered by shareholders and creditors of bankrupt firms, and also are associated with the liquidation and redeployment of economic resources. All of these costs are easier to bear with a growing economy. Economic expansion supplies new jobs for the unemployed, it enlarges the tax base for government revenues, and it ensures new economic opportunities for investors and lenders. A stagnant economy, in contrast, sharpens the pain associated with bankruptcy.

Capitalist markets require some kind of bankruptcy law but the substance of bankruptcy laws can vary considerably. How bankruptcy law deals with financially distressed corporations reflects public policy choices about how to manage the costs associated with bankruptcy while encouraging economic growth. Consider the choice between a bankruptcy law that encourages corporate liquidations, on the one hand, and a law that facilitates corporate reorganizations, on the other.[6] The latter seems like a better way to encourage the retention of jobs, for liquidation of a firm leads to the layoff of all workers. According to Elizabeth Warren, one of the virtues of Chapter 11 of the 1978 Bankruptcy Code was that it encouraged reorganizations and reduced the incentive for politicians to try to bail out troubled firms: "The bankruptcy system also forces greater internalization of costs by providing a mechanism to deal with failing companies and the enormous claims against them in a manner that discourages the parties from demanding a public bailout" (Warren 1993: 365).

In the discussions leading up to the 1978 US Bankruptcy Code, John Ingraham, a Citicorp banker with considerable bankruptcy experience, spoke before the House judiciary committee. Ingraham reminded the Congressmen of the social, and ultimately political, costs of a bankruptcy law that did not work well:

---

[6] Reorganization and liquidation represent two ends of a spectrum of changes in a firm's structure and relationships, but there is sometimes a blurring of the lines between them. A reorganization frequently involves selling off or closing down unprofitable divisions, while liquidations can mean the continued operation of some part of an insolvent company under new ownership. See LoPucki and Whitford (1993*b*: 612). In England, however, a liquidation leads to the entire breakup of the firm and very rarely allows for the continuation of any part of it (although parts might be sold off as going concerns).

There's also the question of jobs, and social cost. And it seems to me that, when you present the final version of H.R. 8200 to your colleagues in the House . . . there's a very practical question that I hope some of your colleagues remember. And that is: If you look at the U.S. economy, and the expansion and contraction that takes place periodically, and the fact that some companies just don't make it, but we (banks) do try to give—at least in the financial community—a borrower, or a company that gets into trouble, a second chance. But it's very difficult, in some cases, to give them an effective second chance—which may mean that some companies, in the next business cycle, may go out of business. Particularly, if you have a cumbersome, lengthy, process. . . . And I know jobs and employment are a significant item that every congressman, every one in the United States is thinking about.[7]

By encouraging reorganizations over liquidations, even a conservative government firmly committed to free markets (and reluctant to fund generous welfare benefits) can ameliorate some of the social and economic costs of bankruptcy.[8] As Flaschen and DeSieno put it:

. . . if a nation wishes to preserve as much job security for employees as possible, its law should be designed to foster reorganizations . . . If, on the other hand, a nation wishes to encourage foreign investment as much as possible by promoting creditors' rights, its law should foster liquidations, permitting creditors relatively quick access to the assets of the financially troubled business in order to satisfy their debts (Flaschen and DeSieno 1992: 671).

Financial distress need not always lead to high unemployment, or to greater demands for social services. A reorganized firm may have to shed 50 per cent of its workforce, but that means lower unemployment than with a liquidated firm, which must lay off 100 per cent of its workers. "Thus, bankruptcy laws give large companies the opportunity to reorganize. Along with this opportunity come the hopes that creditors will eventually be repaid, tort victims will be compensated, and employees will be able to keep their jobs—all without subsidization from the taxpayer" (Warren 1993: 367). A law that facilitates reorganizations helps a government enjoy the benefits of market competition and

---

[7] *House Hearings on H.R. 8200*, p. 211.

[8] Countries for whom capitalism, mass unemployment and bankruptcy are new experiences have been mindful of the costs of liquidation. Russia's new bankruptcy law, for example, is necessary for the transition from a command-style to a free market economy. Nevertheless, it has still not been applied widely, despite the sorry state of many Russian economic enterprises. The government recognizes that rigorous application of the law would lead to many liquidations, more unemployment and further economic dislocation. See Campbell (1994: 343–95).

accommodate some of the costs without having to undertake extensive and expensive social programs.

However much shifting corporate bankruptcy law away from liquidation and toward reorganization can ameliorate the costs of bankruptcy, such a change is not without its opponents. In general, such a shift is supported by managers, employees, and shareholders, but opposed by creditors. It is the latter who may lose even more money if the reorganization is unsuccessful for reorganizations generally risk creditors' money.[9] Managers, shareholders and employees, in contrast, have little left to lose. A successful reorganization will save their jobs and investments whereas failure can make matters no worse.

Within the strictures of a conservative economic policy that sanctifies the free market, it is possible to shape a bankruptcy law in response to the costs of bankruptcy. As more and more markets become competitive, either through deregulation or privatization, insolvency and bankruptcy become increasingly common. Furthermore, as social welfare programs become more restricted, the ability of the government to soften the blow of bankruptcy diminishes. What conservative governments can do, however, is adjust the balance of bankruptcy law so as to favor reorganizations over liquidations. Although such an adjustment may hurt creditors, it can help to save jobs.[10]

THEORIES AND PROFILES OF INFLUENCE

It is one thing to realize how a bankruptcy law that favors reorganizations can help protect workers and others from economic duress, but quite another to argue that this explains how and when major changes in bankruptcy law occur. Our analysis considers the politics of bankruptcy law-making through two sets of ideas. The first asks which political actors wield influence, and the second considers how they wield that influence.

---

[9] In practice, there is no hard and fast distinction on this matter as creditors can sometimes be both secured and unsecured. If a bank loan worth $1 million is collateralized by an asset worth $500,000, then the bank's interest in risky gambles is mixed. If the gamble pays off, the bank will receive more of the unsecured portion of its debt back. If the gamble fails, however, the secured portion of the debt will be endangered.

[10] Part of the logic of reorganization, and certainly its rhetorical defense, rests on the prospect that in the long run reorganization will be beneficial to all creditors. Even if they must write off old debt, the prospect of future business may encourage them to support reorganization rather than liquidation, especially if they can obtain stronger security.

Theories of Influence

Political scientists and sociologists have generated at least four theories relevant to financial law-making—theories of financial and party dominance, and state and professional dominance. Implicitly, or explicitly, each of these pits one class of political actors against the rest and supposes that the outcomes of legislation—"who gets what," in Harold Lasswell's famous aphorism—turn on the dominance of that actor.

Financial Dominance

Political sociologists strongly influenced by Marxist thought propose that financial legislation will be a creature of the major institutions of finance capitalism—large investment, commercial or merchant banks, trading banks, insurance companies, and similar financial institutions. For these scholars, the state and political parties fundamentally dance to the tune of finance capital. This need not take the form of earlier Marxist instrumental theories of the state, in which finance capital directly controlled the state as if it were a puppet. Just as theories of corporate control distinguish between bank control, in which banks intervene often and intrusively into a company's affairs, and financial hegemony, in which banks exert a distant pressure that only becomes overt in times of crisis, so too theories of financial law-making distinguish between the universal, immediate, and definitive influence of finance capital on reform processes and more remote involvement on points of greatest threat to financial institutions. Theories of financial dominance would therefore predict a span of substantial legislative influence, ranging from a strong, virtually instrumentalist role, in which financial institutions comprehensively craft reforms, to a pattern of influence in which they intervene sparingly, but decisively, on matters of greatest moment to their long-term interests (Glasberg 1989; Kotz 1978; Mintz and Schwartz 1985, 1990).

Political Ideology

Opposed to these notions of a hidden financial hand guiding political choices is the idea that political ideology, channelled and mobilized through political parties, will prevail in "non-technical" law-making. This latter qualification matters, for it is arguable, as we shall observe below, that certain kinds of technical legislation (including bankruptcy law) fall below the horizon of party ideology and thus fail to activate its formidable forces. However, a pervasive, powerfully articulated ideology, such as that formulated by Prime Minister Thatcher, can embrace even so arcane a subject as bankruptcy. When the Conservative Party, backed by an overwhelming majority in Parliament, embraced matters such as championing privatization, down-sizing public administration, expanding corporate reorganization, defining the morality of markets, and ensuring the probity of directors, then almost any opposing political forces were bound to be vanquished. Of course, party dominance does not preclude the powerful influence of finance capital, for the Conservative Party itself represented those interests far more than the Labour Party. But it does not make the party in power the servant of financial interests, for on occasion party and financial interests will diverge, and party interests may prevail as we shall observe in the English case. A theory of party dominance, therefore, predicts that a powerful party ideology, with strong electoral support, and embracing some of the main elements of financial law-making, will dictate the outcomes. In the absence of party ideology, or its relevance to the provisions of a draft statute, the pattern of dominance will lie elsewhere.

State Officials and Agencies

Recent theories of the state contest the idea that civil servants and government agencies write legislation in due obedience to their political masters or implement legislation without regard to either the interests of civil servants themselves, or the imperatives of the agencies and institutions in which they work. State agencies and officials have interests of their own. These may coincide with those of legislators, political parties, and outside interest groups, but often they do not. If party ideology dictates down-sizing state agencies or the privatization of state functions, public officials and government agencies have powerful incentives to modify, subvert, and even block proposals that will entail loss of administrative powers, civil service jobs, or status. Moreover, public administrators develop their own perspectives about which policy works. They may have the face-to-face contact with creditors, managers, debtors, and other parties in bankruptcy that their political masters do not, whether it be the experiences of the Securities and Exchange Commission with large public companies, the Inland Revenue with long overdue taxpayers, the Department of Trade and Industry with incompetent or fraudulent directors, the judiciary with hapless small creditors, or the court registrars with unprofessional workers. It should be anticipated, therefore, that financial legislation that threatens government agencies or officials, or that presents great opportunities, will produce energetic mobilization of state officials. Moreover, to the degree that legislation actually originates and is shaped within government departments, the influence of state officials rises sharply.

Professional Dominance

Finally, technical legislation in law and finance has attributes conducive to dominance by professions. Professional influence will be at its greatest under five conditions.[11] First, professions exert greater influence when they can attain exclusive technical authority. By convincing policy-makers that an issue should be classified as the proper domain of a particular knowledge specialist, competing interpretive frames are held at bay.[12] Second, professions will be more influential when they can translate substantive policy issues into technical terms. Here the problem is less to keep other professions at bay and more to convince policy-makers that policy changes are really a technical issue that should not trouble political interest groups. It is a matter of converting a substantive issue into a technical one (Halliday 1982; 1985). Third, professions may expand their influence when they can persuade political authorities that expert recommendations embody central cultural values. Values of efficiency, freedom, preservation of life, economic growth—all grant professions some ideological cover from undue scrutiny or skeptical appraisal (Brint 1990). Fourth, professions exert greater influence when states are weak and have limited resources, or states have not yet penetrated certain policy domains, and private experts are the logical groups on which to depend. Fifth, professional power increases the greater a given profession's credibility, credentials, and capacity for political mobilization. Because bankruptcy legislation is both infrequent, seemingly non-ideological, not of great electoral interest, and highly technical, it appears to be a site particularly amenable to professional dominance.[13]

---

[11] For a more detailed account of professional influence, see Halliday and Carruthers (1993*a*).

[12] Such an exclusive grant will not always be possible, especially when complex issues clearly involve different experts. If professions cannot successfully claim exclusive authority, therefore, it is a sensible and often effective strategy to form alliances with other experts—but often these, too, are defined in contradistinction to other occupations.

[13] This proposition must be qualified historically. Bankruptcy law-making in the 19th century was closely linked to economic crises and it generated strong political interest, with significant regional differences in orientations to the law. Its political controversiality can

Each of the preceding theories focuses on the power of a particular actor or class of actors. Each new site of political contention triggers latent conflicts so that long-standing foes again march to battle along well-trodden paths using well-worn techniques. An excellent example comes from one of the few efforts by sociologists to treat law-making in a theoretically systematic way—William Chambliss's proposition that major changes in law occur in response to fundamental social contradictions. Chambliss criticizes pluralist and orthodox Marxist accounts of legal change, but follows the latter in claiming that the most central contradiction in capitalist society exists between labor and capital. Chambliss views major changes in labor law (for example, the Wagner Act of 1934) or law encouraging regional economic development (for example, Britain's Special Areas Acts of 1934, 1936 and 1937) as a reaction to capitalist contradictions (Chambliss 1993: 3–35).[14] Given the centrality of bankruptcy to market society, Chambliss's argument suggests that dramatic changes in bankruptcy law are driven by the same core contradictions within capitalism. We would expect to see a conflict between organized labor and organized business over the terms of statutory law. For instance, business liquidations through bankruptcy lead to higher unemployment, and consequently put downward pressure on wages. Declining wages are good for employers and bad for workers. Hence, labor groups ought to push for bankruptcy laws that minimize straight liquidations. Yet the contradiction of interests is not always so neat; cross-class alliances muddy the picture of a simple labor versus capital difference. For example, the workers, managers, and shareholders of an insolvent firm all share a common interest in having the firm reorganized rather than liquidated. This generally pits them against secured creditors (usually banks) rather than each other. Bankruptcy can be a highly conflictual setting, which nevertheless does not simply mirror the conflict between labor and capital.

be seen by the on-again/off-again character of law-making, which was enacted and repealed, enacted and repealed, several times during the century (Warren 1935). While the 1938 legislation took place in the wake of the Great Depression, the role of experts was much more prominent. By 1978, however, there was comparatively little economic pressure or political controversy and, under these conditions, professionals thrived. They got rather less a free hand when economic changes stimulated pressure groups to take a much closer interest in the legislation of the 1980s and early 1990s.

[14] See also chs. 2 (on criminal law), 7 (on worker safety law), and 9 (on immigration law-making).

Political conflict is also well institutionalized between conservative and liberal political parties, between consumers and businesses, and between state agencies and private financial institutions. Each of these conflicts can be triggered by a legislative change that affects commerce. They should be intensified in the field of bankruptcy law where, by definition, not all creditors can be satisfied fully. But as we have also observed in the previous chapter, legislative disturbances can also unsettle well-demarcated areas of work. Professions and occupations, with reasonably settled understandings about what occupations controlled what areas of work, can be thrown into confusion, and emerge battling over who should be in control. In other words, the latent tensions among occupations over where their boundary markers lie can suddenly break into open warfare if attacks are launched on work jurisdictions or new work jurisdictions open up. The bankruptcy legislation threatened to do exactly this, and thus we can expect that cross-cutting struggles among long-standing rivals will provide a political backdrop to the drives for dominance by finance capital, parties, state agencies, and professions.

Profiles of Influence

Influence on law-making follows two general patterns—global and targeted. On the one hand, some actors exert comprehensive influence over all facets of a given piece of legislation. They have a generalized interest in every element of a statute or group of statutes, usually because the law effectively regulates or empowers their commercial, administrative, or occupational interests. Such political actors understand the law as an integrated whole, and any change in one or another element affects the relations among all the elements. They seek some sort of equilibrium, a balancing of interests, of costs and benefits, in which no aspect of the proposed statute is irrelevant to the functioning of the whole. For example, every change of any consequence whatsoever in the Tax Code affects the Internal Revenue Service. If the entire Tax Code is subject to meta-bargaining, then no change will be irrelevant to the interests of the Government's primary tax collector.

At least three sets of actors seek a global influence on financial legislation. The first is the government department or commission, or legislative committee with primary responsibility for formulating, drafting, negotiating, and implementing a statute. The second is the occupation, or occupations, whose work depends on the size, wealth, intrinsic interest, status, and administrative organization of an occupational field. The third is any commercial, or non-profit, or governmental entity whose core interests are regulated by the legislation.

Political actors with these profiles will try to enter the reform process at the earliest stages of agenda-setting, to influence commissions or reform committees, to present comprehensive sets of submissions on all aspects of the proposed legislation, to form alliances and obtain front and back channels of communication and influence, and to remain fully engaged throughout the process until its final resolution. These actors will seek to manipulate the temporal and political structure of proceedings to the degree that their resources, and countervailing political forces permit. These are classic insider politics, frequently based on long-standing personal and professional ties among individuals who stand on opposite sides on questions—regulators with the regulated, professionals with civil servants—individuals who have had to work with each other in the past and must do so in the future. But they are also politics that require any actors' resources to be spread thinly over a very wide domain.

The great majority of political actors, in contrast, follow a more finely targeted strategy. The putative reform affects them intensely in very specific areas. Since resolution of a few issues will satisfy them, and they have no particular concern with everything else in the bill, their attitude is less systemic than particularistic. So long as an important provision here or there conforms to their interests, they care little about its ramifications across other areas of the bill.

These actors can afford to follow a quite different strategy of influence. While their concerns may warrant ongoing surveillance of the reform process, at certain key moments they mobilize swiftly and powerfully, bringing great force to bear on a narrow point. In the US bankruptcy reforms, for instance, the federal judges reserved their greatest energies until the bankruptcy bills reached the Senate, where federal judges have especially close ties to the senators who nominated them. In England, the Confederation of British Industry exploited its connections with peers in the House of Lords, to try to change provisions that adversely affected company directors. In other words, targeted influence manifests itself as both a specific target in the scope of an entire bill, and as a narrow band of time at particular moments in the reform processes. Since these actors are not responsive to arguments in favor of "package deals" or "global balancing," and because they can afford to pour enormous resources onto a narrow target, their interventions in reform processes can frustrate systemic approaches to comprehensive reforms. Irrespective of content, therefore, a fundamental tension exists between the single-interest, highly-motivated, heavily-resourced actor with a narrow target to hit and the globally-oriented, systemically-inclined, total-package solution of actors with broad policy goals.

In the following sections we present, first, a brief narrative of each reform process, and second, a more detailed accounting of the actors and their profiles of influence. We conclude by assessing the extent of influence that seems likely, given the ways that actors mobilized.

UNITED STATES

The Path to Statutory Reform

Unlike the major bankruptcy acts of the past 150 years, the 1978 Bankruptcy Code did not spring from a severe economic downturn or depression (Klee 1980). By long term historical standards, the failure rate for enterprises preceding the 1978 reforms showed none of the sharp peaks of the 1930s, late 1890s, late 1870s, or the early 1860s (see Fig. 3.1). If anything, the very long-term historical trend in business failures was downward. And while the rate increased for the twenty years from the mid-1940s through to 1965, it had actually begun to

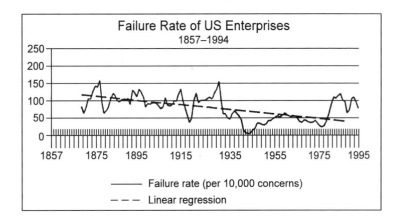

FIG. 3.1:   **Failure Rate of US Enterprises**
Sources: Statistical Abstracts of the United States (1996) and The Statistical History of the United States (1976).

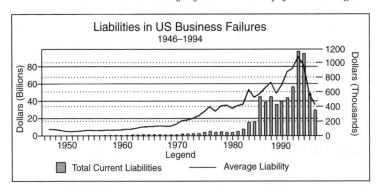

Fig. 3.2: **Liabilities in US Business Failures**
Sources: Statistical Abstracts of the United States (1996) and *The Statistical History of the United States* (1976).

decline in the decade preceding the Bankruptcy Reform Act. However, this rate is deceptive, for it masks a more relevant trend: the quite sharp increase in the average size of company liabilities in business bankruptcies, which increased some 400 per cent from 1965 to 1975 (Fig. 3.2), a threshold that was maintained at some $20 billion for the decade and then doubled again, to $40 billion of total liabilities by 1990. Even if the country as a whole were not in depression, therefore, the bankruptcy system experienced growing pressure due to the expanding liabilities of businesses in default and increasing pressure on creditors in the ten years preceding the Act. Growing economic pressure was punctuated with some highly visible corporate failures. The government's bailout of Chrysler and the reorganization of the Pennsylvania Central Railroad, for instance, demonstrated that business failure could reach the most irreproachable of large, blue-chip companies. Coincidentally, it also drew attention to the creaky machinery of bankruptcy law and administration that seemed increasingly out of touch with the times, or with the demands of mega-business failures.

Within the small community of bankruptcy specialists, opinions differed significantly over the maladies of the bankruptcy system. For those collections' lawyers, trustees, and bankruptcy judges who comprised the so-called "bankruptcy ring"—collecting debts, liquidating companies, managing small bankruptcy estates—the current system worked tolerably well. Yet even many of these could echo the litany of complaints that came from law professors, practicing bankruptcy lawyers, credit companies and financial institutions, and judges about many aspects of bankruptcy law and practice. As we shall observe in later chapters, all the players in the bankruptcy field complained about the high priority in the recovery of assets from bankrupt companies that bankruptcy law gave to the Internal Revenue Service. The Securities and Exchange Commission (SEC) bore the brunt of charges that its heavy hand in large corporate reorganizations did more harm than good. Large credit institutions and corporate bankruptcy lawyers bemoaned the confusion among three different chapters (X, XI, XII) that governed corporations in bankruptcy; they vented frustration over confusion in jurisdictions of the court, and the ensuing problems of interminable litigation as parties to bankruptcy appealed from the derivative, low-prestige, limited-powers bankruptcy court to the high-status federal district courts. Elite lawyers, law professors, and judges pointed at grey areas of bankruptcy practice, where favoritism, benefits to lawyers rather than clients, and the most rudimentary of legal skills cast a cloud over the entire bankruptcy field. Said Congressman Butler, himself a practicing lawyer who became the Republican leader in the House subcommittee that handled the bankruptcy bills:

[T]he bankruptcy system was not working very well. It was run by a bankruptcy ring of not very qualified lawyers and judges, just a bunch of guys getting up there and trading it off with one another, using up all the assets to take care of attorneys's fees and trustees' fees...[a] process that was not quick, and did not lend itself to quick reorganization and salvage. It was more of a discharge operation that anything else.... The system was oppressive and not really accomplishing much for the individual debtor.[15]

While many of these issues were being canvassed during the 1960s by professional groups, the genesis of the United States Bankruptcy Commission came from complaints from constituents to Senator Burdick of North Dakota. Although individual debtors supposedly received a discharge of their debts from the bankruptcy courts, and therefore could no longer be pursued by creditors, consumer finance companies had found a loophole which enabled them to keep pressing debtors for repayment. At the time, Senator Burdick was chair of the subcommittee of the Senate Judiciary Committee that handled bankruptcy. He had discussions with academic and other experts about the various deficiencies of an Act that had not been comprehensively reformed since 1898—problems of bankruptcy administration, the functioning of bankruptcy referees, as well as the difficulties facing consumer debtors. Since Sena-

[15] US Interview 91:04.

tor Burdick was "dissatisfied with the piecemeal approach to corrective legislation," those he consulted concurred that it would be more satisfactory to undertake a comprehensive appraisal of bankruptcy law that could be pursued in a governmental Commission.[16]

Following hearings conducted by Burdick's subcommittee in 1968, Congress established The Commission on the Bankruptcy Laws of the United States (the Bankruptcy Commission) to investigate practices and recommend changes in the content and administration of individual and corporate bankruptcy law. The Commission, which included nominees by the President, the Senate, and the House, had substantial resources, and access to the best bankruptcy practitioners and academics in the country. It canvassed widely, not only consulting such specialty organizations as the National Bankruptcy Conference, the National Conference of Bankruptcy Referees, and the Commercial Law League, but also holding public hearings, conducting substantial surveys, and deliberating for some forty-five days (see Table 3.1 for a summary of the legislative steps).[17] In the meantime, the Brookings Institution published a major report in September 1971, which excoriated the personal bankruptcy system and made a startling proposal for the establishment of a new government agency, the US Bankruptcy Administration, to remove small-scale bankruptcies from the hands of the "bankruptcy ring" (Stanley and Girth 1971).

The Commission Report, which was presented to Congress on 30 July 1973, came in two parts. The first systematically reviewed the main components of bankruptcy law and administration, both for consumers and companies. It made recommendations about the restructuring of the bankruptcy system; it introduced innovations in consumer bankruptcy; and it provided new mechanisms for corporate reorganizations. Moreover, it also restructured the delivery of legal services in bankruptcy by providing substantial incentives to induce "the best and brightest" corporate lawyers to enter the bankruptcy field. Most controversially, the recommendations proposed a radical reformation, and

[16] US Interviews 91:02, 92:01. For accounts of the legislative process by those involved in it, see Kenneth Klee (1980), who was minority counsel for the House Subcommittee; Caldwell Butler (1980), who was the Republican minority leader in the House subcommittee; Vern Countryman (1985), who was integrally involved as an academic observer from the Commission through the legislative debates; and Peter Rodino (1990: 329–38), former chair of the House Judiciary Committee, and Alan A. Parker, former General Counsel, Committee on the Judiciary, House of Representatives.

[17] See *Report of the Bankruptcy Commission*; US Interviews 91:04; 92:01; 96:03.

TABLE 3.1:   **A Time-line of the US Bankrutpcy Reform Act of 1978**

Commission Stage	1968	Senate subcommittee hearings to establish a commission to study the US bankruptcy laws.
	July 24, 1970	Commission on the Bankruptcy Laws of the United States established by an act of US Congress.
	July 30, 1973	Commission files its report with Congress.
Congress	1975	Bankruptcy bills introduced to House (H.R. 31 and H.R. 32) and the Senate (S. 235 and S. 236).
	February 1975– May 1976	House Subcommittee on Civil and Constitutional Rights engages in over 35 days of hearings on the bankruptcy bill and Senate Subcommittee on Improvements in Judicial Machinery holds 21 days of hearings.
	July 11, 1977	Clean, revised bill H.R. 8200 introduced to the House to supersede old bankruptcy bills.
	October 27, 1977	House begins debate on H.R. 8200.
	October 28, 1977	Congressman Edwards temporarily removes H.R. 8200 from House consideration.
	Febrary 1, 1978	House resumes consideration of H.R. 8200. The House passes H.R. 8200.
	February 8, 1978	H.R. 8200 is sent to the Senate.
	September 7, 1978	The Senate considers S. 2266. With a few amendments, it is passed and offered as a substitute for H.R. 8200. The Senate then requested a conference with the House to work out differences.
	September 28, 1978	The House passes an amended form of H.R. 8200 worked out as a compromise between House and Senate. Chief Justice of the United Statses, Warren E. Burger lobbies to prevent passage by the Senate.
	October 5, 1978	The Senate passed the bill with a list of amendments.
	October 6, 1978	The bankruptcy reform bill passed the House.

Continued

Continued

October 25, 1978	Bill is transmitted to the White House. Chief Justice of the United States urges a presidential veto.
November 6, 1978	President Jimmy Carter signs the bankruptcy reform bill into law.

upgrading, of bankruptcy courts and judges. The recommendations were accompanied by a draft bill.

Congressmen Don Edwards and Charles Wiggins, who were members of the Commission and of the House Judiciary Subcommittee on Civil and Constitutional Rights, introduced the Commission Bill in 1973 at the same time as Senator Burdick introduced it in the Senate. Since the House and Senate Committees were heavily preoccupied by the impeachment hearings of President Nixon in 1973, and subsequently the Voting Rights Act, the Commission Bill, in the form of H.R. 31, did not come back to Congress until 1975. In the intervening eighteen months, the respective House and Senate Committees appointed lawyer-staffers to examine carefully the Commission Bill and its relationship to a parallel and "competing" bill, H.R. 32, which had been drafted by the bankruptcy judges, who had been excluded— reportedly by the Chief Justice—from participation on the Bankruptcy Commission.[18]

Extensive public hearings—thirty-five days in the House and twenty-one days in the Senate—took place on the Commission and bankruptcy judges' bills from February 1975, through May 1976. A large number of organizations and individuals participated, but lawyers and judges dominated the deliberative process, particularly those identified with the National Bankruptcy Conference and the National Conference of Bankruptcy Judges, the two organizations whose members had a universal interest in all provisions of the draft legislation.

During the hearings, some doubts were raised about whether it would be constitutional to elevate bankruptcy judges and significantly strengthen bankruptcy courts without giving them the full status of federal courts governed by Article III of the United States Constitution—a move later to be fiercely contested by the federal judges themselves. Judge Weinfeld of the Bankruptcy Commission had already signalled the sentiments of the federal judiciary when he filed a minority

---

[18] US Interview 92:01; Klee 1980: 943–4.

report, or dissent, alongside the Bankruptcy Commission Final Report. The Federal Judicial Conference amplified this dissent during Congressional testimony. A caucus of legal experts was asked to advise the legislators on the constitutionality of a bankruptcy court with much enhanced powers and jurisdiction. Although they did not reach a consensus, their views were sufficient to persuade the House Judiciary Committee that there was "substantial doubt" that a greatly strengthened bankruptcy court would be constitutional, if it were *not* constituted as an Article III court (Klee 1980: 944–5; Countryman 1985: 7–8).

Among reformers, it made no sense for two rival bills, which agreed on the broad contours of change, to continue to divide reformist forces. House legislators exerted pressure for the National Bankruptcy Conference and the National Conference of Bankruptcy Judges to settle their differences. Consequently, Congressman Edwards instructed the subcommittee staff to prepare a compromise bill that bankruptcy experts, including members of the National Bankruptcy Conference and the Bankruptcy Judges, studied over Christmas of 1976. The compromise bill, introduced as H.R. 6 on 4 January 1977, was further circulated among bankruptcy lawyers, judges, and law professors. Following some intermediate permutations, a revised bill, H.R. 8200, passed through the House Judiciary Committee and onto the floor of the House for debate, only to confront a relatively hostile amendment from Congressmen Danielson and Railsback, who led a rump group opposed to the elevation of the formerly derogated bankruptcy judges and courts to the status of Article III federal courts. Following defeat on this integral feature of the reforms, Congressman Edwards pulled the bill off the floor (Klee 1980: 949).

Action then shifted to the Senate, where Senator DeConcini, Chair of the Subcommittee on Improvements in Judicial Machinery, Senate Judiciary Committee, introduced in late October 1977 a bill, S. 2266, which closely paralleled the House bill, albeit with some important differences. Both House and Senate subcommittees held further hearings at which the status of the bankruptcy courts dominated proceedings. The Federal Judicial Conference made forceful representations, all to oppose the "dilution" of the status and power of federal judges if bankruptcy judges and courts were upgraded to Article III standing. With his forces re-marshalled, Congressman Edwards took H.R. 8200 back onto the House floor to confront again the Danielson–Railsback amendment. This time the Amendment was soundly defeated, 146 votes for and 262 votes against, thus clearing the way for the Bill to be sent on to the Senate.[19]

With time running short, the Senate Judiciary Committee adopted an amended S. 2266 and passed it on to the Senate Finance Committee to resolve some outstanding questions. The bill finally adopted by the full Senate in late September 1978 was much more sympathetic to the federal judges than the House version, and it differed in several other substantive areas. The House and Senate moved quickly to resolve the differences, with the most important compromise coming in the agreement that the new bankruptcy courts would not have Article III status, but would have substantially greater jurisdictional powers as adjuncts to federal district courts, and their judges would serve for lengthy terms following appointment by the President.[20]

Even this retreat from fully upgrading the bankruptcy courts was too much for the Chief Justice of the United States Supreme Court. He entered a round of intense lobbying by telephone, calling Senators DeConcini and Wallop, who were Senate leaders of the bill, and eventually persuading Senator Strom Thurmond to put a "hold" on the bill. Senator DeConcini refused to negotiate with the Chief Justice, who reportedly had called the Senator and "yelled at me that I was irresponsible" and that he, the Chief Justice, would "go to the President and get him to veto this." In the following week, intense political negotiation brought the Attorney General, Griffin Bell, to meet with House and Senate managers of the legislation, while various interest groups—the commodities industry, the railroads, the Securities and Exchange Commission, and the consumer finance industry—sought last minute concessions (Countryman 1985: 9–11).[21]

With adjournment of the 95th Congress scheduled for 14 October 1978, prospects for passage became progressively bleaker. Eventually the deadlock was broken when someone close to the bill asked David Rockefeller to intervene and press Senator Thurmond to yield. He did, and Thurmond agreed to let the bill go forward. As time ran out, Congressman Edwards was given an ultimatum by Senator DiConcini: accept the Senate version of the bill as it was, or the bill would die in the 95th Congress. Edwards agreed, the bill went forward in the House, and was sent to the White House for President Carter's signature.

---

[19] US Interview 92:01; Klee (1979).
[20] US Interview 92:01; Countryman 1985: 7–10.
[21] *Washington Post*, 3 and 7 Oct. 1978.

At this penultimate moment, the strongest foes of the Bankruptcy Reform Bill, the Securities and Exchange Commission, who had lost considerable control over corporate reorganizations, together with Chief Justice Burger, made one last stand. Both pressed the President to exercise his pocket veto. By doing nothing, the bill would fail and the entire legislative process would need to begin anew in a future session of Congress. According to sources, perhaps apocryphal, the President called his long-time colleague, Attorney-General Griffin Bell, from Camp David for advice minutes before midnight on the final day the bill could be signed into law. The President asked Bell what he should do. Bell replied that so many people had worked so hard on it, the President should go ahead "and sign the damn thing." And so he did.[22]

The Agents of Reform

The primary players who shaped and crafted the 1978 Bankruptcy Code ranged from powerful groups of professionals, to selected interest groups, government agencies, and the legislative committees and their staffers.

The Bankruptcy Commission

All members of the Bankruptcy Commission had been, or still were, practicing lawyers and judges. Of the three appointed by the President, Harold Marsh, chairman of the Commission, was an experienced corporate creditors' lawyer from California; Professor Charles Seligson, of New York University Law School, was styled by one academic colleague as "the dean of the bankruptcy bar;" and Wilson Newman was a lawyer from New Jersey. Senate Burdick, himself, sat on the Commission, together with Senator Marlow Cook from Kentucky. The two appointees from the House were the majority leader in the House Judiciary Subcommittee that would eventually spearhead the legislation, Representative Don Edwards from California, and his Congressional colleague, also from California, Charles Wiggins, who was the minority leader in the House subcommittee. Congressman Edwards was an ex-FBI agent with no experience of practice in bankruptcy law. The Chief Justice appointed two federal judges, Hubert Will from Chicago, who had no special expertise in bankruptcy, and Edward Weinfeld from New York, who had substantial experience on the bench in bankruptcy law.

---

[22] US Interviews 91:02; 92:01.

Who was *not* appointed to the Commission prefigured later political struggles over the bankruptcy courts. Senator Burdick had hoped that a bankruptcy referee or judge would be appointed to the Commission alongside a federal circuit court judge. However, the Chief Justice resolutely resisted the presence of a bankruptcy judge on the Commission, and consequently the bankruptcy judiciary, with arguably the strongest direct stake in bankruptcy administration, was effectively frozen out of the inner circle—a move that made them "very angry" and pushed the bankruptcy judges later to draft a rival bill that did reflect their interests.[23]

Although the Bankruptcy Commission consulted widely, and held public hearings in several cities, professionals dominated the submissions (see Table 3.2). They also dominated investigations by the Commission's staff. The Commission ordered several studies and mailed questionnaires on the principal items on the Commission's agenda to approximately 100 organizations and individuals.[24] Another questionnaire on business bankruptcy issues went to approximately fifty attorneys and law professors.[25]

The Commission organized a one day conference of economists, and consulted extensively with three associations of lawyers and judges—the National Conference of Referees in Bankruptcy, who formed a liaison committee to work with the Commission; the National Bankruptcy Conference, which consulted extensively with the Commission; and the bankruptcy committees of the American Bar Association. The Commission received formal and informal reports from the principal organization that represents unsecured creditors—the National Association of Credit Management.[26] The Commission consulted widely with legal and business academics on everything from business reorganization to the role of the SEC in business bankruptcies and the relation of the Bankruptcy Act to the Internal Revenue Code. Some twenty scholars undertook small research projects at the behest of the

---

[23] US Interview 91:02.

[24] Studies included those on the organization and costs of bankruptcy administration in the United States, (undertaken by the Rand Corporation); the operation of the dischargeability legislation of 1970; the impact of wage garnishment on consumer bankruptcy rates; the relationship between state bankruptcy rates and the bad debt losses suffered by consumer creditors; the effects of Chapter XIII as compared to straight non-business bankruptcies in Tennessee; a study of business failures; and a study by The Institute for the Future on the relationship between the social environment and bankruptcy law.

[25] *Report of the Bankruptcy Commission*, pp. xi–xiii.

[26] *Ibid*, pp. xiii–xiv.

TABLE 3.2 **Submissions to the Public Hearings held by the Bankruptcy Commission**[a]

State
General Accounting Office
Administrative Office of US
  Courts
Department of Transportation

Labor
United Auto Workers
United Steel Workers of America
AFL–CIO

Judiciary
National Conference of
  Bankruptcy Judges
Judicial Conference of the US

Financial Industry
Dearborn Federal Credit Union
American Federation of
  Community
Credit Unions
California Bankers Association
Bank of America
Walter E. Heller and Company

Professionals
National Association of Chapter
  XIII Referees
National Legal Aid and Defender
  Association
lawyer/trustee (numerous)
lawyer (numerous)
Commercial Law League
National Conference of Referees in
  Bankruptcy
law professor (numerous)
Dr. Hempel, Washington
  University (economist)

New York Bankruptcy Lawyers
  Bar Association
Boston Legal Assistance Project
Chicago Legal Aid Bureau
Committee on Bankruptcies and
  Reorganization, Chicago Bar
  Association
Dr. Yeager, School of Commerce
  and Finance, St. Louis
  University

Consumer
National Consumer Law Center

Credit Organizations
Credit Counselling Centers, Inc
National Association of Credit
  Management
Fireside Thrift Company
Minnesota Association of
  Collection Agencies

Other
Brookings Institute
Mrs. Connelly
National Council of Higher
  Education Loan Programs
New Jersey Board of Higher
  Education

[a] *Bankruptcy Commission Report*: pp. vii–xi

Commission. All these activities were orchestrated by a staff of twenty-seven members under the direction of Frank Kennedy, a law professor at the University of Michigan, and an expert in bankruptcy law.[27] Through its personal and organizational networks the Commission effectively had access, opined a senior Congressional staffer, to "every bankruptcy brain in America."[28]

Compared to its British counterpart, it is notable that the American Commission included no direct representatives of either the financial industry or corporate debtors, or for that matter, of workers or consumers. Yet commissioners and later reform participants did not perceive it to reflect any distinctive ideological hue. The Commission's recommendations, themselves, have been characterized as pro-debtor. Most obvious from the composition of participants is the overwhelming dominance of lawyers and judges and the extensive mobilization of technical expertise. The Commission's recommendations can therefore be expected to bear the imprint of professional and pragmatic values, as well as differences among professionals. At the very least, the heavy investment of legal expertise guaranteed that matters of work jurisdiction would be integrally connected to substantive distributive reforms.

While the Commission's consultative style blurred the boundaries, its composition reflected the difference, between the center and periphery of bankruptcy practice. Inside the Commission were law professors from distinguished universities, leading practitioners, and federal judges. Outside the Commission lay the bankruptcy referees, the collections' lawyers and the bankruptcy ring. A penumbra of specialist organizations consulted closely with the Commission, but here, too, there were important differences. The National Bankruptcy Conference, a small organization of elite practitioners, professors, and judges, not only made formal submissions to the Commission, but several of its members served as commissioners or staff. Other judges' and lawyers' organizations were involved, but they possessed less status or their interests were too nakedly self-serving. Noticeably absent at this stage was the formal input of the Judicial Conference of federal judges, perhaps because it expected its views would be well represented by its two members on the Commission.

The Commission effectively set the agenda for the political revision of the Bankruptcy Code. The general philosophy that underlay the Act,

---

[27] *Report of the Bankruptcy Commission*, pp. xiii–xiv.
[28] US Interview 91:05.

which stressed rehabilitation, efficient and expert judicial administration, high quality legal professionals, and a limited role for the state, can be found in the Commission's Report. Major innovations in the Act are prefigured in specific recommendations for a combination of the three previous reorganization chapters into one single chapter; greater reorganization powers to corporate management (debtors-in-possession), coupled with stronger protections for secured creditors; a limit of the state's priority for unpaid taxes; a new incentive structure for professionals; and a new approach to judicial staffing and administration.

The Congressional Committees

Lawyer-legislators with varying degrees of practical experience occupied all seats in the House and Senate subcommittees which managed the legislation. Here party ideology might have inserted itself, for Don Edwards and Robert Drinan on the House side had impeccable voting records on liberal issues and identified clearly with the small debtor.[29] By contrast, Congressman Butler, who succeeded Charles Wiggins as minority leader, was perceived as a "very conservative Republican" (though he voted for Richard Nixon's impeachment). Nevertheless, while all the actors can point to one or another aspects of the various bills that appear more liberal or conservative, sometimes favoring small debtors, sometimes large creditors, in fact, the Bills generated by the House committee steer a more pragmatic course. All the core participants from either side of the aisle concur with one staffer's conclusion that "the substance of the bankruptcy law was not terribly political in terms of party ideology." Part of this was simply good politics. As the Republican leader in the House subcommittee put it, "we were conscious, if we never said it, that if you lean too far one way or the other, it won't work." This pragmatism was reinforced on the corporate side by the strongly procedural character of the reforms. Of course, procedure, too, enhances some interests at the expense of others. But, even here, little of the benefit could be systematically aligned with the party platforms or political ideology of the Democrats in the House or the more conservative disposition of the Senate as a whole.[30]

If it was not ideology that moved legislators to commit years of their lives to technical financial legislation, what did? It certainly had few votes in it. Even if Congressman Edwards had real sympathy for the fate of consumer debtors in bankruptcy, and Senator Burdick could solve the

---

[29] US Interview 91:04.   [30] US Interviews 91:04; 92:01.

problem of discharges for some of his constituents, bankruptcy law was too remote and too arcane for the ordinary voter to care or comprehend. And if the law would count little at the ballot box, neither is there evidence that its primary legislative sponsors were acting as agents, directly or indirectly, for dominant corporate interests. At specific moments, one or another legislator would respond directly to an interest group, whether the bankers, the federal judiciary, or the SEC. But these were the exceptions that proved the rule—neither the dominance of party ideology, nor the electoral interests of major Congressional sponsors, nor the power of the financial industry cast a dominant shadow over the entire Code. Whether from the political left or the right, the consensus remains that the United States Bankruptcy Code was for the legislators a classic instance of "good government" at work. This conclusion does not deny that legislators themselves got the satisfaction and derived parliamentary stature from successfully guiding a major bill through Congress. But it parts company from any explanation that insists that either political ideology, electoral prospects, or the power of finance capital dictated the reform process.

Omnipresent, however, were lawyers. The committees appointed lawyer-staffers as midwives for the legislation. The Monday following President Nixon's resignation, Charles Wiggins, ranking Republican on the House subcommittee, appointed Kenneth Klee to his staff and set him to work analyzing the Commission and Judge's bills. Klee had recently graduated from law school and had never practiced, but the long hiatus between Watergate and passage of the Voting Rights Act gave Klee some eighteen months to scrutinize the two bills that had been introduced in 1973. Chief Counsel to the Judiciary subcommittee, Allen Parker, had some prior bankruptcy experience as a law clerk and in private practice. When he saw that Don Edwards was about to become chair of the subcommittee with responsibility for the new bill, he called Edwards and offered his services. Edwards initially appointed him to his congressional staff, and then as chief counsel. Parker in turn appointed Richard Levin, recently graduated from Yale Law School. Klee and Levin worked so closely and effectively together, they were collectively designated as "Klevin" and received high plaudits from leading reformers. Said one senior staffer, "they were exceptionally bright young men."[31]

---

[31] US Interview 91:04.

Legislative impetus and expertise was concentrated in the House committee. Partly this followed from the institutional advantage of the House to undertake detailed technical legislation that requires intensive staff commitments. The Senate was concomitantly more sensitive to powerful lobbies, the most notable being the federal judges, as well as more vulnerable to individual vetoes that a strong ethos of collegiality gives any Senator, as Senator Thurman's "midnight hold" on a later bill dramatically demonstrated. The institutional character of the respective chambers led to a division of labor in which general distributive and finely balanced bills emerged from the House subcommittee to be confronted with the *realpolitik* of mobilized interests in the Senate, where an intensely focused campaign could halt a bill in its tracks.[32]

The House and Senate subcommittees organized testimony in which staffers, in consultation with the committee chair, set out the main issues, proposed how they would be sequenced, and decided who would get to testify. Although "no legitimate point of view" was turned away, said the staffers, a review of those who testified demonstrates two things: first, professionals and their organizations dominated proceedings in sheer length of time and breadth of appearances; and second, many groups who would be significantly affected by the legislation showed little interest in it (see Table 3.3). Time and again, legislators and staffers repeated the refrain that "very, very few evidenced any interest in bankruptcy legislation," or that given groups were "asleep at the switch." For instance, business interests were conspicuously absent. Said one key player, "one of the problems we have with American bankruptcy legislation, I think, since the 1970s, is that there has been no effective debtor lobby." The National Association of Manufacturers or the Business Roundtable were nowhere to be found. No business leaders testified to argue for the greater discretion and powers of managers and directors in a reorganizing company. This was done for them by lawyer–policy makers. Of course, directors in the United States have no personal liability for the failure of their companies, so one incentive that was present in England did not apply in the United States. Further, business treats corporate failure like a contagious disease. Business leaders are loath to be associated with it in the public mind, and even in the worst case, a given business leader is unlikely to be a frequent repeat player in the game of corporate reorganization.[33] The large creditors—banks, insurance companies, and

---

[32] US Interviews 91:04; 91:02, 92:01, 92:02.   [33] US Interview 92:01.

TABLE 3.3 Number of Appearances Before Congressional Committees by Interest Groups on Topic Areas

	Bankruptcy Commission	Bankruptcy Administration	Status of Bankruptcy Judges	Labor Issues	State as Creditor	Personal Bankruptcy	Business Bankruptcy	Municipal Debt	Agricultural Issues	Railroad Bankruptcy	Financial Institutions	Technical Issues	Miscellaneous
Financial	4	17	7	—	3	13	28	2	—	3	7	5	9
Labor	—	—	—	5	1	—	—	1	—	1	—	—	—
Bankruptcy Judge	11	29	28	—	1	3	7	1	—	2	1	3	6
Federal Judge	3	13	13	—	—	—	—	—	—	1	—	—	2
Academic	5	10	8	—	1	6	7	2	—	—	—	2	2
Attorney	3	11	5	—	6	11	9	4	—	—	—	4	7
Government	8	9	—	—	12	6	13	1	—	5	—	4	1
Special Interest	1	—	—	—	2	—	—	—	—	2	—	—	3
Non-financial	—	—	—	—	—	—	—	—	—	—	—	—	1
Railroad	—	—	—	—	—	—	1	—	—	9	—	1	—
Agriculture	1	—	—	—	—	—	—	—	1	—	—	—	—
Bankruptcy Commission	1	6	5	—	—	—	1	—	—	—	—	—	—
National Bankruptcy Conference	4	2	7	—	—	6	10	—	—	7	—	—	4

the like—were the primary representatives of industry, and they, of course, had very particular views about their interests in the legislative package.

The House staffers caucused privately with those individuals and groups that did appear, mostly directly after the morning hearings, to ensure they understood entirely the testifier's priorities and to sense where they might be flexible. Throughout 1976 to 1978 they were in continuous contact with leading bankruptcy specialists, and particularly so after the hearings when drafting the bill. For a period of weeks they broke the draft bill into sections and then invited small groups of lawyers and judges (some twenty to thirty in total), to meet in Washington for intensive discussion of each section of the bill. Strongly partisan players—the federal judges and SEC—were excluded, because they were viewed not as conciliatory, but as "spoilers."[34]

Professions

Professionals—almost entirely lawyers and judges—permeated every facet and stage of the reforms. They participated in three main capacities: as members of formal bodies, such as the Commission or the legislative subcommittees; as members of professional societies or associations; and as experts at large. We have considered their formal involvement in the proceedings. What of the other two?

Three key groups spearheaded the involvement of professionals in the passage of the 1976 Code: the National Bankruptcy Conference, the National Conference of Bankruptcy Referees, and the Commercial Law League. They were followed by the Judicial Conference of the US.

(a) National Bankruptcy Conference

The National Bankruptcy Conference (NBC) described itself as a non-profit, voluntary organization composed of representatives of different groups who are interested in the administration of bankruptcy law and practicing attorneys who specialize in this area.[35] The self-perpetuating elite of judges, academics, and lawyers had been formed in the 1930s to advise Congress during passage of the Chandler Act, and thereafter it continued as a general advisory group on bankruptcy legislation. More

---

[34] US Interviews 96:01; 96:02.

[35] Commission to Study Bankruptcy Laws, 1968, Hearings on S.J. Res. 100 before the Subcommittee on Bankruptcy of the Senate Committee on the Judiciary, 90th Cong., 2nd Sess. (1968), p. 84.

than once, informants described it as a "debating society" or "a brain trust" which scrutinized bankruptcy law and practice and drafted legislation to improve it, a function that was evident in its role in the minor revisions of bankruptcy law in 1966 and 1970.

Yet insiders differ over whether the NBC was the "hidden hand" behind the reform process from the start, and that in turn depends on whether the actions of NBC members should be attributed to the impact of the NBC as an organization (Aaron 1980: 201). One senior staffer asserts categorically that the initiative for the Bankruptcy Code originated with the NBC, which was composed of "the leading practitioners" and the "cream of the crop" in bankruptcy practice and education.[36] Many of the key players in the reforms were also members of the NBC: Charles Seligson, a member of the Bankruptcy Commission; Frank Kennedy, the Director of the Commission staff; Lawrence King, professor at New York University; J. Ronald Trost and George Treister, experienced bankruptcy practitioners from Los Angeles; Vern Countryman, Harvard law professor; Conrad Cyr and Joseph Lee, bankruptcy judges, among others who were specialists in such areas as international bankruptcies (John Honsberger) and tax matters (William Plumb). These and other members repeatedly appeared on a wide range of issues (see Fig. 3.3). They consulted with the Commission and the legislators and their staffs. Moreover, the experts with whom the House staffers consulted closely in the private drafting sessions from October through December of 1976 were almost entirely members of the NBC.

The collective representations of the NBC were influential, not only because of its distinguished membership, but because the NBC brought together in a non-political context a set of experts—some more sympathetic with creditors, others with debtors—who sought "consensus building." They were committed to a global view of bankruptcy law as a whole, and while some viewed them as elitist and unrepresentative of consumer bankruptcy practice (unlike their English counterparts), they effectively acted as a private "law revision council." They were one of the very few groups who were considered ideologically neutral about party politics or debtor/creditor orientations, expert in theory and practice, and holistic in their conception of substantive and procedural law. That combination gave them great authority. Furthermore "individual members of the conference," said one staffer, "were extremely influential in not only the technical side—in getting us to understand

---

[36] US Interview 91:05.

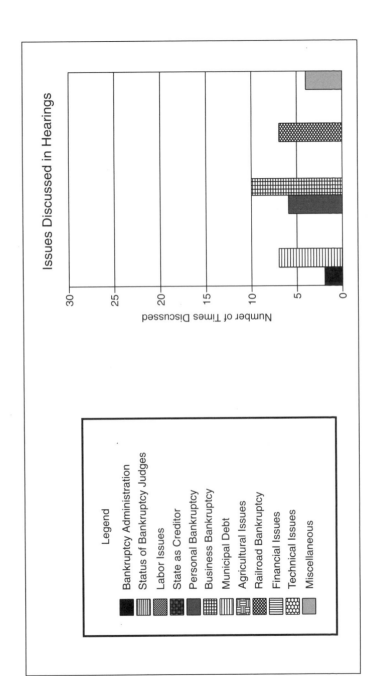

FIG. 3.3: **National Bankruptcy Conference: Frequency of Appearances on Issues**

what the issues were on the technical side—but also the policy issues and the implications of the policy issues." A leading academic reformer, who was also a member of the NBC, contested the notion that it was the "hidden hand" behind the reforms on the grounds, and that it was the individual members acting in their own right, rather than the NBC acting collectively, that had the greatest impact. Even here, however, bankruptcy experts testifying and consulting in their individual capacities had been influenced by the "consensus building" that had taken place inside the NBC.[37]

(b) National Conference of Bankruptcy Referees

If the National Bankruptcy Conference most closely approximated a private legislature which balanced the tensions intrinsic to bankruptcy, the National Conference of Bankruptcy Referees (later retitled Bankruptcy Judges (NCBJ)) straddled the divide between technocratic neutrality and interest group politics. Of a much lower status than the NBC, the NCBJ nevertheless had some distinguished leaders—Conrad Cyr, Asa Herzog, Joe Lee (all of whom were also members of the NBC)— and it was positioned in practice to offer a broad view of the legislation. In this respect they paralleled the NBC.

At the same time, the NCBJ represented the interests of bankruptcy specialists for whom the legislation either threatened loss of jobs or promised upward mobility. On matters concerning judicial status, salary, methods and terms of judicial appointment, court powers—any facet of the legislation that had an impact on their own status position and power in the bankruptcy field—they acted like "trade groups protecting their own personal interests."[38]

Since the bankruptcy bills offered the best opportunity for decades to advance their collective fortunes, the NCBJ mobilized with great effectiveness. They had been excluded from the Bankruptcy Commission, but they counter-attacked with their own rival bill. They hired an effective lawyer-lobbyist, Murray Drabkin,[39] and they exploited their local

---

[37] In retrospect, several of the reform participants indicated that a major change had taken place—that the National Bankruptcy Conference's legislative influence had waned since 1978 as powerful interest politics congealed around specific aspects of the Act. "Now that it (bankruptcy law) is on the front pages and every special interest group has got somebody watching it all the time, they have a much smaller influence because good government doesn't run these issues any more. Now it is special interest politics that runs these issues."US Interviews 91:05; 92:02; 92:01; 91:02.

[38] US Interview 92:01.

[39] Drabkin previously had served as a staffer on the House Judiciary Committee.

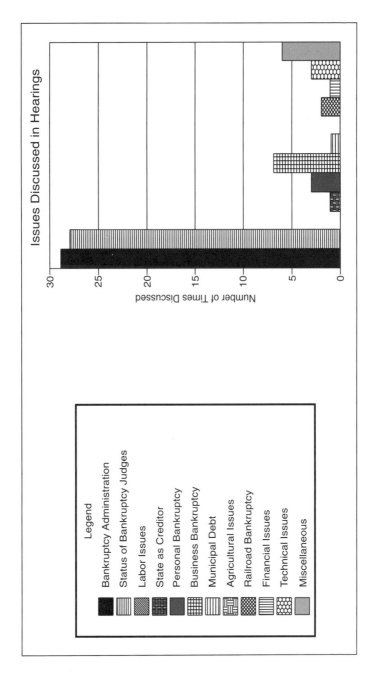

FIG. 3.4: **Bankruptcy Judges: Frequency of Appearances on Issues**

political connections across the nation to advocate their distinctive view of bankruptcy administration. While they would not have been politically strong enough to have pushed through provisions narrowly beneficial to themselves, they did have sufficient strength to slow or stop the forward momentum of the legislation. Because they could "put the brakes on" and threaten the entire bill, they forced political leaders to co-opt them. As a result, the Bankruptcy Act vastly improves the conditions of work, powers, and status of bankruptcy judges. We will see that this was not only in the interests of the judges themselves; many other groups pushed for improved judicial administration. But without a compromise in favor of the judges, the bill would likely have died in committee. This is not to say that the bankruptcy judges had no interests in other areas, for Fig. 3.4 demonstrates they did make submissions on business bankruptcy and several other issues. But these were dwarfed in proportion to the number of times they appeared before Congress on matters of bankruptcy administration and the status of bankruptcy judges.

(c) Commercial Law League

The Commercial Law League (CLL) represented the interests of those lawyers wryly described by one of its leaders as the "bankruptcy ring." However, it was not purely a lawyers' association. Founded in 1895 to "keep pace with the rapid strides of commerce and the development of the credit system of the nation," the CLL brought together three parties to commercial transactions, as an expanding national economy made "buyers and sellers become strangers" to each other. In addition to lawyers, who acted as agents for companies and traders who extended commercial credit, the CLL included publishers of law lists, which provided lists of attorneys who could handle collections' work in towns and cities across the nation, and credit collection agencies.[40] Sometimes

---

[40] In their own words, CCL members acted as attorneys for petitioning creditors, attorneys for debtors, and attorneys for trustees. A past-president readily acknowledged that a "commercial lawyer" was a debt collector, "but what lawyer is not?" Commercial law was concerned with debtor–creditor relations between businesses in several areas: "(1) Contracts for the sale of merchandise; (2) Contracts for the borrowing of money, usually secured by Chattel Paper, Conditional Sales Contracts, Trust Receipts, and so forth; (3) Claims for the damage of merchandise in shipment or otherwise; (4) Claims for damages due to delay in shipment, and subsequent loss of profit; (5) Contractual claims for services performed by one business unit for another business unit such as construction work, repair work, credit services, insurance premiums, architectural services, advertising services, and so forth." A good deal of work involves bankruptcy. "It is a volume practice. The average fee per case is small..." See Morris (1976: 19ff.).

disparaged as "debt collectors," even "down and dirty, in the trenches, collections lawyers," it was CCL members who were the butt of the 1930 Donovan Report on bankruptcy in New York, and it was their members who fell disproportionately into the categories of practice so excoriated by the Brookings Report. CLL members disproportionately served as trustees in the patronage relations of bankruptcy referees and trustees deplored by Brookings and the Commission.

Members of the League described themselves as a "creditors' rights" organization. They represented unsecured trade creditors—businesses that loaned money when they sold goods or services. Consequently, they were strongly opposed to innovations that would extend exemptions or discharges available to individual debtors, as they were apprehensive about wholesale changes to a form of bankruptcy administration in which their members had been primary beneficiaries. Despite their effective mobilization, and their involvement in each phase of the reforms, some staffers on the Hill perceived them "as a straight organization protecting their own interests."[41]

Other professional organizations made representations to the Bankruptcy Commission and Congressional committees. A bankruptcy group within the Business section of the American Bar Association made representations as did some smaller bar associations.

(d) Judicial Conference of the United States

The professional group that thrust itself prominently into the later phases of legislative passage was the Judicial Conference, the organization for federal district court, appellate, and Supreme Court judges. The federal judges were represented on the Bankruptcy Commission and they testified in the 1972 hearings, but until late 1977, when the Bankruptcy Bill looked increasingly likely to pass, the Judicial Conference remained largely mute. Its interests in bankruptcy law did not display the breadth of the National Bankruptcy Conference, or even the National Conference of Bankruptcy Judges. Because federal judges are nominated by Senators and often have had close connections with politicians and their parties, the Judicial Conference had unusually strong influence in the Senate. Principally in the Senate, the Judicial Conference engaged one issue only, and so effectively that their opposition put the entire bill in jeopardy (see Fig. 3.5). It was the status of bankruptcy courts, their jurisdiction and powers, together

---

[41] See Weisman (1976); US Interviews 93:02; 92:01; 92:02.

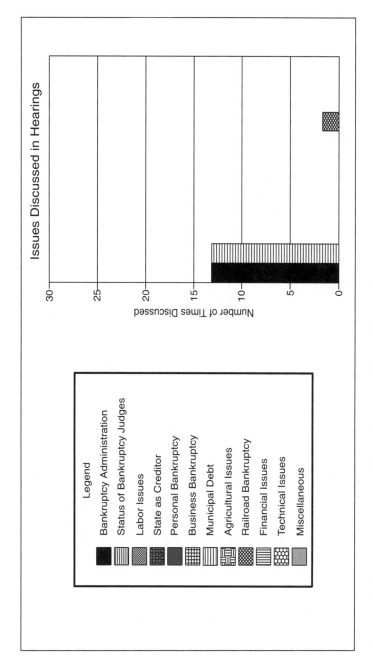

FIG. 3.5: **US District and Appellate Judges: Frequency of Appearances on Issues**

with the standing of bankruptcy judges, that gripped the Judicial Conference. For twelve months, from November 1977 to November 1978, they fought collectively and individually—most notably in the person of Chief Justice Burger—to block the proposals that bankruptcy courts and judges be raised to the same status as federal district courts.

Financial and Non-Financial Industries

Although one senior banker admitted that the bankruptcy reforms caught the financial industry "with its pants down," the peak associations of the financial industry displayed far greater activism than other industries.[42]

(a) Financials

Figure 3.6 indicates that the financial industry featured prominently in appearances before congressional committees and their interests ranged widely over most fields of bankruptcy. Three groups dominated. Alongside the generic American Banking Association, a trade association of banks, stood the Robert Morris Associates, a national association of more than 6,000 bank loan and credit officers, who could boast that they represented some 1,650 banks holding 78 per cent of all US commercial banking resources. In case their political weight was under-estimated, they informed each subcommittee of Congress that their banks lent in excess of $190 billion to business firms. Joining the banking groups was the American Council of Life Insurance, which also reminded Congress that they spoke on behalf of 473 life insurance companies which carried more than 90 per cent of life insurance in the US. Their assets exceeded $312 billion and they had $87 billion in private pension plans, quite apart from the $265 billion they held in corporate securities, mortgages, and other loans.

The submissions by the Robert Morris Associates illustrate the significance of problems bankers saw in the legislation before Congress in 1975. Without amendments, warned a senior banker, the proposed bill could "adversely affect the willingness or ability of banks to undertake certain kinds of risk," seriously impair "the allocation of capital to certain segments of industry with great needs, such as small businessmen," further erode "the already weak position of secured creditors", and hinder capital formation more generally. Not to put too fine a point

---

[42] US Interview 91:01.

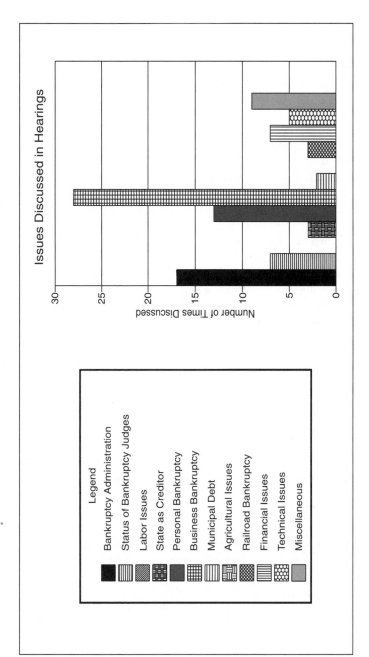

Issues Discussed in Hearings

Number of Times Discussed

Legend

Bankruptcy Administration
Status of Bankruptcy Judges
Labor Issues
State as Creditor
Personal Bankruptcy
Business Bankruptcy
Municipal Debt
Agricultural Issues
Railroad Bankruptcy
Financial Issues
Technical Issues
Miscellaneous

FIG. 3.6: **Financial Industry: Frequency of Appearances on Issues**

on it, the submission stated that for lower grade borrowers, "the proposed laws may amount to a virtual 'kiss of death' ".[43]

Of even more importance to the financial sector were their forms of security over loans. For instance, many creditors and the Bankruptcy Commission were concerned about the priority given to those lenders who had real estate liens—or legal claims to a borrower's property as collateral—and who would enforce them, and reclaim their property, when none of the other creditors could share in the proceeds.

The bankers had a related concern: how easy it would be for bankrupt corporations to use or sell their property during a reorganization. The financial sector feared that during attempts at rehabilitation, those few assets that the company had would be run down, depleted, or sold, and the creditors would recover even less of their loans. Financial institutions therefore recommended that managers in control of bankrupt companies should not be able to use or sell property on which there was a lien, without a court hearing and protections for the assets' value. In other words, the creditors' fear of losing more of their assets clashed with the corporate managers' needs to have flexibility in the use of assets to rehabilitate the company.[44]

The American Bankers Association and the Robert Morris Associates also argued in favor of their right of "set off." When a bank lends money to a customer who also has a savings or checking account at the bank, if the customer defaults, the right of "set off" enables the bank to seize the money from the customers' bank accounts and pay off part or all of the loan. This means that other creditors do not get to share those assets of the bankrupt, and it therefore gives financial institutions a special advantage. Because the proposed law threatened to weaken this privilege, the bankers argued vigorously for its retention.

(b) Non-Financials

Non-financial corporations played no role in the formulation of the 1978 Bankruptcy Code, except in the very limited case of leasing companies.[45] Apart from the special interests of the railroads, which, it

---

[43] *Bankruptcy Reform Act Hearings on S. 235 and S. 236*: 2484–6.

[44] See, for instance, the statements of the National Commercial Finance Conference, Inc. (NCFC) (*Bankruptcy Reform Act Hearings on S. 235 and S. 236*: 511–12, 517–18). The NCFC's positions were typical with respect to a secured creditor's views of the use of collateral by a debtor in bankruptcy.

[45] *Senate Hearings on S. 2266 and H.R. 8200*: 802–11.

could be argued, were involved in the hearings for historically idiosyn-
cratic reasons (Stearns 1990), and agriculture, which was interested in
only one chapter, the great body of American companies completely
ignored legislation that could significantly affect them.[46]

Unions

Organized labor had a direct interest in corporate bankruptcies because
workers can be given priorities in the distribution of a bankruptcy
company's assets for past wages and benefits still owed. Moreover, the
success of company rehabilitation affects jobs, though rehabilitation
frequently also requires concessions by workers. Labor's limited contribution to the reforms focused on benefits to workers in bankruptcy. The
chief legal counsel of the Garment Workers Union, Max Zimny, led the
charge on behalf of organized labor and the AFL/CIO (American
Federation of Labor/Congress of Industrial Organizations). But it was
a limited push on a narrow front. And even though Zimny himself
recognized that bankruptcy legislation might be used to break agreements with unions on wages and benefits, the union movement stirred
itself little until Continental Airline's union-busting use of the Bankruptcy Code galvanized organized labor to close this loophole in the
reforms of 1984.

State Agencies and Others

The state has a direct interest in bankruptcy law. On the one hand,
bankruptcy law affects the viability of the credit economy, the level of
entrepreneurial risk-taking, and economic growth. On the other hand,
the state has a narrow pecuniary interest in bankruptcy, for it usually
holds a high priority for taxes and social security payments that have not
been made by an insolvent company. Moreover, state agencies contest
domains of work like any private sector occupation.

Within the court system court administrators allied with judges to
keep bankruptcy administration within the judiciary. Within the

---

[46] The leasing companies were concerned that their equipment receive special treatment when bankruptcy proceedings began. For instance, the American Association for
Equipment Lessors maintained that companies in bankruptcy could only continue to use
leased equipment (covered by a lien) if it could be demonstrated to the court that the
leasing company's interest in the equipment would be protected. Leasing companies feared
that their equipment would be seized by other creditors, or that it would be poorly
maintained, or that the bankrupt company would use the equipment without continuing
to pay the lease. *Senate Hearings on S. 2266 and H.R. 8200*: 802–5.

executive, contrary movements took place, for, on the one side, the Internal Revenue Service and the Securities and Exchange Commission lobbied hard to maintain, respectively, their high tax priority and their official role in corporate reorganizations. On the other side, the Justice Department fought energetically to keep new administrative responsibilities for bankruptcy administration *out of the executive branch* and in the courts. As Table 3.3 shows, appearances by state officials were reasonably extensive. Yet this indicator under-estimates the powerful, and ultimately unsuccessful, lobby undertaken by the SEC, which pursued its behind-the-scenes maneuvers to maintain some control over corporate reorganizations all the way to the White House.

Consumer representatives did very little. Credit managers and collection agencies, whose interests aligned most closely with the Commercial Law League, were more involved but their limited actions affected corporate bankruptcy law very little.

ENGLAND

The Path to Statutory Reform

Like the United States, the origins of the 1986 Insolvency Act cannot be found in a purely economic explanation of rising bankruptcy and insolvency rates, although these surely increased the pressure for policy changes. For the decade before establishment of the English Insolvency Reform Committee in 1977, both individual bankruptcies and corporate insolvencies (voluntary and compulsory) had risen and fallen in two five-year cycles. Although 1970 may have been one of the worst years for bankruptcies since World War Two,[47] they eased off from 1970 to 1973 when they began to climb again, this time to a new peak.

Corporate insolvencies in 1976 occurred at more than twice the level of 1973, and individual bankruptcies almost kept pace. Both declined until 1979 when they began a dramatic climb, especially for corporate insolvencies, which peaked in 1985–an approximately three hundred per cent increase over 1979–and the year in which the Insolvency Bill was before Parliament. While these rising failures do not explain the appointment of an insolvency committee, the figures for the mid-1980s certainly help explain why the government earned some political capital

---

[47] *The Times* (of London; hereafter cited as *The Times*), 10 Aug. 1971.

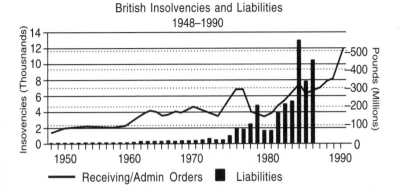

Fig. 3.7: **British Insolvencies and Total Liabilities of Insolvent Companies**
Source : *British Business* (company liquidations series).

by confronting boldly an extreme level of corporate failure. The rise in liabilities underline pressure on the government even further (see Fig. 3.7).

England had its share of high profile corporate failures. The collapse of Rolls Royce in 1971 symbolized the decline of an exemplar of British manufacturing excellence. The 1969 crisis of the Handley Page aircraft company with debts of £14 million and 4,000 employees, and Brentford Nylons in 1976 with some 3,000 jobs and debts of £15 million, were dwarfed by Britain's biggest property failure in 1974. Owing some £170 million to thirty-three financial institutions, the Stern Property Group could have precipitated a ripple of insolvency that pushed £1,000 million of real estate onto the property market, setting off a dive in property values, and quite possibly the collapse of major banks and insurance companies. Other companies that were household names— Massey Ferguson and International Harvester—experienced severe financial difficulties. But since these companies had no debentures, they had no recourse to the English institution of receivership, in which an accountancy or insolvency firm could step in and reorganize a firm while creditors were kept at bay. Insolvency law did not cater to the reorganization needs of a large class of companies.[48]

The downfall of major companies invariably embroiled the Government and the financial institutions of the City, including the Bank of England. Post-war government policy of financial intervention to prop

---

[48] See Cork (1988: 71–8, 95–102, 195, chs. 4–6). UK Interview 89:01.

up failing private companies became increasingly controversial until the Conservative Government finally broke the post-war policy consensus in the early 1970s with its announcement that it would no longer rescue "lame-duck" companies. But the government found it difficult to hold its course. It permitted the bankruptcy of the Mersey Docks and Harbour Board in 1970, but it rescued Rolls Royce in 1971, and salvaged the Upper Clyde Shipbuilders that same year. Each notable case of failure re-ignited fierce debate and brought problems of corporate reorganization and rescue even more forcefully into public consciousness.[49]

At the same time, the major investing institutions of the City of London, together with the Confederation of British Industry, the Law Society, the Institute of Chartered Accountants, the Stock Exchange, and the British Insurance Association, recognized the devastating consequences that followed from the standard practice of financial institutions to withdraw all credit from troubled companies. With some prodding from the Bank of England, they began to discuss setting up a specialized institution to aid in the management—and turnaround—of problem companies in ways that would have eased the difficulties experienced by such major collapses as Rolls Royce (1971), Vehicle and General Insurance, The Mersey Docks and Harbour Board (1970), and Upper Clyde Shipbuilders (1971).[50]

Individual bankruptcy caught the public eye most sensationally with the case of John Poulson, which broke into the news in July 1972, and transfixed the British public in the following months with revelations of political corruption. Poulson had begun an architectural firm in 1932 and by 1968 it was the largest architectural practice in Europe, with 750 employees. When the company ran into financial difficulties, Poulson was subject to the English practice of a public bankruptcy hearing. Aggressive examination by Muir Hunter, QC, a distinguished bankruptcy barrister, revealed that Poulson had given gifts and moneys to several highly placed politicians and civil servants and their families. It was alleged he paid £22,000 into a favorite charity of the wife of the Home Secretary, Reginald Maudling, an allegation that brought the Liberal leader to table a motion in the House of Commons asking for an immediate Government inquiry into "allegations of financial corruption

---

[49] See, for instance, the article by Nicholas Ridley, MP, "How the lame ducks came home to roost", *The Sunday Times*, 21 Jan. 1974, p. 53.

[50] *The Times*, 16 Mar. 1972, p. 21; 17 Mar. 1972, p. 17; 3 Aug. 1972, p. 19.

in public life." The revelations continued throughout the summer and autumn, naming a senior civil servant in the Scottish Office, several MPs, and municipal councillors. Nor was the Labour Party immune from criticism. A former Labour cabinet minister, Anthony Crosland, had been given a coffee pot by Mr Poulson, after Crosland had opened a school built by Poulson.[51]

The political row spilled over into professional circles. Leaders of the Inns of Court, England's ancient societies of barristers, were approached by several Members of Parliament who called for an investigation of Muir Hunter on the grounds that he may have gone too far in his aggressive pursuit of Poulson's dealings. In response, the Professional Conduct Committee of the Bar Council, which governed British barristers, instituted an inquiry into Muir Hunter's conduct in his investigation of Poulson's affairs. Eventually, Hunter was entirely exonerated but the tremendous political pressure on the Bar signalled the potential fallout of public bankruptcy hearings for national, commercial, political, and professional leaders.[52]

The more substantial outcome of the Poulson hearings was the call for reform of bankruptcy law. *The Times* editorial stated that it was "high time the Bankruptcy Acts of 1914–26 were brought under the kind of review to which Lord Salmon's commission subjected tribunals of inquiry." An upshot of the Poulson affair was a Commission on Standards in Public Life, chaired by Lord Salmon.[53] Papers reported that practicing lawyers and lawyer MPs began to advocate a commission of inquiry into the Bankruptcy Acts that had stood substantially unchanged for over fifty years. These were echoed in Parliament.[54]

Consumer pressures provided added impetus to reform. Consumers, consumer associations, together with consumer programs on radio and television, exposed an ugly underside to the ways some company directors and liquidators dealt with weaker creditors. The public labelling of "rogue directors," "cowboy liquidators," and the "Phoenix syndrome" signalled dissatisfaction with company directors who exploited limited liability and loopholes in company regulation to defraud customers, and with liquidators of companies, who were retained to sell off the company

[51] *The Times*, 30 Jan. 1973, p. 1.

[52] *The Times*, 1 Feb. 1973, p. 1; 5 Mar. 1973.

[53] Lord Salmon, it might be noted, was a barrister who was head of chambers in which Muir Hunter served and David Graham subsequently entered.

[54] *The Times*, 31 Jan. 1973, 1 Feb. 1973, p. 1. See Lord Hale and the Lord Chancellor, *The Times*, 9 Feb. 1973.

assets, but who lacked professional qualifications, regulation, or ethical controls, and who conspired with directors to drain companies of assets and relieve hapless individuals of their prepayments or deposits. The conspiracy of directors and liquidators was symbolized in the Phoenix Syndrome, a practice in which directors bled companies of assets, declared bankruptcy, sold the remaining assets at vastly reduced prices to a trusted family member or friend (with the connivance of a friendly liquidator), and then set up a new company with a very similar name to engage in a similar business. The new assets of the company were bought at "knock-down" prices from the family member or "friend" who had bought them from the liquidator at deeply discounted prices. Consumers had no recourse and, on occasions, even got caught up in the new business, unknowingly ripe for further loss. As the economic downturn intensified in the early 1980s, the level of consumer disquiet caught the attention of government ministers and MPs.

What began as a rather technical enterprise had by 1984 metamorphosed into a politically sensitive issue for the government and opposition. It was politics, not professionalism, that converted high-minded and rational reforms into political will.[55]

The "bad odor" cast upon all insolvency work by "rogue liquidators" underlined the problems that can arise when areas of potentially lucrative work are not regulated by professions or the state. Since the tail-end of insolvency practice dragged down the reputation of the entire field of work, many qualified or licensed accountants who practiced insolvency work, and unlicenced liquidators who had built reputable practices, began to push for some government intervention to regulate the field,

---

[55] The awareness of growing consumer pressure for political action became apparent not only to professionals who were advancing their reform packet, but to politicians, civil servants, and consumer groups. (UK Interviews 90:04; 91:07; 91:17; 90:09; 91:16; 90:16). As one senior civil servant, who worked closely with government ministers, described the pressures: ". . . in addition to the Cork Committee, the items which particularly influenced ministerial minds, or politicians generally, had what have been called . . . the delinquent directors and the rogue liquidators, and to a lesser extent, the Phoenix Syndrome . . . various consumer bodies, various consumer television programs. . . . So consumer programs were aware of the level of complaint, ministers were aware, both through the consumer programs and through their own post bag from constituents complaining." (UK Interview 91:17). Said Sir Kenneth Cork, about the government's sudden rapid push for legislation in 1984, "The Tories came in (in 1979) and they said that to implement our report would take a whole session of Parliament, and there were no votes in insolvency. . . . And then they found there were a lot of votes lost because they wouldn't deal with the fraud and troubles that were going on, and the House of Lords was also shouting for implementation." (UK Interview 90:04). More generally, see Chapter 6, on the moral imperatives to "clean up markets," which also propelled reform.

principally through professionalization. Elite and specialist professionals had strong reputational interests in the regulation of insolvency work, and a general review of insolvency law offered a perfect moment at which to advance that cause.

It did not require the bad odor of scandal to persuade leading bankruptcy lawyers and accountants that English law, which had remained substantially unchanged since the late nineteenth century, was in need of modernization. In 1975, Justice, the English branch of the International Commission of Jurists, released a report, which asserted that "the essential features of bankruptcy law are long overdue for reconsideration and reform and they coincide with an upsurge of public interest in the whole subject of insolvency generally and bankruptcy in particular." The allusion to an upsurge of public interest had a delicious irony, since one of the report's authors was none other than Muir Hunter, QC, briefly darling of the Press and embarrassment to the Bar.[56]

Cases in which bankruptcy law seemed to act particularly harshly on individuals drew the attention of Justice and prompted its investigation of bankruptcy. Its further inquiries disclosed a "general dissatisfaction" over aspects of bankruptcy in practice—cases where bankruptcy had been pursued against individuals who were solvent, or where proceedings had seized belongings in an oppressive manner and "deprived the bankrupt of his self-respect, or where a bankrupt's assets were sold off at much less than their true value." Bankrupts could be refused a discharge by the court for many years, which placed them in a kind of no-mans-land for the extension of credit. Moreover, the law rather indiscriminately lumped together debtors who were "victims of misfortune," and deserved fair treatment, and debtors who were guilty of fraud or reckless behavior, and arguably deserved firmer punishment. Further, the members of the Justice Committee recognized the injustice in the ways that different creditors were treated, most especially in view of the preferences given some classes of creditors (government departments) against others, especially employees.[57] Justice therefore set out with three aims: (a) to reduce the number of debtors forced into bankruptcy; (b) to

---

[56] *Bankruptcy*, by Justice, the British Section of the International Commission of Jurists (London: Stevens and Son, 1975), p. v. The bankruptcy bar was a small world. Muir Hunter's junior in the Poulson case was David Graham, who was a member of the Justice Committee with Muir Hunter, and later still became a close advisor to Kenneth Cork in the Insolvency Law Review Committee.

[57] Justice (1975); UK Interview 90:21.

alleviate the harshness of bankruptcy proceedings on certain bankrupts and their families; and (c) to protect small creditors, such as employees "from the activities of unscrupulous debtors." Its report made a substantial number of modest recommendations, though they fully realized that they were offering something much less than "a comprehensive review of bankruptcy law."[58]

Several of these provisions were implemented in a small piece of legislation in 1976. A sympathetic Labour minister in the Department of Trade and Industry, which housed the Insolvency Service, pushed through several amendments. One would permit automatic discharges for some categories of bankrupt individuals. Another introduced the idea of disqualifying company directors in egregious cases.[59] While these changes were modest, the so-called minor reforms generated a great deal more lobbying and political by-play than the minister, Clinton Davis MP, had anticipated. It became readily apparent to government officials that the legislation was simply scratching the surface. Given the pressure to do more in the bill than the government intended, and its difficulty in obtaining passage through Parliament, a deal was struck in which the political pressure for more extensive reforms would be suspended in exchange for a commitment by the minister to undertake a full-scale, comprehensive inquiry into bankruptcy and insolvency law.[60]

The Labour Government appointed a committee on 27 January 1977 headed by Kenneth Cork with a fourfold charge:

(1)   to review the law and practice relating to insolvency, bankruptcy, liquidation and receiverships in England and Wales and to consider what reforms are necessary or desirable;

(2)   to examine the possibility of formulating a comprehensive insolvency system and the extent to which existing procedures might, with advantage, be harmonized and integrated;

---

[58] Justice (1975: v, 1, 36–9).

[59] Insolvency Act 1976.

[60] UK Interviews 90:2; 90:04; 91:07; 91:10; 89:01. According to an informant who was involved in the 1976 legislation, "we caused enough trouble to disrupt the government's legislative program . . . which of course the government could never allow to happen. Far more important bills are in the pipeline. And the result was that some sort of deal had to be done and the deal that was done, in effect, was that the government would set up a review committee which would review the whole of the law on insolvency." England's law already looked hopelessly outdated, and England lagged behind the United States, Canada, Australia, and New Zealand, all of which were revising their insolvency law (UK Interview 91:14).

(3) to suggest possible less formal procedures as alternatives to bank-ruptcy and company winding up proceedings in appropriate cir-cumstances; and

(4) to make recommendations.[61]

The Cork Committee's charge, including the concepts of harmoniza-tion and comprehensive reform, resulted not only from shortcomings in domestic practice, but from the "Europeanization" of law that was effecting greater economic integration of the European Economic Com-munity. A Draft EEC Convention on Bankruptcy, including a Uniform Law on aspects of commercial bankruptcies, was produced by a Euro-pean Working Party that sought to resolve the special difficulties of reciprocal enforcement of bankruptcy judgments through the EEC. Following Britain's admission to the EEC in 1972, the Department of Trade and Industry appointed in 1973 an Advisory Committee, under the chairmanship of Kenneth Cork, "to consider the terms of the Draft EEC Bankruptcy Convention and to advise the Department upon the effect of the implementation of the Convention in its present terms and to recommend such modifications as they consider necessary and prac-ticable." Or, put more idiomatically, "could our domestic law of insol-vency... be made to fit European requirements?"[62]

Cork's appointment as chair of both committees signalled the Gov-ernment's recognition of two changes in the insolvency field: the grow-ing importance in public policy of corporate reorganization as an alternative to liquidation; and the accompanying shift in the professional field from lawyers to the accountancy profession.

While the Insolvency Law Review Committee (Cork Committee) was conducting its hearings and deliberations, Margaret Thatcher's Con-servative government came to power in 1979 with a political commit-ment to reduce government intrusion into the economy and to stimulate private solutions to public problems. The new government immediately

---

[61] *Cork Report*: p. iii.

[62] *The EEC Preliminary Draft Convention on Bankruptcy, Winding-Up, Arrangements, Composi-tions, and Similar Proceedings*, (London: HMSO, 1976). Cmnd. 6602., pp. 1–5. See also U.K. Interview 90.21. The members of the committee were Kenneth Cork (chair), A. E. Anton, P. H. Armour, P. G. H. Avis, C. L. Dodd, and Muir Hunter. Trevor Traylor, a civil servant, was Secretary. The Committee sent a Consultative Paper to some 850 organiza-tions and individuals, and received back 300 memoranda or letters. The memoranda from organizations numbered less than 30. Professional associations dominated, but memor-anda were also submitted by the main banking associations, the British Insurance Associa-tion, chambers of commerce, the Institute of Directors, and government departments (See Appendix 4, p. 135.).

asked the Cork Committee to produce an interim report on its recommendations to reduce the manpower and financial burdens of bankruptcy administration. In its 1980 report to the Minister of Trade and Industry, the Cork Committee acknowledged that bankruptcy proceedings had been used frequently and unnecessarily for minor debt collection in cases involving small traders and consumer debtors.[63] These high volume, low complexity, low asset cases mostly burdened the Government Insolvency Service and the Official Receiver's Office housed in the Department of Trade and Industry. The interim report therefore proposed a modest set of new measures that would remove minor cases from bureaucratic agencies.

Simultaneously, in an unusual move, the Government published a "Green" discussion paper that took a much more drastic and controversial position.[64] Essentially it called for a radical privatization of bankruptcy administration. In personal bankruptcies most public functions would be shifted to the private sector. Private practitioners would take over responsibilities for discovering and obtaining a debtor's assets, interviewing the debtor, going through the debtor's records, making inquiries of creditors, advising the debtor in the preparation of court papers, and filing a report with the courts.

The Government's proposals to devolve public functions onto the private market—essentially redrawing the boundary of state responsibilities—drew scathing criticism, especially from insolvency practitioners. An academic commentator wrote that "legislation along the lines of the Government's current proposals for 'privatization' of civil bankruptcy would be an unmitigated disaster for all interests concerned: those of debtors and creditors, and those of the public at large." All the principal professional groups involved in bankruptcy administration similarly attacked the government's position. The Insolvency Practitioners Association (IPA) stated that the new proposals would adversely affect the public interest and the business community. Both the IPA and the Consultative Committee of Accountancy Bodies (CCAB)—the peak association of the accountancy profession—roundly criticized the

---

[63] *Bankruptcy: Interim Report of the Insolvency Law Review Committee.* HMSO. 1980. Command Paper 7968. (*Interim Cork Report*).

[64] *Bankruptcy: A Consultative Document.* 1980. Command Paper. No. 7967. HMSO. (*Government Green Paper*). A "green paper," in British political parlance, allows a government to float some of its ideas before the general public and obtain some sense of its reaction, before the government commits itself to a particular policy or legislative agenda. If the reaction is adverse, the Government can back away from the Green Paper with limited political cost, as it did in the insolvency case (Zander 1994, UK Interview 91:17).

discretion this would give to debtors, calling it a "charter for unscrupulous debtors."[65]

The "public outcry" was so great, according to a senior civil servant, that the Government did not follow through with the Green Paper proposals. Yet it may have served a salutary effect, for it alerted the Cork Committee that no expansion of the state's involvement in bankruptcy administration would be tolerable and, indeed, that privatization of bankruptcy work would be highly desirable. Put bluntly, if the Cork Committee wanted its recommendations enacted, it should be sure they were consistent with the main lines of Tory policy to downsize the state and to stimulate private initiative.[66]

After extensive public hearings and submissions on both its original charge and the government Green Paper, the Cork Committee presented Part I of its final report to the Minister on 30 April 1981, and Part II in February 1982. The report was tabled in Parliament on 9 June 1982. The Government's response was suitably neutral to the effect that it was a fine piece of work and would warrant serious consideration, without any commitment from the Government about its legislative intentions.[67]

Despite the technical nature of insolvency law and the stigma connected with bankruptcy, the Cork Report received a notable reception in the Press. Undoubtedly the timing helped, for England was experiencing the highest levels of corporate insolvencies since the Great Depression.[68] News coverage of the Cork Report featured changes in insolvency practice, with special attention to company turnarounds, the problem of cowboy liquidators, and the professionalization of receivers and liquidators. Editorials, reports by financial editors, two-page spreads on the outlines of the recommendations—none of these approximated the drama of the Poulson affair, but they were hard to miss.

Cork had told the press at the inception of his committee that many more companies would be saved if outside administrators with stronger powers could be brought into companies which did not have a loan structure that permitted the appointment of receivers.[69] It was precisely

---

[65] Fletcher (1981: 85). Cmnd. 8558. *Cork Report.*

[66] UK Interview 91:17.

[67] UK Interview 91:10.

[68] Undoubtedly another factor that helped was the concerted effort made by the Cork Committee to produce a document in fine, simple English. The Committee hired a writer and editor to ensure the Report was more accessible to the general reader.

[69] *The Times*, 26 Feb. 1977, p. 15.

this innovation that *The Times* featured in several articles both before and after the Cork Report was published. Anticipating the Report, a *Times* article felicitously titled, "Careful Surgery for Company Surgeons," styled Cork's recommendation for an administrator as a "new type of company doctor" which would be created by the law. Since the big business disasters of the 1970s, including Laker, Stone Platt, and DeLorean, the major banks had become "a much more sophisticated breed in spotting cancers needing surgery before they became terminal." Accountants had played a big role in "company intensive care" as banks asked them for independent views of the company's affairs. Undoubtedly they had "nursed many businesses through difficult times." But for many more, the economic downturn had caused collapse. Therefore, stated *The Times*'s Financial Editor, the problems of business failures, lost jobs, and unscrupulous practices could be partially solved by several of Cork's recommendations, including the invention of "a new receiver-like figure called an administrator who could carry on the business when present law does not permit a receiver or manager, and who might be appointed at an earlier stage than present receivers so that there is more of a business left to save."[70]

If a new set of capacities were to be mobilized to save businesses, then it was critical that higher standards be established for professionals acting as liquidators, receivers, and administrators. Earlier a reporter had "predicted" that "the rules governing liquidators—regarded as the undertakers of the industry—and receivers—credited with the slightly more glamorous title of brain surgeons—are about to be given a big theoretical shakeup." The Cork Report recommended that the substantially unregulated field of insolvency practice be subject to strict professional regulation, following the Government's preferred model of private, self-regulating professionals within a statutory framework. Therefore, improvement of "the standard of administration of insolvent estates" and the prevention of "abuse" would be achieved by minimum qualifications for individuals acting as receivers.[71]

---

[70] *The Times*, 4 Apr. 1982; 13 June 1982, p. 49; 18 Aug. 1983, p. 15.

[71] *The Times*, 4 Apr. 1982, p. 49; 10 June 1982. Anticipating the Government's White Paper, Stephen Aris featured its contents with an article on "Rounding up the Cowboys." According to Aris, the government would seek to "stamp out 'cowboy' liquidators", a move widely welcomed (*The Times*, 5 Feb. 1984, p. 54). See also Graham Searjeant, Financial Editor, on the expectation that the White Paper would "tackle the problem of 'cowboy' liquidators" who "cooperate in selling assets cheaply to failed directors, or associates, at the expense of small creditors."

The Cork Report included much more: a unification, so far as possible, of individual and corporate bankruptcy law. It recommended that the Government's high priority in the disbursement of assets from a corporate estate be reduced. It also proposed measures, such as "wrongful trading," to compel company directors to get help as early as possible for their companies, or find themselves *personally* liable for its debts. The Report made several recommendations to protect consumers and trade creditors in bankruptcy. And although it protected the banks' most hallowed security, the floating charge, nevertheless banks were persuaded to be more flexible in the appointment of administrators to run companies in favor of all the creditors, and not just themselves.

The Cork Report was delivered in two stages, but its reception was interrupted by the election in the summer of 1983. A cabinet reshuffle brought a new Secretary of State, Cecil Parkinson, and a new junior minister responsible for insolvency activities, Alex Fletcher. Both were chartered accountants. "One of the messes on their outstanding agenda was, in short, what are we going to do with the Cork Committee Report."[72] To outside observers, government action on a bill seemed unduly delayed. Kenneth Cork believed that initially the government felt that there were not enough votes in a piece of legislation that would take up a whole Parliamentary session. Cork, himself, lobbied government ministers for action occasionally joined by Lord Benson, a sometime advisor to the Bank of England. Said Cork: "He's a very big man with a bloody great fist...I can remember him sitting in the Department of Trade hitting the table with his fist and everything jumping up and down."[73] The Press also began to play up the issues, sometimes abetted by Cork, whose persuasiveness had been honed from years of meeting with obstreperous creditors, and in City of London politics.

In response to this confluence of forces inside and outside government, the Insolvency Service of the Department of Trade and Industry (DTI) set up a "Bill team" which went about crafting a Government White Paper to express the Government's intentions. The Insolvency Service Division in the DTI provided the home base for the Bill, where a Working Group went through the Cork Report paragraph by paragraph. Officials formed an interdepartmental committee, so that other interested departments, such as the Treasury and the Lord Chancellor's Department (responsible for the judiciary) could advance their views. After reaching general agreement on major issues, a draft White Paper

---

[72] UK Interview 91:17.   [73] UK Interviews 90:04; 91:07.

was circulated among departments until the minister was sufficiently satisfied that he could present it to the cabinet committee. This White Paper, itself, "had green edges," since there were aspects of the legislation on which ministers wanted further comment before proceeding.

The Insolvency Service knew it could not implement the entire Cork Report. Some of its elements were not accepted by the Insolvency Service itself. Others were anathema either to another government department (the Inland Revenue did not want to lose its tax priority; the Lord Chancellor did not want a new specialized insolvency court) or ran awry of Government policy (anything that increased government expenditure). Then again, the DTI, like any government department, was given a set of size limitations for the bill. Said a senior civil servant, "we knew from the start that Cork had more than they could handle. The DTI was told that the bill couldn't be bigger than a given number of clauses," since it could occupy only so many days of parliamentary time. That forced the Insolvency Service to prioritize its legislative ambitions.[74]

The White Paper, released in February 1984, had "green edges" around it, substantially because a legislative opening came earlier than the Insolvency Service had anticipated, and ministers wanted more reactions before proceeding.[75] The DTI knew it had a slot for financial services legislation in 1984–5 and for insolvency in 1985–6. But when drafting of the financial services bill fell behind schedule, a slot opened up for a major bill, and the Minister for the DTI persuaded the cabinet that the insolvency bill was ready to go—a year earlier than had been expected.[76]

The bill's timing depended on more than an opening in the legislative calendar. Pressure on the Government had been building as bankruptcy rates shot up. The "ugly face of capitalism" got a human dimension as scandals related to business failures and liquidators received widespread publicity on Esther Rantzen's Sunday evening consumer affairs program on BBC TV, Robin Cook's investigative radio program, as well as in the press. Of course, a government can ignore a commission or departmental report, but "if it has popular appeal, they do so at their political peril." Somewhat to the surprise of the Government and the reformers, the economic downturn, and its media coverage, slowly

---

[74] UK Interview 91:17.

[75] Since Governments released "Green Papers," as documents to stimulate a discussion over policy options, and "White Papers," which were statements of legislative intent, a White Paper with "green edges" suggests that it still has unresolved policy issues contained in it.

[76] UK Interview 91:17.

turned a marginal area of technical law into a matter on which voters began to vent their feelings. It was one thing if the professions and the City (London's financial center) had an interest in new legislation, as they did. It became quite another when "MPs started to get more and more complaints in their mail."[77] Progressively, insolvency legislation started to look like good policy to government ministers. It became even more compelling when the Government realized that an insolvency bill could be harnessed to the Government's general mandate to "clean up" markets and legitimize privatization. Any provisions that would save companies, save jobs, root out corrupt or incompetent liquidators, or reckless and fraudulent directors, created political capital—and this bill offered to do precisely that. Behind the scenes, Kenneth Cork lobbied all the way to the Prime Minister, Mrs Thatcher, that the Government should act on his report.

The Government's statement of its legislative intentions was contained in a White Paper (*A Revised Framework for Insolvency Law*) tabled in Parliament and released to the public in February 1984.[78] Given the pressure to fill its legislative slot in the next Parliamentary session, it gave the public only two months to respond. Even though several recommendations in the Cork Report were omitted, initial reaction was generally favorable. The Government accepted the need to create a new insolvency practitioner's profession, which *The Times* agreed would "give creditors confidence in the persons they appoint to administer insolvent estates and to reduce the amount of supervision required by the DTI."[79] Observers lauded the new procedures that might save companies and they welcomed the features of the White Paper that would severely punish directors for not taking full responsibility for the financial circumstances of their companies. Consumers got relatively little out of the White Paper, and the Government had no intention of surrendering its high priority for claiming back taxes and unremitted social security withholdings by employers.

During the period between the release of the White Paper and until introduction of the bill to Parliament there was a steady stream of meetings between the minister, and his civil service advisors, and such interest groups as the CBI, Institute of Directors, consumer groups, professional bodies, and banking groups. If the minister agreed in principle to a path of action, interest groups would be drawn into the

---

[77] UK Interview 90:02.   [78] *Government White Paper.*
[79] *The Times*, 1 Mar. 1984, p. 23.

consultative process with department officials preparing the legislation. The time constraints were very tight. The White Paper came out in February 1984, amendments were agreed to within the government by April, and instructions were forwarded to the Parliamentary draftsmen by May. However, the draftsmen could not immediately get to the Insolvency Bill, so that when it was introduced in the First Reading to Parliament in November 1984, even the civil servants responsible for the bill had not seen the draft legislation in its entirety.[80]

The Bill was introduced for its First Reading in December 1984 and set down for its second reading, when the debate over the legislation would begin, in mid-January 1985.[81] The Insolvency Bill was introduced into the House of Lords, rather than the Commons, for two main reasons. First, Parliamentary scheduling dictates that bills be distributed between the Commons and the Lords. If all bills are introduced first to the Commons, then the Lords face a lengthy period in the early part of the session with little to do. Second, the Bill itself was not considered particularly partisan or contentious. But it was highly technical, and could profit from the expertise resident in the Lords, where there were numbers of distinguished lawyers, law-lords, accountants, and business leaders. Moreover, internal rules of the Lords allow legislation to be more thoroughly debated, with the result that the Bill that reaches the Commons will be in "more perfect condition," and therefore take less time.[82]

---

[80] UK Interview 91:17. Some commentators on the Insolvency Bill argue that many of its faults came from the hasty manner in which it was prepared. But the official draftsmen's office disagreed. It was true that they drafted the bill in four months—June, July, September, and October, 1995—but this was no more rushed than usual. The Insolvency Bill was the major government bill that year and therefore it had no option but to introduce it early in the session: "... if the department has got the slot at the beginning of the session they are hardly going to want to spend three months polishing the bill and sorting out everything. Because that means that the chances are they won't get the bill by the end of the session and they will have to reintroduce it the next one again if they get a vote in the program. So what are they going to do? Introduce it, you know, warts and all and debate it." (UK Interview 91:18).

Secondary legislation was being prepared in tandem with the primary legislation. The Labour leader in the Lords took exception to how much secondary legislation was not seen by Parliament. But the draftsmen maintain that it is inevitable, otherwise the Bill would have not been more than 200 pages, but more than 1,000 pages, which would be very difficult to get through Parliament. The draftsmen adopted an approach which sought to get the central principles of the Bill into the Act, and to put the details into the subordinate legislation. (UK Interviews 91:18; 91:10).

[81] The first reading is a purely formal announcement of the title of a bill and it sets a time for the second reading, when the bill will be debated. On statutory law-making in Britain, see Zander (1994).

[82] UK Interviews 91:16; 91:04.

TABLE 3.4:   A Time-line of the 1985 English Insolvency Act

Review Committee Stage	January 27, 1977	Insolvency Law Review Committee (Cork Committee) appointed by Secretary of State for Trade, Labour Government
	October 1979	Cork Committee submits an Interim Report, published July 1980
	July 1980	Government publishes Green Paper, *Bankruptcy: A Consultative Document*
	April 30, 1981	Part I. *Insolvency Law and Practice: Report of the Review Committee*, submitted to the Secretary of State for Trade
	February 1982	Part II. *Insolvency Law and Practice: Report of the Review Committee*, submitted to the Secretary of State for Trade
White Paper	February 1984	Government publishes White Paper, *A Revised Framework for Insolvency Law*
Parliament	*House of Lords*	
	December 10, 1984	1st Reading of the Insolvency Bill
	January 15, 1985	2nd Reading of the Insolvency Bill; Committee of the Whole House
	April 16, 1985	3rd Reading of the Insolvency Bill; Passed and sent to Commons
	House of Commons	
	April 16, 1985	1st Reading
	April 30, 1985	2nd Reading
	May 14–	
	June 20, 1985	Bill debated in Standing Committee E
	June 20, 1985	Report submitted with amendments
	July 18, 1985	3rd Reading; Passed
	House of Lords	
	July 22–31, 1985	Received, debated, amendments accepted, some rejected; Returned to Commons
	House of Commons	
	October 24, 1985	Received
	October 28, 1985	Agree to House of Lords amendments
	House of Lords	
	October 29, 1985	Agree to amendments
	October 30, 1985	Royal Assent

Lord Lucas, a junior minister in the Department of Trade and Industry, led for the Government, supported by Lord Cameron, the Lord Advocate. Labour's leader was Lord Bruce, a Scottish accountant. Debate proceeded through all clauses of the Bill until early April. But it was not without controversy. While both parties agreed with the general principles of the legislation, there was sharp disagreement over two matters, and on both, the Government suffered an unaccustomed defeat.

First, the Government had announced in its White Paper that it intended to compel directors to be more vigilant about the financial situation of their companies. If companies were in financial difficulty, directors should take steps to obtain new capital, co-operate with creditors to reorganize, or voluntarily go into liquidation. If they failed to take these steps, and were forced into bankruptcy, then they would be automatically disqualified from acting as directors of any company for three years. They could apply to the court for relief.[83] The business community attacked this provision with great fervor and eventually, with the support of insolvency practitioners, prevailed upon Parliament to remove the provision for automatic disqualification and to leave the possibility of disqualification up to the discretion of a court.[84]

Second, the Government enjoyed a high priority in the collection of unpaid taxes from insolvent companies. In the House of Lords this special position won no favor, except from Government benches. After a long debate, the opposition forced a vote on an amendment to limit the Government's priority—and the Government lost.

Following the Bill's third reading in the Lords, it was sent to the Commons. After debate on the general principles of the Bill in full House, the Bill was sent to a Standing Committee of MPs, who worked their way through it, clause by clause, before returning it amended to the full House for a third reading. The Standing Committee functions somewhat like a subcommittee of Congress. It is composed in proportion to the number of seats each party holds in the Commons, so the Conservatives had a strong majority. Some members are appointed effectively as whips, others because they are ministers or shadow ministers in the relevant area, and others because they are back-benchers with interests or expertise in the area. Unlike its American counterpart, however, there is no opportunity for interested groups or individuals to make formal representations to the committee itself. These must all be

---

[83] *Government White Paper*   [84] See ch. 6 below.

made indirectly through members of the Standing Committee who may then raise concerns for those by whom they are being briefed. In fact, this informal influence may be quite systematic. The minister, Alec Fletcher, was being briefed constantly by his civil servant advisor, Philip Pink, who was in the room, just as other MPs were receiving less obvious advice, amendments, and arguments from barristers David Graham and Peter Farmery. For instance, Nevil Trotter MP, an accountant and insolvency practitioner who sat on Standing Committee E, was briefed throughout by the Insolvency Practitioners Association, while Alfred Goldman and David Graham briefed the Labour leaders, Brian Gould and Gerald Bermingham, MPs.[85]

The Bill went back to the Lords, where debate was relatively limited. After a record 1,200 or more amendments, most of which were quite inconsequential, the Bill passed in both houses and received Royal Assent on 30 October 1985.[86]

The Agents of Reform

There are some similarities, but a number of differences, in the English approach to reform of insolvency law. Significant differences lie in the form and function of the respective commissions that advised the government. Moreover, interested parties to insolvency legislation were visible at different moments, and sometimes barely visible at all. For instance, the only systematic record of English organizations that mobilized to influence the law-making process comes at the "pre-legislative" stage—those organizations which presented evidence to the Cork Committee (see Table 3.5). Because the Department of Trade and Industry makes available no record of the organizations which made submissions following the publication of the White Paper, and because Parliament does not convene open hearings for interested parties that are ubiquitous in Congress, it is a significant challenge to plot the array and impact of organizations and individuals active in the politics of insolvency. Much of parliamentary politics, therefore, is the politics of insiders,

---

[85] UK Interviews 91:16; 91:17; 90:02; 90:19; 90:21.

[86] Although the passage of the Act represented the most wide-ranging reform of insolvency law in a century, there were two subsequent developments—a consolidation of the Insolvency Act with part of the Companies Act to produce the Insolvency Act 1986; and another consolidation and slight amendment of provisions on director disqualification from the Companies Act 1985 and the Insolvency Act 1985 in the Company Directors Disqualification Act 1986.

and for information we must rely on interviews, private papers, and non-official sources.

The differences in type and timing of mobilization notwithstanding, the array of actors in England was generally similar to the United States. Professions played an enormously influential role, the financial industry was closely involved at all stages, though non-financial industries and trade associations were more centrally involved than in the US. As in the United States, organized labor made representations, but on a small scale, presumably because labor's interests were entirely familiar to the Labour Opposition in Parliament. Unlike the United States, consumer groups acted much more vigorously, for they were much better organized. Utilities, too, made strong representations. And like their American counterparts, state agencies—the Insolvency Service, the Inland Revenue, the Treasury, and other departments—were actively engaged from the first hearings of the Cork Committee through to final enactment.

The Cork Committee

While its function paralleled the Bankruptcy Commission in the United States, the composition and methods of the Cork Committee led to a very different pre-legislative politics. That the Cork Committee was appointed by a Labour Government was of little relevance, for all observers agree with a civil servant that "... it was a fairly politically neutral committee within the left–right sort of spectrum. It was a committee of experts in the field, rather than political appointees."[87] The only obviously "political" appointee was Geoffrey Drain, a former trade union leader. Like its American counterpart, there was a strong representation of professionals. Oddly, given the dominance of accountants over insolvency and bankruptcy, the only accountant on the Committee was Kenneth Cork.[88] By contrast, it included four lawyers: Alfred Goldman, a solicitor who specialized in personal bankruptcy; Edward Walker-Arnott, a London corporate solicitor, Muir Hunter, QC, arguably England's leading personal bankruptcy barrister; and Peter Millett, a barrister with some specialty in corporate insolvency, who would later become a silk (Queen's Counsel), then a judge on Court of

---

[87] UK Interview 91:10.

[88] Cork pushed for other insolvency practitioners, but the Department of Trade and Industry refused (UK Interview 90:04). There were three members co-opted to the Committee, one of whom, Gerry Weiss, was an accountant. The others were David Graham, QC, a barrister, and J. R. Endersby, who was a solicitor with the Midland Bank.

Appeal, as Lord Justice Millett. At the time, Millett had been acting as legal counsel to the Department of Trade and Industry.[89] The Government appointed two members of the lower judiciary with extensive experience in day-to-day bankruptcy practice: John Hunter, who was a Northern Irish bankruptcy master; and Ritchie Penny, who had served in Kenya as a magistrate and was a registrar in a county court.

Unlike the Bankruptcy Commission, the Cork Committee included no politicians. But it incorporated representatives of four major repeat-players—organizations or institutions that repeatedly engage in a practice such as bankruptcy law and practice. The Government had approached the banking industry for names of a banker who could sit on the committee, and it appointed Peter Avis, from the Midland Bank, who maintained liaison throughout with the Committee of London Clearing Banks.[90] The unions were represented by Geoffrey Drain, a barrister who had been general secretary of a local government officers' union and had served as a director of the Bank of England. He was closest to a Labour Party appointee on the committee. Duncan McNab, who had been the general secretary of a co-operative society, understood consumer interests, and John Copp, an executive with a large industrial company, was familiar with the views of large corporate creditors.

Cork balanced these interest group representatives by appointing three legal and accounting experts to sit with the Committee, and by forming two consultative panels of experts—one of lawyers, one of accountants—to provide feedback and creative solutions to the formulation of new ideas and policy principles advanced by the Committee.[91] Despite the disproportionate presence of professionals, Cork believed that the Review Committee required access to greater academic and professional expertise. Chaired by Cork's long-time colleague at the insolvency firm of Cork Gully, and a close advisor, Gerry Weiss, the Accountants' Panel included leading members of the Insolvency Practitioners' Association, reorganization specialists from large accounting firms, including Mark Homan from Price Waterhouse, and academics. Chaired by Cork's close advisor, Alfred Goldman, the Lawyers' Panel included such distinguished law professors as Roy Goode, several solicitors, and another close advisor to Cork, barrister David Graham—later to become a Queen's Counsel and member of Cork's firm. A planned consultative committee on insurance never came about.

---

[89] UK Interviews 90:01; 91:07.   [90] UK Interview 91:13.
[91] *Cork Report*: 1. UK Interviews 90:04; 89:01; 90:21.

In practice, the Cork Committee relied substantially on the Consultative Panels. It used them as sounding boards for new ideas. It asked them for solutions to policy initiatives being considered by the Review Committee. And it requested detailed reactions to specific proposals, and later, draft recommendations to incorporate into the final report. Cork himself expected the legal panel to undertake some preliminary drafting of new measures, because he believed this would hasten implementation. But they were also expected to produce creative solutions to thorny legal issues. Because two trusted Cork advisors chaired the respective committees, and the Secretary of the Review Committee, Commander Trevor Traylor, acted as secretary for the Consultative Committees, their discussions were closely integrated—some said tightly controlled—into the discussions of the primary committee.[92]

The Cork Committee centered on a tight inner circle of professionals who already were very familiar with each other.

> ... [T]he insolvency world then, even more so than now, was a very closed circuit of people. You know, there were a few accountants doing it, a few solicitors, private practice, a few bank solicitors ... and the odd banker who was heavily involved in it. We all knew each other, and it was just when you turned up at the Cork Committee it was ... very clubby. I mean there were some people who weren't in the club who were involved.

The Cork Committee had strong overlap with its predecessor organizations. Of the six members of the Advisory Committee on the EEC Draft Convention on Bankruptcy, which had reported in 1976, three were also appointed to the Insolvency Review Committee (Cork, Avis, Muir Hunter). The chair of both committees was Kenneth Cork and the secretary of both was Trevor Traylor. Of the six individuals who gave oral evidence, three (David Graham, John Hunter, and Gerry Weiss) were closely associated with the Insolvency Review Committee, which for good reason came affectionately to be characterized by insiders as

---

[92] One informant, who was close to the lawyers' committee but not on it, styled the Consultative Committees as places for those who could have been on the main committee and were not, for whatever reason. The lawyers' group itself, he said, was the "most high powered" technically, a "powerhouse" which generated new ideas. It benefitted enormously from the leadership of David Graham, who "at that stage was probably the most impressive living intellectual insolvency practitioner in the country." (UK Interview 91:08). The legal panel met 21 times and produced 23 working papers and 37 miscellaneous working papers. The accountants' panel held 24 meetings and produced 24 working papers and 56 miscellaneous working papers.

Cork II.[93] Moreover, the group that produced the report, entitled *Bankruptcy* by Justice, the British Section of the International Commission of Jurists, included several closely associated with the Cork Committee, including Professor R. M. Goode, Alfred Goldman, David Graham. Muir Hunter, QC, and Gerry Weiss. Its secretary was Michael Crystal, who participated in the Joint Working Group of the Law Society and Bar on the Cork Report.[94] In the three reformist groups formed in the 1970s—the EEC Advisory Committee, the Justice Group on Bankruptcy, and the Insolvency Law Review Committee—three expert professionals (Muir Hunter, Graham, Weiss) served on all three, and several others served on two (Cork, John Hunter, Peter Avis, Trevor Traylor).[95]

After setting out its own general agenda for reform, the Cork Committee solicited opinions from hundreds of interested parties in industry, government, consumer organizations, professions, unions, and others. A large number provided written responses, and of those, a smaller number were selected to appear in oral hearings. Groups were often asked to elaborate upon criticisms or proposals and were themselves questioned about ideas the Cork Committee had begun to formulate. Table 3.5 lists those organizations that gave written and oral evidence.

Table 3.5: **Organizations that made Submissions to the Insolvency Law and Practice Committee (Cork Committee)**

Professional Associations and Firms	The Hundred Group of Chartered Accountants
Arthur Young McClelland Moores & Co.	*Insolvency Practitioners Association*
The Association of Authorised Public Accountants	The Institute of Chartered Secretaries and Administrators
The Association of Certified Accountants	Issuing Houses Association
The Association of Corporate Trustees	*The Joint Contracts Tribunal for the*
The City of London Solicitors' Company[a]	*Standard Form of Building Contract Inns*
The Consultative Committee of Accountancy Bodies	*of Court and the Bar and the Law Society*
	Joint Working Party of the Law Reform
	Committees of the Senate of the Inns of
	Court and the Bar and the Law Society
Ernst & Whinney	Justices' Clerks' Society
Hall Brydon	

[93] EEC Preliminary Draft Convention. Cmnd. 6602. P. 129. Appendix 1.

[94] London: Stevens and Son, 1975.

[95] So close were the connections that David Graham was the "junior" (a supporting barrister) to Muir Hunter QC, in the Poulson case, and Michael Crystal, later secretary of the Justice Report, was a pupil (and cousin) of Graham's. (UK Interview 91:08; 90:21).

Table 3.5 *Continued*

Kidsons
The Law Society
The Law Society of Scotland
The Senate of the Inns of Court and the Bar
The Society of Conservative Lawyers
Spicer and Pegler
Stoy Hayward & Co.
Touche Ross & Co.
Watkins Nayler & Co. Ltd.
John Williams of Cardiff Ltd.

Non-financial Businesses, Trade Associations
Aerialwork Ltd.
British Aerospace
British Airways
ATA Advertising Ltd.
BAT Industries Ltd.
BM Building Fabrications Ltd.
Bradstock, Blunt & Thompson Ltd.
BPC Ltd.
Carley & Co.
Chloride Group Ltd.
Brooke Bond Oxo Ltd.
Building Industry Consultancy Service
Courage Ltd.
The Delta Metal Company Ltd.
Elf Oil (GB)
Equipment Leasing Association
Esso Petroleum Company Ltd.
Freshfields
Gallaher Ltd.
Girsby Management Services Ltd.
Guest Keen & Nettlefolds Ltd.
John Laing Ltd.
Phoenix Assurance Company Ltd.
The Plessey Company Ltd.
Wm. F. Prior & Co.
Quardon Electronics (Semiconductors) Ltd.
Royal Dutch/Shell Group of Companies

Saville Tractors Ltd.
J. R. Sharpe (Skeet & Jeffes) Ltd.
Slough Estates Ltd.
Stewart Wrightson (Credit Management) Ltd.
Thorn Electrical Industries Ltd.
Trade Indemnity Company Ltd.
Trust House Forte Ltd.
Tube Investments Ltd.
Woodbridge Timber Ltd.

Commercial Trade Associations and Chambers of Commerce
The Association of British Chambers of Commerce
The British Constructional Steelwork Association
Committee of Associations of Specialist Engineering Contractors
City EEC Committee
Confederation of British Industry
Exeter & District Chamber of Commerce & Trade
Hastings and East Sussex Trade Protection Society
Federation of Associations of Specialists and Sub-Contractors
The Federation of Wholesale and Industrial Distributors
The Hire Purchase Trade Association
Maidenhead and District Chamber of Commerce
The Mail Order Traders' Association of Great Britain
Metal Window Federation
National Association of Trade Protection Societies
The National Council of Building Material Producers
National Federation of Builders' and Plumbers' Merchants

Table 3.5 *Continued*

*National Federation of Building Trades
    Employers*
National Federation of Self Employed
    and Small Businesses Ltd.
The Nottinghamshire Chamber of
    Commerce and Industry
The Rating and Valuation Association
The Retail Consortium
Sheffield Chamber of Commerce
United Kingdom Pilots' Association

**Financial Institutions and Trade
    Associations**
American Banks Association of
    London
The British Bankers' Association
British Insurance Association
The Committee of London Clearing Bankers
The Building Societies Association
British Insurance Association—
    Investment Protection Committee
The British Insurance Brokers'
    Association
Corporation and Committee of
    Lloyd's
Finance Houses Association Ltd.
Institute of Credit Management
London Personal Finance Association
Midland Bank Ltd.
Northern Ireland Bankers'
    Association
The Stock Exchange—Quotations
    Department

**Government Departments,
    Quangos, and Judiciary**
Board of Inland Revenue
*Department of Employment, Economic Policy
    (Manpower) Division*
Department of Health and Social Security
Department of Trade, Companies Division
Department of Trade, Insolvency Service

Court of Session, Edinburgh
The Eggs Authority
English Tourist Board
HM Customs and Excise
The Judges of the Chancery Division
The Judges and Registrars of the
    County Courts: (Birmingham,
    Blackburn, Bow, Cardiff, Croydon,
    Exeter, Gloucester, Halifax, Kings
    Lynn, Leeds, Maidstone, Reading,
    Sunderland, Wandsworth, Courts
    of the South Eastern Circuit)
Law Commission
Office of Fair Trading
The Post Office

**Consumer Organizations and
    Non-Profits**
The Birmingham Settlement Money
    Advice Centre
Consumers' Association
*Kent County Council, Consumer Protection
    Department*
*South Yorkshire County Council, Consumer
    Protection Department*

Local Governments
Association of District Councils
Association of Metropolitan
    Authorities
District Council of Brentwood
Metropolitan Borough of
    Knowsley

Unions
Furniture, Timber & Allied Trades
    Union, London District No. 18
*The Institution of Professional Civil
    Servants*
*Trades Union Congress, Economic
    Department*
Under Sheriffs Association

Table 3.5   *Continued*

Utilities	Capstick-Dale & Partners
British Gas Corporation	Humphreys & Parsons
The Electricity Council	Lucien A. Issacs & Co.
	Thomas Mackie & Sons Ltd.
Other/Unclassified	Little & Co.
R. A. Axtell & Partners	T. J. Newman & Co.

[a] References in italics signify organizations that made both written and oral submissions.

The Cork Committee contrasted sharply with its American counterpart in its approach to evidence. Whereas the US Bankruptcy Commission had the financial resources needed to mount surveys, empirical studies of the bankruptcy process, and conferences, the Cork Committee had none and satisfied itself completely with evidence from the experience of its inner and outer circles of committee members, supplemented with evidence from government agencies and private organizations. Hence the English reformers had no systematic information about any of the behaviors about which they were proposing remedies. Their final resort was experiential and pragmatic.

In a series of seventy-one meetings between 1979 and 1982, the Cork Committee formulated its report. Delivered of its charge, the Committee officially dissolved, but some of its members continued to lobby for action, as did Kenneth Cork in his repeated efforts to press the government to legislate, or to advise government ministers and members of parliament, as the Bill wended its way through Westminster. David Graham QC, and particularly Alfred Goldman, advised Lord Bruce in the Lords and the Labour Party leaders on this bill in the Commons.

The structure of private representation to the Cork Committee bore strong similarities to that in the United States. Like the American experience, interest groups divided into two: one class focused its activity narrowly on particular provisions, such as corporate governance, directors' responsibility, utilities, and taxes; another class engaged the entire spectrum of the reformist agenda with repeated briefs, commentaries, and reports. The dominant professional bodies exemplified this latter pattern of consistent, long-term, comprehensive coverage of the entire reform agenda and process.

The Professions

If a small group of professionals sat at the center of the bankruptcy reform circles, they were integrally connected to major, sustained initiatives by the leading societies of lawyers, accountants, and insolvency practitioners.

(a) Lawyers

Representations from the legal profession were co-ordinated through the Joint Working Party in Insolvency Law of the Law Reform Committees of the Law Society and the General Council of the Bar. The Law Society had a committee on insolvency in place from the mid-1970s. The Joint Working Party overlapped with lawyers who had worked on the draft EEC Bankruptcy Convention and the Justice group on personal bankruptcy. Operating autonomously from the general leadership of the Bar Council and the Law Society, the lawyers focused on technical aspects of the law and produced sixty briefs for the Cork Committee on recommended reforms. Reports from the Joint Working Party were also directed to the Department of Trade and Industry and the lawyers' counterpart in the accountancy profession. Except for some individual efforts, the Working Party did not transform itself into a lobbying or pressure group after the Cork Report. Its political posture remained low.[96]

(b) Accountants

The accounting profession, too, used a peak working group, the Consultative Committee of Accountancy Bodies (CCAB), to co-ordinate all representations of the main accounting bodies.[97] The members of the CCAB group on insolvency covered the spectrum of specialties from receiverships and corporate insolvency to personal insolvency. The CCAB divided into subcommittees and prepared an extensive set of submissions to the Cork Committee and the Department of Trade and Industry. Their engagement spanned the entire life of the reform process through the Government White Paper and the parliamentary debates,

---

[96] UK Interviews 90:11; 91:08; 91:01.
[97] The CCAB included the Institute of Chartered Accountants in England and Wales, the Institute of Chartered Accountants of Ireland, the Institute of Chartered Accountants of Scotland, the Chartered Association of Certified Accountants, the Institute of Cost and Management Accountants, and the Chartered Institute of Finance and Accountancy. See oral testimony to the Cork Committee by the CCAB, 24 Nov. 1990. *Public Record Office*.
[98] UK Interviews 91:02; 91:03.

where they informed and directed their thinking through Neville Trotter, an MP who was also an insolvency practitioner.[98]

Much of the accountants' interests centered on the professionalization of insolvency practice. Since both the government and the Cork Committee were intent on regulating the field of insolvency work, the accountants had a powerful incentive to ensure that they would have access to this work and that current practitioners could reasonably qualify. At the same time, they also had some interest in excluding other professions, such as the lawyers, from competing in what could be a lucrative field of practice. But their representations far exceeded pecuniary interests. Said one leader of the CCAB:

The professional interests differed in breadth from interest groups: our interest, the accountancy bodies and the IPA's interest, was right across the board in insolvency. And looking at the other people here, the bankers, the Inland Revenue—very capable people—but they were interested in a certain aspect and not the whole scene. We were interested in the whole scene.[99]

The peak accountancy body overlapped heavily with the Insolvency Practitioners' Association (IPA), an association of licensed and unlicensed accountants who specialized in bankruptcy and insolvency. The IPA had grown out of a discussion group formed in the 1960s and its reconstitution as a professional association immediately preceded the series of insolvency reforms in which it expected to register a voice.[100] In the politics of insolvency, the overlap was so complete that "the representations were often written by the same people and the same committee (for the respective organizations). They were almost word for word the same. There was no divergence really between the views of the IPA and the views of the CCAB." In fact, said a leader of both, "I found myself appearing twice and saying the same thing twice (for the respective groups)."[101]

Nevertheless, for the political mobilization of accountants, it made good tactical sense to multiply influence through representations to government by several overlapping organizations. The accountancy bodies included many insolvency practitioners who were not IPA members and whose interests should be represented, and unlicensed

---

[99] UK Interview 91:02.

[100] See Chapter 10.

[101] UK Interviews 91:02; 91:03; 90:14. Exemplifying the overlap was Mr Samwell's invitation in the same year to chair both the IPA law reform committee and the CCAB committee on insolvency.

accountants would not have been represented without the IPA. Moreover, there was significant advantage for the somewhat marginalized insolvency practitioners to borrow the prestige of the established accounting bodies, for "traditionally the chartered accountants were the premier accountancy body in the country and the government always asked their opinion."

(c) Judges

The virtual absence of judges from the reform process in England represents the most radical difference between the politics of bankruptcy on either side of the Atlantic. Judges adhere to a longstanding tradition that proscribes collective action on prospective legislation. The Judges of the Chancery Division did make some limited contributions in response to a request from the Cork Committee, and there were personal contacts between barristers on the Cork Committee and their judicial colleagues, but these were limited in scope. No formal representations of any magnitude occurred at any point.[102]

However, the Lord Chancellor's Department had much to say about Cork's proposals for the creation of a specialized Insolvency Court. English judges could wage a quiet campaign to maintain the court system they preferred. Whereas American judges were compelled to debate in open congressional hearings the merits of proposed changes in the American judiciary, their English counterparts were spared any appearance of politics. Inside the Government the Lord Chancellor simply informed his cabinet colleagues and the Department of Trade and Industry that he rejected Cork's proposal for a new insolvency court and the matter went no further. Of course, parliamentary amendments might have been proposed that an Insolvency Court be established. More than one peer or MP expressed regrets during the parliamentary debates that the Government had not seen fit to incorporate a specialized court system in its bill. But the Lord Chancellor had taken this proposal off the agenda following Cork, and none brought it back on.

Financial industry

Alongside the professions, the financial industry—clearing banks involved in retail banking, building societies, savings banks, finance houses—had the strongest general interests in insolvency reform. The

---

[102] UK Interview 91:14.

centralization of English retail banking into five major banks, each with many local branches on the "High Street" of every parliamentary constituency, should in principle ensure a strong basis for political mobilization. In fact the divisions within the English banking industry and the late entry of retail banking into parliamentary politics granted no automatic veto to retail bankers. Historically, the Bank of England advised the Government on matters of public policy that had far-reaching implications for financial stability, and would intervene in particular instances of financial collapse that might destabilize English financial institutions. But it had very little involvement in the insolvency legislation.

(a) The Clearing Banks

English banking divides along functional lines which correlate with the social class origins and networks of bankers themselves. Merchant bankers (or investment bankers in American terms) traditionally "have regarded themselves as the *crème de la crème* and socially several cuts above" retail bankers. "The merchant bankers regard themselves as the ex-public school boys (that is, private schools), and the ex-grammar school boys (that is, public schools) worked in the clearing (or retail) banks." In virtue of their class location, the merchant bankers maintained strong ties with the political elite.[103] But the tight networks between merchant bankers and Parliament had little consequence for insolvency, because "the merchant banks couldn't care less about insolvency. They really didn't do much lending anyway. It wasn't really a big deal for them. . . .[T]he only people who are really interested in insolvency were the clearing banks and the finance houses."[104]

The United Kingdom's largest retail banks—Midland, Lloyds, Barclays, the Royal Bank of Scotland, and National Westminster—are co-ordinated through the Committee of London Clearing Bankers (CLCB), an organization originally constituted to provide oversight for the clearing of transactions among banks. Until the early 1970s the CLCB had functioned more as a service organization for joint discussions and common activities. It deferred on legislative matters to the Bank of England. The turning point for the clearing banks came in 1974 when

---

[103] UK Interviews 91:13; 91:06. "The Old Boy network is between the merchant bankers and Westminster. The clearing banks did banking for the multitudes, whereas Barings (a venerable merchant bank later to be brought to its knees by one of its Singapore traders) did banking for governments and superpowers" (UK Interview 91:13).

[104] UK Interview 91:13.

"the banking industry was caught with its pants down" over a bill before Parliament on consumer credit and truth in lending. At this "watershed moment," the banks realized that disengagement from Whitehall or Westminster could be costly and they moved to bolster their influence as a representative body. They began by getting to know key civil servants and ensuring that the CLCB was on the consultation lists of all government departments related to banking. They also turned their sights on Parliament, said a CLCB official, by establishing

this program of getting to know likely members of Parliament, principally a lunch program...and we would generally try and find a peg to hang the invitation on. I would read Hansard every day...and I would see who had been talking in any way about banks, or had mentioned banking, or seemed to know something about banks and banking, and we set up a program to get them along and get them interested.[105]

But the CLCB, whose member banks serviced virtually every citizen and company in England, perceived itself to be relatively powerless in Westminster. In contrast to the Old Boy ties of the merchant bankers, during the mid-1970s there was not a single retail banker in the Commons for them to work with, and in the Lords, only one. According to another banker close to the insolvency reforms:

(Well, in my) experience the bankers haven't been particularly successful in their lobbying of Parliament directly. They have a very mixed success in that sort of thing. Their views are invited as the views of any other trade body or interested group. But their record isn't particularly good...[106]

Nonetheless, the clearing banks were consulted about putting a member on the Cork Committee and they formed a Working Party to liaise with Peter Avis, their nominee. The CLCB made submissions to the Cork Committee and its members generally monitored Cork's deliberations and the subsequent steps taken by the Government. On at least one occasion the Cork Committee sought reactions from the CLCB on proposals it was considering.[107] While the CLCB maintained a much lower profile than the professional organizations, its representations had considerable efficacy within the Cork Committee. It might well have been true that "any suggestion of the bankers' hidden hand of the power of the banking lobby" was misconceived, but the fact remains that on three crucial issues—changes to the floating charge security,

---

[105] UK Interview 91:13.   [106] UK Interview 90:03.
[107] *Minutes of the Cork Committee*, 11 July 1978.

changes to the controlling role of banks in receiverships, and changes in the retention of title security—the banks were largely, if not entirely, successful in protecting their privileged position, as we shall demonstrate in later chapters.[108]

Non-Financial Industries and Trade Associations

Table 3.5 shows that English industry and trade associations mobilized much more extensively than in the United States. But the listing is deceptive, for it disguises the fact that industry tackled the insolvency legislation selectively, on only a few highly contentious matters. Virtually all the individual firms wrote only a single letter, spurred by The Hundred Group of Chartered Accountants, to protest a rumor that the Cork Committee would recommend that parent companies be responsible in certain circumstances for the debts of subsidiaries. For insolvency practitioners, who sought to draw as many assets as possible into the estate of an insolvent company, it made good sense to target the assets of parent companies.[109] But corporations found the concept distinctly chilling, and they wrote, sometimes almost identically, to head off any attempts to reach into the pockets of parent or holding companies.

Many chambers of commerce and trade associations responded to a narrow set of issues. All deplored the abuses of insolvency practice by unlicenced practitioners and they endorsed the professional regulation of insolvency practice. Several expressed outrage at the "Phoenix Syndrome," in which unscrupulous company directors dissolved their companies, freed them of creditors' demands, and started up a new company in a similar or identical trade.[110] Most protested the floating

---

[108] For example, Peter Avis (along with several other committee members) wanted the security of trade creditors—retention of title clauses—outlawed in insolvency, but eventually it was maintained, with some restrictions. *Minutes of the Cork Committee*, 8 Mar. 1978.

[109] Kenneth Cork told his Review Committee that he thought "there was great demand for a holding company to be made responsible . . . for the debts of the subsidiary, but if the holding company becomes insolvent those debts should be deferred to creditors of the holding company." *Minutes*, 25 Sep. 1980. See also *Minutes*, 20 Aug. 1980, which reviewed briefs from the Accountants' Panel and Legal Panel, along with proposals for reforms in New Zealand, and comments from the One Hundred Group of Chartered Accountants and the Confederation of British Industry.

[110] In the House of Lords debates, Lord Denning described this process as follows: "A man acquires or forms a private company in which he holds a majority of the shares. He himself may be a director—he and his wife and one or two friends. What do they do? They incur debts; they milk the assets; and within a year, perhaps, the company goes into voluntary liquidation. A liquidator is appointed and the liquidator proceeds to sell the

charge, which allowed large banks to seize assets of insolvent companies with an arbitrariness and unfairness that angered other creditors. And trade creditors pressed strongly that their security, the retention of title, be respected in corporate insolvency, because it enabled trade suppliers to retain ownership of their goods after delivery and until they had been paid.

The Confederation of British Industry and the Institute of Directors generated the most headlines. Neither organization took very seriously the opportunity to present their views to the Cork Committee. But when the White Paper announced the Government's intention to sanction miscreant directors, through automatic disqualification and the prospect of civil actions brought by creditors against director's personal assets, both acted swiftly and decisively.

Representing the interests of the larger publicly-held companies, the Confederation of British Industry (CBI) maintains a public presence on matters concerning the general state of the economy, the nature of economic policy, and the concerns of big business. The White Paper galvanized the CBI to appoint a young barrister-lobbyist to sharpen the efforts of its Company Law Panel, which prepared CBI policy positions that opposed the Government. The CBI not only undertook the normal sorts of consultations with the civil servants and minister responsible for the bill, but it mounted a genteel campaign of education and pressure, especially in the House of Lords. With a core of interested peers on side, including Lords Benson, Bruce, Caldecote, and Mottistone, the CBI shadowed the peers during the debates in the Lords, preparing briefing materials, drafting amendments, conducting brief post-mortems after the important sessions—all to ensure the defeat of the government's most objectionable measures.[111]

assets; the liquidator is not necessarily a qualified man at all. A good buyer comes on the scene. The director who has been running that company gets a new company. He buys it 'off the shelf' by buying the shares of the company, and he buys the assets of the former company from the liquidator at a giveaway price. So he gets the assets of the first company into the hands of the second company. He changes the name of the second company to be very like the name of the first, so that people get mixed up between the two; and then having got this second company going, he goes through the whole process again. He incurs debts and gets such assets as there are; and he winds up the company. In each case he leaves a trail of creditors behind him." (H.L., vol. 458, 15 Jan. 1985, col. 901.)

[111] UK Interview 91:09. The fact that peers attended meetings and were briefed did not necessarily, in their minds, make them spokesmen for either the CBI or Institute of Directors. Lord Benson, for instance, stated that while his views were consistent with the two organizations, he did not consider that he spoke on their behalf. (UK Interview 90:01).

The lobbyist for the Institute of Directors candidly acknowledged that "we waited until late in the day (a few months before the bill was introduced to Parliament) because our political intelligence was not as good as it should have been."[112] When the Institute did spring into action, its Policy Unit joined forces with its Company Affairs Committee to defeat automatic disqualification of directors and personal liability of directors for company debts. Like the CBI, the Institute directed its efforts to the House of Lords, where it briefed the Earl of Buckinghamshire and Lord Noel-Buxton, together with a former chairman of the Institute and President of the Board of Trade. Although the Institute also briefed MPs who sat on Standing Committee E, their most "effective work was done in the House of Lords," where they had numerous members who were peers. They concentrated their efforts in the Lords for two reasons. The Institute of Directors believed that the Commons had formidable barriers to amendments. "Whips are much more heavily applied in the Commons, and the job of back bench members of standing committees is to shut up, write their letters, and vote when they are required to." It took a "very strong case" in the hands of a "very strong personality" to make headway. Not only did party whips deal a gentler hand in the Lords, but much company legislation is introduced there precisely because "you can probably find someone there who knows what they are talking about, without any particular axe to grind. . . . An amendment with a reasonable technical case stands a reasonable chance of getting pushed through in the Lords."[113]

The CBI formed a loose alliance with the Institute of Directors, more through shared information and a common cause than joint submissions. The Institute of Directors reached out to work not only with a number of smaller bodies representing business, including The Association of British Chambers of Commerce, but they even found common cause with unlikely allies, the National Consumer Council and the Consumers' Associations, on a couple of matters.

In the event, their results were mixed. While the Lords voted down automatic disqualification of directors, the major peak associations of business and directors could not derail the impetus to make directors personally liable for company debts, if they failed to act soon enough to protect themselves and their creditors.

[112] "In hindsight," he observed, "we would certainly have treated it much more seriously . . . we simply didn't pick it up in time to do anything significant with the committee."

[113] UK Interview 90:08.

Consumer Groups

Consumer issues had been a stimulus for reform from the beginning and consumer groups continued to push strongly for changes in the law that would protect consumers and allow them to recover prepayments, deposits, and other losses commonly experienced by unsecured creditors. A national consumer organization, the Consumers' Association, published a magazine, *Which?*, with a circulation of more than two million. Yet its political influence came not from mobilizing its national constituency,[114] but from joining hands with the media, forming alliances, and finding sympathetic sponsors at Westminster.

The Consumers' Association had long supplied Esther Rantzen's popular BBC TV program, "That's Life," with legal advice, subjects and data. It complained early to the Cork Committee about ways that weak creditors were victimized in bankruptcy law. Together with the National Consumer Council it advocated protections for consumer prepayments as well as strong sanctions against reckless or callous directors. The two organizations had identical positions and they took advantage of their substantial cachet to provoke media attention to the insolvency bill, while they lobbied and briefed MPs and peers, such as Lord Taylor and Lord Mottistone. On some issues—reducing the government's priority in the queue for assets—they formed a surprising alliance with the Institute of Directors and Confederation of British Industry, but their views diverged sharply over sanctions against company directors. Nevertheless, more than one peer invoked the Consumers' Association and the National Consumer Council in support of some way of protecting consumers' prepayments, but without success. The Consumers' Association took some heart, however, from the reduction in the government's claims for back taxes, and while automatic disqualification was voted down in the Lords, the provision on directors' personal liability for company debts remained a measure strongly advocated by consumer groups.[115]

Unions

Since the Cork Committee was appointed by a Labour Government, it is not surprising that the Government appointed a member with union

---

[114] The Consumers' Association had considered American-style write-in campaigns which would mobilize the subscribers to *Which?*, but decided that the strong system of party whips in the Commons would effectively defeat such initiatives (UK Interview 90:16).

[115] UK Interview 90:16.

credentials. Geoffrey Drain, its nominee, might well have championed measures that would have favored workers. But his participation in the Cork Committee was so minimal—he effectively stopped attending after the 7th committee meeting[116]—that he could do little to support those initiatives that would improve the standing of workers in bankruptcy.

The Trades Union Congress mounted a strong team, headed by Lord Allen, chairman of the TUC Economic Committee, which made both written and oral submissions to the Cork Committee. Organized labor wanted workers' wages to be given preferential treatment in bankruptcy. It also pressed for wider, earlier consultative relations between management and labor when a company experienced financial difficulties, a proposal that generated some warm exchanges between the panelists, most of whom resisted any obligation for insolvency practitioners to consult workers before management received court protection, and the unionists, who believed workers should know that all avenues were being pursued to keep the business going and workers employed. Unionists also struck out at the receivers appointed by banks, by urging that they "have a duty to take into account employee interests."[117]

However, English employment legislation softened the bite of unemployment. Largely in response to pressure from the European Community, provisions in the Employment Protection Act provided compensation for employees who lost their jobs because their employer became insolvent. Under the Act, the Department of Trade and Industry created a redundancy fund. When an employer became insolvent, the fund would quickly pay employees their back wages and holiday pay up to a limit. The DTI then would seek to "claw back" those moneys from the estate of the insolvent company. For workers, this had the advantage that it was quick and saved them having to act as creditors, for the government essentially stood in their place.[118] Part of the debate over labor, therefore, occurred more over what statute would offer particular protections, than whether or not they would be offered at all.

A more intriguing manifestation of "labor" that has no equivalent in the United States came from the Institution of Professional Civil Servants (Insolvency Service Branch), a white collar, non-party affiliated, union of civil servants, who in this case were also higher ranking members of the Insolvency Service. Indeed, Philip Pink, who made a notable

---

[116] He attended nine meetings of the seventy-one held by the committee.

[117] Oral Testimony by the Trades Union Congress, *Public Record Office*, 11 May 1978.

[118] Employment Protection Act. UK Interview 91:17.

impression on the Cork committee members, headed the Institution's delegation and subsequently headed the civil service policy team that spearheaded the insolvency legislation.[119] In their guise as members of a civil service professional body, the civil servants proceeded entirely as experts, informing the committee of their objections to certain practices by banks and directors. Pink and his team protested deleterious effects of banks' floating charges and urged that company directors be exposed to criminal and civil actions if they had engaged in fraudulent trading, calling for "a complete rethink about what . . . [is] sometimes called white collar fraud." The civil servants came into play again in 1980, this time in direct conflict with the position taken by their own department. When the Government published its controversial Green Paper, which proposed to privatize a large amount of previously government work, the Institution of Professional Civil Servants made representations to Cork which effectively undercut, indeed on some points flatly contradicted, the position taken by their colleagues who were responsible for the Green Paper. Thus professional organization within the civil service permitted government insolvency experts to express their points of view free from bureaucratic imperative or government muzzles.[120]

---

[119] A key player inside the Cork Committee recalled the express sentiments of others as he also indicated the strong internal connections that occur in the professional core of this statute: ". . . the other person who impressed us was the representative of the staff side of the Department of Trade, Philip Pink. And came over very strong, very sensible, and very perceptive. . . . Little did I know that he would become the chief policy maker or head of policy . . . for insolvency . . . and was the minister's right hand man throughout the passage of the legislation" (UK Interview 90:21).

[120] Oral evidence from the Institution of Professional Civil Servants (Insolvency Service Branch), 13 June 1978. Comments by David Graham. *Public Record Office*. It should be noted, however, that a strong set of conventions governs when civil servants can differ from views taken by their superiors or their ministers. Civil servants who are actually on a bill team and directly engaged in the conception and drafting of legislative proposals cannot step outside their obligations to their departments or the minister, short of withdrawing from the team or resigning. However, other civil servants, at arms length from legislative proposals, may use their union to express points of view independent of their departments and the policy positions of government ministers. One civil servant on the team described how "we gave our evidence not in respect to the department but in respect to the views of the staff rather than the views of the department." Refining the point, he stated that "where as a civil servant you are in a very impartial role, you administer the law as the law is. And you take direction from your ministers on policy and possibly interpretation of the law in certain instances. But then there is the individual. You have got your own views. In theory, we are constrained in expressing views that aren't the party, the government, views. But in these sort of consultation exercises, and particularly where in this instance the unions took a view that the Green Paper was going completely in the wrong direction, as a union rather than as individuals, you can express contrary views. It happens quite often." (UK Interviews 91:10; 91:17).

Organized labor continued to monitor the Insolvency Bill through to enactment. It maintained contact with Labour leaders in the Commons and Lords. But there is no evidence that it played a particularly powerful role in a Conservative-dominated legislature other than to lend what support it could for preservation of workers' preferences. The bolder concepts of worker consultation at earlier stages of corporate decline fell away at the beginning of the reform process and never returned with any force.

Government Departments and Agencies

Unlike the United States, English government departments, especially the Department of Trade and Industry's Insolvency Service, were integrally involved in the reform process from beginning to end. The Review Committee was a child of the Department of Trade and Industry which also determined its terms of reference. All of the minutes of the Cork Committee meetings were forwarded to the Inspector General of the Insolvency Service (with rare exceptions), so at all times he was briefed on the directions taken by the Committee. The mid-course correction forced on the Committee by the 1980 Green Paper came from the DTI, impelled by the arrival of a Conservative Government concerned about the resources of public administration, and the final report was submitted to the DTI.

The DTI drafted the White Paper, which set out the Government's legislative intentions. From the time of Cork's Report until the introduction of the Insolvency Bill, the DTI policy team sought to accommodate interests outside and inside the Government. Following the Cork Report, and even more so, the White Paper, civil servants and the minister received submissions and met with interest groups and individuals who wanted changes of one or another measure. At the same time, the DTI orchestrated the differing interests of government departments, which not infrequently clashed over the principles and recommendations of the Cork Report.

The most direct conflict occurred between the DTI and the revenue-collecting departments. The DTI's Insolvency Service had an interest in rehabilitating businesses and therefore pressed to keep as many assets as possible in the pool to finance corporate rehabilitation. This led the DTI to press for a reduction in the special preferences that creditors, including tax authorities, were given in the assets of an insolvent company. But the Inland Revenue, Customs and Excise and the Treasury more generally used insolvency proceedings as a method for collecting unpaid taxes.[121] As a senior civil servant put it, "the Chancellor of the Exchequer doesn't want to give up anything."[122] Consequently, substantial differences among government departments can be found in the oral submissions to the Cork Committee made by the Inland Revenue, the Department of Employment, the Department of Trade, and Customs and Excise. Moreover, at a time when Mrs Thatcher was pressing government departments to downsize, any changes in administrative arrangements for insolvency, which shifted the burden from one department to another, brought them into conflict. Insofar as the insolvency legislation involved the courts, the Lord Chancellor's Department also was involved.[123] Cork's recommendation for the creation of a specialized insolvency court was killed by opposition from the Lord Chancellor.[124]

Many of the provisions in the White Paper and the subsequent Insolvency Bill, therefore, represent agreements within government between civil servants and ministers. In fact, one of the Government's stinging defeats in the House of Lords resulted from exactly such a settlement. The Department of Trade and Industry argued long and unsuccessfully with Treasury for a reduction in the taxes that would be owed from insolvent corporate estates. Neither the White Paper nor the Insolvency Bill, therefore, incorporated this recommendation of the Cork Committee. But the House of Lords did concur with Cork and the DTI's earlier position and it voted down Treasury's preference—the Crown preference—in the Bill. Ironically, therefore, the defeat suffered by Lord Lucas, the minister leading for the DTI in the Lords, put back into the statute provisions his department had failed to win on the playing field of intra-governmental politics.

POLITICAL MOBILIZATION AND PATTERNS OF INFLUENCE

At the outset of this chapter, we proposed that law-making can be understood in terms of the distribution of power in temporal and

---

[121] In their Oral Testimony to the Cork Committee (21 Oct. 1980), officials from the Inland Revenue estimated they were creditors in some 30 per cent of all bankruptcies.

[122] UK Interview 91:17.

[123] Oral Submissions to the Cork Committee by the Inland Revenue Department (21 Oct. 1980), the Department of Employment, Economic Policy (Manpower) Division (21 Oct. 1980), Department of Trade, Companies Division (22 Oct. 1980), Customs and Excise (10 Nov. 1980). *Public Record Office*. Along with preferences on betting and gaming licenses, Customs and Excise administered the VAT (Value Added Tax), which involved the department in some 9,000 bankruptcy cases a year in which it recovered some £6 million.

[124] UK Interview 91:17.

political structures, in terms of ideas about political dominance, and in terms of distinctive patterns of influence. We now return, in reverse order, to these frames and draw some provisional conclusions about the general structure of influence in making bankruptcy law. These will be elaborated and refined by the empirical materials presented in Parts II and III.

Profiles of Influence

The schematic analysis of the principal players in the United States reforms sustains the proposition that there were two contrasting profiles of influence. On the one hand, professional specialists pervaded every stage and every element of the reforms (Tables 3.2, 3.3). Epitomized by the National Bankruptcy Conference, bankruptcy lawyers, judges, and academics formed a relatively tight circle of some twenty to thirty individuals, variously representing themselves and their professional associations. Even here there were gradations. At the core was a circle of Commissioners and staffers, House staffers, and members of the NBC and NCBJ, who worked in close consultation for more than eight years to produce the Code. A second circle was comprised of frequent and fairly broad-based representations by the American Bar Association and Commercial Law League. A third circle, exemplified by the federal judges, confined itself to a narrow range of issues, but acted on them forcefully. On the other hand, there were non-professional groups that acted vigorously, most notably, the financial industry. They, too, were engaged fairly broadly and through several phases of the process. It was the creditor interests, and not the debtors, that dominated; capital and not labor, which defined its interests very narrowly.

The "repeat-players"—the financial industry to a lesser degree and the professionals to a pronounced degree—favored a general philosophical approach to the comprehensive reforms that would present a global package of changes, finely balancing all interests against the others in pursuit of an overall goal. Professionals could claim that their goal was to serve the public good, the more so when their representative associations or putative motives could be seen to be disinterested. Of course, professionals had jurisdictional interests in almost every aspect of the reforms, and these were manifest. Those aside, the legitimacy of professional influence rested on the relative ideological neutrality of the legislation and balance that professionals, representing all parties in bankruptcy, could strike among themselves. In this sense, a meta-bargain among professionals prefigured a meta-bargain amongst all parties to bankruptcy law reform (cf. Halliday 1987: ch12).

The general "packet" advanced by the inner professional circle, and effectively negotiated with the strongest interest groups, resulted in a series of trade-offs, all in service of the ideal of rehabilitating corporations or saving businesses. The state (IRS) gave up some of its priorities in bankruptcy, and the SEC lost most of its control over corporate reorganizations. Bankers gave up some control over their assets in reorganization in return for strong guarantees to protect their assets. Corporate directors and managers—debtors-in-possession—obtained greater discretion to reorganize their companies, free of creditor harassment. Legal professionals were given strong new incentives to practice bankruptcy law in a deal-making style, and with much greater rewards. And bankruptcy courts and judges were drastically upgraded.

To a remarkable degree, the general configurations of interest on the English side virtually mirror the experience in the United States, with some national variations. The inner core of English professionals, many of whom spanned the entire eight years from 1977 to 1985, was even more tightly knit. The core group of lawyers and accountants in the Review Committee had long-standing personal and professional relationships, they had served together either in Justice or on "Cork I," the Review Committee on European bankruptcy law, and they overlapped with the primary professional associations which most comprehensively engaged the reform efforts—the Co-ordinating Committee of Accountancy Bodies, the Joint Bar and Law Society working group on bankruptcy, and the Insolvency Practitioners' Association. This group of ten to fifteen lawyers and accountants, and a slightly wider circle of compatriots in the respective professional bodies, canvassed every aspect of insolvency law, and they did so from the inception of the Cork Committee through passage of the Insolvency Act, with some attenuation of efforts once the political process got under way in 1984. In contrast to the United States, the Insolvency Service within the Department of Trade and Industry was the other "universal" actor for it initiated the Review Committee, drafted its terms of reference, monitored its activities, reacted to its report, drafted the government's legislative intentions, and molded them into the bill, which it helped shepherd through Parliament. Here again a very small number of key individuals predominated.

Both the professional circle and the government department took a systemic approach to the law. Any higher priority ranking given to one party necessarily had an adverse effect on another. Indeed, the Cork Committee itself was explicitly conscious of a deal it was seeking to effect between secured creditors (and especially banks) and unsecured creditors. It sought to increase the flexibility available to insolvency practitioners who were attempting to rehabilitate a company without trampling the property rights of trade and other creditors. Its systemic approach was informed simultaneously by values of equity and pragmatism. For instance, the Cork Committee agreed that floating charges used by banks frequently produced inequities and disproportionately hurt weak creditors; yet they also knew that a full-scale assault on the floating charge could so alienate the banks that their legislative support would be withdrawn. Similarly, they were in conflict over the rights of trade creditors, who on the one hand wanted to maintain ownership of their goods until they were paid for, but on the other hand could frustrate the ability of insolvency practitioners to act decisively and save a business. The Department of Trade and Industry also had a global orientation, though its emphases differed somewhat from those of the Cork Committee.

Few other political actors in England spanned the full range of bankruptcy concerns. The financial industry, substantially through the internal interventions of its nominee on the Review Committee, did mobilize on a broader front than most other organizations, although it concentrated its fire on critical provisions to do with the floating charge and its ability to control corporate reorganization. Several political actors had highly focused strategies and they mobilized vigorously to remove offensive or include neglected provisions. The Consumers' Association, the Institute of Directors, the utilities—each had a relatively narrow target and they focused on it intensely. The Consumers' Association followed a focused course of action over the entire period, but their reliance on the press and on sympathetic legislators made the last two years the most critical. The Institute of Directors stayed outside the process until the year the government announced its legislative intentions. It might have exercised influence earlier and its late entry was inadvertent. The Confederation of British Industry, by contrast, deliberately waited until the late stages of reforms, quietly assured that it could block anything too objectionable through its powerful connections in the Lords.

The contrast between political actors with global versus focused types of engagement in statutory reforms crystallizes differences in the mode of politics either can practice. Global players have more room for negotiation, or degrees of freedom, on any given issue, because they have an "inventory" of many issues among which they can do trade-offs. One-issue and focused players, by contrast, have no such freedom. They may have some limited ways of packaging some divisible elements of their narrow interests, but they are much more constrained in the options they have for give and take. Inevitably they appear more rigid and arguably they more quickly have recourse to raw political power, threatened vetoes, and the like. Invariably they appear unreasonable and obdurate. Because global players can yield or trade-off on particular points, they can negotiate with greater flexibility and look more reasonable in the process.

Patterns of Dominance

Do these contrasting patterns of influence affect dominance in law-making? Before the evidence is adduced in subsequent chapters, a definitive answer to this question is premature. However we may advance some preliminary observations about four theories of dominance—respectively, financial, political, state agencies and officials, and professionals.

The evidence in this chapter on the financial industries does not establish their dominance of bankruptcy law-making. In neither country did the financial industries mobilize across the full spectrum of the legislation, though they did exert influence on a broader front than most special interest groups. In both countries the financial industry concentrated particularly on protection of their property rights and in minimizing risks to dissipation of their assets during corporate reorganization. Both had some interest in bankruptcy administration: the English bankers supported regulation of insolvency practice and the American bankers argued forcefully for radical reforms of the bankruptcy courts. On none of their issues did they lose heavily, but neither did each industry act with instrumental power to impose solutions on all other players in the reforms. More likely, the bankers set some parameters around the legislative process and some minimum thresholds for settlements they could accept. So long as no party sought to abolish a key security, or to rob banks of any control or protection of their assets in reorganization, they were prepared to let the reform process run its course.

Political ideology took quite different forms in each reform process. In the United States, it effectively was absent altogether. In Britain, however, a set of circumstances, including rapidly rising bankruptcy rates and rising public dissatisfaction, brought the apparently technical legislation of insolvency into the broader currents of Mrs Thatcher's policies to downsize government, to privatize industry, to stimulate entrepreneurship, and to clean up markets so they would be safe for ordinary investors. Whatever its technical complexities, it is inconceivable that the English Act can be understood without comprehension of the powerful ideological undercurrents that variously sought to champion reorganization, privatize bankruptcy administration, professionalize insolvency practice, and discipline company directors. While professionals and their technical interests were pervasive in the English reforms, the particular cast of the insolvency reforms, and the very fact of their parliamentary passage, testified to the affinity between professional agendas and wider party ideology.

Considerable evidence has already been adduced to indicate the influence by state agencies and officials. The institutional structure of legislative bodies in the US and Britain leads to a significant difference in roles among governmental entities. In the US the draft legislation came in the form of two bills, one from a government-appointed commission and the other from a private association of bankruptcy judges. While these permitted staffers on congressional committees some discretionary opportunities, and while federal agencies did make representations in a fashion not dissimilar to private interest groups, neither evidenced anything like the pervasive influence of the English civil servants later in the reform process. The legislation in Britain emerged from a government department as it adopted, selected, and adapted the various provisions from the Review Committee the department had initially appointed. In fact, the government department effectively co-ordinated the entire reform process. It is not easy to distinguish actions by civil servants that demonstrate views independent of their political masters or the interest groups and Review Committee. Nevertheless, especially in the matter of work jurisdictions, we shall show a strong point of view expressed by civil servants with some measure of success.

It can already be observed that professionals pervaded all stages of British and US reforms. They did so in substantial part precisely because bankruptcy legislation has several of the attributes most conducive to expert influence (Brint 1994; Halliday 1983, 1987). Without much deliberate politicking, professionals on either side of the Atlantic successfully drew a mantle of technical complexity over the distributive features of the legislation and so diverted many legislators, interest groups, and affected constituencies from the potential impact of their recommendations. Of course, both reform efforts canvassed opinion fairly widely, but it is notable that several major sets of interests either did not see or did not care about the issues placed on the table by reformers, who were preponderantly professionals. And we shall see that not all major interest groups remained at bay throughout. Some sprang into action very late in the day, but with great vigor and some little success.

The infusion of professionals through the reform processes begs the question of the guise in which they are acting. Professionals may mobilize on their own behalf, as they compete for wider jurisdictions of work, higher status and monetary rewards, more interesting and influential sorts of practices, and the like. Professionals may act collectively or individually as agents of their clients, who remain discreetly out of sight. And then again professionals may act with a civic consciousness, admixing their own interests, and those of their clients, with some concept of a public good. Our study will show much evidence of public goods at the moment of their creation. But public goods are mixed in most complex ways with contests for jurisdiction over larger or more desirable areas of work.

Finally, this chapter has presented evidence that the market power and political power of actors in the politics of bankruptcy are not identical. Powerful actors in the market, such as the financial industry, or utilities, could not always translate market dominance into political pay-offs. Ironically, as the utilities in England discovered, great strength in the market can trigger a political backlash. Obversely, weakness in the market can be compensated by political strength. Consumers in either country were vulnerable in the market, but obtained considerable force in the political arena, if not always successfully.

PART 2

Reconstituting Property Rights

Introduction

The goal of rescuing business courses through both the British and American reforms. From the outset of reforms to their enactment, politicians and professionals repeat the refrain that a new bankruptcy law should help "save business," give companies a "second chance," rehabilitate companies unfortunate enough to be caught by an economic downturn or sudden cash-squeeze, and reorganize companies whose finances or debt-structure have become unmanageable.

Two things must happen to achieve the rehabilitation of corporations. First, more funds or assets must be brought into the estate (the "basket" of resources available to the agents of reorganization) so that reorganizers have the means to turn the company around.[1] Second, more flexibility and control must be given to the agents of reorganization. Both of these presuppose a "freeze" or a "moratorium," or a "stay" on the rush of creditors to seize assets and remove them from the control of the reorganizers. Companies and their agents of rehabilitation must be given a "breathing period" in order to take stock, appraise the situation, and develop a plan for reorganization that can be executed without having to fight constant rearguard battles with creditors eager to seize company assets.

More funds in the estate, and more control by reorganizers can in turn be achieved by two broad courses of action. First, more funds can be made available for saving businesses by: (1) taking assets away from the strongest creditors, such as banks, the state, and utilities, and putting them into the estate to swell resources available for reorganization; (2) permitting strong creditors to retain their property right over assets, but persuading or compelling them to delay seizing the assets and to relax their control over use of the assets; and (3) providing incentives to

---

[1] The agents of reorganization in the United States may be either the managers of the bankrupt firm or trustees. If the creditors approved, *managers* of the pre-bankruptcy firm can remain in control of the company, and are designated "debtor-in-possession" (DIP). They may act in consultation with the creditors' committee and in a manner consistent with the plan for reorganization accepted by the bankruptcy court. If the court or creditors decide to displace current management, they can appoint in its stead an "independent or disinterested" *trustee*, who would be proposed by the United States trustee and affirmed by the court. The agent of reorganization in the UK is a new position invented for this purpose—an *administrator*, is proposed by a firm's managers or creditors and affirmed by the court. Otherwise the secured creditors with a floating charge appoint a *receiver* who may or may not liquidate the business.

creditors so that new moneys will be made available to finance reorganization.

Second, more flexibility and control over assets can be achieved by a combination of two approaches: (1) reducing the discretion of strong creditors, like banks or the state, to liquidate a business or seize assets at will, or to be unduly intrusive in the reorganization itself; and (2) creating agents of reorganization, and/or endowing agents of reorganization with greater discretion and bargaining power.

Part II analyzes the ways that British and American players in the bankruptcy reforms sought to bargain their way around the trade-offs required to change the law on company reorganization. Chapters 4 and 5 treat three sets of strong creditors, whom virtually all other parties to the reforms sought to weaken. The secured creditors, overwhelmingly banks, sought to protect the strong property rights they had bargained with companies against attack inside bankruptcy. Politicians, professionals, weaker creditors, and the agents of debtors all knew they must loosen the grip of secured creditors over their property or the ideal of rehabilitation could not be attained.

Chapter 5 reveals that the state had even less friends. Every interest group and constituency in bankruptcy politics, including the secured creditors, circled around the revenue agencies of the state (the Internal Revenue Service, Inland Revenue) looking for points of weakness so that moneys for back taxes, previously seized by the government, could instead be channelled into reorganization, or to weaker creditors, or maybe proportionately to all other creditors. Similarly, Chapter 5 shows how monopolies, such as utilities, found themselves besieged by other creditors and debtors who resented their practices of jumping the queue of creditors by threatening to turn off the power, water, and gas unless debtors paid them (first).

Chapter 6 analyzes the metabargaining over legal changes that might enable managers and administrators to use their swollen basket of assets with greater flexibility to turn a business around, if the tight grip of banks, revenue authorities, and utilities over assets could be loosened. Who should have the power to reorganize a company? Its former managers? Private professionals? Civil servants? And how can bankruptcy law facilitate their efforts while protecting the property rights of creditors? We shall see that British and American reformers took radically different views about the competency and efficacy of who the law should designate as the optimal agent of reorganization. Indeed, the two countries differed sharply in how intrusively they imagined bankruptcy law might penetrate into constructing the morality of markets.

Then there are the weak creditors: consumers, trade suppliers (companies that supply goods to other companies), and workers. Chapter 7 identifies a strong impulse in both countries to do something for weak creditors in corporate bankruptcies. But the story of weak creditors is more than a struggle of the Davids of small business and defenseless widows against the Goliaths of vastly powerful retail banks and the overweening state. Weak creditors draw attention to a fundamental antinomy that flows through the bankruptcy reforms.

There are two logics interwoven in the law-making: a political logic and a market logic. At the level of bargaining in the market, a logic of efficiency prevails in rhetoric, if not always in practice. According to this logic, market efficiency is best served when assets in a corporate bankruptcy are taken from failed companies and re-allocated to successful companies. A strict application of this logic to bankruptcy would presume that firms in financial distress should be liquidated (and, more doubtfully, reorganized) so that scarce resources of capital should flow to the most competent managers. If this logic were to be applied in the political arena, then the only point at issue would be how best to shift moneys or control from strong creditors, the state, and utilities, to managers or professional agents of reorganization.

At the level of metabargaining, however, a different logic comes into play—that of equity, fairness, or justice. Politicians cannot simply ignore the fallout from a strict adherence to efficiency. In their calculus of political trade-offs, they must weigh the market principle of pragmatism against concepts of equity, no matter whether rehabilitation would be best served by ignoring weak creditors. Legislators attuned to the sensibilities of constituents, especially for political parties close to weak creditors, like consumers and workers, know that any solution for corporate creditors must include the fact or appearance of concessions to weaker players in the market and politics (though the two are not necessarily identical).

In the political arena, liquidation of companies does not sell well. Business failure, lost jobs, closed plants, depressed communities, domino-effect collapses of more fragile dependent businesses—none play well in local political constituencies. Saving business, on the other hand, has a much more constructive ring and stakes a claim to a more defensible moral high ground. Saving businesses, coupled with better protected weaker creditors, compounds political capital. Metabargaining consequently overlays the market logic brought into the political arena by conventional players in day-to-day bankruptcies with a political logic that demands the balance of efficiency with the values of equity and fairness, the muscle of large economic actors with the vulnerabilities of small individual consumers. The political arena brings new players along with competing principles.

The chapters in Part II thus reveal the often awkward juxtaposition of market strength and weakness with their political counterpart. With saving business as the goal, for instance, the strong creditors of Chapter 4 will not get far with their stated preference to turn companies around *outside* bankruptcy and with themselves, or their agents, in control. While they must find a rhetoric suitable for political theater, they must also be weakened in some degree. But they hold a strong hand: politicians and reformers know, or believe, that at once they must whittle away some of the strong creditors' rights without triggering an adverse reaction that might sink statutory reforms altogether. Unless political reformers can find a proper balance between the re-allocation of assets and the principle of efficiency, they will doom a metabargain to failure.

The state and utilities, on the other hand, can be attacked in the political arena with relative impunity. Indeed, an assault on the prerogatives of the state, and its disproportionate grab for assets at the expense of other players in the bankruptcy game, resonates well with the audiences to the reform debates. Forging an alliance against revenue authorities comes easily and at low political cost. To every other actor, a solution that weakens the state in bankruptcy seems both equitable and not a little efficient. Hence the state itself, ironically enough, proves a soft target for the moral entrepreneurs who seek to save businesses.

The pragmatics of strengthening the hand of reorganizers—management, administrators, trustees—convey a constructive tone whose public appeal vindicates its own rationality. Surely it is better to save a business than to destroy it. And if it can be done in a way that enables every party to benefit, then economics and politics succeed simultaneously. But politics does not require the strict accounting of success or failure that economics demands. Therefore enabling managers in statutory law may yield a political dividend very substantially more than its actual economic consequences will impart.

The weak creditors we observe in Chapter 7 bring the market and political logics most acutely into tension. To protect weak creditors, to redistribute resources to consumers, to allow trade creditors to frustrate reorganization, to give workers substantial benefits—all may hinder the prospect of a successful turnaround for a company. Not only the diversion of assets, but the transaction costs of accommodating large numbers of small creditors, can impede reorganization. Yet weak players in the market may turn out to be powerful players in politics and to forge strong alliances in metabargaining. Thus, claims of equity that play well in the political arena can be mobilized through political action. By the same token, however, the equity claims of weak creditors may threaten a successful metabargain every bit as much as the efficiency claims of strong creditors. Hence the fine line negotiated by reformers who seek to strike such an overall bargain must be to negotiate between the politically appealing claims of the weak for a larger share of assets in bankruptcies, and the voracious claims of reorganizers and secured creditors for assets sufficient to produce a successful reorganization.

As a result, the politics of metabargaining over the rules that govern corporate reorganizations are about the micro-politics of bargaining over the norms of individual reorganizations. On the one hand, the logic of bargaining in the market does not translate seamlessly into a political logic, and thus the politics of bankruptcy law are in part a clash of competing logics on a playing field defined more by politics than the market. That will produce a dynamic, a set of players, and number of outcomes perceptibly different from what might have occurred in a private settlement among economic actors. On the other hand, the bankruptcy reforms represent a struggle over rules of the game in everyday practice. The political settlement in Congress or Parliament sets the rules, weights the handicaps, and designates the players, in all subsequent market settlements.

4 Weakening the Strong: Banks and Secured Lenders

By Bruce G. Carruthers, Terence C. Halliday, J. Scott Parrott

A large scholarly literature attributes considerable economic and political power to banks. They do not simply collect deposits and make loans, so the argument goes, but help to co-ordinate investment, influence markets, and shape the overall direction of economic development. Mintz and Schwartz, for example, argue that: ". . . a substantial proportion of the discretionary decision making of the most significant enterprises in our economy is conditioned by decisions made by the leadership of financial companies" (Mintz and Schwartz 1985: 70).[1] They go on to claim that banks exert themselves most vigorously during corporate bankruptcies, when they can dominate a creditor's committee and shape the reorganization of troubled firms: ". . . chapter 11 bankruptcy is a legally mandated form of bank control involving the subordination of corporate policy to bank dictation" (Mintz and Schwartz 1985: 83). In their view, bankruptcy is a crucial setting for the exercise of bank power.

Of all the organizations in the credit network, financial institutions are among the most sophisticated at crafting debtor–creditor relationships in order to protect their own interests. Consequently, they usually possess the strongest and most enforceable property rights.

For banks, freely negotiated contracts set property rights. The property rights held by financial institutions are primarily determined in financial agreements that lenders and debtor-corporations negotiate privately and consensually, within a statutory framework of contract and debtor–creditor law. Rarely do legal statutes directly specify such property rights. As Bratton describes it, "contracts governing corporate debt instruments—trust indentures in the case of bonds and debentures, and loan agreements in the case of privately placed notes and long-term bank loans—are generally viewed as the only meaningful source of rights and duties in corporate debtor–creditor relationships." (Bratton 1984: 371).

---

[1] See also Stearns (1990), Glasberg (1989), Kotz (1978). For a strong dissent against this argument, see Roe (1991).

Financial intermediaries enforce their claims through the use of a variegated repertoire of forms of security, enforceable in commercial law. Lenders also insert a variety of protective covenants into their debt contracts. Like other creditors, banks acquire property rights in the collateral of debtors as a way to reduce their financial risk. If the debtor defaults, the creditor can seize the collateral and liquidate it in satisfaction of the debt. Contractually obtaining a secured interest is therefore one of the most basic and reliable ways for lenders to protect their own financial position. With the strongest legal rights, banks are best able to recover their money when companies become financially distressed.

Banks have a further advantage over most other creditors. Banks and other financial institutions repeatedly play the game of financial risk, consistently assuming the creditor position. Most other for-profit corporations, in contrast, simultaneously function as both debtors and creditors (borrowing from some and lending to others) and so their economic interests are subject to cross-cutting pressures: a legal change that benefits debtors, for example, will help corporations in some respects but hurt them in others. Their response to legal proposals gets mitigated by their mixed interests.[2] Yet financial institutions almost always enter bankruptcy court as creditors wishing to recover their money.

Given their strength in the market, the apparent purity of their interests as creditors, their easy access to the best legal advice and accounting services, and their enormous financial resources—not to mention the vast sums they have at stake in the stability of markets—banks and other financial institutions should be in a strong position to impose their will on statutory reforms—an expectation perfectly consistent with bank control and financial hegemony theories of corporate control (see Mintz and Schwartz 1985). Moreover, their political strength should be magnified in direct proportion to the relative weaknesses of other parties in meta-bargaining—weak creditors and debtors for instance. Said one leading American reformer: "... you don't have a debtors' lobby. Debtors are debtors, they're not an organized group of people—you don't know you're a debtor until you're in difficulty."[3]

In fact, however, we shall observe that banks did not dominate the reform process. Market power and political power are not identical.

---

[2] Even firms with clear-cut debtor interests rarely involve themselves in bankruptcy reform as debtors. The opprobrium associated with bankrupt debtors is not something a corporation wants to invoke.

[3] US Interview 91:02.

Indeed market power proved to be something of a political liability to the banks in both countries, for the very privileges and powers they enjoyed made them a target of reform. Thus the strong position of banks in bargaining over financial property rights did not automatically translate into equivalent force in political metabargaining over property rights. Moreover, the relative clarity and simplicity of their position in everyday corporate defaults or bankruptcies did not translate into precise, comprehensively articulated interests at the outset of the reform processes.[4] Banks came to define the terms of their interests in particular forms of security as they weighed the points of political sensitivity and public disquiet that emerged in the course of the metabargaining.

In both countries the everyday distributional struggles that pitted one creditor against another, and creditors as a group against the debtor, were translated into a larger political debate over the outcomes to be achieved by bankruptcy reforms. Distributional conflicts centered in both countries on the tension between the ability of a firm to reorganize, on the one hand, and rigorous enforcement of creditor's rights, on the other. The latter often precluded the former. Freedom of contract, therefore, confronted imperatives of public policy that directly threatened in bankruptcy what had been freely contracted outside it.

LENDING AND SECURITY

Sophisticated lenders use a number of contractual devices to stake out and defend their financial position. Not only do they insist on protective covenants that prescribe and prohibit a variety of behaviors on the part of the debtor (in effect, attaching legal strings to the money they lend), but they acquire a property interest in assets belonging to the debtor. In addition to the protections afforded by positive and negative covenants, when a debtor defaults, a secured creditor can seize and liquidate collateral to satisfy the obligation.[5]

A creditor's first impulse in lending money is to attach as many conditions as possible to prevent debtor misbehavior. If a debtor nevertheless gets into financial difficulty, a creditor's second impulse may be to try to use those contractual conditions to manage the debtor. Yet,

---

[4] Of course, even in everyday bankruptcies their interests are not entirely straightforward. Depending on the value of collateral, a creditor-bank could assume the role of secured lender for part of its loan, and unsecured lender for the balance.

[5] For a practical discussion of collateral from a lender's standpoint, see Larr (1994).

however tempted a creditor may be to direct a troubled debtor, too much control poses its own dangers. A creditor that exerts excessive influence can become liable to the corporate debtor or to third parties for losses incurred on account of the creditor's involvement (see, generally, Douglas-Hamilton 1975). At the very least, under American bankruptcy law a creditor may be classified as an "insider" and have its claims subjected to more stringent tests than other creditors or even subordinated. Thus, creditors must guard against becoming too influential over the affairs of troubled debtors, even when there is money at stake. It is sometimes better to remain "at arm's length."

Secured loans are extended within the context of a bilateral financial contract between debtor and creditor. When a debtor defaults, however, this bilateral relationship unfolds into a more complex multilateral situation in which creditor actions affect not only the debtor but also the other creditors, and vice versa. Bilateral contracts do not manage multilateral interactions very well, especially contentious ones. Creditor interests directly clash because the greater the proportion of debtor assets that go to one creditor, the less there is for all the others. Thus, creditors must fight over a finite pie. The conflicting claims of creditors are adjudicated by law and, according to Alan Schwartz, are regulated within American law by three priority principles of the Uniform Commercial Code (UCC):

First, if the first creditor to deal with the debtor makes an unsecured loan, it shares pro rata with later unsecured creditors in the debtor's assets on default. Second, if this initial creditor makes an unsecured loan and a later creditor takes security, the later creditor has priority over the initial creditor in the assets subject to the security interest. Third, if the initial creditor makes a secured loan, it generally has priority over later creditors in the assets in which it has security (Schwartz 1989: 209).

Thanks to the operation of these legal principles, secured creditors almost always do much better than unsecured creditors when a debtor defaults. Brealey and Myers (1984: 656) note that in business bankruptcies, secured creditors get back roughly thirty-one per cent of the value of their claims, compared to the eight per cent that unsecured creditors receive.[6] Clearly, collateralizing a loan protects the creditor when the debtor defaults.

---

[6] Using different data, Stanley and Girth estimated an even starker contrast: secured creditors received an average of 66 cents on the dollar, versus only 7 cents for unsecured creditors. See Stanley and Girth (1971: 21–2).

Security helps a creditor in relation to the debtor but equally important, protects a creditor from other creditors. Jackson and Kronman observe that in the American context: ". . . the value of a security interest depends upon the degree to which it insulates the secured party from the claims of the debtor's other creditors" (Jackson and Kronman 1979: 1143). Exactly the same principle applies in England. The Cork Committee opened its discussion of fixed charges with the observation that: "The object of the creditor who takes security for the debt due to him is to obtain priority over other creditors in the event of the debtor's insolvency" (*Cork Report* 1982: 338). A security interest fends off encroachment by other creditors.

Security protects creditors when the debtor defaults. To default is not the same, however, as going bankrupt or becoming insolvent. In a default, the debtor has typically failed to make a loan payment when due, and the affected creditor is provided by debtor–creditor law with a range of legal weapons to enforce his or her rights. Most importantly, the secured creditor can repossess collateral and sell it to recover the debt. Debtors, however, can default on some loans but not on others, and so debt-recovery still occurs within a specific bilateral debtor–creditor relationship. In contrast, insolvency in Britain and bankruptcy in the US affects the entire set of bilateral relations. When a debtor becomes bankrupt under US law, for example, the automatic stay imposed by the court halts *all* actions by *all* creditors to reclaim and liquidate collateral, enforce liens, and recover property or setoff debts (Rome 1979: 392–3). Even the normal protections enjoyed by secured creditors are suspended by the bankruptcy court, and so: "Bankruptcy is the acid test for the secured lender. It is in bankruptcy court that any flaw or imperfection in the secured party's claim will most likely be revealed, perhaps with disastrous results" (Koch 1982: 788). In the terminology of Chapter 1, rights modification rules can dramatically transform the arrangements constructed on the basis of rights specification rules. American bankruptcy and British insolvency both interrupt the normal processes of debt recovery and repayment. However carefully or prudently a creditor has constructed its position, things can be very different in the post-bankruptcy situation.

Given their financial and legal sophistication, banks are usually careful to lend money on a formal contractual basis. This distinguishes banks from many other businesses, for in a classic study, Stewart Macaulay (1963) found that a surprisingly large number of commercial transactions among Wisconsin manufacturers occurred outside of contracts, without the legal formality and certainty that a contract provides (see also Bratton 1984; Gordon 1985; Macaulay 1985; and White 1982). Such transactions are conducted on the proverbial "handshake basis," and have the advantage of considerable flexibility and open-endedness. Other researchers (for example, Bernstein 1992) have found a similar pattern in other markets (for example, the New York diamond industry), yet it would be a mistake to overgeneralize from Macaulay's results. Contractual formality varies from situation to situation: some markets are generally more informal than others. Among banks, there appears to be considerable insistence on contractual rectitude, on ensuring that all "i" 's are dotted and "t" 's are crossed. Bankers' handbooks, for example, repeatedly insist that loan agreements be as formalized, explicit and complete as possible, and that as little as possible be left on an informal or tacit basis (see, for example, Larr, 1994; Simpson 1973; Simmons 1972; Alexander and Downey 1988: 661; Stroup 1986; Grimmig 1986). This requirement is very much predicated on the possibility of debtor insolvency. Unless the legal formalities are fully taken care of, a lender will likely lose its secured status and therefore an additional proportion of its money. Informality is a dangerous luxury which a bank can seldom afford, especially if there is any chance that one of its clients may some day become bankrupt.

Given the obvious economic advantages of secured loans, it is reasonable to ask why all creditors do not "collateralize" when they lend. There are two basic reasons. First, the extent and nature of security depends on the deal agreed to by debtor and creditor, and hence on their respective bargaining positions. A large corporate debtor with unimpeachable credit, whose business many banks pursue, can insist on more favorable terms: lower interest rates and weaker or less intrusive security. As one British insolvency expert put it: "... you could say that the blue chip companies who are the ones best placed to borrow from the banks are also the ones best able to say to the banks: we're not prepared to give security. If you, Barclay's, insist on security, we'll go to Lloyds."[7] Smaller, weaker borrowers typically must concede more to their lenders. In addition, obtaining security means negotiating an elaborate and specific loan agreement, and it involves subsequent monitoring of the debtor to ensure ongoing compliance with the terms of the agreement (Larr 1994). It entails what economists call "transaction

[7] UK Interview 96:01.

costs." Secured loans bring benefits to the creditor, to be sure, but they also involve costs. When the latter are non-trivial, it may make sense to negotiate a less stringent or detailed agreement. In deciding whether to make a short-term unsecured loan, for example, a bank can use the current financial status of the borrower to estimate the likelihood of repayment. If the borrower wishes a long-term loan, however, its current status may be a poor indicator of its ability to repay the loan five or ten years hence. Given higher uncertainty, the lender will want to secure the loan as fully as possible.

Creditors' actions vary depending on which of two kinds of debtors they deal with. First are consumer debtors—people who have borrowed money to purchase a commodity which may range in value from dishwashers and stoves to automobiles and houses. Individual borrowers are relatively unsophisticated and generally at a disadvantage when it comes to bargaining with banks or finance companies. Second, and in contrast, business borrowers tend to be relatively knowledgeable and experienced. They are more cognizant of the legalities and contractual minutiae of debtor–creditor relations and bargain with lenders on a more equal basis.

The revision of bankruptcy and insolvency laws reflected these differences between borrowers. We shall later show that many reformers sought to provide some protection for innocent or ignorant or relatively powerless consumers, while leaving business borrowers to fend for themselves on the grounds that they could do so more easily. Some reformers recognized differences within the business community, with small firms operating at a lower level of sophistication than big firms. A number of them in both countries wanted to use the law to equalize the imbalanced relationship between sophisticated creditors and unsophisticated debtors. Furthermore, it was clear that rigorous enforcement of the rights of sophisticated secured creditors would make it much harder to engineer a successful corporate reorganization. A British expert stated that: "If a company needs to be able to get rehabilitated then you can't just give a free hand to secured creditors to come in and enforce their security."[8] Meta-bargaining therefore offered a site where inequities and inefficiencies in everyday practice might be corrected by redirecting the force of securities and changing the rules of bargaining. Meta-bargaining also brought into sharp relief costly trade-offs between the efficiencies needed for successful reorganization of firms and the equity

---

[8] UK Interview 96:01.

of balancing the relative strengths and weaknesses of creditors and debtors.

On either side of the Atlantic, therefore, the making of new bank-ruptcy law focused on several economic issues. Both countries struggled with distributive equity among creditors, weak and strong. Both coun-tries sought a new balance between, on the one hand, the rights of banks to secure their credit using preferred instruments on terms that they negotiated freely with debtors, with, on the other hand, the power of bankruptcy courts or statutorily-mandated procedures to alter those rights for the purpose of corporate rehabilitation. Both countries wit-nessed concerted efforts to redress grievances that other creditors and debtors had over the practices of banks when corporations were in distress or became bankrupt. The particulars of those political struggles varied significantly. The problem of "setoff" in the US did not arise to the same degree in the UK. Nor did the powers of debtors-in-possession in the United States find any favor with British reformers. But even there, both countries sought new ways to protect the collateral of secured creditors, while granting some flexibility to the agents of reor-ganization, whom we discuss in Chapter 6.

Yet the politics of secured creditors varied markedly between the countries. While both groups were involved from the outset through the final stages of reform, the American bankers vigorously defended their interests over a wide set of issues. Those issues ranged from substantive law to procedural and administrative reforms. While the sheer scope of their engagement led to some early uncertainty about the particulars of many interests, the complex and global nature of their interests allowed banks to make political deals and trade-offs, gaining in some respects while losing in others. They seldom faced direct opposition from other interested parties, for most of the pressure to restrict or weaken their rights came from bankruptcy reformers who believed that strong creditor rights interfered with corporate rehabilita-tion.

In the British case, banks directly confronted reformers and several interest groups (like trade and unsecured creditors) whose interests directly conflicted with their own. The range of issues was narrower, but the political confrontation was more explicit and sharper than in the United States. Attacks on the bankers took place within the Cork Committee, in the press, and in Parliament, over the rights endowed by the powerful floating charge security held by banks, which allowed them unilaterally to seize company assets, almost regardless of the cost to other creditors.[9] Because the confiscation of assets by secured creditors usually destroyed the company, it significantly impeded corporate reconstruction and diminished any hope of company rehabilitation. The operation of floating charges clearly posed the trade-off between company liquidation and reorganization.

SECURED CREDITORS IN THE UNITED STATES

The interests and behavior of secured creditors in the political sphere are more ambiguous than either formal models of rational economic actors might predict, or empirical observations of everyday behavior in bankruptcies might imply. Ambiguity abounds in circumstances where group interests have not been comprehensively engaged or evaluated for many decades. The political process compounds uncertainty because the set of players, and their particular concerns, cannot be predicted reliably, and many political and ideological interests that are quite external to bankruptcy itself can intrude in unpredictable ways. Moreover, when powerful creditors come to the meta-bargaining table, they may not fully comprehend their own interests until they are arrayed against the interests of others. Because other groups may similarly be seeking to define their priorities in relation to others, meta-bargaining permits, even encourages, ambiguity around the general parameters that groups may consider at the outset to be their bedrock interests.

The ambiguities of meta-bargaining for secured creditors resulted not only from the complex array of substantive interests they had in the strength of various forms of security, which protected their capital, but also from a compelling desire to improve the administrative process in bankruptcy. While the latter did not have direct substantive implications for the relative strength of one security versus another, the "procedural rationality" of the bankruptcy system itself—courts, judges, trustees, lawyers, rules and procedures, legal jurisdictions and appeals— influenced significantly the confidence of bankers that the courts could protect their assets, facilitate liquidation or reorganization, and minimize the transaction costs for either.

Secured creditors therefore entered the political arena with two general concerns that were related in complex ways: there were the pre-

---

[9] The issue of setoff also arose in Britain, but not in connection with banks. Rather, as we show in Chapter 5, it related to Crown rights of setoff.

dictable substantive interests in strong legal securities; and there were the procedural and administrative facets of bankruptcy practice. Substantive interests were well captured by the concept of absolute priority, which held that creditors with higher ranked securities, that is, senior creditors, should have their claims satisfied in full before any creditors with lower ranked securities, or no securities at all, should obtain any part of the bankrupt company's assets.[10] And, notably, the absolute priority rule determined that creditors should be satisfied in full before any shareholder retained *any equity* interest in the company. However fair the standard of absolute priority, it put a powerful brake on the scope of bargaining over reorganizations, for the rule sharply constricted room for movement by stronger creditors to trade some of the assets they had secured for concessions and flexible adjustments by weaker creditors, debtors, and stock-holders.

The strength of the securities of major creditors, and the fidelity with which courts applied the absolute priority rule, made little difference if the transaction costs of resolving conflicts in the courts or reorganizing companies so depleted a company's assets that little remained to distribute to creditors. Since bankers had become highly disgruntled with the operations of the bankruptcy system, a subject we shall consider in some detail in Chapter 10, their own position at the meta-bargaining table entailed potential trade-offs between uncertain changes in substantive law and unproven changes in administrative procedures. This introduced a degree of ambiguity that could only be resolved in the give and take of political bargaining around the entire range of interests they had previously perceived and came to perceive in the process of the reforms.

The trade-off between substantive advantages and procedural rationality played out over issues of control over assets in three different circumstances. First, there were negotiations over collateral that was *owned or secured* by a bank, but *controlled* by the debtor. How should this collateral be adequately protected when banks had an interest in preserving their assets, and managers needed to use (and thus risk) assets for an effective rehabilitation of the company? Second, there were negotiations over collateral that the *debtor owned*, but the *bank controlled*—the practice of setoff. How should legislation balance the *de facto* control that banks exercised over a company's liquid assets that were held in bank accounts, with the *de jure* ownership of those assets by the debtor company? And, third, *what degree of control should courts exercise* over bar-

---

[10] For a history of absolute priority, see Markell (1991).

gaining around reorganization? Were courts bound by the decisions of the parties to bargaining in bankruptcy? Or could courts step in and "cramdown" a decision against the will of key creditors, most notably, the banks?

By focusing on the issues of collateral in reorganizations, setoff, and cramdown, we shall see how secured creditors came to define and resolve their interests in a trade-off between substantive principles and procedural practices.

Context of the Reforms

The bankers entered the reform process with a very modest and narrowly crafted statement to support establishment of a Bankruptcy Commission. Their four-paragraph comment on Senate Joint Resolution 88, which sought to create a commission, placed its emphasis on "steps to reduce bankruptcies which do so much to disturb the moral fiber of those Americans that become involved" and that increase the cost of credit. The American Bankers Association sought—unsuccessfully—to add to the Commission two powerful financial figures—the Secretary of the Treasury and the Chairman of the Federal Reserve Board. But their most direct substantive comment focused on individual bankruptcy, where they called for a greater reliance on Chapter 13 to rehabilitate wage-earner bankrupts. Only in their comments on two related bills, H.R. 6665 and H.R. 12250, did they hint at their unhappiness over the jurisdictional inadequacies of bankruptcy courts, the "multiplication of suits," and the need "to secure expeditious administration of bankruptcy proceedings."[11]

By the time the Commission's Bill reached Congress, the financial industry's broad dissatisfaction over the administration of bankruptcy and corporate reorganization had been shaped into a comprehensive formulation of substantive and administrative change. In contrast to the British banks, which fought most strongly over substantive legal instruments such as the floating charge, the financial industry trade associations in the United States balanced their emphasis on who would obtain the largest share of the bankruptcy pie, a matter of substantive equity, with heavy emphasis on the inordinate waste of the pie itself because the bankruptcy system performed so inefficiently. American bankers

[11] Creation of a Commission to Study Bankruptcy Laws, Hearings on S.J. Res. 88 and H.R. 6665 and H.R. 12250 before Subcommittee No. 4 of the House Committee on the Judiciary, 91st Cong., 1st Sess., October 1, 1968, p. 86.

rejected any piecemeal improvement of bankruptcy law or administration in favor of a far-reaching restructuring of the law and the institutions that administered it. The bankers called for nothing less than a holistic reform in which they traded off some legal protection of assets for a thoroughly reconditioned bankruptcy system that embraced courts, judges, lawyers, and legal jurisdictions.

The sentiments of the bankers were well expressed by a referee in bankruptcy during the hearings for establishment of the Bankruptcy Commission. When asked by a Senator about the activities of some groups to improve the existing bankruptcy laws, he replied:

Well, as far as I know, those groups are devoting themselves to the present structure of the act, to plug the loopholes in the present structure. I see this Commission, the proposed Commission, as going well beyond a repair and overhaul and finding some new concepts, some new approach to bankruptcy entirely. This Bankruptcy Act was written in the horse and buggy days and we are in the jet age today.[12]

Bankers concurred that a piecemeal improvement of the law was not capable of solving the magnitude of its problems. Thus property rights might be defended directly, through the protection and fortification of security instruments, or indirectly, through reduction of the transaction costs of bankruptcy administration. In current bankruptcy practice, a reorganization or liquidation could be protracted and expensive. Several factors contributed to the problem: the low status of bankruptcy courts and their consequent inability to attract the best legal talent, their limited jurisdiction, the tendency for "shopping" among different chapters in the Bankruptcy Act, and the ubiquitous potential for appeals, delays and other procedural maneuvering. All of these problems could lock up the collateral of a secured creditor for a long period of time and lead to substantial dissipation of the assets.[13]

From the very beginning of the reform process, the American Bankers Association was concerned that, because of the complexity of a bankruptcy case, the jurisdiction allotted to bankruptcy referees would not provide an adequate forum for bankruptcy cases to be decided. Unless the court was given adequate authority, a single bankruptcy case

---

[12] Statements of Referee in Bankruptcy, Asa Herzog, before the Commission to Study Bankruptcy Laws, 1968, Hearings before the Subcommittee on Bankruptcy of the Senate Committee on the Judiciary, 90th Cong., 2nd Sess., 1968, p. 9.

[13] A more detailed analysis of bankruptcy administrations, its failures and prospects, will be presented in Chapter 10.

could result in a "multiplicity of suits."[14] Suits themselves were subject to delaying appeals. The banking associations forcefully demanded that the status of bankruptcy courts be upgraded and their jurisdiction be expanded to the status of full-fledged federal courts with the powers enshrined in Article III of the US Constitution.

Banks also affirmed one of the central criticisms enunciated in both the Brookings Report and the Bankruptcy Commission: that bankruptcy courts were too influenced by a local "ring" of lawyers and judges. Such arrangements created both the possibility and the appearance of favoritism towards "insiders." Since national financial institutions did business in many communities and local markets, they were often the "outsiders," and bankers worried that they could not receive a fair hearing.[15]

We reserve until Chapter 10 a detailed discussion of administrative reforms. It is enough here to recognize that consideration of procedural rationality, of jurisdictional and administrative issues, lent a distinctive context to the negotiations of secured creditors over substantive property rights. Because property rights depended in part on jurisdictional rights, US banks accepted the possibility of trade-offs in meta-bargaining between substantive protections and administrative improvements. Indeed they demanded that the legislation not confine itself to substantive law alone. At a moment when the bankers perceived that Congress might retreat from wholesale changes to bankruptcy administration, John Ingraham, spokesman of the American Bankers Association, warned that:

We in the lending community fear that the proposed revision of the bankruptcy laws is on the verge of becoming a revision of *substantive* bankruptcy law, which revision will not be well received unless accompanied by the promised reform of the bankruptcy *court system*.[16]

Banks therefore defined their interests expansively. Although their complex procedural and substantive interests made political trade-offs all that more complex, nevertheless the breadth of interests permitted banks to bargain with more flexibility across substantive and procedural domains. Hence the negotiating positions of banks on property rights—use of collateral, setoff, cramdown—can be fully comprehended only in

---

[14] Creation of a Commission to Study Bankruptcy Laws, Hearings on S.J. Res. 88 and H.R. 6665 and H.R. 12250 before Subcommittee No. 4 of the House Committee on the Judiciary, 91st Cong., 1st Sess., October 1, 1968, p. 86.

[15] *House Hearings on H.R. 8200*, pp. 205–6.

[16] *House Hearings on H.R. 8200*, 12 Dec. 1977.

the context of bankruptcy administration, the jurisdictional reach of bankruptcy courts, and the jurisdictional power of bankruptcy judges.

Relaxing Absolute Priority

The absolute priority rule anchored the rights of secured creditors in a bedrock of legal priority. Yet, while absolute priority protected contracts entered into before bankruptcy, it could undermine bargaining among creditors, and diminish the power of courts to effect company reorganizations. The absolute priority rule therefore embraced issues of ownership and control over assets that directly affected the prospect of a "fresh start" for financially distressed companies. The concern of secured creditors to protect their assets, and the drive of many reformers to save companies and protect unsecured creditors, pointed to lines of incipient conflict from the outset of the reform process.

A central tension ran through the reform process: the contradiction between freedom of contract, on the one hand, and the vulnerability of small creditors and the desirability of firm rehabilitation, on the other. Freedom of contract dictated that bankruptcy courts should recognize and enforce the prior agreements freely negotiated between debtors and creditors. If in such financial contracts some creditors obtained security while others did not, then the court should acknowledge the difference and enforce the superior rights of secured creditors. In this view, courts should not rewrite contracts or redistribute property rights after parties had come to a mutually satisfactory bargain. In effect, this position meant that rights modification rules should not substantially alter the arrangements contracting parties reached using rights specification rules.

Freedom of contract may be desirable because it facilitates mutually advantageous exchanges,[17] but in practice it can conflict with the uncertain realities of commercial life and the hardships of corporate extinction. For example, the parties to a contract do not always bargain as equals. Agreements may reflect a measure of coercion as well as consensus. Moreover contracts that seemed desirable before bankruptcy may later prove to be burdensome. Contractual agreements sometimes need to be revised or adjusted after the fact in order to ensure that small creditors are not left completely destitute, or to salvage troubled corporations rather than liquidate them. Nonetheless, adjustments to

---

[17] For many arguments in support of freedom of contract, see Posner (1986).

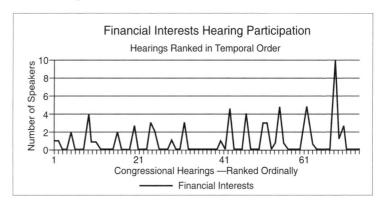

Fig. 4.1:   **Financial Interest Temporal Participation in US Congressional Hearings**

previously negotiated contracts amongst creditors and debtors most often harm those who enjoy the most favorable contractual arrangements, namely, the banks.

It is not surprising, therefore, that financial interests made more appearances before congressional committees on the issue of business bankruptcy than on any other (see Table 3.3 in Chapter 3). They entered the reform process early, and stayed late. Figure 4.1 shows that the peak associations of the financial industry participated from the beginning and their volume of activity increased perceptibly as the bankruptcy bill moved to its final stages. Not only did the financial industry embrace all stages of legislative passage, but Fig. 3.6 shows that their interests spanned everything from personal to municipal debt, from state preferences to railroad bankruptcies. Dominating their political involvement, however, were business bankruptcies and bankruptcy administration, which tower above all other issues.

Although the Brookings study examined many facets of the bankruptcy system, Stanley and Girth (1971) had little to say about secured creditors except to note that although they enjoyed a highly privileged status (pp. 16–17), most of the creditors in a typical business bankruptcy were unsecured (p. 113). Obtaining a secured interest may have been advantageous, but evidently it was not costless, otherwise all creditors would have done so. Expert commentary by Professor Countryman from Harvard University Law School criticized secured creditors for obtaining too much of a legal interest in debtor property, and thus ensuring that in the event of bankruptcy, and after the liquidation of debtor assets, little or nothing would be left for unsecured creditors, who did not "deserve" to get so little (Countryman 1971: 35).

Deficiencies of the "absolute priority rule" were thoroughly canvassed by the Bankruptcy Commission. When applied under Chapter X of the 1938 Bankruptcy Act, the rule determined that a reorganization plan "must fully compensate classes with senior rights in the debtor before junior classes can be given any value in the reorganized company" (Treister et al. 1988: 411). Senior claims (for example, those of secured creditors) had to be completely satisfied before anything could go to junior claims (unsecured creditors, or company owners). In other words, if a bankrupt company owed fully secured creditors $1 million out of a $1.5 million estate, the secured creditor must receive all $1 million before any other creditor received anything at all. And all creditors must be fully paid before shareholders received anything at all. The stringent application of this rule clearly favored secured creditors, but its inflexibility could undermine a potentially successful corporate reorganization. In particular, the rule interfered with the ability of creditors to bargain among themselves and negotiate deals in which all or most creditors got something, even if this meant that senior creditors did not receive payment in full (Broude 1984). In other words, the price of a bargain amongst creditors, and even stockholders and managers, sometimes turned on the prospect that every party would get something. In these circumstances, secured creditors might be happy to yield a little on absolute priority if this flexibility encouraged other creditors to support a reorganization plan.

Furthermore, Bankruptcy Commissioners observed that the impact of the rule in practice often depended on the projected future earnings of the reorganized company. Using optimistic projections, a reorganization could proceed on the belief that there would be enough money to cover all senior claims, with sufficient left over that junior secured creditors or unsecured creditors would receive some of the assets. But if earnings projections were lower, then junior claimants would go unsatisfied and receive little or nothing. Thus, whether or not junior creditors or shareholders received anything or had a stake in the reorganization depended on speculative financial projections and valuations.[18]

The Bankruptcy Commission therefore debated some modifications in the absolute priority rule. Commissioners recognized they would face substantial opposition from the powerful Securities and Exchange

---

[18] See US Bankruptcy Commission Minutes, 22–4 Feb. 1973, p. 55.

Commission (SEC), which was opposed to any relaxation of the rule. Yet a relaxed rule, stated Congressman Wiggins, might facilitate successful corporate reorganizations by allowing greater flexibility in bargaining among the parties involved in the bankruptcy. Moreover, said Judge Weinfeld, bankruptcy law should recognize that larger interests were at stake in corporate reorganization than just those of creditors and share-holders of a particular company. The blow felt by local suppliers and employees when a firm collapsed could spread to the rest of the community. Whole communities would generally be better off if a troubled corporation were reorganized, and thus continued operating.[19]

These arguments persuaded the Commission that bankruptcy law must take a more flexible approach to the absolute priority rule. In current practice, observed the Commission, rules outside of bankruptcy determined a fixed priority ranking of creditors. Within bankruptcy such a ranking was counterproductive, particularly if it could not be adjusted or modified. The absolute priority rule had a "rigidity and an illusory precision which cannot be justified" (Commission Report 1973: 27). The Commission recommended that the rule be more flexible and take into account the interests and circumstances of other creditors, the shareholders, and the employees who would be affected by the liquidation of a firm.

Thus it is both infeasible and unwise for the bankruptcy process simply to adopt the external rules of creditors' rights to carry out a policy of fair and equitable treatment of creditors' claims. Instead, internal standards of two kinds are required: *distributive standards* that take into account the legal status of claims and *allocative standards* that reflect the social and economic consequences of the burden of loss.[20]

The Commission recognized that a relaxed rule would allow the law to treat senior creditors differently within bankruptcy than without.[21] Yet the expediency of successful bargaining in the marketplace warranted some retreat from a pure distributive rule that ultimately harmed junior and weak creditors, the company itself, and the community in which the company was located.

When the Commission Bill reached Congress, the bankers' organiza-tions rallied against the proposed assault on their strong securities, for

---

[19] US Bankruptcy Commission Minutes, 22–4 Feb. 1973, pp. 56–8.
[20] *Report of the Bankruptcy Commission*: 77, emphasis added.
[21] Outside bankruptcy, it stated, "... a creditor obtaining a lien interest in property of the debtor prevails over any other creditor's interest in the same property that becomes effective subsequent to actual or constructive notice of the prior lien." *Report of the Bankruptcy Commission*: 76.

they clearly realized that assets over which they had obtained control, at cost to themselves, might now be diverted to other creditors, or diminished by the managers of the debtor company. While rehabilitation of companies was a fine ideal, it was not always practical. In the long run, it might do more harm to the circulation of credit.

The American Bankers Association professed mixed feelings about the proposed changes in standards for business reorganization. Reorganizations forced the law, and those who would modify it, to reconcile conflicting principles and to weigh "... philosophical considerations bearing on the rehabilitation of a temporarily distressed debtor against legal concepts rooted deeply in the protection of property rights, contract rights and security interests".[22] Robert Grimmig, a bank spokesman, conceded that debtors sometimes deserved a second chance and that a bankruptcy reorganization could be one way to provide that chance. Yet the subversion of property rights carried considerable risks.

[W]e recognize that in the commercial credit economy in which we currently function, the continued availability of credit to business enterprises is their lifeblood, and to assure free flow of credit at reasonable cost and in adequate amount, the safeguarding of contracts, property rights and security interests is essential."[23]

The Robert Morris Associates (RMA) also professed support for debtor rehabilitation, but was clearly opposed to many of the measures in both the Commission and Judges' bills which were supposed to encourage reorganization and rehabilitation. The RMA claimed that these proposals ignored an important fact:

... massive rehabilitation efforts are frequently made prior to the commencement of a bankruptcy proceeding. Consequently the initiation of a proceeding by a debtor is a clear indication that out-of-court rehabilitation efforts have been unsuccessful. ... The pending bills explicitly support the continued allocation of financial resources to those who are demonstrably inefficient in their use of such resources.[24]

By the time a company ends up in bankruptcy court, said the RMA, usually there have already been many informal reorganizations, many renegotiations between debtor and creditors, and so to provide in bankruptcy yet one more opportunity is to prop up a debtor in what is

---

[22] *Bankruptcy Reform Act Hearings on S. 235 and S. 236*: 458.
[23] *Bankruptcy Reform Act Hearings on S. 235 and S. 236*: 459.
[24] *Bankruptcy Act Revision Hearings*: 2486.

obviously a hopeless situation. The costs of this additional and undeserved chance would be born by the creditors.

Yet secured creditors in the political sphere could not ignore political and redistributive sentiment in favor of weaker creditors, and so they felt compelled to mitigate the potential political liabilities of an appearance of narrowly self-interested lobbying. Consistent with the tactics banks employed with weak creditors, they sought to show how the proposals they opposed would damage others besides themselves. Like many other secured creditor groups, RMA claimed that hurting secured creditors was short-sighted because it would also eventually hurt debtors.

> For prime borrowers, the impact of the enactment of either the Commission Bill or the Judges' Bill is likely to be minimal in terms of either cost or availability of funds. But for lower grade borrowers, the proposed laws may amount to a virtual 'kiss of death'.[25]

Passage of either of these bills would lead, the RMA direly predicted, to a permanent change in secured lending. What hurt creditors, said the American Bankers Association, would indirectly hurt debtors, because creditors would be forced either to curtail credit, or to charge higher rates of interest, or both. Such a restriction of credit would damage marginal debtors, or debtors in a precarious financial situation—precisely those debtors that the new reorganization provisions were supposed to help. Banks pressed the case that strong creditor rights, not ones weakened to facilitate reorganizations, would serve the general interest.[26]

To weaken the absolute priority rule would give undue weight to allocative standards that threatened to weaken in bankruptcy the strong position that secured creditors had negotiated outside of bankruptcy. Rights modification rules could dramatically undo the work of rights specification rules.

Three allocation rules or practices exercised banks most strongly: (1) debtor use of collateral, (2) banks' right to setoff, and (3) cramdown. The first issue concerned the debtor's use of property formally owned by the bank but controlled in fact by the debtor. The second issue concerned the banks' appropriation of property formally owned by the debtor but controlled in fact by the bank. The third issue concerned the bankruptcy

---

[25] *Bankruptcy Act Revision Hearings*: 2486.

[26] Secured creditor groups maintained a vigorous internal discussion of the proposed legislation. Francis (1974), for example, summarized many of the provisions of the Commission Bill that affected secured creditors, while Justman (1976) sharply criticized the proposals in the Commission Bill about setoff.

court's "trump card" that could force rival groups of creditors to come to an agreement on the bankruptcy reorganization plan. In all three of these issues, the principle of absolute priority was to be modified. Even though the secured creditors realized that a rationalized bankruptcy system might well require them to modify their claims to absolute priority, the banks were not prepared simply to yield their strong ground without some balancing of their complex interests. That balance would be achieved, proposed reformers, through a guarantee of "absolute protection" for a secured creditor's assets, a substantive protection to be anchored in a reorganized, empowered, and upgraded bankruptcy system.

Use of Collateral

Collateral is one of the main devices secured creditors use to protect their interests: they acquire property rights in some asset of the debtor. So long as the loan is being repaid, the debtor possesses and can use the collateral. In the event of a default, however, creditors usually have the option to take hold of collateral and sell it in order to recover their money. Collateral can be taken in almost any kind of property, but in bankruptcy reorganizations, the two most crucial types of collateral are inventory and cash.[27] Inventory gets converted into cash as a company sells its products in the ordinary course of business. Inventory before filing for bankruptcy becomes cash as sales continue inside bankruptcy. Cash is key. Those responsible for turning the company around need the cash to keep the business alive. But secured creditors see cash as a particularly vulnerable asset, a piece of "soft" collateral, that can easily be frittered away. Agents of reorganization need the liquidity; secured creditors want protection. Should the collateral consist of a fixed asset which is critical to the operation of the debtor (for example, specialized machinery), then seizure by the secured creditor can completely halt the debtor's productive activities and shut down the business.

If the goal in bankruptcy is to reorganize the company, then seizure of critical assets by collateralized creditors cannot be tolerated for it would completely defeat the purpose of the reorganization. Collateral therefore must stay in the hands of the debtor (or debtor-in-possession), or some agent who is charged with saving the company, whether it be a lawyer, trustee, or insolvency practitioner. But since the secured creditors had property rights in the collateral, and since it played such a central role in the protection of their financial interests, it was important to consider

[27] US Interview 96:04.

how and under what circumstances the debtor should be able to use collateral that contractually belonged to someone else (due to default or bankruptcy).

Whether a creditor could reclaim the property that the debtor had put up for collateral, or whether the debtor could use, sell, or otherwise dispose of property which a creditor had secured as collateral, were both affected by the *automatic stay*. The automatic stay is a powerful device which stops all actions by creditors to recover their moneys or assets from debtors. It is designed to forestall a rush by creditors to reclaim assets and to produce some temporary order—a respite—in which an orderly plan of action can be implemented. A banking lawyer acclaimed the power of the automatic stay to halt all private remedies, and all civil and even criminal proceedings, on grounds that

you have a chaotic situation where everything is flying apart at once. The reason for an automatic stay, rather than a series of temporary restraining orders ... is the very practical one that you just do not know everything that is going on. . . . I see the stay as a real advantage and something that is at least going to hold things together.[28]

While an automatic stay can protect debtors from a scramble for company assets, creditors can also be harmed if the stay permits debtor-managers or trustees to use the collateral in ways that diminish its value. Banks may continue to have liens against a company's equipment or a security in their accounts receivable, but securities do little good if the underlying value in the collateral dissipates away.

The Bankruptcy Commission recognized that it must negotiate a fine line between two conflicting values: continued use of collateral was often critical for the success of a proposed corporate reorganization; but the credit industry relied on collateral to secure loans to smaller companies. While the Commission sought to provide companies a "second chance" for workouts, it did not wish to interfere with the extension of credit. To persuade banks to leave their assets in the control of the very managers who had run the company into financial difficulties therefore required safeguards that would adequately protect secured creditors.[29] Or as bankers preferred to construe it, "one of the most difficult tasks" facing Congress was "balancing the important public policy favoring a second chance for worthy and viable debtors with the equally important public policy of maintaining the integrity of the debtor's previous transactions

[28] *Bankruptcy Act Revision Hearings*: 1773.
[29] US Bankruptcy Commission Minutes, 17–19 May 1973, pp. 48–50.

with its creditors." And this should be achieved without "significant inroads upon creditor's rights."[30]

By that standard, the bills introduced by the Commission and Judges failed. Bankers objected vigorously to the solution adopted in the Commission's bill, which gave debtors considerable discretion in the use of property in which secured creditors had an interest. While they had no particular objection to a comprehensive automatic stay, which kept creditors from seizing collateral, the Commission's and Judge's bills permitted, in their view, much too much opportunity for debtor-managers to squander assets. While publicly bankers continued to express support for reorganization, they sought strenuously to shore up their strong property rights, even if these interfered with reorganizations.

In their submissions to the Congress, bankers asserted that the situation of secured creditors, and the use of collateral, were of "paramount concern to the banking industry." In the first place, the bills permitted debtors to use secured property and its proceeds *without notice* to the security holders. Collateral could dissolve without the knowledge or possibility of compensatory action by secured creditors. In the second place, the bills allowed debtors to use collateral, and especially "perishable collateral," like cash, *without permission* of the secured creditors. As a result, said the American Bankers Association:

Apparently the trustee, receiver or debtor would be free to use self-liquidating collateral such as accounts receivable, chattel paper, contract rights and inventory in the operation of the business, effectively depriving the secured creditor of his collateral. No provision is made to protect the property interest of the secured creditor or to provide compensation during the [automatic] stay for what will be an almost certain loss.[31]

The bankers buttressed their objections in fundamental terms. "We believe that these provisions constitute a serious impairment of contract rights bargained for at arm's length and for which the secured party gave full and adequate consideration." The provisions were unconstitutional for they deprived the secured creditor of property without "due process" protected by the Fifth Amendment. "The creditor would be denied a substantial property right without prior notice or hearing as to the propriety of that denial." Moreover, a "stronger objection" was that

---

[30] *Bankruptcy Act Revision Hearings*: 1756.
[31] Testimony of the American Bankers Association before *Bankruptcy Reform Act Hearings on S. 235 and S. 236*: 460.

the collateral itself may be consumed in the process without any determination of whether the secured creditor will be damaged, and without any automatic provision for protection of the secured creditor's value. That, we suspect, is a taking which would violate the just compensation clause of the fifth amendment.[32]

Another industry group which specialized in business credit, the National Commercial Finance Conference (NCFC), added to the complaints about the Commission and Judges' bills. It argued that seizure by secured creditors of some types of collateral, in particular "self-liquidating" or liquid forms of collateral, should be exempt from the automatic stay. Like the American Bankers Association, it opposed any use of collateral by debtors or the trustee of the bankrupt estate unless they first received permission from the relevant secured creditor.[33]

The American Bankers Association and Robert Morris Associates proposed that no collateral be used without notifying the secured creditor and without actively seeking permission from the secured creditors or the court. The burden of proof should lie with debtors to show that they had "good cause" to use collateral and they could do so without dissipating it. "Good cause" standards might include:

[a] that there is no significant prospect of impairing the value of a secured creditor's value; [b] that the credit is necessary...to operate the business; [c] that credit cannot be obtained without granting a priority position; [d] that reasonable efforts have been made to obtain credit from other sources; and [e] that there is a likelihood that the debtor can be rehabilitated within a short period of time.[34]

Moreover, a court must be persuaded that secured creditors would receive "adequate protection" for the secured creditor's property rights. "With respect to 'adequate protection,' the statute should offer specific guidance to the court such as the making of cash payments, the giving of alternative or additional security, the giving of a priority...or such other means as will adequately and fairly protect the secured creditors' rights."[35] In addition, adequate compensation for the value of their securities should be appraised at the "going concern value" of the security. In sum, said the bankers, "we can support a statute which would permit the treatment of secured creditors in that fashion against

---

[32] Testimony by Patrick Murphy on behalf of the American Bankers Association before *Bankruptcy Reform Act Hearings on S. 235 and S. 236*: 473–4.

[33] *Bankruptcy Act Revision Hearings*: 1811–12, 1817.

[34] Testimony by Robert Grimmig on behalf of the American Bankers Association before *Bankruptcy Reform Act Hearings on S. 235 and S. 236*: 461.

[35] *Ibid.*

their will as long as the treatment is completely compensatory of their position."[36] Significantly, while bankers conceded the value of a "second chance" doctrine in the new Bankruptcy Act, they argued that the interests of creditors required that standards of adequate protection and "good cause" be written into the Act, and not simply left to the vagaries of judicial decisions. Patrick Murphy, a member of the ABA Bankruptcy Task Force, said to the House subcommittee, "I . . . feel very strongly that there are protections that should be required and they should be set forth clearly, both in a procedural and substantive sense, in the statute itself."[37]

Both the House and Senate Committees heard the bankers' representations on collateral without much contest. While they sought clarification about some specific details of the bankers' proposals and the strength of their interests, legislators gave every indication of accommodation. No debate was joined directly from other interest groups.

If Congress were to relax the absolute priority rule and make assets available to other creditors and managers, it needed simultaneously to permit flexibility for use of assets while protecting the banks, whose steadfast opposition could imperil the entire bill. The House therefore proposed a compromise: while the automatic stay would not permit secured creditors immediately to seize their assets, their collateral would be carefully protected in terms we return to below.

Setoff: A De Facto Security to Protect a "Perishable Commodity"

Setoff is a *de facto* security of special concern to banks. Typically, corporate debtors and bank creditors both have claims on each other: the company owes money to the bank (in the form of a loan) while at the same time the bank holds money for the company (in the form of a bank deposit). What the company owes to the bank is usually worth much more than the bank's debt to the company. In the event of bankruptcy, the practice of setoff allows the bank unilaterally to seize the company's bank deposits to offset and hence reduce the debt owed to the bank. In effect, the bank can reclaim some of its money without having to share any of the proceeds with other claimants, and thus it enjoys a de facto priority.

Furthermore, setoff allows a bank to seize the debtor's most liquid asset, making a successful reorganization much harder to accomplish. Exercising setoff rights made banks privileged creditors, a status which

---

[36] *Bankruptcy Reform Act Hearings on S. 235 and S. 236*: 475.
[37] *Bankruptcy Act Revision Hearings on H.R. 31 and H.R. 32*: 1764–1765.

they endeavored to protect. Other creditors, including reformers who believed that creditors should be treated equally, and advocates of the rehabilitative ideal, sought to constrain, restrict or otherwise attenuate the banks' de facto priority.

In practice, bankers often moved preemptively, in the days before the filing of a bankruptcy petition, to setoff their outstanding loans before the courts became involved and bankruptcy law strictly regulated the activities of creditors. Said one reformer, "prior to the Code, what a bank would do was say 'well, you're going to file chapter XI tomorrow, we're going to settle up today.' "[38] For the most part, it was generally accepted under the prior Act that banks could exercise their right to setoff immediately before a bankruptcy petition or after it. However, a Supreme Court case, *Baker v. Gold Seal*, gave the green light for some lower courts to apply a standard long used in railroad reorganizations that forbade setoffs in bankruptcy. Hence reformers faced a somewhat muddied case law that had disturbed conventional practice.[39]

The terminology used in the debate signalled the strength of commitment that banks had in their de facto priority. While liens against real property were referred to as "interests," the creditors' ability to exercise setoff was referred to as a "right". Unlike "interests", which, assuming equity in value, are more or less substitutable, and therefore negotiable, a claim to "rights" heightens the stakes in negotiations.

The Bankruptcy Commission was sharply divided over the "right" of banks to exercise arbitrary control over deposits by offsetting loans with cash deposits in other accounts. For proponents, setoff was not only framed as a "right" of banks (and other creditors) but, according to one member of the commission, was "so deeply imbedded in American law that the Commission should not undertake to disturb it".[40] A corporate lawyer on the Commission defended the banks on the grounds that since setoff rights figured in a bank's original decision to extend credit, restricting or eliminating those rights would force banks to think twice before lending money. Banks would make fewer loans and would be forced to precipitate involuntary bankruptcy sooner when faced with a financially troubled debtor.[41]

[38] US Interview 96:04.

[39] Trost and King, 1978, p. 519; *Baker v. Gold Seal Liquors, Inc.*, 417 U.S. 467 (1974).

[40] US Bankruptcy Commission Minutes, 15–17 Mar. 1973, p. 30.

[41] Minutes, 13–14 Nov. 1972, pp. 41–3; 15–17 Mar. 1973, pp. 28–30; 15–17 Mar. 1973, p. 32.

Taking a contrary position, Judge Will and Professor Seligson argued that setoff rights should be not be allowed at all in bankruptcy, for they gave banks an unfair advantage over other creditors. Moreover, the banks' ability to setoff their claims against the debtor was a "mere fortuity;" the bank was in a different position from other creditors only because it happened to possess the debtor's deposits.

When a vote was taken to formalize a position on the "right" to setoff, the vote evenly split the Commission. Eventually a compromise solution distinguished between setoff in liquidations and setoff in reorganizations. The right to setoff might be retained in straight liquidation cases.[42] But where the goal was to reorganize the business as a going concern, setoff could only occur with court approval. In other words, as a price of keeping their de facto security, banks must cede some of their control to the discretion of the court.

In its Report, the Commission grounded these recommendations on the principles of sympathy with the plight of small creditors and with society's general interest in corporate reorganization. Setoff directly hindered reorganization and indirectly harmed the remaining creditors. According to the Report,

the exercise by a bank in which the debtor has a deposit account of a right of setoff immediately after the filing of the [bankruptcy] petition frequently deprives the business of any available cash to continue its operation and thereby preserve its going concern value pending the formulation of a [reorganization] plan.[43]

A bank holding the debtor's money on deposit could be ordered by the bankruptcy court to release that money to the debtor, instead of simply appropriating it to offset a debt. In exchange for the cash, the creditor was to receive "adequate protection" of its assets, something which secured creditors viewed as a poor alternative to ready money, but certainly better than nothing at all.

Claims of the debtor against third parties, which are subject to setoff against mutual claims against the debtor may be ordered to be paid to the trustee or debtor to be used in the operation of the business in appropriate cases, but that the court adequately protect the party having the right of setoff.[44]

When bankers had an opportunity to air their views before Congress, they justified their "right" to setoff as a "secret" security granted to

[42] Minutes, 15–17 Mar. 1973 pp. 31–2.

[43] *Report of the Bankruptcy Commission*, p. 24.

[44] *Report of the Bankruptcy Commission*, p. 28.

banks which allowed them to lend on a more flexible basis.[45] With some of the debtor's cash in hand, as a kind of informal collateral, a bank could lend more generously with lower interest rates and thus a lower price of capital. For financially distressed companies, said Robert Grimmig of Chemical Bank, "the right of setoff is a very, very important banker's tool in any workout."[46] Inside bankruptcy, bankers feared that "cash in the hands of a financially troubled debtor may be a far more perishable commodity" than other forms of property.[47] "We are not opposed to the debtor utilizing setoffs. What we oppose is that the setoff moneys be simply taken and utilized without placing upon the debtor the burden of establishing that he is not going to the races with it."[48]

Faced with the criticism that a *de facto* security should not be enforceable *de jure*, the American Bankers Association responded that a bank's possession of deposits to offset a loan was no "mere stroke of luck," but instead the result of deliberate choice. The amount of credit a bank was willing to extend to a customer was calculated on the average balances of the debtor's accounts over an extended period of time.[49] The use of setoff as a kind of informal basis of lending was reinforced in a later subcommittee hearing by the Robert Morris Associates. By the time a debtor company declares bankruptcy, said the bankers, they usually have already been involved in a long workout process with their major creditors. Banks usually offset the debtor's deposits against their debt to the bank. Then they lent the same money back to the debtor, but this time bankruptcy law allowed them to give the new loan a priority as an administrative expense of the reorganization. Thus, they argued, the bank's right to setoff did not really limit the amount of cash available to the debtor corporation, but rather afforded the banks the ability to lend informally when they could, and yet shift those loans onto a more formal basis when they had to.[50]

---

[45] The fact that it was a "secret" security was a source of irritation and uncertainty to other creditors for they could not know how large the cash deposits were in bank accounts. Banks might be sweeping cash into bank accounts as a hedge against financial failure, but this would be invisible. US Interview 96:07.

[46] *Bankruptcy Act Revision Hearings on H.R. 31 and H.R. 32*: 1772.

[47] Testimony of James Ingraham, Robert Morris Association, *Bankruptcy Act Revision Hearings on H.R. 31 and H.R. 32*: 2490.

[48] *Bankruptcy Act Revision Hearings on H.R. 31 and H.R. 32*: 2506.

[49] *Ibid*: 1772.

[50] *Ibid*: 2510. Klee points up the inequity of setoff: "Does not the setoff enable the bank to receive a higher percentage of its claim than other creditors similarly situated [with respect to security] but who do not enjoy a right of setoff?" (p. 2507).

Some staffers and lawyers on the House subcommittee wanted to abolish setoff altogether, but they acknowledged the *realpolitik* that it was politically unacceptable to the banks.[51] They therefore offered a carrot and stick alternative. When the bill was reported out of the House Judiciary committee it incorporated responses to most of the banking industry's reservations about changes to their "right" of setoff. Essentially banks retained the right they inherited from the prior Act, but they were offered a set of inducements—positive and negative—not to setoff. Put more picturesquely, "what the setoff section does . . . is to say, 'Yes, we know you can setoff today, but these are the goodies we are going to give you if you don't setoff today. And this is the risk you're going to take if you do setoff today.' "[52]

The positive inducement was that banks would get stronger protection for their "perishable" assets, such as inventory and cash. Any cash collateral coming into the company after the bankruptcy petition could not be used by the debtor without the permission of the secured creditor or a court hearing, in which the debtor would bear the burden of proof (Lake 1982; Trost and King 1978, 520).[53] The negative inducement followed from an important limitation on the creditor's ability to employ setoff, which was kept in the House version: setoff was retained within the definition of a "transfer" so a court might compel the creditor to make those funds available for reorganization. The House effectively said, "you can keep the right, but if you use it before bankruptcy, if you setoff before bankruptcy, we'll penalize you, because we want the money kept in."[54] The court would look back to the cash balance ninety days before filing. It would then compare that figure to the cash balance on the day of filing. If the latter were higher, and the banks had improved their position (and presumably had been building up cash reserves), the banks would be compelled to contribute the "improvement" back to the debtor for use in reorganization. In fact, this potential penalty produced two forms of ambiguity. Banks, themselves, would not necessarily know exactly when a company would file for bankruptcy, and thus they could be caught with temporarily high balances. Moreover, the wording in the Code was ambiguous and it was not clear whether the improvement would be paid as a cash transfer, or as an unsecured loan.[55]

[51] US Interview 96:05.
[52] US Interview 96:04.
[53] *Ibid.*
[54] US Interview 96:05.
[55] US Interview 96:05; see Section 553 (b) of US Bankruptcy Code Pub. L. No. 95–598, 92 Stat. 2549. 124 Cong. Rec H11047, daily ed, September 28, 1978.

These compromises amounted to a trade-off between the financial interests' claim that setoff was a "right" and the position that funds available for setoff were to be treated like any other form of collateral and used in saving the business. Banks were thus pressured not to setoff, to leave their cash in control of reorganizers. In return, secured creditors were assured of some formal safeguards (for example, they had to be "adequately protected" if their collateral were used or sold, and reorganization plans had to be "fair and equitable" (see Freeman 1980; Weintraub and Resnick 1983; Rosenberg and Sattin 1979)) by negotiating the fine line between protection of interests securely held by banks and the need of funds by companies that were seeking to reorganize. Effectively some measure of control shifted from banks—which could no longer make automatic transfers from deposit accounts to offset loans—to courts—which could weigh the relative needs of a company for cash against the "rights" of the banks.

Cramdown

The relative control of the courts in bankruptcy recurred as an issue in a discussion over their ability to impose a reorganization plan if parties could not reach an amicable agreement. In reorganizations, debtors and creditors must negotiate an agreement over a plan that not only lays out how a company will rehabilitate itself, but also indicates how financial restructuring will benefit various classes of creditors.[56] The plan identifies the problems that got the company into difficulties and indicates how the business can be made profitable again. And it redefines the relationships the company will have to its various creditors in the future. Once a plan has been proposed to the court, creditors vote on whether to accept it. Voting on plans presents an opportunity for recalcitrant (usually secured) creditors to reject *any* plan under which their collateral would be used in the ongoing rehabilitation of the company. Moreover, the threat of continued rejection would effectively allow secured creditors to hold the firm hostage to their interests. The longer the delay, the less probable a successful reorganization.

---

[56] Creditors are divided into classes for purposes of voting on plans. Each secured creditor is in a single class. Trade creditors and unsecured creditors may be in a number of classes. Since voting is by class, a single secured creditor could vote against a plan because he does not get the treatment he wants. Hence the advent of cramdown as a method of dealing with dissenting creditors who would frustrate an otherwise acceptable solution to the vast majority of creditors and the court. For a history of claims classification, see Markell (1994–5) and Markell (1991), n. 9.

Cramdown permits a bankruptcy judge to appraise the merits of a plan and, if circumstances warrant, "cram down" a decision on dissenting creditors, even if some secured creditors remain opposed to it. The importance of the cramdown provision rested in the general perception by reformers and the secured creditors that cramdown was a means of empowering the unsecured creditors and debtor/trustee so as to free up resources which might otherwise have been restricted as "secured assets" for ongoing operation during reorganization proceedings.[57] Cramdown provisions therefore enhanced the probability of a successful reorganization, but at the expense of creditors' rights. In the judgement of one expert participant: "It [cramdown] strengthens the debtor's position in seeking reorganization and weakens the secured creditor's position..."[58] Given this incipient conflict, it again put secured creditors on the defensive and might reasonably have sparked significant legislative controversy.

Surprising enough, the issue generated little commentary from interest groups, including those it would benefit. Of the over 100 groups that testified in Congressional subcommittee hearings, only four discussed cramdown. Three of those four represented secured creditors: the American Bankers Association, the Robert Morris Associates, and the Municipal Issuers Service Corporation (an association of insurance agencies that guaranteed municipal bonds). They well understood how cramdown would affect their interests. In the words of the representatives of the American Bankers Association and Robert Morris Associates, "Simply put, the concern that creditors have is that the cram-down language is and will be...used as a device to divert values to junior interests."[59]

Nevertheless, secured creditors exerted themselves little to oppose cramdown. At least two reasons account for their relative inaction. First, by the time reform reached the subcommittee stage (1975–78), it had been underway for eight years. The American Bankers Association had been involved on behalf of secured creditors from the beginning. Since they had helped frame the issues, and strongly believed that bankruptcy law and procedure needed to be updated, they were loath to derail legislation they had helped to formulate from its earliest stages. Instead of the secured creditors coming to the table as outsiders, a select

[57] US Interview 92:01. See also the joint statements of the American Bankers Association and the Robert Morris Associates (*Senate Hearings on S. 2266 and H.R. 8200*: 577.)

[58] US Interview 96:03.

[59] *Senate Hearings on S. 2266 and H.R. 8200*: 577.

group of powerful representatives of the banking industry was co-opted into the reform process from its outset.[60] Only if the law were irredeemably and fundamentally flawed would bankers have criticized it vigorously, for to do so could have risked the entire reform process and endangered their wide-ranging calls for improvements in bankruptcy courts, bankruptcy administration, and the bankruptcy bench. Furthermore, secured creditors possessed the kind of global interests that permitted trade-offs across different aspects of the legislation, including cramdown. Banks could accept cramdown if the judge and courts in which it occurred were highly competent, neutral, and efficient.[61]

Second, a version of cramdown with a relatively narrow application had been part of Chapter X of the Bankruptcy Act since 1948 and had emerged as a practice, recognized in case law, since the early 1970s. It had arisen as a means to facilitate successful debtor reorganizations by neutralizing secured creditors' attempts to veto a debtors' reorganization plan.[62] Thus, case law had already made cramdown something of a fact of life for secured creditors, where it played a role consistent with the principle of corporate rehabilitation favored by many of the reformers. Barring a major political effort on the part of banks, cramdown seemed almost inevitable: it already existed in practice and fit in rather well with the rehabilitative goals of legislative reform. Thus the best strategy for banks was to accept cramdown but seek additional protections.

There were two protections advanced by the banks. First, banks were concerned that the method of appraising the value of their collateral fairly represented its worth. Value could be established in two ways: (1) by appraising the worth of assets if they were sold piecemeal in a breakup or liquidation of the company. For instance, a piece of custom-made machinery against which a bank had a $1 million claim, might be worth, say, a tenth of that if sold by itself on the market. Or (2) value could be established when collateral was appraised as part of an ongoing business concern.[63] Since the latter was usually much higher, it

---

[60] The list of US banks whose personnel were involved in the bankruptcy legislation under the auspices of the American Bankers Association include such financial institutions as Citibank, Chemical Bank, American Security Bank, Bank of America National Trust & Savings Association, and First National Bank of Boston.

[61] See Chapter 10.

[62] According to Small (1979), the two cases most often cited in court with respect to cramdown were *Wachovia Bank and Trust Co. v. Harris* (455 F.2d 841 [4th Cir. 1972]), and *In re Pine Gate Associates, Ltd.* (Bankr. Ct. Dec. 1478 [N.D. Ga. 1976]).

[63] A more technical formulation of their position can be found in the representations of the American Bankers Association and the Robert Morris Associates: "At a minimum, if

was also much preferred by the bankers, and it was this standard that was accepted in the negotiations over cramdown.

Secondly, bankruptcy law provided that when a reorganization plan was confirmed over the objections of secured creditors, a bankruptcy judge would have to recompense dissenting creditors with other forms of property. Secured creditors were concerned that such property could variously include stock, notes, and bonds. A deal in which equity was exchanged for debt would in effect reduce a secured creditor to unsecured status. Thus, banks wanted restrictions placed on the kind of property with which dissenting creditors were to be recompensed.

Congress responded favorably with several important provisions for secured creditors in a cramdown situation: (1) a plan could be "crammed down" only if the secured creditor was able to retain its lien on the property whether the property was retained by the debtor or transferred; (2) the secured creditor was entitled to have the entire amount of the debt related to the property secured by a lien even if the value of the collateral is less than the amount of the debt (for example, the secured creditor is allowed to claim the entire amount of the debt even if the value of the property against which the creditor has a lien has fallen below the amount of the debt); and (3) the secured creditor could be recompensed only with an "indubitable equivalent" of his claim. Practically, this meant that unsecured notes or equity securities of the debtor would not be the indubitable equivalent of a lien on real property. Thus, the secured creditor could not be reduced to the status of unsecured creditor. The net result, said one academic-reformer in retrospect, was that cramdown bought flexibility for reorganizers without impairing the rights of secured creditors concerning their collateral or their rights to get fair payment. "What it basically affects, I think, is simply the time when they get the payment."

> [T]hey're going to get complete payment of their secured claim with a current present value—and that's going to be a function of what interest rate is used and how long a stretch out period would be, and, in the meantime, they would maintain a lien on the collateral. So that, in effect, it seems to me that the basic rights of a secured creditor are not being changed.[64][65]

the rights of secured creditors are to be abrogated as a part of a rehabilitation process, the valuation of secured creditors' collateral should be on a going concern basis since an ongoing business venture is the only legitimate basis for invoking the broad powers inherent in cram-down." Bankruptcy Reform Act of 1978 (Senate Hearings), p. 577.

[64] US Interview 96:04.

[65] Bankruptcy Reform Act of 1978, section 1129(b)(2)(i); section 1111(b)(2); section 1129(b)(2)(iii); section 553, 101(40) under the definition of "transfer."

Thus, consistent with their positions on use of collateral and setoff, the banks demonstrated that they were willing to modify the principle of absolute priority, given two sorts of protections: clear statutory language that institutionalized the protections for their rights; and administrative improvements to courts in which they could have confidence. Both issues, valuation and recompense, constituted ways in which secured creditors accommodated themselves to the reality of cramdown.

Giving Adequate Protection

To attain the balance they sought between the rights of secured creditors and flexible use of collateral, the House legislators developed a formula for "adequate protection" that they believed would satisfy the strong reservations expressed by the financial industry, and thereby sidestep a potential landmine to passage of the bill.

The substantive concept of adequate protection, promulgated by the Bankruptcy Commission, and subsequently adapted by Congress, assured banks that losing some of their control over the timing and realization of assets would not harm the underlying value of those assets.[66] While the courts were the ultimate guarantors of this assurance, the reformers knit together a variety of procedural measures that would satisfy bankers that their rights so carefully negotiated outside bankruptcy would not be treated carelessly inside bankruptcy.

Cash that came into the company after the bankruptcy petition, for instance, could not be used by managers or a trustee unless they obtained permission from the secured creditors or the court. Adequate protection of banks' collateral might be extended by giving them new security or additional security, or even an administrative priority—typically the first expenses that are paid to creditors out of an estate are the administrative fees it cost to liquidate or reorganize a company.[67] (Trost and King 1978: 543) All of these were to be appraised against a standard, that of the "indubitable equivalent" value of assets. Although its meaning would remain to be defined more precisely by the courts, the concept was drawn from a line of cases that sought to ensure that secured creditors were adequately compensated for depreciation in the value of their collateral during a reorganization.[68] If the banks were

---

[66] Bankruptcy Reform Act of 1978, sections 362, 363. "Adequate protection" existed in Chapter X of the Bankruptcy Act, but was little used (Markell 1991).

[67] *H.R. 8200*, S 361.

[68] Lake (1982: 1157), n. 37.

to have the value in one kind of asset paid in another kind of asset, the two would have equivalent value. No longer could banks with collateral in a company be "cashed-out" at a level that the lenders believed was much lower, and with no recourse to obtain that "real" value.[69] Then again, in a cramdown secured creditors were offered protection, for if a court confirmed a plan despite their objections, the court must ensure that secured creditors received compensation for the property at a value equal to that of the asset at the time the plan went into effect.[70]

Secured creditors had difficulties with *timing*. Even if banks were given the right to obtain relief from a court to protect use of their collateral, this would mean little if courts delayed action until the collateral had diminished in value. Therefore later versions of the bill included a provision that if the secured creditor asked for relief from the automatic stay, then the court had thirty days in which to act. If the court did not act in that window of opportunity, then creditors obtained "automatic" relief, and debtors could not use their collateral.[71]

Secured creditors had difficulty with *notice* and *the burden of proof* for they wanted at least to be advised if their collateral was under threat and to have a chance to protect it from "taking" by the debtor. The House responded by insisting that debtors must either obtain permission from the creditors or from the courts to use soft collateral, such as cash. Moreover, the burden of proof that cash collateral needed to be used would sit on the shoulders of the debtors who wanted to use it, not the creditors who wanted to protect it.

Secured creditors also had problems with *valuation* of their claims. The Commission had initially proposed that the secured creditor be considered adequately protected when the collateral was valued in terms of its liquidation value.[72] The secured creditors argued that it should be valued in light of its part in an ongoing concern.[73] The final bill left the determination of the value of the collateral up to the discretion of the court on a case by case basis.[74]

---

[69] US Interview 96:04, see Section 1111(b) and 1129 legislative notes.

[70] West Publishing 1988, Bankruptcy Code, historical and revision notes.

[71] See Schimberg (1979: 57); Trost and King (1978: 538). Also c.f. §362(d), (e) of H.R. 8200, 95th Cong., 2nd Sess.

[72] H.R. Doc. No. 93–137, 93d Cong, 1st Sess., pt. 1 (1973) p. 237. This was apparently based on a development in the case law: *In re Penn Cent. Transp. Co.*, 494 F.2d 270 (3d Cir. 1974).

[73] *Senate Hearings on S. 2266 and H.R. 8200*: 575–7.

[74] Trost and King (1978: 543). See Schimberg (1979); Rome (1979); Lake (1982).

All of these discussions took place within a climate of uncertainty over the specification of what "adequate protection" would mean. When the term "adequate protection" appears in the text of the hearing transcripts, it is often placed in quotes by the secured creditors, intimating their doubts about "adequate" or "protection," whereas a term like 'ordinary course of business' is not. It was precisely the substance of this term that was being contested. No one argued that banks did not need to be adequately protected, but secured creditors argued that the bills did not go far enough in developing clear standards, enshrined in statutory law, that would lay out those protections with some precision.[75] Bankers' concerns had some basis: a string of common law cases in the early 1970s gave increasing ability to the debtor/trustee to use the secured creditor's collateral.[76] Consistent with the press for flexibility, H.R. 8200 left the definition of adequate protection up to the discretion of the court.[77] This in turn gave all the more reason for secured creditors to ensure that the substance of legal reform was accompanied by major improvements in the staffing and administration of bankruptcy law in the courts.

Although the bankers had urged Congress to specify in the statute itself such notions as "good cause" for using collateral,[78] lawyer-legislators adhered to more general principles in statutory drafting. Staffers argued that developing "bureaucratic" lists were too rigid and not sufficiently inclusive. It was much better to leave matters in the hands of the court, which could decide specific problems, often hard to anticipate by precise rules, on a case by case basis. Thus practice would emerge from the accumulation of cases drawn from real-world experience. While this of course is a fine common law principle, it made it all the more imperative for bankers to ensure the quality of the bankruptcy judiciary.

Outcomes

The secured creditors came to the meta-bargaining table at its inception. Their wide-ranging interests wove integrally into a process in which their

---

[75] As we have seen, both the National Commercial Finance Conference and the American Bankers Association offered revisions of the Commission and Judges bills that spelled out what "adequate protection" might be understood to mean (*Bankruptcy Act Revision Hearings on H.R. 31 and H.R. 32:* 1754 (American Bankers Association); 1821–22 (NCFC)).

[76] Trost and King (1978: 539–40).

[77] Trost and King (1978: 542–3).

[78] See p. 177ff above.

co-operation was encouraged and their potential for veto effectively acknowledged. Yet bankers approached the 1978 reforms with a larger agenda than substantive rights alone. While they remained keenly engaged in any diminution of their rights in law and practice, they balanced these with a concern for procedural reforms. To anticipate Chapter 10 of this book, their drive for procedural rationality included a radical simplification and clarification of jurisdictions in bankruptcy law, a substantial expansion of the powers of bankruptcy courts, and a perceptible improvement in the qualities and powers of bankruptcy judges. Were these procedural improvements to be attained, secured creditors were prepared to show more flexibility in the relaxation of their substantive rights, and the ceding of control over the preservation and use of assets to newly upgraded bankruptcy judges and courts.

Banks therefore argued strenuously and fought tenaciously for Article III courts in bankruptcy and this they virtually attained—at least before the 1978 Code's provisions on the status of the bankruptcy courts were struck down by the Supreme Court. So fundamental were their concerns over procedure, and so powerful was the rehabilitative movement, that they were prepared to relax the standard of absolute priority so long as they received adequate protection. In each case of control over their assets—use of collateral, setoff, and cramdown—the secured creditors were prepared to settle for something less than watertight security, if judges and courts protected their assets. In other words, they ceded a measure of control to courts.

More generally, to protect small creditors and encourage successful corporate reorganizations, Congress was willing to let freely negotiated contracts be modified in bankruptcy, and to weaken the claims of secured creditors. These were not minor concessions. A Congressional staffer underscored the enormity of the changes wrought in secured creditors rights:

> ... before the 1978 code, with some case law exceptions ... the secured creditor power was enormous. For the 1978 code to come along and give every Chapter 11 debtor the power to alter secured debt was an enormous policy change—an enormous substantive change in the law.[79]

Bankers realized the high stakes of trading their strong security for greater procedural efficiency and flexibility. Yet they may not have comprehended in 1978 the full scope of their concessions. Looking back some fifteen years after the Bankruptcy Code became law, another

---

[79] US Interview 92:01.

Congressional staffer concluded that ". . . secured creditors generally took a bigger hit than they realized they were taking."[80] As we shall see with organized labor, in complex meta-bargaining of the sort represented by the bankruptcy reforms, key players may not only misperceive their interests at the outset, but they cannot predict the outcomes of their political settlements with any great degree of accuracy. It is in this disjunction between law in practice as it enters the political realm, and the politics of law-making that shape law in practice, that innovation thrives.

SECURED CREDITORS IN ENGLAND

In England, discussions of the rights of secured creditors, most notably the commercial banks, broke out beyond arid technicalities amongst experts to engender vigorous, even passionate, exchanges among a wide array of creditors, debtors, and policy-makers. English law had long favored creditors over debtors, and secured interests over unsecured interests. English banks, and other secured creditors, could "take a pledge over physical movables . . . and a mortgage or charge over almost every conceivable kind of asset, tangible or intangible."[81] Many of the tensions in the English reforms centered on the justice and pragmatism of such a favored status for secured creditors, and most especially, on the security that was the darling of banks—the floating charge.[82] Described by one banker as "a lynchpin of bank lending," the floating charge nevertheless could wreak havoc with other creditors, with financially struggling companies, and with efforts to rehabilitate a business. In the final stages of the insolvency reforms, Lord Denning said, ". . . judges from the earliest times pointed out the injustices of the floating charge," but the banks had remained indifferent to those injustices.[83] The largest English banks learned very quickly that the insolvency review committee intended to look closely at remedies that could threaten the viability of their security in favor of other, weaker creditors, and of professionals engaged in corporate reorganization.[84]

---

[80] US Interview 91:04.   [81] Goode (1990: 51). UK Interview 96:01.

[82] Floating charges were used principally for working capital, and loan capital was provided under fixed charges that were attached to particular assets. *Minutes of the Cork Committee*, 1 Mar. 1977.

[83] Denning (H.L., vol. 459, 7 Feb. 1985, col. 1223).

[84] The floating charge was not the only issue problematic for secured creditors. One banker-reformer says setoff was a matter of "great concern," as was a threat to impair the bank's ability to used fixed charges over book debts. U.K. Interview 91:06.

The Floating Charge on the Defensive

Devised by the Court of Chancery in the 1860s, the floating charge had become a staple of English lending. A floating charge possessed three essential characteristics. First, it secured assets that companies held at present and will hold in the future. It effectively provided a security over the entire assets of the debtor company. Second, the charge "floated" above the assets. Because it was not attached to any particular asset, the debtor could buy and sell and continue trading with assets in the ordinary course of business without any need to go back to the bank for permission to dispose of assets or to renegotiate terms of the loan. Third, the floating charge might "crystallize" or fix on the particular assets in the company either when it went into liquidation, or when the charge-holder (the bank) decided to appoint a receiver (normally an accounting firm to liquidate the company), or when some event specified in the loan agreement was triggered. When the charge crystallizes, if the charge covers all the company's assets, "the practical consequences are extremely inconvenient," for "the company cannot deal with its cash balances, pay any debt, or sell any stocks without the debenture-holder's consent."[85]

The terms of the floating charge were freely negotiated between the bank-creditor and the corporate-debtor.[86] They operated mostly with middle range companies, since the largest companies were financially strong enough that they did not have to give floating charges in order to obtain credit, and it was more trouble than it was worth for the banks to use this security with smaller companies.[87] But much of the contention around the floating charge, and the "debenture holder" (the institution that held the charge), arose because banks could and did enforce their security outside insolvency law, thus avoiding the constraints of insolvency law, and pre-empting other junior or unsecured creditors (Goode 1990: 76). If companies breeched the terms of the security, banks could

---

[85] *Cork Report*: 355, paras 1571–2. In the words of the Cork Report, the floating charge "(a) is a charge on a class of assets of a company both present and future; (b) those assets are of a kind which, in the ordinary course of the business of a company, would be changing from time to time; and (c) it is contemplated that, until some step is taken by or on behalf of those interested in the charge, the company may carry on its business in the ordinary way, and dispose of all or any of those assets in the ordinary course of business." (*Cork Report*: 31).

[86] American banks also used the equivalent of a floating charge to secure their loans. These did not, however, prove to be politically controversial, probably because the issue had previously been settled in the negotiation of article 9 of the Uniform Commercial Code, concerning secured transactions.

[87] UK Interview 91:11.

step into the company, appoint a receiver, and grant him the powers necessary to satisfy the bank's claims. If this required liquidating the company and selling its assets, as it usually did, then such was the cost of business failure.

When the government appointed a review committee to examine bankruptcy and insolvency, "it came out fairly early on that the floating charge...was under attack." The banks soon realized that a consensus was developing within the review committee "that the banks—and their all-enveloping floating charges—should no longer have such an advantage in insolvency."[88]

Floating charges, and their use by the banks, produced disquiet, frustration, and a sense of inequity among numerous groups. The Cork Committee stated that it had "...received more evidence both oral and written on this one subject from those whom we have consulted than on any other".[89] Company managers and other creditors complained that the banks frequently acted precipitously, often well before the condition of a company warranted the kind of drastic intervention that came with appointment of a receiver and liquidation of a company's assets. Floating charges, too, effectively reserved an insolvent debtor's assets solely for the holder of the charges, and so their use hurt many other classes of creditors, who were left with little or nothing. Thus the National Federation of Building Trades Employers, a peak association of the construction industry, spoke on behalf of an industry which experienced frequent defaults and insolvencies. Construction companies typically were unsecured creditors and so often suffered because of a bank's superior secured claims on an insolvent firm. They attacked the floating charge, and suggested that banks should instead rely on fixed charges to secure their debts.[90]

Even more aggrieved were those trade creditors that supplied goods to companies *after* a floating charge had been taken over a company's assets. As Peter Millett put it to the Cork Committee:

The trouble was that it [a floating charge] sweeps into the security future goods, goods which are not owned by the company at the date when the money was borrowed but were bought later and not paid for.[91]

---

[88] UK Interview 90:03.
[89] *Cork Report*: 34.
[90] First submission of the National Federation of Building Trades Employers to the Cork Committee, *Public Record Office*, 3 Feb. 1978.
[91] *Minutes of the Cork Committee*, 16 Apr. 1980, p. 3.

When trade suppliers observed banks seizing goods that the trade suppliers had supplied, but for which the company had not paid they considered themselves palpably wronged. Both the Insolvency Practitioners Association and the Institute of Professional Civil Servants (Insolvency Service Branch) expressed their unhappiness with floating charges because of such effects on unsecured trade creditors.[92]

Anticipating some of these familiar attacks, the banks mounted a strong defense of their prerogatives and practices.[93] The Committee of London Clearing Banks (CLCB), which represented the largest half-dozen retail and high street banks in England, told the Cork Committee that the floating charge was "an integral component in the range of security available to Banks".[94] Indeed, by the mid 1970s floating charges secured an estimated £2,000 million in English commercial debt.[95] The many virtues of this security included its informality, flexibility, cheapness and speed.

The British Bankers Association told the Cork Committee that "in our view the floating charge is a well tried instrument which has stood the test of time and is very well suited to a legal environment." One of its great merits for businesses, "to a greater extent than any other security arrangement," is that it "enables a bank to adopt a very flexible attitude towards the facilities it agrees for a company." As sales increase, it is easy to expand the size of the loan. Most importantly for business, "the customer has complete freedom to deal in his assets in the normal course of his business without constant reference to his banker." Because the loan "floated" over a basket of assets, the assets themselves could change so long as their underlying aggregate value remained. This provided a much more flexible arrangement than a series of fixed securities in particular pieces of equipment, particular lists of inventory, or particular pieces of real estate. A rigid security device requires greater involvement by banks, more distraction for managers, higher transaction costs in time and money to conclude new loan agreements, with the net result that capital becomes more expensive and companies have "less freedom to deal with the day to day running of the business." Without the

---

[92] Oral Testimony of the Insolvency Practitioners Association and the Institute of Professional Civil Servants (Insolvency Service Branch) to the Cork Committee, *Public Record Office*, 13 June 1978.

[93] For instance, in the early days of the Cork Committee, BBC 2 aired a program entitled "The Liquidators," which criticized receivers and the conduct of receiverships along lines that rang true to the Committee (*Minutes of the Cork Committee*, 28 Apr. 1977).

[94] CLCB Memorandum: 1.

[95] Oral submission to the Cork Report, British Bankers Association, 8 Mar. 1978.

floating charge, said the Midland Bank, banks would be forced to rely on other, more rigid forms of security, "which would hamper companies in the conduct of everyday business."[96]

In addition, the floating charge actually served the customer, said the bankers, because it was relatively cheap for banks to administer. The banking spokesman on the Cork Committee told his peers that "the floating charge was the cheapest and most convenient method of financing when margins were generally low."[97] If the floating charge were abolished, it would only hurt those most in need of credit. Corporate borrowers would suffer from increased restrictions and the final result would be "greater cost all round, and more difficulty by some companies in borrowing at fine rates of interest."[98]

Neither were the banks prepared to be scapegoats for the harm done to other creditors. In elaborating its defense, the CLCB denied that floating charges tended to "scoop the pool" of assets and leave little or nothing for ordinary creditors. In fact, ordinary or trade creditors were often in a better position than the banks to monitor the fortunes of a company and to protect their assets. The CLCB memo sharply criticized Romalpa clauses, which is not surprising given that banks and trade creditors struggled over the same debtor assets, using floating charges and Romalpa clauses, respectively.[99] Said one banker, "Retention of title . . . was the matter of great concern."[100] The CLCB was: ". . . not convinced of the need for or desirability of the concept of reservation of title," and argued that its widespread application led to ". . . distortions as between one type of ordinary creditor and another."[101] Banks claimed that ordinary creditors were generally better positioned to know the true financial state of companies they traded with, and already had other adequate methods, such as insisting on cash on delivery, to protect themselves.[102] Unlike ordinary trade creditors, it was the banks that needed special treatment, said the bankers!

---

[96]   *Public Record Office* 15 Aug. 1977; CLCB, *Public Record Office* 4 June 1979; Midland Bank, *Public Record Office*, 7 Sept. 77.

[97]   *Minutes of the Cork Committee*, 8 Mar. 1978.

[98]   CLCB, Memorandum, *Public Record Office*, 1979: 2.

[99]   Romalpa clauses, or retention of title, were contractual devices used by trade suppliers to ensure that the goods they supplied to companies remained the property of the supplier until the company had fully paid for the goods. In other words, if a floating charge crystallized on the company's assets, which might include those goods, they could not be easily repossessed by a receiver.

[100]   UK Interview 91:06.

[101]   CLCB, Memorandum, *Public Record Office*, 1979: 10.

[102]   See Midland Bank to the Cork Committee, *Public Record Office*, 20 June 1977.

In sum, claimed the banks, both they and their customers benefited from floating charges: "...we did feel that the floating charge was a very helpful instrument both to the customer and to the banks." The abolition or "emasculation" of floating charges would be nothing short of "deplorable."[103]

The clearing banks were not without their allies. The British Chambers of Commerce, the Law Society, and the accountancy bodies favored the continuation of floating charges.[104] According to Kenneth Cork, accountants liked the floating charge because they believed it might actually facilitate rehabilitation of a business since "it enabled the appointment of a receiver at the drop of a hat. The receiver had complete authority to run the company...so you've saved the company." This support was scarcely disinterested since the receiver was usually an accountant. The City of London Solicitors Company went so far as to argue that floating charges were much better for debtors than fixed charges because to collect the latter, the security holder had to destroy the debtor company, thus ending all chance at a successful reorganization.[105] And representatives from the Department of Trade and Industry worried that measures directed against banks could result in fewer loans to firms.[106]

The Cork Committee reflected this diversity of opinion about secured creditors. There were those, like Muir Hunter, QC, who were convinced that "the only way in which modern industry could be financed was by the floating charge." Several preferred it to stay in place, with perhaps some careful adjustments to mitigate its worst effects on company rehabilitation. Others, like Peter Millett, Alfred Goldman, and Richie Penny, recognized the "long standing grievance" that trade and unsecured creditors nursed towards what they considered was an inequitable legal device.[107]

Given both strong support and strong opposition to floating charges, the Cork Committee declared in the final report "that the floating charge has become so fundamental a part of the financial structure of

---

[103] UK Interview 91:06.

[104] First submission of the CCAB to the Cork Committee, Dec. 1977, Oral Testimony of the City of London Solicitors Company 7 Feb. 1978, Submission of the Association of British Chambers of Commerce to the Cork Committee, 7 Feb. 1978.

[105] Oral Testimony of the City of London Solicitors Company: *Public Record Office*, 7 Feb. 1978.

[106] Oral Testimony of Department of Trade and Industry, Companys' Division, *Public Record Office*, 22 Oct. 1980.

[107] *Minutes of the Cork Committee*, 8 Mar. 1978; 16 Apr. 1980.

the United Kingdom that its abolition cannot be contemplated. But we are equally convinced that reform is needed." If the floating charge should persist in insolvency, it must be reformed substantially, particularly in light of how it affected the unsecured trade creditors of an insolvent company.[108] The Committee therefore proposed that all creditors "participate" more equally in the "distribution of the proceeds of those assets comprised in the charge." Its most notable innovation was the proposal to compel a secured creditor to give up ten per cent of the value of its floating charge to be set aside for distribution to unsecured creditors.[109]

While the Committee recognized the general unhappiness that this proposal engendered in the banking world, its attenuation of the floating charge, through the Ten Percent Fund, could only be understood in the context of a larger set of revisions. While taking testimony from representatives of the Consultative Committee of Accountancy Bodies in November of 1980, Kenneth Cork stated that:

What we are proposing is a package. First, the almost total abolition of preferences; secondly, restrictions on the reservation of title; thirdly, creditors having fixed charges to be restrained from realizing their security for 12 months after the appointment of a receiver.... Therefore it seems fair to some of us ... to give the unsecured creditors a stake, say 10 per cent, in the net realizations of the receiver.[110]

In other words, as we shall see in subsequent chapters, the Cork Committee sought radically to reduce the moneys going to some preferred creditors, such as utilities and government tax authorities. With these moneys kept for the estate of the insolvent company, the Committee hoped to be able to make more assets available for all the other creditors, including banks. The banks also should benefit from some restriction over the use of retention-of-title clauses by trade suppliers, thus putting still more assets back into the pool. At the same time, secured creditors (whether their security was based on a fixed or floating charge) would have their claims weakened. The Committee sought to

---

[108] As one member of the Cork Committee put it: "You know, it came down to freedom of contract. If I want to give you a special sort of security, I can give you a special sort of security. We absolutely looked at that, and we were absolutely mad against that sort of really very serious legislation making enormous inroads into freedom of contract" (UK Interview 90:20).

[109] For a more extended discussion of the Ten Percent Fund, see Chapter 7. *Cork Report*: 34, 335, 345, 354.

[110] *Minutes of the Cork Committee*, 24 Nov. 1980, pp. 2–3.

set aside a Ten Percent Fund for the sole benefit of unsecured creditors. It was the view of the Cork Committee that without other modifications, a weakening of preferred creditors, such as the Inland Revenue, would simply put extra money into the pockets of the large secured creditors, and unsecured creditors would realize no benefits at all.[111] Shifting money from one set of deep pockets to a different set of deep pockets hardly seemed fair. That was why the package of changes was seen as so important: it all fitted together.

Alerted to these proposals well before the Cork Report was published, the banks expressed strong opposition to the Ten Percent Fund. Were such a measure to pass, the CLCB insisted, it would only mean that banks would lend less money and on more stringent terms. The CLCB underscored their opposition by asking rhetorically: "...why it is that the debenture holder alone should be singled out for this compulsory reduction."[112] In oral testimony before the Committee, the CLCB worried that 10 per cent could just be an "opening bid," and might in subsequent years get enlarged to 12, 15 or even 25 per cent, effectively confiscating a greater and greater proportion of banks' claims.[113] As one person expressed it: "Well, I think they saw that the recommendation...it could be ten per cent today and a higher per cent tomorrow ...it is a foot in the door."[114] Moreover the bankers were quite skeptical that the Government would give up its priority for taxes, social security payments, and the like. Banks hardly wanted to be in a position where they gave up ten per cent of their proceeds in the expectation of a Government concession that never came. Even if the entire package of proposed changes were enacted into law, big secured creditors like banks could expect a gain of uncertain size as they, along with all the other creditors, shared the assets pried from the pockets of preferred creditors. They could also, however, expect with certainty a loss of considerable magnitude if floating charges were undercut or if the Ten Percent Fund went through. It was this clear downside that seized their attention and added to their general wariness about many of the ideas developed by the Cork Committee, a fact which the Committee itself acknowledged.[115]

---

[111] *Minutes of the Cork Committee*, 27 Sep. 1978, p. 6.

[112] CLCB, Memorandum, *Public Record Office*, 1979, p. 9.

[113] Oral Testimony of the CLCB, *Public Record Office*, 8 Sept. 1980.

[114] UK Interview 90:03.

[115] "We discussed our approach in general terms with representatives of the banking community and some other witnesses who gave evidence before us. Not surprisingly, it was less than enthusiastically received" (*Cork Report*: 346).

Government Policy and Opposition Dissent

Despite the banks' self-declared expressions of relative ineffectiveness in the political realm, the Government essentially took the side of the banks. The 1984 White Paper agreed with the Cork Committee that floating charges were a fundamental fact of British financial life and that they should not be abolished. And the Government opposed the Ten Percent Fund, arguing that in practice such a measure would not materially improve the situation of unsecured creditors.[116] The reason, the White Paper explained, was that fixed charge creditors would still have first claim over the assets, and creditors who currently used a floating charge to secure their loans would simply switch to fixed charges.[117] That is, lenders would respond to a new law so as exactly to offset and undermine its intended effects. These "Coasian" expectations recognized the sophistication and adaptability of banks, and their ability to "contract around" legal changes, even if a recourse to more fixed securities would introduce higher transaction costs for all parties and more rigidity in the system of lending.[118]

When the Insolvency Bill was introduced to the House of Lords, the Government's timid treatment of the floating charge, and its failure to advocate the Ten Percent Fund, drew fire from Labour and independent peers. Lord Bruce, who led for Labour, pointed out the failure of the Bill to deal with the "ruthless" behavior of receivers, as agents for the banks in the realization of assets covered by the floating charge.

One of the problems to which the Cork Committee addressed itself was the undue power that was apprehended in the hands of a receiver for the debenture holders [secured creditors]. Complaints were laid, and complaints continue, that very often receivers for the debenture holders apply themselves quite ruthlessly to the realization of assets in order to satisfy the charge comprising the debenture with, in some cases, scant regard either to the future of the business itself or even the plight in which creditors further down the line might find themselves.[119]

Distinguished lawyers buttressed the assault on the government in language that was none too temperate. Quoting a case from 1897, Lord

---

[116] *Government White Paper*, p. 17.

[117] *Government White Paper*, p. 18.

[118] Coase (1960) argued that in situations with zero transaction costs, private parties can simply contract around whatever distribution of resources or property rights initially obtains. Thus, statutory redistributions are unlikely to have any real effect as the parties can contractually compensate for them.

[119] H.L., vol. 459, 4 Feb. 1985, col. 851.

Mischon reminded his fellow peers of Lord MacNaghton's opinion that "everybody knows that when there is a winding up, debenture holders generally step in and sweep off everything, and a great scandal it is." Mishcon continues, "if a great scandal it was in 1897, it has not lost its quality of being scandalous in 1984."[120] Lord Denning, former Master of the Rolls, concurred that judges had long pointed to the "injustices" perpetrated by the floating charge: "Although those injustices have been caused to no end of people, nevertheless, the banking community and the commercial community have said, 'We cannot interfere with the general principles of these floating charges, however grievous may be the injustices that are inflicted by it.'..."[121] But the Government remained unmoved. The influence of the banks on the government's position was hardly a mystery as Lord Lucas publicly insisted that: "We must also take account of the views of the banking community on this matter. Their judgment is that the effect of reducing the flexibility they currently enjoy would be harmful."[122]

Much the same argument recurred in the House of Commons. Labour members suggested that Government leaders "have been perhaps too solicitous of the banks' interests," noting that "one of the major shifts in emphasis between the report and the Bill is that the banks have managed to ensure that nothing will happen to disturb their preferences." Indeed, one Labour MP, Mr Wrigglesworth, went so far as to claim that the Government's insolvency bill did not simply leave the status quo untouched but actually strengthened the banks' position.

Despite the arguments, attempts to restrict substantially the operation of floating charges failed in the Commons. Opponents could not rally support for unsecured creditors comparable to that which would be marshalled over taxes and company directors. With their considerable political resources, and a good relationship with the Tory party, the banks successfully defeated what would have been a major blow to one of their preferred financial devices.

BARGAINING IN THE MARKET, META-BARGAINING IN POLITICS

Banks possess considerable sophistication in the financial game of debts and credits. They are repeat players who have accumulated vast

---

[120] H.L., vol. 458, 15 Jan. 1985, col. 919.
[121] H.L., vol. 459, 7 Feb. 1985, col. 1223.
[122] H.L. Debs, vol. 459, col. 1221.

experience, and they employ tried-and-true legal devices whose complexity and completeness would baffle an ordinary individual borrower. Banks are among the most able and powerful bargainers in credit markets. Generally, when banks lend money they also obtain security—they acquire an interest in the property of their borrowers. That interest may be specific, as when a lender holds a lien on a particular asset, or it may be general, as when a bank obtains a floating charge over a changing pool of assets. Outside of bankruptcy, their security puts banks in a strong position in relation to the debtor. If bankruptcy occurs, their security also gives them a strong hand in relation to all the other creditors. Security protects the lender's economic interests. More generally, collateralization is central to the ways banks manage credit, and so any legal change which threatens to attenuate, restrict or otherwise modify security interests has the potential to undercut the profitability of banks and other secured lenders.

The strong position that secured creditors enjoy in the market, in bilateral and multilateral bargaining over terms of financing, cannot be assumed to hold within political institutions. Of course, there are plausible grounds for expecting that economically powerful actors who are organized into national peak associations, should exert significant influence on policy-making. And alongside that collective influence stands the dense web of personal and institutional ties that can occur among bankers, banks, politicians, and parties. But politics introduces new players, uncertainties, and ideologies that require their own analysis, and which do not simply reflect market circumstances. If politics makes a distinctive contribution to the outcome of meta-bargaining, then the differences in political institutions and dynamics between countries should lead to differences in the solutions of problems common to both markets.

Politics introduces new players to financial bargaining, most notably political parties, legislators, and professionals who are not identified primarily as agents of one or another adversarial principal. Thus the political conflicts over property rights did not simply reproduce the cleavages commonly found in other policy arenas—labor facing capital, workers versus management, businesses seeking to extricate themselves from burdensome government regulation. The conflicts of secured creditors in the political arena instead occurred within the business sector, as one relatively organized group of capitalists (banks) struggled within another less organized group of capitalists (all other business creditors, and debtors). In the United States, however, representation of debtors' interests came not from business organizations, but from professionals and other reformers who were acting in the stead of debtors, seeking to gain them greater flexibility in reorganization, and greater autonomy from the unilateral action of banks. While representatives of British debtor organizations—the Institute of Directors, the Confederation of British Industry—did become involved in the reforms late in the day, their engagement concerned more the protection of individual directors than the prerogatives of management in business reorganizations. Effectively, British debtors were unrepresented on all but the narrowest issues, and that did not include debates over the floating charge.

As we shall find in Chapter 7, politics may also configure interest representation in ways that compensate for the powerlessness of individual actors. Thus the unsecured interests of small businesses, or the grievances of trade creditors, or the complaints of consumers, were variously articulated through Chambers of Commerce, trade associations, and consumer groups. More important than any of these, however, was the representation of their concerns by groups of reformers, who were insiders to the Commission and Review Committee, or expert advisors and consultants to reform organizations. Like the banks, their interests were global. Unlike the financial industry, they appeared to express a "general interest:" attacking the unfairness of powerful secured creditors who seized assets inequitably from weak unsecured creditors; and stressing the importance of protecting jobs and encouraging economic growth. However, whereas that "general" interest led to recommendations in the United States for transfers of powers from secured creditors to debtors-in-possession and courts, it led to recommendations in Britain for transfers of assets from secured creditors to other creditors, but certainly not to managers, and the courts were kept at bay. A legal culture sympathetic to debtors manifested itself in Congressional politics in a manner quite perplexing to English creditors and politicians.

Parties and ideologies intervene in the political realm to confound expectations about bargaining in everyday financial transactions. Reformers and politicians in both countries were gripped with a powerful rehabilitative ideal to save businesses, an impulse so strong that banks could seek only to contain and accommodate it. In Britain and the United States, coalitions of reformers and creditors pushed to weaken the freely contracted property rights of strong creditors, once a debtor had become insolvent. The Cork Committee and the Bankruptcy Commission offered proposals that clearly threatened the banks. Reformers offered a similar rationale in both cases: secured creditors were too powerful—in a liquidation they claimed too much of an estate's assets, and they often stood in the way of a successful reorganization. Their economic gains came at the expense of others, resulting in an unacceptable contrast between winners and losers. The market power banks enjoyed made them politically vulnerable to criticism that they were too powerful. Secured creditors' vigorous protection of their own narrow interests could in some situations unjustifiably hurt the interests of other creditors and the larger community. If firms are liquidated rather than resuscitated, local economies shrink, jobs are lost, and tax revenues decline.

The political domain therefore included all players with an ideology of corporate reconstruction, of saving businesses, or giving companies a second chance. This ideology did not accord with the operating model of bankers, who protested frequently that they were committed to "workouts" and rehabilitative ideals outside the strictures of bankruptcy law or the long arm of the courts. The political forum effectively rebutted the working premiss of banks that their efforts at workouts in the private market were tantamount to reorganizations beneficial to all parties—companies, other creditors, and the community, as well.

The ideology of rehabilitation set in motion negotiations and disagreements over the relative balance that new law would institute between the freedom of contract and the rehabilitative ideal. While banks could valorize the purity of property rights exchanged in the open market, a shift in the direction of rehabilitation—where it was seen to serve a general, not particular, interest—necessarily demanded that banks must loosen their control over property, and delegate some of their discretion to others. In the United States, this meant greater discretion to debtors and more powers to courts. In Britain, this was construed as a loosening of the arbitrary bite of the floating charge. One form of "loosening" in fact would have led to reallocation of ten per cent of the value in the assets to weaker creditors or to insolvency practitioners so they might corral assets for the insolvent estate. Another form of loosening, as we shall see in Chapter 6, would lead to greater discretion in the hands of a new agent of reorganization—the administrator—a private practitioner appointed by the court to act on behalf of the general interest of all creditors. In either case, banks fought strenuously to protect the value of their underlying assets. "Adequate protection" became the underlying imperative, and in America the rallying cry, of bankers everywhere.

Since banks could not depend on their market power in the political realm, and since the rehabilitative ideal put their tight control of assets under threat, their political meta-bargaining strategy became critical. Banks in both countries offered a similar response to attacks on their strong position. They cautiously resisted the criticism that their preferred solution of reorganizations outside bankruptcy was fundamentally antithetical to the interests of other creditors or the prospect of saving businesses. And they regularly affirmed that they supported, in principle, the ideal of saving companies, even if they preferred that to occur outside bankruptcy law. Bankers in both countries offered a similar response to measures that encroached on their securities, arguing that changes intended to help weak creditors or save troubled debtors would in fact damage them. What hurt banks would also hurt their customers, albeit indirectly. They explained that weakening a bank's security or undercutting a floating charge would force them to change their lending practices by hiking interest rates, rejecting more loan applications, or using less flexible forms of security. If banks had to incur higher loan-losses, for example, they would simply pass on the higher costs to their customers. In effect, banks claimed that they could adapt to legal changes by contracting around them and so subvert the intentions of the new law. Their hands would be "forced," of course, but the net outcome would not be what reformers intended.

Reformers in their turn recognized that they needed the acquiescence of the banking community if either piece of legislation were to surmount the obstacles to passage that can bedevil technical legislation with little political payoff. On the American side, from the beginning, the congressmen and staff of the House Judiciary Committee's Subcommittee on Civil and Constitutional Rights took a strategy of keeping the bankruptcy legislation low profile.[123] Bankruptcy law had no "natural" constituency—no committed political or social groups willing to apply political pressure in favor of the bankruptcy legislation. Members of the subcommittee believed that if the bankruptcy initiatives were opposed by a powerful lobbying group, there would be no counter-force and the legislation would die.[124] Pragmatically, this meant that the potential for conflict had to be defused both within the political arena as well as within the market.

---

[123] Members and staffers alike on the House subcommittee observed that the bankruptcy legislation was intentionally kept low profile, both in the political institution as well as in the market. (US Interviews 91:04; 92:02; 92:01).

[124] UK Interview 91:04.

A low profile can be assured by persuading interested parties that the reforms are not especially ideological or substantive. The proponents of the American bankruptcy legislation actively tried to frame their work as "a legislative statement of case law that had developed over the years."[125] The legislation was introduced as "simply" procedural rather than substantive; that is, reforms would not make any radical changes in the legal landscape. In addition, members of the Subcommittee on Civil and Constitutional Rights worked actively to head off as much conflict in the Congress (and the government generally) as possible. By managing the low profile of the bankruptcy legislation in the political arena, the framers were able to avoid activating conflicting political interests.

Because initial pressure for revising the bankruptcy law (especially in corporate bankruptcy law) came from outside the market, congressional subcommittee staff were more in control of which market actors could help formulate the new legislation. Thus relatively few market players had information about what was going on concerning bankruptcy law, and of those who did, very few perceived the law as directly germane to their routine operations. It was only those market players who were most often in the position of creditor (and thus were likely to deal with problems of debt repayment on a regular basis) who participated in the framing of the bankruptcy law. Effectively, only the peak organizations of the financial community participated in the Congressional hearings. So, it was in this setting that the potentially controversial propositions for restructuring security within bankruptcy—cramdown and setoff—were negotiated in low key.

Similarly in Britain, while the call for reactions to insolvency reforms was widely distributed, the reform committee sought to establish cordial ties and regular private channels to the retail banking industry. And while the Cork Committee did not concede entirely to the bankers, it made diligent efforts to compensate any weakening of their securities with some more acceptable trade-off.

The concept of "balance" or of a "package" solution was the principal technique used by reformers to redistribute the assets of the estate to weaker creditors, or to move control over assets away from secured creditors. To produce more flexibility in reorganizations, American reformers simultaneously gave the courts more discretion and strengthened the hands of judges while allowing debtors-in-possession more latitude in turning their companies around. But this shift in powers

---

[125] UK Interview 91:04.

away from secured creditors could only succeed if the reformers could persuade the banking industry that secured creditors would get increased protections of their assets.

> The purpose behind all of these provisions...the automatic stay...adequate protection...was to balance out—it's hard to say equally, but as equally as possible— the rights of the secured creditors as against the estate:...giving to the court some discretion, more discretion, giving to the debtor more ability to reorganize, but at the same time affording protection to the secured creditor and all of these kind of worked that way, I think. That's a very important concept underlying the code.[126]

The "package" solution in Britain had a similar logic: if secured creditors benefitted from larger estates, because many preferences would be eliminated, then secured creditors should give some proportion of their assets—ten per cent—to weaker creditors. Thus bankers ceded some control, so long as they could be assured that their underlying value was protected.

In the American case, however, the balancing of interests spread across a wider front, for American financial institutions demanded procedural and administrative reforms every bit as strongly as other creditors demanded substantive concessions. Hence American bankers were prepared to concede some control over collateral, including setoff, if they were confident that a new, unified, bankruptcy court, with clear jurisdictions, and a highly qualified judiciary, were to be exercising the discretion that substantive concessions would require. The recommendations of the Bankruptcy Commission, and later Congress, for a near-Article III court satisfied them that what they yielded substantively and distributively might be balanced by what they gained through administrative and judicial efficiency.

In neither the English nor American cases can the banks be considered hegemonic in their political power. It is true that they, like many other actors, carried effective veto power over passage of unacceptable legislation. It is also true that they soundly defeated the Ten Percent Fund in England and maintained their floating charge in insolvency. Furthermore, American bankers obtained a bankruptcy system much more to their liking along with substantive and procedural protections of their assets. However, neither financial industry was assured at the outset that key securities would survive unscarred, and neither escaped without significant concessions, especially on the American side.

[126] US Interview 96:04.

Political-institutional differences between the US and the UK favored the British banks in the politics of meta-bargaining. The Insolvency Act was unquestionably a product of Thatcher's Conservative government, and there was no need for bipartisanship in order for the bill to become law. With a secure majority in the Commons, the Tories had wide discretion in the legislation they could push through Parliament. The banks had an affinity with the Conservatives—despite their own protestations of political impotence—and so could use their political connections to defeat measures they found particularly onerous. Furthermore, as Peter Hall has argued (1992), British governments became increasingly beholden to financial capital during the 1970s, as growing public indebtedness made the government more dependent on bankers and financiers. American banks had no comparably close relation with a party in complete control of government, and the massive deficits of the 1980s came after bankruptcy legislation, not before. In the US, by contrast, highly partisan legislation would run into trouble if members of the opposing political party exploited the "checks and balances" to bottle up or defeat objectionable legislation. Bipartisanship was necessary to get the legislation through.

Professionals, acting as much as agents of a public good as a private interest, mediated the efforts to attenuate strong property rights and to increase flexibility. Several of the innovations that effected such trade-offs emerged from creative solutions by professionals inside the reform causes— "adequate protection" and the Ten Percent Fund, the most notable cases in point. But if professionals were constructing a rehabilitative regime that was good for business, it turned out also to be beneficial for professionals. More cash available to managers, more flexibility in bargaining in the shadow of bankruptcy law, more reconstruction inside bankruptcy—all ensured that the bargain made in the political arena would stimulate bargaining, in which professionals were integral, within the market. From these reforms, judges, lawyers, and accountants all emerge with significantly larger jurisdictions of work, greater powers of reconstruction, and greater rewards, both extrinsic, via fees, and intrinsic, via the intellectual stimulation of new law. While these benefits can hardly be understood as conspiracies of market expansion and control, it nevertheless remains the case that weakened secured creditors led directly to strengthened professionals—not the outcome that any parties foresaw at the outset of reform.

5 Restraining the State and Utilities

Creditors can enjoy a strong position in bankruptcy and reorganizations by virtue of statutory law. That is, they are legally empowered and prioritized so that their property claims get satisfied ahead of others. We call this *de jure* strength. But even when their legal position is not especially strong, creditors can exploit other resources in order to gain an advantage inside bankruptcy. They might, for example, use their powerful market position to push ahead of other creditors. This we call *de facto* strength.

This chapter contrasts these two types of strength as they are exercised in bankruptcy by the state and utility companies. In varying-degrees, these two monopolies—one over coercion and the other over markets for critical services—share an attribute in common: their sheer institutional power affects the probability of rescuing businesses, for in exploiting their economic strength either may confound the efforts of professionals or managers to turn companies around.

While the state takes on many guises in bankruptcy law and practice, its role as a creditor affects, at the very least, how much cash is available for corporate reorganizations, not to mention other creditors in a liquidation. Utilities, too, can determine the difference between life and death for a struggling company. If they monopolize the supply of water, power, and phone services, then companies cannot do business without them. A threat to discontinue service represents a powerful lever for utilities to pursue their own narrow interests in ways that can doom reorganizations and effectively jump the queue over the legal rights of other creditors.

Meta-bargaining over property rights in bankruptcy therefore embroiled many classes of creditors, and reformers, in complex negotiations over ways to reconcile discrepancies in law and practice that surfaced in public hearings and inquiries over the equity and effectiveness of these two powerful actors.

THE STATE AS PLAYER AND REFEREE

The state is a singular creditor in bankruptcy. When a corporation goes bankrupt,[1] the state is frequently one of the creditors. Financially

---

[1] We use the expression, "going bankrupt," as a shorthand for several different legal "states," including voluntary filings by managers and directors to obtain protection of

troubled firms and individuals typically fall behind on their tax payments, and when they finally become bankrupt, the total amount of back taxes can be substantial. The state often is the first creditor firms stop paying, not only for taxes, but also for moneys employers are collecting on behalf of the state, such as social security deductions. Insolvent companies have a habit of using social security deductions to try and remain solvent.

The state is therefore caught in the same zero-sum distributional struggle that ensnares all other creditors of a bankrupt company: there are not enough assets in the pool to satisfy every one, and the more one creditor gets, the less there is for others. Like other creditors, if the state insists on immediate and total repayment of sums owed to it, fewer assets will be available for company rescue. Like all the other creditors, the state is also subject to the bankruptcy rules that rank creditors and give some priority over others. And like the others, it too would prefer a higher ranking and a longer arm to reach more assets. Once a company has become bankrupt, state revenue agencies have strong incentives to reach back in time, and to reach widely in scope, to capture lost taxes and social security deductions. The state's unique institutional strength potentially conflicts with all other creditors, who may resent having to compete for assets with such a powerful entity.

Unlike all the other creditors, however, the state occupies a dual position as both a player and referee in bankruptcy law. At the same time as the state competes with banks and small firms and consumers for unpaid debts, the state devises and enforces bankruptcy law. It creates the legal framework that will subsequently determine its own position as a creditor in bankruptcy, relative to other creditors. Its own conduct, and that of all other creditors, will be governed by rules that the government helps to create. It determines the rights and obligations of every party affected by financial failure. In this uniquely advantageous situation, it seems likely that governments will try to ensure a high priority to state claims, and will endeavor to ensure that their revenue interests would be satisfied as completely as possible (Plumb 1973: 309). The state will push its own property rights ahead of others.

Furthermore, given the power of the state, its concentration of expertise, and its enormous capacity for mobilization, we can expect that its

---

bankruptcy law, involuntary bankruptcies when a company is "pushed" by a creditor into liquidation, or in the English case, when a secured creditor decides to appoint a receiver to act as its agent in order to seize collateral which usually leads to the sale of a company as a going concern, or to liquidation.

advantageous position as a referee should readily be converted into a privileged situation as a player. The fact that many other creditor groups, such as small businesses and consumers, suffer from debilitating capacities at political mobilization, reinforces the state's advantages. In short, the institution with a monopoly over coercion in a society should be able to impose its will on bankruptcy law and institutionalize a privileged standing.

A number of scholars have argued that states in general try to maximize their revenues (see, for example, Levi 1988; Nelson 1986; and North 1981).[2] In bankruptcy law, this means that state claims should prevail over the claims of other players. Were any other group of creditors given license to write the bankruptcy code, they would undoubtedly treat themselves just as favorably. If lower priority creditors will lose in proportion to the gains of the state, it seems probable that they would oppose any strengthening of the state's position, and indeed would prefer to see that position weakened. As tax-expert William T. Plumb reminded bankruptcy lawyers, "...the principal and most formidable competitor of your clients for the assets of an insolvent debtor is the federal tax collector" (Plumb 1973: 309).

There are many ways in which a state can be the creditor of a bankrupt corporation or individual, just as there are many ways in which the state's interest as a creditor can be strengthened or weakened. Taxes come in many forms and their status in bankruptcy differs. Tax authorities collect at least two quite different kinds of moneys from taxpayers. On the one hand, they impose taxes on individuals or companies which will become part of the general revenues of the state, and these vary widely from income and corporate taxes to customs and excise taxes. On the other hand, as an administrative convenience and efficiency, companies may collect the taxes owed by employees to the government as well as social security payments that will go into government pension funds for citizens. These latter moneys can be considered as "collector taxes," where the company simply collects moneys that are held in trust or quasi-trust. In addition to general taxes and social security taxes, states also impose fees and penalties, they offer direct loans and loan guarantees (and thus expect interest payments) on all measure of activities, and these, too, may go into general revenues or into earmarked funds.

---

[2] Along similar lines, the doctrine of sovereign immunity protects that state from liabilities that it usually would be subject to, were it an ordinary private individual.

Different classes of money collected by the state have a somewhat different moral status, a status differential that becomes especially salient in bankruptcies. Regular taxes do not attract the same degree of "peculiar sanctity" as "collector taxes" or withholdings by the state for individual employee's income taxes or, even more, for social security purposes. And as we shall see, many parties to the bankruptcy reforms argued vigorously about differences in treatment that should follow from these differences in moral status.

Moreover, state taxing authorities are wont to draw an important distinction between *consensual* and *non-consensual* credit. Most private creditors reach agreement on the extension of credit through consensual bargaining. All parties consent to put their signatures on the loan documents. State taxing authorities, however, argue that their claims are in a special class because they do not consent if a company fails to pay its taxes and so incurs an obligation. The debtor company acts unilaterally in keeping the money. The state therefore may engage in special pleading that it is a non-consensual creditor who deserves special provisions to compensate for its non-consensual status.

The strength of government claims can vary significantly along a number of different dimensions. First, state authorities get more out of an estate when their claims are granted a high priority in the ranking of repayments. Second, claims vary in the duration of the reach-back period. The longer a government can reach back in time, the more unpaid taxes it can claim out of the bankrupt company's estate. Suppose a firm has underpaid income taxes for five years. The bankrupt estate will owe the government much more in taxes if the reach-back period covers the full five years than if it only goes back one year. Third, state authorities have their own forms of security, such as tax liens, which give revenue departments a security interest in the property of the debtor, and the right to seize the collateral in satisfaction of the debt.

Each of these dimensions represents a way in which the government's overall position as a creditor could be strengthened or weakened.[3] Each therefore represents an opportunity for other creditors to enhance their own position by attacking that of the state. The lines of conflict between the state and other creditors are thus sharply drawn: any loss for the state is a potential gain for all other creditors. In this well-defined

[3] Other ways to maintain the government's strong position as a creditor include: the validity of tax liens would not be affected by bankruptcy, and prior tax recoveries would not be considered voidable preferences.

distributive conflict, meta-bargaining on the terrain where a state is the referee seems bound to lead to an outcome in its favor. But the politics of bankruptcy law provided a surprise of their own.

Fiscal Strength and Political Liability in the United States

Traditionally, the government has been a favored creditor in bankruptcy. As Plumb put it: "The absolute, or near-absolute, priority of the sovereign over other creditors has deep historical roots, tracing back to early English precedents" (Plumb 1973: 309). Under pre-1978 US bankruptcy law, all tax claims received a high priority. Taxes ranked fourth, after administrative expenses, wage claims, and certain creditor expenses (see Table 2.1). Taxes were not dischargeable for individuals, so even after going through bankruptcy an individual still owed his or her taxes. Tax authorities could reach back to reclaim unpaid taxes for three years prior to the bankruptcy. Furthermore, federal tax liens gave the government a security interest which attached automatically to the debtor's property, and in bankruptcy this interest was accorded the highest priority (Marsh 1967: 682–3). The state therefore effectively offered itself a double security:

For over a century it has been the view of Congress that it is not enough to rely, for the collection of taxes, on a mere right of priority, however absolute, in the assets remaining in an insolvent estate. Congress has felt the need for a lien that exists regardless of insolvency and follows the property even into the hands of third parties acquiring interests between the time when the tax is assessed and the time when the enforcement machinery can be brought to bear. The law provides, therefore, that a lien on all the property of the taxpayer, real and personal, tangible and intangible, shall automatically arise when any federal tax is assessed, if the tax is not paid on demand. (Plumb 1974*b*: 1000)

Ironically, this privileged, well institutionalized position in law became a political liability. Harold Marsh, later to become Chairman of the Bankruptcy Commission, laid out an angle of attack that was premissed on the state's double-dealing as both referee and player in the field of bankruptcy law.

Does the traditional rule which has granted priority to all tax claims, at least over all general non-priority creditors, rest upon anything more than a naked assertion of power based upon the fact that this particular creditor happens to be writing the rules of distribution? (Marsh 1967: 729)

The state's position as a creditor had been weakened in some minor amendments to the Bankruptcy Code in 1966.[4] In a precursor to the 1978 reforms, creditor groups such as the National Association of Credit Management and the American Bankers Association joined the National Bankruptcy Conference to support amendments that were intended to benefit unsecured creditors that the Treasury department opposed. The amendments made dischargeable some tax claims that preceded the reachback period and also invalidated some tax liens.

The Brookings Report argued that high priority tax claims took a large proportion of the total assets available for unsecured creditors, but that the contribution these claims made to total government revenues was minuscule. According to their calculations, in 1964 federal tax claims alone consumed about eleven per cent of the assets of bankrupt estates undergoing liquidation (and about one-third of the amount paid out to unsecured creditors), but these tax claims constituted only 0.005 per cent of the federal government's total revenues (Stanley and Girth 1971: 131). A small gain for the government cost unsecured creditors a great deal. Furthermore, Stanley and Girth condemned the priority accorded taxes for being based on: "... dubious logic and indefensible social policy" (Stanley and Girth 1971: 4). Their report recommended that tax claims should be put on an equal status with unsecured creditors, which effectively would drop them to the lowest level of claims to the bankrupt company's estate (Stanley and Girth 1971: 5, 209). They recommended that the state should give up its seemingly invulnerable position and surrender some of its very strong property rights.

In its deliberations, the Bankruptcy Commission expected that the Treasury would argue against making taxes or any other government claims dischargeable, even before the Treasury had said anything officially.[5] Following the logic of his law review article, Harold Marsh, chairman of the commission, proposed a radical change in public policy—to abolish all tax liens and priorities on the grounds that the: "... amount realized was insignificant in light of the total revenues.... [T]he Justice and Treasury Departments spent far more attempting to collect by use of the priority and lien provisions than was realized."[6]

---

[4] See Marsh (1967). H.R. 136 and H.R. 3438 were signed by President Johnson on 5 July 1966.

[5] See *Minutes of the Bankruptcy Commission*, 30–1 Jan. 1972: 20. In fact, as the Commission noted in its report, the Treasury never did formally express its views, despite requests to do so. See *Report of the Bankruptcy Commission*: 1: 216.

[6] *Minutes of the Bankruptcy Commission*, 11–12 Sept. 1972: 23.

Which is to say that the transactions costs of collecting unpaid taxes actually exceeded the revenues finally recaptured by the state. Marsh also argued that when taxes enjoyed a high priority, they were in effect paid by the other creditors.[7] Marsh's views encountered some resistance within the Commission by members who argued that tax claims should continue to enjoy priority status.[8] Mr Newman, for example, worried that a reduction would encourage more vigorous and extensive tax audits, and he joined Judge Weinfeld in opposing further restrictions on tax claims. In the final analysis, the Commission could not reach consensus and decided by a majority to keep a government priority in place, but to reduce its reachback from three years to only one year's taxes.[9]

The final Commission Report recommended that government claims be reduced in a variety of ways. The Commission found middle ground in its commitment that individual and corporate bankruptcies could better lead to rehabilitation if the state's privileged position were to be significantly reduced. For individuals, said the Report, the nondischargeability of taxes frustrated the rehabilitative goals of bankruptcy: no bankrupt debtor could enjoy a "fresh start" if still encumbered by pre-bankruptcy tax liabilities. Thus non-dischargeable taxes should be reduced from three years down to only one year.[10] The Commission proposed that taxes should not enjoy a blanket priority, but that only specified taxes be granted this privilege. And since the use of statutory tax liens often gave tax claims an even higher priority in practice than that specified in the law, the Commission recommended that the enforceability of such liens be curtailed.[11] Finally, the Commission resolved that trustees should not have to pay taxes on the income of the estate, particularly when the estate was simply being liquidated.[12] As for the non-tax claims of the government, the Commission felt that these should not have any priority status at all.[13]

Taken together, the 1966 revisions, the Brookings Report, and the Commission Report consistently sought to cut government claims in bankruptcy down to size. Both the Commission Bill (H.R. 31 and S.

---

[7] Marsh (1967: 24).

[8] *Minutes of the Bankruptcy Commission*, 13–14 Nov. 1972: 30.

[9] *Minutes of the Bankruptcy Commission*, 13–14 Nov. 1972: 31.

[10] *Report of the Bankruptcy Commission*: 1: 176; Plumb (1974*b*: 1028,1050–51). This meant that taxes owed from the year before bankruptcy would be nondischargeable, as opposed to those owed from the previous three years.

[11] *Report of the Bankruptcy Commission*: 1: 214–15; Plumb (1974*b*: 992, 1003).

[12] *Report of the Bankruptcy Commission*: 1: 277–8; Plumb (1974*a*: 937, 948).

[13] *Report of the Bankruptcy Commission*: 1: 217–18; Plumb (1974*b*: 992).

236) and the Judges' Bill (H.R. 32 and S. 235) reinforced the alliance against the state through identical provisions that would reduce the priority of taxes from 4th to 5th place. Both would also curtail the government's ability to secure tax obligations under bankruptcy.[14] Reformers concurred that the government possessed an undeservedly privileged position.

Although the federal tax departments had said nothing officially to the Commission during its deliberations, they finally responded to the proposals after the reform process moved to Congress. Speaking for the Tax Division of the Justice Department, Scott Crampton voiced strong opposition to the Judges' Bill:

We wish to emphasize, at the outset, those proposals which we oppose as having a serious and detrimental effect on enforcement of the tax laws and on debtor attitudes toward bankruptcy. These are the wholesale invalidation of tax liens, the proposed drastic reduction in the priority accorded tax claims, and the increased dischargeability of tax claims.[15]

Crampton listed three detrimental consequences of the proposed changes:

First, it destroys the tax debtor's incentive to satisfy his tax obligations and encourages the use of tax money to finance failing businesses. Second, it would have a substantial impact upon the confidence of the public in the fairness of the tax collection system and thereby would endanger voluntary compliance, the cornerstone of that system. Third, by destroying the safeguards with respect to tax collection which exist outside of bankruptcy, it creates new incentives for creditors to put the debtor into bankruptcy and thus increase their potential distributions. The inevitable result will be a serious decline in revenue collection, and an increase in both voluntary and involuntary bankruptcy petitions, if these proposals are adopted.[16]

Crampton sidestepped the fact that the value of bankruptcy collections was negligible in relation to total government revenues, by suggesting that voluntary compliance, upon which the US tax system depended, would be threatened by the changes. His ominous prediction suggested that tax collections in bankruptcy might be small now, but if the proposed changes were put in place, tax collections in general would be sharply undermined: "Their general effect would be not only vir-

---

[14] For the provisions of both bills on tax priority, tax liens and tax dischargeability, see *Bankruptcy Act Revision Hearings on H.R. 31 and H.R. 32*, Appendix: §4–405, §4–506, §4–606.

[15] *Bankruptcy Reform Act Hearings on S. 235 and S. 236*: 782.

[16] *Bankruptcy Reform Act Hearings on S. 235 and S. 236*: 782.

tually to eliminate taxes as a substantial factor in bankruptcies, but to erode taxpayer compliance outside of bankruptcy".[17] Even a small change could lead to large consequences.

Crampton's main arguments were echoed by the Commissioner of the Internal Revenue Service, Donald Alexander, who underscored the point that the government was not a voluntary creditor.[18] Alexander argued that banks and other voluntary creditors are able to take into account the possibility of debtor-bankruptcy in their credit decisions. Should the risks be deemed too great, they can refuse credit, and they can pass the costs of bad credit onto others. But people and firms can decide on their own not to pay their taxes, and therefore can force the government to extend them credit. The government has no choice in the matter, and as an involuntary creditor it therefore deserved special consideration.[19] Alexander buttressed his case with comparative examples, for he pointed out that the proposed changes were "inconsistent" with bankruptcy laws in other major commercial countries, including Great Britain, Australia, Canada, West Germany, France, and Belgium.[20]

Revenue officials conceded the point that tax claims on bankrupt companies were not a major part of public revenues. They acknowledged that a minuscule sum for government could mean life or death for a small company. But they insisted that important principles were at stake. First, there was the principle of equity; it was unfair to expect a large creditor like the state to subsidize small creditors simply because it was large. Second, and more importantly, there was the principle of legitimacy; because public revenues rely heavily on voluntary compliance, any symbolic breach in the obligation to pay taxes could potentially erode the revenue base of the state. The second principle essentially reached to the viability of the state itself, for a state unable to collect revenues without substantial public compliance puts its central functions at risk. A Treasury official, Dale Collinson, underscored how much the tax system depended on the voluntary self-assessments of taxpayers, and how large a threat the proposed changes posed for the state: "We believe

---

[17] *Bankruptcy Reform Act Hearings on S. 235 and S. 236*: 788.

[18] *Bankruptcy Reform Act Hearings on S. 235 and S. 236*: 789–96.

[19] See also the testimony of Dale Collinson, of the Treasury Department, which reiterates the uniqueness of the US government as an involuntary creditor (*Bankruptcy Reform Act Hearings on S. 235 and S. 236*: 797–9).

[20] *Bankruptcy Reform Act Hearings on S. 235 and S. 236*: 21.

that adoption of the proposals...would substantially and seriously undermine the integrity of the voluntary assessment system.[21]

Congress remained largely unmoved by testimony from tax officials, for successive bills continued to propose a reduction in the government's position as a creditor. Expert witnesses echoed the criticisms made by Brookings and the Commission. Vern Countryman, a Harvard Law professor, said that: "...even a full priority [for tax claims] contributed only a small drop in the bucket of the federal fisc, but took a very large share of all dividends distributed to creditors in bankruptcy cases."[22]

Treasury officials, among others, countered that this was not the point. Although William Plumb fully understood that the state priority rested on centuries of tradition, nevertheless it had a convincing warrant of its own.

The Federal tax system...is largely dependent on voluntary self-assessment, and taxpayers' awareness of even relatively isolated instances in which smart tax-payers have found ways to escape paying their taxes impairs the willingness of others to cooperate in the self-assessment process...[23]

Plumb warned that the Commission's evidence completely underestimated the potential negative effect of a change that struck at voluntary compliance. But like most counter-factual arguments, it was impossible to show how drastic the consequences might be. Other witnesses bolstered the government's assertion that the proposed changes would seriously undermine the tax system.[24]

Despite the vast financial power of the Treasury, in Congress it faced political impediments even more severe than those of strong private creditors. Said one staffer close to the political bargaining, "In our country there is no great vote for the Internal Revenue Service (IRS). They are not very popular."[25] Another reformer explained why:

...virtually everybody benefits if the IRS isn't benefitting. So no matter who you are in the [bankruptcy] system you are benefitting if the IRS isn't getting that fourth priority let's say. See everybody else gets that money then. So it is the whole world against the IRS.

Moreover the broader political context constrained the leadership of the IRS, for its Commissioner, Donald Alexander, was under wide

---

[21] *Bankruptcy Reform Act Hearings on S. 235 and S. 236*: 797.

[22] *Bankruptcy Reform Act Hearings on S. 235 and S. 236*: 5.

[23] *Bankruptcy Reform Act Hearings on S. 235 and S. 236*: 800.

[24] See the Nov. 1977 testimony of Donald Lubick, Deputy Assistant Secretary for Tax Policy, Treasury Department (*Senate Hearings on S. 2266 and H.R. 8200*: 554–72).

[25] US Interview 91:05.

public scrutiny over the allegations that President Nixon's administration had been using the IRS to persecute its political adversaries. Much of the time that might have been committed to fighting for tax priorities was instead devoted to the fierce personal politics surrounding President Nixon and his political tactics. Even after Nixon resigned, the residue of distrust in the IRS did little for its political efficacy.[26] A Republican reformer summarized the political situation,

Keep in mind you had a Republican administration during the early years. You had Ford, and then you had Carter at the beginning of '77, '78. But you had Nixon/Ford during the evolution of the Commission and the initial hearings on the Hill. And you had a negative . . . you had a very bad relationship between the branches right then. So nobody . . . people don't like the IRS anyway. Not only that but it is a Republican IRS.[27]

Nonetheless, the state taxing agencies did not surrender easily. They gained some ground in the House bill, H.R. 8200, and even more in the Senate bill, S. 2266, where the government fought back to a stronger position than the Commission had sought.[28] A Deputy Assistant Secretary of the Treasury, Daniel Halperin, noted that: ". . . S. 2266 differs significantly from the House-passed bill, H.R. 8200. We want to particularly emphasize our strong preference for the Senate bill as opposed to the House bill in a number of areas."[29] For instance, as compared with S. 2266, H.R. 8200 would limit the priority and nondischargeability of certain types of taxes. Halperin sharply distinguished taxes that a debtor was directly liable for from those for which the debtor acted as a kind of collection agent for the government. The latter, he argued, ". . . are different from other taxes paid by the debtor. They are held in special trust for the Government. They are not the debtor's liability, but are the liability of employers or customers."[30] The Senate bill recognized the distinctive character of such taxes whereas the House bill did not. In addition to public testimony, the IRS quietly applied pressure behind the scenes and out of the public glare, where its position held little popular appeal.[31]

---

[26] US Interview 91:07.

[27] US Interview 91:03.

[28] As one former staffer said to us: "You saw what the commission bill did. It was far less priorities than what we came up with" (US Interview 92:02).

[29] *Senate Hearings on S. 2266 and H.R. 8200*: 10.

[30] *Ibid.*

[31] One person summarized the IRS's low-profile political tactics: "They [the IRS] mobilized behind the scenes. They mobilized in private" (US Interview 92:02).

The final political settlement knocked the state back down the rank order of privileged creditors. The 1978 Bankruptcy Code reduced the priority of tax claims from 4th position to 6th position.[32] Certain non-priority tax claims became dischargeable, tax liens could be invalidated, and the rules against preferential transfers (so-called "voidable preferences") became applicable to governmental units.[33] The final outcome also reflected the state's strong view that moneys it withheld for social security should be treated with particular sanctity. In the government's mind, said a legislative staffer, "that's sacrosanct and we'll never give a penny on that."[34] Social security taxes, therefore, were not discharge-able in the new Code, and remained due no matter how long they had remained unpaid.

In the event, the revenue agencies of the state proved to be remark-ably vulnerable, especially in the unsettled partisan politics of the 1970s. The philosophical shift away from state privilege, if not revolutionary, nonetheless evoked historic imagery:

the '78 code reduce[d] the government from its status of "the King shall do no wrong, the King shall be first paid" to the status of an ordinary creditor . . . it was really to make things more equal rather than playing God and saying, "the state will be paid first, and then we will pay people in all these separate orders."

But, asserted this staffer, if that was the theme, he saw it as "a non-partisan theme."[35]

The state, it transpired, had few friends to rally and few resources to mobilize, other than its inside politics on the Hill—which did bring it some relief. The argument for taxpayer compliance won it few converts, especially when measured against the move towards greater distributive justice. Simultaneously, the new Code reallocated property rights away from the strong and towards the agents of corporate rehab-ilitation.

Mrs Thatcher's Defeat

Her Majesty's Government occupied a position of privilege little differ-ent from its former colony. The state had strong preferences and stronger powers. Moreover, unlike its American counterpart, English

---

[32] The drop from the 5th position recommended by the Commission to 6th position will become clear from the politics of weak creditors in Chapter 8.

[33] See Bacon and Billinger (1979: 76–80).

[34] US Interview 92:02.

[35] US Interview 92:01.

revenue authorities regularly used bankruptcy law as a form of debt collection for unpaid taxes. The government pushed debtors involuntarily into bankruptcy in order to collect back taxes. Neither did the government have qualms about seizing assets ahead of small creditors, at the bottom of the priority list, who were anxious for repayment. Somewhat to the government's surprise, therefore, it discovered how unfair most other players judged the taxman's special advantages.

The Insolvency Review Committee

When the Labour Government appointed the Cork Committee in 1977 to review bankruptcy law, it set the mandate of review broadly enough to include state preferences. In its investigations, and from submissions to the committee, members of the committee were reminded that, under the status quo, the Crown preference was of "great antiquity"[36] and the scope of its preferences ranged broadly. Priority debts included general rates (for example, to municipal authorities), income taxes, corporation taxes, capital gains taxes, PAYE (Pay As You Earn) deductions (in which taxpayers could have their personal taxes removed from their regular pay checks by the employer), VAT (Value-Added Tax) deductions (a sales tax that is added at each stage of most business transactions), car taxes, social security and redundancy fund contributions, and other miscellaneous duties and license fees that were due over the year before insolvency or bankruptcy.

The Cork Committee had begun its deliberations with a sentiment akin to zero-based budgeting. In their case, many of its members, including the chairman, began with the presumption that all preferences should be abolished.[37] Preferences worked against principles of equity and harmed the weakest creditors. And preferences diverted resources from reorganization. More than a year before they heard from revenue authorities, members of the committee looked for ways to reduce privileged government claims.

Some of the notions to abolish preferences for the state flowed from the earlier Cork Committee's recommendations on harmonization of English bankruptcy law with those in Europe. According to David Graham, there was a movement afoot in other European countries to "rationalize if not eliminate the system of preference and we were

---

[36] *Cork Report*: 318, 319.
[37] *Minutes of the Cork Committee*, 12 Apr. 1978: 22.

coming to the conclusion in Cork Part One that it wouldn't be feasible to have harmonization of insolvency laws if you had an imbalance over preferential claims. . . ."[38]

The Cork Committee recognized that not all claims were of the same kind. Regular taxes—income and corporation taxes—no longer warranted their privileged status.[39] The government could offer no principled basis for its standing ahead of smaller creditors. The existence of the preference proved most vexing to ordinary creditors.

. . . [I]t is obviously very galling when there is an insolvency and by its very nature the creditors are going to get less than fifty pence in the pound, and to find that forty pence of that goes to the Inland Revenue direct—payment in full—whereas every other creditor who has also extended funds to the company without security finds itself scrambling for what then becomes much less than fifty pence in the pound.[40]

Moreover, if the Cork Committee was seeking a "package" solution, and they wanted the large banks to give up ten per cent of the moneys secured by the floating charge, it seemed quite reasonable to ask the government, another creditor with deep pockets, to also make a contribution to reorganizations and weaker creditors.[41] Part of the deal with the banks depended on their belief that the government would also make its contribution to the betterment of the estate and weaker creditor. "We made it a package with the floating charge, because . . . we didn't see why the crown should give up its preference merely for the bank to pick up the money."[42]

The Government had a stronger case for keeping "trust" or "quasi-trust" monies, such as the VAT and PAYE taxes that companies collected as administrative conveniences. These should continue to enjoy priority status, but the committee proposed to reduce the reachback period from one year down to as little as three months (in the case of PAYE).[43] These moneys never had belonged to the employer or company but were merely collected by the employer on behalf of the state.[44] Cork's committee agreed with other witnesses that the government was "pretty lazy" in collecting taxes that had accumulated over many years. They should act diligently to obtain these "quasi-trust" monies in a period of months, not years.[45]

---

[38] UK Interview 90:21.   [39] *Minutes of the Cork Committee*, 12 Apr. 1978: 26.
[40] UK Interview 91:16.   [41] UK Interviews 90:04; 91:08.
[42] UK Interview 91:14.   [43] *Minutes of the Cork Committee*, 10 May 1978: 16.
[44] *Minutes of the Cork Committee*, 18 Mar. 1980: 30–1.   [45] UK Interview; 91:09.

Despite such strong initial impulses, the Committee decided to wait until after hearing from the Inland Revenue before resolving these issues.[46] When representatives of the government revenue departments at last appeared before the Cork Committee, Cork himself summarized the Committee's current thinking that: "...there are far too many preferential claims in liquidations and bankruptcies, and that it is unfair to the ordinary unsecured creditor that a whole lot of things that he cannot see in the balance sheet come before him getting some share in the pot." What we are trying to do, said Cork, was to "set a fair balance between you (the revenue authorities) and the unsecured creditors."[47]

In this less than propitious climate, the officials sought to counter assaults on government tax claims in terms that are familiar from across the Atlantic. First, said one official, "we consider that the Crown preference should be continued" on a "historical argument" that "the tax is a debt to the community which ought to be paid by everyone, all of whom share in the benefits of paying taxes, whatever those are."[48] By shifting the target, Crown officials reminded the panel that a loss of the Crown preference robbed not the government, but ultimately the community on whose behalf the government was collecting taxes. The benefits of government spending should not be disassociated from the obligations of paying taxes.

Second, far from being a privileged creditor, in fact the government itself did *not* enjoy certain advantages of other creditors.

[I]n the nature of things the Crown is at a disadvantage in the collection of debts, because compared with a trade creditor the Crown has to be later as a rule establishing the actual size of the debt.... [T]he trade creditor can choose basically with whom he deals. If he does not think the credit of any particular customer is good, then he can avoid dealing with that person. The Crown has to deal with whoever comes along, and we have no choice in this matter at all.[49]

Both parts of this argument rested on the ground that the government cannot screen a taxpayer for creditworthiness before extending involuntary credit. Nor can it determine the size of its involuntary "loan." The Government is compelled to take all comers, bad creditors with the good, and at whatever levels of credit the taxpayer determines, before the government's enforcement apparatus gets into motion.

---

[46] *Minutes of the Cork Committee*, 5 Oct. 1978: 7.
[47] *Oral testimony to Cork Committee by Customs and Excise*, 10 Nov. 1980.   [48] *Ibid.*
[49] *Ibid.*

Moreover, said the government officials, the current system of law and its favorable pattern of preferences significantly enabled collections of bad debts. Said one official:

...in the current year for six months we have recovered 95.5% of our recoveries from preferential creditors and 4.5% from our non-preferential claims. This is over the whole field of compulsory liquidations, voluntary windings up and receiverships. *Question:* So obviously your preferential claim is very valuable to you. *Answer:* Indeed it is, yes.[50]

The Committee was barely moved by these representations. It restated its distinction between "trust" revenues and other state claims, and it took a strong view about the use of bankruptcy law for debt collection, something that plainly worked against reorganization. Committee members were particularly skeptical of the implicit premiss in the government's case that it needed several years to reach back to collect unpaid taxes. It was one thing to complain that the government was an unwilling party to a loan, for it did not get to give its consent. But the government showed itself to be administratively inept by allowing unpaid back-taxes to build up without either monitoring them or taking earlier action.

After attending to the arguments from the Inland Revenue and other government taxing authorities, the Cork Committee returned to its initial impulses and recommended that the state's priority be cut back sharply. Summarizing the entire issue of preferential debts, the Cork Report stated that:

We have received a considerable volume of evidence on this subject, most of it critical of the present law, and much of it deeply hostile to the retention of any system of preferential debts. We are left in no doubt that the elaborate system of priorities accorded by the present law is the cause of much public dissatisfaction, and that there is a widespread demand for a significant reduction, and even a complete elimination, of the categories of debts which are accorded priority in an insolvency.[51]

The Cork Report opposed preferences on the grounds that they hurt ordinary unsecured creditors, and offered two specific objections to the ancient "claim to preference for unpaid tax."[52] The first was that all creditors should share a priority in proportion to the extent of their credit. This was the classic argument from equity. The second was that

---

[50] *Minutes of the Cork Committee*, 10 Nov. 1980: 28–9.   [51] *Cork Report*: 317.
[52] *Cork Report*: 319.

the debts owed to the state were insignificant in proportion to the total state revenues, but could make a big difference for the other creditors or the debtor. The Report recognized that the state was an involuntary creditor (although not the only one), but insisted that it had recourse to some exceptional remedies that were unavailable to other creditors in general.[53]

On grounds of equity, therefore, a large and powerful creditor like the state should not be diverting moneys it did not need from smaller and weaker creditors whose needs proportionately were much greater. On pragmatic grounds, the Crown's preference snatched money out of pools that could be used by insolvency practitioners to rescue businesses.

The Cork Report further rejected entirely any preference for local rates or municipal taxes. It recommended that preferences be abolished altogether on direct taxes (income, corporation, and capital gains taxes). For "collector taxes", where the employer collected on behalf of government an employee's tax, national insurance and Redundancy Fund contributions, or where a firm collected value-added taxes, the Report recommended that preferences should be retained, but that the reach-back period for arrears should be limited. These proposed changes, it argued, would simplify the administration and disposition of insolvent estates, and thus make the whole process much quicker.[54]

Like banks, the state also has the prospect of off-setting moneys it is owed by debtors with moneys it controls. The English state had a favored status over setoff for a very long period.[55] "It has been a principle of the law of bankruptcy for nearly 300 years that where there are mutual debts existing between a creditor and a bankrupt, the smaller debt is to be set against the larger debt and only the balance is to be accounted for by the creditor or to be proved for in bankruptcy."[56] Should there be any mutual debts between departments of government and an insolvent firm, the state had the right to set-off the debts, and deduct what it owed to the firm from what the firm owed to it.[57] The Cork Committee sharply criticized setoffs as they applied to the state:

We agree with the criticisms we have received that the present practice is most unfair to the general body of creditors. There is no mutuality between different

---

[53] *Cork Report:* 320–1.   [54] *Cork Report:* 324.
[55] For a brief summary of the Crown's setoff rights, see Arnull (1984).
[56] *Cork Report:* 304.   [57] *Cork Report:* 304.

taxes which are not of the same nature, or between taxes and other impositions and liabilities arising under contract. Furthermore, the present practice operates only in favor of the Crown, never against it. The taxpayer for his part is unable to set-off a sum owed by him to one revenue department against a debt owed to him by another revenue department.[58]

The Political Response

Predictably, the Conservative government was unpersuaded by the Cork Committee's recommendations on Crown preferences. The White Paper which set out the Government's legislative purposes rejected all the recommendations that would have lowered its state tax priorities. Said the Government, tax debts were different because they were "imposed by law" whereas others were "incurred by agreement". As for collector taxes, they "represent monies which a debtor has deducted or collected, acting as agent for the Government, but which have been diverted for his own purposes instead of being paid over to the Exchequer."[59]

The White Paper in turn was heavily criticized by the financial community, consumers, and trade creditors, among others.[60] Accountancy organizations attacked government departments for not taking measures that would allow them to monitor arrears more carefully and thus forestall the need for such drastic measures as pushing companies into bankruptcy in order to collect unpaid taxes.[61] With their high priority and substantial reachback periods, said the accountants, state agencies could tolerate sluggish collections because they knew they would eventually get most of what was owed them. Administrative improvements would have allowed the government to shorten the reachback period for taxes along the lines proposed by the Cork Report.

In the face of these broad-based criticisms, the Tory government conceded very little.[62] The bill introduced into Parliament rejected most of the Cork recommendations on state preferences and it took little heed of interest group calls for a more generous stance by revenue agencies. In this, the government badly underestimated the opposition. In the Lords, a coalition of opposition and independent peers, together

[58] *Cork Report*: 306.
[59] *Government White Paper*: 18.
[60] See Fletcher (1984: 304–7). In Britain, the Insolvency Reform Committee, the financial community, consumers, and trade creditors all pressed the government hard to contribute more to the pool of assets available to smaller creditors.
[61] *Financial Times*, 19 Apr. 1984, p. 10.
[62] *Financial Times*, 3 Nov. 1984, p. 1.

with some government back-benchers, rejected the government's position and pushed for an amendment that would conform the bill more closely to the Cork Committee's recommendations.

Out of concern for small creditors, the Labour leader in the Lords, Lord Bruce of Donington, took aim at Crown privileges: "If the unsecured creditors in a company liquidation are to receive a better deal than they get at the moment, it will, I think, be necessary for us to revise Schedule 5 to the Bill, which deals with the whole question of preferential debts, notably debts due to the Inland Revenue, to local authorities and to others."[63] The stark contrast between the rights of small unsecured creditors and the imposing prerogatives of the Crown only served to make the latter look illegitimate. One peer commented that:

...I have a brief from the National Farmers' Union and they have said that they think this is disgraceful. The point is, why on earth should the Government, who have lots more money than the small creditors, have any preference over the small creditor?...it really is jolly unfair of the Government to continue to look after themselves.[64]

Stated Lord Denning:

Sir Kenneth Cork and his colleagues said how ordinary people are outraged that the Crown and the tax people should have this preference over everybody else and get their debts in full before unsecured creditors get anything....But the Government look after themselves. In this Bill they say, We do not want any of that. Let the Crown keep its taxes....I should like to see an amendment which would be in accordance with ordinary justice to the effect that Crown debts and other debts all rank together....The Crown should not take one pound while the unsecured creditor has one shilling. They should all be equal.[65]

Moreover, it was not simply a matter of equity but of practicality. At a small cost to itself, the state could greatly improve the situation of other creditors. Lord Noel-Buxton said: "...the loss to the Government on a single insolvency is minuscule compared with their total income. The loss to an individual or company, by contrast, can be substantial or even fatal."[66] Another peer claimed that: "More often than not the recovery of the VAT debt by Customs and Excise will wipe out all that is left of the assets of the wrecked company. The effect of this on the other business creditors can be devastating."[67]

---

[63] H.L., vol. 458, 1 Jan. 1985, col. 887.   [64] H.L., vol. 458, 1 Jan. 1985, col. 912.
[65] Lord Denning, H.L., vol. 458, 1 Jan. 1985, col. 903–4.
[66] H.L., vol. 459, col. 1245.   [67] H.L., vol. 462, col. 629.

Moreover, the government had not provided any convincing case about why it should keep its preference. It was relying entirely on its overwhelming majority in the Commons to avoid altogether any serious encounter with the issue. According to Lord Meston:

There has been no reasoned justification for Crown preference, other than that it has always been there. The underlying theory which has supported it is that the Crown is an indivisible whole. The reality, of course, is that the Crown is many distinguishable parts and it is quite wrong to treat all categories of tax as one single category.[68]

Most critics of the Government's position agreed with Cork's distinction between regular and collector taxes. Preferences for the former should be abolished altogether, the latter greatly reduced.

Opposing peers invited the Government to offer its own response to criticism, and initially it demurred. Pressure mounted when an amendment was introduced by Lord Noel-Buxton essentially to insert the Cork recommendations into the Bill. Recognizing the rising opposition to its Bill, a senior minister, Lord Cameron, rose to assure the House that the Government had heard the objections and had decided to give up its preference for "assessed taxes," though it wanted to maintain its preferential position on "collector" or quasi-trust taxes. While some peers, like Lord Denning, thought the Government should go all the way and abolish all Crown preferences of every sort, most accepted that the "Government have made a genuine and real offer of a generous compromise," and in anticipation of the Government's amendment to effect its new position, Lord Noel-Buxton withdrew his.[69]

But the matter did not end there, for when the Government introduced its own amendments, it abolished preferences for income taxes, corporate taxes, and local municipal taxes, but kept the reachback period for collector taxes—PAYE and VAT—at twelve months, not the three months that Cork had recommended. Otherwise, said the Government, it would put too much pressure on the collection procedures by "revenue-collecting departments."[70] Labour peers renewed their attack on VAT preferences and when the Bill came back for a Third Reading, Lord Mottistone, who was taking advice from the Confederation of British Industry, introduced an amendment to reduce preferences on the VAT tax to within six months of the insolvency,

---

[68] H.L., vol. 459, col. 1253.   [69] H.L., vol. 459, 7 Feb. 1985, cols. 1243–54.
[70] H.L., vol. 462, 2 Apr. 1985, cols. 172–8.

though he noted his own spirit of compromise given strong views that it should be abolished altogether.[71]

Sensing an unaccustomed defeat, the Government leader on the Bill in the House of Lords called upon senior Government peers to enter the debate and seek to forestall an impending defeat. But it was not to be. Since the Government refused to yield, Lord Mottistone pushed the amendment to a division, which the Government lost by 101–90.[72]

The Government's unaccustomed defeat in the Lords might have been remedied in the Commons, where the Conservative majority was absolute. But interest groups maintained their political pressure and the Government discovered a mild revolt among its own back-benchers. In retaining preferences for PAYE and VAT, the Lords had set different reachback periods: a year for PAYE and six months for VAT. The opposition in the Commons now proposed to remedy this inconsistency and set both periods at six months, thus further reducing the extent of the Crown preference.[73]

In response, the government argued in favor of strengthening the preference: "One of the most telling arguments for a full and unrestricted period of preference is that a person may continue to collect taxes from others and use that money for his own purposes."[74] VAT collections, protested the government, did not really belong to the insolvent debtor, although they might have been used by the debtor. Moreover, said the government, in an argument reminiscent of bankers, the very move to reduce the government's reachback period could do harm to debtors. Shortening the reachback period, said government MPs, would only make the revenue departments more stringent and less flexible in their treatment of taxpayers:

As business men rejoice in the changes relating to Crown preferential debts, public bodies which lose preferential status may decide to move more quickly

---

[71] *Financial Times*, 17 Apr. 1985. In successfully amending the government's bill, Lord Mottistone concluded that: "It will be clear from this example that the whole process of VAT debt recovery can take place comfortably within six months, even allowing for reasonable extensions of time at each stage" (H.L., vol. 462, 16 Apr. 1985, col. 635.

[72] H.L., vol. 462, 16 Apr. 1985, cols. 628–39.

[73] Mr Gould stated: "The Minister may recall that when in another place their Lordships forced upon the Government their amendment on VAT, which reduced the preference period from 12 months to six months, the Minister who led for the Government in that debate argued in advance of the vote that it would be most curious to have VAT and PAYE treated differently in terms of the period during which the preference should operate" (H.C., Standing Committee E, 7th Sitting, 11 June 1985, col. 305).

[74] H.C., Standing Committee E, 7th Sitting, 11 June 1985, col. 314.

and be less lenient when debts become outstanding. With the loss of preferential status, such bodies may chase for their money harder than before. [75]

The final outcome turned on a strange serendipity. Labour introduced an amendment in Standing Committee E to set both PAYE and VAT taxes at six months. During the debate in committee, one of the Labour MPs, Gerald Bermingham, who supported the Amendment, went down the hall to attend another House committee hearing. When a division was called on Labour's amendment, the doors of the committee room were locked before Bermingham could return. While he knocked to be let in, the Committee voted, and with back-bench crossovers, the vote was tied. Following custom, the Chairman voted with those who rejected the amendment, and it was lost, notwithstanding the energetic protests of Bermingham when he was finally admitted after the door was unlocked.[76] Thus, the Commons effectively left intact the amendments in the Lords despite extensive debate in Committee and in the House itself (Sealy and Milman 1988).

But while the Insolvency Act substantially reduced state preferences, the state did not lose all of its advantages. In the Commons, the opposition offered several amendments to curtail Crown setoff rights. First, they proposed that, for the purposes of setoff, government departments should be treated not as elements of the state as a whole, but each department effectively should be considered as an individual creditor. It should not be possible that the taxes unpaid in one department should be set-off against the payments due taxpayers in another.

Bryan Gould, Labour spokesman in the Commons, stated:

... not for the first time the Crown finds itself in a uniquely privileged position. That position arises because the Crown operates through a range of Government Departments each of which has its own ability to enter into tax raising and commercial transactions with a debtor or trader. As the rule stands, it is possible for the Crown to set off, as it were, a commercial debt against a debt which the debtor owes to the Department in respect of tax. It is able to take advantage of that arrangement, but to deny any disadvantage. ... It seems equitable to me that the Crown, for such a purpose, should be unable to do that and that each Department should be compelled to make a set-off arrangement individually so that it is not able to take advantage of the arrangement or the possibility in one case, but not in another.[77]

---

[75] H.C., vol. 78, ser. 6, col. 152.

[76] H.C., Standing Committee E, 7th Sitting, 11 June 1985, cols. 304–23; UK Interviews 91:17; 90:02.

[77] H.C., Standing Committee E, 10th Sitting, col. 398.

Later, the opposition tried to restrict setoffs by allowing them only among obligations of a like nature, but this amendment was also rejected by the Tories.[78] At the end of the day, "despite considerable pressure, neither the Bill nor the Act interferes with the system whereby debts due from one Government department are set off against those due to another, irrespective of whether these debts are for taxes or commercial transactions" (Phillips 1985: 6).

Nevertheless, by the time that the Insolvency Bill had wended its way through Parliament, the Government's defeat on tax preferences had proved the state politically vulnerable on its own ground. The Conservative Government lost face and lost the state its priority. Its decision not to overturn the Lords' amendment in the Commons further signalled its awareness that it had lost the moral high ground.

But why did the Government not yield the point without public repudiation? Given the Thatcher government's philosophical commitments to small governments and vibrant markets, a reduction of government claims, in exchange for an increase in private claims, would seem an attractive proposition. After all, what better way is there to engineer small government than through the public fisc? The government was forced, initially against its will, to concede the changes and weaken state preferences. The Thatcherite political program combined strong markets with a strong state, and the latter meant a fiscally strong state (Gamble 1989). Her Treasury was most reluctant to surrender its moneys.

RESISTING "BLACKMAIL" BY MONOPOLY SERVICES

However much the behavior of debtors and creditors is shaped and constituted by law, those disadvantaged by law on the books may seek to evade the law or compensate for its perceived inadequacies by exploiting in practice its various lacunae and ambiguities. Parties may try to achieve *de facto* what they have failed to accomplish *de jure*.

The discrepancy between statutory law and law in practice is neither stable nor static. As the number of actors who violate the spirit of the law

[78] Again, Mr. Gould proposed the amendment: "The new clause would reduce the effect of these advantages by providing that set-off would be permissible only between obligations of a like nature—between statutory obligations on the one hand and contractual obligations on the other. It is therefore a relatively modest attack on Crown privilege and advantage in this respect, as it leaves many other rights of set-off untouched" (H.C., vol. 83, ser. 6, col. 571).

increases, or the scope of evasion expands through loopholes in the letter of the law, then politicians and legislators may come under political pressure by disadvantaged parties or public interest groups to modify formal laws, clarify the ambiguities, shore up the weak spots, and close the loopholes. For a time the disjunctions between law in practice and on the books may be reduced. But legal and professional creativity thrives on uncertainty and ambiguity. That creativity opens up the gap between law on the books and law in action, just as professional creativity serves also to narrow the gap.

On either side of the Atlantic, utility companies sought to use their monopoly position in the market to construct a de facto preference which they did not possess in law. As creditors with sole control of a critical resource, they sought to strengthen their claims on debtors' estates and extract all they believed was due to them, whether it conformed to legal priorities or not. What they had lost in some earlier meta-bargaining, they sought to regain in everyday bargaining.

Legal reforms motivated by concerns for equity, especially on behalf of weak creditors, and by a pragmatic approach to company rehabilitation, could not avoid confronting those creditors whose unilateral exercise of market power imperilled both. In either country, therefore, professionals and policy-makers sought to bring utilities into conformity with a standard that did not allow them to strike their own private bargains with debtors outside the rules that governed all other parties to reorganization.

England

Gas, electricity, water, and telephone companies are frequently among the creditors of an insolvent company. Their claims had no priority in insolvency law, and they were treated as unsecured creditors. But because they were sole providers of necessary resources, they could act like preferential creditors. Before Thatcher privatized a number of the public utilities, utility companies enjoyed a monopoly by Act of Parliament. In exchange for their monopoly privileges they were statutorily required to provide service to eligible customers. This did not mean that customers had an unconditional right to service, for when a customer's payments were in arrears, the utilities could discontinue service. Given the necessity of utility services for even the most basic level of organizational functioning, insolvent customers could not do without service. Utilities frequently took advantage of their critical position by insisting that all debts be paid in full by the insolvent company if utility service were to continue or be resumed.

Experienced bankruptcy and reorganization specialists knew well the coercive threat that loomed from enormous utilities.

> There is one type of creditor who, although unsecured and non-preferential, is often able to insist upon and obtain payment of his debt in full from a company in insolvent liquidation or receivership in priority to other creditors. This is the monopoly supplier of goods or services, such as gas, electricity or water, which are essential to the carrying on of the company's business. It is the common practice for each public utility, on the insolvency of a customer, to threaten to cut off supplies unless the outstanding account is paid in full. Where the supply is essential for the preservation of assets, such as livestock or frozen foods, or to maintain a continuous production unit, the liquidator or receiver has no choice in the matter; he must pay the statutory authority its debts in full.[79]

Cork illustrated the intransigence of a utility company and its devastating effects from his own experience:

> ... [T]here was an example I had when I was appointed receiver of a glass works, a modern glass works and it was heated by electricity or gas, I've forgotten which, and that they said you owe us God knows how much money, and I said that I haven't got any. They said if you don't pay us, we will cut out the gas and I said you will freeze the whole flaming equipment. They cut it off and froze the whole of the equipment. The whole thing became useless, all the glass congealed in the pipes and the whatever you make bottles out of.[80]

If the Cork Committee had limited sympathy for any type of preference, it had none for these powerful utilities that impeded company rescue and muscled aside weaker creditors. In this view the Committee received significant support from many of the groups testifying before them. A number, including the Consultative Committee of Accountancy Bodies and the Association of British Chambers of Commerce, called upon Cork to remove de facto preferences illicitly enforced by the utilities.[81]

In response to these attacks, both the British Gas Corporation and the Electricity Council defended their right to cut off insolvent customers. The latter met the opposition head on:

---

[79] *Cork Report* 1982: 330.   [80] UK Interview 91:07.
[81] See the third submission of the CCAB, *Public Record Office*, Apr. 1978, and the submission to the Cork Committee of the Association of British Chambers of Commerce, *Public Record Office*, 28 June 1977.

I would like to deal principally in this letter with one aspect of the insolvency law which particularly effects electricity and which in our experience has sometimes given rise to misunderstandings. I believe that it also applies in the case of other public utilities, such as gas, but I will deal with it mainly in the context of the electricity legislation. It arises from the fact that the electricity boards are under a statutory obligation to give supplies, and hence credit. They are also given corresponding powers to discontinue their supplies if, in stated circumstances, payments by the consumer are in arrears . . . Though questions are raised from time to time about this power, it is in our view essential for the maintenance of a proper financial regime. . . . Though liquidators and others have sometimes raised queries about this position, it is, in our view, fully justified for the reason that the statutory obligations of supply continues until there is a new occupier for the premises, and the boards, unlike other traders, are thus left with no discretion to discontinue supplying a customer whose credit may be suspect. It is also usually beneficial to the general body of creditors that supplies of electricity should be continued. But it seems unreasonable that this should be done without payment of the anterior debts, and thus ultimately at the expense of the general body of consumers.[82]

But since there was no popular outcry against the utilities, and certainly no groundswell of support in their favor, the Cork Committee was largely free to follow its own mind about what to do.[83]

The Cork Report took the side of utility company critics and charged that the Electricity Board, British Gas Corporation, Water Authorities, British Telecommunications (the telephone company), and even the Post Office engaged in practices which Cork himself characterized simply as "blackmail."[84] The Review Committee proposed instead to treat the insolvent or reorganizing company as a *new* customer, with an unencumbered right to receive utility services:

We recommend that, once a winding up or liquidation of assets has commenced, or a receiver or administrator has been appointed, statutory undertakings should be required to treat the liquidator, administrator, etc (as the case may be) as a new customer with a statutory right to receive supplies, separate and distinct from the customer whose account is in arrear.[85]

[82] Submission to the Cork Committee from the Electricity Council, *Public Record Office*, 26 July 1977. Also see the submission from the British Gas Corporation, *Public Record Office*, 16 June 1977.

[83] A leading reformer recalled: "I don't think there was a lot of opposition, there may have been lobbying, but there wasn't a lot of opposition to the utilities" (UK Interview 91:07).

[84] UK Interview 91:07.

[85] *Cork Report*: 331–2.

As a "new customer" the insolvent estate would be under no obligation to pay the old debts of the "old customer" and thus could not be threatened by the utility company.

The Government ignored altogether this recommendation in its White Paper. However, on introduction of the Insolvency Bill, the Government announced its intention to amend the bill so that "essential utilities should be prevented from ensuring more favorable treatment than other creditors on the insolvency of a customer."[86]

In the Commons, several members applauded the Government's amendment. Michael Hirst, who as a former accountant had considerable experience with corporate insolvencies, echoed some of the Cork Committee's criticism:

I cannot overlook the position of the public utilities, which invariably find themselves in a position to blackmail insolvency practitioners by use of their monopoly powers. It is frequently the case on an insolvency appointment that the first telephone call that the insolvency practitioner receives is from the gas board, the electricity board or the telephone company stating that it refuses to reconnect the supply until the outstanding account is paid. In my view, that gives the public utilities an improper advantage over all other unsecured trade creditors.[87]

The problem was most acute for insolvency practitioners trying to "turn around" an insolvent company when they faced the demands of utility companies for payment of old debts. In response, Alex Fletcher acknowledged that the government "...fully intend[s] to take away what is in fact a bogus preference with regard to the monopoly utilities...."[88]

In June of 1985, Standing Committee E returned to the question of utilities, and Alex Fletcher delivered on his promise by proposing an amendment that would: "...prevent the major utilities providing essential services to businesses from securing more favorable treatment on insolvency than other unsecured creditors."[89] The amendment covered the gas, electricity, water and telecommunications utility companies. The new measure provided that: "...the utilities mentioned shall not make it a condition of providing a supply to an insolvency practitioner who is

---

[86] H.L., vol. 458, 15 Jan. 1985, col. 876; *H.C., Standing Committee E*, 11th Sitting, 18 June 1985, cols. 435–41.

[87] H.C., vol.78, 30 Apr. 1985, col. 186.

[88] H.C., vol.78, 30 Apr. 1985, col. 187.

[89] *H.C., Standing Committee E*, 18 June 1985, col. 437.

trying to maintain an insolvent individual's business that any charges unpaid at the date of his appointment must be met. That has the effect of placing the practitioner in the position of a new customer with the same right to supply as any other new customer."[90] The measure gave insolvency practitioners the right to legal action if they were denied service.

Labour MPs were in general agreement with the proposed amendment, with the exception of one feature which the government included as a concession to the utility companies. Fletcher's amendment also proposed that "in return for new rights granted to practitioners, the utilities will be entitled to ask them to guarantee payment for post-insolvency services." Insolvency practitioners could be made *personally liable* for payment of post-insolvency utility supplies. In other words, the provision would weaken the ability of a utility to secure payment of past debts, but would strengthen its ability to ensure payment for current and future supplies to the insolvent company. The Labour members and the one insolvency practitioner in Parliament, Neville Trotter MP, brought an amendment to remove personal liability but it was voted down.[91]

The United States

The American reformers confronted a very similar situation. The Bankruptcy Commission considered whether: "... something is needed in the Act to deal with the right of a public utility to cut off services. There seemed to be general approval of the notion that a public utility should not be empowered to use its monopoly position to compel payment of prepetition bills as a condition to continuing the rendition of service."[92] Meeting no objections, the Commission recommended that:

... any public utility be prevented from cutting off service to a debtor undergoing rehabilitation because of the nonpayment of past bills, provided adequate assurance is given of the payments for current charges. The practice of public utilities in terminating or threatening to terminate service has merely been a method to coerce the giving of a priority to the utility not provided for in the Bankruptcy Act.[93]

The Commission's dissatisfaction with this state of affairs was predicated on its commitment to the "equality of treatment of unsecured

[90] *Ibid.*
[91] H.C., Standing Committee E, 12th Sitting, 18 June 1985, cols. 436–41.
[92] *Minutes of the Bankruptcy Commission*, 17–19 May 1973: 56–7.
[93] *Report of the Bankruptcy Commission*: 24.

creditors."[94] Significantly, however, the Commission included similar language to that used earlier to mollify the banks—not the *adequate protection* offered the banks, but its cousin, *adequate assurance* of future payments.

Both the House's H.R. 8200 bill and the Senate's S. 2266 followed along the same lines, with some minor differences in the wording. In §366 of the former, the House bill reads: "(a) Except as provided in subsection (b) of this section, a utility may not alter, refuse, or discontinue service to, or discriminate against, the trustee or the debtor solely on the basis that a debt owed by the debtor to such utility for service rendered before order for relief was not paid when due."[95] The following subsection permits the utility to cut off service if the debtor (or trustee) has failed to provide adequate assurance of payment for service rendered after the order for relief. In effect, §366 required utilities to continue service unless they are not likely to receive payment for postbankruptcy service. The Senate version of this section was only slightly different, and favored the utility companies a little more.[96]

These proposals generated little reaction, even from the utility companies themselves. The American Public Power Association, for example, said nothing about §366, although it objected strongly to various provisions in §363 of S. 2266 and expressed them to the Senate.[97] Consumer groups also failed to take up the issue. Aside from minor differences about how exactly to rein in utility companies, there seemed to be a general consensus that that should be done. §363 passed into law with very little comment or controversy.

TWO CASES WITH ONE PATTERN

Spearheaded by professionals, the bankruptcy reforms in either country surprised two of the strongest actors in meta-bargaining, for whether their strength lay in politics or the market, they both found their resources diverted to other creditors or the debtor.

---

[94] *Report of the Bankruptcy Commission*: 213.
[95] *Senate Hearings on S. 2266 and H.R. 8200*: 73 (insertion of a Committee Print, Comparison of H.R. 8200, as Reported, and S. 2266, as Introduced).
[96] In both bills, utilities may cut off supplies if they did not receive "adequate assurance." In the Senate version, trustees or debtors had only 10 days to offer such assurances, whereas in the House version they had up to 30 days.
[97] *Senate Hearings on S. 2266 and H.R. 8200*: 1232–37.

Taxes are equivalent to the property rights of the state. Moreover, they are property rights that must be renewed constantly. The mechanisms of fiscal extraction, therefore, become critically important in the capacity of the state to carry out one of its most basic functions. Its capacity to capture lost or delayed revenues should not have been impaired in the area of bankruptcy law for the state was not only the most powerful of creditors, but the ultimate arbiter of the rules by which all creditors played. As a referee, it could enhance its capacity as a player. Yet the strong attacks launched on the taxation authorities in both Britain and the United States demonstrated that this dual position proved to be a fiscal asset, but a political liability.

Because the state has such "deep pockets," all other creditors had powerful incentives to reduce the priority, size, and period of reachback for state claims. Doing so would inflict a small cost on the state, but grant relatively large benefits to the other creditors.[98] Ironically, in both countries, the ostensibly most powerful of all creditors was compelled to weaken its own claims. And unlike private actors, such as utilities, the state could not recover de facto what it had lost de jure. Less readily could it informally circumvent or evade its own rules.

Why was the state unable to maintain itself as the first among equals in the scramble for the assets of a bankrupt debtor? First, neither government won any sympathy from the private sector over its long delays in collecting back-taxes. Such rank inefficiency merely confirmed to private creditors that government needed stronger incentives to keep abreast of taxpayer delinquency. Second, revenue departments found it difficult to find allies. The increase in revenue was not connected with any discernible public good. It was revenue collection for its own sake, not because it funded health or education or defense. Consequently, the Inland Revenue and Internal Revenue Service attracted few supporters. Third, the state as creditor found itself locked in a struggle with every other creditor—not only consumer groups and professionals, but the entire financial industry and major business groups. With negligible support, and massive opposition, it could only have appealed to political party support. But there was no political mileage for party leaders in supporting the most unpopular agency of government, when opponents

---

[98] The political outcome is unusual given the pattern of costs and benefits. Collective action problems frequently mean that policies or reforms that have widely distributed benefits, but concentrated costs, do not get enacted. Each of the potential beneficiaries has an incentive to "free ride" on someone else's effort to push through the reform, and thus do not contribute to the cause.

to the revenue departments happened also to be major supporters of the Democratic and Conservative governments in power.

In addition, utilities had major problems in translating their power in the economic arena into politics. While they might capture executive branch regulatory agencies, they found themselves relatively friendless in the legislative arena. No allies spoke on their behalf. Like the state, few reformers believed that such powerful corporations required any special protection and not a few practitioners resented their bullying tactics in the market.

With some variations, three principles explain why the state and utilities failed to sustain their advantaged positions in the distribution of assets in bankruptcy. Surprisingly, the most compelling argument advanced on behalf of the state turned on institutional morality and it came not from Britain, where the morality of the market was part of political discourse, but from tax authorities in the United States, where a discourse of institutional morality was almost entirely absent. American officials advanced a not unreasonable thesis, based on a sociological premiss, that taxation in a modern society relies on a culture of compliance. Any attenuation of sanctions on debtors to pay back taxes would begin a general unravelling of tax compliance. Thus a government should not readily surrender its privileges in bankruptcy, not because it needs the funds, nor because they belong to the community (though that is more persuasive), but because states themselves depend upon certain institutional moralities, which are bases of legitimation, and without which they could not function.[99] Yet this argument was not at all persuasive, for it clashed with two more compelling criteria.

The principle of compliance faltered in addition because it came into conflict with a more compelling principle of equity. Both the utilities and the state were vulnerable to the charge of unfairness. In the distributive justice of reallocating property rights, it seemed entirely wrong that the state, with all its powers of coercion, should get priority over other creditors. The state's enviable position as a creditor was unfair because in effect it got to write its own rules, and grant to itself strong claims on an estate. Similarly, utilities were perceived to be acting unfairly because they informally circumvented the letter of the law in order to benefit themselves, and consequently to hurt other creditors. Bankruptcy reformers unanimously agreed that such unfairness warranted a special effort to update the law so as to reduce both the state and utility

---

[99] See Levi (1988) on quasi-voluntary compliance.

companies to their rightful, and weaker, position. Both strong actors fell victim to strong currents of opinion, particularly in the UK, to redistribute the balance of power in bankruptcy in favor of weaker creditors. The grounds of resistance by the state seemed stronger because of the special status of certain taxes (for example, the "trust" monies for social security in the US, and VAT and PAYE in the UK) and because the state was an involuntary creditor. Utilities, however, could make no such appeals. As one of British participants put it: ". . . none of these people were involuntary creditors, they could always ask for deposits beforehand, and yet to be able to just cut off the supply and refuse to reinstate it unless you paid all the arrears."[100] Perhaps that is why state preferences were reduced less sharply than the claims of utility companies.

Most important, however, in either country and for both the state and the utilities was the drive to rescue companies, and that rested on a premiss of proportionality. It was plain to all creditors that what was a minute proportion of revenue to the government could be a major amount of revenue for small creditors, mostly small businesses. And, indeed, at this point the contradictions in the states' own positions became manifest, for few disputed that an insistence on paying government first could dampen the very entrepreneurial activity that Mrs Thatcher's government, in particular, was bent on stimulating. To rescue companies requires assets, particularly liquid capital. By demanding payment of back-taxes for extended periods, substantial amounts of cash are diverted from reorganization into the public treasury. Demanding back payment for utility bills has a similar result. Neither can companies move forward without capital or the necessities of electricity, gas, water, or telecommunications. When these two elements of the argument were combined—keeping resources available to reorganizing companies, and the greater value of those resources to debtors than creditors—then the dominance of the rehabilitation ideal demanded that the state and utilities, like the banks, be compelled to free resources to turn companies around.

Professions played a critical, though often invisible, role in these debates. First, the original ideas to limit state preferences came out of reform commissions that were dominated by professional experts. Second, professions acted as "conceptual ideologues" by providing the intellectual apparatus and theoretical argumentation that was carried into the legislative debates and made available to opponents of the

---

[100] UK Interview 90:14.

state's position. They knew the history and theory of bankruptcy law and could construe its contemporary relevance in convincing ways. And third, professions had a singular capacity to draw on what might be called "practical reason." Because they were intimately involved in every kind of bankruptcy at every level of consumer and corporate insolvency through every region of either country, they could speak with convincing authority about how things worked in practice. Their portrayals of economic and social cost to weak creditors were irrefutable. But then, too, the agents of corporate reorganization—lawyers and insolvency practitioners—could only practice their art of reconstruction with the resources controlled by powerful financial institutions, the state, and the utilities. The professional power in everyday practice to turn companies around required the means to do so. Chastened utilities and a less greedy state freed resources to rescue companies. That was the ultimate vindication for the lawyers and accountants who pervaded the reform proceedings.

6 Enabling and Constraining Managers

Insolvent companies confront two fates: one leads to closure and corporate death, the other to reorganization and corporate rebirth. If the former occurs, the firm ceases to function as a going concern. Its assets are liquidated and distributed to pay off creditors, and most if not all of its employees lose their jobs. When firms are reorganized, in contrast, they get another chance at life. Not all their assets are liquidated and most workers remain employed. A successful corporate reorganization benefits almost all interested parties. With a return to profitability, shareholders preserve their wealth, creditors get their money back, suppliers retain a customer, and employees keep their jobs. Such success brings political benefits as well. Unlike liquidated firms, corporations that rebound contribute to economic growth and investment, and hold down the rate of unemployment. Successful reorganizations therefore benefit the elected politicians who in modern capitalist democracies are largely held responsible for the state of the economy (see Block 1987). But if the benefits of a successful reorganization are shared, the risks of failure are not. Should a firm fail a second time, it is the creditors who will lose additional money. A corporate reorganization is like a gamble in which shareholders, creditors, managers, suppliers, and workers all win with success, but where only creditors bear the costs of failure. It is a "can't lose" situation for the former groups, and "can't win" for the latter. Creditors therefore tend to be less enthusiastic about reorganizations than the others.

This rather uneven distribution of benefits and costs affects how different parties view the choice between liquidations and reorganizations. Consequently, it also affects how they view bankruptcy laws which do, or do not, encourage reorganizations. In general, secured creditors favor liquidations. They are more reluctant than others to support a reorganization because they gain the least if it succeeds, and they lose the most if it doesn't. Furthermore, should a reorganization occur, secured creditors will want to control the proceedings so that they can protect the collateral assets that secure their loans, and minimize the potential for further losses. This leads fairly directly to political pressure to make reorganizations hard to initiate, and to subject them to close creditor control. In contrast, shareholders, managers, and workers generally favor reorganizations because they have little to lose and everything to gain. Liquidation leads to certain job loss and worthless shares, but reorganizations can protect jobs and preserve equity value (although they may eventually lead to liquidation later on if the reorganization fails). Despite these interests in support of reorganizations, such groups tended not to mobilize politically around the issue of bankruptcy law. Shareholders and workers were hard to organize and possessed more pressing legislative priorities, and corporate managers were reluctant to lobby as "managers of insolvent firms" for fear of becoming publicly associated with failure. Someone else would have to battle secured creditors if laws were to be revised to encourage more reorganizations. Conveniently, in an era of fiscal retrenchment and laissez-faire economic policy, politicians find reorganizations a tempting possibility that is hard to resist. With no need for difficult public buyouts, deficit spending, or expensive state subsidies or other interventions, market activity continues at a higher level with minimal job loss and hence less voter unhappiness.

Since successful reorganizations generally make everyone better off, the problem for legal reformers is how to design bankruptcy laws that encourage success. The general question for such institutional design concerns who to put in charge: who should control a reorganizing firm? Which persons should invoke the provisions of bankruptcy law that lead to reorganizations? Who ought to decide between liquidation and reorganization? Whatever is optimal in theory, laws must also recognize that troubled corporations begin with managers in control, and so if it seems better to put someone else in charge, then managers will have to be ousted. Once the control question is settled, the next issue concerns how much power the person(s) in charge of the reorganization should have to modify the structure of a firm and reduce creditors' claims over it. Strong powers engender radical changes which can increase the likelihood of success but which also violate creditors' property rights.

Whoever is put in control, and however free they are to remake a corporation, reorganization can be a heavily professionalized undertaking. That is, protracted legal negotiations about revisions in complex financial relationships require considerable input from legal and accounting professionals. By comparison, simply "pulling the plug" on a firm by liquidating it generates much less work. Corporate reorganization work therefore offers lucrative possibilities for professionals, and raises jurisdictional issues about who will perform it.

As we will see, these various questions were answered very differently in the two cases. In the US, the problem was how to encourage successful reorganizations with the "debtor in possession," that is, with current management remaining in charge of the corporation. Little thought was given in the US to the possibility of ousting management. In the UK, the idea that the same managers who led a firm into insolvency should stay to oversee its reorganization seemed absurd. Thus, the English problem was how to reorganize without a "debtor in possession." What to do with corporate management therefore became a vexing issue in both countries, especially given its effect on reorganizations. Britain also differed from the US in embracing a much more "creditor friendly" philosophy that sought to protect creditor rights as much as possible.

In addition to being the object of much scrutiny and analysis in both countries, particularly insofar as they figured into corporate reorganizations, managers themselves possess political and economic interests which they can pursue in the context of statutory reform. Managers of large corporations are the captains of industry, key decision-makers who in a capitalist economy shape investment, employment and economic growth. Hence, they possess considerable power in the market. They are also a group who feature prominently in some theories of legal change, precisely because of their position within the "most basic contradiction" in a capitalist society (see Chambliss 1993: 14). William Chambliss argues that the process of law creation comes out of social contradictions, and that under capitalism, the contradiction between workers and capitalists is fundamental. Such contradictions create tensions and dilemmas that people try to solve through law. Chambliss's argument suggests that managers, as the foremost agents of capital, will play a prominent role in bankruptcy law making, and shape how such laws manage the tension between corporate liquidation and reorganization.

THE QUESTION OF CORPORATE CONTROL

Who controls the modern corporation when it is wounded, dying, and in need of resuscitation: managers, shareholders, or creditors? The state, workers, or community interests? One might begin to answer this fundamental question by considering who controls a corporation that is not bankrupt, but even here the answer is not simple. The obvious response, that *owners* control corporations, was first cast into doubt in

Berle and Means's *The Modern Corporation and Private Property* (1932) where they argued that the shareholders of a large, widely held, and publicly traded corporation were so dispersed and hard to organize that they had limited control over corporations. By default, corporate control was ceded to top managers, who were relatively autonomous from shareholders. Weakened control by shareholders freed managers to maximize their own interests, sometimes at shareholders' expense. Managers might pursue growth strategies, such as "empire building," which maximized their power and status even if it reduced dividends for shareholders.

More recently, some researchers claim that the US has witnessed a resurgence of *shareholder* control over the corporations they own (for example, Useem 1993). The rise of large institutional investors such as pension funds and mutual funds marked the emergence of more sophisticated and better-organized shareholders who care about the long-run performance of corporations and who are able to put pressure on managers. Their size and ability to "move the market" means that institutional investors cannot simply sell their shares if they are unhappy with company performance or management policy: the mere fact of selling so many shares will depress the market price and cause them to lose money. Since the "exit" option is no longer viable, they must rely on the "voice" option and use their rights as shareholders to express their dissatisfaction.[1] In recent years in the US, institutional investors have become very active in forcing managers to improve short-term company performance, and have strongly advocated changes in corporate governance that tie management compensation more closely to share prices and dividends.[2] The resurgence of shareholder power has forced managers to modify corporate policy so as to maximize shareholder value (see, for example, Abowd 1990).

Still other researchers agree with Berle and Means that shareholders have little control, but object to the thesis of managerial autonomy. Instead, they point out that firms are often highly dependent on *financial institutions* and other outside lenders for capital. Internal sources of financing (for example, retained earnings) are often insufficient to meet the demands of a large corporation. But reliance for financing

---

[1] See Blair (1995: 163); and Hirschman (1970). For more on the connection between exit and voice in relation to shareholders, as well as a less sanguine assessment of institutional investor activism (see Coffee 1991).

[2] The shift from straight salary for Chief Executive Officers (CEOs) to salary and stock options reflects this change.

on banks and other lending institutions can weaken managerial control because lenders can combine their high degree of organization with concentrated control over financial resources to influence corporate management. As a result, managers are less influenced by shareholders and more influenced by bank creditors, particularly when the corporation is heavily dependent on outside funding sources.[3]

If the issue of who controls solvent corporations is complicated, then matters become even less clear as corporations approach bankruptcy. Whatever claims shareholders possess over a solvent company, it does not necessarily follow that they should control an insolvent company. In bankruptcy, shareholders are the residual claimants over a corporation with no residual value; assets do not cover liabilities and so the value of their interest is zero or negative. This suggests that management should no longer be answerable to shareholders and instead should protect creditors' claims. Yet the fact remains that shareholders and managers share a common interest in seeing that the insolvent firm continues to operate as long as possible. Such a corporation is running on creditors' money and if it undertakes risky but rewarding projects, then it may earn enough money to return to financial solvency. Management and shareholders share an incentive to gamble since they will enjoy whatever gains accrue while corporate creditors will bear the losses. Shareholders may have only weak controls over management, but insolvency cultivates a strong alliance between these two parties. Since financial institutions supply the credit on which companies depend, and their decision to "pull the plug" determines whether monetary resources will continue to flow, they face two broad options: to pull their secured assets out of the company, at whatever cost to the company itself or other creditors; or to maintain a continuing presence, but with some assurance that who controls the corporation will protect their interests.

The fact of insolvency introduces two other sets of actors, in addition to shareholders and managers, that potentially confound control over liquidation or reorganization. At the moment of filing for bankruptcy, *the state* immediately becomes a key player, whether through the supervision and adjudication of the courts, or the intervention of executive agencies as diverse as revenue authorities, financial regulators, and government bankruptcy specialists. Thus, who controls the corporation in bankruptcy depends on what role the state plays in bankruptcy law.

---

[3] See Glasberg (1989: 181–3). Gilson and Vetsuypens (1994) discuss in particular creditor control over financially distressed corporations.

Furthermore, corporate control sometimes depends on parties that have little or no role outside of bankruptcy—future claimants, who are prospective victims of corporate malfeasance, and towns, cities, and even national governments, that may assert an interest in the form and function of a company whose decisions affect jobs, community well-being, and national economic and political interests.

Control in bankruptcy varies greatly depending on whether companies will be liquidated or reorganized. Generally, firms that are hopelessly insolvent are simply liquidated, in part or in whole. They may be broken up entirely, or some parts sold as going concerns. If the company is liquidated, governance is much less of an issue because the firm is dismantled, and nothing is left to govern (surviving pieces are controlled by their new owners). By contrast, firms that retain some economic potential may be reorganized in the hope that they can return to solvency. If a firm is reorganized, governance takes on much greater importance, for the success of reorganization will turn in large part on the competency of incumbent managers or whoever is in charge of the firm.

Thus, the choice between liquidation and reorganization partly reflects the severity of insolvency. Firms generally get into a little financial trouble before they get into a lot, and so for reorganization to have any hope of success, the firm must be rescued or rehabilitated before it is too late. Timing, in other words, is crucial. And timing depends substantially on the actions of managers, for they know better than anyone else just how far downhill a firm has gone. Who controls managers during financial decline of a company, and the incentives and constraints they experience before and after bankruptcy, significantly affects the odds of successful reorganization.

Managerial Incentives in Financial Distress

The alternative fates of ailing companies differentially affect groups and how they mobilize around bankruptcy. A simple liquidation favors secured creditors and other parties with strong claims since they are likely to get most of their money back. Unsecured creditors and shareholders frequently get nothing and so bear the brunt of the firm's losses. Furthermore, liquidation usually leads automatically to job loss among company management and the other employees (LoPucki 1982: 336). For this reason, managers have little incentive to liquidate the company voluntarily—their hand usually has to be forced by outside creditors.

The incentive for managers to keep their jobs and maintain control of the company influences the timing of bankruptcy. If managers automatically lose their jobs when their firm tries to reorganize in a bankruptcy court, then it is tempting for them to postpone filing as long as possible. At the same time, if the firm is heading towards insolvency, that very delay may forestall any possibility of a successful reorganization and make liquidation the only possible outcome. Moreover, the longer the delay the less money there will be for distribution to creditors. The incentives facing managers therefore are a key element in the success of reorganizations.

The importance of managerial incentives for corporate reorganizations can be seen in differences between two chapters in pre-1978 United States bankruptcy law. Firms could be reorganized under either Chapter X or XI. Although Chapter XI had been originally intended for small debtors, it became the preferred reorganization vehicle for most corporations for one principal reason: the debtor, or the managers, remained in control of the company during a Chapter XI reorganization.[4] Debtors could initiate Chapter XI proceedings at their own discretion, they could organize classes, and only debtors could propose a reorganization plan.

In Chapter X, on the other hand, an independent trustee was usually appointed by the court to control the company. The trustee could change the rights of secured and unsecured creditors as well as shareholders. Furthermore, Chapter X involved a fairly stringent application of the absolute priority rule, which reduced the likelihood that the shareholders of an insolvent firm would receive any value.[5] Indeed Chapter X was itself introduced during the 1930s precisely to take business reorganizations out of the hands of management, or their close allies, and to put them under the control of independent trustees because policy-makers believed that managers were unwilling to investigate and pursue certain financial claims that their firm had against others (Dodd 1938: 225). An independent trustee, they anticipated, would act more vigorously and thus enlarge the pool of assets. Managers strongly favored Chapter XI over X because it left them in charge.

---

[4] See the *Report of the Bankruptcy Commission*: 244–5. The Brookings study found that bankruptcy referees (the precursors of bankruptcy judges) strongly preferred to leave debtors in possession in a Chapter XI bankruptcy. See Stanley and Girth (1971: 133).

[5] See *The Bankruptcy Commission Report*: 27, 255.

It is important to distinguish among (a) the interests and incentives that structure behavior before bankruptcy occurs, (b) those incentive structures that occur under the regulation of bankruptcy law, and (c) a wider set of public interests.

Before bankruptcy managers seek to continue trading as long as possible, if they know they will lose control by filing for bankruptcy, in the hope of a turnaround, especially given that it is the creditors' assets they are risking. Managers also want maximum flexibility for their use of company assets, and so will prefer fewer legal constraints of the sort that are triggered by bankruptcy law. And since timing is always an issue, managers will want to control how and when to file for protection under bankruptcy law. Corporate managers and directors are frequently resisted by creditors who press for stronger security or collateral for their loans. Creditors will prefer maximal discretion to seize back their assets and to control when to file for bankruptcy and under what provisions of the law, if legal alternatives exist. Shareholders tend to share the interests of managers although they are not identical.

After bankruptcy, issues of control are also critical. The comparative and historical range of bankruptcy laws shows that the options are almost as broad as the parties involved: control may reside predominantly with managers, or debtors in possession, as it has done since the 1978 Bankruptcy Code; control may be vested in public officials, such as official receivers in England; control can be vested in creditors, such as a debenture holder operating through a receiver; or control may be vested in private practitioners, whether lawyers or accountants, who are acting as agents for private or public interests. The relative primacy of any of these at a particular historical moment depends on an amalgam of historical experience and theoretical expectations.

Bankruptcy law results not only from interest group politicking among the parties in the credit network, but also from *wider public interests* that are formulated and expressed through party ideology, or public debate. Both the US Bankruptcy Commission and the Cork Committee affirmed a general commercial interest in saving companies, if at all possible, a view that generally requires intervention earlier rather than later in the declining fortunes of a company. An even more general interest in the functioning of markets was expressed by the Bankruptcy Commission's commitment to foster an "open credit economy" that ensures the provision of credit for economic development, a value that requires assurance for creditors that the extension of credit will be adequately protected—which influences the flexibility given managers in reorganizations. The general interests in market reconstruction articulated by Thatcherism embrace even more expansive ideals—not only a greater technical efficiency and carrying-capacity of markets, but their moral regulation and normative upgrading, a "cleaning-up" of market behavior in order to encourage greater investments by wider publics. And then there is a public interest in protecting the weak, in this case those individual and smaller unsecured creditors who are relatively defenseless in conflicts among the titans of the state, large financial institutions, and major corporations, not to mention opportunistic smaller debtors who can disappear from sight, taking unsecured creditors' assets with them.

Meta-bargaining

The contest for control over insolvent corporations plays out at two levels. At the level of individual firms, parties with a substantial interest in the company's fate bargain (or fight) for control before and during liquidation or reorganization. At the level of public policy, statutory law-making precipitates political meta-bargaining over the relative powers of managers and creditors in bankruptcy and the incentives that will shape their actions. Since more power to managers may reduce the power of creditors or shareholders, control can become a flash-point for conflict among all the actors in the credit network.

As an instrument of public policy, one purpose of a bankruptcy statute will be to institutionalize incentives that try to ensure appropriate courses of action and optimal allocations of company assets. Companies with no hope of survival, for instance, whose managers appear incompetent, should be liquidated and their assets placed in the hands of competent managers as quickly as possible. Those companies that have suffered only a temporary set-back, and require a brief respite from creditors in order to get their house in order, should be encouraged to restructure and become competitive again. And those companies that initially looked like good candidates for reorganization, but proved to be in more trouble than was first realized, should be given the means to dissolve themselves.

Bankruptcy law, then, is frequently viewed by students of public policy as a giant incentive scheme to encourage companies to follow the best course of action. We, however, view bankruptcy law more as an arena for struggle among creditors, managers, professionals, and shareholders. Who controls the corporation depends not only on the outcome of political conflict, but also on sets of assumptions and taken-for-granted orientations about models of corporate management, theories of firm failure, cultural frames of debtor–creditor relations, and wider political ideologies. In a sense, therefore, incentive systems in bankruptcy law lie embedded within broader theories of occupational performance and managerial culpability.

At one level, debates in the US and Britain over managerial control turned on incentives—how to encourage managers or stakeholders to choose the "correct" or "efficient" course of action that adequately distinguished between hopeless cases (liquidations) and hopeful ones (reorganizations). If capitalist markets are essentially the same the world over, such incentive models ought to produce relatively similar bankruptcy regimes across different countries. At another level, however, the political struggles over managerial control differed radically between Britain and the US because, in the former, insolvency legislation was assimilated to a larger Tory political project of economic reconstruction, whereas in the latter, bankruptcy reorganization involved a more limited adjustment to a problem of corporate adaptation in order to facilitate the "open credit economy." Both technical and moral attributions were redolent in the English case, whereas only technical attributions featured in the American case.

The reforms of the 1978 US Bankruptcy Code and the 1986 English Insolvency Act demonstrate two radically different ways of allocating control in corporate liquidation and reorganization. Each mode of control assumes a different theory of managerial motivation or incentives and a set of structural mechanisms to implement those incentives. Each role in turn derives from contrasting attributions of technical and moral responsibility and their relationship to wider economic and political ideologies. Bankruptcy law reforms may be contrasted as a concern in the US with market efficiency and a concern in Britain with market morality.

Our approach focuses particularly on the role of professionals in the changing balance of power between debtors and creditors. Since professionals—whether lawyers in the US or insolvency practitioners in Britain—are integrally involved in corporation liquidation and reorganization, they have their own strong interests in the substance of bankruptcy law. At the level of what we call jurisdictional rights, professionals legitimately exercise control over domains of work, including corporate reorganization. It is reasonable to expect they will use their expert influence to ensure that who controls the corporation in bankruptcy offers an expansive role for expert authority. They can also, however, represent a public or community interest, and consider or advocate the perspective of those who do not represent themselves in political bargaining. Whatever interests they represented, their own or someone else's, professionals were involved in all facets of legislative reform.

CORPORATE GOVERNANCE IN THE US

Corporate governance has been an important and ongoing issue in American bankruptcy law. In the discussions leading up to the Chandler Act in 1938, scholars and bankruptcy specialists recognized that corporate control was central in determining whether corporate insolvency could lead to a successful reorganization (that is, one that repaid creditors most or all of their money) or liquidation. In 1934, Congress directed the newly-established Securities and Exchange Commission (SEC) to investigate corporate reorganizations. Reporting back in 1936, the SEC study recommended that a qualified and disinterested trustee be appointed to oversee corporations undergoing a reorganization, and that corporations not be left in the hands of incumbent management (the "debtor in possession"), or in the hands of a trustee too friendly to management. The reasons for the proposed change were, first, the demonstrable incompetence of managers (that is, they had led the firm into insolvency) and, second, that only an independent trustee would aggressively pursue corporate claims on insiders like directors, managers or their associates (see Dodd 1938: 226; and Swaine 1938: 257–8). In short, a pall of corruption hung over debtors in possession. Furthermore, the study indicated that creditors' committees were frequently dominated by management and investment bankers, and consequently that they failed to serve those they were supposed to represent (Dodd 1938: 254).

Under the Chandler Act, Chapter X was designed partly in response to the SEC report, and targeted large, widely held corporations. In Chapter X, the bankruptcy referees ordinarily appointed an independent trustee to assume control of the corporation and the reorganiza-tion plan had to comply with the absolute priority rule. Not coincidentally, the SEC played an official role in such reorganizations, advising bankruptcy referees on the merits of proposed reorganization plans. (Swaine 1938: 260).

In contrast, a Chapter XI reorganization did not require a trustee, nor strict conformity with the absolute priority rule. It was originally intended for reorganizing small, closely held corporations and was initiated voluntarily. In practice, however, most reorganizations of both large and small corporations occurred under Chapter XI and so Chapter X was rarely used.[6] In retrospect, the popularity of Chapter XI is easy to understand: without the appointment of a trustee, managers were more likely to hang on to their jobs, and without the absolute priority rule, shareholders had a better chance of keeping some of their money (Altman 1993: 30–1). Managers and shareholders of troubled firms pushed together for the Chapter XI option. Nevertheless, secured creditors often contested the use of Chapter XI (since they fared better under Chapter X) and so courts expended considerable time deciding which was the appropriate chapter to file under. Although Congress intended for Chapter X to apply to big corporations, and Chapter XI to small debtors, the statute provided little direct guidance to courts over who should file where, and so insolvent corporations made their own choice (Rostow and Cutler 1939: 1362). In a Chapter XI proceeding, the debtor proposed a reorganization plan which, if it were unacceptable to creditors, meant that either the proceeding was dismissed or converted to a liquidation (Trost 1979: 1326). Thus, there was only one chance to secure agreement.

The 1960s Brookings study provided one of the few systematic empirical investigations of how corporate reorganizations actually worked under the old bankruptcy system. In general, Chapter XI failed to do its job. The report found that only about one-third of firms were still operating two years after their Chapter XI proceedings closed (Stanley and Girth 1971: 115). With so few of the reorganized firms surviving, the report concluded that: "...the Chapter XI proceeding cannot be considered an effective mechanism for business rehabilitation." (Stanley and Girth 1971: 146). The Report recommended that business reorganizations be put under the control of a to-be-established bankruptcy agency in the executive branch.

The US Bankruptcy Commission quickly decided that the three separate reorganization chapters created by the Chandler Act needed consolidation. In a memorandum to the Commission, Professor Lawrence King proposed to combine Chapters X, XI, and XII into a single

---

[6] Chapter XII was intended for unincorporated debtors, and like Chapter X was in practice rarely used.

chapter dealing with all business reorganizations, and thus to eliminate the time and litigation wasted on selecting and contesting which chapter to use.[7] The combined chapter borrowed features from both Chapters X and XI, although as the former was thought to be cumbersome and overly-elaborate, it was not emulated too closely.[8]

Consolidation of bankruptcy chapters was one way to speed up proceedings, but the Commission felt that other changes were also necessary to facilitate successful reorganizations. For instance, the Commission discussed a reduction in the role of the SEC. Some members recognized that the SEC would resist a termination in its participation in reorganizations or witness a diminution of its powers. J. Ronald Trost, a Los Angeles attorney who worked closely with commission staffers, strongly condemned the SEC and urged that its role be eliminated entirely. Mr Trost stated that the SEC's participation was worthless on the West Coast: "The SEC representatives are not available for investigation when needed; they pick the cases in which to be involved on the basis of glamor, location, and the like; and they are not imaginative but are totally inflexible on the absolute priority rule." [9] Some Commission members spoke in favor of the SEC but the Commission's overall sentiment was in the direction of reducing SEC involvement.

The Commission considered the relevance of the absolute priority rule. Some argued against its retention, claiming that it was difficult to apply, that it required speculative valuations of corporate assets, and it lacked the kind of flexibility necessary for successful corporate reorganizations.[10] Ronald Trost submitted an analysis of the absolute priority rule to the Commission and called for its replacement by two weaker alternative standards (the relative priority rule and the best-interests-of-creditors rule). Commission members were unmoved by Trost's arguments and continued to assert that the absolute priority rule had a place in reorganizations.[11]

Another way to facilitate reorganizations was to loosen creditor control over collateral. One of the Commission staffers, Gerald Smith, pointed out that: " . . . not infrequently a debtor's right to continue

---

[7] *Minutes of the Bankruptcy Commission*, 1 May 1972: 15–16. One Commission member published an article in which he worried about the absence of statutory guidelines for the choice between a Chapter X and Chapter XI proceeding. See Seligson (1971: 101).

[8] *Minutes of the Bankruptcy Commission*, 22–4 Feb. 1973: 34.

[9] *Minutes of the Bankruptcy Commission*, 22–4 Feb. 1973: 46.

[10] See, e.g., *Minutes of the Bankruptcy Commission*, 22–4 Feb. 1973: 55.

[11] *Minutes of the Bankruptcy Commission*, 7–12 June 1973: 78–80.

using equipment or other property subject to a security interest is crucial to the hope of any possibility of a reorganization."[12] If secured creditors seized their collateral, it could doom the corporation. Somehow it was necessary to protect the interests of the secured creditor without denying use of critical assets to the reorganizing debtor. What concerned the Commission was how to devise reasonable safeguards for creditors.[13]

Mindful of the problems caused by costly procedural delays, the Commission's decision to consolidiate the three chapters was intended to prevent much "pointless and wasteful litigation as to which chapter should be utilized in a particular case."[14] Following somewhat the direction of the old Chapter X, the Commission also felt that courts should in each case consider whether an independent trustee was appropriate, or whether the firm should continue in the hands of the debtor-in-possession. The Commission felt that trustees should be presumed for large reorganizations (that is, cases involving debts worth more than $1 million or firms with more than 300 shareholders). Thus, management of large insolvent firms would likely lose control of the corporation.

The SEC and the absolute priority rule were linked in the minds of Commission members: "Enforcement of the absolute priority rule in Chapter X has been primarily the task of the Securities and Exchange Commission. Unfortunately, the rigidity of the rule has frequently resulted in the destruction rather than the protection of interests of public investors."[15] While careful not to criticize the SEC directly, and firmly committed to the idea that some kind public administrative input was needed for large reorganizations, the Commission nevertheless proposed to strip the SEC of its formal role and bestow its oversight and advisory duties on an administrator from the to-be-established Bankruptcy Administration.[16] With the SEC out of the picture, it would be easier to apply a more flexible distributive standard than the absolute priority rule, and make reorganizations easier to accomplish.

Commenting on the reorganization provisions of the Commission Bill, Merrill Francis alerted bankers to the fact that " ... the new Act obviously substantially increases the number of situations in which the

[12] *Minutes of the Bankruptcy Commission*, 17–19 May 1973: 48.

[13] *Minutes of the Bankruptcy Commission*, 17–19 May 1973: 48–50.

[14] *Report of the Bankruptcy Commission*: 23.

[15] *Report of the Bankruptcy Commission*: 256. This connection was apparent from the beginning of the SEC's role in bankruptcy reorganizations. See Rostow and Cutler (1939: 1335–6).

[16] *Report of the Bankruptcy Commission*: 26, 249.

rights of secured creditors may be affected" (Francis 1974: 3). In his discussion of the Commission Bill, Trost posed the tension in sharp terms:

> ...the reorganization facilitating powers with which the Chapter VII (the reorganization chapter of the commission bill) debtor or trustee will be empowered should permit reorganization of any business that is truly viable. Debtors and unsecured creditors will regard these powers as corrective of undue prebankruptcy leverage held by secured creditors. Others (e.g., secured creditors) may characterize the reorganization facilitating powers as an unconstitutional impairment of the right of contract.[17]

Bankers valued the flexibility and speed provided by Chapter XI and although Chapter X adhered to the absolute priority rule (which benefitted secured creditors, such as banks), the automatic appointment of a trustee and the inflexible and protracted nature of the proceedings made it unpopular with banks.[18] As Harold Marsh, the chair of the Bankruptcy Commission, explained in Senate testimony:

> The reason that most creditors, including most senior creditors, as well as most debtors, prefer a Chapter XI as at present is because of the usual interminable proceedings that go on to have the trustee get acquainted with the business that he has never even seen before and to have a valuation made of the going concern value and to wait sometimes quite a while for the SEC report.[19]

The differences between the Commission Bill and the Judges' Bill were less stark on the matter of business reorganizations than on other issues, but even so they were hardly identical. The Commission Bill proposed to combine Chapters X, XI and XII into a single chapter, while the Judges' Bill recommended only that Chapters XI and XII be combined, and that Chapter X be continued as a separate venue for reorganization (Lee 1975: 38–9). This difference reflected the bankruptcy judges' belief that the old Chapter XI needed only some modification to be satisfactory, and that to force all businesses to use one

---

[17] Trost (1974: 129). Trost recognized that the most controversial of these powers were those which affected the interests of secured creditors (Trost 1974: 132–3).

[18] See the 1975 testimony of Robert J. Grimmig, (*Bankruptcy Reform Act Hearings on S. 235 and S. 236*: 465), and his 1976 testimony on behalf of American Bankers Association: "...we are most concerned with certain aspects of Chapter 11 of S. 2266 which would return major corporate reorganizations to a two-track system with the expense and delay of a mandatory trustee and absolute priority standard in each case" (*Senate Hearings on S. 2266 and H.R. 8200*: 575). See also Ingraham's comments (*Bankruptcy Act Revision Hearings on H.R. 31 and H.R. 32*: 2489).

[19] Senate Hearings on S. 2266 and H.R. 8200: 490.

reorganization chapter was a "punitive measure" that ironically could lead to the "demise of debtor rehabilitation under the auspices of the bankruptcy court."[20] The same difference carried over into the contrast between H.R. 8200 and S. 2266, with the latter following the Judges' Bill. Furthermore, the Judges' Bill continued the advisory role of the SEC, and unlike the Commission Bill did not propose to shift that role to a new bankruptcy agency (Lee 1975: 46–7). In other respects, the Judges' Bill followed the lead of the Commission (Coogan et al. 1975: 1150).

When it began its deliberations on the Commission Bill and the Judges' Bill, Congress followed the Commission in recognizing that reorganizations were generally preferable to liquidations, and that to encourage them it was necessary to target corporate management. Politicians agreed that liquidation was an unhappy economic and political event. One staffer involved in the passage of the 1978 Act summarized Senate committee thinking:

There was a general philosophy in favor of reorganization, in favor of getting companies in while there is still something to save rather than too late. And I think everybody understood that you need to protect management if you are going to do that. People don't willingly sign their death warrants. . . . [I]f you tell people that the only way they are going to reorganize is if they sign their own death warrant, they'll try and tough it out until there is nothing left. And then there'll be liquidations and nobody will get anything.[21]

A basic disagreement over managerial control broke out during Congressional testimony. On the one hand, some groups believed that in order for corporate reorganizations to succeed, management would have to submit voluntarily to the bankruptcy court. And the only way to encourage management to do so would be to give it a sufficient inducement. L. E. Creel III, representing the Dallas Bar Association, argued in favor of the Judges' Bill, with its multi-chapter reorganization provisions:

---

[20] See Lee (1975: 40). Members of the American Bar Association Committee on Commercial Bankruptcy reported that the Judges did not feel strongly about their differences with the Commission and so would be willing to concede ground on reorganizations. See Coogan et al. (1975: 1154, 1160).

[21] See US Interview 92:02. One banker observed that: "It came down to (I think) philosophically, if we could bring 'em back alive (the old second chance doctrine), we felt at the time that a debtors possess(ion) provided a better vehicle, ex-fraud, than a Chapter X trustee which seemed to motivate people to want to sort of stay with a sinking ship much beyond the point of logic." US Interview 91:01.

... chapter XI is motivated by the business itself: it is only because management is able to end up with something that they are interested in going through the pain and turmoil of rehabilitating, trying to rehabilitate a problem business chapter X is trustee motivated, creditor motivated; the motivations are different, therefore the chapters should be different because the goals are different. If you eliminate management motivation, you essentially eliminate the chapter XI approach, and that is not practical.[22]

Creel understood that managers would not file voluntarily if it ensured the end of their control over a company.

On the other hand, bankers regarded managers of insolvent companies much less charitably. Not only did they blame incompetent managers for most bankruptcies,[23] but it seemed unnecessary, and even foolish, to extend to managers yet one more chance to reorganize their firm. Thus, bankers expressed considerable reservations about the reorganization philosophy behind bankruptcy reform. Speaking on behalf of the Robert Morris Associations, John Ingraham, a Citibank vice-president, argued that:

It is clear to us that the pending bills presume that the rehabilitation of debtors through proceedings under the bankruptcy laws is a worthwhile policy objective. This presumption appears to us to ignore a vital point, that massive rehabilitation efforts are frequently made prior to the commencement of a bankruptcy proceeding. Consequently the initiation of a proceeding by a debtor is clear indication that out-of-court rehabilitation efforts have been unsuccessful. Any law which impedes the efficient allocation of the scarce resources of the nation should recognize this fact. The pending bills explicitly support the continued allocation of financial resources to those who are demonstrably inefficient in their use of such resources.[24]

According to Ingraham, a formal bankruptcy reorganization was simply the last in a long series of unsuccessful reorganizations that previously had been attempted outside of bankruptcy. Given this succession of failures, he saw no reason to give an insolvent firm or its incompetent managers yet one more opportunity to save themselves.

In the face of attacks on its role, the SEC Commissioner nevertheless understood well the stakes of reorganization: "At issue between S. 2266 and H.R. 8200 is who shall control the reorganization process."[25]

---

[22] *Bankruptcy Act Revision Hearings on H.R. 31 and H.R. 32*: 1661.
[23] See the testimony of John Ingraham, *Bankruptcy Act Revision Hearings on H.R. 31 and H.R. 32*: 2488.
[24] *Bankruptcy Act Revision Hearings on H.R. 31 and H.R. 32*: 2486.
[25] *Senate Hearings on S.2266 and H.R. 8200*: 621.

Commissioner Loomis strongly defended the role of the SEC and the effectiveness of Chapter X reorganizations, and tried to undercut some of the criticisms directed at his organization as exaggerated and self-serving: "Management and large creditors, however, had a great incentive to try to use Chapter XI whenever possible, and sometimes when it really was not possible. They complained about the delay, expense and disruptions which they thought were involved in a Chapter X case."[26] But the SEC and the absolute priority rule it had traditionally enforced were besieged from many directions.[27] The experts of the National Bankruptcy Conference reinforced the Commission recommendation that the three reorganization chapters be merged into one chapter, and singled out Chapter X for particular criticism:

Sophisticated creditors, as well as debtors, avoid present Chapter X because experience has shown that it takes too long, costs too much, and the radical nature of the surgery, even if skillfully performed, may kill the patient.... There are at least two inherent difficulties with this rule [the absolute priority rule]: (1) it rejects the notion that fully informed and well represented senior creditors and stockholders may, for reasons satisfactory to themselves, negotiate for a reorganization that does not need the inflexible requirements of absolute priorities; (2) the rule depends for its application on the court's evaluation of the business based on a capitalization of future earnings, a tedious and expensive process of crystal ball gazing at best.[28]

In the event, it was the advocates of a second chance and the critics of the SEC that won the day. The 1978 Code replaced Chapters X, XI and XII with a single reorganization procedure, Chapter 11. To allow for more flexibility, the absolute priority rule was replaced by a weaker standard and the SEC's role largely eliminated (Trost 1979: 1310). Congress recognized that if it wanted to encourage more timely reorganizations it was necessary to persuade the managers of a troubled corporation to act voluntarily. Unlike the old Chapter X, there was no automatic appointment of an independent trustee. Such a person could, of course, be appointed, but the presumption was that the debtor would continue "in possession," and thus that current management would stay in control. Furthermore, Congress was less likely than bankers to view

---

[26] *Ibid.*

[27] Herbert Katz, a bankruptcy judge, claimed that: "The so called Absolute Priority Rule in present Chapter X proceedings is a creature supported by the Securities and Exchange Commission which, in the writer's opinion has haunted the effective use of Chapter X proceedings for years" (*Senate Hearings on S. 2266 and H.R. 8200*: 667).

[28] *Senate Hearings on S. 2266 and H.R. 8200*: 833.

corporate insolvency as proof of the incompetence of management. Rather, a combination of honest mistakes and a downturn in the business cycle played an important role (Klein 1979: 10). Even if previous informal reorganizations had failed to resuscitate the firm, a Chapter 11 bankruptcy would provide one final opportunity.

The filing of a bankruptcy petition acted as an automatic stay of all collection proceedings against the debtor, thus giving it much needed "breathing room" in which to effect a successful restructuring (Fig. 6.1).[29] Furthermore, under Chapter 11 the debtor could borrow in the ordinary course of business, without the specific permission of the bankruptcy court. Such post-petition debts enjoyed first priority, and so from a creditor's standpoint were a good risk. Ironically, a "bad risk" borrower suddenly became a much more desirable customer after becoming officially bankrupt. As soon as practicable after the filing, the court had to appoint a committee of unsecured creditors to help oversee the debtor's operations. The court could also appoint additional committees (of shareholders, or additional creditors) if it saw fit.

If the debtor stayed in possession, it had the exclusive right to file a reorganization plan within 120 days after the bankruptcy petition. If the debtor did so, it then received an additional sixty days in which to secure agreement from the creditors. After the debtor's exclusivity period was over, creditors could then propose their own reorganization plan but clearly the debtor could drag out the proceedings, if it wished to. Whoever devised it, each plan had to group creditors into different classes on the basis of their claims, and propose how to modify those claims so as to make the firm viable again. Firms were given substantial power to alter their own structure and obligations so as to revive their prospects: executory contracts could be assumed or rejected, assets could be sold, contracts modified, and the corporate charter modified (Trost 1979: 1327–8). After a plan was devised, it was communicated to the affected creditors in a disclosure statement, and the creditors voted to accept or reject the plan. Unanimous agreement was not, however, necessary. A class of creditors was deemed to have accepted a plan when a numerical majority of creditors, with two-thirds of total claims, had voted in favor. Furthermore, a class that was not impaired by the plan was deemed to have accepted it, while a class that was to receive nothing under the plan was thought to have rejected it. Once a proposed plan

---

[29] Among other things, the stay prevented banks from seizing the contents of bank deposits in order to setoff the monies owed them. Thus, the debtor could hold on to its cash reserves. See Moller and Foltz (1980: 887).

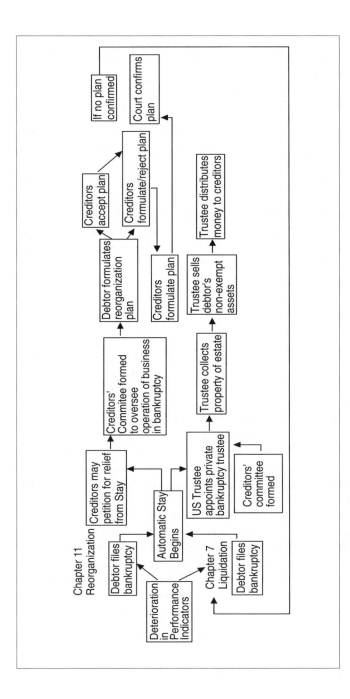

FIG. 6.1: **Schematic Representation of US Bankruptcy Procedure: Post-1978**
Sources: Collier on Bankruptcy, 14th Edition (1978) New York: Matthew Bender. Epstein, David G. (1995) *Bankruptcy Law in a Nutshell*, St. Paul, MN: West.

had been accepted by the creditors, and if it satisfied various other requirements, then it could be confirmed by the court. It could also be confirmed over the opposition of creditors if the court was persuaded to use the "cram down" provision of the bankruptcy code.

One informant summed up the philosophy of Chapter 11:

And under the old act, by the time you could file under Chapter 11 it was usually too late, you were too far gone. It was a rare business that got saved. And the whole idea ... the driving force behind the new Chapter 11 was to make certain that you could get businesses in there early on, and save them, and reshape them, and let them go on and do business.[30]

The enactment of Chapter 11 turned again the cycle that reflects considerable ambivalence about the role of managers in American bankruptcy law. Before the Chandler Act of 1938, reorganizations had been mostly led by corporate management, the equivalent of debtors-in-possession. The SEC report written by William O. Douglas had criticized such reorganizations, arguing that management frequently abused its power.[31] In response, the Chandler Act had created Chapter X to take reorganizations of large publicly traded companies out of the hands of management and put them under the direction of an independent trustee (LoPucki and Whitford 1993*a*: 674, 691). In the decades following, corporate managers frequently evaded this SEC-inspired attempt to curtail their powers by switching to Chapter XI for reorganizations. Ironically, therefore, Congress in 1978 returned again in certain respects to the role of managers in reorganizations that they had played before the Chandler Act.

Many of the changes made in bankruptcy law were based on implicit predictions about how the provisions of the new law would work. To evaluate how it operates in practice, asset distributions under Chapter 11 have been compared to what would occur under the absolute priority rule. Several studies find that creditors indeed concede payments to shareholders, even though creditors have stronger legal claims that are not fully satisfied by available assets. In other words, equity holders receive money in situations where, according to the absolute priority rule, they ought to get nothing. Nevertheless, as a proportion of the total amount of assets distributed, the deviation from the absolute priority

---

[30] US Interview 91:05.

[31] The SEC report was consistent with the picture of managerial autonomy drawn by Berle and Means. Whether in bankruptcy or out, it seemed that corporate managers served their own interests first, with little effective control from anyone else.

rule tends on average to be small (Betker 1995: 162; LoPucki and Whitford 1990: 126; Whitford 1994: 1382). Inside the bankruptcy court, shareholders may receive value that they would not be entitled to outside of bankruptcy but the magnitude of that value is not large. Since Congress gave Chapter 11 reorganizations more flexibility for distributions than the old Chapter X possessed, in this respect Chapter 11 succeeded. Chapter 11 has also offered some surprises. One is that although the chapter was intended to speed up reorganizations, in fact it appears to have had little effect on the duration of reorganizations for large, publicly traded companies. According to LoPucki (1993), the median time for a reorganization of a large company has not changed much.[32] The median time for smaller companies has, however, increased and is now much closer to that for large companies (LoPucki 1993: 745). It appears that having one chapter for all reorganizations, large and small, has led to a convergence of reorganization times.

Perhaps the biggest surprise is the fact that corporate managers tend to disappear at a high rate, even though a Chapter 11 bankruptcy filing does not automatically push them out of office or install a trustee (as the old Chapter X did). As "debtors in possession," managers stay in charge of the insolvent corporation as it enters into bankruptcy, but in many instances they do not remain there for long. Gilson (1989, 1990), LoPucki and Whitford (1993*a*), and Whitford (1994) found high rates of turnover among CEOs and senior managers of financially distressed firms.[33] Job loss was a practical likelihood if not a legal certainty, and so Chapter 11 is clearly not a safe haven for management.[34] Yet the difference is crucial, for Chapter 11 confers enough leverage so that even tainted managers can negotiate for a more favorable exit rather than simply be fired.[35] Their bargaining strength has risen. In sum, as one reformer reflected on subsequent development management did

---

[32] LoPucki offers several estimates for pre- and post-1978 median times, with 20 months for pre-1978 reorganizations and 18 to 24 months for the post-1978 period. See LoPucki (1993: 743–4).

[33] Gilson (1989: 250–1) goes on to argue that such management changes are usually initiated by bank lenders, and almost never by public bondholders. See also Whitford (1994: 1383).

[34] This may vary by corporate size. Kerkman's (1987) study examines a sample of smaller firms in Chapter 11 reorganizations, and concludes that debtors remain very much in control.

[35] Betker (1995: 171) speculates that management's leverage derives from its ability to delay resolution, which can hurt creditors. LoPucki and Whitford (1990: 149) agree but argue that the threat of foot-dragging isn't sufficient to explain deviations from absolute priority.

very well: "... At the business end, you know, at the Chapter 11 end of it, I think the debtor in possession—which is the big business debtor—came out very very well.... I mean he just got all kinds of power that he could retain. And then he got... He didn't have the SEC looking over his shoulder."[36] It matters a great deal to managers whether job termination is guaranteed or merely probable. Thus, Chapter 11 still offers sufficient incentives to induce corporate managers to file sooner (while the firm is salvageable) rather than later (when it isn't) (Warren 1993: 372).

The security of incumbent managers, at least in the short-run, helps to explain another unanticipated outcome of the 1978 Code—the rise of strategic bankruptcy. The original intention behind Chapter 11 was to help save firms that were in serious economic difficulty. Yet solvent firms have filed for Chapter 11 bankruptcy to take advantage of the considerable powers incumbent managers have to remake the corporation, undo its commitments, and reduce its obligations. Scholars like Kevin Delaney have analyzed in some detail the variable uses to which a Chapter 11 reorganization can be put: to settle a mass tort liability or legal judgement, reduce labor costs, reject pension obligations, or resolve toxic waste-related liabilities (Delaney 1992, 1996). In many cases, the reorganizing firm was not insolvent, and may in fact have been performing rather well. Such creative adaptations of Chapter 11 by innovative bankruptcy lawyers was completely unanticipated by its designers.

ENGLAND: REHABILITATING THE MORALITY OF THE MARKET

The debate over corporate control in England embraced a much wider range of issues than its American counterpart. The British reforms centered on the behavior of directors preceding insolvency and the powers of professionals as agents of rehabilitation following corporate insolvency. While these concerns affected the centrality of financial institutions in the determination of companies' fates, they were subsumed under the wider policy commitments of Thatcherism, and its orientation towards the state and market. In Britain, corporate insolvency was not simply understood as a matter of the neutral purging by an impersonal economic institution of its less fit member organizations, or the release of poorly managed assets to more effective managers.

---

[36] US Interview 91:03.

Instances of economic failure generated normative attributions and stimulated moral discourse which shifted the framing of economic failure away from a purely technocratic perspective. For this reason, the revision of insolvency law presented to the Tory government an opportunity to rehabilitate the morality of the market and affirm key Conservative values in the process.

Political meta-bargaining over corporate control during insolvency revolved around four recurring sets of problems. First, media reports, professional complaints, and politicians shared a consensus that too many company directors acted incompetently, or recklessly, or even fraudulently, and so put at risk the assets of investors and lenders. Second, the reformers' inner circle, and especially the professionals, believed that the floating charge held by large financial institutions gave them so much control over insolvent firms that the business and most other creditors were adversely affected. Third, control over directors and companies suffered from incompetent and occasionally fraudulent activity by unregulated, non-professionalized liquidators and insolvency practitioners. And fourth, most reformers agreed that English law had some large gaps that prevented rescue or reorganization of companies when it would have most benefitted the business and the entire body of creditors.

All of these particular complaints came to be absorbed into the government's larger agenda to redress the technical and moral failings of effective markets. Throughout the 1970s and the early 1980s, the British public had been subjected to successive waves of bad news about the workings of the economy. The steady media reports of rising insolvency rates, which reached epidemic proportions in the recession of the early 1980s, punctuated by company collapses symbolically more unsettling because of their magnitude, and the government's changing attitudes to intervention, signalled the dangers in the "discipline" of the market (Gamble 1994: 110). The public was stunned by the 1971 failure of Rolls Royce—a venerable symbol of British manufacturing prestige. This event impressed laypeople and professionals alike that no-one was safe from insolvency. For the front rank of insolvency practitioners, Rolls Royce demonstrated that how much—and how little—that could be done to effect a reorganization, without going into liquidation, under the prevailing law. In 1974 Britain's biggest property failure occurred as the Stern Property Group, which owed some £170 million to thirty-three financial institutions, threatened to dump up to £200 million of his properties onto the property market, thus triggering a chain reaction of secondary business failures (Cork 1988: 96–102). At the same time, the "Fringe Bank crisis" unsettled the financial community and consigned a raft of companies to commercial oblivion, while others tottered on the brink (Cork 1988: 93–5, 194–5). Property companies "went to the wall," and many influential people experienced for the first time what it was like to be defrauded.[37] Moreover, each time a major public company faced collapse, Government came under tremendous pressure to rescue "lame-duck" companies with public funds—an expedient it became increasingly reluctant to take. Privatization, therefore, offered a different way out. But for privatization to work, Thatcher's government had to ensure that the market would do its job, and so the state would have to effectively "police the market order" (Gamble 1994: 41).

This was not only a matter for large corporations. The chairman of the Insolvency Reform Committee was convinced that television programs critical of insolvency practitioners and directors alike had a substantial impact on public attitudes. Both featured cases where consumers were duped by companies that accepted prepayments and then disappeared, declared insolvency, and then revived in a new company with a very slightly changed name. Travel agents sold tickets for foreign holidays, and then went broke, not only depriving customers of their payment, but often stranding them overseas as well. Other business scams sought large deposits for the double-glazing of windows, goods that were never delivered.

Developments in the markets were not simply understood as matters of economic efficiency, the purging by an impersonal institution of its less fit organizations, or the release of poorly managed assets to more effective managers—the standard interpretive frames of economic theory. When firms failed in the market, they produced not simply a technocratic analysis of financial shortcomings, but sets of moral and normative interpretations of behaviors and actions. Furthermore, corporate insolvency was itself an instance of failure-in-the-market that raised moral issues of culpability, responsibility and blame. And for the English, culpability began with company directors, not only in terms of their technical competency, but against the standard of moral rectitude articulated by the Government and reformers alike.[38]

---

[37] UK Interview 90:04; Interview with Kenneth Cork 1988.

[38] While problems with insolvency practitioners had a direct effect on the regulation of directors, more detailed discussion of their professionalization comes in Part III.

The politics of English insolvency law took a two-pronged approach to save businesses. Reformers pushed for the use of negative sanctions to improve the quality of management outside bankruptcy and to compel directors to use insolvency law before their companies reached the terminal stage. In a complementary move, a strong reform initiative pressed for new mechanisms within insolvency law to increase the probability of saving companies. In both, the control of companies by managers was the pivotal decision point. We analyze, first, the measures proposed to regulate company directors before their companies became insolvent, and second, the innovations to save companies through enabling provisions of insolvency law.[39] The former sparked the liveliest interest group and party politics in the entire reform campaign. The latter was heralded as one of the Insolvency Act's principal innovations.

Regulating Company Directors[40]

The Attribution of Blame

In the British insolvency debate, managerial culpability for corporate failure effectively was classified into three categories: (1) honest mistakes made in the course of usually efficient and competent business activity, which received general approbation; (2) excessive risk-taking and commercial recklessness, which attracted statutory regulation; and (3) fraudulent or criminal activity.[41] For each of these, reformers proposed different sanctions, ranging from preventive measures through restitutive and retributive legal regimes. The sanctions varied in their reliance on civil actions by private or state parties and criminal interventions by the state.

(1) Incompetence

The competence of company directors presented a formidable hurdle for Government aspirations to increase the capacity of markets, a concern that coincided with the complaints aired by consumers and various

---

[39] It should be observed that directors in English companies will usually include inside directors, such as the managing director, who is usually the company's chief executive, and outside directors, who are not engaged in day-to-day management.

[40] For a more extended account of the regulation of company directors, see Halliday and Carruthers (1996).

[41] The dynamics of framing and reconstructing a normative order extend to any institutional setting. For another case where distinctions between errors of judgement and blameworthy actions order a normative system, see Bosk (1979) on the management of medical error in hospitals.

trade associations. By the time the Insolvency Bill reached Parliament in 1984, a cross-party consensus had emerged that some proportion of company directors—its estimated size varied depending on ideological dispositions—were well-meaning but essentially unfit to manage. In debate, parliamentarians accepted that companies frequently failed to maintain minimal standards of business accountability either for themselves or for their various constituencies. A Labour spokesman in the Commons asserted that hundreds of thousands of companies regularly failed to file their company accounts with the government.[42] Accountancy bodies had advised the Cork Committee that failure to keep proper accounts was a major sign of impending company failure, and penalties for not filing annual financial reports with the Companies office were, according to the Institution of Civil Servants, "derisory." The Government was convinced that many company failures occurred because directors were not adequately informed about their own company's financial situation.[43] And there was little opportunity for prospective investors to discover how often directors had been in companies that became insolvent on previous occasions, a complaint that had earlier been registered by accountants, the insurance industry, the British Steelworkers Association, and the National Association of Trade Protection Societies, among others.[44]

Even more vexing were perceived failures in financial and governance structures. Members of Parliament echoed insolvency practitioners' observations that company collapses frequently followed from lack of start-up capital and inadequate continuing capitalization. Fragile capital structures were compounded by widespread lapses in corporate governance. The Government took a dim view of what it considered to be the casual manner in which many prominent individuals accumulated multiple directorships, thus making it difficult to pay adequate attention to any one company. In the face of considerable disquiet from business circles, the government proposed to bolster responsibilities for non-executive or outside directors. Said Lord Lucas, "we wish to encourage people to consider carefully before they join a board, whether it is in the capacity of a 'doctor' or as a non-executive director, because,

---

[42] Bryan Gould, H.C., vol. 458, St. Comm. E., 16 May 1985, col. 58.

[43] Alex Fletcher, Minister of State for Trade and Industry, H.C., vol. 458, St. Comm. E., 21 May 1985, col. 100.

[44] Written Submissions by the British Steelworkers Association, the National Association of Trade Protection Societies, the Association of Certified Accountants, and the Cork Committee, *Public Record Office*.

in our eyes, whatever prefix you put before the word 'director' the responsibilities are exactly the same."[45]

The Opposition pressed the Government even more strenuously on unacceptable practices by company directors: cases where directors took disproportionate monies out of their company for personal use;[46] difficulties of reaching shadow directors who governed companies through proxies and who could not be held accountable by clients, suppliers, or the state;[47] and cases of parent companies which acted as shadow directors, instigating their subsidiaries to trade recklessly or wrongfully, but confident that limited liability shielded them from legal action.[48] In their submissions to the Cork Committee, the Association of British Chambers of Commerce, a small-business trade group, had criticized the practice of failed directors starting up new companies, but with their wives, or other family members, as "mock" directors who immediately then "employed" their spouses in supposedly advisory capacities.

(2) Recklessness

Failures in basic corporate governance shaded into ethical failures via commercial "recklessness." The most frequently recounted tale concerned prepayments, particularly in the travel and construction industries. Without complete confidence they could deliver goods or services, companies solicited advance payments for holiday tours, blinds, clothing, records, furniture, or deposits on home building, only to discover that they were insolvent. Consumer organizations, television programs, news reports, and Labour politicians pressed the government to act on complaints about "paying deposits to the . . . cowboy builder, deposits for greenhouses, deposits for kitchen units, paying fifteen hundred pounds for double glazing, we'll come along and fix it next month, and next month comes, and they don't."[49] According to a senior civil servant, government was strongly prodded by consumers "to ensure that

---

[45] Lord Lucas, H.L., vol. 459, 25 Jan. 1985, col. 604.

[46] Bryan Gould cited the instance of a man whose mail order firm went into liquidation owing £700,000. He had paid £187,000 to himself as personal expenses, and on a £119,000 loan he had charged his own company 100% interest (H.C., vol. 458, St. Comm. E., 23 May 1985, col. 149).

[47] "To take a classic example, a man called Stone set up garden gnome firm in the Midlands. . . . Nominee directors were used but the management of the business lay in his hands. Stone was an undischarged bankrupt" (Bermingham, H.C., vol. 458, St. Comm. E., 4 June 1985, col. 166). These directors could be "hired" by service contracts.

[48] See, for example, Alex Fletcher's comments to Standing Committee E (H.C., vol. 458, St. Comm. E., 6 June 1985, col. 214).

[49] UK Interview 91:17:35.

the necessary firepower was there to cope with those who took people's money in advance and didn't supply the goods and services."[50]

(3) Malfeasance

The notorious "Phoenix Syndrome" helped to mark out the moral boundary dividing incompetence and recklessness from outright malpractice. Echoing the media, the discussions of the Government and the Insolvency Review Committee were replete with references to "rogue" directors, "dishonest" directors, "fly by night traders"—directors, in the view of one senior policy-maker, who deserved to be "hammered into the ground."[51] Through collusion between directors and liquidators, the Phoenix Syndrome allowed directors of companies in financial difficulty to liquidate the company and sell its assets at a very low price to an accommodating liquidator, who would then sell the assets back at knock-down prices to the directors whose new company had risen like a Phoenix from the ashes and was ready to trade again, now free from all its debts. Collusive deals where "rogues" agreed "to take in each other's washing," instances of how "Johnnie Smith for the umpteenth time has let the firm go under and for the umpteenth time has arranged to buy back from the friendly neighborhood liquidator the contents of the firm to start up again," the widespread grievance "about directors who seemed to run their companies into the ground and walk away scot free"—all seemed to bear witness that "the market wasn't working in the sense that directors were not behaving well."[52]

The inability to control unethical and dishonest directors represented a failure of criminal and commercial law.[53] Unscrupulous directors could walk away from their liabilities and the economic and personal wreckages left in their wake, because the legal mechanisms were fundamentally flawed. The law had provisions to prosecute directors for fraudulent trading, but:

. . . there was never a prosecution of a director. Never. Practically never for fraud or trading insolvently. People would start off solvent, then just go on trading, and their hope springs eternal, they would just go on trading, so they'd then trade more and

---

[50] UK Interview 91:17:15.

[51] UK Interview 91:17:35.

[52] H.C., vol. 458, St. Comm. E., 14 May 1985, col. 18; H.C., vol. 458, St. Comm. E., 16 May 1985, col. 58; UK Interview 91:14:29.

[53] In classic socio-legal terms, critics of the government complained that this was not simply a problem of law "on the books," but of the ways that government had chosen—or had the capacity—to mobilize compliance measures.

more insolvently. And they would trade insolvently with other people's money. And . . . this was dimly considered acceptable by the business community.[54]

In all of Britain, there were only thirteen prosecutions in 1976, twenty-two in 1980, and forty in 1983.[55] While the Opposition insisted that the problem lay partly in the reluctance of government to use weapons already in their hands, lawyers and accountants agreed with the civil servants that the need to prove an *intent* to defraud almost inevitably doomed any prosecution which, a leading insolvency barrister confirmed, "you could never get off the ground."[56]

The prevalence of fraud and repeated company reincarnations raised the stakes of insolvency reform as some began to attack the core concept of company law that seemed to permit such abuse—limited liability. Introduced formally into English law in the nineteenth century, limited liability was intended to stimulate the formation and risk-taking of companies by sheltering investors from personal liability for the debts of their company. By the 1970s, even the Institute of Directors was prepared to concede that directors were "able to walk away from liabilities" and that limited liability itself "was being abused."[57] Numerous interest groups petitioned the Cork Committee for a law that would breach, under certain circumstances, the protection of limited liability so that directors could be held personally responsible for company debts.[58]

Whether it was incompetence, recklessness, or fraudulent behavior, the defects of management had ramifications that extended far beyond the shareholders and direct creditors. "Continuing to trade after the company was insolvent," contended Sir Kenneth Cork, "was giving the market a bad name and it was giving companies a bad name and capitalism a bad name."[59] In other words, the Tory government confronted the efficiency and morality of markets as a political project.

A push to reconstitute market morality emerged from insolvency reform. Two elements of the Cork Report provided the centerpieces of the government regulatory legal framework. One concept, *wrongful*

---

[54] UK Interview 90:04:1–2.
[55] Lord Bruce, H.L., vol. 459, 29 Jan. 1985, col. 600.
[56] UK Interview 91:14.
[57] UK Interview 90:08:7.
[58] Written Submissions by the Nottinghamshire Chamber of Commerce and Industry, Midland Bank, Association of British Chambers of Commerce, Finance Houses Association, Equipment Leasing Association, Institution of Professional Civil Servants, British Constructional Steelworkers Association, and National Association of Trade Protection Societies to the Cork Committee, *Public Record Office*.
[59] UK Interview 90:04.

trading, was directed at directors' behavior which lay in the grey area between honest mistakes by a competent director, and criminal acts by a fraudulent director. This intermediate area lumped together blatantly incompetent and careless directors with reckless and excessively risky directors, and subjected them to punitive and restitutive sanctions which exposed their personal assets to civil liability. The other concept, *director disqualification*, was oriented towards incorrigibly incompetent directors, as well as to the worst cases of reckless trading, and to all cases of fraudulence. Quite apart from possible criminal sanctions, director disqualification enacted prevention by banishing directors *qua* directors from the market.

Punitiveness and Restitution: Exposure to Limited Liability

Lawyers and accountants in the reform circle recognized that current laws on fraudulent trading did not work, either because there was little incentive to activate them, or more probably because the legal standard of proof was unattainable in practice. If the Cork Committee needed any stronger reasons to reform the law, it could draw support from civil servants, financial associations, chambers of commerce, and the accountancy bodies, all of whom found common cause with the Inland Revenue's pronouncement that:

> ...it is wrong that a director can shelter behind that limited liability creature of his in such a way as to pay least with near fraudulence, when he is deliberately setting out to take money from people for goods and services that he has no intention, or very little intention, of providing...and still worse, to escape from the situation only to repeat it all over again with a fresh corporate creature.[60]

If proving fraudulent intent neutralized current law, and if lack of incentive hobbled any potential agent of control, then reformers faced a threefold task: to find a juridical criterion for recklessness or fraud that dispensed with intent; to lower the criminal standard of proof; and to build into law reform a set of incentives—especially to private parties— that would activate legal weapons against directors. Perhaps most importantly, the reformers felt constrained to reach cases of recklessness or high risk-taking that may not have involved dishonest or criminal fraudulence.

After extensive deliberations, the reform committee invented a new civil action for "wrongful trading" that would permit creditors to sue

---

[60] Oral Submission by the Inland Revenue Service to the Cork Committee, *Public Record Office*, 21 Oct. 1980.

directors personally for monetary compensation of creditor losses. The Cork Report proposed that wrongful trading would occur when (a) "any business of the company is carried on with an intent to defraud creditors of the company;" or (b) "at a time when the company is insolvent or unable to pay its debts as they fall due, it incurs further debts or other liabilities to other persons without a reasonable prospect of meeting them in full."[61] If a director knew that the company was trading wrongfully, he or she could be personally liable for company debts.[62]

Characterized by the Committee as a "radical" extension of previous law, the wrongful trading concept made it possible for creditors to reach the personal assets of directors who acted recklessly or unreasonably by normal business standards. Congenitally optimistic directors, or high stakes risk-takers, would not escape liability if they "unreasonably" believed that "there was light at the end of the tunnel," or that "the dark clouds had a silver lining," and they continued to trade regardless.[63] As Cork, himself put it, "we almost added the phrase: 'limited liability is a privilege; if you abuse it, you lose it.'"[64]

Wrongful trading involved two changes in the sanctioning of directors. First, it promised to shift social control of directors from criminal to civil proceedings. Cork explained that:

We realized that you could never write a law in this country where a jury will convict a man of fraud when all he had done was continue to trade. We had to take it out of the criminal law and make the responsibility a financial one inasmuch as he lost his immunity—limited liability.[65]

Wrongful trading also changed the burden of proof from a subjective standard, where it was necessary to show intent to defraud, to an objective standard, where the test was "what a reasonable businessman would have done in all the circumstances."[66] No attributions or proofs of intent needed to be demonstrated, only the objectively established conditions of whether the company was insolvent and whether it continued to trade.[67]

---

[61] *Cork Report*: paras.1781, 1806.
[62] *Cork Report*: para.1783.
[63] *Cork Report*: paras.1782, 1790.
[64] UK Interview 90:04.
[65] UK Interview 90:04.
[66] UK Interview 90:21.
[67] There is an extensive scholarly literature on this new concept, but very little research on how it works in practice. To date, relatively few cases have wound their way through the courts. See Sealy (1989), Goode (1990), Flynn (1991), Dine (1991a, 1991b).

While personal liability for company debts might be a powerful sanction against directors, it was intended that a successful wrongful trading suit would also help replenish the estate of an insolvent corporation. During the Parliamentary debates, for instance, government minister Alex Fletcher characterized wrongful trading as "a collective remedy" in which the liquidator would bring a suit against directors, the proceeds of the successful suit to be deposited in the general pool of assets from which all creditors would benefit.[68] By making more assets available to distribute among the creditors, restitution provided a powerful monetary incentive for liquidators and creditors to initiate wrongful trading actions. However, the Government limited the scope of the Cork Committee's recommendations by deciding that applications for wrongful trading actions should be restricted to insolvency practitioners, thus forestalling the much larger number of direct actions that might have been started by distressed creditors.[69]

Prevention and Retribution: Banishment from the Market

Under the Insolvency Act 1976, a court could disqualify a director if he or she had served in two companies that had gone into insolvency within five years and if he or she displayed unfit conduct. Similar provisions were contained in company legislation.[70] Disqualification effectively banned company directors from serving on any boards for the duration of the disqualification period, which could extend up to fifteen years. But specialists on company law at the Institute of Directors acknowledged that "disqualification of directors was a joke."[71] There was little incentive for anyone to "pull the trigger." "The creditors would get what they could out of the insolvency and then wash their hands of it. They wouldn't want to be bothered say with spending more money to bring proceedings to get a director disqualified."[72] For that reason, among others, it was scarcely used.

[68] H.C., vol. 458, St. Comm. E., 4 June 1985, col. 172.

[69] The Government departed from Cork in its refusal to allow the court as much discretion in how it disbursed assets brought back into the estate by a successful wrongful trading suit. And the Government resisted the Cork proposal that directors could go to court and get an "anticipatory declaration" that their current course of action would not render them liable for wrongful trading. See Hansard, 1 Apr. 1985.

[70] For example, under section 93 of the Companies Act 1981, a director could be disqualified if he had been convicted of an offense in connection with company failure, or if he had persistently failed to satisfy certain basic obligations to file accounts, or he had been guilty of fraudulence in certain circumstances (*Cork Report* para.1812).

[71] UK Interview 90:08:12–13.

[72] UK Interview 90:11.

The Review Committee had ample support from civil servants and several trade associations to tighten disqualification sanctions; some proposals were draconian in the length of sentences and the severity of offense.[73] But Cork's Committee took a measured approach, extending the circumstances in which disqualification occurred and providing courts with a range of more or less discretionary approaches. Proceeding from the principle that "a director who, when judged by current standards of commercial morality, is found to have abused the privilege of limited liability, will forfeit that privilege," the Report recommended that it would be mandatory to disqualify a director for two years if there had been wrongful trading after only one insolvent liquidation. The court would have the discretion to increase the length of disqualification by up to fifteen years. Discretion could also be exercised to disqualify directors if "it was expedient in the public interest"—an enormous extension of court powers.[74]

Whatever the laws on the books, their efficacy depended on agents of control. On the basis of Tory ideology and prior departmental experience, the Government made it clear that it had little interest and less capacity to pursue delinquent directors through state agencies. Cork, therefore, widened the agents of control by suggesting that both liquidators and creditors could apply for disqualification. Moreover, without any economic incentives to pursue directors, Cork wanted an obligation to be imposed on liquidators to report to the Insolvency Service on any directors who warranted disqualification. Finally, the public could check on the status of any director by referring to a national register of all disqualified directors to be located at the Department of Trade.[75]

The Government embraced both the principles and concepts of director disqualification. Consistent with its posture on wrongful trading, it restricted applications for disqualification to liquidators. But its most remarkable amendment to Cork made its proposals the political lightning rod of the legislation. Contained in the Government's White Paper were provisions that *all* directors of *any* company that was pushed into compulsory liquidation would *automatically* be disqualified from

---

[73] The National Consumer Council recommended that there be "an automatic ban on any director of two or more companies which became insolvent of each other in five years" (Farrar 1983: 424–30). During the latter stages of the parliamentary debates, Mr Trotter, a Member of Parliament who was also an insolvency practitioner, wanted the possibility of disqualification for life "for reckless and criminal directors" (H.C., vol. 458, St. Comm. E., 23 May 1985, col. 154).

[74] *Minutes of the Cork Committee*, 15 Oct. 1980; *Cork Report*, paras. 1807–21.

[75] *Cork Report*: paras.1816–25.

acting as a director for three years, subject to relief from the courts. Directors had three months in which to persuade the courts that they should not be banned from management.[76]

Although few interest groups were prepared to concede it, the Government's position possessed a certain legal logic and bureaucratic rationality. The Department of Trade and Industry policy unit that produced the legislation pointed out that an individual who becomes bankrupt "is automatically disqualified anyway.... In general, company failures are more serious than bankruptcies, so it follows logically that a person who has failed whether it is in a bankruptcy or in a company should be treated the same."[77] This consistency further harmonized the personal and corporate wings of bankruptcy law, a primary purpose of the reforms. More telling was the bureaucratic impulse behind the measure. Lord Lucas, the Government leader in the Lords, unapologetically agreed that "it was a very economical way to get a lot done with limited manpower." Less benign was the judgment of his Opposition counterpart, who opined that a measure that automatically disqualified directors "shifted the onus of proof" onto a director to prove his "innocence" and demonstrated a "disinclination" of the Government "to go to the trouble and expense of initiating prosecutions."[78] Moreover, automatic disqualification seemed perfectly designed to advance the purification of markets; disqualification was a legal form of prevention—it removed from the market precisely those managers that diminished its repute and endangered its moral climate.[79]

The Government had in mind a more expansive concept of managerial responsibility that welcomed disqualification as a necessary stimulus. Broader responsibilities, the Government hoped, would lead to improved corporate governance. In the opening debate on the Insolvency Bill in the House of Lords, Lord Cameron summarized the Government's thinking about the connection between the quality of business leadership and insolvency law:

---

[76] *Government White Paper*: ch. 2.

[77] UK Interviews 91:10; 90:05.

[78] UK Interview 90:09; Lord Bruce, H.L., vol. 459, 15 Jan. 1985, col. 885.

[79] In a case subsequent to passage of the Insolvency Act, the Vice-Chancellor, Sir Nicholas Browne-Wilkinson opined that the primary purpose of the section on disqualification "is not to punish the individual but to protect the public against the future conduct of companies by persons whose past records as directors of insolvent companies have shown them to be a danger to creditors and others." *In Re Lo-Line Electric Motors Ltd & Ors* (1988) 4 BCC 415.

Automatic disqualification for directors involved in insolvency compulsory liquidation is designed to help ensure that directors carefully monitor the financial position of their companies at all times and thereby avoid the need for compulsory liquidation. It is the duty of all directors, non-executive as well as executive, to take timely action to minimize loss when financial difficulties arise or can be foreseen. Where the directors of a company have allowed it to get into such a state that the court has to intervene in its affairs, it is right that their fitness to act as directors should no longer be taken for granted.

As a result, there will have to be changes in the way some directors approach their duties. Existing and prospective directors will have to be careful to familiarize themselves with their companies' financial affairs, and to make arrangements to monitor their progress regularly. Those who come on to the board as part of a rescue operation (sometimes known as "company doctors") and the providers of risk capital are strongly placed to do this. There may be individuals who will have to limit or even reduce their commitments so as to devote sufficient attention to their companies.[80]

Put another way, automatic disqualification was designed as a sharp prod to British corporate managers. Not content with placing directors' personal assets at risk, the party of business-in-government declared its readiness to deprive directors of their livelihood altogether if they fell into a compulsory liquidation. From the point of view of market morality, the Government's manifest intentions seemed entirely valid. Automatic disqualification, it believed, would compel directors to seek professional advice earlier in the financial slide towards insolvency, force directors to sit only on those boards on which they could participate intelligently, and pressure directors to scrutinize company operations more diligently.

However impressive these reasons seemed to the Government, they were not compelling either to business or to the professions. The chorus of protest began with publication of the White Paper and continued relentlessly onto the floor of the House of Lords where it was definitively resolved. Six major objections featured in resistance to disqualification.

Ironically, pointed out Government critics, automatic disqualification would defeat one of the primary purposes of the legislation. First, directors would become so nervous about the possibility of being caught for wrongful trading or subject to disqualification that they would "jump ship" from boards prematurely and doom a company to failure.[81] Second, "company doctors" with specialist knowledge would be

---

[80] Lord Cameron, H.L., vol. 459, 15 Jan. 85, col. 878–9.
[81] Lord Marsh, H.L., vol. 459, 29 Jan. 1985, col. 613.

frightened away.[82] Mr Thurnham MP predicted that: "there is a danger that if someone is asked to join the board of a company which is in some difficulty, he will back off and not join because he will be in danger of being caught by this legislation."[83]

Thirdly, automatic disqualification also smacked of injustice. The distinguished accountant and former advisor to the Bank of England, Lord Benson, averred that this was against natural justice and amounted to "conviction without trial." And Lord Denning, formerly Master of the Rolls, and one of England's most outspoken jurists, concluded that "it was wrong to put the burden of proof on the director."[84]

A fourth objection had to do with costs: directors would be financially penalized, even if they were innocent, because clearing their names in court would be costly. And critics of the measure imagined its use for much more malevolent purposes, such as blackmail. Petitioners—creditors or liquidators— could privately threaten directors that they should "pay up personally or I will push you into disqualification by petitioning the court."[85]

A sixth objection also pointed to the irony that by solving one bureaucratic problem in one branch of government, the Bill would create a much bigger problem in another branch. Lord Meston reckoned that courts would be overwhelmed with directors seeking to exonerate themselves. Indeed, a little simple arithmetic and an assumption or two projected that some 15,000 directors would descend on the courts for relief each year.[86]

The proposal brought down a storm of criticism from the business community, led by the Institute of Directors and the Confederation of British Industry. Unwilling to back down, the Government pressed the disqualification clause until it was finally defeated—much to the shock of its legislative leaders—in the House of Lords.[87] It judiciously chose not to reinsert the offending clause in the House of Commons, where it had an overwhelming majority.

---

[82] See H.L., vol. 462, 1 Apr. 85, cols. 23–4.

[83] Thurnham, H.C., vol. 458, St. Comm. E., 14 May 1985, col. 87.

[84] Lord Benson, H.L., vol. 459, 29 Jan. 1985, col. 606.; Lord Denning, H.L., vol. 459, 29 Jan. 1985, col. 610.

[85] See Lord Meston, H.L., vol. 459, 29 Jan. 1985, col. 613; Lord Bruce, H.L., vol. 459, 29 Jan. 1985, col. 626.

[86] In any year, 10,000 liquidations would produce 20,000 directors who were automatically disqualified, 75% of whom might be expected to seek relief. See Lord Meston, H.L., vol. 459, 29 Jan. 1985, col. 614.

[87] UK Interview 90:09.

Even without automatic disqualification, the combination of personal liability for wrongful trading and disqualification for unfitness represented an important change in the moral regulation of English commerce. Wrongful trading and automatic disqualification, stated Lord Denning, "are the great new remedies brought into our law."[88] Equally important from the viewpoint of moral reconstruction, English company law for the first time put "sins of omission into the same category as sins of commission" (Sealy 1989: 39). Until 1985, directors were expected to be honest and conscientious; now the normative framework of company management introduced standards of competence and skill.

Cork's recommendations that insolvency practitioners have an obligation to file reports on those directors that they considered to be deviant had been accepted by the Government and incorporated into its Bill. The Government's original proposal was that insolvency practitioners would have a duty to report on directors where there was evidence of malfeasance. Reporting, in other words, would be discretionary.

In Parliament, however, members doubted that insolvency practitioners would take this seriously, and thus "pull the trigger" often enough for the sanctions to really take effect. Skeptical MPs pressed the Government for stronger action. The Earl of Buckinghamshire proposed that "in every winding up, whether voluntary or compulsory, the liquidator would be obliged to report whether or not in his opinion the Secretary of State should seek a qualification order."[89] In the Standing Committee debates in the Commons, Labour MP Gerald Bermingham introduced an amendment requiring insolvency practitioners to file a report on every director of an insolvent company, indicating whether there were any grounds for disqualification or potential actions for wrongful trading. This would, asserted Bermingham, benefit the standard of management and professional practice.

Such action would put the cowboy liquidators out of business because they would always be subject to scrutiny. If they were known to be involved in a liquidation, the Department would know that they had to report.... If liquidators failed to report, it would give the Department a further sanction because it could say to the liquidator, "you have not reported. What is the position".[90]

---

[88] Lord Denning, H.L., vol. 459, 15 Jan. 1985, cols. 900, 904.

[89] H.L., vol. 459, 15 Jan. 1985, col. 898.

[90] Amendment No. 22 to Clause 7; H.C., vol. 458, St. Comm. E., 14 May 1985, cols. 54–7. In a later stage of debate, Alex Fletcher, the Minister responsible for the Bill

Acceptance of this amendment by the Government ensured the universal monitoring of all directors in insolvent companies—thus vastly increasing the reach of regulatory control. This was not a privilege desired by insolvency practitioners. It required more forms to be completed and it was unrecompensed. Moreover, it operated as a secondary monitor over the professionals themselves, whose records could be periodically checked to see if they had found miscreants in the course of their work.[91] It was, in other words, also a way to regulate the regulators.

The wrongful trading and disqualification provisions ensured that regulation of directors would receive ample press. Beyond even the Government's wildest dreams, however, the socialization of directors about their new duties—and vulnerabilities—diffused widely across English company management, especially of middle-sized and larger companies. Business organizations, such as the Institute of Directors, hastened to develop and revise guides for directors that alerted them to the new standards and dangers contained in the Insolvency Act.[92] This could be as much a benefit for the association as its members. The CBI, for instance, earned a lot of money by educating members,

setting up and having seminars and going on road shows around the country. And it also shows we are interested in the members. Don't forget that. We are telling them what we have done on the bill or the act, how successful we have

in the Commons, indicated that the Department of Trade and Industry will "receive reports on all directors who have been involved in insolvency proceedings. The reports will form part of the data base which will gradually be built on all directors who have been involved in insolvency proceedings" (see H.C., vol. 83, 18 July 1985, cols. 581–88).

[91] In its 1993–94 Annual Report, the Insolvency Service sought to steer between two orientations: (1) its enforcement of guidelines that set out monitoring responsibilities of insolvency practitioners: ("...during the year a system of monitoring (insolvency practitioners') reports was implemented to ensure quality and completeness of reporting. Where practitioners fell below acceptable standards they were notified..." and followup advice was given) and (2) the Service's recognition that they could impose an administrative burden on practitioners ("...the system will be developed and refined further during 1994/95, supported by a revised report from introduced to reduce the burden on practitioners...."). Annual Report, 1993–94, The Insolvency Service, DTI Publication 133/3K/7/94.

[92] The Institute of Directors' Corporate Governance Series published a thick handbook on Directors' Personal Liabilities, including substantial sections on insolvency and disqualification. See also its Guidelines to Directors, London: Institute of Directors. More generally on directors' duties and sanctions for failure to perform them, see Souster (1987, 1990).

been, and these are the things to watch out for. Then they pay their subscriptions the next time round.[93]

Accountancy and law firms followed suit, outbidding each other in the vigor of their efforts to educate clients about their risks under the Act. For one of the primary intentions of the Act, evidently realized in subsequent practice, was to push business much closer to the legal and accountancy professions. Lord Lucas made clear that "it is the Government's view that if there is any doubt in the director's mind about the correct action to take in a particular situation . . . then his best course is to consult his professional advisors."[94] Thus, providing directors with incentives to use professionals earlier and more extensively may have been one of the most important consequences of the Act.[95] [96]

Administering Failed Corporations

If one solution to the problem of corporate control sought to improve management outside bankruptcy, another tried to facilitate recovery within the provisions of insolvency law. Outside bankruptcy, new incentives were intended to force directors to save companies and jobs by saving their own livelihoods and personal assets. Inside insolvency law, protagonists would argue for new rules that would pressure directors of failing companies to rescue those companies. Before 1986, English insolvency law did not provide very satisfactory mechanisms for the turnaround of ailing companies. It was one thing to push directors towards rehabilitative solutions. It was another thing to create a legal framework that helped to rescue companies, especially when control over the reorganization process was likely to be strongly contested. English insolvency law did rather better with liquidation of companies than reorganization. Thus company rescue featured prominently in reform discussions. Underlying all those discussions were tacit and manifest expectations over who should control the faltering company once it came under the protection of insolvency law.

At the onset of reform in 1976, companies in financial distress had three main alternatives:

[93] UK Interview 91:09.
[94] Lord Lucas, H.L., vol. 462, 1 Apr. 1985, col. 20.
[95] UK Interview 90:14.
[96] Disqualification orders in 1992–93 totalled 341 (disqualifications for 2–4 years), 100 (disqualifications for 6–10 years), and 5 (disqualifications for 11–15 years); and in 1993–94, 266 (2–5 years), 120 (6–10 years), and 13 (11–15 years). Annual Report, 1993–4, The Insolvency Service, Department of Trade and Industry, pp. 8–9.

(1) *Deeds of Arrangement.* A company in distress needed the agreement of a substantial proportion of its creditors for a binding arrangement, sanctioned by the court, to reschedule its debt. In a variant on the court-sanctioned method, it was possible to make an arrangement outside the court if the company could obtain agreement from 75 per cent (in number or value) of all its creditors.

(2) *Winding Up or Liquidation.* Through compulsory or voluntary methods, a company entered an orderly process for dissolution, either under control of a court, or without direct involvement of the court.

(3) *Receivership.* A secured lender with a floating charge could appoint an accountant or insolvency practitioner as a "receiver" to take over the business and take whatever steps served the best interests of the lender, whether to continue the business, or liquidate it and distribute the assets to the highest ranking creditors, most notably the bank that appointed the receiver.[97]

Neither schemes of arrangement nor receivership provided strong incentives or mechanisms for anyone to rescue companies. Indeed, the law seemed to frustrate efforts by directors, banks, or insolvency practitioners to turn insolvent companies around.

English legal culture holds little sympathy for directors and managers who run their companies into the ground. In the creditors' culture that pervades English commercial law, the failure of a company results not from general macro-economic forces, industry shake-outs, or market downturns, but specifically from managerial incompetence and misfortune.[98] Company rescue cannot therefore be entrusted to directors. Indeed, the very first step in any effort at reorganization will be to supercede the authority of the current managers. English insolvency practitioners were nonplussed by approaches to reorganization that left managers in control, or debtors in possession, of their companies. A former president of the Insolvency Practitioners Association said: "Our main objection to the Chapter 11 procedure (in the United States) is that you are leaving the company in the hands of the guys who got it into a hell of a mess in the first place." Stated another leading practitioner, "... the one principle of leaving the debtor in possession is abhorrent. They failed once, what makes you think they are going to make good a second time. In fact the second time they will probably do it even worse

---

[97] For a more precise and detailed description of alternatives for liquidation and reorganization, see *Cork Report*: 46–52, 97–101.

[98] For instance, the Cork Report states "... the majority of debtors are considered to be incompetent...." *Cork Report*: 64.

than they did the first time. And the costs involved are horrendous." Put more pungently, "a debtor maintaining control of his or her corporation certainly could not work here. It an open door to abuse."[99] If English insolvency law displaced managers inside insolvency, it offered perverse incentives for them to continue trading as long as possible before insolvency, in the hope of a turnaround.

Schemes of arrangement offered little hope. None of the mechanisms in place provided what a company beset by creditors needed most: a binding hold or moratorium on debt collection by all creditors. Unless there was a floating charge in place, "an absolute hole" in the law did not permit directors or insolvency practitioners to "stay" claims by all creditors and give the company some "breathing space" for reconstruction.

There were numerous companies going through difficulties which didn't happen to have a debenture under which someone could appoint a receiver. And so there was no means in that awful twilight world where there's a vacuum, where nobody's got any information, the creditors are issuing writs, they've got judgments, they are petitioning, in which the company just folds. . . . There was just no way in which it could be done.[100]

Consequently, directors had no way of stopping a rush by creditors to the assets. Those measures in place took too long and were too complicated.

The problem was compounded many times in insolvencies where huge companies had large numbers of creditors spread over many countries. Since very large companies could often obtain credit without strong securities, such as a floating charge, a threatened collapse left few effective mechanisms for restructuring debt or the company.

A particularly good example that was current at the time of the Cork Committee, was the Massey-Ferguson collapse. . . . Sir Kenneth himself was masterminding recovery for that group world wide. But, there was no machinery there. It was just a bunch of talking to all the lenders, "Don't you pull the rug. Don't you file the petition for liquidation." It was grandly orchestrated meetings of all the creditors . . . of the major creditors to get them to hold back and permit the survival of Massey-Ferguson. . . . It was orchestrated without any legal machinery whatsoever. It was all done by consensus among the creditors and the company itself.

Cork, himself, expressed great frustration at the law's inability to save Rolls Royce, which "should never have gone into liquidation," but should have been turned around short of insolvency. But Rolls Royce

---

[99] UK Interviews 90:14; 90:12; 90:21.   [100] UK Interviews 90:20; 91:20.

merely symbolized a vastly greater problem.[101] If only professionals could get into companies at an earlier stage of financial decline, then they could take action to save the company. Cork believed that if only he had been able to deal with companies earlier, "four out of five never needed to have been insolvent." The lack of legal provisions to save a company short of insolvency simultaneously encouraged directors to keep trading, delayed the introduction of experts who might have turned the company around, and gave rogue creditors incentives to break ranks of informal moratoriums over debt collection. All militated against company rescue.

Even in those cases where a floating charge was in place, and lenders could appoint a receiver (a private accountant or insolvency practitioner) to run the company, rehabilitation of the business was hardly assured. Indeed, one recurring complaint by managers and unsecured creditors centered on the roughshod ways that secured lenders asserted their rights, liquidated a company, recovered their assets, and gave little consideration to losses incurred by more junior creditors. After all, receivers looked out for the interests of the bank that appointed them, not the interests of the business or the other creditors.

Cork and all always liked to say that when you put in receivers, it was a way of saving the business. But actually, the first thing the receiver does is say, "how am I going to get my appointor's, my debenture-holder's, money back?" A bank is owed 10 million, you put the receiver in, the receiver's job is to find 10 million, and it often did lead to liquidation.[102]

Bankers and some receivers contested the notion that receivers looked out only for the interests of the secured lender. "We think the better receivers say they have a duty to the company, and the banks acquiesce at the moment," stated a member of the Cork Committee to government witnesses. And as the representative of the Committee of London Clearing Bankers asserted, "we would like to place emphasis on the receiver/manager turning a company around, which happens so very often, if not totally, certainly in viable parts. . . . " Nevertheless, said the bankers, while receivers might have some regard for the interests of members, employees, and creditors, their prime responsibility is to the holder of the floating charge.[103] Furthermore, a floating charge can

[101] UK Interviews 90:04; 91:07.

[102] UK Interview 91:20.

[103] Oral testimony of the Committee of London Bankers, 8 Sept. 1980, *Public Record Office*; Oral testimony from the Department of Trade, 22 Oct. 1980; Oral testimony of the Committee of London Bankers, *Public Record Office*, 4 June 1979.

make charge-holders more permissive towards directors and allow them to continue trading beyond the point when unsecured creditors would be paid in full, because the floating charge-holder can still recover his assets.[104]

Banks that enforced their security not infrequently vindicated the proposition that security enforced in a fragmentary manner "will realize less than if it can be sold off collectively."

It's nice if you can sell the chaise along with the engine, along with the body. We had a phenomenon referred to as "feeling blue chips." These were all blue chip companies without a floating charge—with fixed charges. When they got into difficulty or faced acute problems of collective behavior, the fixed charge-holders appointed their receiver, realized the security, and ran. [105]

If banks did not have floating or fixed charges, they were often unsecured creditors and therefore as vulnerable as any other unsecured creditor. The floating charge was affixed most often to middle level, not very large or very small, companies. But even in circumstances where many banks held floating charges in the assets of a large company, there was potential conflict and confusion over how to coordinate a recovery operation.

As a result, the law offered no framework for rescuing companies before they were technically insolvent. It gave a very limited mechanism, in the role of the receiver, for some creditors to effect a reorganization. And it left a void, before and after insolvency, for outside experts to hold creditors at bay while they scrambled to turn around the company. In short, the problem of control manifested itself in scattered ways: consensus decreed that directors could not remain in control; no one could be sure of control short of bankruptcy; secured creditors might obtain control once a company was insolvent, but that didn't help creditors who remained at arms length, and it helped not at all in situations where there was no security and thus no mechanism for anyone to push for reorganization.

Proposals for Company Rescue

Cork and several members of his committee initially intended to create new legal mechanisms to save businesses and give unsecured creditors a better deal. But they were not alone. In mid-1977, the British Bankers

---

[104] Oral Testimony, British Chambers of Commerce, *Public Record Office*, 28 June 1977.
[105] UK Interview 90:14.

Association wrote to the Cork Committee that "a procedure for the appointment of a manager and for a moratorium amongst creditors short of winding up would . . . be a useful innovation. Many companies get into difficulty through a shortage of cash at a particular time and some method to bridge the gap covering a cash shortage would be of immeasurable value." The Committee of London Clearing Bankers liked that idea, too, when there was no floating charge and no way to appoint a receiver. The professions agreed. During oral testimony through 1978, the City of London Solicitors recommended a "moratorium system" that would hold all creditors at bay while an independent administrator attempted to sort things out, a view supported by the Joint Working Party of solicitors and barristers. The joint accountancy bodies expressed general support for a short term moratorium. The British Chambers of Commerce also liked a "speedy process" that would produce a moratorium on debt collection.[106] Although banks claimed that they did try to take other creditors into consideration, organized labor argued strongly that insolvency law should impose a duty on receivers to take employee interests into account.[107]

The Cork Committee told the Committee of London Clearing Bankers that they were "considering the idea that a receiver appointed under a floating charge" should have a "statutory duty" to look after the company, its members, and employees. Similarly, committee members signalled to the Department of Trade and Industry that it intended the receiver in control of the insolvent company "should act as much as it can for the community." Receivers should have a statutory duty "to realize assets for the benefit of all."[108]

With such fairly broad-based support for a new mechanism to produce company turnarounds, the Cork Committee proposed creation of a new office, new procedures, and new opportunities to rescue businesses before either the directors were culpable or the business was

[106] Submission by British Bankers Association, 15 Aug. 1977; Oral testimony of the Committee of London Clearing Bankers, 8 Sept. 1980; Memorandum from the London Solicitors Company (undated) and subsequent oral testimony, 12 Oct. 1978; Oral testimony, Joint Working Party, 12 Nov. 1980; Written submission by British Chambers of Commerce, 28 June 1977; Oral testimony, *Public Record Office*, 24 Nov. 1980.

[107] Indeed, the TUC recommended that the receiver give particular attention to maintaining employment of workers and they recommended a "committee of control" which would include workers, a suggestion that got a cool reception from several members of the Committee. TUC, oral testimony, *Public Record Office*, 11 May 1978.

[108] Oral testimony, Department of Trade, Company's Division, 22 Oct. 1980; Oral testimony of the Committee of London Clearing Bankers, 8 Sept. 1980.

beyond hope. Appointments of receivers by holders of floating-charges provided the model. In those cases, a receiver could take control of a business, "slim it down," and sell the business as a going concern, which could save a lot of jobs. So the Cork Committee pursued the idea "that even if there isn't a debenture (floating charge), let's try and get the same results," albeit with some important modifications.[109]

The Cork Report recommended that in cases where a company was in, or near insolvency, then the company, or directors, or creditors, or the government could apply to the court for appointment of an administrator, who would be a qualified insolvency practitioner. At the appointment, a moratorium would be imposed on all efforts by creditors to enforce their security or collect their assets, and so gave the administrator much-needed breathing room. The administrator would be given a period of several weeks to examine the companies affairs and develop a general strategy for the company's rehabilitation. If creditors approved, reorganization could proceed. If not, the company could go into liquidation. Once the creditors approved the administrators' proposals, he would take control of the company and attempt to turn it around. If he succeeded, the administration order could be dissolved and control would return to management. If there was no prospect of rehabilitation, he could put the company into liquidation.[110]

To the Cork Committee, administration had many merits. First, it gave managers a positive incentive and credible mechanism to seek protection from disqualification and wrongful trading suits. "What are our directors to do when they are faced with a situation where they may feel that liquidation is no longer avoidable? And their answer is that they ought then to consider administration." The punitive measures on directors provided a trigger to push companies to obtain outside help earlier. "There was not much point in having wrongful trading if you didn't give them a way out, so the way out was to apply for an administration order." A related inducement made administrations more attractive to managers, for they could retain, or imagine they might retain, some measure of control. "... [T]hey think they can beat the rap. First of all they might persuade the creditors to go along with something less than a full blown insolvency where the truth might be discovered. Secondly, they are able to nominate straight away the

---

[109] UK Interview 91:14.

[110] *Cork Report*, ch. 9. For a lucid analysis of administration orders under the Insolvency Act 1986, see Goode (1990).

insolvency practitioner of their choice who might be more friendly" than an unknown person.[111]

Secondly, administration was good for professionals. Indeed it was designed to bring in professional advice earlier in the process of financial decline, partly to inform directors, partly to obtain expert advice, and partly as a form of insurance, for the early involvement of professionals offered a positive defense against wrongful trading and disqualification. Said one member of the Cork Committee:

[I]t was terribly important in terms of saving businesses and giving people time to think in that awful panic-stricken world of "we're nearly bust, what the hell are we going to do," to introduce a simple way in which you get in a professional, you go to court, the professional is made the boss, there's a stay on everything and he has about three months to see if he can work it out. [112]

Thirdly, the freeze on efforts to collect debts solved two problems simultaneously: administrators had time to take stock and act deliberately without the enormous pressure of losing assets to creditors; and it solved the collective action problem of enforcing security in a fragmentary manner. Like many collective action problems, a race to seize assets might work well for the first creditors to enforce their security, but such a race frequently toppled the business as a going concern and harmed unsecured creditors. However, unsecured creditors sometimes included banks, and on those occasions when they, too, had little or no security, a device that did not disadvantage them seemed appealing. And since the role of the administrator looked quite like a receiver, bankers felt some comfort in this new machinery.[113]

Finally, Cork explicitly defined the administrator as an agent of *all* the creditors:

not just one set of creditors, not just another set, they are doing the best for the whole. And they are not beholden to the old management, they are not beholden to their appointor. They are a court appointed individual and they do it as they see best.

---

[111] UK Interviews 91:14; 90:21.

[112] UK Interview 91:14.

[113] According to one banker close to the Cork Committee, "it [the administration order] was always seen primarily as a remedy for the failure of very big companies. Not your medium sized British company, but very big ones where there was no security.... the administration seemed to provide a useful way of organizing the rescue. So, there was no particular problem, particularly if they saw that the role of the administrator was not vastly different from the role of the receiver." UK Interview 91:06.

While the idea of an administrator found much favor among professionals, banks were more ambivalent, since they were usually secured creditors (although some portion of their claims might be unsecured), and had a right to appoint their own receiver. The innovation threatened their power to appoint who they wanted when they wanted. The Committee mollified the banks by proposing that holders of floating charges must be notified of an application for an administration order. If the floating charge covered most or all of the company's assets, then the holder of the charge had the right to appoint a receiver in preference to an administrator. If the receiver had a charge over a limited proportion of the assets, he might then be appointed as an administrator.[114]

The administration order gave companies and secured creditors more flexibility to respond to financial problems. Since there are "a wide range of reasons that companies get into difficulties," the administration order provided secured creditors with some motivation to distinguish between "that family of situations that is terminal from that family of situations that are curable."[115] Indeed, while the Cork Committee anticipated that banks and secured creditors would usually choose to appoint their own receivers, there could be circumstances in which they would waive that right in favor of administrators. The Confederation of British Industry took a rather more guarded approach to the concept. While they were not opposed to the idea, they did not think it would be used much in practice.[116]

Public Debate over the Cork Report and Government Bill

Major newspapers, well-briefed by Kenneth Cork, endorsed the new measures. If saving businesses was a central goal of the Cork Report, then the creation of "a new corporate fireman" with powers to "keep firms afloat" was a significant innovation. *The Times* featured the administrator as a "key recommendation" of the Cork Report and endorsed the concept that "a new type of company doctor should be created by the law in an attempt to staunch the record-breaking torrent of company failures."[117] The papers accompanied their reports with Cork's repeated statements that administration orders offered a way of formalizing earlier informal efforts at intensive care—with legal teeth to solve the problem of co-ordinating multiple, cross-cutting claims by creditors.

---

[114] *Cork Report*: para. 504, 118.   [115] UK Interview 90:14.
[116] UK Interview 90:06.
[117] *Financial Times*, 6 Oct. 1982, p. 11; *The Times*, 4 Apr. 1982, p. 49.

Cork and the papers clearly construed administration orders as a problem of control. Cork viewed the prospect of administration orders as a way that creditors could "apply to the courts for control of a company long before it goes bankrupt," a sentiment echoed by the *Financial Times*. Cork saw this explicitly as a revolt of shareholders or creditors against the directors.[118]

The Government White Paper and subsequent bill assimilated most of the Reform Committee's recommendations for the appointment of administrators, with a critical deviation. While the Government asserted its commitment to "a more effective method of achieving rehabilitation or reorganization," it proposed that administrators might only be appointed when the company actually "is insolvent or close to insolvency." This was not at all what Cork had in mind:

> ...the Department of Trade, I couldn't persuade them to do it. In my report, you could have an administrator even if the company was not insolvent. My idea was that go back to Rolls Royce, which should never have gone into liquidation. Rolls Royce ought to have gone into administration, and we wouldn't have the trauma of this famous British company going broke which was ridiculous. It wasn't even insolvent, it paid twenty shillings a pound.... I wanted a provision in the Act where the shareholders, or the Department of Trade could say, "Look, this company is going down with a loony body of directors." Apply to get an administrator without it being insolvent....I never intended the administrator should be an act of insolvency. But the Department of Trade, particularly the OR, as we call the receivers department, couldn't understand how anything could happen when it wasn't insolvent.[119]

The Cork Report reads more ambiguously. On the one hand, it proposes that "the Court should have power to appoint an Administrator whenever it is satisfied by evidence that it is expedient to do so." On the other hand, it moves immediately to specify the prospect of appointing an Administrator in the more precise conditions of (a) "jeopardy to the general body of creditors," and (b) insolvency, with (c) the giant catch-all in reserve, "the public interest." In all cases there should be some reasonable expectation that reorganization will succeed.[120]

When the Bill was introduced in the Lords, the Government featured as the fourth principal purpose of the legislation its "new insolvency mechanism, known as company administration, specifically designed to facilitate company rescue and reorganization." Although the Govern-

---

[118] *Financial Times*, 21 Apr., 1982, p. 20; UK Interview 90:04.
[119] *Cork Report*: 19; UK Interview 90:04.   [120] *Cork Report*: para. 506, 11.

ment's "business rescue scheme" obtained general support from both parties, it attracted a number of amendments in the Lords and the Commons. Some sought to specify various financial standards—a balance sheet test, contingent and prospective liabilities, a cash flow crisis—under which an administrator could be appointed. More pointed were amendments over control: whether a floating charge holder could block an administrator (this provision was retained on grounds that a "very delicate balance" needed to be struck with the debenture holders), or a committee of creditors would be functioning in a "supervisory" capacity, and thus actively intervening in managerial decisions being taken by the administrator (the Government changed the language and insisted that creditors' committee had the power to accept the proposal for reorganization by the administrator and thereafter only "to raise questions and to receive answers.")[121]

In the Commons, the Government explicitly cast the administrative provisions in terms of control and thereby sharply contrasted its new rescue provisions with Chapter 11 in the US Bankruptcy Code, where management remains in control. The Minister claimed that the English approach is "bolder and more radical" for "there must be a change of control" and the administrator must have "the power to dismiss directors and appoint new ones and generally to take personal control of the business."[122] Successful corporate reorganizations required a change at the top.

While the Opposition welcomed the new procedures, it vainly raised two concerns. Bryan Gould introduced an amendment to place at least one worker on the administrator's committee. In addition, "the administrator should be under a clear statutory duty to consult and inform the work force. He should have a general duty as well to safeguard employment." Echoing the debate in the Lords, the Opposition attacked the veto power given to floating charge-holders, who could exercise their right to install a receiver rather than the administrator. Charging that the Government has been "perhaps too solicitous of the banks' interests," the Opposition introduced an amendment that gave courts the right to override holders of floating charges, if their interests would be protected by an administrator, and if the court determined it would be better to appoint an administrator to satisfy "wider objectives."[123] That,

---

[121] H.L., vol. 458, 15 Jan. 1985, col. 876; H.L., vol. 459, 4 Feb. 1985, cols. 847–78.

[122] H.C., St. Comm. E, 20 June 1985, col. 450.

[123] H.C., vol. 78, 30 Apr. 1985, col. 156; H.C., St. Comm. E, 20 June 1985, cols. 468–75. Note that the Administrator can deal with or dispose of property subject to a

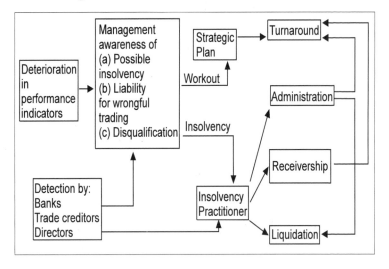

Fɪɢ. 6.2: **Schematic Representation of UK Insolvency Procedure: Post–1986**
Source: Adapted from Campbell and Underdown, *Corporate Insolvency in Practice* (1991)

too, lost in committee. In the event, the Bill permitted administrators to be appointed readily when no floating charges were in place, but it made far more contingent the prospect of an administrator when there was a floating charge in place.

Although there were initial "teething troubles" and a slow start in use of the new provisions (see Fig. 6.2), many of the reformers expressed surprise at how often banks with floating charges did permit creditors to appoint an administrator.[124] The reasons were varied. Banks could avoid some of "the stigma of putting in a receiver," or of "suffering the odium of putting the company into liquidation," if they were confident that a good administrator would do as well for them as a receiver—indeed, it might well have been the same person. Moreover, banks could secure some goodwill from unsecured creditors, whom several observers believed were better off with the new regime. And if

floating charge, given that the floating charge holder has declined to appoint a receiver. (H.C., St. Comm. E, 20 June 1985, cols. 451–2).

[124] An early survey by Mark Homan has been seen as evidence that the new measures were successful in the survival of a majority of companies that were reorganized by an administrator. In 40 per cent of cases in this survey, floating-charge holders permitted an administration when they could have appointed their own receiver (Homan 1987; Goode 1990: 112).

tough measures needed to be taken, banks might prefer the administrator and not their receiver to be the object of criticism.

MARKET EFFICIENCY AND MARKET MORALITY

Political meta-bargaining over corporate reorganization dealt with two
issues. For the general architects of public policy, the stakes turned on
the political, social and economic costs of high rates of corporate failures. The magnitude of such costs favored new laws that would help to
save troubled firms. For the central actors in the credit network, the
stakes turned on who would control either the choice about whether to
attempt rehabilitation, or how to rehabilitate a company if it seemed a
likely option. The two sets of issues, of course, interrelate because a
decision about which actors are most likely to produce effective company turnarounds then becomes the basis for a policy to place greater
control in their hands.

That the stakes are high can be gauged from patterns of mobilization.
Three parties predominated on either side of the Atlantic. The financial
institutions in both countries fought to protect their secured assets,
especially when their own agents were not in control of an insolvent
debtor corporation. Yet, in the face of a considerable push to encourage
reorganizations, financial institutions were prepared to yield control to
managers (in the US) or administrators (in the UK) if they retained some
rights to present their own candidates to run a company (receivers in the
UK) or their own plan for its reorganization (creditors in the US).
Essentially their negotiating positions were similar: both were under
pressure not to send companies to premature graves, and thus each
was prepared to tolerate new mechanisms of company rescue, so long as
their security was maintained or preferably even strengthened. State
agencies mobilized strongly in either country—the Securities and
Exchange Commission (SEC) to retain its privileged position in the
reorganization of large public companies, and the Department of
Trade and Industry in its interest to discipline directors and produce
company rescues—without new burdens of responsibility to be placed
on civil servants.

But it was the professionals whose influence was pervasive, within
constraints set by the banks and the state. English insolvency practitioners and lawyers invented the concept of administration orders and
administrators, an innovation adopted by the government and written

into the legislation. Lawyers and judges in the United States vigorously pressed alternative models of company reorganization, and thus debated among themselves almost as strongly as with the banking industry. And in both countries, it was the experts on the Commission and Review Committee who endorsed most strongly the shift from corporate liquidation to reorganization. We reserve until Part III a fuller treatment of jurisdictional interests, but it should be noted that the shift from liquidation to reorganization also created considerable demand for professional accounting, financial and legal services.

Notably absent in the meta-bargaining were the managers and directors themselves and representatives of shareholders, despite their central role in the conflict between labor and capital, the basic contradiction in capitalist society (Chambliss 1993). In the United States, no organization of managers or business mobilized to carry their banner. In Britain, the Institute of Directors and Confederation of British Industry mobilized only when direct assaults on hallowed institutions—limited liability, personal assets of managers—put all directors potentially at risk. The championing of company directors in the United States, therefore, came not from their own lobbies, but from lawyers.

The centrality of company control and the autonomy of managers as issues in the bankruptcy reforms can also be observed in the conflicts that broke out around them. Resistance by the SEC to the Bankruptcy Bill was one of the two great hurdles that almost unsaddled the entire statutory package. Automatic disqualification of directors and suits against directors for wrongful trading absorbed more Parliamentary time than any other measure and cost the Government an embarrassing defeat in the House of Lords.

Who, then, controls the insolvent or near insolvent company? In the United States, managers or debtors obtained the protections necessary to escape pressure by creditors, to obtain breathing space to develop a reorganization plan, and to rehabilitate their companies with themselves at the helm. It did not matter that managers might not last through their tenure as debtors-in-possession under the protection of Chapter 11. The reforms offered them strong incentives to file early, save their companies, and protect their positions. Nevertheless this discretion was bounded with two sets of constraints: the permission of the courts; and the need to obtain credit. In the UK, directors might control the timing of the double-edged protection given by the Insolvency Act. They could choose when to file for an administration order, and might even succeed in the appointment of their administrator of choice. But undoubtedly their discretion was limited by banks' willingness to suspend their right to appoint a receiver, if they had a floating charge, and more radically, by the rights of an administrator to dismiss them and run the company at will, subject to various limits. In short, while the state provided the procedural parameters, and the financial institutions set credit parameters, American managers had the prospect of remaining in control of their companies during reorganization, while English directors were expeditiously removed from control.[125]

A comparison of these two industrial capitalist powers displays some unsurprising similarities but also a radical difference. Common to both was commitment by almost all parties (with the possible exception of banks) to rehabilitation as a constructive value, and consequently to the incentive schemes that would locate corporate control with those best able to return a company to profitability. Yet designations of which party—the state, managers, creditors—was best equipped to produce the turnaround, and how to ensure that they controlled the company, diverged sharply. Given the substantial similarity between the two countries in terms of capital market structure and the nature of those operating in them (companies, managers, creditors, shareholders, etc.), one might expect reorganization rules to converge to a single, optimal form. Because they diverge so sharply, the explanation must lie somewhere among differences in other economic forces, or differences in theories of managerial motivation, firm behavior, political or economic ideology. Put another way, differences in bankruptcy incentive structures, their ends and means, are embedded in wider economic, institutional, and cultural frameworks.

Since the English were well aware of Chapter 11, and yet chose explicitly to reject it, the English case suggests how models of corporate governance in bankruptcy derive from cultural forces and ideologies.[126] The English divergence grew out of intermediate level theories of firm failure and macro-economic and social ideologies about the market as an effective institution.

The Cork Committee adopted its new reorganization regime fully aware of the sharp contrast with Chapter 11 in US bankruptcy law, which left managers in control. As Cork himself noted, "we studied

---

[125] The contrast looks stronger than it is in practice. American managers turn over at a high rate during bankruptcy. English directors may stay through administrations and emerge as managers in control on the other side.

[126] This possibility clearly relates to the kind of analysis done by Frank Dobbin (1994) on national/cultural differences in business and industrial regulation.

Chapter 11. We had the advantage that the Bank of England did too," for it had a department that monitored businesses "going broke" and it was "very keen" on Chapter 11. But after a team visited the United States, its leader told Cork "it is totally against our principles [b]ecause it leaves the debtor in possession." [127] Two reasons seemed to lie behind this emphatic rejection of the US Chapter 11 approach.

First, incumbent managers and directors represented the shareholders, and with an insolvent company, shareholders simply had no more stake in the company: their interest had diminished to zero. Thus, corporate control should shift into other hands:

But... once a company is insolvent and is carrying on business at a loss (lets assume the two are combined), who does it really belong to? And the answer has to be the creditors. The shareholders no longer have any financial interest at all. And I think the whole attitude of English law is... once that stage has been reached for goodness sake it must be up to the creditors to decide what to do.[128]

Whoever might lead a reorganization, this analysis suggested, it should not be someone acting on behalf of shareholders.

Leaving incumbent management in control was ill-advised for another reason: the blame for insolvency lay squarely at management's door. Poor managerial decisions led to financial disaster. With their shortcomings so amply demonstrated, it made little sense to keep them in place if the intention was to save the company.

... the key thing which strikes me is the weakness of Chapter 11 ... is what we over here sometimes refer to as shutting the fox in the hen house. You put the debtor in possession and either the debtor has no experience in insolvency proceedings, in which case he does not know what to do once Chapter 11 occurs, and he has got a crisis to manage with no experience of the framework within which he has got to manage in. Or alternatively, he's been the manager of so many bust companies that the best you can hope for is that you have got an experienced debtor in possession who is going to screw up so many properties that he has got a lot of experience. That strikes us as crazy.[129]

English insolvency experts averred that an independent outsider—like themselves—could certainly do no worse than management, and would most probably do better.[130]

[127] UK Interview 90:04.
[128] UK Interview 91:14.
[129] UK Interview 91:11.
[130] Another insolvency expert put it thus: "But certainly that approach [Chapter 11] to rehabilitation was not the English way. We saw the need for a more sophisticated remedy,

Cultural and structural factors may also have played a part in the solid English rejection of Chapter 11. Peter Graham QC believes that the "pioneering spirit" so admired in the United States supported entrepreneurial risk, whereas the English did not "encourage people to go out on a limb." The English did not applaud unlucky failures, even if they had made a good try. Structurally, the great dispersion of large American companies over many states and the fragmentation of the banking industry favored leaving managers in place who understood the complexities of their own industry and organization. In the UK, smaller companies drew most of their financing from only five or six national banks. The concentration of banking and the less complex form of companies lent themselves to decisive intervention by banks and to quick appraisals and formulation of business plans by independent professionals.[131]

Finally, even lawyers close to the Cork Committee agreed that it was highly desirable to keep lawyers at bay and the courts at arms length during reorganizations. "Chapter 11 is very much a court driven process," said a leading English barrister, "with the lawyers having a predominant role. Administration is designed to work without automatic access to the court, and to be run by a chartered accountant." The transaction costs exacted by disputes among parties represented by lawyers would "eat up huge amounts of money" that could otherwise be directed to reviving the company.[132] Lawyers showed no sign of breaking the professional consensus in favor of new procedures that would draw more heavily on their services.

Finally, English reformers were convinced that a strong administrator or receiver could act far more decisively and swiftly than Chapter 11 permitted. Without the need to go back to the courts for rulings, and with few constraints by current management, the administrator could quickly appraise the scope of the problem, sell off parts of the enterprise, release staff—all without encumbrance by employees, directors, creditors, or courts. Professional dominance of corporate affairs would ensure rapid turnaround, if turnaround was possible. If speed of turn-

---

if there was the possibility of saving the business as a going concern, but even so, our experience of the adequacy of . . . managers, particularly if they've got the company onto the rocks, was that it was best to bring in a new broom, a new approach, a new individual. And that is I think the English philosophy." UK Interview 90:21.

[131] *Ibid.*
[132] UK Interviews 91:14; 91:08.

around was the primary indicator of efficiency, the English expedient seemed clearly superior.

These pragmatic alternatives to the American solution were embedded in the long English history of suspicion about debtors and an equal ambivalence about the relative primacy of the state or private practitioners in dealing with their failures. But the particular solutions institutionalized in the Insolvency Act sprang also from the political and economic ideology of Thatcherism, as it appropriated and adapted the inventiveness of English professionals.

Thatcherism demanded a fundamental re-ordering of the relations between the state and the market, between the public and private sectors (Joseph 1976; Gamble 1988: 4). In so far as the Conservatives were ideologically committed to shifting public goods onto the private market, they confronted the task of reconstructing market institutions so that they were capable of handling responsibilities devolved from the state, and persuading the public of the appropriateness of the market for functions previously thought indissolubly the domain of the state. Privatization demanded both structural and cultural transformation.

Structurally, privatization entailed shifting assets through the withdrawal of government from the ownership and management of state industries and state-owned housing. At the same time, privatization was directed to the provision of services by making users pay for government services, contracting public services out to private firms, breaking monopoly powers and enforcing competition, and withdrawing the state entirely from the provision of its previous responsibilities. Rolling back the state, dismantling of monopolies, deregulation, and competition were the catchwords of the new political order (Gamble 1989).

But privatization of industries previously nationalized by earlier governments also committed the Government to fundamental changes both in public attitudes and behavior—a cultural transformation in public understanding of markets and their functions. Mrs Thatcher aimed "to create a mood where it is everywhere thought morally right for as many people as possible to acquire capital."[133] The minister responsible for privatization pronounced that it would "produce an irreversible shift in attitudes and achievement which will bring lasting benefits to the United Kingdom." And in her closing speech to the 1985 Conservative Party conference, Mrs Thatcher beckoned Britain to "come with us then

---

[133] See Wolfe's (1996) discussion of the Thatcherite rationale for privatization, namely to broaden share ownership in Britain and obtain wider political support for market based decision-making.

towards the next decade. Let us together set our sights upon a Britain...where owning shares is as common as having a car...."[134] Yet confidence in British markets was at a low ebb. Since the beginning of the 1970s and into the next decade, reports about the sorry state of the economy repeatedly confronted a public who had witnessed at close hand the long-term decline of British industry.

In the context of the insolvency legislation, talk of market morality sprang from all the parties to law reform. Reformers believed they knew what market morality was not, even when they were unable to articulate what it was. As a government "committed to the expansion of private enterprise," commented a Conservative backbencher, the Conservatives were "very much sensitive to the kind of arguments that were somehow being suggested by the socialists to the effect that private enterprise was by definition morally less defensible that state enterprise." To the extent that the opposition could point to flagrant abuses of market morality, "then the arguments in favor of privatization would always be seen to be morally deficient."[135] As a matter of party politics, quite apart from shifting economic culture, the Government felt compelled to lay moral foundations on which a market edifice could be constructed.

The revision of English insolvency law offered Mrs Thatcher's Government an unusual vehicle to address problems that extended far beyond the technicalities of liquidation and corporate reorganization. Conservative ideology committed the Government to reduce the size of the state and reinvigorate markets. Privatization demanded public trust and confidence in a discredited institution. Trust and confidence, believed the Government, could be instilled only if markets were seen to be efficient and market actors were perceived to be accountable. During the debates in the House of Commons, Sir Brandon Rhys Williams perceptively captured governmental intent to create trust through sanitized markets: "This Bill is part of the strategy that (the Government) are pursuing to make the capitalist system on which we rely for the creation of wealth, more effective, cleaner, and altogether a healthier system, in which people can entrust their savings" as investors.[136] Insolvency reform presented an unlikely path towards a renovation of market morality, which the Government nevertheless followed.

---

[134] *The Economist*, 19 Oct. 1985; *The Times*, 12 Oct. 1985: 4; Hall, P. (1992: 111).

[135] UK Interview 91:16:10–11.

[136] H.C., vol. 87., St. Comm. E., 30 Apr. 1985, col. 202.

But if the English aspiration to reconstitute market morality far exceeded the pragmatics of market efficiency in the American statute, both stood on common ground in a critical respect—the centrality of professions. Not only were professionals integrally engaged in the reformulations of corporate control in bankruptcy, but they emerged as the primary agents of rehabilitation in each country. When placing debtors in possession of company reorganizations, US reformers assured that rights of creditors would be protected by lawyers and judges in the courts. As a result, as the English critics pointed out time and again, the price of greater discretion for company directors in the United States was a sharp increase in the transaction costs of legal representation of all parties to a Chapter 11 filing. As we shall show in Chapter 9, economic incentives built into the 1978 Bankruptcy Act were intended to attract the best and brightest lawyers into the bankruptcy field. It is not without some merit that Father Drinan called the Bankruptcy Act a "full employment bill" for lawyers.

The English legislation can similarly be interpreted as a significant opportunity for insolvency practitioners to lock into place a domain of work, so that informal workouts now became formal, and persuasion of creditors became coercion in the form of a legal moratorium. The invention of the administrator permitted English insolvency practitioners to move away from the odium that can accompany zealous advocacy of the interests of one party to insolvency proceedings. Like banks, receivers too recognized the unpopularity of liquidations where floating-charge holders reclaimed their assets at the cost of other creditors. In the face of a backlash against the banks, the new administration orders permitted insolvency practitioners to distance themselves from close identification with secured creditors into the more defensible and classical position of relative disinterestedness that professions typically claim for themselves.

In short, while states in both countries sought forms of control that would save more companies, and while the banks yielded a little control over management so long as they retained strong control over their secured assets, the primary architects of the new regimes in England and the United States—the professions—repositioned themselves with greater centrality in broader domains of lucrative work. Whoever controls the corporation in bankruptcy, professionals remained in control of bankruptcy.

7 Empowering The Weak: The "Forgotten Class"

Shield International Corporation sold books, records, and horoscopes. It advertised widely in national magazines, and sold its wares through the mail. In the final year of its descent towards insolvency, complaints about *Shield International* began to appear frequently in the in-boxes of consumer protection agencies, for it had perfected the doubtful art of accepting and cashing customers' checks without sending the merchandise they had paid for. When *Shield International* filed for protection from creditors in the southern district of the federal district court in New York, on 8 May 1970, it listed 4,616 customers who had paid in full for goods they had not received. The size of the claims ranged from $1 to $50, with the average about $7. The referee appointed by the district court judge to manage the case advised all the short-changed customers that court proceedings would look into the affairs of *Shield International*, and they were invited to file claims of proof, a form to be completed and filed with the court that laid out the nature of the customer's claim to recapture his moneys or his goods. Only 87 of the 4,616 filed. In the final analysis, however, it was those that did not file who seemed wise to the ways of bankruptcy proceedings. Neither those who filed nor those who did not—none of the 4,616 who had prepaid for their goods—received anything at all.[1]

Corporate bankruptcy presents an arena where the most powerful financial actors—the state, the financial industry, large corporations—are pitted against all other creditors, including the comparatively weak. The fate of *Shield International*'s customers represents in microcosm the typical fortunes of many weak creditors in bankruptcy proceedings. They get little or nothing from the corporate bankruptcy estate. "Weakness" is, however, a deceptively simple concept, for creditors may be weak in their everyday bargaining within the market or work place, weak in the capacity to mobilize politically, or weak in their legal standing when corporations fail. These different types of weakness are frequently related, but not simply or predictably.

---

[1] Reported in Schrag and Ratner (1970: 1147); for the case file see *In re Shield Int'l Corp.*, No. 70 B 323 (S.D.N.Y., filed petition 8 May 1970).

We examine three sets of variations on the theme of creditor weakness: individual consumers, trade creditors, and workers. These three groups varied in their ability to bargain in the market, and meta-bargain in the polity. Consumers could do little to protect themselves in the marketplace, and were not well-organized politically. In both the US and Britain, they rarely mobilized on their own behalf and were in effect represented by others involved in the reform process. Representation by someone else was undoubtedly better than no presence at all, but these self-appointed advocates frequently had their own professional and jurisdictional interests to consider as well. Trade creditors had somewhat better recourse in the market than consumers, particularly in Britain, but were also politically disorganized. The fortunes of workers in either place, market or polity, depended very much on whether they were unionized or not. Unionized workers can bargain more effectively in the market and also possess considerable political resources. How well they meta-bargain depends very much on how clearly they can foresee the impact of legal alternatives on their interests.

Consumers and Trade Creditors

Individual consumers account for a heavy volume of business transactions, and in many of these they effectively extend credit to a firm through some sort of prepayment. This occurs for mail order business on clothing, footwear, do-it-yourself equipment, household goods and the like. The service sector commonly takes prepayments for insurance, holiday and travel business, correspondence courses, and shipping and removals. In Britain some of the most publicized problems were centered on the building and home improvements industries, where consumers put down large deposits for central heating, insulation, double-glazing of windows, and plumbing, and then the companies went into insolvency.

Trade creditors supply goods to buyers, such as manufacturers, expecting that they will be paid within thirty days, or so. Like ordinary consumers, they do not view themselves as creditors, though in practice they are "unwitting, unprotected purveyors of loan finance in the form of credit for other companies" (Wheeler 1994: 86).

Individual consumers and trade creditors comprise two sub-sets of a larger set of unsecured creditors. The remaining unsecured creditors vary enormously, from small businesses that engaged in transactions on the basis of a handshake, through major banks that lent to the most financially robust corporations without bothering to take a security interest or collateral in their property. Not infrequently a bank may find itself both a secured creditor on the collateralized part of its loan, and an unsecured creditor on the remainder of the loan, often because the collateral has diminished in value and thus only protects a proportion of the original loan.

Consumer creditors, whose primary extension of credit occurs through prepayments for goods and services, and trade suppliers, whose credit-making activities occur when they supply goods for which they have not yet been paid, both suffer major impediments in corporate bankruptcy. First, these two groups possess unclear or weakly secured property rights. For the most part they do not use legal devices that would enable them to seize back some part of the debtor-company's assets if it goes into bankruptcy. One reason is that the transaction costs of negotiating a price, hiring a professional, signing and exchanging papers far outweighs the size and frequency of the transaction. Individual customers are usually one-shot players, and so do not build up any fund of experience in dealing with insolvency law or insolvency practitioners. Thus they suffer from both limited experience and limited access to expertise. It may also be that they prefer legal informality, regarding contracts and "legalese" as impediments to good business relations (see Macaulay 1963). Trade creditors are frequently in a better position, because if they have regular trading relations with a company, as "repeat-players" they might have a stronger incentive to create standard form contracts that give them some measure of security.

Second, weak creditors suffer from ignorance: they know less and have fewer resources than other creditors to find out about the declining fortunes of a company. Anyone who walked into a furniture store and asked to see the company accounts would be laughed out of the store. And since so much commerce is done at a distance, and through the mail, it is that much more difficult to discover the financial reputation of a merchant. In Britain, there was no credit reference agency easily available to a consumer, although Better Business Bureaus in the US and the like can be useful for purchases that require a deposit. Nor do consumers have ready access to company reports or trade magazines. Of course, a trade supplier may be in a better position than an individual to discover a company's financial situation, or at least to learn of its reputation, especially if it is a repeat player in a local community, where sources of information multiply rapidly. But even here the information will be more reputational than technical.[2]

Third, a power imbalance puts small firms and individual consumers at a disadvantage in relation to larger creditors or debtors. The consumer cannot bargain for collateral since the size of his transaction is usually too small and he has no easy way to increase that bargaining power. This is compounded in bankruptcy proceedings where it is a handful of the largest creditors which get to sit on creditors' committees and influence the course of the reorganization.

Fourth, time works against weak creditors: if their margins are slim, they cannot wait years to reclaim assets that are tied up in bankruptcy court or in a reorganization, even if waiting meant a higher return on their dollar. Major changes in the law that might facilitate corporate turnarounds are only good for those who can afford to bide their time for the turnaround to occur.

Finally, weak creditors are disproportionately vulnerable because the credit they have extended is a larger proportion of their own assets or income than that of major secured creditors such as the state and large financial interests. For the consumer, the loss cannot be passed along to customers and must be borne entirely by the consumer. Nor can it be set off against profits or tax liabilities.

Some of these problems can translate into equal difficulties with collective action in political meta-bargaining. Weak creditors in the ordinary course of business will also face severe problems of collective action when the legal rules are formulated for governing corporate failure and asset distribution. Moreover, unsecured creditors are a divided and heterogeneous lot: some are very powerful, such as banks who are seeking to protect the unsecured portion of their loans, while most others have quite limited capacities. As their more general interests diverge, there is little hope of a common alliance.

Yet weak creditors were not entirely without advocates or political recourse, as this chapter will demonstrate. Consumers found advocates not only in private consumer organizations, such as the Consumers' Association in Britain, but in government bodies, such as the Office for Fair Trading in the UK, and consumer protection agencies in American

---

[2] In Britain this close proximity of trade suppliers to the companies buying their goods supported an argument made by financial institutions that suppliers should not get any special treatment in bankruptcy. Since trade suppliers were in closer touch with the day to day dealings of the buyer, said the bankers, they should be more acutely attuned to financial reversals and take the appropriate action to protect themselves.

state governments. In addition, "horror stories" make good press and compelling tele-journalism. It is a relatively short step from aggrieved public opinion to pressures for action from MPs or congressional representatives. Trade suppliers have rather more of a problem, because their great diversity militates against collective action through representative associations, and their plight does not provoke the same affective reaction as stories of consumer distress.

Wide-ranging legislative reforms opened up the possibility of a redistribution in favor of weak creditors. The crucial question in the politics of redistribution lies in the linkage between the market and political spheres. If the relative weakness of unsecured creditors in the ordinary course of business translates into similar weakness in the political sphere, then the likelihood of redistribution remains low. If, however, weak creditors, at certain moments and in favorable political circumstances, have access to different forms of leverage in the political domain, then the prospects brighten for empowering the weak. Since the plight of consumers and some other weak creditors edges close to political interests of elected politicians, it seems likely that party politics will intrude more deeply into this aspect of the technical legislation than most others. We should not expect that weakness in the market will necessarily engender weakness at the political level of meta-bargaining over bankruptcy rules.

Labor

While individual workers appear particularly vulnerable to corporate failure, workers have two powerful means to bolster their position. If they are unionized (or even if they are not but can "free-ride" on benefits won by unions), then workers have a mode of collective action readily available in either the marketplace, through collective bargaining, or in the political arena, through active lobbying. In addition, workers in most Western countries identify strongly with labor, socialist, or left-of-center political parties. Hence they are assured either of direct organizational representation before a sympathetic parliamentary party, or they can expect a sympathetic response from legislators who depend on their political support.

In several respects, workers have certain advantages over consumers and trade creditors in the ordinary course of business, for they are sufficiently close to a firm's behavior to sense its economic viability; the asymmetry in power on the shop floor can be balanced by unionization; and they have a proximity to political power that can translate into forceful meta-bargaining. For all these reasons, in both countries workers already had statutory priority in the allocation of assets from the estates of bankrupt companies. Meta-bargaining over the principles of bankruptcy law therefore gave workers something to defend as well as opportunities for something new to gain. Nevertheless, workers' well entrenched position in prior bankruptcy statutes proved something of a liability, especially in the United States, for it locked organized labor into a conceptual frame that blinded it to dangers that only became fully apparent after the Bankruptcy Code had been enacted.

Bankruptcy is a stage upon which the classical conflict between labor and management can be re-enacted. To be sure, it is not center stage, for bankruptcy is not at the very core of industrial relations (unlike union–management negotiations, strikes, lockouts, and so on). Nevertheless, among the conflicting interests activated within a bankrupt firm, are those which pit workers against their managers. Since both of these groups are politically organized outside of bankruptcy, and since both are frequent national political actors, it seems quite possible that their longstanding struggles should be re-enacted in the bankruptcy reforms.[3]

The workers' position in bankruptcy is twofold, depending on whether the firm is being reorganized or liquidated. On the one hand, a firm that is in financial trouble will often fall behind on its wage payments, or will fail to make payments into an employee pension fund. When workers are owed back pay or benefits by a bankrupt firm, they become creditors. As such, their financial claims over the pool of assets compete with those of all the other creditors. But, unless workers are unionized or otherwise organized, they may have only limited access to legal and accounting expertise, and will be hampered by collective action problems.[4] Their ability to enforce their claims may be inadequate, even though they are among those hardest hit by a liquidation. To compensate for these weaknesses, workers usually receive a strong statutory priority in the distribution of assets during liquidation. They are paid ahead of the unsecured creditors. While the priority is strong, however, the amount is capped at a limited sum which may not cover back wages and rarely compensates for the catastrophe of

---

[3] Chambliss's (1993) emphasis on the role of contradictions for law making certainly underscores this possibility. For him, the most basic contradiction is that between labor and capital.

[4] In other words, there will be a tendency for workers to want to "free ride" on another worker's attempt to get his or her share of the assets.

losing one's job. When bankruptcy law is being revised, we can expect an interest by workers in maintaining or strengthening their statutory priority, and in increasing the maximum sum to which the priority status applies.

On the other hand, workers occupy a different position as one of the major costs that reorganizing firms seek to reduce. A company that is trying to recover its competitive position typically cuts costs by renegotiating its debts, lowering labor costs, and selling off unprofitable divisions. Obviously, employee compensation comes under severe pressure during a bankruptcy reorganization, and workers' ability to resist pay cuts is heavily dependent on their bargaining position, their degree of organization and how easily their employment contracts can be modified. Long-settled labor relations can become unsettled during bankruptcy, along with many other of a firm's commercial ties.

Since failure will mean the loss of their jobs, it seems that workers, like management, have an interest in a successful reorganization. But here interests became more uncertain for too much protection of jobs, wages, and benefits may jeopardize the viability of the firm as a whole. Workers will want to resist pay cuts, but not so strenuously as to endanger the firm. And while workers as a whole prefer a reorganization that cuts some jobs but not all, those whose jobs are likely to be cut may not find this a very palatable solution. Moreover, the power of organized labor on the shop floor can be undermined if any jobs go or benefits are lost. Thus labor, we expect, will want the burden of cost-cutting to fall on other shoulders (for example, those of the creditors, or suppliers).[5] Since workers are a reducible cost, they will want to ensure that the law prevents modification or cancellation of their employment contracts. The more unyielding such contracts are, the more likely it is that the burden of reorganization will have to be shifted elsewhere. If they cannot be modified at all, however, it becomes harder to reorganize successfully.

Liquidation and reorganization bankruptcies are both redistributional exercises in which workers, along with all others who have a stake in the firm, can be either winners or losers. Furthermore, bankruptcy law sets the terms of the redistributional game. In either capacity, as creditors or as costs, the ability of workers to protect their position during bankruptcy reform is not likely to be great. To intervene in the process of legislative reform is an expensive undertaking that requires

---

[5] In general, the parties who constitute the "costs" in a reorganizing firm will try to protect their position and encourage others to make concessions first.

political and organizational resources, and so only when politically strong unions deal with sympathetic governments can workers hope to strengthen their position.

Nevertheless, the role of workers in the bankruptcy reforms demonstrates again that interests cannot be taken for granted, and that traditional manager–worker conflicts can lock both sides into interpretive frames in which neither anticipates problems that can significantly alter their fates in corporate failure. Especially in the United States, labor understood its interests in historical terms as they were defined in prior bankruptcy law. They fought to maintain or improve their priority in relation to other creditors, and they pressed for minor expansion in the benefits those priorities endowed. But organized labor in the United States badly underestimated the import of some provisions in the 1978 Bankruptcy Code. Indeed, neither labor nor management anticipated the advantages which the new reorganization provisions of the bankruptcy code conferred upon management. And despite the significance of bankruptcy law for an "open credit economy," virtually no organizations representing American management showed interest in bankruptcy reforms or in proposed provisions for executory contracts. In this, management and labor stood on equal ground: both failed to comprehend the import of substantive and procedural changes in the law that would permit creative lawyers to use the 1978 Bankruptcy Code to change radically labor–management relations.

We argued in Chapter 2 that property and jurisdictional rights in bankruptcy are indissolubly linked. The creativity, power, and control of work domains by professionals affects directly the substance of meta-bargaining over bankruptcy, the subsequent rules of bargaining among parties within the framework of bankruptcy law, and the ability to mobilize bankruptcy law for the solution of problems that extend beyond the limits of corporate bankruptcy itself. The battlegrounds over weak creditors exemplify the integral politics of jurisdictional rights in settlements over substantive property rights.

Not only does the situation of weak creditors affect distributions of property rights in bankruptcy, but the allocation of jurisdictional rights to professionals in bankruptcy substantially affects the real returns to weak creditors. Since the cost of accessing expert advice habitually excludes weak creditors from recapturing their assets, any statutory measures that increases the incentives for professionals to act on behalf of individuals or classes of consumers will simultaneously create work for professionals and empower weak creditors. Thus the structure of representation incorporated into the legislation—access to lawyers, costs of expert advice, the ability to aggregate many small claims into large class claims—directly affects returns to the weak. Put another way, the distribution of jurisdiction rights influences the effective allocation of property rights.

Augmentation of jurisdictional rights characteristically benefits professionals, and because it is the professionals themselves who are primary advocates for expansion of their own sphere of influence in bankruptcy work, changes in property and jurisdictional rights depend significantly on forms of professional mobilization. Thus our account of statutory reforms on behalf of weak creditors must also attend to the modes of professional collective action, to evidence of professional innovation, and to the dynamics of negotiation between professions and state authorities—recurring themes in our accounts of the contingencies of expert power in legal change. We might expect that for consumers and trade suppliers, professionals will mobilize in favor of expanded rights using mechanisms that concurrently expand the size of their work jurisdictions.

Yet professionals, too, act from complex motivations which belie any simple-minded conception of rational maximization. We have argued that professionals are one of the few groups in bankruptcy that think globally about the entire packet of distributional and procedural reforms, for they embrace in their work the entire territory of bankruptcy practice. While they will not be indifferent to the consequences of reform for occupational status, power, and financial returns, some also attend to distributional equity and procedural justice. Moreover, since innovative solutions to technical and distributive problems are the substance of much professional work, we will expect to observe professional innovation in the crafting of the legislation, and be certain of its appearance in the implementation of that legislation, when stakes—and rewards—are particularly high.

In bankruptcy law the potential measures that are available to aid weak creditors fall into two main classes. The first and most obvious class comprises the adoption of *direct measures* to ensure consumers, trade suppliers, and unsecured creditors obtain a larger share of the pie. These in turn may be subdivided.

On the one hand, weak creditors could be ranked as preferred creditors in the statute itself. After the secured creditors recovered their assets, a priority on behalf of consumers or workers would rank them so that they would receive a distribution ahead of all unsecured creditors and some other priority creditors. The political question turns on whether this particular class of creditors can establish a compelling case that they be given special status and, if so, how high they should be ranked. If, for instance, they are ranked ahead of government tax authorities, they can expect a reasonable recovery of assets; but if they are ranked behind the government, much less will be available to redistribute. Since the government is the priority creditor that usually takes the largest bite of the pie, weak creditors are inevitably pitted against one of the strongest actors in a zero-sum game. Weak creditors might also be given a leg up on others—even including other secured creditors—if they can lay claim to a form of security which permits them to retain property rights in their prepayments or the goods they have supplied.

On the other hand, weak creditors can be helped by *indirect measures*. These can be grouped into three subclasses, all of which rely on the same presumption: if more funds are swept into the estate, then everyone, including unsecured creditors, will benefit. This is the bankruptcy analogue to trickle-down economics. The more proximate of the indirect measures rely on reducing the claims of other large creditors. The more limits are placed on the claims of the Internal Revenue Service or Inland Revenue, the more will be available for everyone else. The less de facto priority given to utilities, the larger the size of the estate for other creditors. However, these benefits are likely to be relatively smaller than priorities, less certain, and longer lived in their realization.

Weak creditors will also receive indirect benefits if companies can be reorganized in such a way that creditors will receive more from the sale of a streamlined business as a going concern than if the company is simply liquidated, or broken up, at its lowest financial ebb. Again this is a distant hope, and depends on the faith that rescheduled debt, better management, and selective corporate reorganization will permit an ailing company to re-emerge as a competitive business. Rehabilitation, however, means that many of the most vulnerable creditors may have to wait years to get their money back. Moreover, consumers and trade creditors seldom get much voice in a reorganization, so their ultimate stake may be impaired by their lack of representation in negotiations over the restructuring of debt.

The least direct benefit to weak creditors comes through the reduction of victimization of the weak by businesses and professionals. If legislation or market mechanisms can exert tighter controls on company directors and managers, then scams, frauds, reckless trading, and even poor business practice should be reduced with the result that all consumers will be that much better off. Since professionals, too, have been accused of preying on the weak to fatten their own wallets, tighter professional regulation should have a similar result.

The outcomes of the Insolvency Act and Bankruptcy Code are instructive for more than their distributive consequences for weak creditors. In any legal change which pits strong groups against weaker ones, how do the strong justify and make rhetorically acceptable their opposition to reforms that might protect the weak? After all, while the politically weak suffer enormous impediments of collective action, there is an important sense in which they hold the moral high ground—the sense that it is right and just to help the poor, the weak, the hungry, the vulnerable. This puts the strong, who already hold most of the political resources, at a curious disadvantage: if they oppose a redistribution of resources to the weak, they must find rhetorically acceptable ways to justify a symbolically callous position.

Statutory reform therefore reveals some of the incipient conflicts between what we call the *logic of resistance* and the *rhetoric of critique*. The logic of resistance refers to the underlying grounds of opposition that strong players have to proposals that would empower the weak. The rhetoric of critique expresses the logic of resistance in forms that are politically acceptable and can thereby neutralize the moral disadvantage of the strong. A successful outcome for the strong will present a rhetoric of critique that is both persuasive and sufficiently detached from the logic of resistance that it does not compromise the political standing of the strong. This interpretive frame, therefore, juxtaposes sharply the strengths of strong and weak creditors in market relations and the political arena respectively. Market institutions and political institutions each have their own "morality." Being able to play the game of economic or political morality becomes a determinant of power in either institutional domain. The case of weak creditors illustrates that dominant players in either domain cannot take for granted their dominance in the other.

The Triumph of the Weak: Consumer Creditors in the United States

The fortunes of consumer creditors in corporate bankruptcy did not make it onto the reform agenda until amendments were offered to the bills introduced to Congress in 1975. Despite the Brookings Institution's political identification with the Democratic Party, the Brookings Report documented the problem for unsecured creditors in general, without identifying the needs of consumer creditors in corporate bankruptcy. Stanley and Girth reported on two sets of data. In a study conducted by the Administrative Agency of the US Courts on straight bankruptcies between 1965 and 1968, the total claims of creditors in cases where there were any assets totalled $431 million each year, of which $70 million, or 16 per cent, was received by creditors. While secured creditors accounted for only 11 per cent of claims against the assets, they actually received 66¢ on the dollar; priority creditors held 9 per cent of claims and received 35¢ on the dollar; and the largest class of creditors, the unsecured creditors, held 80 per cent of claims, but received about 7¢ on the dollar (Stanley and Girth 1971: 21).

Brookings' own study of reorganizations found that about 60 per cent of the debt was unsecured in corporate bankruptcies and Chapter XI cases. Secured creditors were paid in 80 per cent of cases and realized 31¢ on the dollar; priority creditors received 36 per cent of their claims; unsecured creditors had 44 per cent of their claims allowed, but only received about 8¢ on the dollar for those claims. Stanley and Girth observed that "the largest bite from what unsecured creditors would otherwise receive was taken by priority claims (35%), and the largest portion of this bite (at least 13% of the total distribution) was taken by the Internal Revenue Service (IRS)" (Stanley and Girth 1971: 112–3). However, the Brookings Report did not identify consumer creditors as such and therefore made no recommendation about alleviating their plight.

While the Brookings Report appeared to overlook consumer creditors in the larger problem of bankruptcy administration, the same cannot be said of the Bankruptcy Commission, which had in its hands an articulate statement of the problem, and some recommendations for a solution, but nonetheless excluded this class of creditors from its agenda altogether. The Bankruptcy Commission initiated many studies and academic inquiries into various aspects of bankruptcy law and practice. One study focused explicitly on consumer creditors and led to a submission, later published as a law review article, which surveyed the fortunes of weak creditors with great clarity. Since Schrag and Ratner's article laid the groundwork for subsequent debates on this topic, we present it in some detail (Schrag and Ratner 1970: 1149).

Schrag and Ratner premised their article on the proposition that the 1898 and 1938 Bankruptcy Acts had little interest in small, non-commercial creditors in commercial bankruptcy, and therefore that they are "the truly forgotten parties in bankruptcy proceedings." The magnitude of the problem was hard to gauge because data were not available on all companies, and many companies did not individually list their consumer creditors in bankruptcy filings. But they speculated that the bankruptcy of a department store would create 500–5000 out of pocket consumers; and the bankruptcy of a major national consumer business could create hundreds of thousands. A consumer representative later extrapolated that millions of consumer creditors were affected each year by commercial failures, a sense reinforced by such examples as *Shield International Corporation,* and *FAS International, Inc.,* which operated a set of correspondence schools nationwide. When they filed for bankruptcy in 1972, 114,000 customers nation-wide had already paid in part or in full (Schrag and Ratner 1970: 1149–50; note 12, 1149).

Consumer creditors in corporate bankruptcies suffered from two problems: their substantive rights were limited; and procedural problems subverted what few rights they did have.

1   The Substantive Rights of Consumer Creditors

Consumers who had prepaid for future services got no priority and therefore shared equally with the other unsecured creditors, which meant they generally got nothing. In principle they could recapture losses on two theories—both of which posited that the monies in question still belonged to the creditor and not the bankrupt company. One theory argued that the creditor never really relinquished ownership of the money but that it was only held in trust by the debtor. However it was extremely difficult to prove this. The second theory was that the transaction took the form of a future services contract, and since there had been misrepresentation by the company, it should be rescinded. But because this course of action entailed the tracing of moneys, an exceptionally onerous undertaking, it was not very satisfactory. Prepayment for goods was also subject to law on trusts and tracing. If the consumer wanted his goods back, he had to prove they belonged to him and were not part of the bankrupt company's estate, but this required identification of specific goods and was subject to very restrictive procedural rules which rendered it "an illusory promise to the prepaying consumer."[6]

[6] Schrag and Ratner 1970: 1159. Goods could be pursued through section 2–502 of the Uniform Commercial Code. State statutes might give consumers rights when a company

2 *Procedural Problems*

Even if substantive rights were activated, most consumer creditors would be defeated by the procedures surrounding bankruptcy administration and courts.

The hopelessness of the consumer's situation only begins with the inadequacy of the substantive law. If a consumer did have any rights, they would not know about them and would therefore not press their claims. If they knew of them, they would be hard put to assert them unless they had counsel, or at least substantial business sophistication. If they tried to obtain counsel to represent their small claims in bankruptcy proceedings, they would probably not be able to find lawyers willing to undertake the task. And if they had rights, knowledge, stamina, and counsel, they would still frequently be denied any recovery because no money would be found in the bankrupt's estate.[7]

Furthermore, consumers usually didn't know that a company was bankrupt, at least in a timely enough fashion to act; nor could they easily find the location of the company headquarters or where the bankruptcy court was located. Given that failing companies tend also to keep poor records, consumers would not receive notice of the bankruptcy proceedings; even if they did, they could not comprehend the document that came from the court, since its language was in heavy legalese, and without counsel it would be difficult to attend and participate in hearings before the bankruptcy referee or the creditors' committee (Schrag and Ratner 1970: 1149).

Even within the then extant system, Schrag and Ratner believed weak creditors could get a better deal if they had strong professional representation. In the market for legal services, it would be relatively simple to allow attorneys to be retained on a contingent fee basis and initiate class actions on behalf of many small claimants. However, Ratner drew on his own experience as Consumer Advocate for the City of New York to propose that Departments of Consumer Affairs actively solicit consumer claims on major cases that came to their attention, thereby effectively constructing classes of consumers who may not even have known about their rights.

Even if the government did not take so proactive a role, at least a strong consumer agency could file a proofs of claim on behalf of *all*

went into insolvency, but this was actually a disguised priority and therefore would be invalid, according to the best legal authorities. Consumer protection statutes might help in theory, but they tended not to cover property interests and offered only money damages instead. Schrag and Ratner 1970: 1163.

[7] *Ibid.*

consumers who were listed as creditors in a bankrupt company's filing. Government resources could be quite effective in the vigorous pursuit of funds, and by auditing the books of the company, and monitoring the trustee: "An institution can do for consumers what they cannot economically do for themselves, and take actions that no other party is inclined to attempt." Schrag and Ratner demonstrated further that more money could be available to consumer creditors if an institution could defeat some of the claims made by secured creditors. In the case of *Vigilant Protective Systems, Inc.*, which sold burglar alarms on an installment plan, the New York Consumer Affairs Department was able to demonstrate that many of the secured claims made by banks could not be sustained because their security instruments were deficient. This made the banks unsecured creditors and thus forced them to share distributions of a much larger pie with consumer creditors.[8] Moreover, public interest lawyers could organize consumer creditors so they could effectively vote their claims and attempt to have a creditors committee appointed in which they had some standing.

Efforts at reorganization placed consumers in an even more vulnerable position because neither the debtor nor the creditors committee had an interest in acknowledging unsecured creditors' claims. The celebrated features of reorganization—the continuation of business, the halting of litigation, and the rescheduling and reduction of debt—might be of "great practical value" to lawyers, but Schrag and Ratner dismiss them as a "debtor's picnic" that presents "enormous" hazards for consumers (Schrag and Ratner 1970: 1184–7).

Since it "is unfair and inefficient to require isolated consumers, agencies, and referees to bear alone the burden of reform," Schrag and Ratner made three sets of recommendations to the US Bankruptcy Commission. First, *substantive reforms* should include (a) a provision that consumers could recover all prepayments for undelivered goods and services before any other distribution of the estate; (b) some relief of prepaying consumers from the tracing requirement in current law; (c) a means whereby referees could take an executory contract approach and complete the seller's performance under the contract, thereby providing a stronger form of security; and (d) reforms at the state level so that

---

[8] Schrag and Ratner 1970: 1176–82. See *In re Vigilant Protective Systems, Inc.*, No. 71 B 729 (S.D.N.Y. filed petition July 27, 1971). The Department also sued the company for engaging in consumer fraud (*Myerson v. Vigilant Protective Systems, Inc.*, No. 40652 (S. Ct., N.Y. Cty. April 27, 1971).

sellers were compelled to put in their contracts that prepayments would be held in trust until the conditions of the sale are fulfilled.

Second, *procedural reforms* should mandate that (a) no formal claim procedures should be necessary up to a fixed amount (for example, $300); (b) retailers should be compelled to list all consumer creditors so that they could be easily contacted in case of bankruptcy; (c) if consumer creditors had to file a proof of claim, a much simplified form and procedure should be devised; and (d) legislation should make it clear that class actions are permissible in bankruptcy.

Third, a set of *institutional reforms* should be implemented. Every United States Attorney's office should have one assistant committed to consumer affairs in bankruptcy. And every bankruptcy court should have an attached Small Claims Part, patterned on a successful Small Claims Part of the Tax Court for claims of trade creditors, wages by non-unionized workers, and consumers (Schrag and Ratner 1970: 1187–91).

Finally, Schrag and Ratner raised one intriguing suggestion that briefly anticipated one of the most innovative and controversial features of the English reforms. More money could be brought into the estate to be shared among all creditors if the corporate veil of limited liability could be pierced.

> ... [W]ith respect to insolvent corporations, a hole has already been bored. Wisconsin has recently enacted a comprehensive consumer protection code that prohibits a wide range of corporate misconduct, and ... provides that "damages or penalties" that cannot be collected from a corporation "by reason or dissolution shall be recoverable against the principal agents of the corporation including, but not limited to officers, managers and assistant managers who knew of, should have known of or wilfully participated in ... a violation."

Presciently, the authors observe that "this type of protection may, in the long run, be more important than any amendment to the Bankruptcy Act itself."[9]

Schrag and Ratner's submission fell on completely deaf ears, at least in the Commission. While their study was acknowledged in the final Commission report, no mention of it occurred in the body of the report,

---

[9] Schrag and Ratner (1970: 1190). See Wis. Laws ch 239, §425.310 (1972). This direct anticipation of wrongful trading in the English Insolvency Act 1986 (see pp. 388ff.) never recurs in the American reform debates and the English are quite unconscious of its existence in the United States—despite its revolutionary significance.

nor was the problem of consumer creditors even discussed in the Commission meetings.[10]

The reception of Schrag and Ratner's powerful analysis of a problem with direct political overtones, and its subsequent publication in the prestigious *Columbia Law Journal*, presents an intriguing case on the political efficacy of professional expertise. Since the authors were an academic and a consumer advocate, the article had twin auspices, which simultaneously protected it from charges that it identified a practical problem without understanding the legal technicalities, or that it offered an academic analysis that was too remote from pragmatic concerns. Yet the fusion of legal expertise with pragmatic knowledge was not sufficient to compel a response from the Bankruptcy Commission. What, then, did it take to protrude the rights of consumer creditors into the bankruptcy reforms?

Legislative Initiatives: Leaving Consumers Out

When H.R. 31 and H.R. 32, the Bankruptcy Commission's bill and the Judges' Bill respectively, were introduced to the House of Representatives, neither contained anything that addressed the problems of consumer creditors in corporate bankruptcy, nor did they incorporate any of the central recommendations made by Schrag and Ratner. For all intents and purposes, the consumer creditor issue had never been raised.

Distressed by the neglect of consumer abuses in current bankruptcy law, and in the bankruptcy bills that had been introduced to replace it, the Hon. Millicent Fenwick, Congresswoman from New Jersey, pushed consumer interests onto the policy stage by introducing a bill, H.R. 11871, that would provide direct remedies for consumer creditors. In three days of testimony before the Subcommittee on Civil and Constitutional Rights, consumer advocates pressed their case before ambivalent politicians, staffers, and interest groups.[11]

Elinor Guggenheimer, Commissioner of New York City's Department of Consumer Affairs, testified that:

Consumers lost many thousands of dollars in New York City last year, not because they were careless with their money or because of frivolous investments. These were average consumers who, in good faith, paid in part or in full for

---

[10] A comprehensive search of the Minutes of the US Bankruptcy Commission yielded nothing on consumer creditors and trade creditors. Discussion of priorities treats only wage, tax, and administrative priorities.

[11] *Bankruptcy Revision Act Hearings on H.R. 31 and H.R. 32*: 1723–74.

goods and services which they never received. It's outrageous, of course. But perhaps what's even more outrageous is that it is legal—because the business with whom these consumers were dealing had filed for federal bankruptcy relief.[12]

Guggenheimer took pains to underline that although these problems disproportionately hurt those of lower and moderate incomes, they were a much larger problem because some 75 per cent of all furniture sales required deposits. For New York State alone some $158 million a year was going into unprotected retailers' bank deposits.

The bankruptcy act has it backwards. It punishes those who are the most vulnerable and who proportionately have the most to lose, while it rewards those who—even though their loss be considerable—are best able to insulate themselves from disaster.

Not only is the "hapless consumer depositor at the bottom of an empty barrel," but he loses virtually everything because "the Federal Government has been far too greedy in satisfying its appetite at the expense of the little man."[13]

Guggenheimer proposed statutory changes that would (a) permit a state lien on the assets of a business for consumer depositors, thus making them secured creditors; (b) grant that this lien have some priority over other security interests; (c) compel companies to inform consumers that they are in Chapter "XI"; and (d) ensure that the automatic stay not be applied to consumers who wanted to continue legal actions on warranties, and the like. Consumers should be given simple forms, or no forms at all. Retailers should be compelled to list all consumer creditors in their bankruptcy filings. Moreover, Guggenheimer advocated the right of consumer agencies to represent consumer claims and "*to be compensated for doing so out of the costs of administration.*" Finally, the commissioner urged that: "Where consumers are not listed, the claims should be a charge on the assets of the officers, directors and major shareholders where it can be established that they could have been identified if reasonable care were exercised."

Fenwick agreed with the general premiss of the legislation that the 1938 bankruptcy provisions in the Chandler Act needed over-hauling. The *Shield International* and *FAS International* cases exemplified the need to give consumers a priority. Yet this proposal flew in the face of the much

---

[12] Testimony of Elinor C. Guggenheimer, *Bankruptcy Act Revision Hearings on H.R. 31 and H.R. 32*: 1699.

[13] *Bankruptcy Act Revision Hearings on H.R. 31 and H.R. 32*: 1701.

hallowed principle of *pari passu*—that all creditors in the same class should be treated equally. Fenwick argued that this doctrinally imposed equality affronted the realities of unequal access to information and differing abilities to mobilize.

... [T]he major creditors in a bankruptcy are usually well-organized interests like banks and insurance companies, who would be able to represent their own interest more than adequately. Consumers, who are most often unorganized and ignorant of their rights in bankruptcy procedure, would undoubtedly lose out to these interests if all were given a strictly "equal" opportunity.[14]

While Fenwick's proposals, even her examples, show a strong resemblance to the case made by Schrag and Ratner, her ace-in-the-hole was her ability to mobilize politically.[15] First, she chose to formalize her ideas in a separate bill, a strategy not unlike that adopted by the bankruptcy judges. In addition, she began to mobilize Attorneys General from across the US to write in support of her proposals. Her congressional testimony was therefore buttressed by letters from the Attorneys General in Massachusetts, Wisconsin, California, and New Jersey. The correspondence multiplied stories of customers who had lost moneys to the Land Auction Bureau, the Old Colony trust, Paul Bunyan Fences, International Health Spas, Freshness Industries, Camera Hut Ltd., and Koscot Interplanetary, Inc., among others.[16]

Committee members mostly acceded to Guggenheimer and Fenwick's analyses, acknowledging that "... it is a fair statement that we have not approached the bankruptcy law from the point of view of the consumer, and Congress never has." Committee chair, Don Edwards, indicated he would take a long hard look at the problem. Congressman Badillo even suggested expanding the scope of the bill to incomplete services and faulty goods that have been paid for as well as to rental housing security deposits.[17]

Responses to Fenwick's proposals diverged sharply. One reaction expressed sympathy with the concept and sought only to obtain more information on the operation of similar ideas elsewhere and a greater

[14] *Bankruptcy Act Revision Hearings on H.R. 31 and H.R. 32*: 1723–5.

[15] Congressman Drinan later stated his view that it was the Schrag and Ratner article that created sufficient attention to bring about Fenwick's bill (*Bankruptcy Act Revision Hearings on H.R. 31 and H.R. 32*: 1732).

[16] *Bankruptcy Act Revision Hearings on H.R. 31 and H.R. 32*: 1725–8.

[17] Congressman Butler, *Bankruptcy Act Revision Hearings on H.R. 31 and H.R. 32*: 1711.

[18] Father Drinan asked whether other states had adopted similar measures and if there were any hard statistics on consumers creditors. He also wondered about the feasibility of a bankruptcy administration that made the effort to realize $7.50 for a claim of $10. One of

awareness of the magnitude of the problem.[18] Another reaction was more querulous. Committee staffer, Kenneth Klee, launched into a blunt attack on Guggenheimer's deviation from strict equality of disbursements. The bankrupt estate is a pie that has to be split up amongst creditors and that is a "zero sum situation." If one creditor gets more, other creditors get less. By asking for consumer creditors to be given a priority, the consumer commissioner effectively was asking businesses and government—that is, "the citizens of the United States"—to "subsidize consumer creditors." Klee had little sympathy with the notion that consumers are hapless customers at the mercy of more powerful market actors: "To the extent the government does not get 100 cents on its tax dollar what you have is every citizen of this country who pays taxes subsidizing those citizens who have been imprudent enough to deal or invest with a failing business."

Klee's confidence in the level playing field presented by markets is reflected in his rhetorical question: "Is not the answer to the problem a system of total disclosure to enable the consumer to act with total information so that notice of the status of a business is given?"—a recommendation, presumably, that subverts those companies in reorganization. Congressman Butler, a Republican, expressed reservations about informing customers that a company was in Chapter XI. That would erode confidence in the business and compound its problems. Guggenheimer dismissed the notion of total disclosure as "simply not a practical concept."[19]

More qualified were arguments that consumers are better dealt with at the states level. Butler argued that this was a matter for the states, who could put money in escrow. He could not understand why states had not already done it. Fenwick replied that if states could do it they would; the fact that 16 states asked for a change in the bankruptcy law indicated that they thought it was a federal matter. Butler retorted, "I suspect that they are asking us to do something that they are unwilling to ask their States to do because they are not willing to buck the retail merchants associations."[20] Klee would also push the remedy onto the states and have them create a consumer lien, a proposal in turn rejected by the Commissioner and her legal advisors on the grounds that such a lien

---

the co-authors of the Brookings Report did not help the cause of the consumer creditors. When asked if it had surfaced as a problem in their research, Marjorie Girth said that they did not find any abuse. *Bankruptcy Act Revision Hearings on H.R. 31 and H.R. 32*: 1731.

[19] Kenneth Klee, *Bankruptcy Act Revision Hearings on H.R. 31 and H.R. 32*: 1714–16.

[20] *Bankruptcy Act Revision Hearings on H.R. 31 and H.R. 32*: 1734.

would not stand up in federal court (presumably because it was a de facto priority, which permitted states to give their citizens an advantage over the citizens of other states).

Direct resistance did not come in public hearings from the Treasury or businesses. It was the representatives of the American Bankers Association who had most to say, but that was not very much, nor very intense. Asked the leading question by Mr Butler—did they have "any compassion for the consumer?"—a vice president of the Chemical Bank responded, "... the consumer, represented by the strong advocates, state or local, gets a very fair hearing, and at least in my experience, seems to get a piece of the action, even if it is out of a secured creditor."

But it was reorganizations of companies that was principally on the minds of the bankers. By a strange coincidence, two members of the Bankers Bankruptcy Task Force appearing before the House Subcommittee indicated they were counsel in the *Famous Artists Schools* (FAS) case, which had been a leading case quoted by Fenwick and cited by Schrag and Ratner. This case demonstrated not so much, they contended, that students were left holding the bag, but that a successful Chapter XI reorganization permitted the students to come out well— they "received exactly what they had bargained for, because the debtor persuaded the court, and the secured creditors, that fulfilling the lesson commitments would return more to the banks than a straight liquidation." But if reorganizations were to run this successful course, the bankers raised the pragmatic problem that obtaining consent from large numbers of small creditors could subvert new debt arrangements. Had that been necessary in the FAS arrangement, it would not have worked. Therefore it was vital to ensure that the smallest creditors did not have to be canvassed. One banker opined that states could create trusts on layaway funds, a solution that drew no demurrers from his colleagues.[21]

The National Bankruptcy Conference (NBC) approached the problem of consumer creditors only indirectly and principally through procedural mechanisms aimed at smaller unsecured creditors. For instance, the NBC resisted the idea of a single creditors committee made up of the largest unsecured creditor. It endorsed proposals in H.R. 31 to allow the

---

[21] Testimony of Robert J. Grimmig, Vice President, Chemical Bank, Member, The American Bankers Association's Bankruptcy Task Force, accompanied by Jack Gross of New York and Patrick A. Murphy of San Francisco, *Bankruptcy Act Revision Hearings on H.R. 31 and H.R. 32*: 1759–60.

formation of other unsecured creditors committees in order to forestall abuses and broaden participation and representation. Moreover, while the NBC was mindful of difficulties in orchestrating reorganization plans when there were large numbers of claimants within a creditors' committee, it pushed for no minimum dollar limit in size of claims. In some cases $100 would be too high a limit, in others too low. The case administrators, subject to court supervision, should have discretion to set the minimum. This would help to solve one of the collective action problems at the center of company reorganizations—getting agreement within a class of creditors for a plan.[22]

The NBC also signalled that the new powers given debtors and trustees to facilitate reorganizations, including "cramdowns," should be understood as a way of re-balancing the undue powers of secured creditors in favor of debtors and unsecured creditors. Similarly, relaxation of the absolute priority rule, which determines that the claims of higher ranked creditors must be satisfied in full before any claims of the lower ranked are satisfied, also helps "junior" or unsecured creditors, which the NBC strongly endorsed.[23] As for the complexity of filing claims, the NBC applauded the measures in H.R. 31 and H.R. 32 that simply accepted the debtor's listing of creditors as effective claims. It would only be necessary to file proofs of claim if they were disputed, contingent, or unliquidated.[24] But on the matter of consumer priorities, the NBC was silent.

Legislative Initiatives: Writing Consumers In

The introduction of H.R. 8200 in the 95th Congress reflected Congresswoman Fenwick's push to include a priority for consumer creditors. H.R. 8200 mandated that in reorganization proceedings the court appoint one or more committees of unsecured creditors. But for small consumer creditors, the new section in the bill on consumer claims registered a direct response to the advocates orchestrated by Fenwick, the fifty-nine members of the House who co-sponsored the consumer priority amendment, and the endorsements of the Consumer Federation of America, the National Association of Attorneys General, and the

---

[22] Statement of Harvey R. Miller, William J. Rochelle, Jr., J. Ronald Trost on behalf of the National Bankruptcy Conference on Business Reorganizations, *Bankruptcy Act Revision Hearings on H.R. 31 and H.R. 32*: 1879–90, 1920.

[23] *Bankruptcy Act Revision Hearings on H.R. 31 and H.R. 32*: 1915–16.

[24] *Bankruptcy Act Revision Hearings on H.R. 31 and H.R. 32*: 1879–90.

New York State Bar Association. A new fifth priority was created that would come after administrative expenses and wage claims, but, of greatest importance, *before* taxes or Treasury claims. Each individual creditor could claim up to $2,400 and would apply uniformly across all the states. This high priority would virtually assure consumer creditors of getting back some proportion of their deposits and prepayments.[25]

While Fenwick expressed great satisfaction with the inclusion of the consumer priority, she registered continuing concern that H.R. 8200 did not solve the problem of consumer representation.

> Mr Chairman, I believe . . . it is imperative that the bankruptcy rules be modified so that attorneys general, and perhaps State and local consumer protection offices as well, will be allowed to intervene on behalf of consumer creditors. This should not be left to judicial discretion. It should be clearly spelled out in the rules. In my view, the attorney general should also be allowed to initiate an adversary proceeding in a bankruptcy case.[26]

But the victory was not secure, for the bankruptcy bill introduced into the Senate, S. 2266, included the consumer priority at a lower rank— sixth—and, most critically, behind the fifth priority for taxes. The hearings before the Senate Subcommittee on Improvements in Judicial Machinery therefore moved the struggle to a new battleground for a change in the ranking of priority and for enhanced representation of consumer creditors by states' attorney generals. Appearing before the Senate Subcommittee, an Assistant Attorney General from Massachusetts proposed further amendments on behalf of the National Association of Attorneys General (NAAG), and its Consumer Protection Committee.[27] First, the NAAG made "a strong recommendation" that state attorneys general be given a right to intervene on behalf of consumers in bankruptcy cases. Second, the NAAG pushed energetically

---

[25] Report of the Committee on the Judiciary, House of Representatives, 95th Congress, 1st Session, Report No. 95–595 (to accompany H.R. 8200), 8 Sept. 1977, pp. 91–3, 235–6 (hereafter *Report on H.R. 8200*): "Paragraph (5) is a new priority for consumer creditors— those who have deposited money in connection with the purchase, lease, or rental of property, or the purchase of services, for their personal, family, or household use, that were not delivered or provided. The priority amount is not to exceed $600. In order to reach only those persons most deserving of this special priority, it is limited to individuals whose adjustable gross income from all sources derived does not exceed $20,000. See Senate Hearings on S. 2266 and H.R. 8200: 848–9. The income of the husband and wife should be aggregated for the purposes of the $20,000 limit if either or both spouses assert such a priority claim."

[26] Remarks, Congressional Record, House, 27 Oct. 1977, H 11700.

[27] Statement and Testimony of Paula W. Gold, *Senate Hearings on S. 2266 and H.R. 8200*: 689–98.

for consumers to rank *before* the government. If not, consumers would get little or nothing and the priority would be cosmetic.[28] Third, the NAAG proposed that a consumer be given a lien on some assets in the debtor's estate. In a supporting statement from the Attorney General of Wisconsin, Bronson La Follette added that the new bankruptcy law should enable state consumer offices to enforce actions against debtors who defraud the public and then shelter behind bankruptcy. La Follette reiterated that consumer creditors were "the forgotten class" because they were not recognized in law or practice as creditors. Furthermore, in a national economy where multi-state sales are the norm, bankruptcies always result in court proceedings far removed from the physical location of most consumer creditors, effectively stopping them from knowing and acting in their own interests.

But it was fraud, and the market's immorality, that exercised him most strongly:

> ... the silence of the Rules of Bankruptcy Procedure to give the state attorneys general the right to intervene in bankruptcy on behalf of consumers in their states prevents even this remedy from being utilized except in the most extraordinary cases. If thousands of consumers are defrauded by a single bankrupt, it would be both practical and efficient for a state Attorney General's Office to be able to intervene in bankruptcy proceedings on behalf of all affected consumers in the state, since the issues would most likely be similar and grouped together in one litigatable form.

Indeed, La Follette extended his critique of fraud to relations between consumer and trade creditors.

> The failure to include consumers as a creditor class denies the existence of the sole definable group without which no business could exist. To bar consumers from priority status yet grant it to trade suppliers is gross discrimination ... it encourages trade creditors to either actively or passively assist in the fraud since consumer dollars are a ready source of cash to make sure that the bankrupt's estate has enough to pay their preferred claims.

La Follette importuned the Senate committee to adopt three key provisions advocated by the NAAG: give consumers a priority ahead of taxes;

---

[28] Gold argued that consumer creditors are different from other creditors, and therefore should be treated differently. First, they have much less bargaining power over merchants than do lenders. Second, they do not intend to become creditors, and usually do not realize that they are. Third, other creditors are compensated for their risk, through higher interest rates, and the like. And in addition, the consumer creditor feels the loss more keenly, since he or she cannot create a "bad debt reserve." Moreover, the IRS can look after itself, since it has extensive powers to create and enforce liens. *Senate Hearings on S. 2266 and H.R. 8200*: 689–98.

provide a consumer lien in bankruptcy; and empower states' attorney generals to intervene on behalf of consumers. In addition to the heightened priority, he argued that the $2,400 limit for each consumer in the House bill be substituted for the diluted $600 limit in S. 2266.[29]

The organized bar had little to say about the consumer priority, other than the opposition from the chair of the Dallas Bar Association's committee on bankruptcy.[30] The bill was reported out of Senate Judiciary Committee on 14 July 1978 with the consumer creditors' priority not only intact, but ranked more highly than government tax priorities—the crucial decision for consumer advocates. As enacted, the Bankruptcy Act provided that the unsecured claims of individuals of up to $900 are allowed for deposits in connection with the purchase, lease, and rental of property, or the purchase of services. But the new Act did not solve the collective action problem so energetically pursued by the States' Attorneys General.[31]

Labor's Myopia: Investing Short and Risking Long

As a creditor, organized labor stood on stronger ground than consumer creditors at the outset of the bankruptcy reforms. Its priority was well institutionalized in the 1938 Bankruptcy Act (Table 1.1). Labor was also well organized and able to mobilize in defense and expansion of its creditor position. Nevertheless, while labor's pointman sensed threats that could embroil labor well beyond its position as a priority creditor, organized labor gambled that those threats would not be realized, and if they were, labor's political power could resolve them in Congress. Thus, in the bankruptcy reforms, organized labor invested much more in conventional protections of workers as creditors, than in hypothetical vulnerabilities based on the modifiability of executory contracts.

Workers as Creditors

Workers had a priority position as creditors in the old Bankruptcy Act. Pre-1978 US bankruptcy law provided for the financial claims that workers might have against the assets of a failed company. But those

[29] Statement of Bronson C. La Follette, *Senate Hearings on S. 2266 and H.R. 8200*: 698–700.
[30] Statement and testimony of L. E. Creel III, Study Committee Chairman, Dallas Bar Association's Section of Bankruptcy and Commercial Law, *Senate Hearings on S. 2266 and H.R. 8200*: 811–49.
[31] An Act to Establish a Uniform Law on the Subject of Bankruptcies, Public Law 95–598, 92 Stat. 2549, November 6, 1978.

claims were capped. Past-due wages, up to a maximum amount of $600 and over the period of three months before the bankruptcy filing, received a high priority, coming right after administrative costs in the ranking of claims for distribution. The $600 limit was originally set in 1926, and so by the mid-1970s its real value had diminished substantially because of inflation. In addition, the priority covered only wages and left out benefits or other forms of deferred compensation (for instance, pensions, annuities, health plans, etc.). As a result of a 1959 Supreme Court decision,[32] it was clear that the priority accorded wages did not extend to pension contributions or other benefits. In the post-World War II period, employee compensation increasingly consisted of both wages and benefits, but the latter claims were unrecoverable under the old bankruptcy law.

The erosion of the value of workers' claims and the inappropriateness of excluding benefits or deferred compensation were both quite obvious. In their study of bankruptcy, Stanley and Girth (1971) recommended revising the old priority ranking of creditor claims. They did not, however, suggest any change in the status of wage claims. The Bankruptcy Commission then took up this issue, and although one member questioned whether there should even be a priority for wages, the Commission resolved to keep the priority and extend it to include benefits.[33] It recognized that the old $600 limit was inadequate, but there was some disagreement over which of the several proposed increases was better (up to $1,200 or to $1,500).[34] In its final report, the Commission proposed to revise the ranking of claims, but insisted that employee claims retain their high priority because workers are involuntary creditors deserving of special treatment. Furthermore, the Commission Report recommended that the ceiling for claims be raised from $600 to $1,200, and that this enlarged sum cover up to $300 worth of benefits.[35]

In general, organized labor had limited interest in bankruptcy law and so bankruptcy reform gained little attention from the unions. In part, labor may have been distracted, for it was heavily involved with bills such as the Employee Retirement Income Security Act (ERISA), which passed in 1974 with the strong support of organized labor, and the Labor Law Reform Act, which unions tried to get passed in the late

---

[32] *United States v. Embassy Restaurant Inc.*, 359 U.S. 29.
[33] *Minutes of the Bankruptcy Commission*, 11–12 Sept. 1972: 22.
[34] *Minutes of the Bankruptcy Commission*, 13–14 Nov. 1972: 31–5.
[35] *Report of the Bankruptcy Commission*: 21–2, 213–14.

1970s (Goldfield 1987: 32). It is true that labor had encountered bank-ruptcy directly in the 1975 revision of municipal bankruptcy law, which followed in the wake of New York City's financial distress. In fact, labor's capacity to "shut down the city" exercised reformers, particularly on the political right.[36] But organized labor did not perceive its interests as being centrally involved in the bankruptcy process. Said an insider to the reforms: "Labor surprised me, because they were awake in 1976.... And then when we came to the comprehensive reform, while labor was certainly there and they testified, they just...were sort of asleep at the switch." While labor did address closely the situation of workers as creditors—wages, retiree benefits, pension plans—when "you look at all the other areas where bankruptcy law interfaces with other areas of federal law, most people were just sort of apathetic"—and that included labor.[37]

One measure of labor's relative indifference was evident in the deci-sion of the AFL-CIO to hand over leadership of labor's involvement in the reforms to the general counsel of the International Ladies' Garment Workers' Union (ILGWU), Max Zimny. Because of perpetually high rates of corporate bankruptcy within the New York garment industry, Zimny was thoroughly familiar with the problems of bankruptcy for workers. Zimny referred to his efforts at the time as "singular."[38] Testifying before the Senate in April of 1975 on behalf of the AFL-CIO, the United Auto Workers, the Amalgamated Clothing Workers and his own union, Max Zimny asserted that: "The major focus of the ILGWU and our sister unions is with the treatment of employee wages, both direct and indirect, in S. 236 [the Commission Bill]."[39] The emphasis on wages and benefits was reproduced in virtually the only contemporaneous published comment on the new 1978 legislation: "AFL-CIO interest in this legislation was to improve protection for employee wage claims, particularly fringe benefits, when their employer invoked bankruptcy proceedings."[40] No mention was made of executory contracts or collective bargaining agreements. Yet the labor press was not technically correct on this account. Although wages and benefits occupied center stage, Zimny was not unaware of dangers lurking in the provisions on executory contracts.

---

[36] US Interview 92:01.   [37] US Interview 92:01.   [38] US Interview: 92:06.

[39] *Bankruptcy Reform Act Hearings on S. 235 and S. 236*: 255.

[40] *Labor Looks at Congress 1978*: 23.

Zimny proposed in his submission to the Bankruptcy Commission that priority status be extended to cover benefits and pensions, arguing that the benefits and pension contributions lost through bankruptcy were a real hardship to employees. He suggested that the 1959 Supreme Court decision, *United States v. Embassy Restaurant Inc.*, (subsequently reaffirmed in 1968) was a mistake that invited legislative correction. He also argued that the amount and period of wage priority be increased from the $600 and three-month limits up to $3,000 (or more) and one year, and contended that the $1,200 limit proposed by the Commission was inadequate.[41] Other labor representatives testifying before the Senate subcommittee elaborated on Zimny's arguments. Jeffrey Gibbs, from the Industrial Union Department of the AFL-CIO, pointed out that shortly after the Second World War, fringe benefits constituted only about 16.1 per cent of employee compensation, but that this proportion was up to about a third by the early 1970s, and thus that the exclusion of benefits from the priority status was detrimental to workers.[42] He also complained that the $1,200 limit proposed by the Bankruptcy Commission was still much too low.

House and Senate bankruptcy proposals diverged over these provisions. H.R. 8200 proposed that wages and benefits receive a priority ranking for all claims up to a total of $2,400, whereas S. 2266 set the limit for claims at $1,800. The final Act settled on a limit of $2,000 and specifically remedied the *United States v. Embassy Restaurant* decision.[43] H.R. 8200 and S. 2266 also differed over the extent of the priority reachback period for employee benefits. The House proposed a full year, whereas the Senate proposed ninety days. The final Act settled on ninety days.[44]

Aside from organized labor, no one else expressed interest in the priority granted to wages and benefits, or in the ceilings on amounts. More for workers meant less for others, but other creditor groups did not take up the issue. Although organized labor's legislative proposals are frequently opposed by business organizations, such as the US Chamber of Commerce and the National Association of Manufacturers, they made no representations about bankruptcy law to Congress on these bills.

---

[41] *Bankruptcy Reform Act Hearings on S. 235 and S. 236*: 257–9, 265.
[42] *Bankruptcy Reform Act Hearings on S. 235 and S. 236*: 268.
[43] Public Law 95–598, §507(a)(3)(B).
[44] Public Law 95–598, §507(a)(3)(A).

Workers as Costs

Workers' interests as creditors matter when the bankrupt firm is simply to be liquidated, and the pool of assets is split up among the claimants. When firms are reorganized, however, workers' position in terms of costs becomes more salient. A reorganization tries to adjust the commitments, obligations, and structure of the firm so as to make it financially viable again. Cost-cutting is, of course, a major part of this, and in many instances labor costs come under heavy pressure. Just as creditors in a liquidation try to displace the burden of losses onto someone else, so the parties who contribute to the costs of a reorganizing firm try to shift the burden of cost-reduction onto someone else. To give a simple example, suppose a troubled firm has two costs: wage payments to its workforce, and interest payments on a loan from its bank. Such costs are determined by the specific terms of employment and loan contracts. To reorganize successfully, the firm must somehow lower its overall costs, either by reducing wages, or by negotiating better terms with its bank, or both. The workers and the bank all want the firm to reorganize successfully, but in addition, each has an interest in seeing that more of the brunt of cost reduction falls on the other party. Workers would rather see the interest rate lowered and repayments stretched out than a big cut in their salaries.

Which costs can be reduced, and how easily, results from a complex bargaining situation whose parameters are shaped by bankruptcy law. In post-bankruptcy negotiations, how easily the contractual relations of the firm (to its workforce, bank, suppliers or whomever) can be altered is of crucial importance, and the easier that changes can be made, the greater the chance of success. A unionized workforce is typically in a stronger bargaining position than one which is not, and so will make it harder for the reorganizing firm to cut its wage costs. Equally important, however, is the legal resilience of the collective bargaining agreement that binds a unionized workforce and their employer.

In a reorganization the troubled firm's structure and contractual relationships are altered to make the firm financially viable. Among the most important of these is the relation between the firm and its employees (Countryman 1974: 492). After filing for bankruptcy, a reorganizing company operates either under the old management (as debtors-in-possession) or under a court-appointed trustee. A reorganization plan is proposed detailing specific changes to the company and its contractual obligations and then negotiated among the interested parties. If there is no agreement among the parties, another plan might be proposed (and perhaps "crammed-down" by the bankruptcy judge), but more than likely the company will be liquidated.

Under the pre-1978 statute, the trustee or debtor-in-possession was empowered to reject any executory contract as part of the reorganization.[45] According to Countryman, an executory contract is: "... a contract under which the obligation of both the bankrupt and the other party to the contract is so far unperformed that the failure of either to complete performance would constitute a material breach excusing the performance of the other" (Countryman 1973: 460). This allowed the firm to avoid burdensome obligations, and thus enhance its financial prospects. For example, a firm may be bound by an expensive long-term lease, and to reorganize it may be desirable to reject the lease and rent cheaper office-space elsewhere.

The Brookings Report criticized the old law for not encouraging distressed corporations to rehabilitate themselves. It found that failing corporations continued to operate past the point of salvageability until the only possible outcome was liquidation, and that most reorganizations ended up in failure (Stanley and Girth 1971: 115, 212–14). Legal change was necessary to encourage reorganizations earlier on, so that they would be more successful.

The Bankruptcy Commission also took up the issue of how to encourage more reorganizations. In the Commission's deliberations, most members took the position that executory contracts should be rejectable by trustees or debtors-in-possession, and there is no indication that anyone anticipated a novel or substantial impact on collective bargaining agreements. The 1973 Commission Report proposed substantial changes with respect to reorganizations. It criticized the multiple reorganization chapters of the old act because: "... each of these chapters has detailed and overlapping rules regarding its availability which frequently produce pointless and wasteful litigation ..."[46] The Report recommended that all reorganization provisions be consolidated into a single chapter, and made a number of proposals for how to make reorganizations more effective.[47] It recognized that the incentive for

---

[45]   On the old provisions for executory contracts, see Finletter (1939: 222–41). A labor contract between employer and employee is one type of executory contract. The power to reject is a relatively crude instrument since the contract must be accepted or rejected in its entirety. Trustees or debtors-in-possession cannot accept some provisions and reject others.

[46]   *Report of the Bankruptcy Commission*: 23.

[47]   *Report of the Bankruptcy Commission*: 23–9.

management to file for bankruptcy and reorganize the firm depended on who was to be in control of the reorganizing firm: the debtor (that is, management), or a court-appointed independent trustee.[48] Managers are less inclined to reorganize if it means they will be replaced by a trustee, and, not surprisingly, the absence of a trustee was one of the main attractions of the old Chapter XI.[49] Following prior law, the Report also suggested that reorganization trustees, or debtors-in-possession, retain the power to accept or reject executory contracts.[50] The goal of all these proposals was to encourage corporations to reorganize *before* their situation became hopeless, and to give the reorganizer sufficient flexibility to be able to reestablish the viability of the firm.

The Commission's proposals for reorganization were generally uncontroversial. In particular, the provisions that granted to trustees and debtors-in-possession the power to reject executory contracts, subject to court approval, were reproduced through every version of the bankruptcy bill, up to and including the 1978 Act.[51] For ordinary executory contracts, the traditional test for court approval was the "business judgement" test: if rejection would benefit the estate financially, it was approved (Miller 1984: 8). The parties hurt by rejection of the contract could claim damages, but their status as unsecured prepetition creditors made their claim a weak one (Countryman 1974: 545). The courts recognized that labor contracts were not ordinary executory contracts and so they usually applied a more stringent standard than the business judgement test (Gregory 1984: 561). There was some disagreement, however, over what exactly was an appropriate standard.

The assumption or rejection of a collective bargaining agreement by a reorganizing firm was potentially subject to two legal jurisdictions. On the one hand, under bankruptcy law, trustees and debtors-in-possession were empowered to reject executory contracts. On the other hand, collective bargaining agreements were subject to the terms of the National Labor Relations Act (NLRA), which prohibited a company from unilaterally altering the terms of such agreements. The question

---

[48] *Report of the Bankruptcy Commission*: 243–4.

[49] *Report of the Bankruptcy Commission*: 247.

[50] *Report of the Bankruptcy Commission*: 248.

[51] The Commission Bill, Judges' Bill, H.R. 6, H.R. 8200, S. 2266, and the final Act all had virtually identical provisions for executory contracts. H.R. 8200 and S. 2266, for example, both stated that: "... the trustee, subject to the court's approval, may assume or reject any executory contract or unexpired lease of the debtor" (Subcommittee on Civil and Constitutional Rights of the House Committee on the Judiciary, 95th Cong., 1st Sess., Committee Print No. 6, July 1977: 67).

arose over whether there was a conflict between bankruptcy law and labor law over this issue, and if so, how it was to be resolved.

In one frequently cited case, *Shopmen's Local 455 v. Kevin Steel Products*,[52] the debtor-in-possession successfully petitioned the bankruptcy court for permission to reject its collective bargaining agreement with a union. The National Labor Relations Board then argued that rejection of the agreement by the debtor-in-possession violated the NLRA. The court decision in favor of the union, and against rejection, was later overturned by the Second Circuit Court of Appeals, which argued that a Chapter XI reorganization created a new business entity, one which was not bound by the obligations of the pre-petition firm. The Second Circuit ruled that, as executory contracts, collective bargaining agreements could be rejected, but that the standard for rejection had to be much stricter than for ordinary executory contracts—a court could allow rejection only after determining that it would benefit the estate, but also after a "careful balancing of the equities on both sides" (Becker 1981: 398; Gregory 1984: 561–3). The "new entity" theory was reaffirmed shortly thereafter by the Second Circuit in the case of *Brotherhood of Railway Clerks v. REA Express Inc.*[53] In this case, the court elaborated an exacting standard for rejection—that unless the agreement were rejected, the firm would collapse and the jobs would be lost (Gregory 1984: 563–5).

Neither of these cases concentrated the minds of any in the reform circle, including organized labor. Labor witnesses focused upon the priority rank accorded wages and benefits.[54] One reason for labor's prior neglect was that management groups also showed little interest. Labor and business groups are frequent political opponents and had fought just before the period of bankruptcy reform over the Employee Retirement Income Security Act of 1974.[55] Yet organizations like the US Chamber of Commerce and the National Association of Manufacturers made no presentations during the hearings over bankruptcy law

---

[52]　519 F.2d 698 (2d Cir. 1975).

[53]　523 F.2d 164 (2d. Cir. 1975), *cert. denied*, 423 U.S. 1017 (1975).

[54]　For example, the testimony of Elihu Leifer, from the Office of the General Counsel of the Building and Construction Trades Department, AFL-CIO, made no mention of executory contracts. Like the other labor representatives, he discusses the priority rank given employee wages and benefits under bankruptcy (*Bankruptcy Reform Act Hearings on S. 235 and S. 236*: 279–83).

[55]　This measure involved the regulation of private pension programs and the establishment of a Pension Benefit Guaranty Corporation to insure them. Business opposed ERISA, and its passage was viewed as a victory for labor.

and did not mobilize very energetically in other ways. In their publications, they manifested little interest in the reform process, and certainly showed no appreciation that the ability to reject collective bargaining agreements would subsequently prove to be a powerful management tool. In recalling whether or not management tried to influence the reform process, organized labor's representative recalled:

I have no recollection of a committee or a Chamber of Commerce or other similar groups coming in and testifying in other ways.... I'm sure there were a number of key congressmen that communicated with the Chamber [of Commerce], probably much more with the NAM [National Association of Manufacturers]. The chamber is much more active than the NAM and is much more (from my point of view) right wing on an issue like this. I am sure there was communication. But they never came in with heavy pressure...because they never took it very seriously.[56]

The business groups that did testify were mostly from the financial, banking and credit industries.[57] In bankruptcy, these groups were in the position of creditors (frequently secured creditors), not that of debtor-in-possession, and so they were not so concerned about the ability to reject labor contracts.[58] Their main goal was to protect their own financial claims. Obvious management support or interest in these measures could have at least suggested to labor that the matter was worth investigating further.

Another reason for labor's neglect may have derived from the role of the National Labor Relations Act in regulating union–management contracts. The NLRA prohibits an employer from unilaterally altering its employment contracts (Bordewieck and Countryman 1983: 297–9; Countryman 1974: 494). Without union consent, an employer cannot modify or terminate a collective bargaining agreement (Pulliam 1984: 1–2). By NLRA standards, to do so is to engage in an unfair labor practice (Gregory 1984: 545; Rasnic 1986: 637). With NLRA protection, labor groups may have felt that the executory contract provisions of bankruptcy law posed no real threat. Where labor law and bankruptcy law conflicted, organized labor thought the former would prevail.

[56] US Interview 92:06.
[57] For example, representatives of the National Association of Credit Managers, the American Bankers Association, the American Life Insurance Association, and the National Association of Bank Loan and Credit Officers testified at various times.
[58] As Trost points out, banks, savings and loan associations, and insurance companies are not eligible for relief under the reorganization chapters of the bankruptcy code (Trost, 1979: 1312).

Significantly enough, Max Zimny, who carried the flag for organized labor in the 1978 reforms, was aware that the provisions on executory contracts were a potential time-bomb in the legislation for labor. Not only was he aware personally, but he argued the point with his labor colleagues that there was a danger that should be addressed. In fact, the third of labor's proposals in its submission to the Commission pointed out that ambiguity about executory contracts could, in principle, be used against labor contracts and this misuse should be anticipated and blocked. Yet the probability of labor contracts being abrogated by a court seemed so remote, and the importance of back-wages and fringe benefits so immediate, that labor made a tactical choice to emphasize wages and fringe benefits over executory contracts.[59]

Thus while labor's chief lobbyist in the bankruptcy reforms recognized "a serious need" to ensure that a court did not consider a "collective bargaining agreement like any other commercial agreement," he had relatively little confidence that it would win favor in Congress, and thus did not warrant the kind of political mobilization that might imperil a strong push to expand wages and benefits for workers in the new Code. Quite why labor did not push its case more forcefully remains a puzzle, since the leading representatives on the Democratic side, such as Congressmen Edwards and Drinan, had strong credentials as labor supporters. Moreover, a moderate Republican on the House side opined, in retrospect, that

[I]f labor had said, "You are giving an awful lot of power to the bankruptcy court over union management contracts," that ... an exception would have been written and grafted on the bill so fast it would make your head swim.... I am saying if labor asked for it, and we had denied it, that would have killed [the bill].[60]

In other words, had unions raised strong objections *before* the law passed, the provisions in regard to executory contracts would have been rewritten to satisfy them. Yet labor did not see collective bargaining as a prime issue for the same reason that neither management nor staffers gave it close attention: the probability of its occurrence seemed sufficiently remote that it should not clutter the legislative agenda. The 1978 Act was scarcely mentioned in union publications, and no mention was made of executory contracts.[61] Moreover, from labor's standpoint, there

---

[59]   US Interview 92:06.

[60]   See the two paragraph description in the *AFL-CIO Convention Proceedings, 13th Convention* 1979: 256. US Interview 91:04.

[61]   The only one we have found consisted of a neutral comment, four paragraphs long, in *Labor Looks at Congress, 1978*: 23–4.

was always the expectation that if a major problem arose, labor would have the political force to push through subsequent legislation to defend its interests.

In February 1984, labor's incipient fears were realized. In the case of the *National Labor Relations Board v. Bildisco & Bildisco*, the Supreme Court ruled unanimously that a collective bargaining agreement was an executory contract subject to the terms of section 365 of the Bankruptcy Act of 1978.[62] Trustees and debtors-in-possession could legitimately reject collective bargaining agreements during a reorganization. The court also set forth a standard for rejection that went beyond the business judgement test but short of the standard proposed in the *REA* case by the Second Circuit. Finally, by a five to four majority, the justices ruled that a firm which rejected such an agreement before securing the permission of a bankruptcy judge was not guilty of an unfair labor practice (Levit and Mason 1984: 177; Hermann and Neff 1985: 622–3, 625–30). The lesson of *Bildisco* was clear: Chapter 11 reorganizations threatened unions.

The 1978 Act was such a success in encouraging more corporations to reorganize earlier, that some companies pushed the envelope of the law and filed even though they were having no trouble meeting their current obligations and were, from a balance sheet perspective, solvent (Hermann and Neff 1985: 621). Not until the early 1980s did large corporations file for Chapter 11 primarily in order to reduce their labor costs. The most publicized examples were Continental Airlines and Wilson Foods, both of which in 1983 used Chapter 11 reorganizations to cut their unionized labor costs by a substantial amount.[63] When companies began to use "strategic bankruptcy" to alter their labor contracts, it finally became clear to organized labor that the provisions for executory contracts posed a serious danger.

The unanticipated nature of these consequences is clear from interviews with reform participants. According to one congressional staffer: "We never dreamt, I guess at the time, anymore than we dreamt

---

[62] *National Labor Relations Board v. Bildisco & Bildisco*, 104 S. Ct. 1188 (1984). See Begin and Beal 1985: 306.

[63] Wilson Foods Corporation filed under Chapter 11 in April 1983, repudiated its labor contracts covering 6,000 of its 9,000 employees, and reduced wages between 40% and 50%. In 1983, Wilson earned $12 million in profit, and at the time of filing had a net value of about $67 million. Evidently, the company was not insolvent. See Gregory (1984: 542), Delaney (1989: 646), Browning (1984: 60), "The Bankruptcy Laws May Be Stretching Too Far," *Business Week*, 9 May 1983, "Wilson Foods: Nine Days to Chapter 11," *Business Week*, 30 May 1983, and "Management by Bankruptcy," *Fortune*, 31 Oct. 1983.

somebody could file a Johns Manville as Chapter 11, that you could unilaterally abrogate an executory contract with a union." According to another staffer: "I don't thing anybody could really foresee Bildisco and Continental Airlines to the extent it developed."[64] The *Bildisco* decision resolved the legal ambiguities surrounding the status of collective bargaining agreements in bankruptcy, and so labor's vulnerability became manifest.[65] It was perceived as part of: "... an overall assault upon national labor policy" (Simon and Mehlsack 1984 : 6). For example, at its 15th convention, the AFL–CIO resolved that: "Misuse of the bankruptcy laws to destroy workers' wages and working conditions is the latest, and one of the most pernicious, in the long list of union-busting devices." This decision galvanized organized labor into pressing for statutory changes to overturn the court's decision, and the 1982 Supreme Court ruling that the 1978 Bankruptcy Code was unconstitutional (a ruling reached on other, unrelated, grounds) provided a convenient political opportunity.[66] Said a labor spokesman:

I think that things like the first Continental [Airlines] bankruptcy, when they went into bankruptcy courts to specifically reject the collective bargaining... it made a lot of headlines. It sensitized the AFL-CIO and other unions of what they should have been sensitive of a long time before then. And then when Bildisco came along and said, yeah, they clearly can do all of these things there was a lot of pressure put on the AFL-CIO to lead the charge.[67]

After an intense effort, labor allies in the House managed in 1984 to pass a bill that would have made it more difficult to reject labor contracts (Pulliam 1985: 396–7; *Congressional Quarterly Almanac* 1984: 266–7). The Senate was lobbied by business groups and resisted the House measure. None of the proposals contested the right to reject an executory contract, nor the fact that collective bargaining agreements were executory contracts. They did, however, try to make the test for rejection a stricter one. The question was: how much stricter? (Rasnic 1986: 634). Eventually, the 1984 revisions to the Act specified a series of steps that an employer in Chapter 11 bankruptcy must undertake before it can reject a labor agreement.[68] Unlike the politics of the 1978 Code, this

[64] See Pulliam (1985: 395). US Interview 91:05; US Interview 92:01.

[65] Wilson Foods' unions filed unfair-labor-practices charges against the company after it rejected its union contracts in Chapter 11. Whether or not such rejection was an unfair practice was one of the key issues settled by *Bildisco*.

[66] *AFL-CIO Convention Proceedings, 15th Convention* 1983: 100.

[67] US Interview 92:06.

[68] These steps were set forth in section 1113, and were part of the Bankruptcy Amendments and Federal Judgeship Act of 1984, PL 98–353. See Hermann and Neff (1985:

legislative episode took on the form of politics as usual: pro-labor and pro-management legislators mobilized around competing legislation that favored their respective constituencies.[69]

Therein lay two significant differences from the 1978 Code: labor and management's interests were clearly articulated in classical opposition form; and both mobilized to secure their respective interests. Furthermore, before 1978 labor's position as a creditor took precedence whereas after, its contribution to a firm's costs became a more important issue partly because the Act so successfully encouraged reorganizations. The 1984 Act serves to sharpen the juxtaposition with the 1978 politics of expertise in a long undisturbed legislative arena, where interests were opaque, threats were vague, and mobilization—or its lack—reflected both.

ENGLISH INSOLVENCY REFORMS

Victory to the Strong: Consumers and Trade Creditors

Several members of the Insolvency Reform Committee viewed the overhaul of bankruptcy law as a rare opportunity to redress an imbalance between the big institutions—the banks, the state, the utilities—and the small and weak creditors. Three issues directly influenced the potential of insolvency reforms to strengthen the weak: a special fund to set aside money for small creditors in bankruptcy; the threat to abolish a method, called the retention of title, for securing the goods supplied by trade suppliers; and a move to create protections for prepayments made by consumer creditors.

The Ten Percent Fund

As in the United States, corporate insolvencies too often left unsecured creditors with meager left-overs, if anything at all. And as on the other side of the Atlantic, this alienated consumers and small businesses from

---

634–7). Labor commentators believed that 1113: "... effectively prohibits unilateral abrogation by the debtor of its labor agreements and establishes standards for rejection which include good faith negotiation as a necessary precondition to an application to the court for authorization to reject" (Simon and Mehlsack 1984: 6–44).

[69] Both the AFL-CIO and the Air Line Pilots Association were very active, and their proposals were strongly resisted by Continental Airlines and the National Association of Manufacturers. See Hermann and Neff (1985: 630–4); and "A Last-Minute Deal to Keep the Bankruptcy Courts Alive," *Business Week*, 26 Mar. 1984.

the entire process of corporate reorganization and liquidation. The Cork Committee invented an ingenious solution by proposing the establishment of a "Ten Percent Fund," (TPF) in which banks would waive their right to ten per cent of the proceeds of their security, and this money would be distributed among the unsecured creditors.[70]

The Ten Percent Fund was one element of a bigger "package deal" proposed to all parties in bankruptcy by the Cork Committee. On one side, Cork offered a deal in which government preferences—all the moneys owed by companies to government—would be severely limited, thereby putting more money in the pot for small creditors as well as for other unsecured creditors (which often included banks). On the other, the banks would be expected to put aside ten per cent of the value of the assets they had secured with a floating charge holder for distribution among ordinary unsecured creditors.

While on balance the banks would likely have been better off with the total packet, they vigorously opposed the TPF. As a result, the government rejected the idea altogether and it appeared neither in the government's Green or White Papers (1984), nor in the Insolvency Bill (1984) introduced to Parliament. However, the Fund caught the imagination of the Labour Party, which tried to insert it into the legislation.

The TPF polarized parties to law reform. Within the reform committee, the main proponents for redressing the imbalance between weak and strong had been lawyers, liquidators, and a county court registrar, who were motivated strongly by equity concerns. Said a member of the committee: "I loved that fund. It dealt with my sense of justice tremendously," a judgement that corresponded to the equity position taken by the Labour Opposition in both houses of Parliament. Its advocates felt strongly that the Ten Percent Fund corrected glaring weaknesses in the ways banks acted against weak creditors at the back and front end of the extension of credit. Not only did the floating charge perpetrate injustices that deserved to be remedied, but the Ten Percent Fund offered a

[70] The idea was raised initially by Mr Goldman as a limitation on floating charges. The debenture holder should be allowed no more than 90 per cent of the realization of the assets. Ten per cent should be kept for unsecured creditors. The debenture holder would rank as an unsecured creditor for the balance. This would support acceptance of the idea that the receiver was working for everyone, not simply the debenture holder. This idea, it was agreed, "would go a long way to solving the problem of the unsecured creditor and would make the recommendations more likely to be acceptable to the politicians." Goldman prepared a paper for consideration by the committee and transmission to the Committee of London Clearing Bankers for comment. (*Minutes of the Cork Committee*, 27 Sept. 1978: 6.) See generally, section 1538, on "The Ten Percent Fund," in ch. 35, "Fixed Charges," *Cork Report*: 347–51.

correction against wanton approaches to lending. One reformer observed that:

... a lot of us felt that banks and lending institutions were a lot of rather stupid people who were lending money that should never have been lent—this business of banks chucking credit at private individuals and then clobbering them if they don't pay displayed a callousness of banks with "hopeless and incompetent individuals."[71]

As opposition mounted to the TPF, its principal proponents within the Cork Committee, and subsequently its sponsors in Parliament, shifted their arguments from an initial appeal to principles of general equity and the redress of distributive injustices to a more pragmatic approach. Since redistribution for its own sake found little support on the Tory benches, the reformers converted the concept of the TPF as a redistributive device into that of an instrumental mechanism, retooling its purpose and recasting its defense. In the place of the TPF as a *compensation to weak creditors* came the TPF as a *"fighting fund"* for the professionals.[72]

The fighting fund had three main virtues. It would give insolvency practitioners the financial resources—for their own fees and those of other professionals—to engage in "hot pursuit" of debtors who were hiding monies or creditors who had smuggled out assets before they got into the estate. With a floating charge, the banks in control had little incentive to enlarge the pool beyond what was necessary to repay the money owed them. One MP explained:

The view taken by myself and others was that if you set aside 10% of the assets you could at least fund your liquidator without your liquidator having to go, or your receiver having to go to his paymaster who is the floating charge, the bank, for permission to pursue. Because very often banks and other people took the view, look we've got enough to satisfy us to hell with everybody else, we will not pursue. Now had there been a pursuit or a hot pursuit trading policy, in a number of cases you may well have recouped monies. So as the little creditors you were going to get something out of it.[73]

---

[71] UK Interview 90:13.

[72] In the House debates in Standing Committee E, Labour spokesman, Bryan Gould indicated they would introduce an amendment on the TPF. Alex Fletcher replied that he had spoken to Cork, and Cork had agreed that its purpose was to produce a fighting fund, not a dividend for unsecured creditors. Gould observed that there had been a slight shift of position, but that the fighting fund was a stronger premiss. (H.C., vol. 78, 30 Apr. 1985, cols. 157–8).

[73] H.C., vol. 78, col. 156, 166. UK Interview 90:02.

"All of us know," stated a barrister-MP, "that time after time we came across a situation where a pursuit could lead to substantial recovering. Without the pursuit everyone loses."

Hot pursuit also entailed a heightened degree of moral regulation, particularly of company directors, because, "it would act as a deterrent to some of the shysters we had hanging around." Deviant company managers would quickly come to recognize that competent and well-funded professionals now had the financial backing to track them down, either to demand the return of assets, or to bring them into civil or criminal court to answer for reckless or fraudulent practice.[74] The net result would be to increase the size of the pie, and a bigger pie meant that unsecured creditors could expect a real return.

It was an opportunity whereby some of the funds in the debenture could be used in a way that may gather more income which enabled the small investor or the small creditor, and perhaps even the shareholder, at the end of the day, to recoup something from the debacle.[75]

The TPF might have benefitted weak creditors. But it was guaranteed to help professionals: it ensured more fees to fund "hot pursuit;" but it also hinted at a measure of autonomy from the bankers, or debenture holders, who were normally the paymasters of insolvency practitioners. In theory, the TPF could actually be turned against the debenture holders, for the scope of the floating charge itself might be challenged by the insolvency practitioner.

The bankers "really fought hard" against the TPF, said Sir Kenneth Cork, because they foresaw dire consequences for the way they did business.[76] While they feared an immediate ten per cent reduction in the assets protected by their floating charge, they were even more anxious that ten per cent might be the thin edge of a larger wedge. Like income tax, it would start small, and grow inexorably. Moreover, bankers had little stomach for a loss of control over their agents, the

---

[74] Following the logic of the English legislation more generally, the use of the Ten Percent Fund as a fighting fund for private practitioners represents the analogue for solving the collective action problem of weak creditors to the proposals in the American legislation that government officials, such as the states' Attorneys General, be given the power to initiate class actions on behalf of weak creditors.

[75] UK Interview 90:02.

[76] Said Cork, "the Ten Percent was the only thing they [the large banks] really fought" in the entire legislation. "Everybody [at the banks] was saying that it was outrageous the fact that they should lose ten percent of their money." UK Interviews 90:04; 91:07.

insolvency practitioners, who might add insult to injury and take some of the lost ten per cent and turn it against them.[77]

Part of the bankers' resistance stemmed from the dilemma in which the reformers placed them. The reformers presented a "general package" where everyone got something, but most had to give something away. If nobody broke ranks, then the banks would be better off because the reforms would drastically cut down on high-ranked Crown preferences—moneys going off the top of the estate to the government to pay unpaid taxes. But the bankers were "extraordinarily cynical," by their own description, that the government would give up any of its own Crown preference, and they feared a situation where they would yield ten per cent, but the government would yield nothing. Without confidence that all parties would maintain solidarity with each other, the bankers took the more cautious route and refused to be a party to the TPF.

This conservatism also reflected practical concerns. Although the concept of the "fighting fund" was a noble notion, no one had any idea how well it would work nor how many assets it would bring into the estate. Moreover, the TPF threatened to lift the veil on banking practices for it would require bankers to share more information with third parties. To identify the ten per cent, the banks would need to give an accounting of the proceeds in the estate to a wider constituency than had been their wont, an unveiling of banking practice that was instinctively abhorrent.[78]

But an even more skeptical view was expressed about the motivations of the insolvency practitioners, personified by Sir Kenneth Cork.

Excuse my cynicism for a moment, but I think that at that point in time certainly Cork himself was going for this sort of public position. You know he had started as an ambulance chaser, really, and he was sort of moving into respectability in a big way. I mean he was already Lord Mayor of London.[79]

The bankers found a welcome ally among the civil servants in the Department of Trade and Industry who were drafting the legislation. For them the Fund was politically inexpedient. Already they had pushed the envelope in a big bill that contained much controversy and a great deal of innovation. To get the legislation through Parliament, the government could not make an enemy of the banks.[80] The professionals, and especially the insolvency practitioners, found themselves in a double

[77] UK Interview 91:06.   [78] UK Interview 91:06.   [79] UK Interview 91:06.
[80] UK Interviews 91:17; 91:10.

bind. They could alienate their most important clients, the banks, by supporting the TPF. However, the Fund effectively promised to create a huge pool to finance an extension of lawyers' and accountants' jurisdictions. It *might* help the weak creditors, but it *undoubtedly* empowered the professionals, and they aligned themselves with the innovators and the champions of the weak, whose agents they might become, given enough resources.

What rhetorical devices did the opponents of the Fund deploy to block its adoption without being accused of callous disregard for the weak? The bankers offered a graduated response whose central message was that the Fund would do more harm than good, even for the parties it was intended to benefit. The banks painted a bleak scenario of the ways that banking practices would need to adapt. Because bankers would be unsure of how much they could secure of a debtor's assets, they would not lend to riskier, more marginal enterprises, a practice that would disproportionately hurt smaller creditors. And if they did make loans, banks would be compelled to charge a higher premium for loans, since they would be taking on more risk, and this, too, would squeeze smaller creditors out of the capital markets. Another means of reducing the risk of lending would produce equally detrimental effects: banks would be forced to employ more fixed securities, where every asset had to be specified and valued, an approach to collateral that would drive up transaction costs through lost time, lost flexibility, and higher legal fees. Overall, banks claimed they would be forced in effect to "contract around" this measure so as to counter its effects.

An even more compelling argument struck at the core of the government's statutory purposes. Since the rehabilitative ideal was at the heart of the Bill—saving companies through timely and expert reorganization—the bankers made the case that the Ten Percent Fund would introduce a harmful delay in reorganizations, because in order to find out the actual monetary value of the ten per cent, it would be necessary to know the full value of the estate, a process that could take months or years. Since delays often make the difference between life and death for a company, relief for weaker creditors might sentence a business to death. And if this prophecy of doom did not suffice, then the bankers countered with a general principle of their own, namely, that the floating charge had become integral to English banking. Tampering with its use threatened to undermine the entire credit system.

In public, civil servants took the view that it simply was not practical. No one knew how it would work. In private, however, one policy-maker mused that the Fund should not have been taken seriously in its own terms for it was itself a rhetorical exercise, a cynical smokescreen by the Cork Committee to distract attention from the fact that it was so pro-banking. "I suspect that the 10% fund was a sort of crumb at the last minute," said a civil servant on the legislative team. While some committee members may have had a genuine commitment to equity, the leading insolvency practitioners offered the Fund as a palliative to disguise the fact that they had sold out to their primary clients—the banks. Not to put too fine a point upon it, the liquidators—even the great Cork himself—once were ambulance chasers. Their conversion to protecting the poor represented a highly publicized bid not only to rehabilitate companies, but their own occupational status—this time not as company doctors, but as altruistic professionals.[81]

When the Insolvency Bill was first introduced into the House of Lords, Lord Bruce, the Labour leader on the Bill, immediately served notice of the Opposition's disappointment that the Ten Percent Fund had not found its way into the Bill. Not only would it serve as a fighting fund, but it would leave something over for unsecured creditors, who "often find that they are left completely out in the cold." Lord Mishcon, a solicitor, tried to link the fighting fund with one of the government's primary goals by arguing that it would reinforce other measures to better regulate business, by ensuring that directors acted properly. "There have been too many scandals . . . we are trying to stop people hiding behind limited liability and carrying on nefarious activities that no decent businessman would countenance." And Lord Mottistone pressed the views of the Consumers Association that special arrangements should be made to set aside sums of money for small creditors, since the large creditors could take care of themselves.[82]

But the Government remained adamant that the Fund had no place in the Bill. In the beginning, Lord Lucas, the government minister in charge of the legislation, simply ignored the calls for amendment in favor of the Fund. But when pushed to provide a rationale for its exclusion, he opined that it was just "emotive in nature," and noted that the Cork Committee itself had not been unanimous. In any event,

---

[81] UK Interview 90:05.

[82] Lord Bruce introduced an amendment that one-tenth of the proceeds of the floating charge should be retained in a trust for the liquidator and for ordinary creditors. Since the striking down of other preferences would increase the funds available, this would not diminish the amount available to other creditors (H.L., vol. 458, 15 Jan. 1985, cols. 887, 912–13, 920; H.L., vol. 458, 7 Feb. 1985, cols. 1222–3).

he said, echoing the bankers, it would be counterproductive: lenders will lend less, charge higher rates of interest, or no longer use the floating charge, all defensive measures that would harm the smaller unsecured creditor. Moreover, it was impractical: it would tie up funds in special accounts and deprive them from the turnaround specialists. Furthermore, for a government seeking to reduce public regulation, the Ten Percent Fund would be "a hugely expensive business" to police, said Lord Lucas, and would require regulators to intrude further into companies' affairs. Helping the poor, he implied, meant big government—and that the voters had clearly rejected.[83]

Nevertheless the final fate of the Fund was a much closer decision than many expected. After extended debate in the Lords, the Opposition forced a division, which they lost by an unexpectedly close vote of 106 to 89. The intensity of feeling in the debate is reflected in the normally judicious comments of Lord Denning, who scathingly concluded that:

I am afraid the Government must have been much influenced by those big bankers.... The banking community want every penny. They want the last 10 percent.... They always want their interest, right to the very top rate. The banking community do not need this 10 percent.... They ought to allow the unsecured creditors a little bit, just 10 percent, that is all.

Thus came the debate full circle, as Denning echoed the very redistributive themes sounded inside the Reform Committee at its earliest deliberations—long before the rhetoric shifted to reward professionals for their valor at seizing back funds that had escaped the estate.

Prepayments

A second major area for weak creditors concerned consumer repayments—people who had paid deposits to companies in exchange for some future supply of goods and services; or consumers who had responded to mail order advertisements and sent money with the order. When the company failed, these people got nothing.

In a letter to the reform committee, the Consumers Association identified two problems. The first was that of unscrupulous liquidators and directors who took the deposits people made for houses, appliances, furniture, and the like, liquidated the company, and started up again, free of all obligations to deliver on the goods. The second was the related but more general problem of prepayments—individuals who had paid

---

[83] H.L., vol. 458, 15 Jan. 1985, col. 92; UK Interview 90:09.

for deposits in the expectation of some future supply of goods and services or had sent money in response to mail order advertisements. Both of these also applied to guarantees built into a purchase, which were not then provided after the purchase. In its oral submissions, the Consumers Association gave some poignant accounts of ways that poor and naive consumers had lost large sums of money with no redress.[84]

To give some idea of the magnitude of the problem, the Office of Fair Trading, a quasi-government watchdog group, listed the businesses that required advanced payments by consumers: (1) the "postal bargain trade" on clothing, footwear, do-it-yourself equipment, household goods, garden requisites, records, typewriters; (2) deposits for electrical appliances and furniture; (3) prepayments in the service sector, including insurance, holiday and travel business, shipping, removals industry; and (4) building services and home improvements, such as central heating, insulation, glazing and plumbing cause many problems. In 1975–76 the Office received 3,994 complaints about these in insolvency.

The Office of Fair Trading catalogued the severe disadvantages of consumers compared to many other creditors. Their losses could not be passed along, but needed to be borne entirely by the consumer, and could not be set off against profits or tax liabilities. It was frequently difficult to investigate the financial reputation of a merchant. And there was no credit reference agency easily available to a consumer. Consumers did not have access to company reports or trade magazines. Neither could they bargain for collateral. Hence there was a major information and bargaining deficit for consumers.

The Office of Fair Trading acknowledged that some codes of practice had been adopted by trade associations, but these did not extend to insolvency.

We conclude that at present the consumer who makes advanced payment to a trader is inadequately protected against the effects of the trader's insolvency.... Yet in spite of this vulnerability the consumer's claims are at present disregarded in favor of those with preferential status, many of which derive from claimants who in their dealings with the trader have been in a far better position than the consumer to judge the trader's financial stability.

At the very least, the Office of Fair Trading called for equal status with other preferential creditors.[85]

---

[84] Submission by the Consumers Association, *Public Record Office*, 27 Feb. 1978.
[85] OFT Submissions *Public Record Office*, 13 Sept. 1977.

Most professionals, however, took a contrary view. It was the general presumption of insolvency practitioners, accountants, and lawyers that insolvency reforms must reduce the number of creditors who got preferred treatment, or preferences, before any of the unsecured creditors. The general accounting bodies were opposed to all preferences except employees' wages and holiday pay. The Joint Working Party of the Law Society and Bar also submitted that preferences should be eliminated or cut down.[86]

At first the Reform committee agreed following its premiss that there should be no preferences whatsoever. Yet its position eventually softened and it agreed that although general payments in advance by consumers should not be preferential, if businesses had set them aside in a special account, effectively in escrow, they would not be included in the insolvent estate.[87]

Prepayments or deposits did not return to the agenda until after the government announced its legislative plans. The Cork Report did not raise at all the possibility of preferences for prepayments or advance purchase consumers. And the Government White Paper had nothing to say about consumer creditors or prepayments, despite the outrage expressed by the government Minister for Consumer Affairs at the way some company directors used liquidation "as a commercial device for the exploitation of consumers." It was a "monstrous abuse" of a trader's responsibility to consumers "who have paid in advance for goods from traders who then go out of business only to carry on the same business under a different name."[88] Yet it was clear that the government preferred to approach consumer concerns indirectly through regulation of directors than by creation of another preferential category.

Effectively, therefore, the unprotected consumer received no support from the professionals, the reform committee, or the government. In mid-1984, however, as the Government released its Insolvency Bill, a public debate broke out between proponents and opponents of special treatment for consumer prepayments.[89]

---

[86] *Public Record Office*, 13th submission from CCAB, Dec. 1980. Joint Working Party of the Bar and Law Society, 7th submission, Oct. 1980.

[87] *Minutes of the Cork Committee*, 12 Mar. 1978: 6; 12 Apr. 1978: 4.

[88] "Vaughan attacks 'abuse' of liquidation," *Financial Times*, 29 Mar. 1982: 6 (the reports on a speech by the Minister of Consumer Affairs, Dr. Gerard Vaughan, to the annual Consumer Congress meeting).

[89] In the chapter on "Preferential Debts" in the Report of the Insolvency Committee, which was released to the public (ch. 32), the possibility of preferences for prepayments or

Here, even more than the Ten Percent Fund, the supporters of a preference for consumers held the high moral ground. The Consumers Association bemoaned the lack of government responsiveness to the needs of individual creditors, for whom current law gave little hope of getting any money back when firms went into liquidation. Government proposals, outlined in the Insolvency Bill,

> will do little for customers who have parted with their money for goods and services they have not received, the protection they should have against losing out when firms go bust. There is, in our view, no good reason why individual consumers should at the end of the day pick up the whole bill for unsuccessful traders.[90]

In both the House of Lords and the Commons, the Labour Party and several independents in the Lords made consumer losses in bankruptcy one of their principal lines of attack on the Tory bill. In his opening speech on the Bill in the House of Lords, Lord Bruce stated his intention to revise the Bill, especially on preferences, to get unsecured creditors a better deal. He similarly called for further steps to protect consumer creditors, who are not creditors in the ordinary sense of the term, and who pay deposits for goods they do not receive. Twice he mentioned the steps taken in the United States to give some preference to consumer creditors.[91] In the same debate, Lord Taylor declared that he had been briefed by the Consumers Association, Justice, and other consumer groups, in order to obtain greater protection for depositors.[92]

In the Second Reading of the Bill, Lord Lucas sought to pre-empt an amendment on prepayments by stating that the Government were aware of the problem, but agreed with the review committee that "the provision of credit in this way was not appreciably different from other forms of credit." Consequently, consumers making advanced payments should not be given any priority over other unsecured creditors. Furthermore, the strict measures being taken against delinquent directors should "reduce the likelihood that consumers will lose their money in the future." He obtained political cover by aligning the Government's position with a discussion paper produced by the Director-General of Fair Trading in which "he suggested that the answer lies probably more

---

advance purchase consumers is not even mentioned (*The Government White Paper*, its announcement of its legislative intentions, has nothing to say about consumer creditors or prepayments).

[90] Consumers' Association Briefing, Aug. 1984.
[91] H.L., vol. 458, 15 Jan. 1985, cols. 887–8.
[92] H.L., vol. 458, 15 Jan. 1985, col. 894.

in increased public awareness of the risk and wider adoption of voluntary schemes..."[93]

Three weeks later, Lord Taylor introduced an amendment to the Insolvency Bill which would have compelled the Secretary of State to issue regulations for companies to account for their handling of deposits and place them in separate bank accounts. This he sought to combine with another amendment which gave consumer prepayments and deposits a priority even over floating charge holders. Supporters of the amendment reiterated their belief that consumer creditors were not ordinary creditors—they do not think of themselves as extending credit at all—and that principles of "fairness and equity demand that a much better deal for consumers should be observed in this legislation." Prepayments were an integral and widespread practice in the modern economy, accounting for at least 15 million transactions each year, and they were a conventional method by which "the small man" equips his family for ordinary living. If the Government were so concerned to protect company directors, "it should be equally sensitive about the small man, the consumer."

Here Lord Denning was joined by other peers to resist a preference to creditors. Following Cork, he doubted that equity should privilege depositors more than other creditors—fairness dictated they not receive special treatment. The Government's resistance rested on three considerations. First, more rules and regulations made companies less competitive. Placing moneys in restrictive accounts deprived businesses of working capital and increased the likelihood of their failure. Second, regulations needed to be enforced, and the Government did not have the resources to do it. And, third, consistent with the Government's general philosophy, it much preferred private and voluntary schemes by business groups to set up compensation funds or make use of bonds. Sponsors of the amendment found little comfort in the Government's wish to push the problem onto market institutions. Neither were they much reassured by the Government's commitment to prosecute criminal fraud when "somebody who is on the verge of bankruptcy accepts money for something they know they can never deliver." Dissatisfied with the Government's response, Lord Taylor pushed the amendment to a vote, which he lost by a margin of 99 to 53.[94]

[93] H.L., vol. 458, 15 Jan. 1985, cols. 879–80.
[94] H.L., vol. 458, 2 Feb. 1985, cols. 837–47.

Advocates of the "little man" tried again when the Bill reached the Commons. Several ideas were presented by Labour members and some Tory back-benchers. Gerald Bermingham MP introduced an amendment to give consumer depositors a priority in bankruptcy. Others urged that businesses keep special accounts for deposits, an idea that had been long supported by the National Federation of Consumer Groups. Both of these were objectionable to the Government, either because the creation of more preferences worked against the current to reduce them, or because keeping special accounts seemed impractical for businesses, and would create an "enforcement nightmare."[95] The junior minister in the House of Commons, Alex Fletcher, conceded he would be glad to help out consumers, but no one—not even the consumers' organizations—could come up with a workable method.

The most intriguing proposal, however, arose in the context of a debate over differences between trade creditors and "deposit creditors," both of whom were relatively weak creditors, but who would be at odds with each other should a consumer preference be adopted. Those opposed to the amendment argued that any preference given to consumers would deprive trade suppliers of funds that might affect their survival. Advocates of a prepayment preference countered with the now familiar thesis that trade creditors had ample opportunity to judge the creditworthiness of their customers and, in any event, they had access to the retention of title, a security that placed them ahead even of banks that held floating charges. Talk of retention of title, or the Romalpa clauses, stimulated a fresh idea that might benefit consumers—a kind of "reverse Romalpa Clause." Explained Conservative MP, Steve Norris,

we are saying that until a depositor who has been sent a cheque to a company gets his goods, he should be treated as though he has retained title in that deposit. He should therefore be able to apply to a liquidator or a receiver and say, "I sent my money. I never had anything in return for it. The company has become insolvent and I should like my deposit back. I retain my claim to it because I have received nothing."

Even this did not change the Government's view that the solution was impracticable. It fell back on its affirmation of voluntary schemes tailored to solve the problems in ways particular to various corners of the economy. Knowing that a division on the amendment would lead to

---

[95] Opposition to the consumer preference did not follow simple party lines. The Opposition spokesman on the Insolvency Bill, Bryan Gould, could not support it (H.C., vol. 78, series 6, 18 July 1985, col. 576).

defeat, Norris withdrew the motion and any real chance for consumer protection disappeared from the legislative agenda.[96]

Most curious in these debates was the position of the insolvency practitioners. None had been especially enthusiastic about a consumer preference. In their reaction to the White Paper in April 1984 they articulated their opposition along now familiar lines: it was impractical to create separate trust accounts for depositors; since deposits are a source of credit for a company, their withdrawal would actually exacerbate the financial difficulties of firms; and there was no reason why this group of creditors should receive any more favor than other (unnamed) groups that might have similar grievances.[97]

By November 1985, when no further legislative action was possible, a radically new image appeared in a release entitled, "Consumer Protection—A Missed Opportunity." The Insolvency Practitioners Association expressed its disappointment that the insolvency legislation was a "missed opportunity" to help consumer creditors. Though it reads most ingenuously, given the earlier response to the White Paper, the IPA announced that its members had been pressing the Government "to afford some measure of preferential status to the ordinary members of the public who lose their money." They noted several television programs, such as "Watchdog" and "That's Life," which evidence "the widespread concern of the sense of injustice felt by ordinary people." Ironically enough, after criticizing the Government for heeding the very views previously expressed by the IPA, in a few short months the insolvency practitioners had switched sides, and now articulated the view of the pro-consumer lobbyists, who had vainly sought to persuade Parliament that:

members of the public are not like other creditors. They do not give credit to a company. They do not get tax relief on the money lost. They do not get VAT bad debt relief. Unlike the trade creditors there is no element of profit in the transaction and the prepayment has already come out of taxed income. To a consumer it is a 100% loss. Similarly the public does not have the knowledge or the resources to assess credit risks.[98]

It is difficult to avoid the conclusion that the insolvency practitioners tried to polish their image by seeking the moral high ground in public,

---

[96] H.C., vol. 78, St. Comm. E., 11 June 1985, cols. 281–303; H.C., vol. 78, series 6, 30 Apr. 1985, cols. 145–6, 153–4, 157–60, 163–6; H.C., vol. 78, series 6, 18 July 1985, cols. 573–9.

[97] Submission to the DTI in response to the *Government White Paper*, IPA, April 1984.

[98] IPA Press conference briefing paper, "Consumer Protection—A Missed Opportunity." 5 Nov. 1985.

after they had effectively helped kill in private the very measures that offered relief to consumers.

Protections for Trade Suppliers (Retention of Title)

Ownership of assets is usually secured when the owner acquires title, evidenced by a legal document that records the transfer of property rights from one company to another. But there are many commercial transactions when the change of ownership is not so unambiguous or so clearly labelled. In British construction and manufacturing, for example, producers sold raw materials, like bricks, or steel, to a buyer, usually on credit. Once they were in his or her possession, statute law usually conferred ownership of the raw materials on the buyer, even if he or she had not yet fully paid. If the buyer became insolvent, the administrator sent in to liquidate the business seized the raw materials, sold them, and distributed the proceeds to all the various creditors—including the original supplier.

Many trade suppliers believed this was unjust. They delivered goods in the expectation of payment; ownership passed to the buyer without payment; and now, after insolvency, they were forced to share the value of the goods with unsecured creditors, and would receive back only a fraction of their money.[99]

In 1976, the English Court of Appeal ruled that the Romalpa Aluminium company retained title on its aluminium until the buyer paid in full, since there was a clause in the contract to that effect. Professor Roy Goode, an academic company lawyer and a member of the Cork Committee Legal Consultative Panel, doubted whether "any case decided this century had created a greater impact in the commercial world" (Davies 1985: 3–5). This ruling effectively allowed trade suppliers to jump from the bottom of the repayment queue, as unsecured creditors, to the top, even ahead of banks with the strongest forms of legal security, most notably the floating charge (McBarnet and Whelan 1987).

The reform committee discussed at great length whether, first, it would seek to modify the floating charge in insolvency, and second, whether it would recommend that suppliers be able to retain title to their goods when the buyer became insolvent. The two issues were

---

[99] For the most detailed work on the law and practice of retention of title, see Sally Wheeler (1991).

interrelated because the priority of devices (Romalpa clause vs. floating charges) determined the priority of those who typically used them (trade suppliers vs. banks).

The Logic of Resistance

The debate over retention of title (ROT) did not have the public appeal of the Ten Percent Fund, but that did not stop a heated debate within the reform committee, where the banks and certain insolvency practitioners had interests quite strongly at odds with those sympathetic to trade suppliers.[100] The contours of that debate help delineate lines of cleavage, the limits of technical law reform, and the character of legislative innovation.

Professional reformers opposed the institutionalization of this new form of security from the outset. In the first place, it ran against the current to abolish all preferences. In the second place, as Sally Wheeler has shown, ROT clauses can be a great nuisance to insolvency practitioners, since it is much harder to keep companies running if suppliers arrive with their trucks to seize back crucial goods (Wheeler 1994). Furthermore, there was a practical problem: raw steel or chemicals or bricks might have become invisible, because they had been incorporated into a new product. If it was impossible to identify the goods, it was difficult to demand payment. Thus there were nuisance problems of identification and proof. Cork told his committee that if every supplier were permitted to insert a retention of title clause in the contract, every business that became insolvent would close down the next day. Moreover, the evidence showed the practice was spreading rapidly, with trade

[100] The most important consultees on this subject, from the vantage point of the Cork Committee, were the City of London Solicitors Company, the British Bankers Association, the Insolvency Service, and the Institute of Credit Management. *Minutes of the Cork Committee,* 17 Nov. 1977. The City of London Solicitors Association would restrict retention of title to original goods, but they were opposed to registration (Oral testimony, 7 Feb. 1978), whereas the IPA would also accept retention of title on original goods, but wanted registration, and some measures to ensure that Romalpa clauses did not force the company to be prematurely closed down (Written submission, Apr. 1978; Oral testimony, 13 June 1978). The Clearing Bankers were generally opposed to the retention of title, but if it were to be retained, then clauses should be registered in a similar way to securities, and goods would need to be identifiable (Written testimony, 4 June 1979; Oral testimony, 8 Sept. 1980). The British Bankers Association shared an aversion to ROT clauses because they created a form of security at a cost to other creditors and they rendered useless methods of evaluating a company's worth. But if they were to be retained, they called for disclosure of their existence, and limits both on how far title could be traced into "mixed" goods and how long the proceeds of sales of mixed goods could be pursued (Written submission to Cork Committee, 15 Aug. 1977) (*Public Record Office*).

groups, such as the Institute of Credit Management urging its members to introduce it. The bankers, too, sensed that it was catching on quickly. Ironically, some banks had begun to ask their customers if they held ROT clauses in their contracts. Alerted by the question, suppliers began to include them![101]

The banks were alarmed about the impact of ROT on lending and reorganizations. ROT clauses were invisible to bank lenders. This, they alleged, introduced a significant degree of uncertainty into lending practices. According to one of the bankers negotiating on behalf of the major clearing banks, it was "horrific...because you wouldn't know what the assets of the company were that you were lending to." More-over, the financial uncertainty induced by invisible clauses in contracts was compounded by a legal uncertainty about the status of ROT clauses under law. The amount of case law was so limited that bankers remained anxious about exactly how much security they retained in the assets of the corporation. And in solidarity with the insolvency practitioners, the bankers anticipated an adverse effect on corporate reorganizations. Said one banker, "you could easily foul up an efficient receivership or admin-istration because the receiver or administrator would have nothing to actually trade with."[102] The often unspoken but most fundamental objection was the expectation that ROT of title would diminish the assets in the estate. Not only could trade suppliers pull out their goods before the floating charge holder got control of the remaining assets, but fewer goods reduced the general estate for unsecured creditors.

This strong viewpoint within the committee led initially to a decision, with some demurrers, that ROT clauses should be rejected in insolv-ency. Since the decision against ROT was taken in the absence of committee member Peter Millett QC, on his return to the committee he pressed for reconsideration, noting that the Law Reform Committee for the Bar Council and the Law Reform Commission had both been hoping for some leadership from the Cork Committee on this vexing matter. Millett persuaded the Cork Committee to permit him to draft a working paper on ROT, which was subsequently passed through the lawyers' and accountants' adjunct committees, and brought back some nine months later to the full Cork Committee with a recommendation to accept ROT, subject to provisions that allayed the major sticking points for the bankers and insolvency practitioners.[103]

---

[101] *Minutes of the Cork Committee*, 27 June 1977: 5–6.   [102] UK Interview 91:06.
[103] *ibid*, 23 Sept. 1977: 2; 11 July 1978: 4.

Millett's compromise, which formed the basis for the Cork Report's recommendations, met the bankers' problems with uncertainty in their strength of security by demanding that retention of title clauses be disclosed in a register so that all future creditors could ascertain if ROTs were already in place. The fears expressed by insolvency practitioners that ROT militated against keeping the business running were countered with the recommendations that sellers could not immediately and unilaterally repossess their goods. They would face a moratorium of up to one year. Nor could they seek to seize goods already incorporated into new products, though they might press for some measure of proportional reimbursement once the new products were sold.[104]

It was, in other words, a Solomonic solution with everyone—trade suppliers, bankers, professionals—getting something, but nobody getting everything. As the Cork Report itself explicitly stated, it weighed significantly on the Reform Committee that the principal beneficiary of abolition of ROT would be the floating charge holders—the banks. Abolition of ROT in insolvency would not benefit general unsecured creditors and it would continue to be a hardship for trade suppliers.

Although the Cork Committee came to a compromise solution, the rhetoric used in the debate is worthy of attention in its own right. Unlike the open political forum, where party ideology, public preferences, and media stories demand a distinctive mode of presentation suited for general audiences, the reform committee engaged in an interior and highly technical form of deliberation.

One expedient, for and against ROT, centered on the lessons of regional and global law and practice. Since several insiders to the Cork Committee had been close to the Advisory Committee on the Draft EEC Bankruptcy Convention, they were familiar with forms of the ROT that were recognized by the original six nations of the EEC. For instance, in the wine industry, a seller of goods with the equivalent of reservation of title clause could recover them, or their cash equivalent, from the bankrupt or the estate. In Germany, according to Gerry Weiss, Cork's longtime expert advisor, ROT was widespread. In distributions, suppliers of goods got back about 64 per cent of the value of their claims, compared to 14 per cent for ordinary creditors. But this empirical evidence attracted radically different interpretations. Weiss believed that the ability of suppliers to walk away with their goods, or cash equivalents, came into conflict with the new ideal of saving

---

[104] *Minutes of the Cork Committee*, 11 July 1978: 4; *Cork Report*, ch. 37.

businesses. Muir Hunter QC, a colorful, outspoken personality, and a member of the Cork I committee, leapt into the fray with his unbridled opinion that the spread of Romalpa, or ROT, would "destroy the English mercantile economy" as it was destroying the German economy. But two could play the comparative game, for Professor Roy Goode, a leading commercial lawyer-academic, noted that the system had worked quite successfully in the US for twenty-five years, in all fifty states, and in two Canadian provinces. Trevor Traylor, secretary of the committee, indicated that if consistency in EEC market—and legal—integration counted for anything it appeared that the UK was preparing to accept ROT clauses, with some restrictions, in the EEC Draft Bankruptcy Convention.[105]

The prognoses from liquidators and bankers centered on the dire consequences for reorganization and extension of credit. Peter Avis, the banking representative on the committee, expressed two objections, which landed in the now familiar bankers' prediction that any change would hurt those it was intended to help—that current practices and instruments worked well, all things considered.

The floating charge was the cheapest and most convenient method of finance and margins were generally low. The banks made inquiries of customers and if there are "Romalpa" type contracts it affects their credit assessment and the amount of funds made available. If the banks see evidence of Romalpa, the companies may not be able to get finance at all; if advances are made they will be at a very different rate and companies will not able to get finance elsewhere at the price now offered by the banks. Business would not be able to cope with the impediment of Romalpa.[106]

And if the refusal of credit and higher interest rates were not sufficiently persuasive, then Avis invoked a sweeping transaction cost argument that recognition of ROT clauses in bankruptcy might produce a rush to securitization for everyone—with the unspoken, but undoubtedly well understood, corollary that lenders and borrowers would both sacrifice fees to lawyers.[107]

The lawyers had their own idiom of expert discourse. In addition to Professor Goode's allusion to the successful American experience, Walker-Arnott, an experienced commercial lawyer, argued in favor of

[105] Report of the Advisory Committee appointed by the Secretary of State for Trade on 27 July 1973 to consider the terms of the Draft EEC Bankruptcy Convention (Cmnd. 6602); Muir Hunter, Goode, *Minutes of the Cork Committee*, 8 Mar. 1978: 4.

[106] Avis, *Minutes of the Cork Committee*, 8 Mar. 1978: 4.

[107] *ibid*, 27 June 1977: 7.

registration of Romalpa clauses by embedding them in the general direction of legal development: the trend in company law, he said, had not been to interfere in contractual rights but to require disclosure. The committee had already accepted security in principle, and Romalpa clauses, were, in commercial terms, a form of security.[108] Professor Goode invoked a strategic argument for ROT that played on the bankers' more fundamental fears about abolition of their favored floating charge.

[T]he floating charge was under heavy attack and suppliers were saying that they should be given the facility to take a security interest. The underlying thought behind the paper was that a lot of pressure would be taken off the floating charge if suppliers were given the means of getting the security interest, provided there was a practical system of registration so that people knew about it.[109]

Pragmatic considerations weighed on this committee of practitioners and practising experts, especially on the problem of registration. The committee anticipated the position that would ultimately be taken privately by the Government: a central registry "would impose an immense burden on government," once again raising the spectre of big government that the Tories would later be at pains to dispell, but in the meantime would be resisted by civil servants who anticipated yet another heavy burden loaded on their shoulders.

Thus the rhetoric here took a much more technical form, where opponents and proponents keep close to their areas of greatest technical knowledge and professional expertise. Predictions about the securitization of financial contracts and the secular trends in commercial law stood alongside conclusions drawn from empirical observations in the other economies and legal jurisdictions. Yet despite the technicality of debate, the underlying generic themes recur. For opponents of the ROT, credit will dry up for those who most need it; inefficient or big government or both will result; saving businesses will falter. For supporters, a shift in the balance of power will produce a more equitable solution in favor of weaker creditors.

The Government was not convinced by the Reform Committee's decision to affirm ROT in insolvency, subject to various limitations and protections. Its proposed Insolvency Bill ignored the retention of title altogether. Effectively this maintained the status quo, though the

---

[108] *Minutes of the Cork Committee*, 27 June 1977; 27 Sept. 1978: 3.
[109] *ibid*, 8 Mar. 1977.

legislation also ignored the committee's recommendations on public disclosure and mixed products, which the banks would have preferred. Partly this reflected the Government's judgement that to disturb the new balance of power among creditors would require too much political effort. But unlike the Ten Percent Fund or the prepayments issue, no interest groups or legislative sponsors stepped forward to champion retention of title in Parliament. In effect, this left the legal status of Romalpa clauses in the courts, and would permit Lord Justice Millett some years later to grapple from the bench with the very issues he had urged Parliament to confront more than a decade earlier.

Neither abolished nor statutorily confirmed in corporate insolvency proceedings, retention of title lives on in common law, as it has been shaped by the courts, and in practice, among suppliers, buyers, floating charge holders, and professionals. Perhaps the last word comes from the voices of subsequent experience. In retrospect, one of the bankers confirmed Wheeler's empirical findings that the doom-sayers in the financial industry much over-dramaticized the impact of retention of title. If Wheeler shows that Romalpa clauses do relatively little for most trade suppliers, the bankers confirmed that it has not proved the "terrible problem" they anticipated. "I mean the world has gone on. It is not the first time that the banks have failed to sway the government that something was going to end the world, and didn't."[110]

Organized Labor: Holding the Line

The Insolvency Review Committee was set up under a Labour Government and received trade union submissions years before Mrs Thatcher's Government created a hostile environment for unions in Parliament. Unlike their American counterparts, English unions recognized the importance of workers in the bargaining that precedes and follows a filing, especially in efforts to reorganize companies and cut costs. But their proposals to be incorporated more fully into decision-making by management and insolvency practitioners came to little. Not only did their more expansive suggestions not find their way into the Government's White Paper, but they did not survive the Cork Committee itself.

In theory, British workers had very similar interests to American workers. In a straight liquidation (or "winding up," as the British call it), a firm's employees often had claims on the firm because of unpaid

---

[110] UK Interview 91:06.

wages and benefits, and they would gain to the extent that their claims had a strong legal standing. In a corporate reorganization, the wage bill is one of the costs that the reorganizer will want to cut if the firm is to be successful again. How frequently and substantially reorganizers can cut wages depends on the legal incentives to reorganize, and also on how easily the firm's relationships with its employees can be altered. In contrast to the similarity of interests, British labor has historically been a stronger political actor than American organized labor, in part because of the power of the Trades Union Congress (TUC) within the Labour Party.[111] The combination of similar interests and greater political power implies that British organized labor would have played a more active role in legislative reform. Yet, in this case, non-insolvency laws and policies served Labour's interests in a variety of ways, and had the effect of diminishing the importance of insolvency law for British employees.

Workers as Creditors

Like their US counterparts, British labor unions showed little interest in insolvency legislation. The Labour government, which appointed the Cork Committee, included within it a trade union official. His level of interest was indicative, however, for he attended only a handful of Cork Committee meetings, and those at the beginning of the process.[112]

To the extent that British labor was interested, its concerns mirrored those of US labor. The Trades Union Congress proposed to the Cork Committee that, under insolvency, employees should have a high priority for wages and salaries, and that there should be no upper limit to the amount they covered.[113] The TUC also argued that workers should participate more fully in decisions about ailing companies and have a voice in company reorganizations. The Cork Committee pointed out in its report that the welfare state and several Employment Protection Acts protected employees extensively, so that they could already obtain arrears of wages, and protection of pension rights.[114] Their claims

---

[111] For example, a simple measure of unionization shows the contrast between the two countries: in 1980, 25% of all non-agricultural US workers were union members, whereas that same year 57% of British workers were unionized. See Goldfield (1987: table 3).

[112] According to the Committee minutes, Geoffrey Drain appeared at 9 of 71 meetings, mostly in the early stages.

[113] See Oral Submission of the Trades Union Congress to the Cork Committee, 11 May 1978, *Public Record Office*, and the *Report of the 114th Annual Trades Union Congress* 1982: 35–6.

[114] The Employment Protection (Consolidation) Act of 1978 extended the definition of wages to cover other non-wage portions of the employee's compensation, so, unlike in the

were paid out of the Redundancy Fund, which is maintained and administered by the state, and is financed by employer contributions. This meant, in effect, that workers' back wages and benefits did not come out of the insolvent company's pool of assets. Workers were not competing with other claimants, and so were in a very different position from other company creditors. As the report explained: "...in the majority of cases probably the whole of each employee's claim is paid immediately out of the Redundancy Fund."[115] One member of the Cork Committee asserted that this strongly influenced what the TUC did politically in regard to insolvency law:

I think at that time... the TUC's natural thought in terms of looking after the employees of a bust company was the government route—the redundancy payments, the protection of statutory rights for money out of the central pocket—and they weren't really (in terms of their principal interest) particularly excited about the rights of the employees in the wreckage.[116]

Cork recommended that all preferences for workers contained in insolvency legislation be replaced with changes in the Employee Protection Act so that workers would be no worse under that Act than under current insolvency law.[117]

The opening speech of Lord Bruce, the Labour leader in the House of Lords, focused on proposals for the disqualification of company directors, and said nothing directly about labor's interests.[118] The TUC also proposed to the Cork Committee that receivers and liquidators should be required to take account of employees' interests, and suggested that company liquidators should be supervised by a committee comprised of creditors and trade union representatives.[119] Neither idea was supported by the Committee, nor by the government, and in fact the TUC did not press them very hard. Thus in the final version of the bill, workers retained their preferences for holiday pay in a section of legislation that attracted no attention in the press and very little notice in Parliament, even from the Labour Opposition.

US, British workers did not have to worry that their benefits would be unrecoverable even if their back pay was recoverable. See Palmer (1991: 174–5).

[115] *Cork Report.* 324. For more on how employees were protected outside of insolvency law, see Benzie (1983), and Napier (1991).

[116] UK Interview 90:20.

[117] *Cork Report.* 319–29.

[118] H.L., vol. 458, 1 Jan. 1985, cols. 882–8.

[119] See Napier (1991: 118–19); *Report of the 114th Annual Trades Union Congress* 1982: 263, 464; *Report of the 116th Annual Trades Union Congress* 1984: 267–8.

Workers as Costs

As in the US, during a British corporate reorganization wages are an important reducible cost, and so wage agreements come under considerable pressure. The difference between the two countries had to do with the legal status of collective bargaining agreements, and the incentive under English law for a firm to try to reorganize. These discrepancies meant that the feature of greatest (albeit unforeseen) consequence in the US, how Chapter 11 affected collective bargaining agreements, was simply not an issue in England.

Under English law, collective agreements between associations of employers and labor unions have no legal standing. They are voluntary agreements with no legal force and with no implication that the parties are acting on behalf of individual employees.[120] There is, in other words, no equivalent to the labor contract as an executory contract. Elements of collective bargaining agreements, however, can be included in individual contracts and it is at the individual level that insolvency provisions have their force.[121] Thus, the possibility that insolvency might be used to alter collective bargaining agreements did not apply in the English case because there was no legal relationship to redefine or overturn. The bargaining power of unions and employers was determined outside of the law.

In addition, British company management was much less likely to voluntarily undertake a formal reorganization. When a British company becomes insolvent, management almost always loses control of the company to an administrator and there are no "debtors-in-possession." Whatever opportunities insolvency offers for restructuring the firm and reducing costs, British managers will be reluctant to seize them unless forced to do so, for their own jobs will also be threatened. The upshot is that there is no English equivalent to "strategic bankruptcy."

THE FORTUNES OF WEAK CREDITORS IN STATUTORY REFORMS

"Weakness" in political meta-bargaining over bankruptcy law manifested itself in a variety of ways. Variations among the representation

---

[120] As one author put it: "Collective bargaining developed in Britain on an essentially voluntary basis, there being no general legal obligation on employers to recognize and negotiate with trade unions, and collective agreements are not legally binding contracts between the signatory parties though their terms may be incorporated into individual employment contracts" (Goodman 1984: 145). See also Kahn-Freund (1954). On the historical background, see Palmer (1991: 137, 158).

[121] See *Chitty on Contracts*: 745–8.

of interests by consumer advocates, trade creditors, and labor reflected different capacities for mobilization in the market and political spheres respectively. Even the question of interests themselves were blurred, for the bankruptcy reforms demonstrate that it cannot be assumed that groups recognize their "objective" interests with any clarity, nor that they have any capacity to mobilize around what interests they do perceive. Since consumers and trade creditors face formidable problems in collective action, their interests were largely imputed and then represented by expert agents—by professionals whose own ideal and material interests became highly salient to the framing of bankruptcy's implications for actors too disorganized or unfocused to think for themselves.

Consumers and Trade Creditors

In both countries, the fortunes of weak creditors were inserted onto the political agenda, in one instance through reformer advocates inside the expert reform committee, and in the other through parliamentary amendment. In both countries, experts allied with political advocates. In the United States, that alliance succeeded for consumer creditors and their position materially improved on the face of the legislation. In Britain, that alliance faltered and ultimately failed on virtually all of its three initiatives.

Since everyday bankruptcy brings all parties into the same arena to settle their competing claims on scarce resources, it is not surprising that the metaphor of a "package" solution, in which every party gets certain benefits in return for yielding on others, applies also to the meta-bargaining in statutory reform. In meta-bargaining, we have seen, changes in the allocation of rights in the overall "package" can be undertaken indirectly or directly. In the end, the British settled on indirect benefits to weak creditors, for the complete failure of the Ten Percent Fund and a prepayments' preference left any other hope for redress in the larger pools of money for unsecured creditors that presumably would result from the proposed reduction of government tax priorities and utilities de facto priorities in the overall package. Trade suppliers arguably did better, for at least the Cork Committee and Government did not erode the new de facto priority they had won in the courts. The US Bankruptcy Code, on the other hand, explicitly rejected arguments for indirect benefits to consumers and built a high, if limited, priority directly into the Act, though it softened the force of that initiative by rejecting recommendations for class actions undertaken by States' Attorneys General.

Both countries grappled also with the relative merits and practical effects of protections given to consumers *before* bankruptcy, versus protections given *after* a company had become bankrupt. Most of the recommendations for protections *before* bankruptcy failed: for example, that consumers should be given sufficient information about company finances so that their contracting for goods and services involved an element of "informed consent;" and that firms be compelled to put prepayments and deposits in special accounts that shielded them from bankruptcy. But protections and possibilities of redress *after* bankruptcy engendered serious discussion. British civil servants avowed that the procedural changes in the law would give weaker creditors more power in creditors' committees and ultimately more money in their pockets, though the critique levelled by Schrag and Ratner at American bankruptcy proceedings in practice would seem to have been apposite to the English case *after* the Insolvency Act as it was to the United States *before* the Bankruptcy Code. The American reforms complemented the direct measures on behalf of consumers in bankruptcy with procedural measures as well, since the new possibilities of representation of unsecured creditors on creditors' committees, and their ability to influence confirmation of a reorganization plan, seemed on paper to give them voice.

Jurisdictional issues were integral to the final outcomes for weak creditors. Lawyers and accountants on either side of the Atlantic made it plain that expanded expert representation would materially benefit ordinary people. Here an alliance against the strong seemed to benefit both professionals and weak creditors. Thus the proposal by the Attorneys General that they be given powers to act on behalf of scattered and disorganized consumers strengthened the standing of Consumer Protection Departments in government and offered much greater likelihood that consumers would realize their formal rights in practice. So, too, the Fighting Fund for English insolvency practitioners promised to swell the coffers of bankruptcy estates, as it would coincidentally create a new pool for professional fees. Whatever the motivations, these initiatives would have partially solved collective action problems for dispersed weak creditors, as they each acknowledged the reality that formal rights without effective representation are meaningless.

Yet the position of professionals was much more complex for the changes they embraced cut two ways, and it was not easy to foresee the net outcome. For instance, professional fees might rise from these initiatives, though in either case that would provoke confrontation from the banks, whose financial claims would be the largest target of consumer claims—and bankers pay best. Of course, neither are professional interests unified. Government Attorneys General might initiate claims against banks, or challenge their strong forms of security, but success would not give any financial advantage to them, though it might well increase the need for more extensive representation by their colleagues in the private bar. English insolvency practitioners as a whole began in opposition to prepayment preferences and to retention of title, both on grounds of philosophical principle and practical experience. Yet several well-placed liquidators and some lawyers took a strong position in favor of weak creditors, and it was they who prevailed in two of the three initiatives within the expert reform committee.

Indeed, talk of financial interests too readily distracts from professionals ideal interests, which are articulated in bankruptcy through such principles as redistribution, rehabilitation and reorganization. Since bankruptcy is substantially a zero-sum game, equity, too, surfaces and is a familiar discourse for English lawyers, for whom equity is one pillar of the law. Thus the cross-cutting interests of professionals frequently brought philosophical principles into conflict. Returns to weak creditors on equity grounds needed to be weighed against a philosophical commitment to company reorganization. Premature insistence on an equitable distribution from a corporate bankruptcy estate might be a Pyrrhic victory, for the company could die as a result and deprive not only creditors of further disbursements, but workers of jobs. If company rehabilitation required maximum flexibility, few priorities, and a moratorium on claims, this might harm consumers in the short term, perhaps even permanently. Yet equity considerations did not readily melt away. Once again, therefore, a short-term certain return was weighed against possible long-term payoffs. Though optimistic reformers might hope that a large number of successful reorganizations would benefit everyone, including weak creditors, the long view was a luxury that strong creditors could more easily afford than weak creditors.

Labor

Before the passage of the 1978 US Bankruptcy Code, the role of labor as a creditor was much more salient than its role as a cost to the ongoing viability of the firm. Organized labor sought, and obtained, an improvement in employees' claims for wages and benefits from a bankrupt employer. No objection was raised by any of the other interest groups. The issue of labor as a cost arose in the context of Chapter 11 reorganizations, in which a firm tries to cut costs and return to solvency. The 1978 Code encouraged reorganizations, but no one could imagine the scope of its consequences for collective bargaining agreements. Had labor gambled on the prescience of its chief lobbyist, who had foreseen some risk, it would have opposed the provisions on repudiating contracts in section 365, but it did not.[122] The pragmatics of its drive for change compromised away an unlikely but potentially disastrous reversal for labor in favor of an imminent and very practical short-term benefit for workers laid off without benefits.

In Britain, the contribution unionized workers' wages made to a firm's costs did not figure prominently in insolvency law reforms. Primarily, this was because collective bargaining agreements had no legal standing in Britain. Thus, they could not serve as a target for cost-cutting corporate reorganizers. However much legal encouragement was given to corporate reorganizations, there was no reason to attack or modify a collective bargaining agreement. The submissions by the trade unions to the Cork Committee, and later to the government, focused almost as narrowly as their American counterparts. Despite its formidable political power, the British labor movement undertook no great effort to shape the course of legal reform.

THE STRENGTH OF WEAK CREDITORS

Weakness and strength, we saw at the beginning of the chapter, are not necessarily constant over economic and political spheres. How economic bargaining unfolds depends on market power. In contrast, meta-bargaining involves political power, and the two do not always coincide. Thus, those with a weak economic position may be much more effective in meta-bargaining than bargaining.

In bargaining situations within bankruptcy, for instance, consumer creditors inevitably have hands so weak they are not even invited to the

---

[122] Not until 1984 was section 365 tempered by section 1113. How effective 1113 was in protecting collective bargaining agreements during a Chapter 11 reorganization is debatable. LTV Corp. filed for bankruptcy in 1986, and employee severance and pension obligations were among those costs targeted for reduction (*Business Week*, 4 Aug. 1986: 24).

table, their individual claims are so small in proportion to their transaction costs that they walk away from their claims (even though when added together they may constitute a substantial sum). Moreover, consumers for the most part have limited modes of collective action, for they are amorphous and hard to mobilize, particularly around an issue such as bankruptcy. Despite this apparent weakness, they found champions in both reform processes, and obtained a voice in legislative arenas and the media. Ironically, for the country which is most celebrated for its intermediate associations, effective collective representation came not from civil society but from government officials in Consumer Affairs departments, and it was their alliance with politicians in the liberal wing of the Democratic Party that produced the new consumer priority. British consumers obtained representation also from the Consumers Association, a private body, and the Office for Fair Trading, a government body. But their best hope at political representation lay more with socially-conscious members of the Cork Committee, and its advisors, and later with the alliance between the consumer associations and the Labour Party. Weak creditors, therefore, did not speak for themselves, but found advocates in the reform groups, non-government organizations, and consumer advocacy groups within government to frame, articulate, and press their interests. Their strength in meta-bargaining over bankruptcy rules proved much greater than their usual marginality in ordinary bargaining. Meta-bargaining in the political sphere held out substantially better prospects for weak creditors, than bargaining in the economic sphere. That was, however, small consolation for British consumers, for neither sufficed to improve their situation through a prepayments' preference or a Ten Percent Fund.

The English case reveals an additional element in bankruptcy politics that we observe in other chapters. Markets and political institutions have a moral logic—rules and principles, norms and values, sanctions and rewards—that variously constrain and empower actors within them. The plight of weak creditors in corporate bankruptcy brought to the surface a struggle over the distributive justice of a system that seemed to reward the strong and to harm the weak excessively. Because this brought into open debate some of the enduring conundrums of economic justice in capitalist societies, it triggered a discourse of moral politics that initially put on the political defensive those actors that are dominant in the market—large, secured creditors, such as banks.

The redistributive outcome turned in part on the interplay between the underlying grounds of resistance by opponents of empowerment measures, and the rhetoric they were able to articulate in defense of causes that lacked the moral high ground. Opponents of the weak employed two strategies to compensate for the moral weakness of their claims. First, their public rhetoric turned heavily on an inversion strategy. The affirmative actions represented by ROT, TPF, and prepayment preferences, said the opponents, will effectively be self-subverting. More than that, they will be counter-productive and assure that the weak actually get weaker. This argument was less plausible for consumers, but compelling on its face to Tory peers and Members of Parliament in the other areas.

Second, the rhetoric of resistance skillfully played off a distinction between direct and indirect measures of redistributing property rights. On the one hand, we saw earlier that property rights in bankruptcy can be redistributed *directly* by giving weak creditors a preferred ranking or by giving them some portion of the assets before other creditors. This can be done through statute, just as the Government and professionals rank above ordinary creditors; or it can be done by some form of legal security, which retains property rights that exclude other creditors. All three measures to aid weak creditors included such direct proposals.

On the other hand, the government argued that these direct actions were redundant, because *indirect* measures would provide the same outcome—and with the added bonus that they did not require large regulatory apparatuses. Some indirect effects would be positive because they would *increase the size of the pie* by limiting other preferences, such as abolition of the de facto preferences of utilities and the government's own preferences.[123] Other indirect effects would be positive because they would *reduce victimization*. For instance, those provisions of the Bill that would exercise tighter controls on directors (for example, making them more vulnerable or liable if prepayments are involved in their default), or would increase regulation of liquidators, were intended to increase market morality (Halliday and Carruthers 1996), thereby lessening the risk of exposure by weak creditors to commercial predators.

Finally, as several Foucauldian theorists of accounting have recently observed, technicality offers a neutral ground on which to retreat in a rhetoric of resistance. If the government's general approach was to concede the fundamental point on ends—that it would be desirable to help the weak creditor—it immediately followed this concession with a pragmatic question on means—how could it be done practically? No

---

[123] See Chapter 7. Cf. *Hansard*, 2 Apr. 1985, col. 180.

one could make a plausible suggestion, or guarantee a satisfactory solution. The problem therefore was translated from something moral, and subject to normative approbation, into something technical, and therefore less exposed to moral appraisal. The will was there, but the way was ostensibly missing.

Moral politics appeared less stridently in the discourse of organized labor in either country. In both cases, labor's positions were well entrenched, and they proceeded on the assumption that workers required protections that other creditors might not need. But it is not clear that organized labor was perceptibly better able to mobilize in the political realm than in the market. In the United States, lower rates of unionization do not give labor great strength on the shop floors of many industries. Yet labor does have a powerful political presence, so much so that at least some politicians in the bankruptcy reforms thought that labor could have derailed the entire bill, had it been disaffected. But on the issue that ultimately came to haunt it some years later—the right of bankruptcy courts to reject collective bargaining agreements at the behest of managers leading a reorganization—labor failed to pursue its own recommendations, effectively overlooking the issue. In Britain the comparative strength of labor in the market did not translate into muscular political action of any great consequence. In substantial part the Trades Union Congress could have expected little sympathy from Mrs Thatcher's government. But even in its earliest submissions, when a Labour Government was in power, its claims were relatively modest.

Several of these legislative episodes in Britain and the United States demonstrate that in an area such as bankruptcy law, where new legislation is both rare and highly technical, actors coming to meta-bargain may discover their interests only in the course of proceedings, and even then, may not comprehend them completely. Short-term returns can overshadow long-term threats. Some parties to bankruptcy, such as consumers, find their interests framed by advocates. And while many reformers on both sides of the Atlantic came to the meta-bargaining table with a disposition to improve the lot of unsecured creditors, it was often during the course of proceedings themselves that bright innovations emerged even if—like the Ten Percent Fund—they did not all triumph.

PART 3

Reconstituting Jurisdictional Rights

Introduction

Saving companies through redistributions of property rights demands expertise. To obtain this expertise frequently upsets the professional division of labor. New opportunities and threats arise for professionals. These not only affect the allocation of work to professionals, but that allocation itself ultimately influences the exercise of property rights. Significant changes in the distribution of property rights therefore precipitate struggles over the demarcation of occupational terrains to produce a complex reconstruction of jurisdictional rights—a redrawing of boundaries and allocations of work.

The significance of jurisdictional rights and the importance of the agents that exercise them rise in proportion to three factors. First, the more kinds of property in which it is possible to obtain rights, and the more complex the portfolios of property rights owned by a particular creditor or debtor-company, the more sophistication will be required to handle them, and the more creativity will be necessary to imagine new combinations, trade-offs, and bargains in the adjustment of rights that accompanies company reorganization. Second, when forms of security are few and simple, it does not require advanced competencies to handle them. As forms of security multiply, and as they interrelate to each other in increasingly complex ways, the greater the need for competent experts who can authoritatively create, adjust, and execute them. And, third, just as multi-party games are more complex than two-party games, so, too, the multilateral bargaining that results from bankruptcies is likely to be proportionately greater around reorganizations with companies that themselves have complex corporate structures, debt structure, and credit relationships.

To the extent that all three—forms of property, forms of security, and multilateral bargaining—have increased in scope and complexity over the past decades, the necessity for commensurate expertise rises correspondingly. Of course, professionals do not simply arise in response to changes in property, security, and bargaining independent of professionals themselves. Jurisdictions increase as much from professionals' own innovative exertions as they do from changes outside their control.

Principles of Jurisdictional Reconstruction

To turn insolvent companies around successfully involves at least four elements of jurisdictional reconstruction.

First, institutional designers of regimes to save companies must ensure the high quality of professionals. The probability of effective reorganizations increases when agents of reorganization have the capacity (a) to decide whether rescuing business is feasible and to advise on alternative courses of action (liquidation, reorganization, creative combinations of these); and (b) to reorganize the company itself, which will usually require adjustments of property rights, altering security, and changing company structure.

Second, a sufficient supply of expert practitioners must be available at a price that reorganizing companies can afford. This requires that public policy (a) motivate high quality professionals to enter the field of reorganization; (b) regulate competition among practitioners so as to ensure some relative balance of supply with demand; and (c) remove financial disincentives (depressed fees) and reduce reputational barriers (that is, company doctors, not undertakers) which would otherwise limit entry of experts into the field.

Third, company rehabilitation presumes that professionals with expertise in the areas relevant to reorganization have rights to practice their craft (for example, accountants, lawyers, surveyors). We do not presume that there is any natural affinity between work and the profession that controls it. Indeed, the sharp juxtaposition of lawyers and accountants, who are the primary professional agents of company rescue in the US and Britain respectively, demonstrates that the relationship between saving companies and particular occupations is much more contingent than is usually recognized.

Fourth, public policy must usually recognize a balance between private and public interests in rescuing business. That is, company rescues have repercussions for the reputation of markets, public confidence in business and the creation of wealth, investment patterns, and extension of credit. Governments as well as business institutions stand or fall on their relative performance and, as we shall see later, the logics of politics and the market do not always present easy solutions to their mutual satisfaction.

Forces of Jurisdictional Reconstruction

While monopoly theories conventionally hold that professionals themselves try to shape the markets for professional services, bankruptcy reforms reveal that political meta-bargaining is much more complex. Indeed, numerous parties to corporate reorganization have interests— often coinciding, sometimes conflicting—in the form of professional services available to turn companies around.

Among these parties-in-interest we can anticipate finding (a) professionals, who care about the scope, complexity, rewards, opportunities, status, power, and degree of control they can maintain over domains of work; (b) fractions of professions, which may take advantage of disturbances in established patterns of work to "usurp" the status of other professionals, or resist incursions by lower prestige segments of their profession; (c) the state, which has a powerful influence not only in the constitution of expertise in modern societies, but endeavors to establish and consolidate "governmentality" and to create professionals as agents of state interest; (d) creditors, whose lending practices depend on the predictability and efficiency of loan devices, contracts, covenants, and dispute resolution mechanisms, all of which are mediated in some degree by professionals; (e) civil servants, who seek to reconcile their responsibilities as executors of public interests with personal career and status concerns; and (f) debtors and business leaders.

Institutional Locus of Work

All these parties-in-interest take a position on the institutional locus for business reorganization. What institutional rules apply? Bureaucratic regulation? Market competition? Or judicial determination? There are three basic alternatives, all in evidence during the bankruptcy reforms. First, reorganization can take place within the state, or under close supervision of state authorities, such as the Securities and Exchange Commission, courts, or special departments like the Insolvency Service that are set up precisely to intervene in bankruptcies. Second, reorganization may be left principally to the market. Private workouts presided over by banks are a prime example. Third, reorganizations may take place substantially in the market, but under varying degrees of constraint, supervision, and intervention by civil servants or judges.

The institutional locus of bankruptcy work has substantial consequences for all parties. It determines the relative weight of public and private interest. It affects what motivations underlie the behavior of professionals. It affects the structure of opportunity for the agents of reorganization. These issues resolve how insulated will be the market from governmental intervention and what mechanisms, such as inspection or self-regulation, governments will initiate or support in order to ensure a public or political interest is served.

In sum, disturbances of the division of labor can precipitate uncertainty, occupational rivalry, and struggles in many directions. Between occupations, struggles to seize new occupational territory from other occupations, or efforts to off-load undesirable work and upgrade the quality and rewards of work, can occur. Within occupations, generalists who want to keep fields of practice open to them conflict with specialists who want work reserved for them; and higher status professionals can find themselves confronted by insurgent movements in their own profession by marginal practitioners or semi-professionals who strive for better work, pay, or status.

Part III untangles the jurisdictional politics of the bankruptcy reforms. Chapter 8 examines the fundamental decision about where to draw the public–private boundary that demarcates bankruptcy work. Since nationalization and privatization constitute the two polar positions open to policy-makers, we show how the boundaries of the state and market came to be negotiated by reformers and professionals quite differently in Britain and the United States. Because debates over the public–private boundary bring technical reforms on financial legislation into the orbit of conflicting political ideologies, we shall observe that jurisdictional politics can intersect with party politics and the general shifts in political consensus that move governments from reliance on state interventions in one decade to private solutions in another.

Once reformers draw the boundaries around work jurisdictions, and allocate work to state officials and private practitioners respectively, parallel occupational dynamics take place in the state and market respectively. Chapter 9 contrasts two radically different ways of restructuring the delivery of professional services for corporate reorganization. The English case demonstrates how the interests of state officials, politicians, and professions can converge to produce a new profession that has state regulatory responsibilities and that advances political ideals for market behavior. The American case, by contrast, demonstrates how statutory changes can alter the basis of professional fees to drastically transform the attractiveness of bankruptcy practice for talented lawyers.

However, the state itself is not immune from jurisdictional struggles. Executive agencies rival each other for responsibilities. The executive branch in one instance may jealously protect its prerogatives from the judiciary, and in another be pleased to yield them. Within the judiciary itself, judges of differing statuses who have legal jurisdiction over bankruptcy cases may find themselves at odds over who should have what kinds of cases and how much scope and power their courts should have over those cases. Nonetheless, the structure of state institutions is scarcely a matter of concern only to state officials. Chapter 10 demonstrates that the quality of public administration and the powers of courts have great salience for the financial industry among others. Hence the politics of professional struggle in the state may be every bit as fierce as that which might be expected in the market.

The eventual settlement of these respective struggles for jurisdictional territory determines at least two things. First, it settles the relative power and perquisites of particular professions and segments of professions in relation to each other. It establishes a new permutation of the system of stratification that organizes expert labor. Second, settlements of work jurisdictions affect substantive and procedural bankruptcy law and organization. The social organization of professionals is not independent of the substantive content of their practice. Thus struggles over jurisdictional rights inevitably affect distributions of property rights, and the flexibility to adjust those rights in favor of creative solutions to rescuing business.

8 Privatization and Nationalization of Bankruptcy Administration

Over the past years, political struggles in many advanced capitalist democracies have centered on the limits of the state. Dramatically exemplified by the policies of Thatcherism and Reaganism, political ideologies of the right have championed the expansion of the market as the most efficient means of allocating goods and services, with a correlative contraction of the state. This general restructuring of the public and private domains has direct and indirect consequences for the field of bankruptcy law and corporate reorganization. The more that the state intervenes directly to administer bankruptcies, the less work remains for private practitioners. Moreover, what kinds of bankruptcy work remain in the market or state affect status and monetary incentives for practitioners. The location of bankruptcy administration over the public—private boundary therefore directly implicates the jurisdictional interests of professionals.[1]

Reforms of bankruptcy law coincided with the exhaustion of Keynesian policies in Britain and disaffection with state interventionism in the United States. Inevitably, therefore, bankruptcy reforms were partially framed within widening policy debates over the relative merits of markets and states as agents of just and efficient public purpose. Indeed, the bankruptcy reforms embraced a rhetoric centered on the appropriate values to appraise market and state performance. Issues of efficiency and fairness co-existed with questions of commercial morality, public interest, protection of citizens, and public order.

---

[1] In the field of bankruptcy, the Thatcher initiatives have a curiously reminiscent tone to legal historians. The central debate over bankruptcy administration in 19th cent. Britain turned precisely on this point: the degree of state intervention in the administration of bankruptcy. In the Victorian era, the location of bankruptcy administration manifested one aspect of the wider political debate over the scope of "officialism." The ambivalence of business and professionals over "officialism," and its benefits or detriments, not only divided government ministers, but resulted in oscillating policies that swung bankruptcy work back and forth between lawyers and accountants in the private market and civil service administration. Indeed, through much of the 19th cent., bankruptcy work represented one of the largest branches of public administration, exceeding the Home Office, and even the revenue departments (Lester 1995).

The goals of bankruptcy law consequently became embroiled with changing definitions of the role of the state in the economy. Greater economic vitality demanded efficient means of reorganizing commercial enterprise. Corporate bankruptcy law offered a means of rehabilitating companies so that they could compete successfully in more competitive markets. Resolution of the tension between efficiency and fairness inevitably produced conflict over privatization and nationalization in both countries.

Bankruptcy reforms, particularly in England, posed in stark relief the irreducibility of critical public functions. The small government philosophy of Tory policy-makers directly confronted professionals with strong views about how far the government could divest itself of its core responsibilities. Disputes over the responsibilities and capacities of governments were compounded by the jurisdictional interests of players themselves, whose views about the state could not be completely disentangled from their interests in controlling the levels and forms of work in their professional domains. Thus conflicts over the placement of public–private boundaries became entangled with debates over the allocation of property and jurisdictonal rights. In Britain a significant struggle occurred over the terms of privatization—the devolution of bankruptcy work from the state to the private market. Obversely, the United States faced a significant impulse in the opposite direction—towards "nationalization"—the movement of bankruptcy administration from the private market into the state bureaucracy.

Expansion or contraction of the state's jurisdiction over work will have different effects on contrasting bankruptcy or insolvency cases. *"Low" property rights* cases are characterized by financial ties with few explicit legal entailments. Because these ties do not rely on densely contracted forms of security, the holders of limited property rights have few legal grounds for defense of their claims. Moreover, there is frequently a great imbalance between the parties in low property rights cases, where consumers or individual bankrupts may face large financial institutions or debtor corporations. Low property rights cases have distinctive professional constituencies. Since there is less property at stake, fees for professional services are lower. And because the economic rewards are limited, bankruptcy work is undertaken by marginal professionals who specialize in low cost, high volume practice. Their principal clients are individual bankrupts, consumer creditors, and small companies.

Most debtors in *low property rights cases* suffer from multiple problems, as we saw in Chapter 7. Because they are so dispersed, and rarely experience bankruptcy more than once in their lives, they have great difficulty in representing themselves politically or speaking with a single voice. Many creditors in low property rights cases are also small, but that is not the case with the government, which finds itself very frequently owed back taxes, or back social security payments. A great asymmetry therefore exists between weak and strong parties in low asset cases. Largely defenseless debtors and creditors must rely on the civic consciousness of reformers to raise issues of fairness, protection from market predators, and constructive rehabilitation.

By contrast, *high property rights cases* involve wide networks of financial ties to a greater range of economic actors, including shareholders, bondholders and investment banks. These actors hold extensive and formal property rights claims with an attendant variety and complexity in forms of security. Greater complexity requires more expertise and time which, when coupled with more property at stake, generate larger fees. The professional constituencies of these cases, therefore, are the elite lawyers, accountants, and insolvency practitioners who serve large corporate clients, such as banks, insurance companies, and large corporations: and they have enormous capacities for political mobilization.

Cross-classifying the institutional locus of work by the scope of property rights frames four cases that exemplify the complex dynamics of bankruptcy law reform: (1) privatization of mundane bankruptcy work in Britain; (2) the movement to empower private insolvency practitioners in Britain; (3) proposals to nationalize low property rights cases in the US; and (4) a drive to upgrade marginalized bankruptcy judges in the US. In this chapter, we describe privatization and nationalization, and in the following chapter, the professionalization of insolvency practitioners and upgrading of bankruptcy judges. Each of these cases helps redefine the public–private boundary; and each demonstrates distinctive ways in which conflicts over jurisdictional rights become entangled with the substantive provisions of bankruptcy law and administration (table 8.1).

Since the politics of meta-bargaining over the public–private boundary embraced corporate and individual bankruptcy, we widen the scope of this chapter to include those aspects of personal bankruptcy that influenced jurisdictional struggles. Many so-called consumer bankruptcies in fact are disguised and transposed bankruptcies of small businesses and small traders that in turn have pushed individuals into bankruptcy (cf. Sullivan et al. 1989).

Table 8.1 **Dimensions of Bankruptcy Reforms in Britain and the United States**

	Institutional Locus	
SCOPE OF PROPERTY RIGHTS CASES	(Britain) Market	(US) State
Low Property Rights Cases	Privatization of Administration	Nationalization of Administration
High Property Rights Cases	Empowerment of Insolvency Practitioners	Valorization of Bankruptcy Judges

JURISDICTION REFUSED: PRIVATIZATION OF MUNDANE
BANKRUPTCY WORK IN THE UK

Mrs Thatcher's Conservative government came to power in 1979 committed to reduce the role of the state in the economy and to stimulate private solutions to public problems. Government ministers immediately issued a directive that all government departments submit plans for potential reductions of between 10 to 25 per cent of their staffs. P. A. R. Brown, the Deputy Secretary of the Department of Trade and Industry, contacted Kenneth Cork and told him that the government was considering a radical privatization of much bankruptcy work. In his subsequent letter, Brown stated:

You will know that the Government is examining many possible ways of reducing the size of the Civil Service; and with the objective of cutting manpower in mind, the Secretary of State is bound to consider the extent to which it is now necessary, and will be desirable in the future, to devote so much official time . . . to the duties currently imposed by the bankruptcy legislation.[2]

Brown requested that the Cork Committee produce an interim report on how its recommendations would reduce the manpower and financial burdens of bankruptcy administration.

Ironically enough, some two years before the advent of Mrs Thatcher's government, the Insolvency Review Panel had already decided in principle to a radical simplification of treatment for bankrupts, which would relieve staffing pressures on the Insolvency Service. The Official

---

[2] *Minutes of the Cork Committee*, 19 Sept. 1979, paras. 6–7.

Receiver's Office in the Insolvency Service had been responsible for conducting the initial stages of personal bankruptcies. It investigated a bankrupt's financial affairs and followed up with public examinations of bankrupts in court. Receivers applied to courts for discharge of bankrupts from their debts. If no private trustee appeared, they took over trusteeship of a debtor's assets, few though they may be.[3] Members of the Cork panel reached an early consensus that a great deal of time, effort, and manpower was being wasted by the Official Receiver's mandatory public examination of every bankrupt, no matter how large the debtor's assets, nor how culpable the debtor's behavior. Committee members believed that current practices failed to distinguish the incompetents, who simply couldn't handle their financial affairs, from the fraudulent and criminal, who had taken illicit advantage of creditors on their way to financial ruin. This position on personal bankruptcy paralleled the distinction it would also make between company directors who were misguided versus those who engaged in fraudulent behavior.

The Committee believed that incompetents, by far the largest group, deserved advice and their cases dealt with speedily. Criminal bankrupts deserved much closer investigation, prosecution, and enforcement. The Review Committee decided to concentrate government attention on the few "bad boys" and to relieve the system of the hapless. This sentiment is well-reflected in Mr Walker-Arnott's reaction to a visit made by the Committee to Croydon County Court:

[T]hose examined ranged from the hopelessly incompetent (where it seemed absurd to have the full panoply of the law) to the man from prison who had fleeced people as an insurance broker (where it was right that he be publicly examined).[4]

Another Cork Committee panelist, who was widely experienced in bankruptcy, picturesquely expressed the Committee's thinking:

One of the troubles was that we were spending too much time on investigating comparatively harmless bankruptcies and not enough time on the really naughty boys, the ones that we really ... very strongly (felt) should not be allowed to get off the hook without being fully investigated, especially where there was the suspicion that assets had been salted away. But there was also the fact that ... there must be adequate machinery for the speedy administration of debtor's estate by an honest and competent trustee for the benefit of the creditors generally. One of the difficulties is with bankruptcy, you get one or two big creditors who dominate them. And the little man who's fighting for his existence

---

[3] *Government Green Paper.*   [4] *Minutes of the Cork Committee*, 17 Oct. 1977, para. 7.

in the little corner shop or in some small business doesn't stand a chance. And I was very keen that the official receiver should be retained as the person who could protect the smaller creditor against the big man who was really not all that bothered about it except he just wanted to tidy it up so he could write off his bad debt.[5]

It made no sense for the full array of government machinery to be set in motion against debtors with no assets and little prospect of paying off their bills. Somehow the law should treat no-asset cases differently from those where there was every likelihood that assets either still existed, and could be distributed among creditors, or that future cash flow would permit creditors to be partially paid off on a time-payment plan.

Moving incompetents and no-asset cases away from costly government interventions would significantly affect staffing requirements in the Insolvency Service and allow over-burdened personnel to devote their attention to serious cases. Not surprisingly, therefore, Cork Committee members reacted with some irritation, even anger, to the government's request that it report prematurely. Especially annoying was the requirement to wrench one small part of the Cork Committee's unified comprehensive plan, thus risking a piecemeal approach to a problem that demanded a holistic view.

Privatization: Modest and Radical Proposals

After some discussion of tactics, and the agreement that it must not be seen to be tailoring its recommendations to the government's manpower projections, the Committee prepared a brief interim report, which it submitted to the Minister of Trade and Industry in April 1980. The Interim Report acknowledged that bankruptcy proceedings had been used frequently and unnecessarily by the government for minor debt collection in cases involving small traders and consumer debtors. Somewhat wryly, the Interim Report observed that if there were a problem, it was partly of the government's own making. Government departments were among the prime offenders for the use of bankruptcy procedures, and the Insolvency Service, to collect back taxes.[6] In effect, the revenue collecting branches of government transferred collection costs to the Insolvency Service, and in the process pushed large numbers of debtors into bankruptcy. All these high volume, low complexity, low asset cases

---

[5] UK Interview 90:13.

[6] *Bankruptcy: Interim Report of the Insolvency Law Review Committee.* HMSO. 1980. Command Paper 7968 (hereafter cited as *Interim Cork Report*).

fell heavily on the Government Insolvency Service and the Official Receiver's Office, which were housed in the Department of Trade and Industry. The Report proposed to remove minor cases from bureaucratic agencies (Fletcher 1982: 78).

The Interim Report acknowledged that the century old legislation in bankruptcy also recognized three types of debtors: (1) those "to be subjected to the full rigours of bankruptcy law;" (2) small consumer debtors and traders who needed no more than an administrative procedure; and (3) debtors who could pay back some of their debts in an arrangement that did not require bankruptcy. But the second option over time had been folded into the first, so that small debtors received full bankruptcy treatment out of all proportion to their assets or behaviors. And the third form, while admirable in intent, became obsolete because it required "cumbrous procedures" and "major obstacles to be surmounted." The Labour Government compounded the problem in 1976 when it significantly raised the filing fee for bankruptcy. Many smaller debtors could not afford—ironically enough—to receive the protection of bankruptcy; and many small creditors could not afford to chase debtors into bankruptcy.

Paralleling its reasoning with company directors, the Cork Committee drew a sharp line between two different groups of debtors. In the largest category were insolvencies where a consumer or small business is not guilty of misconduct, "but rather of a general irresponsibility and muddle on his part."[7] "Failures of small traders arise," said the Report, mostly from the insolvencies of larger businesses to whom they supplied goods and services, and "many are undoubtedly due to an inability to cope with the complexities of the modern business world, or indeed, to sheer incompetence."[8] These groups did not deserve an extensive, expensive investigatory procedure.

By contrast, said the Report, there is another category of debtor "whose actions give rise to a deep sense of public outrage." These "criminals of the credit world", who may be guilty of "serious misconduct, sharp commercial practice, or fraud", must be treated rigorously. They have a deleterious effect on commercial morality and public confidence in business life. For these offenders, and others whose debts are somehow a matter of "public concern", "a disinterested public servant" must question them publicly.[9]

---

[7] *Interim Cork Report:* para. 13, p. 5.   [8] *Interim Cork Report:* para. 15, p. 6.
[9] *Interim Cork Report:* paras. 16, 20; pp. 6–7.

Following this logic of separating mundane from consequential cases of bankruptcy, the Interim Report offered three different approaches to bankruptcy, ranging along a continuum from less to more government intervention, as the seriousness of the case warranted.

For *the small debtor* who could repay more than five per cent of what he owed on an instalment plan, the Cork Committee proposed a new Debts Arrangement Order, or time-payment plan.[10] Either a debtor or creditor could apply to the court for a plan to repay a mutually-agreeable proportion of the debts over three years, up to a maximum of five years. If the debtor fully complied with the Order, his remaining debts would be discharged at the end of the period. In the Committee's view, this innovation "should provide relief at an early stage for the increasingly large number of consumer debtors who become seriously overburdened by debts they cannot immediately repay, particularly where the debtor is affected by some unforeseen catastrophe." Cork anticipated that this new procedure would attract many debtors and creditors to the courts.[11]

A second recommendation, a Voluntary Deed of Arrangement, was tailored to *debtors with significant assets*, but who had been neither reckless nor criminal. By amending present law, the Cork Committee would encourage the appointment of a private professional trustee to administer an agreement between a debtor and creditors for substantial repayments over a period of time. This would seldom involve the courts, and would call on the Insolvency Service to do no more than regulate the activities of trustees.[12]

If the two prior proposals dealt with the incompetent and unlucky, the third tailored its "semi-penal" process to *debtors apparently guilty of misconduct* who deserved "the utmost rigour of the law." When voluntary processes broke down, or debtors were uncooperative, or there were "reasonable grounds for believing that some fraud or serious misconduct" had been committed, then full bankruptcy would swing into motion. The Official Receiver, as a disinterested representative of the public, would conduct a full investigation, and subject the debtor to all the powers of bankruptcy law, including a public examination.[13]

---

[10] The debtor would need to meet various conditions, such as owing between £200 and no more than £10,000. *Interim Cork Report*: 9.

[11] *Interim Cork Report*: para. 8, p. 10.

[12] *Interim Cork Report*: pp. 10–11.

[13] *Interim Cork Report*: paras. 24–5, p. 12.

The effects of these measures appeared initially to increase the numbers of debtors whose financial affairs would fall under the mantle of bankruptcy law. Most of the new voluntary arrangements would move from the Insolvency Service to the courts, or to private professional trustees monitored by the courts. This shift of work out of the Department of Trade and Industry would leave the Official Receiver with a much reduced, but weightier list of cases.

However, in a most unusual move, the Government published a "Green" discussion paper on bankruptcy the very same day it released Cork's Interim Report. The Green Paper staked out a far more controversial position. Essentially it called for a radical privatization of bankruptcy administration. The Government premised its recommendations on its singular characterization of the problem, which ignored much of what Cork's experts thought were pressing issues. According to the Government, most small traders incorporated as businesses. Their financial problems could be dealt with in corporate insolvency law. Personal bankrupts with significant assets were rare. And the Government believed that fraudulent, large personal bankrupts were rarer still. Moreover, by raising the costs of filing for bankruptcy in 1976, the rate of filings had dropped off.[14]

Given this characterization, and its strong commitment to clean up markets, the Government proposed to privatize personal bankruptcy administration and to shift the attention of the department to business regulation. In place of the Official Receiver, the Government proposed that private practitioners would take responsibility for discovering and obtaining a debtor's assets, interviewing the debtor, going through the debtor's records, making inquiries of creditors, advising the debtor in the preparation of court papers, and filing a report with the courts. Since the private receiver would be appointed by the court, both the courts and Department of Trade would maintain supervisory roles.[15]

The proposals to shift work out of government and onto the private markets were justified by government in blunt utilitarian terms: to reduce the size of the Insolvency Service by some 570 positions and to save public expenditure by up to £3 million a year. Moreover, the Government indicated it would tap into market forces and further drive down the demand for bankruptcy, mainly by shifting costs of bankruptcy administration to users—creditors or debtors. According to a senior

---

[14] *Government Green Paper.* 5.
[15] *Government Green Paper.* paras. 7–10, pp. 7–8.

civil servant, it was the Conservative view that "services provided should, so far as possible, be self-financing."[16] The user should pay. Contracting out civil service work, and scaling down the civil service generally, were both consistent with the government plank of privatization.

An economic theory of debtor/creditor behavior lurked close to the surface in the Government's reasoning. Changing the incentive system would have salutary effects, believed the Government. If creditors had to pay for bankruptcy administration, they would probably try and reach private arrangements with debtors out of court, or at least be more careful about whom they pushed into bankruptcy. If debtors had to pay, they would probably file earlier when they had more assets— which would leave more assets to distribute to creditors. Though it did not say how, the Green Paper thought the new procedures would be just as effective in debt collection, as a deterrent to debtors who continued to trade, and to the relief of debtors' loans.[17]

Virtually all these provisions applied to Cork's unfortunate and incompetent debtors. What of the reckless and fraudulent? Private receivers would need to act as public enforcement officers. If they caught a whiff of crime, they should report it to the Department of Trade. As for public examinations, the Government was hard-pressed to think of instances when this would be in the public interest.[18]

The "Privatization" Debate

The Government's proposals to shift public functions onto the private market drew scathing criticism, some genuine puzzlement, and not a little irritation. With genial acerbity, Cork later dismissed the Green Paper as "a lunatic act" (Cork 1988: 193). An academic commentator wrote that "legislation along the lines of the Government's current proposals for 'privatization' of civil bankruptcy would be an unmitigated disaster for all interests concerned: those of debtors and creditors, and

[16] Insolvency Practitioners Association Submission to the Department of Trade and Industry on the Cork Report, *Public Record Office*.

[17] *Government Green Paper*: paras. 12–15, pp. 8–9.

[18] *Government Green Paper*: paras. 17–18, p. 10. The Government did recognize that debtors needed to be treated differently if they had more assets. In cases where assets were sufficient to return moneys to creditors, the private receiver would obtain a court order to collect and disburse funds as a trustee in bankruptcy. All his costs of administration and remuneration would come out of the estate. And if a debtor wanted to make an arrangement with his creditors, he would ask the receiver, who would decide whether to call a meeting of creditors to agree on a plan. If they agreed, the court could approve the scheme after hearing from various parties. *Government Green Paper*: Part B, paras. 10–17, 21, pp. 12–14.

those of the public at large" (Fletcher 1981: 85). All the principal professional groups involved in bankruptcy administration similarly attacked the government's position. The Insolvency Practitioners Association (IPA) stated that the new proposals would adversely affect the public interest and the business community. Both the IPA and the Consultative Committee of Accountancy Bodies (CCAB) roundly criticized the discretion this would give to debtors, calling it a "charter for unscrupulous debtors."

Newspapers revelled in the "split over bankruptcy policies" and the "insolvency law row." The responsible Government Minister, Mr Reginald Eyre, commented that it was not a negative reflection on the Cork Committee that the Government "had radically different views from its predecessor on the responsibilities of the Civil Service." Stanley Clinton Davis, the Opposition spokesman on trade echoed the language of the accountancy profession, by whom he was being briefed, in the view that the Green Paper was an "unscrupulous debtor's charter."[19] *The Times* applauded Cork's efforts to undertake a fundamental reconsideration of insolvency law and to separate "the wrongdoer from the unfortunate or rash." The Green Paper would make bankruptcy less visible and consequently "more open to abuse." Chiding the Government, *The Times*'s editors regretted that the "rushed and incomplete affair" of the Green Paper was more worried about saving jobs than framing a coherent policy.[20]

Justice, the British section of the International Commission of Jurists, weighed in with its denunciation of the Green Paper, indicating that the Government drew its understanding of state responsibility much too narrowly. Because David Graham, one of Cork's key advisors, was a leading figure in Justice's deliberations on bankruptcy, it unsurprisingly echoed the dismay of the Cork Committee that the Green Paper would detract from "the maximum realization of assets for creditors, detecting and preventing fraud, and assuring relief for failed debtors."[21] By early November, the joint accountants' body, CCAB, came out in an attack on the Green Paper, and both they and the Insolvency Practitioners Association met with the Deputy Inspector General of the Insolvency Service and the Minister of Trade to express their complaints.[22] Even

[19] *The Times*, 25 July 1980, p. 17.
[20] *The Times*, 25 July 1980, p. 15.
[21] *The Times*, 30 Oct. 1980, p. 18.
[22] It should be recalled that the mobilization of these several organizations disguises the fact that their memberships were highly interlocking. The leaders of the CCAB on bankruptcy overlapped almost completely with the IPA (See Chapter 3).

Dun and Bradstreet, the financial information firm, indicated that the Green Paper would make it more difficult for small businesses to chase down debtors.[23]

The Times' Editorial of 10 November foresaw the end for the ill-fated proposals. The "chorus of opposition" had been "entirely deserved" for the Green Paper failed almost completely to understand the wider implications of recommendations made on narrow manpower grounds. *The Times* purported to discover a loophole that would allow corporate directors to escape fraud by moving company assets to families and friends. Given the pressure building on the Department of Trade and Industry from other government departments, it was likely the Government would change its mind.[24]

The Government's views are the easiest to understand, because the Green Paper appears consistent, at least conceptually, with small-government, market-oriented policies. Since it is the vitality of the market that animated Conservative policies, the application of a user-pays philosophy seemed simultaneously to lower demand on government and to limit demand for private professional services to those who truly needed them. The sentiment of the Green Paper clearly indicates the Government's primary concern was corporate management and the fraud-free operation of markets. That is where it wanted to concentrate the scarce resources of public administration. Personal bankruptcy it mostly defined away. And it showed little interest in either the vulnerability of weak debtors, or the possibility of humane and efficient ways of reorganizing debt by small traders and individuals. It appeared happy for the hidden hand of the market to sanitize the economy of incompetent small businesses, or hapless consumers.

It is less easy to understand why the Insolvency Service acceded to demands for change that reduced its numbers and compromised its historic functions. In fact, since its three most senior officials were receiving the Minutes of the Review Committee, and must have known about Cork's projected changes, the direction taken by the Green Paper seem more than a little perverse.[25]

In the months following the Green Paper, the Cork Committee held oral hearings in London's Guildhall, for Sir Kenneth was now the Lord Mayor of London. The hearings permitted Cork to direct questions at key interest groups and, not without some political gamesmanship, to stir up a little dissension against those responsible for the Green Paper.

---

[23] *The Times*, 10 Nov. 1980, p. 15.   [24] *The Times*, 10 Nov. 1980, p. 17.
[25] *Minutes of the Cork Committee*, 27 June 1977, p. 9.

Three months after publication of the Green Paper and Interim Report, Insolvency officials had a chance to explain themselves during their appearance before the Cork Committee. While the substance of the Green Paper directly reflected Government policy, they testified that this surrender of work to the private sector was not simply a civil service capitulation to the policy orientations of their Minister. It reflected as much their own very considerable frustration at an inability to satisfy the functions demanded of the Insolvency Service. The Service protested that it just could not provide the "kind of service which the country needs."[26]

For many many years we feel in the insolvency service that we have not been able to provide that service . . . quite simply because we could not get the staff or we could not retain the staff. . . . If you have not got the staff and you cannot get the staff you must give up some of the work.[27]

Higher economic rewards in private industry diverted accountants from government service. If an accountant lived in London, "he can quite literally . . . walk over the road and get a lot more money for doing a similar job."[28] Quite apart from the salary, the Thatcher Government's scathing disrespect for "bureaucrats" could hardly stir enthusiasm for a career in the civil service. Government proposals for contraction of the service fit with civil servants' desire to jettison routine cases and retain responsibility for more serious cases of fraud.

When pressed on how well the Green Paper would permit the use of bankruptcy law for debt collection, the Inspector General of the Insolvency Service side-stepped the issue on jurisdictional grounds. Responsibility for general debt collection did not reside in the Insolvency Service. He believed that the threat of bankruptcy would still be as effective as ever in compelling debtors to pay their debts. Their test was not that bankruptcy serve as a debt collection device, but whether debts would be more difficult to collect if the Green Paper was implemented. "We feel that the proposals will be just as efficient both in their threat and in their application as is the present bankruptcy procedure."[29] If debt collection was not their problem, neither was criminal bankruptcy: ". . . the Insolvency Service itself is not satisfied that the criminal bankruptcy is correctly placed with the Department of Trade . . . . The Insolvency Service is not over-enamoured with keeping criminal bankruptcy."[30]

---

[26] *Cork Report.*   [27] *Cork Report:* 47–8.   [28] *Public Record Office,* 22 Oct. 1980.
[29] *Ibid.*   [30] *Ibid.*

Oral testimony revealed that the Government was headed in a contrary direction to the Cork Committee over the qualifications of professionals in bankruptcy work.

... [W]e will see these receivers coming not from the specialized insolvency firms of accountants from whom we have by tradition drawn our trustees.... I envisage these receivers coming from local firms of solicitors, and perhaps accountants, in the various towns, who would normally act for their clients in any matter.[31]

At first blush this appeared to be a shrewd move, because it not only allowed the Government to externalize costs to the private market, but if debtors themselves could not produce adequate resources to pay for a receiver, they could rely on the goodwill of their long-term professional advisors to carry through the bankruptcy administration. But its shortcomings quickly showed. In contradiction to the Cork Committee's support for specialized and regulated insolvency experts, this policy affirmed the capabilities of generalists. And since they were not specialists, and resided across the length and breadth of the country, consistency of administration would be hard to achieve.

Cork and the civil servants disagreed forthrightly about the need to protect debtors from harassment by creditors. Sir Kenneth asked:

One of the reasons for the Bankruptcy Act (of 1876) was to protect the debtor from his creditors. That was the basic reason we have done away with the debtors' prison ... How will he, the debtor with no assets, get his protection from being hounded every day by creditors and debt collectors and heaven alone knows who will be hounding round his door driving him up the wall?[32]

Mr Armstrong, the Inspector General of the Insolvency Service, took issue with Cork's theory of debtor/creditor behavior. He could not agree that debtors would always spend every penny of their assets before looking to the protection of bankruptcy law. And he certainly did not concede that harassment will increase.[33]

The exchanges revealed the senior civil servants' hitherto implicit view of insolvency service, and wider state, responsibilities. Civil servants accepted that the state and Insolvency Service had a duty to provide a bankruptcy procedure, though the Government was of the view that most of it could be externalized to the private market. Beyond that, the civil servants remained obdurate that "if other people use the bankruptcy procedure for some purpose unconnected with bankruptcy

---

[31] *Ibid.*   [32] *Ibid.*   [33] *Ibid.*

wish to do so (i.e., debt collection by the Treasury), that is entirely up to them."[34] Beyond debt collection, what of the protective function of the state? The proceedings turned a little sour when Muir Hunter QC, England's leading bankruptcy barrister, asked what is a man to do, "if a man has no money at all...with the bailiffs at the door?" Inspector-General Armstrong answered that question with his own: "Is it the responsibility of the state to provide what we might describe as this kind of social service?" Retorted Muir Hunter, "it has been for very many years—four hundred years."[35] This exchange surfaced the government's blind spot, for its own interests were entirely absorbed by companies, directors, trade and industry. As David Graham QC noted, the real problem is that the government failed to acknowledge the problem of the consumer creditor.

Attributions about the civil servants' motivations ranged from authentic to ingenuous to self-serving. One member of the Cork Committee opined that the senior insolvency officials were actually engaged in a brilliant diversion, whereby they showed themselves to the government as avid cost-cutters, knowing all along that the sheer audacity of their recommendations would invoke effective public opposition. A less charitable view had it that these were senior officials bent on knighthoods, or something of the sort, and "they ran along with the government's pressure in the hopes that it would advance their future."[36] More probable is the view that the senior civil servants saw their restrictive concept of the Insolvency Service as a form of institutional self-defense in the face of overwhelming ideological imperatives. Strip the Insolvency Service to its core, and hope to survive with reduced manpower.

The Cork Committee had prepared an ambush for the insolvency civil servants. The day preceding their appearance, the Cork Committee sought to win over witnesses from another government department, Customs and Excise, and perhaps not coincidentally, to sow a little internal discord between departments. Given the Government's interest in revenue, an argument along those lines was likely to be far more effective than some diffuse protestation of general public interest.

Cork had little difficulty in getting the witnesses from the revenue collecting departments to agree to three propositions. In the first place, he touched the traditional raw nerve of tax collectors by suggesting that the Green Paper's proposals would actually *reduce* revenue collected by the state. If there are fewer incentives for individuals to file bankruptcy,

---

[34] *Public Record Office*, 22 Oct. 1980.　　[35] *Ibid.*　　[36] UK Interview 90:13.

then less bankruptcies will be filed. And if less bankruptcies are filed, then the government will lose proceeds that would otherwise come when the bankrupt person's assets were distributed to creditors—including the government. The revenue officials admitted that there would be savings to the Insolvency Service, but only if functions in one department were shifted to another.[37] The officials responsible for the Green Paper pointed to Scotland, where there were no Official Receivers, and the incidence of bankruptcy was much less. But here again, the revenue officials agreed with the Cork panel that debt collection was more difficult as well.

In the second place, the revenue officials agreed that the Green Paper would likely increase their costs, because "presumably (you will) have to bring your own chap along and pay him because there may not be any assets to pay" for private trustees. The debtor would have no funds. Revenue departments could no longer free-ride on the Official Receivers' Office: "it certainly will be more expensive for us of course because we shall presumably have to supply our own receivers."[38]

In the third place, filing a petition of bankruptcy effectively froze or "crystallized" debt. "When they are getting into a poor way financially, the trustees very often will use all the money they can put their hands on in the business to stave off their pressing creditors in order to carry on, and certainly they will use tax money, thereby robbing the government to pay off competing creditors."[39]

Revenue officials shared the Cork Committee's concerns about loss of the state regulatory function:

We are a little concerned, too, with the loss of the regulatory and investigational function that the Official Receiver at present performs. I know that the Green Paper mentions that if the private sector receiver comes across anything that is wrong he will draw the attention of the court to it. We wonder if in fact this will be quite the same thing as an Official Receiver, or Officer of the Crown, who himself has an investigational role.[40]

Officials from the Inland Revenue Department took a similar line, a position Cork was happy to exploit when the Inspector General and Deputy Inspector General of the Insolvency Service appeared as

---

[37] Witnesses from Customs and Excise, *Public Record Office*, 10 Nov. 1980.

[38] *Ibid.*

[39] *Ibid.*

[40] Witnesses from Customs and Excise, *Public Record Office*, 10 Nov. 1980. Note that in the case of directors, the Government clearly envisaged that private practitioners could carry the responsibility of exercising regulatory oversight delegated by government.

witnesses a day later. Putting them on the defensive, Sir Kenneth confronted them with the contrary views of another Department of State:

... [T]he Inland Revenue yesterday gave evidence that the Green Paper proposals will involve a very considerable reduction in the recovery of revenue. I suppose they are about the biggest debt collecting department in the country, and that was their senior officer's view yesterday, that it would involve a great reduction in the recovery of revenue, obviously not in proportion to total revenue but in proportion to the malingerers or whatever you like to call people who do not pay their debts.[41]

In fact, the Inland Revenue representatives expressed some awkwardness about speaking ill of another government department to a third party. Yet they felt compelled to say they were not happy about having to appoint their own receiver and incur heavier administrative costs. As a party in some thirty per cent of bankruptcy cases, they expected to collect less money under the proposed changes. More significant in their eyes, however, was the removal of bankruptcy as an ultimate sanction to use against wayward taxpayers.

A large number of our customers are those people who until that point have shown no response whatsoever to any revenue approaches. They blindly ignore returns or anything like that. At the end of the day, as things stand, a very valuable weapon here in revenue's hands, the ultimate weapon of bankruptcy, is there, not because they want to see the unfortunate fellow fail publicly, but that is an effective way of compelling many people to start treating with the revenue, because until that point is reached, nothing happens.

In short, the jurisdictional shift entailed in the removal of Official Receiver from bankruptcy administration diminished the power of bankruptcy as a collection device, and thereby removed a potent weapon of last resort from the hands of tax authorities.

Following on the heels of their maligned Green Paper, the two civil servants confessed to "tremendous surprise"—and some little skepticism—that the revenue officials had broken ranks and turned against them. But they remained adamant that the Green Paper would reduce jobs in the Insolvency Service even if some were shifted elsewhere in Government. Neither was the Deputy Inspector General "over-enamoured with keeping criminal bankruptcy," which the Insolvency Service would be delighted to contribute to the Home Office.[42]

[41] *Public Record Office*, 22 Oct. 1980, E. G. Harper (Inspector General, Insolvency Service), W. Armstrong (Deputy Inspector General, Insolvency Service), and E. M. Llewellyn Smith (Under Secretary, Companies Division, Department of Trade and Industry).
[42] *Public Record Office*, 22 Oct. 1980.

Defects in the Green Paper, according to the Cork panelists, went beyond jobs, revenue, and added costs. Sir Kenneth suggested that the Green Paper went against the humane progress of bankruptcy law which had abolished debtors' prisons and sought to protect debtors from excessive harassment by creditors. A debtor's petition for bankruptcy would stop creditors in their tracks, bringing welcome relief to someone who had nothing more to give. But if the debtor could not afford to declare bankruptcy, and if he could not retain a private professional to act as his trustee, "How will he, the debtor with no assets, get his protection from being hounded every day by creditors and debt collectors and heaven alone knows who, who will be hounding round his door driving him up the wall?"[43]

But the civil servants disagreed that history vindicated Chairman Cork, for the 1976 legislation had already made it more difficult for people to declare bankruptcy, "so we have 10,000 people in the country today who would have been bankrupt had it not been for the 1976 Act, and there has been no evidence, as far as I know, of harassment."[44]

The lateral conflict that occurred among government departments was one of the jurisdictional disputes over where to draw the state's boundaries.[45] Unexpectedly, however, another fissure opened up within the Insolvency Service itself. The views expressed in the Green Paper and the oral hearings were those of senior management. But unionization permitted other ranks in the civil service to express their views. Comprised of professionals in government, the Institution of Professional Civil Servants invited experienced middle-level specialists in insolvency to send a delegation to the Cork Committee, and they took the unusual step of disagreeing publicly with top managers.[46]

In their appearance, the Institution of Professional Civil Servants affirmed the written submission made three years earlier when they had urged that the Officer Receiver's service be properly staffed, for "it is not desirable or possible for bankruptcy and liquidation to be entirely informal and non-official in view of the continued need for an investigation function.... We feel confident in saying therefore that there is no practical alternative to the retention of a properly staffed and graded official receiver service."[47] They reacted to the Green Paper

[43] *Ibid.*

[44] *Ibid.*

[45] UK Interview 90:13.

[46] UK Interview 91:17.

[47] Submission of Institution of Professional Civil Servants (IPCS) to Cork Committee, *Public Record Office*, Aug. 1977.

with a nineteen-page, highly critical report. The in-house insolvency experts directly contradicted the pronouncements of their senior managers using not the principles of high policy but "practical reason"—their experience in the day-to-day administration of bankruptcy. Admitting that they had not even been consulted about the Green Paper proposals put forward by their managers, the IPCS rejoinder disagreed with the premises of the report, pronounced its proposals to be unworkable, and cast severe doubt on how well their conception of public policy would be served by implementation of the proposals. The middle managers disagreed that fraud was as uncommon as the senior managers alleged. Anticipated savings of staff were exaggerated. And while there might be savings of £3 million to the Insolvency Service, they reinforced Cork's hunch that "it will cost other government departments such as Inland Revenue, Department of Health and Social Security, and Her Majesty's Custom and Excise more to present petitions and it would almost certainly cost the Lord Chancellor's Department in employing more staff. . . "[48] Significantly, they maintained a more expansive notion of Insolvency Service public responsibilities and unveiled their own standards for satisfactory public policy:

Many experienced officers in the insolvency service strongly believe that the proposals are unworkable, that they will weaken remedies available to creditors for collection of debts, remove protection afforded to the business community, and be open to abuse by unscrupulous debtors.[49]

The Cork Committee itself later reacted to the 1980 Green Paper proposals by rejecting categorically the privatization of the Official Receiver, despite the loss of work this would take from insolvency practitioners. The professionals on Cork's Review Committee maintained that the Government proposals for privatization would actually take bankruptcy administration back to where it had been before 1883.

In its final Report, the Cork Committee gave careful attention to the role of the Official Receiver in bankruptcy. After rebutting the Government's 1980 consultative document, most particularly because it focused only on the reduction of public expenditure, the Cork Committee demonstrated that in one country after another "creditors were originally given the primary responsibility for administering the process." This led to "scandal and abuse." Over and over again "exclusive control has been progressively removed from creditors and varying

[48] Submission of IPCS, *Public Record Office.*   [49] *Ibid.*

degrees of official control have been introduced...It has been increasingly accepted that the public interest is involved in the proper administration of bankruptcy."[50] Comparative and historical experience argued for a public official who stood apart from debtors and creditors, who had no financial interests of any kind in the outcome, and who was competent and impartial.[51] All this was necessary for "the preservation of commercial morality" and the general maintenance of law and order.

The Endgame

The Cork Report reinforced its proposals of 1980 by affirming the importance of the new Debt Arrangement Order, which would allow any individuals in financial distress to apply for court protection from creditors and work out a means of repaying their debt, if there were a reasonable prospect of doing so.[52] For particular categories of individuals, such as company directors, professionals, and unincorporated traders, voluntary arrangements could be managed through a private insolvency practitioner, who would act as a trustee of the estate, again with minimal involvement of the courts.[53, 54]

Politically, the Cork Report affirmed two values: government cost-saving and individual financial rehabilitation. The much maligned Official Receivers—the civil servants administering bankruptcy—would become under Cork's new scheme more specialized and limited. Cork estimated that these innovations would reduce the volume of cases dealt with by the government Official Receiver from 3,500 or 4,000 a year to less than 1,000.[55]

The insolvency practitioners' group, comprised principally of accountants, came out strongly in support of Cork's proposals, noting that a "majority of the suggestions" provided by the Insolvency Practitioners Association had been incorporated into the Cork report. Yet they affirmed "our conviction that under any system of insolvency administration it is vital that there should be an Insolvency Service available to deal with certain aspects of public concern," most especially those

---

[50] *Cork Report*: 161–5.

[51] *Cork Report*: 166.

[52] This was the functional equivalent of the new American Chapter 13 individual debt repayment plan.

[53] *Cork Report*: ch. 6.

[54] *Cork Report*: 72.

[55] *Ibid.*

matters concerned with the preliminary investigations of criminal or fraudulent behavior by companies or individuals.[56]

Despite the refusal of insolvency practitioners to accept routine work, Cork's Committee was heavily imbued with the spirit of privatization, advocating the expansion of the market in at least three areas. First, the reform committee provided new opportunities for individuals and companies to take preventive action through "voluntary arrangements" before they became insolvent. Through an expanded use of insolvency practitioners prior to the intervention of the courts, Cork hoped that a great deal of judicial and executive work simply would not materialize. Second, Debts Arrangement Orders and Administration Orders allowed courts to devolve day-to-day administration onto the private sector, though the courts would be more heavily involved in the former. And, third, in cases of individuals with few assets to be distributed, procedures would again reduce state workloads.[57]

When the Government unveiled its draft Insolvency Bill to Parliament in 1984 it was clear that it had capitulated almost completely on its proposals for privatization of insolvency in routine cases. It dropped any further consideration of externalizing fees to debtors. Most significantly, it retreated from the radical diminution of the Official Receiver's responsibilities and, in fact, proved ultimately more conservative in this respect than the Cork Committee.[58] Accepting an irreducible role for Government in bankruptcy proceedings, Mrs Thatcher's Insolvency Bill gave way to the expert reformers by accepting new procedures that would push substantial work into the private sector without radically diminishing public responsibilities.

One notable Cork innovation did not make its way into the Government White Paper. Deeds of Arrangement were dropped, believes its major protagonist, because it too was caught in the campaign for cost-cutting. The Lord Chancellor, government minister responsible for the courts, himself had been under pressure to reduce the size of the London office. The debts arrangement order would have shifted the burden of petty bankruptcy to the courts.

The Lord Chancellor was fighting in his corner, of course, and didn't want any extra work because he was going to show what a good little boy he was to

---

[56] IPA Submission to the Department of Trade and Industry on the Cork Report, para. 9, *Public Record Office.*
[57] *Cork Report.* 169.
[58] *Government White Paper.* ch. 3.

Maggie Thatcher, because he'd reduced the total number of civil servants employed by him.[59]

This struggle over the state/market boundary for bankruptcy administration therefore offers the unanticipated spectacle of insolvency practitioners, both inside and outside the state, *refusing* jurisdiction. Driven by an ideology that championed the efficiency of markets over state bureaucracies, the Conservative Government sought to push routine work onto private practitioners. Surprisingly, the Government found itself allied with senior civil servants who were unable to regulate the supply of their services because they had limited control over departmental budgets and because the private sector provided greater rewards for similarly qualified practitioners. More important than overwork was the quality of work in low property rights cases. As it demanded a very low level of skill and knowledge, a high volume of low property rights cases downgraded both the reputation and the strategic value of government officials. Since the civil servants had neither the personnel nor powers to monitor and control serious cases of corporate and individual deviance, they pressed for a shift away from minor cases to concentrate on complex and morally consequential bankruptcies, a shift reinforced by the powerful moral undercurrents in the 1986 English Insolvency Act.

For their part, private practitioners also resisted responsibility for low or non-paying clients at the very time that a decades-long drive for full professionalization was a realistic prospect. It is true that insolvency practitioners were pressing government for new responsibilities in corporate reorganization—a move that would enhance their reputation and powers. But the Review Committee's specialists were convinced that certain functions must lie with government, because the incentives otherwise placed in private markets would lead to repetition of the very abuses that the reforms were intended to stop.[60]

As a result, each group of professionals—insolvency specialists in the civil service and insolvency practitioners in the private market—sought to avoid a particular category of work. Because the Government required the goodwill of the insolvency practitioners and lawyers, it

---

[59] UK Interview 90:13.
[60] Appleyard, in *The Times*, said of the Green Paper that "its pragmatism is unblushing." He saw it as "denationalizing." Interestingly, he described the Cork approach as "a frankly moral one. It starts from the 'retributive and punitive' elements in existing legislation, which tend to lump together all bankrupts of whatever degree of culpability and on whatever scale. Its answer is a careful and fairly elaborate grading of insolvencies" that would lead to the full rigours of bankruptcy only at the extreme (25 July 1980).

compromised on the export of low rights cases to the market in order to achieve its more important purposes with high property rights cases.

Whereas the primary impetus in the English reforms was to push routine bankruptcy into the private market, a contrary movement took place in the US (Delaney 1989). The discretion given corporate managers to reorganize their companies within Chapter 11 of the Bankruptcy Code readily permits its characterization as a champion of private solutions to business failure. Nevertheless, the origins of the Bankruptcy Code derived less from problems with corporate than with consumer bankruptcies, and the solutions proposed by several leading sponsors of change abandoned private solutions in favor of "nationalization" of key aspects of consumer and individual bankruptcies.

In Praise of Public Administration: Brookings and the Bankruptcy Commission

As David Stanley and Marjorie Girth make clear at the outset of their report, Brookings' primary approach was to "bankruptcy as a governmental process" and the operations of "its institutions, personnel, procedures and financing" (Stanley and Girth 1971). Among other things, the Brookings Report identified a pronounced mismatch between the great bulk of work in bankruptcies, which was primarily administrative, and the organization of the courts, which were primarily adjudicatory (Stanley and Girth 1971: 197). The judiciary was expected to exercise administrative functions it was poorly equipped to handle. The Brookings Report saw a fundamental disjunction between the essentially routine administrative character of the 200,000 or more uncontested cases and the prevailing adversarial system that seemed to add layers of personnel and costs to a process better suited to a bureaucracy (Stanley and Girth 1971: 153ff., 200).

When a debtor filed a petition for bankruptcy, he was automatically declared a bankrupt. The referee (as bankruptcy judges were then called) called a meeting of creditors, though very few usually came. Most delegated the work to their lawyers, and few of them came either. So much for the vaunted "creditor control" of bankruptcy. Stanley and

Girth found that in some 75 per cent of cases the creditors elected a trustee, or the referee appointed a trustee, to handle the assets of the bankrupt person.[61] Usually, the referee appointed a lawyer from a small circle already well known to him. For instance, 43 per cent of referees said they chose their trustee from a small group of no more than five, and 22 per cent used a single "standing" trustee. Most trustees were quite specialized, devoting a majority of their legal practice to bankruptcy. The trustee found and liquidated the assets, which were distributed to the creditors.

Trustees' fees came out of the estate, or assets, of the bankrupt. Indeed, in about 20 per cent of cases, there was no money left over after the trustees had taken their fees, which for the most part, were very limited. The median size of each bankrupt's estate in the Brookings study amounted only to $311, and 86 per cent were under $1,000 (Stanley and Girth 1971: 88).

The Brookings Report discovered that 41 per cent of all money paid out of the estates of bankrupts went to professionals for administrative expenses. Most went to trustees (44 per cent), but some also went to attorneys for the bankrupt (15 per cent) and the attorney for the trustee (11 per cent). As Stanley and Girth put it, "creditors were rarely and meagerly paid" (Stanley and Girth 1971: 92). When the various expenses and creditors were paid, the referee would dismiss the trustee and close the case. The fees for trustees in no or low asset, straight bankruptcy cases were very small. But for Chapter XIII wage-earner cases, where debtors paid back their creditors over time, trustees could earn on commission 5 per cent of amounts paid out. In a high volume business of a thousand cases a year, a trustee could earn substantial fees—certainly much more than the referees who appointed them (Stanley and Girth 1971: 179–80). Fairly close audits did not permit them to make much money on expenses. Other fees were paid to appraisers of automobiles, or household goods, auctioneers, and accountants.

The Brookings' researchers were singularly unimpressed by the operation of this system for consumers and small businesses in straight bankruptcy.

By any rational standard, the present system for handling straight bankruptcies is seriously deficient. Each time a petition is filed, complex quasi-judicial

---

[61] They note, somewhat wryly, that trustees were appointed in 75 per cent of the bankruptcy cases even though only 36 per cent had any assets at all (Stanley and Girth 1971: 77).

machinery is cranked up *as if adversary issues and substantial assets were involved.* Both factors are usually missing. Instead, the referees handle a mass of cases involving uncontested matters and sums of money that are inconsequential from the creditors' point of view (Stanley and Girth 1971: 105 (our italics)).

And the ideology that bankruptcy cases were adversarial proceedings was really "a sham." They were costly and difficult to monitor.

Almost every one of the bankruptcy cases observed or analyzed by the research staff could have been handled with more speed and equal justice as administrative proceedings, with recourse to the courts available in disputed matters (Stanley and Girth 1971: 164–5).

Even more controversially, the Brookings Report alleged that corruption and patronage afflicted the system. According to Stanley and Girth, a system of "mutual accommodations" and "exchanges of favors" brought all players—judges, referees, trustees, lawyers—into a tight coalition of mutually protective practitioners. Their loyalties, charged the Report, lay rather more to each other than to creditors or debtors. Pejoratively labelled a "bankruptcy ring," the clientelistic relationships among practitioners evoked little trust in the probity or fairness of the system. Federal judges appointed referees to act as bankruptcy judges. Distributed across ninety district courts, the 218 referees in turn appointed trustees to sell or abandon the assets of the bankrupt person or company. Trustees, too, had their patronage fiefdoms, since appointments offered a steady stream of work and often some healthy fees, and trustees, too, had discretion to retain other lawyers as counsel, not to mention appraisers, auctioneers, accountants, among others. "A philosophy of 'don't rock the boat' or 'let's take care of one another' prevails," concluded Stanley and Girth (1971: 160, 164, 197, 147, 122–6).[62]

This chain of patronage compromised the perception of fairness in the operation of appeals. For instance, any lawyer could appeal against a decision made by a trustee. But it was quite possible that the appeal would be heard by the very judge who had appointed the trustee in the first place. This did not engender great confidence in the actuality or appearance of strict judicial neutrality. Moreover, the bankruptcy judge had leverage over lawyers both for approving fees and for making new appointments of trustees. There was therefore a strong incentive for

[62] Stanley and Girth reiterated that the judicial branch championed independence of courts at the expense of central management. It was little wonder that "patronage (political or personal) is securely established in the judiciary as a method of personnel selection" (1971: 200).

trustees not to make waves, or to ask for reviews of decisions, which probably helps account for the fact that never more than 2–3 per cent of all cases were appealed.

In the face of this bleak appraisal, the Brookings Report startled the bankruptcy lawyers and judges with recommendations that would replace the "receiver–trustee–lawyer cartel" of patronage with disinterested expertise.[63] In place of courts with "their habituation to patronage, their resistance to co-ordination, standardization, and procedural change", the simple and effective solution was to move most routine bankruptcy work from the courts and create a new bankruptcy administration in the executive branch. One organization could do what previously had involved trustees, receivers, appraisers, accountants, auctioneers, and other personnel. Salaried attorneys, or civil servants, would replace private attorneys. The former tasks of the trustees would be taken over mostly by new bankruptcy analysts. In personal bankruptcies debtors could hire a lawyer, if they wanted representation, but it would not be necessary. In Chapter XIII time-payment plans, the new agency would handle the collection and distribution of monies. Moreover, a government agency could also provide counselling, which might keep the debtor from getting into trouble again. Stanley and Girth went even further and recommended this for many business bankruptcies. The authors of the Brookings Report recognized that their recommendations would not affect creditors' attorneys. But trustees and their attorneys would lose their jobs (Stanley and Girth 1971: 196–218). This nationalization of bankruptcy work effectively would close down the adversarial end of practice, depriving most bankruptcy lawyers of their livelihood. Essentially the courts would retain jurisdiction only for adjudication of disputes.

This reformed system, vowed Stanley and Girth, would "discourage errors, ethical slippages, and waste." It might cost the taxpayer more, but more debtors would be able to pay creditors and taxes. The economic effect would be "negligible." Merit appointment should displace favoritism. And Congress could provide oversight.

The big difference between the current system and the proposed system is one of motivation. The present bankruptcy process is run by the referees, trustees, and debtors' and creditors' attorneys. They have achieved an accommodation of interests under which scandals and spectacular errors are minimized; the rewards are kept high, and but not high enough to provoke severe controls. They are motivated primarily to keep the process as it is, and neither the judges nor the Administrative Office (of the courts) is rocking the boat.

[63] *Minutes of the Bankruptcy Commission*: 1 May 1972.

Officials of the proposed bankruptcy agency would also be motivated by a desire for professional survival, but this would be conditioned on high performance—effective guidance of debtors, maximum return to creditors, rapid and inexpensive processing of cases, and production of valuable information about insolvencies.

"Revision of the law," concluded Stanley and Girth, "would be a memorable achievement both for jurisprudence and for public administration" (1971: 217–8).

The nationalization of bankruptcy work advanced by Brookings was as bold in conception as it was ill-advised in presentation. It replayed again the long-standing belief of high-minded reformers in the superiority of state administration over the capacity of courts to handle vast numbers of petty cases. Civil service norms and meritocratic personnel selection would govern a nationally co-ordinated, uniform system of administration. Lawyers and courts would intrude rarely, and only in the exceptional case.

Like the Cork Committee criticisms of private receivers, a moral tone shades the Brookings report for it is premised on a view that the "bankruptcy ring," and the collusion of mutual accommodations surrounding it, offers professional advantage to lawyers at the expense of helpless debtors. Brookings insinuates that neither of the primary parties—debtors or creditors—benefit so much as the administrators. This is not illegal, but it is extractive. Thus it is bad public policy to support a system whose primary beneficiaries are its administrators.

Moreover, the critique of the private market couples a skepticism about the appropriateness of the adversarial process with the dismissal of fundamental assumptions about incipient conflicts in bankruptcy proceedings. These deep-seated doubts about the functioning of private professional markets, at least in the realm of consumer bankruptcy, are juxtaposed against the administrative and financial rationality of the public service agency. The Brookings analysis, therefore, initiated a series of critiques and defenses of the public and private domains which, in the end, reconstituted the concept of the public in a distinctively American idiom of rights and due process. But buried beneath the rhetoric is a usually tacit struggle over jurisdictional rights. It is a rhetoric that erases the line between property rights and jurisdictional rights and, indeed, makes defense of property rights contingent on the maintenance of an adversarialism only guaranteed by lawyers.

Although it distanced itself from some of the intemperate language, the Bankruptcy Commission endorsed many essentials of Brookings' attack on adversarialism and its replacement by efficient public administration. Influenced by sympathies for the small debtors among the politicians, and the elite lawyers' and judges' distaste for lawyer-trustees hustling for court appointments as private contractors, the Commission concurred that a new bankruptcy administration was needed to provide debtors with expert and independent counselling and advice. It should aid debtors in the formulation of plans for partial repayment of their debts and eliminate patronage. Inside the committee deliberations, the tone of opposition to unnecessary lawyering is captured in the tart comments by the lawyer-chairman of the Commission that it would "be a turn for the good if insolvent debtors dispensed with lawyers" altogether.[64]

The Commissioners concurred with Brookings that collusion and corruption hung over bankruptcy administration. Bankruptcy Commissioners Professor Seligson of New York and Judge Will of Chicago both agreed that there were kickbacks of fees by district attorneys to trustees in New York and Chicago. When this was placed alongside the "unseemly and continuing relationship between the referees and the members of the . . . so-called 'bankruptcy ring'" of specialist bankruptcy lawyers, who were essentially "private contractors seeking business with the bankruptcy court," the entire sphere of practice emitted "a bad odor."[65]

. . . [S]ome referees appoint private trustees because there is no effective creditor participation, and where creditors do vote for a trustee, it is frequently only because law firms solicit such votes as a means of obtaining the business which will be supplied by this trustee. In a number of straight bankruptcy cases, the trustee does virtually nothing to earn his fee, but rather leaves the work to attorneys in the law firm nominally employed by him. In turn these practices lead to law firms seeking favor with referees who control business which the firms will get, and law firms which do receive business tend to monopolize the proceedings in a particular area. Ultimately, the series of actions produces a system which uses expensive legal talent to perform many taks which do not require lawyers' skills and which does not meet the objectives of equal treatment of creditors or of relief to debtors.[66]

Confronted with a system so compromised in its organization and personnel, the Commission echoed Stanley's judgment that minor palliatives would not remedy what needed major surgery. In a series of bold

---

[64] *Minutes of the Bankruptcy Commission*, 4 Oct. 1972: 20.

[65] *Minutes of the Bankruptcy Commission*, 15 Jan. 1973, 42; *Report of the Bankruptcy Commission*: 95; *Minutes of the Bankruptcy Commission*, 13–14 Nov. 1972: 6.

[66] *Report of the Bankruptcy Commission*: 4.

measures the Commission Report redesigned the principal foundations of the system. Like Brookings, it sharply divided bankruptcy cases between those that were best handled administratively, and those that demanded adjudicatory and adversarial proceedings. The routine cases, which accounted for some 70–80 per cent of all bankruptcies, should be handled by a new US Bankruptcy Administration in the executive branch under the general oversight not of the courts, but of Congress.[67] Most adversary proceedings—and lawyers—would become redundant. Thus the new United States Bankruptcy Administration would satisfy four principal objectives in the administration of bankruptcy:

impartial, expert, and speedy performance of decision-making and other functions necessary to bring a case to a fruitful conclusion; economy that avoids waste, duplication, dilatariness, and inefficiency; uniformity in case procedure and in the application of substantive laws throughout the U.S.; and managerial flexibility that can adjust quickly and efficiently to changes in quantity, kind, size, and location of cases.[68]

With the transfer of administrative functions to the executive branch of government, judicial proceedings would handle only contested matters where adjudication was inescapable.

In Defense of Rights? The Lawyers' Retort

This proposed nationalization of a previously private function sharply divided the constituents of bankruptcy law reform. In public hearings before the House and Senate, Commissioners vigorously advocated their model of a Bankruptcy Administration that would be staffed by a permanent corps of civil servant employees, made up of attorneys, accountants, social workers, appraisers, auctioneers, and clerks. In addition to the National Bankruptcy Conference, they obtained some support from key House committee members and staffers, but otherwise few allies stepped forward to support such a radical venture.

John Honsberger, a Canadian lawyer and member of the National Bankruptcy Conference, proved sympathetic to the Bankruptcy Commission, as he detailed the quasi-British form of the Canadian system. Honsberger testified that the United States was converging with Canada's quite successful and substantial reliance on public administra-

---

[67] *Report of the Bankruptcy Commission*: ch. 5. Surprisingly, the Commission actually cited the value of the Official Receiver at a time shortly before the British Government sought to move in the opposite direction—towards privatization.
[68] *Report of the Bankruptcy Commission*: 81.

tion. Like the British, the Canadians had official receivers. Unlike the British, however (at least until the Insolvency Act 1986), Canada had a system of private but licensed trustees who were mostly accountants. A senior civil servant exercised fairly strict control over the private trustees. But nevertheless Honsberger indicated that in Canada "to a large extent creditor control has been superseded by official control." Lawyers chose trustees, and creditors usually confirmed them. The 1970 Canadian Study Committee on Bankruptcy and Insolvency Legislation recommended a continuation of the trend towards even greater public administration of bankruptcy in low asset or no asset cases. Thus a parallel system operated that permitted the appointment of private trustees for those who could afford them or obtain private counsel, and a public system for those who could not.[69]

Honsberger recognized that the system proposed in the Bankruptcy Commission's Bill, H.R. 32, would end up looking much like Canada's. But he pointed out that the US system itself, since the 1898 Act, had gradually shifted from control by creditors and trustees, to "an increase in the administrative functions and responsibility of the court and in the authority of lawyers."[70] In any event, Honsberger gladdened the legislative sponsors of the Commission's Bill, for they applauded his model of a mixed system, complete with an executive agency on the British model to handle mundane, recurrent cases.

By affirming that creditor control was mostly a myth, Honsberger reinforced the view of Brookings that most creditors had little interest in very low asset cases. To chase after minor debts cost more than it was worth. Banks and major creditors simply wrote off some proportion of their bad debts and deployed their staffs more productively. Creditors did not control. They struggled neither with each other, nor with debtors. Control resided in the hands of the trustee, and the trustee, alleged Brookings, used control to channel assets into commissions and allow-

---

[69] John Honsberger, "Bankruptcy Administration in the United States and Canada," *California Law Review* 1975, 63: 1515–45. Testimony by John Honsberger, *Bankruptcy Act Revision Hearings on H.R. 31 and H.R. 32*: 1191–8.

[70] Indeed, Honsberger reminded lawyers and legislators alike that the battle over how much bankruptcy should be handled administratively, and whether in the judiciary or executive, was of long standing. President Hoover broached an option of developing an administrative approach to bankruptcy in the 1930s, but in 1941, the courts headed off any competition from the executive by setting up their own Bankruptcy Division within the court Administrative Office. The Commission Bill opened up a long-standing apprehension by the federal bench that it would be deprived of bankruptcy work—though why it clung to relatively mundane and legally sterile law was not clear. *Bankruptcy Act Revision Hearings on H.R. 31 and H.R. 32*: 1520–1.

ances.[71] Adversarial proceedings made no sense. Too few assets made legal representation uneconomical for most parties. Reflecting the classic British attitude to lawyers in insolvency, Honsberger reported that Canadians resisted the involvement of lawyers in no-asset cases: "we do not need lawyers; lawyers just add to the cost."[72]

Most interest groups, however, took exception to the proposal for bureaucratization of routine bankruptcy work. They were united in resistance to an executive agency. But reasoning differed and consensus fractured over the exact form and functions of an administrative body.

Most vocal in their opposition were the bankruptcy judges, who were alleged by critics to form one segment of the bankruptcy ring. Their National Conference had taken such exception to the Commission's Bill, H.R. 31, that they drafted a rival bill, H.R. 32, which set a different course on bankruptcy administration. Best articulated by Conrad Cyr, bankruptcy judge from Bangor, Maine, the Judges' Bill grew out of a grievance.[73]

Consumer bankruptcy, wrote Cyr, was a primary reason for setting up the Bankruptcy Commission.[74] Despite their role as prime movers, bankruptcy judges were deliberately rejected from seats on the Commission, mostly due to objections from the Judicial Conference, and against the better judgement of Senator Burdick and other legislators. Not only was there no bankruptcy judge, but there was no expert in consumer bankruptcy on the Commission, which had a strong bias towards business bankruptcy. And consumer bankruptcy, protested Cyr, is not simply "a miniature business case," although many consumer bankruptcies are follow-ons from small firm failures.

---

[71] Philip Shuchman concluded from a bankruptcy study in New England that lawyers in no-asset bankruptcies often managed to find enough funds to pay a commission or allowance that well exceeded the low $10 statutory fee, but was not enough to pay anything to creditors. "The trustees are after their fees; the bankrupts want to hold on to their small assets." The general creditors don't participate. So trustee work is lucrative to a stratum of the bankruptcy bar. "What the Bankruptcy Act does in the circumstances we describe is to generate fees for small groups of lawyers who are appointed trustees and to perpetuate a system for most non-business bankruptcies that have no reason for being." Debtors certainly do not get a fresh start, because bankrupts are "stripped clean." *Bankruptcy Act Revision Hearings on H.R. 31 and H.R. 32*: 773, 788.

[72] Honsberger, *Bankruptcy Act Revision Hearings on H.R. 31 and H.R. 32*: 1240.

[73] Conrad K. Cyr, "Setting the Record Straight for a Comprehensive Revision of the Bankruptcy Act of 1898," *The American Bankruptcy Law Journal* 1975, 49: 99–171.

[74] Congressman Edwards introduced H.R. 31 and H.R. 32 to his committee with the statement that the Bankruptcy Commission was established in the first place to deal with the enormous number of consumer filings and "to devise a new method to process the tremendous numbers of consumers who seek the relief of the BR court each year."

The judges strongly challenged the Commission's and Brookings' allegations that there was a bankruptcy ring. Neither body had provided any convincing evidence that law firms curried favor with bankruptcy judges for trusteeships. If anything, studies suggested the absence of a ring. A 1970 study of bankruptcies in Massachusetts' federal courts had not discovered a debtors' bar. Half the bankrupts were lawyers who only did a couple of bankruptcies a year, and thus could hardly be considered experts or even competent.

Cyr objected most vocally to formation of another large executive agency. Invoking time-honored, anti-bureaucratic rhetoric, Cyr charged that it was hard to "contrive a more regressive recommendation for consumer insolvency relief and rehabilitation than the erection of yet another doubtlessly impervious vertical bureaucracy, which is pervaded by a "maze of red tape," providing undifferentiated "revolving door" treatment. A Washington-based national agency would spawn another "dangerous federal bureaucracy which will inevitably multiply and prosper like some uncontrollable malignancy on the shank of the body politic." Cyr buttressed his views with a speech delivered by southern Senator Herman Talmadge to a bankruptcy judges' conference. "One of my primary concerns," said the Senator,

is the creation of yet another government bureaucracy, which no doubt would cost the taxpayers of this country countless millions of dollars. . . . We've had too much of that already . . . Executive agencies . . . in many instances, virtually personify the Peter principle of waste and inefficiency. . . . I understand it has been estimated that the new bankruptcy administration, if it is set up, would cost between $30 and $90 million. But based on the reliability of estimates when other government bureaus have been established in the past, we could look for the cost to run two or three times that amount (Cyr 1975: 142, n. 178).

Not only was more government bureaucracy objectionable, but it did not achieve a primary goal of the Bankruptcy Commission—to separate judicial and administrative functions, ensure that administration was removed from judges ill-equipped to handle it, and eliminate judges' conflicts of interest in administrative and judicial activities. The very problems flagged by the Bankruptcy Commission would be reproduced, predicted Cyr, in the Bankruptcy Administration.

The Administrator would be authorized and at various times required to serve as judge, litigant, counsellor to debtors, advisor and consultant to creditors, appointer of fiduciaries, clerk of the court, trustee, receiver, distributing agent, court advisory, liquidator, appraiser, rulemaker and regulator of fees, as well as the head of an independent federal agency with the Executive Branch of Government (Cyr 1975: 263).

The Judges' Bill therefore proposed that a Bankruptcy Administration be placed within the Administrative Office of the US Courts, where it would work hand in hand with private attorneys. The bankruptcy judges' response thereby rested on skepticism about the inherent efficiency of government executive agencies, and a desire for separation of administrative and judicial functions, but within the judiciary.[75]

The bankruptcy judges drew support from Berkeley Wright, Chief of the Division of Bankruptcy at the Administrative Office for the United States Courts, and his assistant chief, H. Kent Presson, who stood shoulder to shoulder against putting consumer bankruptcies in a new US Bankruptcy Administration.[76] Part of the objection was philosophical. To put bankruptcy in an executive agency indicated that it was "a social program," whereas it more properly should be regarded as "a legal proceeding" where an incipient conflict among creditors and debtors is adjudicated. According to Wright, a loss of property rights was always incipient in bankruptcy, and therefore it was necessary to ensure that due process had been accorded to all parties. Wright drew a clear line on any counselling of debtors by a new agency. This, too, was "a social program and, as such, has no place in a legal proceeding." More properly it should be relegated to private organizations. Anyhow, he was unconvinced that financial counselling would aid rehabilitation.[77] Bankruptcy inherently belonged to the judiciary.

Loss of creditors' rights also drew criticism from Presson, who believed that a Bankruptcy Administration would dampen litigation. Indeed, Presson implies that this nationalization of private bankruptcy work amounted to a sort of de-legalization: the government would give advice rather than private lawyers; and government counsellors would take over work more properly vested in professionals. He remained skeptical that an executive agency "can afford litigants the protection rights they deserve" and would receive if dispute resolution remained exclusively in the courts. And of course the political ace in the hole was cost. Presson dropped the sobering figure of $100,000,000 "without commensurate increased benefits. It would place trustees, appraisers, auctioneers, counselors and attorneys in the civil service."[78]

---

[75] We discuss the internal government struggle over judicial or administrative location of the agency in the following chapter.

[76] *Bankruptcy Act Revision Hearings on H.R. 31 and H.R. 32*: 3–32.

[77] *Bankruptcy Act Revision Hearings on H.R. 31 and H.R. 32*: 9.

[78] *Bankruptcy Act Revision Hearings on H.R. 31 and H.R. 32*: 221–32.

Lawyers' groups similarly resisted nationalization of consumer bankruptcy in the executive branch of government. The administrative ideal, with its repudiation of adversarial proceedings, was anathema to the bar from the outset. The American Bar Association resolved that:

Many of the key features of the bankruptcy proceedings are potentially adversary in nature. Among these are the establishment of the validity of claims and the collection of assets of the estate representing claims against others; the allowance and ranking of, and the recognition of security interest in, claims of others against the estate, the determination of the entitlement to discharge....

Bankruptcy should be kept in the judicial system and bankruptcy representation in the private bar. But they agreed that administrative proceedings could be made more efficient when "adversary contentions do not develop."[79] The Commercial Law League of America, effectively the organizational voice of the purported "bankruptcy ring," contended that an executive agency would create an "all powerful administrator" and would deny representation to debtors who needed private lawyers.[80] And various other representatives of the bar told Congress that a new administrative agency within the executive branch would be "secretive," conducive to "arbitrary and capricious" bureaucratic behavior, and a "far-removed" bureaucracy would bring about a "lack of responsiveness, inefficiency, expense, geographical remoteness, and lack of understanding of local needs."[81]

Nationalization, in other words, would break the tight nexus of association between the lower federal judiciary and private bankruptcy bar. A representative of the Dallas Bar Association invoked all the clichés of big government in his rehearsal of a future Bankruptcy Administration that would have:

...all the efficiency of the United States Postal Service, all the sophisticated business judgment of the Federal Housing Administration, all the public interest orientation of the Bureau of Reclamation, all the heart of the Internal Revenue Service, and all the procedural due process of the Equal Employment Opportunities Commission.[82]

It was not simply that debtors might be deprived of legal advice, but that counselling from within a government agency compromised the quality

---

[79] *Bankruptcy Act Revision Hearings on H.R. 31 and H.R. 32*: 906, n. 5. A letter submitted to the US Bankruptcy Commission following an ABA board decision of 1 June 1973.

[80] *Bankruptcy Reform Act Hearings on S. 235 and S. 236*: 533–52.

[81] *Bankruptcy Reform Act Hearings on S. 235 and S. 236*: 552–78.

[82] *Bankruptcy Act Revision Hearings on H.R. 31 and H.R. 32*: 1652.

of advice that might otherwise be given by a "disinterested" private lawyer. According to attorney Benjamin L. Zelenko, testifying on behalf of Beneficial Finance, the standards against which the bankruptcy proposals should be appraised were "procedural fairness and efficiency, by even-handedness and equitable treatment of creditor and debtor alike."[83] Decoded, this meant "anything but an executive agency."

These objections came not only from the commercial bar, but were echoed by legal aid lawyers. Ernest L. Sarason, a spokesman for National Consumer Law Center, which assisted some 2,300 legal service lawyers that dealt with the poor, maintained that the most important consideration for the consumer bankrupt is not how much he gets to keep, or how much bankruptcy costs, but that the forum afford "legal and equitable due process." An administrative solution is highly defective because in the entire process of counselling, fact-finding, and decision-making, the debtor's best interests are not necessarily served and his rights are not protected without "separate and aggressive representation of the debtor's interests." For instance, if the debtor discloses "potentially embarrassing or inculpatory information" to the administrator, will this be used against him later in the process, or disclosed to others? Therefore discovery of information should be separated from later decisions. In fact, the consumer may need individual legal protection from the administration itself.[84]

Where consumers have insufficient assets for counselling by attorneys, it should be provided for them, presumably by aid lawyers. "What we are fearful of, is if the counseling is in-house as part of the administrative machinery, that it might degenerate into counseling that serves the objectives of the machinery, rather than those of the bankruptcy process and of the debtors."[85] This is both sociologically insightful—bureaucracies do develop interests that may compete with their ostensible purposes—and somewhat ingenuous, since the same argument could be applied to private or legal aid lawyers. Sarason feared that the bankruptcy administration would push clients into wage-earning plans they couldn't really afford, instead of discharging them with a clean slate.

Bernard Shapiro appeared on behalf of the National Bankruptcy Conference and reported on the discomfort of the Los Angeles County Bar with the large number of non-lawyer advisors who were springing

[83]   *Bankruptcy Act Revision Hearings on H.R. 31 and H.R. 32*: 923.
[84]   *Bankruptcy Act Revision Hearings on H.R. 31 and H.R. 32*: 933–45.
[85]   *Bankruptcy Act Revision Hearings on H.R. 31 and H.R. 32*: 951.

up in fields like bankruptcy, probate and divorce.[86] Turning adversarial or advisory functions in the private market into counselling functions in the civil service struck to the heart of a private profession's resistance to "low-skill, low-cost" occupational encroachment. That private lawyers were competing with the government for work did little to assuage their fears.

The National Bankruptcy Conference sought to head off criticism with an amendment on counselling. Any new bankruptcy administration would provide debtors with lists of private attorneys and legal service organizations who would provide assistance at costs no greater than the bankruptcy administration. Or debtors could start with private attorneys if they wished. They would also put a chinese wall between the gathering of information and determinations. So the administrator would not be both "judge and jury."[87]

Both the American Bankers Association and Consumer Bankers Association strongly opposed the Commission's proposals on a US Bankruptcy Administration because conflicts of interest occurred when an administrator acted like a judge. This dual function may create "an impression of impropriety" and "a suspicion that parties will not receive a fair hearing."

It strains trust in human nature to the breaking point to believe that an administrative office can (i) counsel the debtor as to available relief; (ii) serve as trustee; (iii) and then fairly deal with a secured creditor at a valuation hearing.

The objection here is not from the debtors' but the creditors' point of view, since bankers were afraid that the new administration would take the side of the debtor. Instead of the Bankruptcy Administration itself acting as a trustee, they too preferred a private panel of trustees, perhaps on the Canadian model of licensed trustees. The bankers and lawyers made common cause of their belief that counselling more properly belonged to an attorney in a protected, confidential relationship—which in the nature of things would mean attorneys for creditors, but most often not for small debtors.[88] Testifying for the American Bankers Association, Robert Grimmig reiterated support for the Judges' Bill on

---

[86] Bernard Shapiro on behalf of the National Bankruptcy Conference, *Bankruptcy Act Revision Hearings on H.R. 31 and H.R. 32*: 1016.

[87] Testimony of Bernard Shapiro, appearing on behalf of the NBC, *Bankruptcy Act Revision Hearings on H.R. 31 and H.R. 32*: 1016.

[88] Stephen Subrin (Northeastern University) testified that his problem with the administrative agency would be the creation of a two-class, no-asset bankruptcy system, "a rich man's court . . . and an agency handling the mundane work." Most debtors cannot get good

the grounds that "...the entire administrative process lies within the judicial branch of government, where it properly belongs."[89]

Furthermore, the National Consumer Finance Association told Congress that "the rights of a secured creditor...are property rights which cannot be summarily dealt with by administrative decision." Property rights' disputes warranted private representation. Linn K. Twinem, appearing on behalf of the Beneficial Finance Company, urged that debtors preserve the choice to retain a private attorney. "The suggestion that the same agency which undertakes the adjudication, administration, supervision and trusteeship of the estate of a bankrupt should also serve as counsel...is fraught with patent and irreconcilable conflicts." Furthermore, without "opposing attorneys and an impartial judge," more individuals would declare bankruptcy that probably shouldn't, and a bankruptcy explosion could result.[90] Ironically, of course, this suggested that the difficulty and cost of obtaining a private lawyer acted as a disincentive to filing.[91]

Repeatedly, therefore, a connection is drawn between protection of property rights and the clear jurisdictional control of lawyers, and defense of due process in the redistribution or abrogation of those rights. In other words, government could not be trusted to respect the property rights of consumers nearly so much as private counsel. Redrawing the public–private boundary in favor of government agencies abrogated consumers of protections for their property rights as surely it deprived professionals of their jurisdictional rights.

This struggle between segments of a profession evoke the tension between a national legal elite of intellectuals and bankruptcy specialists and the local periphery of the lawyers identified by Dezalay (1992). In historical detail, however, dynamics within the profession defy straitforward characterization. Legal elites themselves were divided: the prestigious National Bankruptcy Conference divided internally over the placement of a bankruptcy administration. And elite federal judges joined forces with the marginal bankruptcy judges, although they were bitterly divided on other issues. The American Bar Association

counsel and will go to the agency. But the major creditors will make proceedings into a contest, that will shift proceedings from the agency to the courts, and that will produce a two-tier system. *Bankruptcy Act Revision Hearings on H.R. 31 and H.R. 32*: 1238.

[89] *Bankruptcy Act Revision Hearings on H.R. 31 and H.R. 32*: 1023–4.

[90] *Bankruptcy Act Revision Hearings on H.R. 31 and H.R. 32*: 905–7. He quotes Judge Cyr's judgment that "the most controversial of the Commission's recommendations is that for the creation of a new independent agency within the executive branch of government."

[91] *Bankruptcy Act Revision Hearings on H.R. 31 and H.R. 32*: 1045.

supported not the Bankruptcy Commission, but the strange alliance of federal judges, bankruptcy judges, and local bankruptcy lawyers.

Confronted by this alliance of bankers, lawyers, and judges, together with the concerted opposition of judicial administrators, the proposal for an executive bankruptcy administration became an early casualty of congressional lobbying. No subsequent bill revived the idea. The powerful lobbies of the federal judges, bankruptcy judges, banking associations, and locally-connected bankruptcy lawyers, overwhelmed the small circle of federal judges, politicians, and leading academic and practicing lawyers who had produced the Commission recommendations.[92]

Nevertheless, the story of professional politics alone cannot explain the ultimate rejection of an executive administrative agency. Congress also killed the proposal at an early stage because, as one legislator put it, " ... from a political point of view, the proposal [the executive branch bankruptcy bureaucracy] will never pass Congress. Congress at this time is not in the mood for creating a new agency."[93] Beginning with the Nixon administration in the late 1960s and early 1970s, and continuing through the Carter presidency, there was growing resistance to the size and cost of the federal government. Congress signalled that creating new agencies was politically out of the question.

Of course, the executive administrative agency might still have persisted if it could have been lodged in another government department. Several reformers proposed that bankruptcy trustees be housed in the Department of Justice and patterned on the highly successful US Attorney Office, which prosecuted cases in federal courts. But Attorney General Griffin Bell, himself a former federal judge and a close confidant both of President Carter and of the Chief Justice of the US Supreme Court, refused categorically, asserting that it would be another conflict of interest because the government is a major creditor in

---

[92] As we shall show in the next chapter, the public–private struggle became transformed into a debate between advocates of a more limited bankruptcy administration to be lodged in an existing executive agency, and the vocal proponents of all bankruptcy work—administrative and adjudicatory—to be housed in the judiciary. The two sets of issues—public/private and executive/judiciary—were not independent, but represented a series of options ranging from complete bureaucratization in a US Bankruptcy Administration, through various mixed public–private options, to the virtual privatization of bankruptcy administration that so exercised Brookings and the Bankruptcy Commission. We shall see that the extreme position staked out by Brookings may well have laid the groundwork for a compromise Act, which introduced an official trustee on an experimental basis, but one housed in the judiciary, and mostly reliant on private services.

[93] US Interview 92:01.

bankruptcy cases. Griffin's real reasons for opposition, informants allege, came from his sympathy with the federal judges' insistence that the judiciary not lose any jurisdiction over bankruptcy work. Essentially, therefore, he refused executive jurisdiction in favor of the judiciary.[94]

The conjunction of congressional opposition to a new bankruptcy bureaucracy, and a strong alliance of judges' and lawyers' groups, eventually forged a compromise with the advocates of administrative reform. The reformers backed away from their insistence on an executive agency in return for a commitment that a trial administrative program be set up in several federal courts, with the anticipation that a successful experiment would lead to a national program.

CREATING A PUBLIC GOOD AND MAKING A GOOD PUBLIC

Ostensibly, bankruptcy law concerns specialized professionals, marginal businesses, unfortunate consumers, and lowly government officials. But the furious debates over bankruptcy administration in two advanced capitalist economies suggest that some visceral element exists in bankruptcy administration, something that reacts forcefully to infringements of deeply felt values and interests.

More extensive in England than the United States was debate over the role of the state in financial extremity. Is there a public good to be delivered in bankruptcy administration? In England, a potent element of protectiveness inspired those Cork Committee members who plainly identified with weak debtors hounded mercilessly by hard-nosed creditors—an ironic position for the committee, given the strong pro-creditor orientation of English bankruptcy law. Nevertheless, panel members revolted against the government's proposed withdrawal from bankruptcy administration in large part because it seemed to leave the weak exposed and vulnerable to commercial predators. A strong state presence in bankruptcy administration redressed the imbalance between resourceful debt collectors and resourceless debtors. When official receivers were involved, the image of the bailiff at the door began to recede, an image imprinted on the English imagination since Dickens.[95]

---

[94] US Interviews 91:03:65; 92:01.

[95] Here, however, the "state's" position was contradictory, for on the one hand, it was charged with a protective role in the orderly liquidation of assets and discharge of debts, while on the other, various government revenue departments in pursuit of back taxes ranked amongst those creditors most likely to push a debtor into bankruptcy.

In both countries, reformers alleged that protection was needed not only from creditors, but from professionals. The Brookings Report attack on adversarial proceedings derived partly from the greater financial benefits that accrued to administrators of estates than the original creditors. Transaction costs exceeded the value of the estate. English reformers revived talk about the invitations to corruption that had accompanied private administration of bankruptcy in the nineteenth century. This resonated with allegations of "bad odor" and patronage deals in the American private practice of bankruptcy administration.

If protection was the most manifest public good delivered by the state in bankruptcy, it was closely followed by a strong sense that the state must provide an orderly means of equitably distributing to creditors what few assets remained in the debtor's estate. Orderliness required sharp bounds on *when* claims could be made against debtors. It decreed *who* could press such claims. The state's ability to freeze debt collection therefore combined orderliness with protection of all parties, whether debtors who were exposed to harrassment by creditors, or creditors who were less able to enforce their claims.

Over the long term, orderliness benefits all parties in a bankruptcy. Debtor rehabilitation and counselling, however, were state concerns that conflicted, in the short term, with the interests of creditors. And some disagreement ensued over the likelihood that the government, itself, would be more generous than some private creditors in the discharge of prior debts, so that consumers could get a fresh start.

The juxtaposition of English and American reforms throws into sharp relief a major difference between the countries over the role of the state. Earlier we saw that Mrs Thatcher's government viewed the Insolvency Act as an instrument of market morality for company directors (Chapter 6). The fierce exchanges over the Green Paper reveal that the private practitioners who dominated the Cork Committee wanted to retain a concept of bankruptcy law as *a regime of moral regulation* for consumers and smaller traders, too. It is true that the trajectory of modern law reform led to a "de-penalization" of bankruptcy law, making it less punitive and more rehabilitative and distributive. Nevertheless, the practitioners on the panel believed that the frequency of recklessness, fraud, and criminality in and about bankruptcy law required a continued state presence. Private professionals would not have the motivation, nor was it clear that it was their responsibility, to investigate breaches of the law. Adjudication and enforcement were inalienable functions of government. When the Cork Committee argued for the retention of public examination of debtors in open court, it signalled that public shaming could serve as a potent sanction for miscreant debtors (cf. Braithwaite 1989). Bankruptcy law should not be entirely decriminalized or swept clean of penal sanctions. If the penal dimension were to be removed, as the government had proposed, then bankruptcy could be turned into an administrative activity that merely distributed assets and paid creditors. For Cork and his committee and most public commentators, however, bankruptcy law was intended to help make citizens good—or at least discourage them from lapsing too far.

In the United States, by contrast, there is virtually no concern with investigative or sanctioning aspects of fraud or recklessness by debtors, nor of the use of bankruptcy law as a sanctioning device. There was concern about incompetence, as was implied in the counselling provisions of the abortive Bankruptcy Administration. But no sense of commercial morality, nor of the government's responsiblity for inculcating or regulating morality, appears during the American reforms. Indeed, it is not too much to say that not only did the Americans give little thought to making a public good, but no one on the American side articulated a coherent concept of the public good.

Debates turned on ideological constructions of the merits of public administration and the justifications of private markets. Bankruptcy reformers divided deeply over the capacities of each. On one side were Brookings and the Bankruptcy Commission, who shared the view of the Cork Committee that markets dealt harshly with incompetents or those who had suffered a major misfortune. Markets had to be tempered by either state regulation of the private market or state take-over of the private market. And the addition of superfluous adversarial proceedings in the United States made a bad situation worse. Carrying the flag for the other side was the Tory government, championing the efficiency of the market and minimizing its proclivity to breed fraud and predatory relationships.[96]

This then precipitated contention over the appropriate standards for appraisal of market performance. They proposed that the supposed gain in efficiency would more than be displaced by the erosion of honest dealings, because private arrangements would foster corruption. They also implicitly argued for equity—equity in uniformity of treatment in

[96] Fairness ran beneath and periodically rose above the surface of debates in both countries, though the appropriate prognoses differed drastically. Its salience intensified with weak creditors, especially consumers with few or no assets left, and limited capacities to obtain good professional advice.

bankruptcy, wherever debtors resided and whatever their means; and equity for treatment of creditors, so that the problem of the common pool would be solved. Without the latter, there will be an uneven rush to the assets, and the largest, strongest, most proximate are likely to prevail. Private practitioners performing public functions breeds special favors, private arrangements, and general suspicion.

Public administration was justified in terms of efficiency, impartiality, and equity, by Brookings, and in terms of probity by opponents of the British government. The value of market efficiency, therefore, clashed with the English reformers' commitment to public order and protection, and the American value of public efficiency (enunciated in the Brookings Report) confronted the singularly American discourse of rights. What began as protestations about market and state efficiency invariably crossed over into disputes over property and jurisdictional rights.

The Jurisdictional Defense of Property Rights

Property rights recur in two guises during debates over bankruptcy administration. In England, it was the state's habit to use bankruptcy law as a form of debt collection, thus ensuring the state's rights to reclaim property it considered its own. In a previous chapter we have shown that the strength of the state's right to back taxes was substantially reduced. The administrative reforms proposed by Cork were also intended to divert the state from overloading the bankruptcy system in pursuit of its property, though state officials complained that this would also reduce their revenue-generating capacities.

In the United States, the rhetoric of property rights bit more deeply and fused with jurisdictional claims by professionals. In contrast to the benign view of the state expressed by their English counterparts, creditors and professionals in the United States suspected that the nationalization of routine bankruptcies heralded some abridgement of individual rights, both of property and due process.

The property rights' discourse is intriguing since it begins with the premiss that bankruptcy is inherently conflictual as it concerns the fair distribution of property among competing claimants. The more property rights come into dispute, the greater the call for an adversarial, representational process in which lawyers provide protection for their individual clients. In other words, according to the lawyer-lobbyists, a natural affinity exists between conflicts over property rights and the allocation of jurisdictional rights in bankruptcy to private practitioners.

But it does not follow that lack of contest over property rights thereby exempts individuals from the need for adversary representation. The spokesman for legal aid maintained that even when consumers do not have many assets, they nonetheless require *private* representation to protect their rights of due process—which, he implied, can easily be trampled by a massive government bureaucracy. The opposition to the counselling service in the Bankruptcy Administration was on behalf of weak debtors who might find the government agency to be judge and jury on their financial affairs. Only a private practitioner could give debtors the confidence that she or he had their interests solely in mind (though this argument solved neither the problem that many debtors could not afford lawyers, nor the Brookings implication that debtors had as much to fear from exploitative professionals as their creditors.)

The great cross-Atlantic irony, therefore, was that where the American lawyers were energetically resisting the loss of jurisdiction on grounds of property and procedural rights, English insolvency practitioners were vigorously refusing jurisdiction on grounds of state responsibility. Nevertheless, the refusal of jurisdiction, in one case, and its defense, in the other, reflects a combination of jurisdictional interest with a concept of what is a proper public function, how best it can be administered, and where it must be limited. The politics of bankruptcy administration became embroiled in questions of efficiency, commercial morality, public interest, public order and protection, and equity—values so fundamental that their abridgement helps explain the emotive tone of debates. At stake was the concept of the public good.

Yet jurisdictional interest was not far behind and can scarcely be disentangled from the fate of bankruptcy administration. For decisions over where the public–private frontier would be drawn also determined whether professional work would reside inside the state, and be the province of civil servants, or in the market, and be the domain of private practitioners. In the struggles over bankruptcy administration, it is equally proper to conclude that boundary disputes over jurisdictional rights came to constitute the limits of public responsibility, just as the ideological disputes over the primacy of markets inevitably provoked jurisdictional skirmishes among professionals on either side of the public–private frontier.

9 Jurisdictional Conflicts in the Market

Major legal reforms, we have argued, significantly disturbed the division of professional labor. Reformist hopes to save companies and reorganize vulnerable firms required reliable and trustworthy experts, whose reputation and skills would encourage managers and creditors to try rehabilitation before giving up hope of corporate revival (Chapter 7). On both sides of the Atlantic, bankruptcy professionals experienced a meteoric rise in their professional identity, their market position, and the rewards accompanying both. This chapter appraises the role of the bankruptcy reforms in professional upward mobility by focusing on two broad questions.

First, what does it take to reconstitute a professional jurisdiction? What mechanisms are available to change the organization of professional services? Many of the most far-reaching reforms of corporate reorganization presuppose competent professionals who command the respect and trust of clients, and other interested parties. How can a professional jurisdiction be thoroughly renovated, therefore, in order for it to function effectively in the reallocation of major property rights? What are the means for stimulating the supply of expert labor in an area of great macro-economic significance?

Second, who crafts the division of labor? Aspirant professions? Reforming governments? State officials? How, then, can we account for the complex interplay between state activism and professional collective action?

Both questions converge on the theory of professionalization. These case studies provide unusual instances in which to observe rapid professional change. And both compel reappraisal of current understandings of professionalization.

ENGLAND: THE ADVENT OF A POLYMORPHOUS PROFESSION

The 1986 English Insolvency Act provides an unexpected moment in which to explicate theories of professionalization. In this case, the reconstruction of market institutions demonstrates how closely professions can be implicated in state purpose. Mrs Thatcher's Government viewed professionalization not simply as a convenient way to regulate a narrow niche in the market for professional services, but, serendipitously, as a means to produce higher "market morality" more generally.[1] We have seen that, by the time the Minister of Trade and Industry presented the Government's 1984 White Paper, Conservative policymakers had appropriated the insolvency bill as one more engine to drive the Tory bid for radical market transformations. The Insolvency Bill introduced to Parliament in the autumn of 1984 contained a powerful thrust towards the upgrading of "market morality," an effort directed towards improving the quality and probity of company management, and to significantly increasing the quality of professional services in corporate reorganization.[2] Although not expressed so baldly, Mrs Thatcher's Government used an unlikely legislative vehicle to further its much broader goal of "cleaning up" markets and making them safe both for investors, and for privatization.

Nevertheless, the advent of insolvency practitioners warrants close scrutiny in its own terms because it presents a model of professional creation and organization that looks quite different from those conventionally studied by scholars. In her bid to improve market morality, Mrs Thatcher's reforms also produced a new specimen of profession with surprisingly comprehensive, regulatory obligations. Government sponsorship of professional regulation climaxed an impetus for professionalization that had been gathering momentum over the preceding two decades. Initiative for professionalization came from four directions, two from the state and two from the private sector. State interests in occupational organization emanated from the Conservative Government and from the civil servants responsible for bankruptcy administration. Private sector calls for occupational regulation came primarily from practitioners in the insolvency field, but secondarily, and significantly, from banks, industrial firms, and consumers.

We have intimated in earlier chapters that the field of bankruptcy work before the mid-1980s had virtually no regulation. Despite the rise in the number and impact of insolvencies, any entrepreneur could hang out his shingle, no matter how doubtful his or her qualifications, experience, or integrity. As the stakes of corporate collapses multiplied, and the private organization of major bankruptcy and accounting firms responded through merger and specialization, the regulatory stakes

---

[1] On professionals and market morality, see a more extended treatment in Halliday and Carruthers (1996).
[2] See Chapter 7.

also rose. Government found itself under attack for permitting vulnerable individuals and companies to be preyed on by incompetents or "cowboys." Leading insolvency practitioners winced from media attacks. Meanwhile officials in the government Insolvency Service were under-staffed and over-worked by trivial cases. Businesses suffered from lack of competent professionals to handle reorganizations. And the economy hurt from unnecessary corporate failures or from excessive creditor caution.

From Corporate Undertakers to Company Doctors: Establishing Collective Organization

These developments, at both the top and bottom of the market for liquidators, catalyzed the impulse of insolvency practitioners towards collegial organization. Since this field was substantially unregulated, and because insolvency had marginal standing in the major English accounting associations, no collegial bodies for practitioners existed until 1961, when a small number of highly experienced practitioners—half from London, half from outside London—formed a group which they called the Discussion Group of Accountants Specializing in Insolvency. Members considered themselves an elite, because they were specialists with at least five years' full-time work in the insolvency field. "Everyone else was playing" at insolvency practice, stated one of its founding members. The Group functioned pretty much as "a gentleman's club" and a "talking group"—essentially "a social grouping which came together periodically with set periods with an annual conference of four or five days." But from the outset some of its leaders had larger aspirations.[3]

Transformations in practice which followed the economic changes of the early 1970s pushed the informal Discussion Group into legal incorporation. By founding in 1971 a small committee on insolvency, the Institute of Chartered Accountants in England and Wales (English Institute) created a potential rival for the Discussion Group, although the English Institute could not represent accountants who were affiliated

---

[3] For instance, members of the Group monitored court cases and regulations on bankruptcy and insolvency. On occasion they also made representations to officials about rules and practices. See Minutes, Insolvency Practitioners' Association, 27 Oct. 1961, 24 Sept. 1965, 27 Sept. 1968, 14 Jan. 1972 (on a subcommittee reviewing insolvency services and the Common Market Bankruptcy Treaty), Archives, Insolvency Practitioners Association, London; UK Interviews 91:08; 91:03; 91:02; 90:14; 91:15.

with one of the other three or four professional societies, nor unqualified accountants. With the greater awareness of insolvency as a social problem, and the expansion of insolvency work at the higher ends of practice, a section of the Discussion Group pressed for formal corporate status. Its secretary maintained that "registration would bring the association within public knowledge and that with its necessary rules and regulations would assist an informal association such as ours in obtaining official recognition by government departments." Registration might also increase the probability that insolvency practitioners could obtain qualification status, such as that conferred on auditors by the Companies Act of 1948.[4]

The new Insolvency Practitioners Association was registered in 1974 and activated as a company limited by guarantee on 1 January 1978.[5] While a major advance over its earlier informal status, this was still a modest step compared to solicitors and accountants. The former had their professional status recognized by Parliamentary statute; the latter were instituted by Royal Charter. Nevertheless, the new legal status of the IPA was accompanied by a raft of "professionalizing" innovations: a formalized committee structure; an elected governance body; the admission of individual members (previously membership had been only by firm); and the development of a code of ethics and disciplinary apparatus for members.[6] By 1977, the IPA incorporated leading insolvency and corporate reorganization partners of all England's top accounting firms, which came progressively to dominate the association.[7]

During the years of the Insolvency Review Committee the professionalization project moved forward on two fronts. Examinations were made a condition of admission for new members. And the engagement of the IPA with Government intensified, climaxing in its intimate involvement with the Cork Committee. After its contributions to insolvency

---

[4] Minutes, Insolvency Practitioners' Association, 20 May 1972 (on a meeting in Eastbourne to consider registration), 31 Mar. 1973 and 15 Aug. 1973 (on advantages and disadvantages of registration), 13 Dec. 1973 (reporting incorporation and registration of the IPA under the Companies Acts 1948–1967, in order to protect its name), Archives, Insolvency Practitioners Association, London, 20 May 1972.

[5] Minutes, Insolvency Practitioners' Association, 11 Jan. 1978 reporting on the general meeting of 28 Oct. 1977 and subsequent meetings, Archives, Insolvency Practitioners Association, London.

[6] Minutes, Insolvency Practitioners' Association, 20 Oct. 1978 (reporting that the IPA had subcommittees on law reform, general purposes, finance, membership, ethics, examinations, publishing, and conferences), Archives, Insolvency Practitioners Association, London. UK Interview 90:14.

[7] UK Interview 91:15.

legislation in 1976, and its regular consultations with the Insolvency Service of the Department of Trade and Industry, the Government acknowledged the IPA as one of two major representative organizations of insolvency experts. The other group was a combined insolvency subcommittee of the Consultative Committee of Accountancy Bodies (CCAB). In the area of insolvency law, however, the two groups were virtually identical in membership and views. By proceeding simultaneously through the Insolvency Practitioners Association and the joint accounting bodies, insolvency practitioners borrowed the cachet of the major accounting societies to multiply their impact on the Insolvency Service and the Insolvency Review Committee.[8]

The Springboard to State Legitimation: Crafting Reputation and Recreating Identity

When the Labour Government set up its Insolvency Law Review Committee in 1977 (Cork Committee), greater prominence for the IPA was assured. And when the Cork Committee called for input from groups interested in insolvency, the IPA and CCAB presented a series of submissions and representations which accompanied every step of the deliberative and parliamentary process through enactment of the statute and promulgation of Insolvency Rules. In sheer volume, IPA and CCAB submissions were matched only by the reports from the joint insolvency committee of the Law Society and Bar Council.[9]

The issue of professional status for insolvency practitioners featured prominently in those recommendations, and had been anticipated in an approach made by the IPA to the Department of Trade in 1976, urging that those persons licensed to act as receivers be limited to members of approved professional bodies (including the IPA).[10] But the DTI deferred action on this proposal to the Cork Committee.

Professionalization was not likely to have a significant economic effect on practitioners at the high end of practice, because they were already doing very well. Leading insolvency practitioners wanted a licensing scheme of some sort, but not for monopolistic reasons. "The accountants were usually so well established that it [licensing] would not affect

[8] UK Interview 91:08.
[9] *Public Record Office.*
[10] Summary of a Memorandum submitted by the IPA to the Department of Trade Insolvency Service, *Public Record Office*, 19 May 1976.

their market position particularly. So licensing wasn't actually going to reduce competition."[11] Licensing would adversely affect the smaller accountants "in the sticks who would have done six or seven a year of these things" and they lobbied hard to retain their access to insolvency work. But their elimination only marginally increased the market for more lucrative services. And most leading insolvency practitioners were already established as professionals through membership in accounting bodies, such as the English Institute.

Status and reputation propelled the drive towards professionalization from the professionals themselves. Even the elite of insolvency practice was tainted by such epithets as "corporate undertakers" and sullied by the unsavory activities of cowboy liquidators such as "Hissing Sid" Caplan and his stylishly-named Chancery Lane Registrars. When the *Sunday Times* intoned that receivers were so unregulated that they could be "convicted fraudsmen," or would not exclude "a deaf and dumb Patagonian fisherman," some dirt stuck (cf. Abbott 1981).[12] And when a lead article on "The Company Vultures" quoted one Barry Calvert's declaration that "some people involved in the liquidation business make second hand car dealers look like angels," it was only a small consolation to be told that "most liquidators are qualified accountants who stick closely to the rules." It was precisely in response to "more cavalier competitors," who gave "their profession a bad name," that the IPA was spurred to form a professional association.[13] And it was statements like Calvert's, reported the *Sunday Times*, that "infuriated" the IPA, which wanted rogues driven out of business, and looked to insolvency reforms to bring about these changes.[14] A President of the IPA observed that it was in the interests of the insolvency profession to "stamp out" unethical liquidators "because it was doing no good to our name."[15] And a member of the Cork Committee recognized that while he "was conscious quite a bit of the time of a 'job for the boys' impulse" that was present among insolvency practitioners, he also noted that legislation

---

[11] UK Interview 91:03.

[12] *Sunday Times*, 14 Dec. 1975, p. 53.

[13] This judgment was delivered in the mid-1980s, suggesting that the reputation of liquidators or insolvency practitioners was still subject to the same biting criticism. In the view of Stephen Aris, an investigative reporter writing for the *Sunday Times*, and author of a book, *Going Bust*, the IPA was formed "to bring some respectability to a business whose image was rather tarnished." *Sunday Times*, 27 Mar. 1985, p. 14.

[14] *Sunday Times*, 22 Nov. 1981, p. 57.

[15] UK Interview 91:03.

which controlled insolvency practice would give "greater dignity to this slightly rather drab end of life in the accountancy profession."[16]

It was true that major firms and "very professional men" were already well-established in the roles of "company doctors,"[17] but few looked with equanimity on the trailing edge of practice that Cork himself disdainfully called "rogue liquidators." For the elite practitioners who controlled the IPA and CCAB insolvency subcommittee, and whose representations were most vocal in the Cork Committee, professionalization of insolvency practice was intended to drive out incompetent, inexperienced, and occasionally unethical and criminal elements. It would stabilize the entire field of work by imposing a uniform normative code of expectations, complete with an enforcement apparatus. And it would guarantee some minimal levels of quality. But its principal direct effects on the elite would be minimal except for a halo that might be cast over the reputation of a specialty within accounting and an occupation outside it. Economics seemed marginal. At the time of the legislation, demand seemed unlimited, and the best practitioners could charge whatever fees the market could bear. According to the *Sunday Times* feature series, there was "a lot of money to be made out of receivership and liquidation. Insolvency, for so long the Cinderella of the accountancy world, is these days a multi-million pound business with an annual turnover.. of more than £50 million."[18] In these terms, professionalization effectively meant elimination of marginal practitioners and control of the low end of practice.

Given the ethos of saving companies, however, reputation was inseparable from responsibility for corporate reconstruction. The status project therefore intertwined with increased powers that Cork and others anticipated should be vested exclusively in licensed insolvency practitioners.[19] But in the meantime, the strengthened IPA had none of

[16] UK Interview 90:20.

[17] UK Interview 90:02.

[18] *Sunday Times*, 27 Mar. 1985, p. 14.

[19] Significantly, the non-specialist insolvency practitioners were effectively disenfranchised in the insolvency reforms, not because they were excluded in principle from giving voice, but because they suffered an irremediable problem of collective action. A rival association entitled the Practicing Accountants Insolvency Association was formed but never got off the ground. The lobbying organs of the accounting societies were controlled by the elites. In this respect, the professionalization of insolvency practitioners paralleled the efforts by 19th century physicians and solicitors to truncate the long tail of subsidiary occupations that were deemed unworthy of professional status (cf. Parry and Parry 1976). Professionalization meant less the rise in status of elite practitioners, than the removal of marginal practitioners.

the features that marked a statutory licensed profession. It was not self-regulatory; and it had no licensing powers. Nor could it influence admission to practice in the area, because there were no enforceable standards. The review of insolvency law, therefore, provided a singular moment in which a relatively low prestige occupation, and a relatively peripheral accounting specialty, could obtain a distinctive identity and state legitimation. Marching towards full professionalization, the Insolvency Review Committee presented an enormous opportunity for unqualified liquidators, in particular, to attain a legally mandated professional status with expanded powers over a protected domain of work.

Curiously enough, however, there is little evidence of extensive formal submissions by either the IPA or the CCAB to Cork on the licensing of liquidators. Not only is this topic not mentioned at all in some submissions, including the oral testimony given by the IPA, but technical aspects of insolvency law and business regulation far outweigh narrower professional concerns in volume or intensity of submissions by the accounting bodies.[20] This may have been restraint tempered by fear of appearing self-serving. More probably, it reflects the confidence among the reformist insiders, who included IPA and CCAB representatives, that recommendations of some sort for professional licensing were assured from Cork's Committee. An unwritten consensus had professionalization on the agenda without any need for collective mobilization.

Clients and Competitors: Ensuring Quality and Jurisdictional Access

It would be wrong to suppose that professionalization of insolvency practitioners was their own doing. Financial institutions and corporations also had an intense interest in what kind of professionals protected their credit or were available to reorganize their debt or companies.

The banking sector was most interested in that part of insolvency practice that touched on their largest loans—the receivers who were called in by the banks to liquidate a company's secured assets and pay off the creditors. The Midland Bank insisted that there should be some

---

[20] Oral Testimony from Representatives of the IPA, *Public Record Office*, 13 June 1978. Significantly, the Accountants Consultative Panel of the Cork Committee spent a great deal of time on technical aspects of the law, including receivers, but there are no entries in their records on the professionalization of insolvency practitioners.

minimal qualification for practice as a receiver, even if a standard would be difficult to apply, but it was chary of an entirely new occupational monopoly and advocated instead the appointment of receivers from several professions. In practice, however, the banks had little need to worry about insolvency practitioners in general, just so long as they could retain their right to appoint receivers of their own choice, and thus enforce their own regime of minimal qualifications. Banks already maintained a black list of those they would not appoint, so even the minimal thresholds of professionalization were not acute issues for them.[21] Most of the major British clearing banks had enduring patronage relations with established insolvency firms.

Business groups supported but did not prioritize professionalization of liquidators. The British Chambers of Commerce did not want a new monopoly either, and they urged that various occupations qualify to act as receivers. But, then again, they also wanted a uniform code of practice and ethics. The Institute of Directors, which arrived belatedly on the scene in 1984, supported professionalization not only because it would encourage corporate reconstruction by competent practitioners, and hopefully "save" companies, but also because a regulated profession could more reliably report on the business fraud which threatened the reputation of company directors. A profession of insolvency practitioners that was charged with the obligation to report on delinquent directors would have the capacity to exercise a control function that the Institute of Directors could not. Moreover, the Institute may have preferred to pass the washing of its dirty linen on to other parties so it could sidestep the need for expanded disciplinary apparatuses within the Institute itself, a function that invariably creates internal conflict within trade associations.[22]

Accounting's potential rivals in a new insolvency occupational order opposed monopolies that excluded them from a burgeoning lucrative practice, notwithstanding the fact that few solicitors, barristers, or surveyors had ever shown much interest in an insolvency specialty. According to the theory of jurisdictional conflict, a conjunction of booming economic opportunities with reforms aimed at controlling admission to a field of work should have precipitated a scramble for jurisdiction (Abbott 1988; Dezalay 1992). But the orientation of lawyers, in particular, was more complicated than this. In the first instance, the main lawyers' groups joined the bankers and business groups by proposing

---

[21] UK Interview 91:06.   [22] UK Interview 90:08.

limitations on who could be appointed as receivers of a company. However, they quietly insisted that restrictions on provision of services should not adversely affect the rights of chartered or certified accountants, and on occasion a solicitor, to be appointed as receivers. For the most part, their case for access to the insolvency market as liquidators or reorganization specialists was not pressed with any vigor.[23]

In addition to proposals which combined minimal standards with some diversity of professional affiliations, the Society of Conservative Lawyers offered a proposal for occupational consolidation substantially more radical than the others either proposed to or emerging from the Cork Committee. The Conservative Lawyers proposed a new profession that would combine and consolidate all the specialist accountancy skills, employed by receivers, liquidators, temporary managers, and trustees, a position effectively adopted by the Cork Committee. They would also consolidate the legal skills of insolvency practice by permitting the newly minted professionals to represent themselves as advocates in court. Hence the legal and accounting functions previously undertaken by solicitors, barristers, qualified accountants, and unqualified accountants would all be rolled into one comprehensive occupational package.[24]

Cork, therefore, confronted an array of positions on the new profession that ranged from complete consolidation of all functions into a single protected profession through the opposite extreme in which any profession currently doing any insolvency work might continue doing so with some efforts at inter-occupational standardization of admissions and norms. Consummate politician that he was, Cork plugged for the middle, though Parliament complicated matters considerably.

---

[23] The most intriguing development in inter-professional competition follows the 1986 Insolvency Act. The Thatcher Government insisted that admission to the new "hybrid" insolvency profession be open to several occupations, thereby encouraging market entrants to drive down prices. But despite their legal right to qualify as insolvency practitioners, virtually no lawyers have done so. Three explanations have been offered for this failure to exploit an enthusiastic invitation to compete for valuable work. First, the boom in corporate failures during the 1980s provided more than enough legal work for lawyers with interests in insolvency, so there was little economic incentive to compete with insolvency practitioners. Second, the start-up costs for lawyers, seemed prohibitive to most. And, third, and most decisively, major insolvency accounting firms let it be known that any law firm which sought to compete with accountants over insolvency work would no longer receive accountants' legal work.

[24] Written submissions of the Society of Conservative Lawyers to the Cork Committee, *Public Record Office*, 18 Jan. 1978.

The Civil Service and the Merits of Self-Regulation

Civil service norms precluded officials who were working on a bill from openly dissenting with their minister. Other officials in the same department, however, could and did exercise their rights of expression through their civil service unions.[25] Consequently, committees like Cork's could receive two sets of submissions from a government department: one represented the official department view in line with government policy; the other represented the expert views of civil servants as they reflected on their experience and projected their personal career and domain aspirations. Frequently these would be identical. Occasionally they would conflict.

But when it came to the licensure of insolvency practitioners, neither the Department nor the civil service union expressed any of the expansionistic inclinations of the sort stressed by state theorists. Officials pressed for some level of expert qualifications, in part because professionalized receivers and liquidators would permit tasks to be shifted from the public to the private sphere, and because properly authenticated private professionals would no longer be required "to come dashing to the department for permission to do this, that, and the other anymore."[26] While they immediately agreed that there should be licensing of professionals in the field of insolvency, when given an option between direct state regulation by a specialized governmental unit (viz, themselves), or professional self-regulation by a private occupational entity, they categorically chose the latter. Administrative rationality and political sensitivities coupled to urge upon the Cork Committee a classical English model of professional autonomy.

Civil servants were fully conscious of their inability to monitor satisfactorily the behavior of company directors. Control mechanisms over company directors in the insolvency field had suffered from a central defect: they relied on overworked government officials in under-staffed departments to bring actions against the tens of thousands of directors implicated in company failures. Furthermore, the Department of Trade and Industry had never managed to strengthen its legal powers to inspect company records or penetrate protective devices that surrounded company liens.[27] But if functions of the Insolvency Service could only

[25] UK Interview 91:10.

[26] UK Interview 91:10. Written submission of the Institution of Professional Civil Servants, *Public Record Office*, Aug. 1977.

[27] Oral Testimony from the Institution of Professional Civil Servants, *Public Record Office*, 13 June 1978.

be passed to a private profession with the fiduciary guarantees of self-regulation, then the DTI itself resisted any responsibility for licensing those individuals or authorizing other bodies to license individuals. Most resistance stemmed from the screening of individuals and groups, which was heavily labor-intensive, especially when the Department was given vague standards of "adequate knowledge and experience" to operationalize. As a senior DTI official explained to the Cork Committee:

I am sure you will be aware of the mine field one gets into with this, and if it is necessary one has to do it. But the Department went through a searing experience last year under pressure from the Institute of Chartered Secretaries to write down qualifications for company secretaries and the companies acts. As soon as you produce a short list of suitable bodies . . . hundreds of people appear pressing their claims. We had people on the doorstep asking to be recognized under the Companies Act. It is a tremendous battle always to agree on what is a suitable short list, particularly if it means that you are cutting people out that have been doing the job before.[28]

Given manpower constraints, the DTI much preferred self-regulation outside government, a preference that also reflected the dangers attached to discriminating among individuals and groups whose claims to professional status were reinforced by political pressures on the Department.

The Cork Committee and the Warrants of Professionalism

Before any submissions from interest groups were solicited, the Cork Committee reached an early consensus "that in future administrators, liquidators, etc., would all be professional men," but without creating a monopoly that confined receiverships to a single profession, such as accounting.[29] The principal issue was the form professionalization would take.

The agreement expressed early in the Cork Committee sprang from a consensus within the tight insolvency practice community. The symbolic geography of professional differentiation placed insolvency practice on the periphery of the accounting professions, the solicitors' profession, and the Bar. None believed that insolvency practice was taken seriously

---

[28] Oral Testimony from the Company's Division, Department of Trade and Industry, *Public Record Office*, 22 Oct. 1978.

[29] *Minutes of the Cork Committee*, 1 Mar. 1977; 24 Mar. 1977; 14 June 1978.

by the leadership of their respective professions. In practice, insolvency accountants had more professional community across the professional divide with solicitors and barristers in the insolvency field than they did with fellow accountants. The same could be said for the lawyers. Much, but not all, of this interstitial terrain was occupied by the collegial association of the IPA. But it did not include lawyers. The hybrid profession that was created by the Insolvency Act was therefore prefigured by an informal, but tightly integrated, community of lawyers and accountants and "unqualified" insolvency specialists. Their concern about this unregulated communal jurisdiction lying between powerful but disinterested professions was imported into the Cork Committee, where the main body and its consultative groups were dominated by experts from the insolvency domain. Mused one of its members:

... the insolvency world then ... was a very closed circuit of people. You know, there were a few accountants doing it, a few solicitors, some private practitioners, a few bank solicitors, and the odd banker who was heavily involved in it. We all knew each other, and when you turned up at the Cork Committee ... it was very clubby.[30]

The Cork Committee, itself, had other reasons for the establishment of a generic profession of insolvency practitioners. One reason was formal. The Committee sought to cut through the complexity of a century of accumulated Bankruptcy Acts by producing much greater uniformity in the law of insolvency and bankruptcy, introducing, whenever practicable, parallel procedures between corporate and individual bankruptcy. This principle in substantive law carried into its administration; a primary purpose of legislation was to rationalize and harmonize the powers and duties of all kinds of insolvency practitioners, including receivers, liquidators, and the administrators invented by the Cork Committee. From the Committee's vantage-point, a new profession of insolvency practitioner represented a form of occupational rationalization, bringing together the various duties that previously were spread among several occupations of differing professional provenance and status.[31]

A further reason was much more pragmatic and far-reaching. Since the City had become increasingly aware of the need to save rather than dissolve companies, banks, insolvency practitioners, and even the Government began to explore methods of corporate reconstruction. Insolvency specialists had pioneered a technique of corporate restructuring

[30] UK Interview 91:06.   [31] *Minutes of the Cork Committee*, 27 July 1981.

called "hivedowns" in which the viable parts of a corporation were repackaged, stripped of their liabilities, and sold as going concerns. Cork undertook his chairmanship of the Review Committee with a strong presumption that some new methods must be found to turn companies around before liquidation became inevitable. The Cork Committee proposed its innovation—which it labelled administration orders— to do exactly this.[32] For this innovation to work, or for it to be politically acceptable, it required highly qualified practitioners to act as administrators. Because both management and creditors would have to be convinced that administratorships were in their ultimate fininical interests, they too would need to have confidence in the capabilities of this new type of professional.

Professionalization, therefore, provided a means of ensuring that a minimum threshold of competence could be guaranteed for courts, management, and creditors. In other words, a change in the status of insolvency practitioners from "corporate undertakers" to "company doctors" could be smoothed by the guarantees implicit in professional status and self-regulation. Professionalization presented a conventional warrant of expert authority to prospective clients. Moreover, it increased the competitive advantage of qualified insolvency practitioners in their struggle with turn-around specialists because access to the courts, and a court order for administratorships, provided more powerful instruments to manage corporate reorganizations.[33]

In its final report, the Insolvency Review Committee recommended the formation of a new profession of insolvency practitioners. The Report urged the adoption of some "minimum professional qualification and control" as a prerequisite for engaging in insolvency practice. An insolvency practioner would need to have been in "general practice" for five years and to be a member of a professional body currently approved by the Department of Trade and Industry. The professional bodies, themselves, must satisfy the department of several prerequisites

---

[32] See Chapter 6 above. Before a company became technically insolvent, it could apply to the court for a moratorium on the payment of its debts, and ask the court to appoint an administrator, who would be an experienced insolvency practitioner capable of turning the company around before its financial circumstances became desperate.

[33] In theory, this argument could be reversed. Insolvency practitioners bent on upward mobility created a demand for their services by formulating the ideal of company reorganization and then offered themselves as the only experts capable of handling it. In other words, professionalization was a classic strategy of market creation and control (cf. Abel 1989 on lawyers). But it is clear that the ideal of "saving companies," while politically convenient for insolvency practitioners, had a much broader well-spring from industry and government.

for approval: (1) that they had a code of ethical conduct; (2) that they had strict accounting rules for moneys belonging to third parties which passed through their hands; (3) that admission to the profession be by examination, including at least an optional paper on insolvency; (4) that the body have "an effective disciplinary body" with powers to deprive members of the right to practice; and, not least, (5) that members be required to renew annually certificates to practice. Further, all insolvency practitioners would be required (6) to have insurance coverage and to be bonded against fraud and negligence.[34]

Finally, proposed Cork, standards of conduct by liquidators or trustees should be measured against a statutorily defined "duty of care" in a manner generally analogous to directors. To minimize the supervisory role of the DTI, control over practitioners would normally be the province of the respective professional bodies. And while the insolvency practitioner should not be personally liable for liabilities he incurred, he should be subject to the wrongful trading provisions introduced to regulate the behavior of company directors. It would be an offence, punishable by a fine, to act as an unqualified practitioner.

Government Interests and Design of Professions

Government interests emanated from three related policy orientations, all to do with changing Conservative ideology on the responsibilities of states and the functions of markets. In the first instance, ideological commitment to reduction of the state foundered on expert and consumer opposition. In the second instance, a contradiction in Conservative policy on professions was awkwardly resolved by the invention of what we call "polymorphous" professionalism. And in the third instance, Government ideology on market solutions received a serendipitous boost through a last minute Parliamentary amendment on the regulatory responsibilities of insolvency practitioners.

The 1980 Green discussion paper signalled the Government's growing realization that its policy of privatization faced serious political difficulty if it could not assure its constituents and the public that the functions previously carried out by civil servants, whose ethos presupposed disinterestedness, could be performed with equal or greater competence by no less disinterested private practitioners. The norms of the market—economic self-interest and the maximization of private gains—

---

[34] *Cork Report*: ch. 15.

ostensibly subverted the Government's purpose. Its preferred alternative, therefore, was to locate insolvency work in the only private market
institution that also espoused disinterestedness—the professions. Moreover, since professionalization in its classical English form also included
self-regulation, professionalization promised to relieve government
departments of their intrusive presence in every phase of insolvency
proceedings. According to a former President of the IPA and a member
of the insolvency panel of the CCAB,

> the Department of Trade and Industry had their finger in everything any
> insolvency practitioner did, which was necessary when there were a lot of rogues
> carrying it on. But once you had established a proper separate profession that
> was properly regulated in its own right, you didn't need all this time-wasting at
> the DTI.[35]

If virtue could be married to efficiency and produce a public good in a
private market, then the Conservatives would vindicate their economic
ideology in yet another realm of market activity, this time employing
professionalization as its primary institutional mechanism.

According to a senior civil servant responsible for developing the
Government's insolvency policy, the ministerial view was that lack of
controls over appointments of trustees or liquidators produced incompetence and dishonesty, so "there was a need for control," and that
fitted comfortably with the Government's policy on professions, which
advocated "self-regulation within a statutory framework." The concept
of statutorily governed self-regulation formed the centerpiece of the
Government's preferred mode of regulating services in the financial
sector—a policy whose effectiveness remains controversial to the present.[36]

The Government's position on insolvency practice sprang from similar philosophical dispositions. In fact, however, political expediency did
not permit, in the first instance, the wholesale removal of bankruptcy
services from the Official Receiver's Office to the private sector. The
opposition that developed to the Government's 1980 Green Paper
precluded privatization of an office that had been founded in the
1880s precisely to forestall the corruption that was rife in earlier market

---

[35] UK Interview 90:14.

[36] Some insolvency practitioners suspected that the government had a subsidiary
motive for keeping ethical regulation of practitioners away from a government department: the work of ethical oversight too readily embroils government in failures of regulation that create political problems for Ministers. UK Interviews 91:02; 91:17; 90:02; 90:09.

models of bankruptcy administration. Moreover, the private profession had no desire to be burdened with a raft of bankrupts with little or no capacity to pay. But resistance sprang not only from pecuniary motives. Insolvency practitioners espoused a concept of professionalization that located the search for bankruptcy fraud firmly in the public domain. For the Cork Committee, the IPA, the CCAB, and non-professional interest groups, the weight of government authority to police the margins of credit consumption was an irreducible public good that should not be alienated from the public sphere. That this argument served also to keep unremunerative bankruptcy work in the hands of government departments reinforced this public good with a private occupational interest.

The treatment of "professional standards for insolvency practitioners" in the very first chapter of the White Paper signalled the priority the Government placed on insolvency practice as a key to the entire reforms. Essentially accepting the Cork Report in all respects, the White Paper reaffirmed the importance of professional competence and the creation of public trust in those who handled insolvencies.

The Lord Advocate, Lord Cameron, opened debate on the Insolvency Bill in the House of Lords with the observation that the legislation was drafted to ensure that "the public should have confidence" in insolvency practitioners.[37] The qualifications the Government sought for insolvency practitioners fell into two classes, which in fact closely paralleled those that it had also championed in the regulation of business. Bryan Gould, Opposition spokesman for Trade and Industry, best identified the Government's intentions by observing that professional qualifications appeared to be of two kinds:

the first relates to professional probity—that is, to a person's honesty, his professional standards and the mechanisms available to provide protection if things go wrong, for example. The second set of qualities relate to competence, experience, the passing of exams, and membership of specialist professional bodies.[38]

Yet there were contradictions in the Government's policy. The Government recognized that the new professional monopoly was a restrictive trade practice, and this forced it to amend the Restrictive Trade Practices Act 1976 to make an exception for insolvency practitioners. And its inconsistency with other Government initiatives in the area of competition policy seemed puzzling to many observers. The Opposition, for

---

[37] Lord Cameron, H.L., vol. 469, 15 Jan. 1985, col. 877.
[38] H.C., vol. 458, St. Comm. E., 14 May 1985, col. 38.

instance, revelled in the Government's discomfiture when Bryan Gould pointed out conflicts in Government policy. The licensing of insolvency practitioners, he noted, was

> one element in a by now very confusing pattern established by the government in their attitude towards professional bodies. On the one hand, we have dereg- ulation for opticians, solicitors, and many other professions; on the other hand, we have the retrenchment of restrictive practices for the stock exchange and in this case for insolvency practitioners. One of these days, will the Minister turn his mind to a coherent competition policy?[39]

Indeed, the Government was pursuing apparently contradictory courses of action. On the one hand, the Tories were determined to pursue in the insolvency field its more general philosophy of "self-regulation within a statutory framework." Lord Lucas states that the Government was frustrated with the disorganization in the insolvency field, most particu- larly in the responsibility for regulation. "Different groups will not come together under one umbrella," he said. They were "all busily defending their own turf." The accounting professions were organized in at least four separate professional associations. The unqualified accountants had no professional regulatory apparatus. Solicitors and barristers engaged in insolvency work were monitored by yet another professional body. And the Department of Trade and Industry had long lost any chance of effective government regulation over professionals. Consequently, at a minimum, the Government wished to consolidate divided professions and to unify the regulatory apparatus to provide uniformity of ethics, regulatory consistency, and a clear locus of professional responsibility. In other words, the Government sought a comprehensive normative sys- tem, complete with policing powers, that operated within precise jur- isdictions. Moreover, it wanted to hold somebody accountable for the quality of its regulatory controls. Concomitantly, of course, because the Government's approach to law making was to draft fairly general legislation, and to fill in the details in secondary legislation and rules, it also needed private organizations that would co-operate in the design and implementation of the new legal and procedural order.[40]

---

[39] H.C., vol. 83., series 6, 18 July 1985, cols. 552–3.

[40] Despite the fact that the Conservatives shifted deliberately away from Britain's well- established post-war politics of tripartite negotiations among government, labor, and business, the rejection of neo-corporatist politics did not go so far as to eschew government reliance on private bodies to effect public purpose. Indeed, Lord Lucas, Government leader on the Insolvency Bill in the House of Lords, indicated privately that one motivation for professionalization was the need for government to deal with unified professional groups in order to better regulate them and their markets (UK Interview 90:09).

Essentially, therefore, the Government had a commitment to the imposition of what looked surprisingly like a cartel in a disorderly corner of the market for professional services. This step, on the other hand, conflicted directly with the Conservatives' much-vaunted ideal of competitive markets and the steadfast opposition of Thatcherism to "closed shops" in other areas of professional services, such as law.

The reform process spawned several conceptions of professionalization. Most interest groups simply had expressed a preference for some minimal requirements for appointments as receivers, without specifying what form those should take. At the other extreme, the Society of Conservative Lawyers proposed the creation of an entirely new occupation that spanned accounting and law. Officials at the Department of Trade and Industry knew what they did not want—individual licensing by the department, vague criteria for admission to practice, and the authorization of professional societies to license indirectly. Eventually they embraced the position that admission of receivers should be handled by professional societies on the basis of relevant professional training and examinations. Although some accountants were not so sure, Cork himself wanted insolvency practice to be kept open to suitably qualified lawyers and even chartered surveyors, a sentiment that was echoed in Parliamentary debates.

This last position resonated most with Government policy-makers and permitted an awkward resolution of the dilemma it faced through its adherence to contradictory principles of monopoly and competition. The resulting *polymorphous* model of professionalization represented a complex solution to these conflicting interests and ideological crosscurrents. The Government's polymorphous model sought to preserve diversity, and defend itself against accusations of creating a "closed shop," within a common framework. The Insolvency Act created the new profession of insolvency practice. All the normal functions of professional associations—admissions, examinations, code of ethics, discipline, continuing education—were delegated to seven professional associations: the Chartered Association of Certified Accountants, The Institute of Chartered Accountants in England and Wales, The Institute of Chartered Accountants of Scotland, The Institute of Chartered Accountants of Ireland, The Insolvency Practitioners Association, The Law Society of Scotland, and the Law Society of England.[41]

---

[41] Insolvency Act 1986, section 391, and The Insolvency Practitioners (Recognized Professional Bodies) Order 1986 (SI 1986 No. 1764).

Associations of lawyers were included principally because the Government was sensitive to criticisms that it was simply strengthening the accounting monopoly, and because it conceded, along with Cork, that there might be occasions when lawyers would be better qualified to act. Since the Government was loath, for reasons of political expediency, to take away work from all insolvency practitioners who were not members of either the accounting or legal professions, and since the IPA demanded minimum entrance requirements far higher than the Government preferred, the Act included an eighth organization that could also license practitioners—its own Department of Trade and Industry which four years earlier had publicly expressed its desire not to have any such powers. Party ideology trumped the preference of its own civil servants, who would administer the regulatory system.

Self-regulation therefore required the consensual regulation of the insolvency field by eight independent organizations who were required to reach agreement on common standards of admission, examinations, codes of ethics, and disciplinary procedures, but would apply them independently. This polymorphous professionalism created new problems of its own. While it seemed on paper to combine the possibility of competition among occupations with threshold standards of competence and ethics, it produced some curious, and other more predictable, outcomes.

Predictable was the pastiche of co-ordinating committees and bodies that sprang up to do the work of producing some consensus on the conventional problems of examinations, admissions, ethics, and representation to government. This in turn lead to some jockeying among the licensing bodies for respect and influence and eventually has produced a new quasi-peak association called the Society of Practitioners of Insolvency, which forms an umbrella organization over all the constituent groups without unduly privileging any (Miller and Power 1993).[42]

Most troubling for leaders of established professions was the need for private professions to obtain the agreement of a Government Department over standards of practice and ethical regulations. In effect, a Government Department now had veto power over private professional codes, a discomforting incursion on traditional professional autonomy. In Standing Committee debates of the Bill, the Minister was asked whether the Department of Trade and Industry would prescribe to the associations of accountants what they should do and thus "interfere in

---

[42] UK Interview 91:15; Archives, Insolvency Practitioners Association, London.

the standards and codes of conduct of those professional bodies."[43] And while the Government believed that its Department provided a safety valve for admissions in case of deliberate efforts by the accounting and legal professions to limit supply of professional services—a classic professional strategy (cf. Berlant 1975)—the professions in their turn suspected that the Department was much more susceptible to political manipulation than private associations. The structural contradiction of the Department's position inhered in its twin status, both as one among eight licensing bodies, and also as the organization which authorized the others and, in the last resort, could withdraw licensing powers from bodies unable to meet "professional" standards.

THE UNITED STATES: THE MAIN-STREAMING OF A MARGINAL SPECIALTY

American bankruptcy lawyers shared one main triumph with British insolvency practitioners: they were catapulted from the edge of professional recognition into the center of corporate practice in less than two decades—arguably the most rapid change in fortunes of any modern legal specialty. But the path of professional progress differed sharply from the insolvency practitioners. While the visible hand of the state was ever-present in the British case, the forces of the market, primed by unobtrusive legislative changes, converged with macro-economic shifts to push corporate US bankruptcy lawyers into the mainstream.

Before the decade of the 1970s, most bankruptcy practitioners existed in a legal backwater, where fees were low and reputations were questionable. The patronage relationships of the "bankruptcy ring," which surrounded the courts, were indicative of a pall that hung over bankruptcy lawyers. The culture of derogation was clearly understood by lawyers advising Congressional committees. A staffer on the House subcommittee, observed that:

One of the principal objectives of the '78 legislation was to bring bankruptcy into the main stream of American law. It was a backwater of American law that was looked at with disdain. Many undesirable elements practised it, and there were bankruptcy rings and charges of corruption. And many of the traditional firms would have nothing to do with it.[44]

[43] Gerald Bermingham, H.C., vol. 83, St. Comm. E., 18 July 1985, col. 527.
[44] US Interview 92:01.

A staffer on the Senate side, concurred that:

> ... bankruptcy practice was not—what is the best and most delicate way to put it—it was a dirty business. You know, people who practiced bankruptcy law were somehow an underclass of lawyers.... None of the big firms, or any of the New York firms, or what I call the "K Street" firms here in Washington, or Chicago—the big firms—none of them had bankruptcy departments.[45]

Stated a leading bankruptcy practitioner from the west coast, "big firms kind of looked down their nose at bankruptcy practice....[T]he vast bulk of bankruptcy practice in this country was in small, five to ten attorney firms." A politician who had practiced some bankruptcy acknowledged that it was "just not that attractive.... People just turned up their nose at a bankruptcy lawyer."[46]

By the late 1980s, the landscape of bankruptcy practice had become unrecognizable, with radical changes in reputation and the structure of practice. Corporate reorganization has taken its place alongside mergers and acquisitions as a revenue-center in the most prestigious corporate law firms. Did the 1978 Bankruptcy Code mediate this fundamental shift in market valuation of bankruptcy practice?

The Amalgam of Two Cultures

Change was already underway in the early 1970s before the the Commission on Bankruptcy filed its report with Congress, and it quickened as legislators deliberated between 1974 and 1978. The landscape of corporate insolvencies changed sharply in the 1960s as the rate of business failures and near failures increased rapidly.[47] Greatly increased demand for expertise in corporate reorganization and liquidation revealed gaps in the organization of legal services. The complexities of large-scale corporate collapses required sophisticated professional advice that spanned many areas of corporate law, tort, contract, and securities—specialties that far exceeded the capacities of boutique bankruptcy firms, and which conventionally were the province of the established Wall Street firms and their equivalents in other cities. Yet the large, elite corporate firms, themselves, gradually came to recognize that their biggest corporate clients demanded legal services that they could not supply.

---

[45] US Interview 91:05.   [46] US Interviews 92:04; 91:04.
[47] See Figs. 3.1 and 3.2.

The growth in demand at the high end of legal practice coincided with two changes in corporate legal practice. From the late 1960s, American law firms began an explosive period of growth, partly in response to economic expansion, but also as a reaction to internal imperatives to provide one-stop corporate services alongside national and global representation (Galanter and Palay 1991). Since bankruptcy work progressively came to look more like other kinds of corporate practice, many bankruptcy boutiques began edging closer to corporate firms, leading to a modest wave of horizontal integration in which bankruptcy boutiques were installed as instant departments on LaSalle and Wall Street.

The mergers rode on the back of a slow cultural revolution occurring in legal practice. Beginning in the late 1960s, elite law schools and elite law firms progressively opened legal careers to Jewish lawyers (Powell, 1991). Since many Jewish lawyers had been concentrated in marginal specialties, like bankruptcy practice, religious integration in the higher strata of the profession combined with the lessening stigma of bankruptcy in corporate America to remove two cultural barriers to professional upward mobility. A series of mergers and acquisitions brought together elite firms, disproportionately dominated by upper class Protestants, with specialty firms historically outside the pale, which were disproportionately Jewish and Catholic (Dezalay 1992).

Major creditors also worked at bridging the two cultures at the center and periphery of legal practice. A senior banker who served on the task-force on bankruptcy created by the banking industry in 1975 expressed the view that effective reforms would only be possible if the two cultures could be amalgamated. On the one side,

bankruptcy up until it became socially acceptable in business was viewed as a sort of arena for a segment of the legal business that was sort of off by themselves. I can describe them in ethnic terms, I can describe them in colorful terms. The old "ten cents on the dollar." But it was a different crowd. They were not the upper class, corporate lawyer. They were not the reorganization expert. These guys were basically known as "I'll take the inventory, you take the receivables, and I'll see you on 37th and 8th avenue".... These guys were good at ringing the necks, ringing some cash out of nowhere from the garment district or the diamond district.[48]

---

[48] US Interview 91:01.

On the other side

you had the Penn Central which involved Sherman and Sterling, Davis Polk, and all your major law firms. Two different cultures . . . So if I were going to try to represent the banking industry I had to bring together both the money center banks and the regional and smaller banks, and I also had to bring together the white shoe, upscale commercial law firms with the traditional bankruptcy experts.[49]

The banking industry had a strong incentive to ensure that the expertise at the top of the bankruptcy bar could be melded with the traditional strength of leading corporate law firms.

Lawyers' Compensation

Underlying all these shifting currents, the rules governing lawyers' fees presented the major impediment to specialization and careers in bankruptcy. Although lawyers hired directly by large creditors, such as banks, could be paid whatever their clients determined, any lawyers whose fees came out of the bankrupt estate were governed by court discretion and legislation. Lawyers for the debtor, lawyers for creditors' committees, lawyers acting as counsel to trustees, private trustees themselves—their compensation was finally determined by the court at the conclusion of the case. Until passage of the 1978 Code, powerful economic disincentives and uncertainties depressed the remuneration of bankruptcy lawyers, discouraging the "best and brightest" from entering the field.

Under the bankruptcy rules before 1979, two provisions governed lawyers' compensation. Because the primary purpose of bankruptcy settlements was to give due consideration to "the conservation of the estate and the interests of creditors,"[50] the governing principle for

---

[49] US Interview 91:01.

[50] Rule 219(c), Bankruptcy Rules. The Bankruptcy Rules were revised by the Judicial Conference in the early 1970s pursuant to 28 U.S.C. §2075. While the Rules are not supposed to affect "substantive rights" or the court's jurisdiction, the Rules do comprehensively regulate court *practice and procedure*. Accordingly, the Rules have a tremendous impact on the day-to-day operation of the bankruptcy court.

According to Treister (1973), Rule 219(c) governing the general approach for determining attorney's (and accountant's) fees was not a major change in the revision of the early 1970s. It was not until the Bankruptcy Reform Act of 1978 that the manner in which professional's fees in bankruptcy procedings changed dramatically.

Pace, however, the statements of a member of the National Association of Chapter XIII Trustees in the Senate hearings on the proposed bankruptcy reform: *Senator Burdick*: " . . . I know something about courts too. And they are rather reluctant to reduce fees." *Mr. Rice*: "If the Senator will pardon me, until the new rules went into effect it was,

decisions on fees was "the spirit of economy."[51] Lawyers needed to persuade judges that their fees were reasonable and did not unduly diminish the value of the estate, and the distribution of remaining assets to creditors. The underlying ethos of the bankruptcy court was that "we are dealing with poor, suffering people and there is not enough money to go around. Therefore you lawyers can only charge 9 per cent of what otherwise you would charge."[52]

Judges adopted very conservative rules of thumb. The most curious norm linked attorneys' fees to those of federal district court judges, who themselves had been smarting from no salary increases for several years. Angry over the failure of Congress to raise salaries, a 9th circuit judge had ruled that it was improper to pay fees to an attorney in a bankruptcy case more than twice the hourly rate of a district judge.[53] Other cases supported the spirit of economy.[54]

Compounding the downward pressure on fees was the uncertainty over what fees lawyers could anticipate. Courts were reluctant to provide interim compensation. Major reorganizations invariably took years. Without interim compensation, firms were forced to carry the cost of services themselves, quite apart from the difficulties this presented for budgeting. Restraints on fees, uncertainty about payment, and long delays until final disposition all dampened enthusiasm for ambitious corporate lawyers to take on major reorganizations.

In one deft and simple stroke, the 1978 Bankruptcy Code changed the professional incentive system. Yet the proposals for change came relatively late in the reform process and occasioned minimal public discussion either in Congress or outside it. Since the Bankruptcy Commission placed heavy emphasis on the importance of corporate reorganization, including the innovations in the new, consolidated Chapter 11, the dependency of reorganization on skilled and prestigious lawyers seemed mandatory. Advocates for an up-graded bankruptcy court, including the Commission, found it absolutely self-evident that courts

---

let's say, unpopular for the local judge to pick on his fellow lawyers. The new rules apparently brought about two things, I think. The rules give them a handle, they have a report, and the lawyer has to state exactly what the fees were and what the basis was. And frankly, the Commission's report to this Congress has made the judges conscious that this is something that they ought to get onto. And they have done so . . . ."(*Bankruptcy Reform Act Hearings on S. 235 and S. 236*: 592)

[51] 3 *Collier on Bankruptcy*, Para 62.12[5] at 1483–91.

[52] US Interview 92:02.

[53] US Interview 92:02.

[54] *Beverly Crest; Massachusetts Mutual Life Insurance Company v. Brock*, 405 F.2d 429, 432 (5th Cir. 1968).

would never be safe for major corporate bankruptcies unless judges were of high caliber. Recruiting top-flight judges depended not merely on the powers of their courts, but on the length of tenure and their salary levels. But the application of analogous reasoning to lawyers fails to find its way into the Bankruptcy Commission's Report, notwithstanding the extensive attention given to fees in personal bankruptcies and salary levels of court and administrative officials.[55]

Likewise, consumer bankruptcy fees featured in submissions to congressional committees by lawyers and the National Conference of Bankruptcy Judges.[56] Rare exceptions were found in Professor Lawrence King's submission that attorneys will have a vested interest in pushing corporate clients towards Chapter 11 reorganizations in the proposal bill, because Chapter 11 permits managers to remain in possession of their companies, and to retain their lawyers.[57] Otherwise, Philip Loomis, the representative of the Securities and Exchange Commission, reported that fees in both the old corporate Chapters X and XI were rising, but that in 1974 they only averaged $36,000 per lawyer for the 300 cases under review.[58]

None the less, the problems of lawyers' compensation had not escaped the attention of the National Bankruptcy Conference, which brought a proposal for reform to the House subcommittee on the bankruptcy code.[59]

The shift came with legislative amendments, which instituted a new principle of compensation. House Bill H.R. 8200 introduced the new standard of "the cost of comparable services." Although lawyers appointed by the court, and acting for creditors' committees, or debtors-in-possession, would need to obtain court approval for fees, section 330 of the bill mandated, in the words of Congressman Edwards, that judges were "to compensate attorneys and other professionals serving in a case under title 11 [the Bankruptcy Code] at the same rate as the attorney or

---

[55] The wording of §4–404(c) of both H.R. 31 (The Commission Bill) and H.R. 32 (The Judges' Bill) is virtually identical to the wording of Rule 219(c)(1) of the Bankruptcy Rules.

[56] Bankruptcy Act Revision Hearings: 1255–1395.

[57] *Bankruptcy Reform Act Hearings on S.235 and S.236: 357–70.*

[58] *Bankruptcy Reform Act Hearings on S.235 and S.236: 713–30.*

[59] In early Congressional testimony, the NBC contended that as a matter of facilitating reorganization, "any claim for personal services by an attorney or insider which exceeds the reasonable value of the services is not allowable." (*Bankruptcy Act Revision Hearings*:1882). Given their later statement that people administering bankruptcy cases (with reference to trustees) are motivated less by benefitting the estate than by "their own financial interests," it seems that the NBC was less concerned about upgrading the quality of lawyers than in reducing administrative overheads generally (*Bankruptcy Reform Act of 1978 Hearings*: 833).

other professional would be compensated for performing comparable services other than in a case under title 11." While Edwards acknowledged that "attorneys' fees in bankruptcy cases can be quite large and should be closely examined by the court," he nevertheless was emphatic in his committee's view that "notions of economy of the estate in fixing fees are outdated and have no place in a bankruptcy code."[60]

Put another way, if bankruptcy services were equivalent in complexity, novelty, quantity, and result, to outcomes in other areas of the corporate law, then the fees should be calibrated accordingly (Butenas 1981:79). Those lawyers who brought millions or billions of extra dollars into the estate should expect to see their industry acknowledged in the size of their fees. By not being confined to hourly billing, the new measures provided a powerful economic stimulus for lawyers who earned high incomes in other fields to enter corporate organization. Lawyers could now be placed on retainer by a client or be hired on a contingent fee basis.[61] The latter effectively linked the compensation of a lawyer directly to the result of his or her services. Finally, lawyers were permitted to receive interim payments every three months.[62]

Building a new incentive system, subsequent events have proved, transformed the bankruptcy bar. Raising the ceiling on fees undoubtedly was the critical change and it was entirely self-conscious. Said a member of the House subcommittee: "We created a bankruptcy bar that is much better in quality and talent than ever was there before. And we bought them. It has gotten to be respectable and fees are better." Or in the terms of one of the House staffers: "Why shouldn't you be able to attract the best and the brightest in this field as in any other field. Now unfortunately, the way we attracted the best and the brightest was with money."[63] Looking back, a Senate staffer claimed that changes in practice proved that better lawyering followed better fees. "Bankruptcy today is prestigious in practice in firms where everything else is not growing but is constricted . . . That came about because they started getting paid real money. Real fees, you know, the same fees that everybody else started getting paid." If the intention was to bring first-rate people into bankruptcy law, it has succeeded. "Today bankruptcy lawyers are at a premium, reorganization lawyers are at a premium. The

---

[60] Congressman Edwards, 124 Cong. Rec. H. 32383, Thursday, September 28, 1978, p. 42. And H.R. 8200, §330.

[61] H.R. 8200, §328(a), after conference report.

[62] H.R. 8200, §331.

[63] US Interview 92:02.

bankruptcy practice has just exploded." Not only absolute size made a difference. Said a reformer, "the feature of the bankruptcy code that probably had the most impact was this thing of letting them be paid early and along the way. Interim compensation and things of that nature has attracted better people to the bar."[64]

None the less, the impact of the Code on bankruptcy practice and organization cannot be separated from propitious circumstances that multiplied its effects beyond the expectations of its designers. While the Code was not born out of economic depression, recession followed immediately on its heels. The Code took effect on 1 October 1979, at a time when the economy had already turned down, and the curve of corporate bankruptcies rose more steeply. Chapter 11 quickly got its own workout, as corporate managers recognized the shelter it provided and lawyers began to understand what great economic and legal stakes were involved. This was not simply a matter of paying more to lawyers already in the field. Chapter 11 cultivated the lawyerly skills of deal-making and negotiation. The highest flying deal-making of the 1980s came in billion-dollar plus mergers and acquisitions (M&A). But when that work declined, it left a vacuum for M&A lawyers, who were accustomed to a free-wheeling, practice that garnered enormous financial rewards, substantially based on the size of the deal. The M&A lawyers "figured, well, we can do deals out of court, we can do deals in bankruptcy as well."[65] As a result, the downturn in the business cycle pushed large numbers of high prestige corporate organization lawyers into corporate reorganization, simultaneously endowing their aura of prestige on bankruptcy law, and releasing their creative energies into corporate reorganization. Combined with the diversification of large firm practices, which found their new growth area in bankruptcy law, the timing of the 1978 Code could not have been calculated more perfectly.

So spectacular were the successes of bankruptcy lawyers in bringing value and creativity to a once-derogated specialty, by 1990 critics turned on this extremely lucrative practice that now seemed to eat large proportions of corporate bankruptcy estates.

Consequently, the 1978 Code combined with developments already under way in the legal profession to transform the occupational landscape of bankruptcy law. The entire field grew in volume of work and lucrativeness of rewards. Mergers of specialist bankruptcy with

---

[64] US Interview 92:01.   [65] US Interview 92:01.

generalist corporate firms, together with the development of in-house bankruptcy and reorganization departments in the most prestigious firms, already signalled the rapid movement of bankruptcy practice from the periphery towards the center of the profession. Setting market rates in bankruptcy that were equivalent to fees generated for other corporate legal services simultaneously upgraded the status, increased the power, and multipled the financial returns of this previously derogated area of legal practice. As Representative Drinan drily commented to a house subcommittee, "I realize it is a full employment bill for lawyers" (Aaron 1980).

Market Morality and Market Incentives: Alternative Models of Jurisdictional Reconstruction

The Insolvency Act and Bankruptcy Code precipitated seismic shifts in the organization of professional work. English legislation excluded some two-thirds of professionals who had been working on bankruptcies in their drive for a fully professionalized, quality-guaranteed, insolvency practitioner. Their expedient was the classical mechanism of state licensing. The results were manifest: the numbers of insolvency practitioners fell sharply, but the average level of experience and, it might be assumed, quality of practice, jumped markedly. American legislation also radically changed the landscape of bankruptcy practice, but without any change whatsoever in government regulation or professional self-regulation. Instead, American legislators relied entirely on the stimulus to expertise that came from direct economic incentives—fees calibrated to the quality of professional service and the magnitude of assets brought into the estate. Even here the state did not disappear altogether. Disputes between creditors and debtors over fees ultimately were mediated by judges, who progressively have cast a more jaundiced eye over expense claims. But for those lawyers retained by large creditors, they could now charge what their market could bear for professional services without judicial intervention.

The irony in Britain was that Mrs Thatcher's Government, which ardently advocated free market solutions to problems historically managed by government, found itself extending government's intervention into market regulation through professional licensing, an irony not lost on the Labour Opposition, as we have seen. In the United States, by contrast, a Democratic President signed into law a set of statutory incentives that solved the quality problem in classic laissez-faire fashion.

Why did Mrs Thatcher's Government adopt restrictive practices that directly abrogated its own first principles of economic freedom? The political problems of insolvency practice provided one necessary condition of action. But even that was unlikely to have been sufficient. The ultimate reason for Government sponsorship of professionalization turned on its readiness to tolerate some restrictive trade practices if that was a price that had to be paid for more efficient, stable, and "moral" markets.[66] The Government did not consider the new profession of insolvency practice to be a complete monopoly, since a license to practice could be obtained through seven professional bodies and the Department of Trade and Industry itself. If, for instance, some of the professional licensing bodies sought to restrict entry to the practice of insolvency work, the Government retained the power to maintain open entry through departmental licensing powers. But most importantly, the Government tolerated restrictive practices because insolvency practitioners were charged with responsibilities to monitor directors in financially distressed companies.

Several members of the Cork Committee had been pessimistic about the implementation of the Cork Report. There were good reasons for low expectations. Insolvency legislation was not a great vote-getter and there were few highly organized interest groups in the insolvency area to exert pressure on the Government.[67] And when the Government seemed loath to move on Cork's Final Report—first to publish it, then to respond in a White Paper—these doubts seemed to be confirmed.

Then, suddenly, in early 1984, some three years after the Department had received the Cork Report, the Government moved with surprising alacrity to present its policy proposals, draft a bill, and rush it through Parliament. Why the abrupt change in attitudes? Several reasons can be advanced, including Sir Kenneth's indefatigable and blunt representations to the Government and the press over the inaction. "Sir Kenneth," said one of his Cork Committee colleagues, "was one of those men that

---

[66] A more conventional explanation was offered by Sir Gordon Borrie (1984: 11–25), Director of the Office of Fair Trading, who instanced insolvency practitioners as an example of "the activities of the uncontrolled professional operator who causes such public scandal that professionalization . . . is advocated in the public interest."

[67] In addition, Mrs Thatcher did not appoint Royal Commissions or Departmental inquiries because, said an Opposition MP, if you already know the correct answer to an economic problem, there is little need to risk convening an independent body to tell you something different. Notable cases of shelved reports sprang readily to the minds of Cork Committee members.

has clout."[68] But the most compelling explanation comes from the Government's recognition rather late in the day that the Insolvency Bill could be saddled with much larger load than liquidation and company reorganization.

In the first instance, the Insolvency Act institutionalized a classic liberal solution to the problems of liquidator competence and probity. Through professionalization, albeit in this strained and architectonic fashion, government could demarcate jurisdictions for insolvency practice (Abbott 1988), legitimate a system of occupational governance, oversee development of an acceptable normative system, regulate admissions, and exert some control over the enforcement apparatuses of the respective licensing bodies. Moreover, the cost of regulation was almost entirely externalized to the professional bodies, thus attenuating government's responsibilities for the sometimes politically embarrassing lapses of failed professional responsibility. This solution was ideologically satisfying, too, because it married the values of efficiency and small government without appearing to erect a new private monopoly.

In the second instance, the Government's sponsorship of professionalization inheres in its consistency with the ideology of privatization. In the Government's view, the emergence of the new profession permitted, simultaneously, a more efficient private solution to market failures and the correlative contraction of the state. We have shown that the two were contingent in the Government's thinking and statutory design: only a form of private institution that was culturally acceptable, with impeccable fiduciary bona fides, could be entrusted with responsibilities previously thought to be indissolubly wedded to the public sphere. The movement of work from the public to the private domains through professionalization yielded a double benefit for public servants. It married the status of their government department to a higher status occupation charged with a higher mandate to reconstruct the leading institutions of capitalist society. Concurrently, it also shifted into the private sphere some of the more mundane and routine tasks that symbolically deprofessionalized civil servants, thus allowing them to adopt supervisory postures and more sophisticated methods of corporate surveillance.

The most notable outcomes of the legislation, however, were the structural innovations that converted professionalism into an agent of

---

[68] UK Interview 91:20. Cork's own private papers contained letters he had written to the Minister of Trade and the Prime Minister, urging action on his Report.

state regulation and moral reconstruction. The Cork Committee handed the Government two weapons with which to assault the failure of business to regulate itself: director disqualification; and director vulnerability to civil suits through wrongful trading actions. On the initiative of insolvency practitioners, a director could be disqualified by the DTI from acting as a director in any company for up to fifteen years. Moreover, the new provisions on "wrongful trading" permitted insolvency practitioners to identify directors who might be made personally liable for the debts of their company.

These extraordinary legal innovations enacted professionalism on two additional counts. They pressured company directors to obtain expert advice more quickly and earlier in the downward spiral of financial distress, and thus they activated more broadly and deeply the professional resources available to the business community. In addition, they pressed non-executive directors of companies—frequently the outside experts, who were not infrequently professionals themselves—to attend more closely to company affairs and to hold full-time managers more accountable. Both outcomes were intended by the Government, and in the view of many observers, have been realized in practice, to one degree or another (cf. Wheeler 1991; 1994). Business leaders and insolvency specialists concur that passage of the Insolvency Act, publicity through trade and professional associations, media attention, and the sharper teeth of court decisions have combined to alter the behavior of directors in large public and medium-sized companies in ways that beatifies professionalism.[69]

But the serendipitous amendment to the Bill as it wended its way through Parliament transported professional responsibilities onto a new plane of regulatory import. Faced with an amendment that charged every insolvency practitioner in a liquidation to write a report on every director, the Government reluctantly accepted that newly minted insolvency practitioners offered a comprehensive means of overseeing directors of all insolvent companies.[70] It allowed the Government to build a national database of directors engaged in more than one insolvency. And, most importantly, it conveyed to directors the message that their decisions and activities were subject to observation and ex post facto examination. In short, the professionalization of insolvency practitioners

---

[69] UK Interviews 90:21; 91:20; 90:08; 91:12; 91:08.

[70] Government resistance stemmed in large part because it was loath to weigh down the Insolvency Service with thousands of reports at exactly the time it was seeking to make government more efficient and to upgrade the seriousness of civil servant responsibilities.

intensified the pressure on business to "professionalize" its own activities through adoption of a defensible code of behavior. And to ensure that this chain of control remained unbroken, insolvency practitioners themselves might be personally liable for the debts of a failed company if they failed to fulfill their professional obligations to file reports, among other things.[71]

Professionalization of insolvency practice therefore presented the Government with a brilliant alternative that at once unloaded costs of regulation onto the private market, essentially as a tax on insolvency practitioners (who resisted this added, unrecompensed, responsibility), and ensured saturation coverage of all defunct companies.[72]

If this extended empowerment of a market profession in its expansive definition of state/principal—profession/agent relations represents the most singular innovation of the Insolvency Act, its spawning of a polymorphous profession represents an intriguing development in the organization and structure of professions. The polymorphism of the insolvency profession has several distinguishing features.

First, the new profession in principle united two, and possibly more, occupations. It melded the insolvency segments of accounting, law, and surveying into a new *second order occupation*. This "layering" of a secondary occupational label and monopoly over an already pre-existing occupational title, most often also endowed with monopoly over a jurisdiction of work, created a new hybrid form of profession with few if any precedents. And while it was a primary qualification for some practitioners, it acted as a specialty qualification for others, essentially segmenting the internal market for accountancy services.

The second, and arguably most notable, attribute of polymorphism in this instance can be found in its awkward *contradictions of regulatory control*. The duality of DTI responsibility has already been noted: at once, the

---

[71] See, for instance, the Minister of State's comment that "at determined intervals practitioners will be required to submit a report on what they have done and what evidence of unfitness has been discovered about the directors of the company concerned during the period reported on. The Secretary of State will thus receive reports on all directors who have been involved in insolvency proceedings. The reports will form part of a data base which will gradually be built on all directors who have been involved in insolvency proceedings." (H.C., vol. 83, St. Comm. E., 18 July 1985, col. 584.)

[72] H.C., vol. 458, St. Comm. E., 16 May 1985, cols. 55–68. Although the amendment was introduced by an Opposition member, it was strongly supported by Trotter MP, an insolvency practitioner, and other Conservatives.

Department is one among equals, responsible for regulating the members it licences as other bodies are for regulating theirs; but then it is also first among equals, for it regulates the regulators. In the case of the pre-eminent English accounting and legal professions, this is likely to count for relatively little. Their prerogatives have been well-entrenched and their powers are formidable. For the smaller IPA, an entirely different dynamic might emerge. But in either case, a government department responsible for registration of professional bodies sat at the same table to negotiate the terms of the normative standards that were to obtain among them. Whatever else it signifies, the regulatory component of polymorphism demonstrates an interpenetration of public and private interest over market transactions that entails a lesser degree of freedom for professional autonomy and more grounds for state control of supposedly autonomous "primary" professions.

Despite its complexity, this hybrid form of professionalism may herald a distinctive and third aspect of occupational organization. It also suggests an alternative resolution of the incipient conflict that can arise when several occupations converge on a single domain of work. When specialists in several professions work together on a presenting problem that presents itself—such as bankruptcy, family disorganization, or urban renewal—stable networks of association are likely to result in the formation of a *trans-professional community*. When the work is highly specialized, and its technicality makes access difficult to non-specialists, the trans-professional community can forge a stronger internal identity than each of its members has with his or her respective professions. (In this sense, of course, trans-professional communities will threaten larger professional communities because they are inherently centrifugal).

Such trans-professional communities are relatively common, and they extend far beyond the professions to many project-based arenas of work.[73] In the past, however, it has been rare for trans-professional communities to be transformed into polymorphous professions with state mandates and protections. Under circumstances where there is pressure for multi-disciplinary partnerships, and progressive specialization in the complexities of organization in the global economy, polymorphous professionalism presents one structural expedient to effect a second-order specialization that breaks out of conventional definitions of professional identity.

---

[73] Compare, for instance, two widely disparate arenas: inter-disciplinary associations of scholars, such as the Law and Society Association in the United States. Full-time lobbyists present another case in point.

This English case suggests that the creation of polymorphous professionalism may not fit easily into prevailing models of professionalization, which postulate too sharp a contrast between market impulses and state interests. The rise of the insolvency profession represents a mutuality of interest between professionals, with varying motives for a new or less tarnished identity, and the state, with its policy objectives of a rejuvenated private sector. In an important sense, the new profession can be viewed as an emanation of the state itself, a projection of state interest into the private market, but with controls by government sufficient to restrain private professions from acting too blatantly in this self-interest. An imperfect cartel, or incomplete monopoly, resulted from government's refusal to grant insolvency practitioners the same measure of autonomy enjoyed by most of its accountant and lawyer members. Yet it was the drive of insolvency professionals themselves that handed government an occupational and regulatory expedient for saving businesses, regulating directors at the margins, and inserting professional advice more centrally into business practice. In Johnson's terms, therefore, the profession and state came to constitute each other, the one obtaining state patronage and protection in return for a reluctant responsiveness to state interests, the other obtaining professional compliance in state regulation in return for jurisdictional control. This image of a profession partially constituting both the market and the state fits uncomfortably with conventional accounts of professionalism. But it may well be that the re-examination of governmentality in advanced societies will force a new account of what professions are about. Insolvency practitioners exemplify one manifestation of this shift.

The American changes not only share a significant restructuring of professional jurisdictions, but they also demonstrate that the so-called laissez-faire forces of the market relied on stimulation by statute. If the market for professional services effectively found a new equilibrium for high-quality, high-cost legal services, the release of market forces depended on statutory intervention. But here the similarity between the two countries ends. For even if both markets required state intervention, in the English case the state itself was a primary agent of change in pursuit of a larger policy goal, whereas the American legislation reflects less a coherent strategy adopted by a political party, than an acquiescence of legislators to an elite interest group's formulation of a new standard of practitioner incentives in the field of bankruptcy law and corporate reorganization.

10 Jurisdictional Struggles within the State

Substantive statutory changes can disturb sovereignty over work by professionals. That conflict breaks out among professions in the market should not be a surprise, since the market itself is created on a competitive principle. It is not nearly so obvious that territorial conflicts over jurisdictional rights should flare up within the state itself. Yet the substance of stratification—the unequal distributions of money, prestige, and power—is equally present within state institutions, though its weighting may lean more heavily to status and power than to money. Since a major statutory disturbance can also dislocate occupations within the state, it seems possible that the reform of bankruptcy laws will lead to disputes in many directions: territorial conflicts between different executive departments; conflicts over the locus of work in the judiciary or the executive; and, in either case, struggles over status and power as work, responsibilities, and rewards are shifted up or down administrative hierarchies.

As in previous chapters on jurisdictional rights, the first line of investigation will be to identify jurisdictional fault-lines and manifest struggles among occupations. The second, and more important, line of inquiry will be to explore how the battles over jurisdictional rights affect the substantive outcomes of bankruptcy administration. Put another way, is the distribution of property rights that results from the Insolvency Act and Bankruptcy Code affected by the disputes among occupations for rights to control certain kinds of work?

ENGLAND: CREATING SPECIALIZED INSOLVENCY COURTS

By contrast to the constitutional dramas and manifold scandals that periodically engulf American courts, the English judiciary conventionally appears as a paragon of virtue. Of course, English judges, too, are assailed from time to time for controversial decisions. But the English judiciary has little of the political immediacy that surrounds lower court elections in the United States; as an institution its constitutional rationale is rarely thrown into doubt; and its judges rarely are tainted by aspersions of corruption or venality. If the American judiciary is a very public institution, with high visibility, and political conflict to match, the

English judiciary melds external ceremony with a norm of discretion, even invisibility. The relative proximity of courts to the political conflicts over bankruptcy reforms reflects these global differences. Whereas the fortunes of American bankruptcy courts and judges accounted for most of the high drama in the politics of the 1978 Code, new ideas about English bankruptcy courts intrigued adventurous lawyer policy-makers, but few others. Yet several of the issues that confronted English reformers echoed precisely the concerns of their American confrères.

The Contours of Complaint

The issue of English bankruptcy administration had been the subject of consideration well before Cork's Insolvency Committee sprang to life. In the course of his efforts to formulate an English response to European initiatives on bankruptcy, Cork and his colleagues developed a fundamental antipathy to what they viewed as the central pathology of Continental modes of handling corporate reorganization—the proclivity of lawyers to race into court. Said Cork: "We are nearer Europe than America, and the whole of insolvency at that time in Europe was appallingly badly done, and it's all done by lawyers in the court. And we were more frightened of that, the EEC, than we were of adopting the American system." The insolvency specialists were "terrified" of placing insolvency in lawyers' hands, not only because "lawyers have the habit of rushing off to the court," but most vexatiously, because judges tended to be cautious: "the easiest thing for him [the judge] to say is, don't do it . . . ." Hence Cork's circle sought to to keep reorganization away from the courts "except for very bad cases."[1]

---

[1] UK Interview 91:07. In the colorful words of a senior English politician: ". . . as soon as you get into court you then bring all the other lawyers in, then you get litigation, all the delays, all the nonsense. No, you want something quick and clean—bang, bang. Don't bugger about in the damn courts." (UK Interview 90:09) And an MP closely associated with the legislation expressed his reasoning for wanting insolvency kept away from the courts:

Informant: "Well, I can see that an American might regard as amazing any society which wasn't a quarter as litigious as the United States. And long may it continue to be the case that we are simply not as litigious! We don't see why the court should be involved in determining points of law, when what is nearly always at issue here is simply the technical management of resources in an organization which is no longer able to meet all its liabilities. It isn't really a matter for the courts, save only of course where you create criminal offenses related to insolvency, where obviously the courts need to be involved. But there would be a cross party view that the courts have only a very subsidiary role to play in this legislation. And that the majority of the legislation should refer to the practioners,

Consequently, a central premiss for all parties throughout the English reforms was that the serious work of company reorganization must be handled by expert practitioners—insolvency practitioners—at arm's length to courts, and with recourse to them only at the outset of proceedings and at the finale of the rehabilitative effort. Administration orders, a key innovation in the Insolvency Act, were designed to permit insolvency practitioners wide discretion and extensive powers to move rapidly and decisively in their bid to save a business. Keeping the courts—and lawyers—at bay was the institutional corollary of a system that prized business experience and efficiency.[2]

Nevertheless, this relative marginalization of courts from day-to-day business rescue did not mitigate problems or dampen aspirations for a considerably more rational, consistent, even efficient system than the one that had grown haphazardly through a century and a half. There were two main issues: could the insolvency courts be rationalized in order to clear up jurisdictional confusion and irrationalities in the allocation of work? And, could the work of the courts be allocated so that expertise was commensurate with the level of complexity and economic stakes in matters before the court?

Rationalizing Courts

Bankruptcy law and administration had a mercurial existence throughout the nineteenth century. The degree of legal intervention into liquidation advanced and retreated, just as the centrality of government

---

those who know about the business, who can actually deal with it far more competently themselves."

Interviewer: "So this is a general consensus of an English legal tradition rather than being an explicit policy by the government to keep things away from the government and in the private sector."

Informant: "Just so. Leave unto lawyers that which has to be left unto lawyers and make sure it is pretty small" (UK Interview 91:16).

[2] A judge with extensive experience in insolvency cases expressed the underlying philosophy of the Cork Committee and the Act as: "Don't bring the courts in." Administrative Orders were intended to permit reorganization without judicial interference and legal conflict: "The appointment of the administrator distances the court. I know we make the appointment. And no doubt we will remain, if he wants approval for things or sanction, or if questions arise which have to be determined. But on the whole the philosophy is 'appoint him, and let him get on with the job'" (UK Interview 91:14). Said a Queen's Counsel who specialized in insolvency work: "Chapter 11 (in the US) is very much a court driven process, with the lawyers having a predominant role. Administration is designed to work without automatic access into the court. To be run by chartered accountant. Very different cultural perceptions inevitably. And there is a great reluctance on the part of chartered accountants, I think rightly, to eat up huge amounts of money in court resolution of disputes that arise in administrations" (UK Interview 91:08).

administration in bankruptcy administration ebbed and flowed (Lester 1995). By the end of the century, "this long series of historical accidents" in bankruptcy administration had produced a system that the Cork Report found relatively little changed by the late 1970s, a system that was not "logical, consistent, efficient, or convenient." Nor was it "calculated to do justice with the maximum economy of resources."[3]

The nation-wide structure of the courts in the insolvency field created what one Cork Committee member called a "ridiculous jurisdiction situation—absolutely crazy." Bankruptcy work was divided between the Chancery Division of the High Court that was centered in London, and County Courts throughout England and Wales. The location of court proceedings depended on a mélange of factors, including the monetary level of an insolvency, the physical location of the bankrupt person or insolvent company, whether criminal or civil matters were involved, whether the Crown entered a petition, and whether matters of law were referred up or down the system by judges or registrars. Moreover, cases could be handled by High Court judges, county judges, or registrars, who handled matters up to a certain point in proceedings and then passed them on to the judge. Various matters could be also delegated from judges to a registrar.[4]

As for appeals, a county court registrar observed that "it was all an enormous jumble." Appeals "sometimes went to the divisional court, sometimes they went to the Chancery division, and sometimes to the Court of Appeals." Individual bankruptcy and corporate insolvency proceedings might also be handled in different courts in different parts of the country, even if the personal and corporate financial failure resulted from the same company collapse.[5]

Nevertheless, despite some of the grumbling over court organization within the Cork Committee, the Committee gathered no systematic evidence on the behavior of courts (although they did visit the Croydon County Court) and few complaints were registered in submissions to the Reform Committee. The clients of the court—the bankrupts and company directors—had no collective voice and expressed no impressionistic reactions, let alone a coherent point of view, on what was wrong or how it should be righted.[6]

---

[3] *Cork Report*: ch. 20, para. 994.

[4] UK Interview 90:13; *Cork Report*: paras. 980, 985–8.

[5] UK Interview 90:13; *Cork Report*: paras. 980, 985–8.

[6] The Cork Committee were aware that legal journals and consultants had complained about the treatment of insolvency in the County Courts. Minutes of the Cork Committee, 2 Sept. 1977.

Thus legal rationalization—through simplification of jurisdictions, improvement in the location and distribution of courts, and unification of procedures between individual and corporate insolvencies—was the project of expert reformers, their consulting committees of lawyers and accountants, and the formal interest groups of the insolvency professionals. All these were integrated by the Insolvency Reform Committee into a new concept—the formation of a dedicated Insolvency Court for all of England and Wales. Yet it was less the organization of the court itself, than the quality of judging that most concerned the professional reformers.

Ensuring Judicial Expertise

Two visions, converging from opposite poles in the legal system, united to form a coherent approach to judicial reform in the insolvency arena. At one pole, many complaints within the insolvency field focused on the theme that "insolvency was a technical subject in which you needed a substantial degree of expertise, and you couldn't get away with an ordinary general knowledge."[7] In County Courts, a registrar might handle insolvencies only ten per cent of the time. The lack of technical knowledge not only led to adverse effects on individual cases (and of course led to appeals), but also contributed to a lack of consistency in the application of the law.

I felt that the Circuit Judges were never going to do enough bankruptcy and insolvency work generally to get the expertise. You see the Circuit Judges, as they now are called, they do every civil jurisdiction, they do every criminal jurisdiction and then they've got their minds on other things. They spend about two thirds of their time in crime, one third of the time civil. So there's no chance they are going to be any good at bankruptcy.[8]

If lack of consistency confused debtors, frustrated creditors, and inhibited development of coherent case law, the thin distribution of insolvency work across many relatively inexperienced registrars and judges induced a loss of confidence that cut two ways. Creditors and debtors could have little assurance that matters treated by different judges in the same court, or by courts in adjacent counties, would have any resemblance to each other—an experience that hardly encouraged recourse to the courts. More significantly for reformers, the new provisions on Administration Orders, with the primary goal of facilitating company rescue, would be defeated by judges whose inexperience

---

[7] UK Interview 90:13. [8] UK Interview 90:13.

robbed them of the confidence to act decisively when swift action stood between general collapse and the possibility of salvage. Both insolvency practitioners and bankers concurred that corporate restructuring would be frustrated if less specialized judges were permitted free play in the insolvency domain. To ensure expertise required concentration of personnel: "we wanted far fewer county court judges dealing with personal bankruptcy in the country."[9]

At the other pole, the pragmatic stimulus to reform coincided with a grander vision expressed by at least one barrister who subsumed insolvency courts in a vision of general judicial reorganization. In contrast to an image of the generalist judge, who was supposedly able to turn his nimble mind to any area of the law, the alternative model posited a semi-specialized court system in which the expertise of judges would be commensurate with the complexity of issues and sophistication of practitioners appearing before them.

Even amongst the lawyers, however, differences in their emphasis on the degree of specialization emerged. Within the Working Party of the Law Society and Bar, there were two views.[10] On the one side were those who valued technical expertise and specialization, and were consequently prepared to restrict the free assignment of judges to any matter within the general areas of civil or commercial law. On the other side were the defenders of the talented generalist. To opt for a specialized court, according to another barrister on the Working Party, "might have meant that you had to have a single judge, or judges, dealing only with insolvency. And that would have been a shame because one of the strengths of the judiciary is that they see cases of a different kind out of different walks of life."[11] A leading insolvency barrister observed that "the Lord Chancellor's Department takes the view that all of its judges should be gifted amateurs rather than specialists at particular fields running specialist courts."[12]

Enforcing Moral Regulation

While technical competence was a priority for effective corporate reorganization, specialization had significant potential repercussions for the

---

[9] UK Interview 91:14.

[10] See Oral Submissions by the Joint Working Party of the Law Reform Committee of the Senate of the Inns of Court and the Bar and the Law Society, Insolvency Law Reform Committee, *Public Record Office.*

[11] UK Interview 91:01.

[12] UK Interview 91:08.

moral regulation exercised by court over debtors. We have seen that moral regulation of directors and insolvency practitioners was woven into the legislation as an arm's-length method for improving market morality. The moral element in the courts involved both investigative and sanctioning elements.

English bankruptcy courts employed a long-standing practice to conduct public examinations of debtors. By forcing debtors to explain themselves, creditors might discover what had happened to their assets, and the court could better judge how to dispose of the case. While the vast proportion of these cases occasioned little interest at all, from time to time a public bankruptcy examination became a national spectacle, especially if a skilled barrister could implicate the rich and powerful in the bankrupt's circle. The most notorious of such cases in the early 1970s concerned one, John Poulson, whose circle of beneficiaries reached into the Cabinet of the British government. Muir Hunter, England's leading bankruptcy barrister at that time, and a member of both Cork committees, assisted by David Graham, a close advisor to Kenneth Cork, turned the media spotlight onto Poulson's financial dealings and those caught in his snare. Hunter, himself, came under heavy criticism, even risking censure by the Bar Council, for his relentless questioning of Poulson, and the political embarrassment it caused politicians and the government.[13] Thus the public examination simultaneously served as a means of eliciting facts that might benefit the court and as a form of public shaming.

---

[13] As we briefly noted in Chapter 3, the Poulson Affair broke as a major media scandal in 1972. John Poulson headed an international architecture firm. During his public examination by Muir Hunter QC, Poulson disclosed that he had donated £22,000 to a favorite charity of the wife of the Home Secretary, Mr Reginald Maudling (*The Times* 4 July 1972, p. 4), allegedly as a means of indirectly compensating Mr Maudling for acting as chairman of a company associated with Poulson. After a motion was tabled in Parliament asking for a government inquiry into "allegations of financial corruption in public life" (*The Times* 6 July 1972, p. 1), it was disclosed that Mr Poulson had paid substantial sums to two MPs and a senior civil servant (*The Times* 7 July 1972, pp. 1, 8; 8 July, p. 1; 10 July, p. 2). *The Times* called for a judicial inquiry (10 July 1972, p. 15; 14 July, p. 2). Mr Maudling resigned as Home Secretary and two civil servants who received payments from Poulson were suspended pending investigation by the Scotland Yard fraud department (19 July 1972, p. 1). More allegations followed that Maudling had received £9,500 a year in director's fees (8 Aug. 1972, p. 1) and that payments, or "handouts," had been made to other public officials, including a member of the Foreign Office, the chairman of the North-Eastern division of the National Coal Board, the mayors of two towns, and the secretary of a regional hospital board (26 Sept. 1972, p. 13). Further evidence accumulated of gifts to influential figures—a silver coffee pot to Mr Anthony Crosland when he was Secretary of State for Education and Science; a gold cigarette lighter to the wife of a senior

Public examination as fact-finding, shaming, or cautionary tale functioned satisfactorily only when a judge was sufficiently experienced in the ways of debtors and creditors that he could "sniff out the true crooks." Ironically enough, since many debtors were repeat players who were appearing before inexperienced judges, neither the technical nor moral functions of the court would be satisfied if dishonest debtors could escape the scrutiny of the judge and the creditors. An experienced bankruptcy registrar observed that:

insolvency was a technical subject in which you needed a substantial degree of expertise so that you couldn't get away with an ordinary general knowledge ... [I]t's possible for bankrupts to run circles by use of these technical things, run circles round the creditors. And I felt that we needed a wider scope of discretion in the judicial hands and a more experienced body of judicial officers presiding so that they weren't misled by these terrible liars and cheats and that sort of thing who come along with plausible stories and they follow it every time and before you know where you are the fellow's got another six months you know ... [Bankruptcy] was getting into the wrong hands with inexperienced people who weren't robust enough in dealing with these chaps. ... [T]here are a lot of the bankrupts—I would say about a quarter to a third of the bankrupts— were dishonest people. The degree of dishonesty varied but [some] were dishonest people and needed to be sorted out. And a fellow coming at it fresh—you just didn't know what was hitting you.[14]

Judges needed technical knowledge so they could match the technical wiles of debtors just as they required worldly experience to sense when "liars and cheats" were seeking to hoodwink them.

But if technical sophistication was a necessary prerequisite for the moral and legal vagaries of bankruptcy cases, technicalities could actually subvert substantive justice. Thus one member of the Cork Com-

Scottish civil servant; and a gift of silver to the widow of Lord Fraser after she opened a hospital (17 Apr. 1973, p. 2).

But Muir Hunter QC, himself, attracted criticism. A *Times* editorial opined that he was carrying out his examination of Poulson with "thoroughness" but at the same time was "showing more than a little carelessness with other men's reputations." *The Times* questioned whether public examinations should be changed so that individuals named during an inquiry could "intervene in court on their own behalf or to put their construction on events."(13 Jan. 1973, p. 15). The Bar Council initiated an inquiry into Muir Hunter's conduct (1 Feb. 1973, p. 1), which in turn was attacked by the Haldane Society of more progressive lawyers (2 Feb. 1973, p. 1). Muir Hunter was subsequently exonerated by the barristers' governing council. Criminal charges subsequently were brought against Poulson and several of his associates, and, in the House of Lords, the Lord Chancellor noted that for the first time the "intricate and highly technical" area of bankrutpcy law had become a "popular subject of discussion." (17 Apr. 1973, p. 6).

[14] UK Interview 90:13.

mittee pressed strongly for powers that would enable judges to override minor technical irregularities—"a fairly minor mistake" in a bankruptcy notice—so long as no important substantive injustice was done.

The critique of judging therefore proceeded from a fear of deception from below, where experienced bankrupts misled naive judges, and a fear of incompetence from above, in those circumstances where bankers sought court interventions only to find that the court ruled unexpectedly or inconsistently. The latter was prospectively subversive, since the Cork Committee's invention of a new reorganization device, the Administration Order, depended for its effective deployment on judges who would act intelligently and creatively to facilitate business rehabilitation. The benefits of the new device, in other words, turned on the efficiency of its administration.

The Reform Committee's "Radical" Proposal[15]

A small group of members—mostly lawyers—within the Cork Committee proposed a new insolvency court system that they believed would solve the problems of expertise and jurisdictional confusion, while ensuring compatability with the interests of the Thatcher Government to move unnecessary work out of the judiciary.[16] With very little debate, but no small measure of skepticism that the Government would accept the recommendations, the Cork Committee committed itself to a rational form of judicial administration significantly different from the status quo.

The reformers proposed creation of a specialist Insolvency Court to handle all matters of bankruptcy and insolvency throughout England and Wales. The court would exist in different tiers of the court system, from the High Court down to County Courts. In the High Court, where there was a relatively large volume of cases, a limited number of commercial judges would be assigned periodically, or on rotation, to "sit" on the Insolvency Bench, so as to ensure some concentration of expertise. County and Circuit Courts would also have their "Insolvency Court," which essentially would take the form of an "empty bench" staffed as needed by specialist judges and registrars. In low volume

---

[15] See *Cork Report*: s. 1001, p. 230: "we have concluded that radical change in the organisation of the Courts dealing with this unified jurisdiction is essential."

[16] Muir-Hunter, QC; Ritchie Penny, former registrar; Edward Walker-Arnott, a commercial lawyer; Peter Millett, QC, Mr Hunter, a registrar from Northern Ireland; and Alfred Goldman. See *Minutes of the Cork Committee*, 13 Dec. 1978.

regions of the country, judges could be rotated in and out, as demand required, effectively "on circuit."[17]

The idea, of course, was to have specialist judges doing it [insolvency work] ... The idea was, partly, to devolve from London—not just the personal bankruptcy (which is done in the county court at the moment), but also the company work and heavier personal bankruptcy work— so that could be tried in the provinces locally. And for that purpose we saw no reason why, let us say, a court in Manchester which had a heavy insolvency case couldn't simply call upon London to have an insolvency judge sent down.[18]

This scheme would achieve greater expertise through specialization, and much greater flexibility of assignment. In fact, this proposal found a palatable middle ground between a concept of complete specialization in bankruptcy, which every English legal reformer rejected (partly on grounds of the boredom it would induce), and the amateur commitment to general "muddling through" by commercial judges in the High Court and any judge in the County Courts.[19] Said one barrister-reformer:

... It's a dream which I hope will emerge one day, even more widely than just insolvency. Because what it really envisioned was that you would set up the local courts which might be unmanned if you like, and just existing in theory as it were. And then if a case could be heard, likely which required expertise, a high court judge with the necessary expertise could be sent down from London to try it. There is no reason why it should be confined to insolvency actually.

Alongside the crisp vertical integration of the Insolvency Courts in one national hierarchy "that would adhere from top to bottom, instead of the present horizontal division,"[20] the Cork Committee proposed the reallocation of work out, up or down the system.

Some non-contentious matters, which were better handled administratively, should be transferred from the judiciary to the Insolvency Service. Important matters, especially involving company reorganization, should be upgraded to specialist High Court judges, whether in London, or on "circuit." But these might also include individual bankruptcies whose moral implications warranted the "full rigours of

---

[17] *Cork Report*: s. 1001–9, pp. 230–2.
[18] UK Interview 91:14.
[19] *Cork Report*: ss. 1016–17, p. 233.
[20] UK Interview 91:14. The same informant later observed that the proposal for a specialized court was a good idea slightly before its time. Proposals in the 1990s to create a Family Court, with different tiers of High Court and County Court judges as part of a single, integrated, nation-wide organization, essentially duplicated in family law what the Cork Committee had proposed for insolvency law.

bankruptcy"—a notion vaguely evocative of medieval practices, but recurrent in these debates from within the Cork Committee to the House of Lords. As the Committee Minutes recorded the discussion, "full bankruptcy would be reserved for the bad cases, and for those who had defaulted in some less rigorous form of administration, and include more severe penalties and full investigation. This was particularly necesssary as it was proposed to deal in this way with delinquent directors."[21]

Whereas more specialized judges would preside over increasingly complex administrations, greater familiarity with business practice at the end of a company's life seemed critical if the two major substantive innovations on company directors were to be effectively implemented. Introduction of "wrongful trading" would set a new standard of business practice *in extremis*. From the courts, this not only demanded experienced judges who had detailed knowledge of directors' practices when faced with financial collapse, but also indicated that the new standards of "unreasonable conduct" and the development of coherent case law would be better achieved by a more specialized judiciary integrated into a coherent vertical system.[22] Moreover, the prospect of disqualifying many more directors also guaranteed that large numbers of cases that required immediate despatch—protection of reputations, lifting of bars to business—would pour into the courts for resolution. Matters requiring less weighty judicial credentials should be allocated to specialized insolvency registrars attached to the Insolvency Court.

The Cork Committee pressed for much clearer legal jurisdictions. It recommended a unified jurisdiction for individual and corporate bankruptcies in the same court. Concurrent jurisdictions would be eliminated. It pushed for other clarifications so that government applications, for instance, should be subject to the same geographical rules as any other creditor.[23]

Political Reactions

Despite the bold simplicity of the Cork Report's new court structure, the Committee had no illusions about its likelihood of succcess. Committee members had previously debated whether their strategy should take the cautious path, and only recommend to government what was likely to

[21] *Minutes of the Cork Committee*, 23 Sept. 1977; 8 Feb. 1978.
[22] *Minutes of the Cork Committee*, 10 July 1978.
[23] *Cork Report*: ss. 1010–15, p. 232.

be implemented, or the bold path, and recommend to government what they believed would be most desirable for effective corporate rehabilitation and public administration. By confronting sharply the government's Green Paper proposals to privatize most simple bankruptcies, the Cork Committee had already displayed its mettle.

It took the same view on the Insolvency Courts.

> We really knew, I think to be fair, we knew it was a dead letter before we even recommended it. We thought, "So what?" We actually had a debate on one occasion. We discussed whether one should put in a report something which one did want to recommend but one knew would never be carried out. And the answer was, "yes."[24]

That prognostication proved entirely accurate. Neither the government's White Paper, nor the Insolvency Bill took any account of the courts, an absence that was noted without much heat by the media, and lamented in Parliament. In the Lords, some perfunctory regrets over a failure to include a specialized insolvency court in the legislation were recorded by Lords Taylor and Hutchinson.[25] Yet most discussion over the courts, to the extent it occurred at all, turned on other matters.

The practice of public examinations of bankrupt debtors—or directors—in court sparked exchanges in the Commons and Lords. By examining bankrupts in open court, the judicial system had the unique capacity to obtain frank responses to questions about financial failure, to uncover facts that revealed fraud or hidden assets or culpable behavior. Yet there was some repugnance to the idea that a person be forced to incriminate himself. And it is more than likely that bitter memories of fallout from the Poulson public examination exercised some members.[26]

Lord Bruce offered an amendment in the Lords to make public examinations discretionary rather than mandatory. Nor should courts force a debtor to incriminate himself. But the Government held the line firmly on the principle that public examination offered an investigative device. Lord Lucas retorted that public examinations would only occur when the official receiver—a government official—applied for it, and that would only occur "where the official receiver cannot obtain relevant information or co-operation from the potential examinee in any other way." Similarly, the amendment against self-incrimination could

---

[24] UK Interview 91:14.
[25] H.L. vol. 458, pp. 875–88, 894–925, cols. 896, 908.
[26] H.C., St. Comm. E., 11 June 1985, cols. 251–8.

not be accepted on the ground that "it could well defeat the purpose of the public examination."[27]

Whether or not the courts remained a stage for public appraisal of business practices, the effects of the new disqualification provisions on the courts attracted more commentary. This was not simply because automatic disqualification of directors would clog already crowded courts—an artful argument that took one element of government policy, automatic disqualification, and demonstrated its adverse effects on another Tory platform, reducing reliance on government institutions.[28] Debates indicated that the new provisions on the behavior of company directors, which were not very well spelled out in the Bill, would flood the courts with "litigation and long arguments about the precise meaning of the expressions in the Bill." Questions about the precise meaning of a director's "unfitness" would be determined by the courts.[29] And if

use is made of the Bill to disqualify delinquent directors from holding office, there must be a great advantage in having a court which has specific powers to develop a body of expertise and experience on what should be the conduct of directors. Moreover, it would be able to judge consistently directors' behavior.[30]

To the Opposition, and to many accountant-parliamentarians, the logic was impeccable: Cork's specialized insolvency court would produce more coherent and reliable law, thus smoothing the implementation of new concepts, such as wrongful trading, or expansion of older powers, such as director disqualification. Altogether, the specialized insolvency court would aid "simplification of inevitably complicated procedures," just as an expert court would "dispense swift justice" and

[27] H.L. 1 Apr. 1985, cols. 74–6, 80. This led to a rather heated discussion where Lord Bruce accused this "wretched Government" of legislating less through "the ordinary democratic machinery of Parliament" and much too much by rules: "this business of legislating *sub rosa* in some obscure background or some obscure office in Whitehall is not one that this House should encourage."

[28] H.L. vol. 458, pp. 875–88, 894–925, col. 918. Cf. Lord Bruce (vol. 459, 29 Jan. 1985, col. 596) who stated that innocent directors will need to consult solicitors, retain a barrister, attend conferences with counsel, swear affidavits, attend court—something that is very costly. Lord Meston (vol. 459, 29 Jan. 1985, col. 614) expressed his belief that that courts were not equipped for the great burden of work, even if the Insolvency Court suggestion had been adopted.

[29] H.L., vol. 459, 29 Jan. 1985, col. 619. According to Lord Denning, there was a need for "the question of unfitness to be decided by the court with guidelines agreed, perhaps, by many interested parties" (H.L. vol. 462, 1 Apr. 1985, col. 23).

[30] This point was made by an MP, Mr Hirst —who had been a partner of Peat Marwick, Mitchell and Co., which had a large insolvency practice—who drew a connection between directors' disqualification and the courts. (H.C. vol. 78, ser. 6, 30 Apr. 1985, col. 187).

"help administrators and liquidators sort out companies in difficulty." Quite apart from good domestic reasons for adopting Cork's administrative modernisation, without a specialized insolvency court Britain would miss an opportunity to join the movement, already evident in Europe and North America, to harmonize personal and corporate insolvency law.[31]

Nevertheless, to members of the Cork Committee who followed Parliamentary debates, these scattered parliamentary maneuvers merely skirted the fundamental reason that the government had years earlier set itself against a new court. That the overwhelming consideration to the Conservatives was cost had become quite evident to the reformers well before the Cork Committee ever put pen to paper. The veto on the concept of a specialized insolvency court came from the Lord Chancellor's Department. At a time when Mrs Thatcher's ministers were under firm instructions to reduce the size and cost of the civil service, any new initiative was viewed with heightened scrutiny for cost-effectiveness. One member of the Insolvency Committee expressed a widely held belief that:

... the instruction came from the Lord Chancellors Department.... This was the high water-mark of Thatcherism, when it was impossible to get anything through that would cost the public money.... [B]efore we even wrote the report, we knew they would never implement it unless we could satisfy them that it would not cost any public money. And we knew we couldn't actually do that. We didn't believe it would. We had long talks with them about it. But we couldn't actually demonstrate it.[32]

This drive to reduce costs in turn led to rivalries between departments because "all of them were pushing to get rid of staff onto somebody else so they could say they had reduced the number of civil servants employed by them."[33] In the concluding debates on the Bill in the House, David Trippier, Under-Secretary of State for Trade and Industry, returned to Opposition attacks on the Government's failure to include insolvency courts in the legislation. The Government rejected Cork's recommendation, he stated, because the review committee "did not establish a strong case for a specialised insolvency court."

---

[31] On the Second Reading in the Commons, Labour Spokesman on insolvency, Bryan Gould, set out a set of missed opportunities in the Bill, among which he included a specialist insolvency court (H.C. vol. 78, ser. 6, 30 Apr. 1985, cols. 157, 165).

[32] UK Interview 91:14. This view was repeatedly stated by civil servants, reformers and politicians (UK Interviews 91:17; 91:08; 90:09).

[33] UK Interview 90:13.

Outcomes

In retrospect, however, many of the strongest advocates for reform of the courts admitted that much of what they had wanted as a matter of law had in fact come about in practice. It was true there had been teething problems. Cork, himself, believed that a specialist court was particularly important in "a bankers' society." And some bankers, in their turn, confessed there had been difficulties where less experienced judges had made wrong decisions. Moreover, for banks to get or permit an administration order, there were costs, delays until a court hearing, and most troubling of all, the uncertainty that comes from inexperienced courts handling the applications.[34]

Yet several of the lawyer-reformers consoled themselves with the recognition, in hindsight, that a *de facto* specialization had emerged, especially in the High Court:

> . . . it is arguable, and certainly the judges take this view . . . that we've now got an insolvency court in practice, although we do not call it an insolvency court as such. If you look at the administration of insolvency cases through the courts, there is to a considerable extent . . . there are exceptions, but the administration tends to be done by the same judges, albeit they may be wearing a different name for the court in which they're sitting. But effectively they are administering the insolvency code in an insolvency court. And there is a considerable amount of integration of the insolvency court. There are exceptions, particularly at the county court system, which I don't think we favor. But although we didn't get our way with the establishment of the court as such, the insolvency court as a parallel for the family court, we sought, we really won that battle in practical terms.[35]

THE UNITED STATES: UPGRADING FEDERAL BANKRUPTCY COURTS

At first blush, the 1978 United States Bankruptcy Code presents an unlikely instance to re-enact the historical struggle over the definition of courts. But within the restructuring of bankruptcy law and administration can be detected a complex change where lawyer-led reforms influenced not only economic behavior, but the wider institutional framework of justice.

[34] UK Interviews 90:04; 91:07; 90:03.
[35] UK Interview 90:21. Said a barrister-MP: the ". . . the division of the High Court which actually covers the question of insolvency is reasonably busy and it has reasonably specialist judges" (UK Interview 90:02).

One movement within the bankruptcy reforms was consistent with the historical trend to reduce political influence and patronage in the functioning of lower courts, whether in state or federal jurisdictions (Halliday, 1987, chs. 6, 7). Indeed, the status of courts threatened to overwhelm all the sweeping substantive changes that were generated by the principal reforms. Another movement had less symbolic notability, but potentially greater practical import—the attraction of courts for corporations as a forum of dispute resolution and a haven for financial reconstruction. As the major financial industry groups explained to Congress, their willingness to aid in the rehabilitation of financially disabled companies turned critically on bankruptcy administration as well as substantive revisions. Major credit institutions signalled their reluctance to use the courts as a forum for saving high risk companies unless the courts made significant changes in the ways they treated business.

We focus on two aspects of the penultimate bills before the House of Representatives, H.R. 8200, and the United States Senate, S. 2266, in which lines of conflict and points of consensus are clearly delineated and all parties were in play. First, we examine the demand by the financial industry for changes in the court system that would ensure the efficiency, neutrality, and competence of commercial courts. These issues quickly generated arguments reminiscent of those from earlier epochs of court reform in which matters of court jurisdiction, patronage influences, quality of judges, and modes of judicial appointment were highly contentious. Second, the legal profession and judges had a pervasive influence on these reforms, but it was highly segmented and often conflictual. The forms and factions of professional politics therefore demonstrate the contingency between the institutional expression of justice and manifestations of lawyers' collective action.

Framing the Problem

The Brookings researchers, Stanley and Girth, recognized that changes in the economy, most particularly the explosive growth of consumer credit, had created an economic environment that built up enormous pressures on a governmental apparatus that threatened to buckle under the strain.[36] Based on several empirical studies, their report

---

[36] Interestingly enough, Brookings overcame conventional parochialism in the US by conducting a brief study of other national bankruptcy systems, but they found "no general cure for the weakness of our system and few ideas for greater efficiency, lower cost, or more equitable treatment of debtors and creditors." Stanley and Girth (1971: App. B., p. 241).

identified deficiencies in bankruptcy administration that were to be echoed incessantly over the next seven years. Without mincing words, the Report bluntly concluded that although the bankruptcy system muddles through, "it is a dreary, costly, slow, and unproductive process. Compared to what the system might be, the present reality is a shabby and indifferent effort." The multiplicity of courts, and the lack of consistency among them produced "baffling inequities" from court to court.

Moreover, with giant corporations, such as Penn Central and Chrysler Motor Corporation, facing radical financial restructuring, it was becoming increasingly clear that a downturn in the economy would require corporate reorganizations of unprecedented size and complexity. The Bankruptcy Commission, in its turn, observed that a great deal of effective financial reorganization goes on outside bankruptcy, which has the merits of "relative simplicity, speed, low costs, and administrative flexibility." But the changing structure of modern business increasingly demonstrated that informal arrangements are much less effective when there are very large numbers of creditors spread over many jurisdictions and a wide territory, and when some creditors refuse to go along.

Criticism of the system penetrated deeply into the core of court organization and practice. The Bankruptcy Commission further directed close attention to the major confusions, terrible time-wasting, and procedural squabbling over the court jurisdictions in which bankruptcy proceedings were held. The Commission was acutely sensitive to problems that provoked lawyers—the sense of bias and conflicts of interest that bedevilled bankruptcy courts and undermined their neutrality. But of greatest relevance to the financial industry, the Bankruptcy Commission recognized that the prevailing system actively discouraged business from using the law for company rehabilitation. Lack of rational order and predictable adjudication ramified through the system.

Confronted with a system so compromised in its organization and personnel, the Commission echoed Stanley's judgement that minor palliatives would not serve to remedy what needed major surgery. In a series of bold measures the Commission Report redesigned the principal foundations of the system.

Lawyers and Bankers in the Reform of Federal Bankruptcy Courts

Scholars who study judicial selection and court autonomy emphasize the incipient conflicts between political parties and their allies in the legal profession, on the one side, and the elite lawyers who historically have controlled bar associations, on the other side. But in the field of corporate law, a third party has a major interest in the character of courts, namely, business and the financial industry.[37] Passage of the 1978 United States Bankruptcy Code was consequently framed by the sometimes confrontational differences among judges, various groups of lawyers, and the financial interest groups on a Congressional terrain effectively controlled by the Democrats.

The potential repercussions of changes in bankruptcy administration for credit institutions brought three enormously powerful financial peak associations into play: the American Banking Association, the Robert Morris Associates, and the American Council of Life Insurance. They faced a judiciary split along lines of power and status. At the lowest rank of judges—forced to fight even to keep this elevated title—the National Conference of Bankruptcy Judges was dedicated to the interests of referees, bankruptcy courts, and the bankruptcy field. Disdainfully confronting them was the federal judiciary, which usually directed its collective activity though its Judicial Conference. The minority report to the Bankruptcy Commission, filed by federal Judge Weinfeld, signalled that an impending attack on proposed changes to judicial administration might be anticipated from the federal judiciary, who vigorously opposed the elevation of bankruptcy courts to the level of federal district courts, whose status was codified in Article III of the United States Constitution.

Practicing lawyers mobilized on three fronts. Leading the charge for the lower bankruptcy and debtor-creditor specialists was the Commercial Law League of America. Having profited from the specialized character of bankruptcy practice, their inclinations were to keep it a relatively private domain of action. Ostensibly representing the bar at large were the national, state, and metropolitan associations, such as the American Bar Association, the Minnesota State Bar Association, and the Dallas Bar Association. Carrying the torch for lawyers who specialized in litigation was the highly resourceful and effective lobbying

---

[37] In some of the earlier campaigns for merit selection, business was an ally of the bar on behalf of merit selection.

organization, the American College of Trial Lawyers. Their implacable resistance to any moves that would segregate specialist courts from general trial courts brought them directly into confrontation with advocates of specialization. Standing apart from the lurking partisanship of respective lawyers and judges groups was the National Bankruptcy Conference (Aaron 1980: 201).

In a bid to bring unity to potentially warring parties within the bankruptcy field—a dispute that could derail the entire reform process—Congressman Edwards of the Bankruptcy Commission, together with the Chair of the House Judiciary Subcommittee responsible for passage of the bill in the House, had urged the National Conference of Bankruptcy Judges to sit down with representatives of the National Bankruptcy Conference and forge a mutually acceptable piece of legislation, especially on the contentious issue of bankruptcy courts and judges. The compromise bill they produced split the differences between them and led—via two intervening bills—to a new legislative proposal that incorporated the compromises into a modified version of the Commission's bill, itself amended by the House subcommittee, to produce H.R. 8200 (Trost and King 1978: 493–5). On 31 October 1977, the Chair of the Senate Judiciary Committee, Senator Dennis DeConcini, introduced a bill into the Senate, S. 2266, which was much more amenable to the federal judiciary.

The House subcommittee and its Senate equivalent invited submissions from interest groups on the bills before their respective chambers. These submissions, and the exchanges between the politicians and the interest groups, reveal both the dispositions of key groups to the prevailing bankruptcy system, and their views on change. Three issues provided the normative battleground on which groups fought for advantage: the efficiency of justice, the neutrality of justice, and the competence of the justice system.

Efficiency of Justice

In bankruptcy cases, delay permits the remaining assets of the bankrupt corporation to run down, or to forestall rapid reorganization, thus impairing chances for corporate turnarounds. Delay and speed in the disposition of bankruptcy cases were affected by: (a) jurisdiction of the court; (b) the constitutional powers of the court; and (c) the degree of court specialization.

(a) Jurisdiction

Among the bankruptcy specialists, the need for broadening of the bankruptcy court's powers was a primary article of faith. The strong representation of lawyers and judges on the Bankruptcy Commission had placed court jurisdiction high on its reform agenda. The awkward delegation of most bankruptcy proceedings to inferior bankruptcy courts, where authority was derivative, resulted in a perpetual uncertainty over the limits of the powers that were delegated to the bankruptcy court. The law made a distinction between plenary and summary powers of the court. The former were the province of bankruptcy courts; the latter were the dominion of the federal district courts. But which was which? "Frequent, time-consuming, and expensive litigation" over this issue made it "one of the most involved and controversial questions in the entire field of bankruptcy."[38]

Moreover, the jurisdictional time-bomb bedevilled any party that required swift resolution of creditors' claims while the assets of the bankrupt ran down. Thus any party that had an interest in delay found jurisdictional issues a godsend because they could trigger appeals all the way through the appellate courts, to the immense frustration of the other parties.[39]

Jurisdictional disputes could also begin with litigation to switch chapters. Since the 1938 Chandler Act permitted various kinds of business bankruptcy to be handled in any of three chapters—X, XI, and XII— their detailed and overlapping rules produced so much "pointless litigation," said an aggrieved complainant, that "the patient will probably die while doctors argue over which operating table he should be on." Hence jurisdictional disputes and delay fed off each other to mire any contested bankruptcy in debilitating obstacles of successive appeals. And as the Commission noted, while delay in any court is a matter of regret, in bankruptcy issues it is especially critical because rehabilitating companies in financial distress depends on the rapid disposition of assets. Decline in value of the estate can be arrested; dissipation of resources can be blocked; creditors can be held at bay; or new agreements can be negotiated. But time and flexibility are key. Moreover, the time value

---

[38] *Report of the Bankruptcy Commission*: XV.

[39] *Report of the Bankruptcy Commission*: 14–17. The Commission notes the problems that companies have previously had with the Act, including the pervasive problem of delay through the use of jury trials, or need to prove acts of bankruptcy, not to mention awkward and costly steps between filing and answer of the petition. All these delays ran down the assets.

of money is compounded by the administrative costs of litigation itself, which can run down the assets available to creditors or for rehabilitation. Jurisdiction, therefore, was central to breaking the logjam.[40]

The problem of court jurisdiction was more than perverseness. A derivative bankruptcy court simply could not exercise powers that the Constitution reserved to federal district courts and presidentially appointed judges.[41] A derivative court, for instance, could not conduct jury trials. Moreover, for a trustee to bring legal actions to retrieve assets for the debtors' estate[42] it was often necessary to scramble from court to court in various parts of the country in order to patch together all outstanding debts. In addition, plaintiffs could bring suits against trustees—and those, too, in courts other than the bankruptcy court. Derivative courts with limited and uncertain jurisdiction consequently multipled confusion, increased delay, and compounded costs in litigation.

In their bill, the bankruptcy judges had offered Congress a stark alternative:

> either (1) a forum of disputed, arguable jurisdictional authority—one operating within the shadow of a supervising court so burdened with other responsibilities and interests as to have neither the time nor expertise to contribute meaningfully, or (2) a forum of clearly defined, true bankruptcy jurisdiction—one operating as a court of identifiable stature equipped with adequate personnel and expertise to give "one-stop" service to the nation's bankruptcy needs.[43]

On this problem, federal district court Judge Shirley Hufstedler agreed: "the idea of requiring poor litigants, bankrupt litigants, to litigate about jurisdiction, to me, is utterly repugnant."[44]

All the lawyers' groups concurred. For the Commercial Law League, vesting the court with complete jurisdiction for all matters that arose in it was "an absolute prerequisite."[45] The corporate lawyers in the American Bar Association agreed that "enlarged powers" of a court with expanded jurisdiction was critical. The professional authority of the elite National Bankruptcy Conference weighed in with the pronouncement that "the present summary–plenary jurisdictional dichotomy is illogical,

---

[40] *Report of the Bankruptcy Commission*: 23, 89.

[41] The difference between Article I versus Article III courts had substantially to do with the breadth of jurisdiction and powers that can be given a court (cf. *Minutes of the Commission*, 17–19 May 1973, p. 3.)

[42] An "estate" in bankruptcy law refers to the total pool of all items of value remaining in the corporation, or that are owed to the corporation.

[43] *Senate Hearings on S. 2266 and H.R. 8200*: 440.

[44] *House Hearings on H.R. 8200*: 87.

[45] *Senate Hearings on S. 2266 and H.R. 8200*: 601.

wasteful, and archaic; it spawns litigation and causes delay and unnecessary expense." It also made for the "uncertainty presently plaguing the system."[46]

Representatives of corporate America offered vivid accounts to enliven their procedural discussions. "If you want delay in the bankruptcy court," stated Stanley Shaw, President of the Bohack Corporation, "the byword is, file a motion and contest the jurisdiction of the court. Everything stops. The red lights go up. And the hearing must be held on jurisdiction.[47] The bankers, too, forcefully demanded "a strong independent bankruptcy court capable of exercising a broad jurisdictional grant."[48]

Only the federal judges demurred. The Judicial Conference were somewhat alarmed by a proposed jurisdiction so broad that it would embrace securities, patents, and civil rights law, among others, thus effectively giving the court a jurisdictional reach identical to the district courts. And their ally in the Department of Justice, Attorney-General Bell, while acknowledging the value of some wider jurisdictions, nonetheless thought it should remain narrower than the district courts. The judges and Bell recognized that a jurisdiction this broad would sustain the call for bankruptcy courts to be raised to full Article III status.[49]

(b) Constitutional Status of the Bankruptcy Court

It was the powers of the court itself, above all else, that aggravated the federal judges. Greatly increased court powers inevitably raised the constitutional status of the court. Four models of a bankruptcy courts were proposed by parties to the reform. First, courts might be given much broader jurisdiction and made independent of the federal district courts, but have a somewhat circumscribed status defined by Article I of the United States Constitution, a standing held by certain specialized courts, such as the Tax Court. This was the model advanced by the Bankruptcy Commission, after long internal debates over the sufficiency of Article I courts to handle the breadth of powers envisaged by reformers.[50]

At the other extreme was the model advanced by the House Judiciary Committee, which decided that bankruptcy courts should be raised to the highest level of Article III courts. This would not only solve jurisdic-

[46] *Senate Hearings on S. 2266 and H.R. 8200*: 831-2.

[47] *House Hearings on H.R. 8200*: 18-27.

[48] *House Hearings on H.R. 8200*: 193. Submissions by the American Bankers Association/ Robert Morris Associates.

[49] *House Hearings on H.R. 8200*: 154-8; oral testimony, Judicial Conference of the US Federal Courts; Attorney-General Bell, *Senate Hearings on S. 2266 and H.R. 8200*: 484.

[50] *Minutes of the Bankruptcy Commission*, 17-19 May, 1973, p. 3.

tional problems, but its standing would attract judges of the very highest caliber and be appealing to business. But it would be a court specialized in bankruptcy alone. Harold Marsh, Chairman of the Bankruptcy Commission, and some of its other members preferred an Article III court. Bankruptcy specialists leaned also in this direction, as did some bar groups.[51] Not unexpectedly, the bankruptcy judges pressed energetically for the Article III model, complete with an appellate division.[52]

The financial community expressed unequivocal advocacy for fully-fledged Article III courts. For the most part, this support sprang from frustration with the cost and delay of endless litigation over jurisdiction. John Ingraham of Citibank declared that:

we do try to help a company, but sometimes it's darn difficult, particularly if you see, from a financial standpoint, that putting new money at risk to a company that gets into difficulty, and where you're going to be tied up in knots, and waltzed around the maypole on appeals...[53]

Moreover, prospective litigation over the constitutional status of Article I courts with exceptionally wide jurisdictions greatly troubled the bankers. Constitutional appeals "will unquestionably paralyze the rehabilitation process.... There are financial interests, who have been largely silent, who really cannot afford to have reorganization efforts delayed while constitutional issues are litigated."[54] In general, said a spokesman for the Robert Morris Associates, "it is hard for members of the banking community with hundreds of millions of dollars invested in debtors who have invoked the jurisdiction of the bankruptcy court, to sympathize with the positions taken by the opponents of Article III status..."[55]

Faced with growing momentum for an Article III court with powers comparable to their own, the federal judiciary at the penultimate moment eventually awoke to the threat posed by this unlikely coalition of law reformers, low prestige bankruptcy judges, and the entire national banking industry. In March, 1977, the Judicial Conference adopted a resolution opposed to Article III courts and it charged a committee of federal judges to formulate a response to Congress (Countryman 1985). Armed with votes from Judicial Councils around the country, and its own hardline document, federal judges appeared before House and

---

[51] *Senate Hearings on S. 2266 and H.R. 8200*: 438; submission by the Commercial Law League; submission by the Minnesota Bar Association, p. 956.
[52] *House Hearings on H.R. 8200*: 166.
[53] *House Hearings on H.R. 8200*: 211.
[54] *House Hearings on H.R. 8200*: 203–4, 210.
[55] *House Hearings on H.R. 8200*: 195.

Senate committees to argue passionately for continuation of the present system, with some modest changes.

The federal judges were not alone in stolid resistance to change. The American College of Trial Lawyers maintained that apppointments of hundreds more Article III judges would dilute the prestige of the federal judiciary. Coincidentally, it would exert great pressure to appoint current referees to the new courts—one reason why they had so vigorously supported the legislation, charged Judge Rifkind, a name partner of a leading New York litigation firm.[56] Welcome support came from the United States Attorney General, who expressed the view that bankruptcy courts should remain in their current status as adjuncts of the district court—the so-called "step-child" status so excoriated by reformers.[57] Most critically, however, key allies of the federal judges emerged from the Senate Judiciary Committee, whose chairman, Senator DeConcini, applauded the Senate Bill 2266, which kept "referees" as adjuncts of the district courts.[58]

(c) Specialization

One element of resistance by lawyers derived from fears of specialization. The American College of Trial Lawyers strenuously resisted any hint of barriers that would exclude generalist litigators from trying cases before a major court. Their spokesman, Judge Rifkind, expressed it most colorfully:

I've watched it all of my professional life—that at the bar there is a parochial hunger which keeps recurring and reexpressing itself periodically for the practitioners in a particular field to get themselves a little courthouse of their own, a little bar of their own, a little judiciary of their own so that they become the ministers of a private temple in which they are the priests and nobody else knows how to function. That gives them a little bit of a monopoly in a field of practice.[59]

According to the American Bar Association, "the entire judicial reform movement in this century has been in the direction of consolidating courts," by eliminating specialized courts in favor of general jurisdiction trial courts.[60] For the litigators, undoubtedly, the preferred solution was a powerful court that would attract litigation, but not so particular a court that their services would be made superfluous.

---

[56] *House Hearings on H.R. 8200*: 9.   [57] *Senate Hearings on S. 2266 and H.R. 8200*: 216.
[58] *Senate Hearings on S. 2266 and H.R. 8200*: 878.   [59] *House Hearings on H.R. 8200*: 16.
[60] *Ibid.*

Neutral Justice

Alongside the need for rapid judgments by an empowered court, lawyers and the banking industry vigorously pressed for resolution of the patronage, partisanship, and conflicts of interest that bedevilled the bankruptcy courts.

This "personal-political-patronage" basis of appointment, as Stanley and Girth styled it, suffused all levels of the system. For instance, when bankruptcy judges were asked how they came to be appointed, 25 per cent said they were recommended by political party officials, 46 per cent were known to the judges, and only 21 per cent applied. In Chicago the patronage link was so tight that referees kept office for only so long as their appointing judge; when he retired, so did they. Compounding the classic conflicts that inhere between patronage in the court system and the vaunted neutrality of justice was a system of "mutual accommodations" and "exchanges of favors" that brought all players in the system into a tight coalition of mutually protective practitioners. Their loyalties, charged the Brookings Report, lay rather more to each other than to creditors or debtors.[61]

Two elements of this "bankruptcy ring" of private practitioners and public officials derogated the bankruptcy court.[62] On the one hand, an appeal made by a lawyer against a referee's decision was decided as often as not by the judge who had appointed the referee in the first place. As two-thirds of these appeals were decided in favor of the referees, it was not surprising that lawyers saw "a natural inclination" of judges to back up their appointees. Moreover, as we have seen, the referee had future leverage over lawyers both for approving fees and for making new appointments of trustees. Lawyers were reluctant to appeal and only a tiny fraction ever did. On the other hand, the Brookings Report saw a fundamental disjunction between the essentially routine administrative character of the 200,000 or more uncontested cases and the prevailing adversarial system that seemed to add layers of personnel and costs to a process better fitted to a bureaucracy.[63]

According to Brookings, the core of the rot lay in the system of political and personal patronage that permeated the lower reaches—

---

[61]   Brookings Report, pp. 160, 164, 197.

[62]   The term "bankruptcy ring" probably was first coined by New York bar associations on insolvency, where they demonstrated that administration of insolvent estates was "cozily distributed" among a handful of attorneys. W. Collier, 1 *Collier on Bankruptcy*, para. 4.03 (14th. edn. 1976).

[63]   Brookings Report, pp. 153ff., 200.

and everyday practice—of consumer and business bankruptcies. In a hierarchy of patronage appointments, prestigious federal district court judges (who themselves were often "political" appointees) had complete discretion to appoint bankrupty judges or "referees," who were then delegated virtually all the 250,000 bankruptcy cases that flooded into the federal courts each year.[64]

Blurred administrative and adjudicatory responsibilities by referees drew condemnation from the Bankruptcy Commission:

> When litigation does arise, there are substantial reasons for not entrusting its determination to bankruptcy judges involved in the prior administration of these litigated estates. It is necessary and important that the adversaries have confidence that their controversy will be determined by evidence adduced by them and present to the tried of the law and the facts. The Commission is convinced that referees' participation in administrative aspects of bankruptcy proceedings tends to impair the litigants' confidence in the impartiality of the tribunal's decision. In particular, adversaries of the trustee in bankruptcy tend to doubt that the referee who appointed the trustee can insulate himself from at least a suspicion of partiality when he may have previously been involved in any and all of a range of prior actions concerning the estate.[65] [66]

Congressional hearings echoed the findings of Brookings and the Bankruptcy Commission that methods of appointment and work organization permitted politics to intrude into the courts in ways that made certain litigants doubt they could get a fair hearing. Stanley and Girth again urged Congress to design a system "free of cronyism."[67] Even

---

[64] Brookings Report, pp. 197, 147, 122–6. Stanley and Girth reiterated that the judicial branch championed independence of courts at the expense of central management. It was little wonder that "patronage (political or personal) is securely established in the judiciary as a method of personnel selection." (Stanley and Girth 1971: 200). See also Chapter 8.

[65] *Report of the Bankruptcy Commission*: 5.

[66] That patronage was pervasive was not doubted by most Commissioners. Chairman Marsh noted that in Los Angeles "demonstrated ability and expertise are not so important as personal relationships to the judges who have appointing authority." And Judge Will agreed that "political factors were significant in referees' appointments in Chicago and elsewhere," a point that the New York lawyers and judges were not so ready to concede. (*Minutes of the Bankruptcy Commission*, 13–14 Nov. 1972, pp. 2, 13.) Bankruptcy Commissioners Professor Seligson of New York and Judge Will of Chicago both agreed that there were kickbacks of fees by district attorneys to trustees in New York and Chicago. When this was placed alongside the "unseemly and continuing relationship between the referees and the members of the … so-called 'bankruptcy ring'" of specialist bankruptcy lawyers, who were essentially "private contractors seeking business with the BR court" the entire sphere of practice emitted "a bad odor." (*Minutes of the Bankruptcy Commission*, 15–17 Jan. 1973, p. 42; 13–14 Nov. 1972, p. 6; *Report of the Bankruptcy Commission*, p. 95.

[67] *Senate Hearings on S. 2266*, p. 1081.

Attorney-General Griffin Bell reminisced that when he was a young lawyer, he was told by an older lawyer that "the bankruptcy court was run for the benefit of the referee and the trustee, and the referees' pension fund.... People wonder who gets all these trusteeships. Whose friends are they?"[68]

Political partisanship melded into localism. Parties who entered a court from out of state, or another community, felt especially vulnerable to the vagaries of local loyalties against "outlanders." In smaller cases, observed the Robert Morris Associates, when a banker-creditor

> leaves his own district, his own home base, he does not believe that he is in a fair court. He may be in a fair court, and it may be that no bias exists or it may be that a bias exists only unconsciously, but the confusion of the roles has led many members of the American Bankers' Association and the Robert Morris Associates to complain of the type of justice that can be meted out in a bankruptcy court context.[69]

Bankers were adamant that they would endorse increased court jurisdiction only if the new court was independent and administrative and judicial roles were segregated. In oral testimony, the spokesman for Robert Morris Associates quoted sympathetically a bankruptcy judge's statement that:

> the bankruptcy court is a departure from the traditional Anglo-American concept of a trial court; an impartial arbiter who receives evidence in accordance with procedure and evidentiary rules of ancient vintage; and who receives no evidence or communication except on the record and in the presence of both parties. The administrator-judge does not and cannot fulfill this image.[70]

---

[68] *House Hearings on H.R. 8200*, p. 224. This was not simply a matter of personal patronage, which could be problematic enough. Professor Vern Countryman, from Harvard Law School, entered a *Boston Globe* article into the Congressional Record to exemplify long-standing complaints about politics and competence in bankruptcy court appointments. US district court judges in Massachusetts had appointed a former US attorney general to the position of bankruptcy judge, even though he had no prior bankruptcy experience. But it was the political overtones that captured the *Globe*'s attention. Mr Gabriel succeeded, reported the article, because he had the backing of US Senator Brook, who had more support for the appointment among sitting judges than his political rival, Senator Edward Kennedy. "Because the district judges are nominated for their own jobs by one or the other United States senator, they are vulnerable to political pressure and may feel inclined to endorse a nominee who has been proposed by their own sponsor.... Ideally, the judges would resist naming hacks to bankruptcy judgeships.... In reality, however, there is no insulation between judges and the political process of nominating and promoting candidates for judicial positions." (*House Hearings on H.R. 8200*, p. 259)

[69] *House Hearings on H.R. 8200*, p. 205–6.

[70] *House Hearings on H.R. 8200*, p. 195.

The American Bankers' Association categorically stated that "we view separation of judicial and administrative functions as a vital part of bankruptcy reform."[71] The refrain of court independence recurred incessantly among all interest groups, except one.

Despite the consensus among the professionals and bankers who wanted an independent court engaged only in adjudication, the federal judges thought the problem was much overstated. So express was their denial of major difficulties in the status quo that the Chairman of the House Judiciary subcommittee responded in frustration that:

> we are in a quandary, of course, because for the last 5 or 6 years we have been hearing witnesses—banks, commercial law representatives, merchants, business people, and the general public—complaining about the referee system. Actually, we have not had one witness, except you gentlemen [federal judges], who have said that it is working well and that we should be proud of it.[72]

Eventually the judges did offer a compromise proposal—that a local bankruptcy administrator be appointed for each court for five years at a time and he would free the judge to engage entirely in adjudication. But this fell far short of Brookings' civil service option, and indeed of a nationally organized system of administration within the judiciary that would avoid any more appearance of patronage and favoritism in appointments of administrative personnel.

Quality of Justice

(a) Caliber of Judges

The Brookings Report had lamented the quality of bankruptcy referees, later to be called bankruptcy judges. The position required no formal qualifications, apart from those common to all lawyers, and it demanded no prior experience in bankruptcy. Even the latter was not a guarantee of quality or respect, as the bankruptcy bar itself was held "in low esteem." Terms of appointment were limited to six years and salaries were low. None of these factors provided inducements to highly qualified practitioners.

Quality of recruitment to the bankruptcy bench was also criticized by the Bankruptcy Commission. Everything conspired against highly qualified bankruptcy judges—patronage appointments, short-term tenure, low salary, and diminished powers of the court, where most of the

---

[71] *Senate Hearings on S. 2266*, p. 574.
[72] *House Hearings on H.R. 8200*, p. 151.

stimulating and far-reaching issues would be siphoned off to a higher court. According to Chairman Marsh,

> fundamentally the public has a right to have issues adjudicated by a full-fledged court and not some subordinate functionary. Perhaps the problem is one of status or maybe pride but in order to attract and hold the right people a new image must be projected.... The community at large ... needs to have confidence in the judiciary. At the moment that confidence rests uneasily on the shoulders of referees.[73]

Accusations of "second-rate justice" and "second class courts" were levelled at the bankruptcy courts by Congressmen Drinan and Edwards of the House Judiciary subcommittee. As the National Bankruptcy Conference put it, the bankruptcy court "is without prestige and ordinarily does not attract highly qualified attorneys to accept appointments on the bench. The best lawyers do not want to be assistants to district judges." All the lawyers' groups supported either life tenure comparable to federal court judges, or very long term appointments of twelve to fifteen years. For most appointees, only two such appointments would bring a judge to retirement. It could serve as a career, thus avoiding the inevitable conflicts of interest that arise in the revolving doors between judiciaries and private practice.[74]

The arguments for life tenure were consistent with those for Article III judges and Alexander Hamilton's original commentary on the US Constitution. Life tenure insulates judges from political control, or as Father Drinan commented during the hearings, it makes judges more courageous. This was more than a rhetorical veneer that permitted the ambitious lawyer-members of the Commercial Law League to proclaim their advocacy of long term appointments for reasons of independence of the courts. Bankers, too, were convinced that the status and method of judicial appointment was "of grave concern to commercial lending institutions throughout the country."[75] In a joint submission, the American Bankers Association and the Robert Morris Associates wanted length of appointment, salary levels, and other benefits sufficient to "guarantee a first rate court."[76] By the time the House and Senate bills came to conference in late 1977, all parties agreed that terms should be at least twelve years in the case of federal judges, and through life in the case of those who favored Article III courts.

---

[73] *Minutes of Bankruptcy Commission*, 4–5 Dec. 1972, pp. 8, 13.
[74] *Senate Hearings on S. 2266*, pp. 950, 98, 831–2.
[75] *House Hearings on H.R. 8200*, p. 194.   [76] *Senate Hearings on S. 2266*, p. 574.

Independence and quality depended as much on who did the appointing as on the length of the appointment. The strongest proposal was for the President to make either life tenure or fifteen year appointments as he did for sitting federal judges and the Article I Tax Court respectively. This not only moved appointments away from local patronage relationships, but it endowed the bankruptcy judge with all the charisma of Presidential recognition. While most professional groups preferred Presidential appointment, the Commercial Law League preferred appointments to be made rather closer to the local situation. They suggested that the local federal Judicial Council or Court of Appeals could do the appointing. This would strengthen the local connection—and their chances of making it to the bench—but it would compromise rather less the relationship between district and bankruptcy court judges.

Here again the dissenters were the federal judges. Since 1960 they had asked for referees' terms to be extended from six to twelve years, and this they had recommended to the Bankruptcy Commission.[77] But they resisted energetically any notion that the appointment process parallel their own. They much preferred to maintain some local judicial control—and thereby perpetuate an attenuated patronage—that most other observers sought to abolish. From Congressman McGlory their position drew the sarcastic retort that: "one very good reason why district court judges don't want to change the system...is that they enjoy appointing the referees.... I'm very sorry to infringe on their very long time enjoyed prerogatives, but I think this is part of the problem we have."[78]

(b) Appeals

The mode of appeals from bankruptcy courts further divided lawyers and judges. While appeals' prerogatives appear as bureaucratic technicalities, like so much else about courts, the structure of the system carried powerful symbolic overtones. As the National Bankruptcy Conference observed, appeals to circuit court judges do little for the dignity of bankruptcy courts. "It is anomalous, and detracts from the dignity of a trial court, for appeals from its orders to run to another single judge court, particularly if that court is essentially a trial court itself."[79] Appeals directly to an appellate court was also the position taken by

---

[77] *House Hearings on H.R. 8200*, p. 115.   [78] *House Hearings on H.R. 8200*, p. 50.
[79] *House Hearings on H.R. 8200*, p. 239.

the Commercial Law League, because perpetuation of the present system simply preserved "both the second class status of bar judges and the unnecessary expense and delay of a 3-tier appellate system."[80]

The financial industry lent its weight to exactly the same end—direct appeals to appellate courts elevated the dignity of the courts and provided an expeditious mechanism to provide prompt relief.[81] For bankers and secured creditors, decisive decision-making that permitted predictable outcomes from the extension of credit was a primary goal for legal change. The principal dissent came again from the federal judges who, ironically, borrowed the bankers' reasoning and turned it against them. In response to an explicit question posed by the House subcommittee counsel, the Chairman of the Ad Hoc Committee on Bankruptcy Legislation of the Judicial Conference wrote that it

recommends that bankruptcy cases continue to be under the jurisdiction of the district courts, with appointment of bankruptcy judges by the district councils. The Committee sees no need for a separate court system which would inevitably create jurisdictional conflicts and would be very costly.[82]

House Bill H.R. 8200 passed on 1 February 1978. Senate Bill S. 2266 passed the Senate in September 1978. But the wide differences between them required intense negotiation between the two chambers to produce several compromises. (1) The expanded jurisdiction sought by virtually all parties was to be lodged in the circuit court of appeals, but bankruptcy courts were directed to use all of that jurisdiction. (2) The bankruptcy court would be retained as an adjunct court to the district court and not attain the Article III or Article I status advocated by the most active interest groups. (3) But to compensate for the loss of Article III, the two Houses agreed to fourteen year appointments that would be made by the President on the advice of the Senate. (4) Salaries were to be substantially improved—only marginally below federal district court judges—and bankruptcy judges would be added to the federal Judicial Conference.

These apparently "watered down" proposals were still too radical for the Chief Justice of the Supreme Court, who intervened directly by calling on key senators to block the bill unless it diluted further three provisions on the status of the bankruptcy courts, presidential appoint-

[80] *Senate Hearings on S. 2266*, p. 601.
[81] ABA/Robert Morris Associates, *Senate Hearings on S. 2266*, p. 574.
[82] *House Hearings on H.R. 8200*, p. 155.

ment, and membership in the Judicial Council. With the Chief Justice's
Senate allies holding the bill to ransom, intense negotiations took place
with the clock slowly running out of legislative time for passage in the
current session. In a last minute bid to find acceptable middle ground,
an amended version of H.R. 8200 downgraded the bankruptcy courts
from adjuncts of appeals courts to ordinary district courts, although the
expanded jurisdiction would remain in place. Moreover, Presidential
appointment would "give due consideration" to any nominees that
might be proposed by local Judicial Councils. With hope gradually
dimming that passage of the bill could make it in the 95th Congress,
the House settled for the compromise and the bill was forwarded to the
President for signature. Again the Chief Justice intervened, this time
calling the President directly to urge that he veto the bill. On the very
last day on which the bill could have been signed into law, 6 November
1978, President Carter ignored his Chief Justice and placed his signature on the bill.[83]

Banking and the Rationalization of the Judiciary

Because the enormous diversity of the American legal profession is
reflected in a profusion of cross-cutting lawyers' organizations, the
bankruptcy reforms display a kaleidoscope of sectional differences.
The "class" divisions between upper and lower strata of lawyers and
judges, and the tension between generalist and specialist practitioners,
replay in this arcane area of lawyers' law many of the same battles over
independence of the courts that have punctuated the history of the
American legal profession. Yet intra-professional conflicts represent
only one dimension of historic shifts in court organization. Less readily
identified by commentators on judicial reforms are the interests of
corporate America in the form of justice offered by the courts.

While the most ubiquitous actors in the bankruptcy reforms undoubtedly were the lawyers' and judges' organizations, it is manifestly clear
that the financial industry saw any modifications of bankruptcy law—
and the arrangements for corporate liquidation and administration—as
integral to commercial lending and practice. We have seen that the
commercial community had decided views on what it wanted from
bankruptcy reforms. Speed and decisiveness depended on powerful
courts with embracing jurisdictions that minimized procedural man-

---

[83] Klee 1980: 281–94; Countryman 1985: 7–12.

euvrings through appeals. Neutrality demanded sharp segregation of politics and personal patronage from judicial decision-making. Quality and expertise of judicial personnel would proceed from presidential appointment of long-tenured judges with benefits comparable to those of the federal bench.

In short, the bankers held Congress to a principle of *implied proportionality* as a condition of their co-operation in riskier corporate rehabilitations. Unless the power and quality of justice was proportional to the scale of financial risk, bankers swore either to handle their affairs outside the reach of the courts, or to foreswear the sorts of commercial risk that economic policy-makers hoped would facilitate corporate reorganization. The courts, in other words, could conform to the expectations of the financial industry, or lose their business. The economic threat was even more palpable: in the face of industry shakeouts in an increasingly competitive economy, the bankers intimated that they could either limit risk and permit widespread company failure, or they could extend credit further and aid reconstruction. The quality of justice was a significant factor in the global strategy of the financial industry.

This powerful impulsion towards court independence and competence melded with a generic impetus towards *rationalization of law*. Bankruptcy judges and lawyers decried the variability among jurisdictions in the ways that judges handled corporate reorganizations. The Bankruptcy Commission Report forthrightly acknowledged that the "open credit economy" demands an "orderliness" which it is a primary function of the bankruptcy system to provide. And the National Bankruptcy Conference insisted that the "inconsistencies, uncertainties, and illogic inherent in the present system of three separate reorganization chapters" needed to be purged and replaced by a rational system consistent with the high dollar value of assets and claims, the need to preserve ongoing value of assets, and the impact of corporate failure on the economy.[84]

Pleas for uniformity and consistency from commercial lawyers found ready response from the financial sector. The American Council of Life Insurance expressed it best with a call for a law that will "assure fair and predictable treatment of claims of long-term lenders and investors. In a free enterprise system where private capital investment is an important component, the law should not provide too many surprises and be so unpredictable that long-term investors cannot cope with the uncertain-

---

[84] *Senate Hearings on S. 2266*, p. 400, submission by the National Conference of Bankruptcy Judges; *Report of the Bankruptcy Commission*, pp. 68–71; *Senate Hearings on S. 2266*, pp. 833–4, submission by the National Bankruptcy Conference.

ties. . ." And to remind legislators again of the stakes, the Robert Morris Associates reinforced their earlier testimony that "we have repeatedly articulated our feelings that the existing structure for reorganizations, particularly Ch. X, overwhelms most corporate debtors, with the result that corporations which could be reorganized die under the surgeon's hand during the pendency of such proceedings."[85]

Invocation of uniformity, consistency, predictability, and legal protection as standards of legal regulation manifestly reflect a principle of formally rationalized law. This resonates clearly with the Weberian propositions that "increased calculability" in the functioning of the legal process, and the "purely formal certainty of the guaranty of legal enforcement," are integral to markets ruled by contract. While not unmindful of law's illogics, nor of antiformal tendencies in the interests of substantive expediency, Weber's depiction of the efficient bureaucracy— with application to the courts—might readily have been submitted to Congress by the financial interest groups: "the utmost possible speed, precision, definiteness, and continuity in the execution of official business" is vital for the modern capitalistic economy.[86]

When commercial enterprises are not confident that they control judicial authorities, and indeed when they suspect that such control might be exercised by rivals, then formal justice and level playing fields represent a more rational expedient. The multiplication of court jurisdictions alongside corporations that operate in scores and hundreds of markets pose enormous difficulties of control over legal and market environments. Formal rationalization of justice, and uniformity of law and practice, stabilize credit environments and facilitate the extension of credit, and predictability about its protection, across multiple jurisdictions.

The safety of courts for powerful commercial interests inverts the conventional analysis of access to justice. Courts only capable of dealing with low level, limited jurisdiction, mundane cases, effectively reduce their appeal to "clients" with high property rights' stakes. In the absence of alternative forms of control, major financial institutions will accept courts as arenas for dispute resolution only when principles of rationality and proportionality are patently operational. Without these assurances, the strong are effectively "disenfranchised" by the courts. Without meeting the criteria implicitly established by the financial community,

---

[85] *Senate Hearings on S. 2266*, p. 855, submission by the American Council of Life Insurance; *ibid*, p. 194, submission by the Robert Morris Associates.

[86] Max Weber (1978, pp. 883); *Max Weber on Law in Economy and Society*, ed. Max Rheinstein (New York: Simon and Schuster, 1954), p. 350.

courts marginalize themselves from powerful actors that demand high expertise and extensive, binding jurisdiction.

Allocations of property rights are intertwined almost inseparably with allocations of jurisdictional rights. Indeed, we have demonstrated that the restructuring of jurisdictional rights among professionals did more than serve abstract principles of corporate rehabilitation. In many cases, they determined, and sometimes frustrated, the realization of those principles. Substantive bankruptcy law, and bankruptcy administration, were influenced as subtly by the machinations of professional politics as by the ideals and politics of reformers.

In the conclusion to this chapter, we provide an analytic disentangling of the complex processes of professionalization we have treated in the last three chapters. We consider three issues: first, the impact of statutory disturbance on the entire terrain of jurisdictional conflicts; second, the effects of professional politics on legal change; and third, the explanations of professionalization. In the process, we shall address both questions raised at the outset of this chapter: what mechanisms are available to radically reconstitute professional services? And, who crafts the division of labor?

Statutory Disturbance and Jurisdictional Conflicts

Legal reforms disturb the professional division of labor. They introduce new threats and opportunities for professional work. This can precipitate struggles within and between professions over jurisdictional rights to control new work. But it does not necessarily do so, as American bankruptcy lawyers have demonstrated. To understand the repercussions, conflictual or not, from a legislative disturbance, it is useful to map conceptually the universe of potential arenas for conflict. This presents a framework for analysis that reveals the complexity of jurisdictional politics and the impact of struggles over jurisdictional rights on the allocation of property rights. Legal change can precipitate jurisdictional conflicts along two cross-cutting dimensions, each of which is subject to political manipulation and social construction.

First, change in the status quo can create uncertainty over the allocation of work within and between occupations. Inter-occupational conflicts sit at the heart of Abbott's analysis (Abbott 1988). But the force of his own theory, and the well developed literature on professional differentiation (Freidson 1970; Bucher and Strauss 1963; Heinz and Laumann 1982; Halpern 1992), make it clear that segments within differentiated professions will recognize inequalities of power and status and mobilize to resist incursions by other specialties or seek to appropriate some of the perquisites of privileged specialities (Parkin 1979). Usurpers form specialty societies, challenge leadership in profession-wide representative associations, and search for innovations that will compete with the alternatives practiced by entrenched practitioners. Defensive strategies include specialty certification to keep out the unqualified, which segment internal markets for professional services, and exclusion of marginal practitioners from representation on boards of professional governance or self-regulatory panels.

The internal cohesion of a profession is frequently implicated in its inter-professional struggles. The peripheral segment of one profession can threaten secession, or a cross-professional alliance, as a means of strengthening its claims within its own profession. And the power of a professional association, or a specialty society, can be eroded by vocal dissent. Consequently, the state of internal professional integration affects cross-professional conflicts and vice versa. A compelling theory of jurisdictional rights must account for both.

Second, legal change determines whether professional rivalries will take place in the state or market. The institutions of the market provide very different terrains for struggle than the state itself. In the former, the competitive pressures of the open market are reflected in competition not only among practitioners and firms, but between associations representing different professions and between firms of differing professionals. The character of market competition is heavily influenced by the relationships between the social organization of practice and its concentration in large firms, on the one side, and the unity of professional voluntary associations, on the other. For instance, in occupations such as the English accounting profession, the alliances among a tiny number of giant firms and the leading accounting societies will allow much more concerted action than the massive dispersion of lawyers among firms and societies in the United States. Within the market, the resources that are mobilized for and against other professions will be disproportionately economic.

It has been less commonly recognized that statutory disturbance can also provoke occupational jockeying within the state apparatus, not only within branches of government, but across them. Most market activities have some regulatory framework, frequently vested in an executive agency. And since all market activity is bounded by law, courts also can be implicated in occupational regulation and change. We have demonstrated that the jurisdictional struggles over bankruptcy law were more bitter and hard-fought inside the state, particularly in the United States, than in the market. But in both countries, reformers recommended changes in the structure and functions of the courts, often shifting responsibility from courts to administrative agencies, or in the case of the United States, from the courtroom to the administrative office of the court. The politics of conflict within the state depend much less on economic resources than on political ties, the hierarchy of power and prestige among state agencies, and the access of judges and senior servants to powerful politicians.

Table 10.1   Dimensions of Jurisdictional Conflict

		PROFESSIONAL CONFLICT	
INSTITUTIONAL LOCUS OF WORK		Within Professions	Between Professions
	Market	English Insolvency Practitioners	—
	State	US Lower and Higher Status Judges	Executive Agencies and Courts (US, England)

Most research on professional jurisdictions concerns conflicts among professions in the market. But the bankruptcy reforms demonstrate that market rivalries among professions were only one of several conflicts that ranged across the occupational landscape. Indeed, the bankruptcy reforms precipitated relatively little struggle against other occupations in the market, although they did produce much restructuring. The complete array of jurisdictional politics are revealed when the two dimensions are cross-classified (Table 10.1). The two axes and four cells point to six terrains on which occupational contests can break out and produce not only significant restructuring of professions, but discernible outcomes in substantive and administrative law.

Demarcating the State/Market Boundaries

Whether in the United States or in Britain, some of the sharpest disputes occurred not within the market, but in delineating the market itself. This was done by determining where work should be located—inside the market or inside the state. The proposal of the Thatcher government for privatization of mundane bankruptcy work, shifting it from the Insolvency Service in the Department of Trade and Industry to private practitioners, expressly followed from a political commitment to reduce the size of government departments and to place work in private markets. Civil servants, too, seized the opportunity to off-load their more trivial, but time-consuming cases, so they could concentrate their resources on large insolvencies and key regulatory functions. Yet the private market, or more precisely its leaders at the high end of practice, resisted a flood of mundane, low property rights cases, with neither much intellectual nor financial reward. The English struggle over the market/state boundary therefore operated at two levels: an ideological dispute over the province of government, and the sorts of public goods that were irreducibly public; and a more utilitarian occupational interest in controlling only work that was interesting and well-paid.

The nationalization proposals of bankruptcy administration and trusteeships in the United States were also about redrawing the public–private boundary, in this case shifting work from the private legal profession to a United States Bankruptcy Administration, staffed by salaried, public servants. The proponents of change were not its beneficiaries—the good government reformers, who wrote the Brookings Report, or the judges, law professors, politicians, and handful of lawyers, who produced the US Bankruptcy Commission Report and its accompanying new Bankruptcy bill. Arrayed against the reformers, however, was the private bar which would suffer most from removal of its work to government administrators. Ideology was quite restrained, and certainly not at the same level as the anti-statist, pro-market vintage of the Thatcher government. American reformers wanted bankruptcy work as a public function to solve the market problems of inefficiency, incompetence, and lack of probity. But US politicians shared with their British counterparts a reluctance to establish any more expensive government agencies, a sentiment that eventually coincided with the concerted opposition of private lawyers and some government administrators to kill the proposal.

Disputes over public–private boundaries among professionals therefore rested on a much more fundamental ideological and policy dispute
over the capacities of markets and the limits of the state.

The case studies generate three propositions: first, the most important
struggles in professions often are not restricted to struggles for control
over work among professional groups within an already defined market,
but occur over how much work is to be available to any contestants in
the market. The drawing of the public–private boundary in a certain
sense precedes the struggles that eventuate once the boundaries are
clearly drawn.[87] Second, conflicts sometimes occur not because
professions are scrambling for more work, but because they want to
refuse it (Halliday and Carruthers 1994). Third, political ideology will be
more prominent in debates over the public–rivate boundary, and this
will advantage groups more sophisticated in playing the ideological
game.[88]

Demarcation of Occupational Boundaries

Demarcation disputes over occupational identities are endemic in the
history of professionalization. For many occupations, this takes the form
of insurgency, where disvalued groups push to obtain acceptance by a
more prestigious or powerful profession (Parkin 1979; Murphy 1988).
Members of this target profession in their turn characteristically try to
repel invaders, or to lop off lower ends of their occupations. This
analytic marker therefore designates the classic struggles over inclusion
and exclusion that are heavily documented in the historical sociologies
of professions (Parry and Parry 1976; Starr 1982; Abbott 1988).

The English insolvency practitioners exemplify three dynamics of
boundary demarcation, two not uncommon, but the third, unique.
First, unqualified insolvency practitioners sought a comparable status
to fully professionalized accountants. While professional status was not
an issue for fully qualified accountants who practised as insolvency
practitioners, it was for unqualified accountants who could claim official
recognition neither as accountants nor as liquidators. Boundary

---

[87] Nevertheless, it is necessary to be alert to a movement of change less from boundaries
to field conflicts, than from field conflicts to redrawing boundaries: a push to change the
public–private boundary may occur precisely because an occupation has outgrown its
jurisdiction and wants to expand its jurisdiction, or shift it.

[88] So critical is the divide between the public and private spheres, that social historian
Harold Perkin (1989) makes it the central divide in the social organization of the middle
class in the modern state.

demarcation on the up-side, therefore, comprised the upward mobility of unqualified practitioners into the new state-mandated status of mostly self-regulating insolvency practitioners.

Second, the leaders of the unlicensed occupation of liquidator or insolvency practitioner used the bankruptcy legislation to chop off the bottom two-thirds of practitioners. This demarcation on the down-side was accompanied by surprisingly little protest on the part of liquidators who fell below the 500 hours per annum of insolvency practice that were necessary to be grandfathered into the new profession. They were dispersed and without an occupational society. Their demise predictably followed from their inability to engage in collective action.

And third, the rise of a *polymorphous* profession points to a new level of professional organization that at once blurs and elaborates occupational boundaries. The disaggregation and rearrangement of specialty occupations has become a new dynamic in the global economy. By creating a new profession, which for some would be a primary qualification, but for most would be a second professional status—and one falling across the traditional boundaries of accounting, law, and surveying—the Insolvency Act simultaneously clarified the monopoly rights of a practitioner in a field of work, but muddied distinctions between professions as they converged on corporate reorganizaiton and liquidation. Rearranging, or simply leap-frogging over, occupational boundaries through multidiscipinary partnerships, or this polymorphic kind of profession, underlines the emergence of a quickening dynamic of occupational reorganization.

Conflicts and Restructuring between Market Professions

This is the modal arena of conflict in the jurisdictional accounts of professional development. Most surprisingly, it was the least conflictual area in the bankruptcy reforms. Dezalay (1992) has argued that the field of corporate reorganization has spawned new firms of company turnaround specialists who threaten reorganization experts in law and accounting. In fact, these exist on the margins, and no sign of them appeared in either the United States or Britain. Nor was there any overt conflict between any of the private professions engaged in corporate liquidation and rehabilitation.

Such a prospect might have been predicted from Thatcher's determination that lawyers, surveyors, accountants, and others could qualify as insolvency practitioners and thereby compete with each other on a level playing field. But despite provisions in the Insolvency Act to encourage competition, it never appeared. Insolvency practitioners with major accounting firms issued the veiled warning that lawyers who intruded on accounting turf could expect to lose the legal business of the accounting firms. But with only a rare exception, lawyers had no interest in qualifying as insolvency practitioners, because they had ample legal work. These cases suggest that conflict between professions in a market situation will be minimized when (a) an expanding market creates opportunities for all professionals, and (b) when another profession in the division of labor has the capacity to sanction intruders by withholding demands for their services.[89]

Conflicts and Restructuring within Market Professions

Professionalization in Britain and the United States displays contrasting mechanisms to create competence and confidence in the market for expert services. Bankruptcy lawyers in the United States were restructured without direct state manipulation of admissions' requirements, licensing, professional education, or professional self-regulation. Economic incentives were adjusted by Congress to allow market forces to raise the quality of professional services, and the change took bankruptcy law from the margins to the center of the profession.

When bankruptcy fees were made comparable to the most remunerative specialties of corporate law, one route to mobility propelled long-time bankruptcy lawyers from their segregated boutiques into the leading corporate law firms. Although this trend had already begun before the new provisions of the Bankruptcy Code began to bite, the Code quickened the pace of mergers and confirmed that bankruptcy law was a new profit center. The other route to the upward mobility of bankruptcy practice was lateral: the large fees to be made in the reorganization of failing firms drew ambitious attorneys in from other areas of corporate law, where work was beginning to slow.

In short, the statutory changes in fees, coupled with broader macroeconomic developments and a restructuring of national law firms, substantially enriched the bankruptcy jurisdiction. An "empty space" that was created by burgeoning demand acted as a pull, just as diminishing work in the mergers and acquisitions area acted as a push. The statutory reforms, therefore, significantly reconstituted the jurisdiction, not by shifting the market/state boundary, or precipitating an intra-

---

[89] There is absolutely no evidence of any conflict between law firms and the large accounting firms in the United States. When the question of inter-professional conflict was put to reformers, it provoked puzzlement, as something beyond comprehension.

professional quarrel, but by expanding the economic incentives, effectively widening and enriching the jurisdiction. The substantive provisions of Chapter 11, which significantly expanded the role of lawyers as advisors to debtors-in-possession and creditors' committees, opened up more sophisticated work that provided its own intrinsic challenge. This was less an issue over how work was to be divided, than how much work, of what sort, could attract first-rate attorneys.

By contrast, we have seen that the British approach to the upgrading of professional services in bankruptcy involved direct state intervention, statutory licensing in the Insolvency Act, state involvement in "self" regulation by placing government officials on professional oversight bodies, and a series of professional responsibilities for surveillance of directors in return for the monopoly over insolvency practice.

Conflicts between Professions within the State
On both sides of the Atlantic, bankruptcy reforms reverberated through government departments and the judiciary. Britain displayed the classic problem of how much rule-making should be administered by the Insolvency Service, an executive agency, and how much standards of directors' behavior, for instance, should be left to the discretion of the court, where legal norms would slowly be established through an accretion of cases. Civil servants wanted greater control over company directors, and they wanted precise standards to be inscribed in the Insolvency Act, or the secondary legislation, rather than relying on court decisions, which in normal circumstances would take some years to accumulate. In principle, the English judges had the enormous advantage that the judges of England's highest court, the Law Lords, sat in the House of Lords, where the insolvency legislation was introduced. The Lord Chancellor, head of the Judiciary, sat in cabinet and in the Lords. Furthermore, various distinguished jurists, such as Lord Denning, former Master of the Rolls, also sat in the House of Lords and participated in its debates. The judge-peers had every confidence that courts could develop a new common law of director disqualification and responsibility. Civil servants had their own access to law-making, because the senior insolvency policy officials advised the Minister of Trade and Industry directly. Compared to the American debates, this was a genteel claim for jurisdiction, with the stakes higher for civil servants than the courts. In the final analysis, the two compromised, with some precise language in the statute, more in the secondary

legislation, but final discretion as to weighting and seriousness of offenses to be left to the courts.

American jurisdictional politics in the state were much more complicated and visceral. We have shown that bankruptcy administration occasioned two conflicts, one over the amount of administration to be moved out of the courts and vested in a bureaucratic agency, and the other over the location of that agency. The first took minor, routine but voluminous work away from bankruptcy judges and vested it in an administrative agency. This move was consistent with the reformers' initiative for a separation of administrative and judicial functions in bankruptcy administration. More volatile was the debate over where the administrative agency should be located—in the courts' own administrative arm, or in an executive agency, either standing alone or in the Departments of Justice or Commerce. The complex politics involved in the shuffling among the options again included an instance of refusing jurisdiction, when neither Justice nor Commerce showed any interest in accepting new responsibilities. In part, this reflected the lobbying power of the federal judges, who prevailed upon the Attorney-General, a former federal judge, to decline any bankruptcy work. Indeed, on this count both bankruptcy and federal judges agreed that administration should stay in the courts and that the court administrative office should be enlarged. Only their reasoning differed: bankruptcy court judges wanted to be more like full federal judges and not to be confused with petty administrators. Federal judges simply resisted the loss of any jurisdiction, in principle, from the courts.

Conflicts within Professions inside the State

Raising the issue of bankruptcy administration in the United States set off an acrimonious dispute between lower and higher court judges. Relatively little of the dispute revolved around salaries, although that was at issue. The heart of the dispute concerned power and status. Because the work of corporate reorganization was every bit as complex and intellectually demanding as most other cases coming before federal district courts, advocates of the bankruptcy judges pressed Congress to upgrade them to the status of federal judges and to give their courts many of the jurisdictional powers of the federal bench. The prestige of Presidential appointment, the security of lifetime tenure on the bench, and salaries high enough to lure fine attorneys out of private practice—all drew the ire of a small, tightly knit federal bench that shuddered at the dilution of its numbers and quality, and recoiled from the notion that bankruptcy law was comparable in any way with the civil suits that came before the courts.

The dispute was fuelled by ingredients of the two cultures ostensible in private practice—a gulf of religion, education, and elite firm experience—as well as a residual stigma that attached to corporate "death" and the odium of a self-serving bankruptcy ring. Federal judges spoke openly of what, in effect, was their fear of attenuating the charisma of their office, with its proximity to White House appointment and the nobility of lifetime tenure through a merger with the lowly, slightly disreputable "referees," as Chief Justice Burger insisted on calling the bankruptcy judges.

In a general sense, the judges reproduced in microcosm many of the dynamics of insurgent–dominant struggles in the history of medicine, law, and accounting. But in a narrower sense, the attitude of the federal judges seemed to reflect a belief that they were playing a zero-sum game: any substantial increase in numbers of bankruptcy judges entailed a proportionate decrease in the stature and prestige of federal court judges. Like any exclusive club, its instant expansion by fifty or one hundred per cent would immediately diminish its cachet.

Unlike the conflicts over the limits of the state, ideology scarcely featured in the internecine judicial debate. The politics of judicial conflict had their own distinctiveness: unlike a market politics where interest group mobilization, and occasional elite networks, presented the main access to power, close ties with the Senate and White House presented federal judges immediate access to veto power in Congress. Capping this was the immense authority of the Chief Justice, who presided over the Federal Judicial Conference, and exercised moral leadership over the judiciary. Bankruptcy judges, too, had political connections, but district by district in the House. Both sides in the dispute therefore found political allies state by state and congressional district by district throughout the nation. But it was the federal judges, all selected and appointed by the Senate and President, whose late engagement in the reforms betrayed a confidence that their veto power was secure, a confidence only partly to be vindicated.

Occupational Politics and Legal Change

Disturbance in the division of labor led not only to a reconstitution of a professional field, but to the reconstitution of organizational fields more generally, and further, to the substance of bankruptcy law itself.[90] In both countries, not only was the organization of expert services transformed, but the very political struggles within and among professions altered the substantive and administrative structure of corporate reorganization. That is, the meta-bargaining over the new rules to govern the corporate credit network was a partial by-product of jurisdictional politics among professions.

We have demonstrated the direct connection between reformist impulses and the expert capacity to implement them. A significant part of this was purposive—a clear instrumental link in the minds of reformers between goals to be attained in saving companies and the professionals to accomplish it. In Britain, competent, sophisticated, and trustworthy insolvency practitioners were a cornerstone of saving businesses, educating and monitoring directors, raising public trust in markets, and liquidating and dispersing the assets of irremediable firms. Reconstructing the division of labor was inseparable from reorganizing business. In the United States, the rising rate of larger, complex bankruptcies demanded a far more sophisticated private bar, more powerful courts, more competent judges, and far greater administrative capacity, untainted by allegations of favoritism, cronyism, and collusion. Thus, reformers in the United States self-consciously understood that more liberal use of Chapter 11 for corporate reorganization would occur if lawyers were induced to advise managers to become debtors-in-possession, while retaining lawyers' counsel throughout. Managers in their turn would take the rehabilitation route if they were convinced that sophisticated turn-around advice could indeed revive their companies.

That these rational means—ends scenarios featured in the thinking of many reformers is undeniable. Yet the full significance of a jurisdictional analysis lies in the unanticipated entanglement of substantive outcomes with professional politics. Legal changes that were initiated by the Insolvency Act and Bankruptcy Code frequently owed as much to the resolution of quarrels among practitioners, as to any rational design of a politics-free social engineer. For instance, the messy resolution of the inter-judicial quarrels in the United States produced a new bankruptcy court that was designated as an Article I court, but seemed to have

---

[90] See Abbott (1988) on the relationship between knowledge claims and advances and the substantive legal outcomes. Dezalay (1992) argues that legal creativity is a prime device for seizing market share. See Powell's (1993) case study of the "poison pill" device in US mergers and acquisitions.

Article III powers. This Solomonic splitting of the difference between bankruptcy and federal judges may have temporarily resolved a seemingly irreconcilable dispute, but it plunged the entire bankruptcy system into crisis only a few years later, when enterprising lawyers found they could challenge the rulings of the bankruptcy court by attacking the very constitutionality of the court itself. Instantly, rampant uncertainty eroded confidence in the settlements of all reorganizations in prospect or in process.

The half-hearted resolution of disagreements over the form of a new US Trustee system also left a residue of uncertainty. The eighteen experiments in a government-based Trusteeship system represented a compromise between the Bankruptcy Commission, which recommended a national system, and the private lawyers and bankruptcy judges, who wanted trustees to be appointed from the bar. But it added another layer of doubt about the long-term structure of the new system, and where it would ultimately settle.

Other outcomes were most subtle, but arguably more consequential. American changes in the incentives to practice in the bankruptcy bar attracted highly talented and aggressive lawyers. They imported much less parochial attitudes to bankruptcy law, viewing it not as an isolated, esoteric area of practice estranged from the mainstream of corporate law, but as a means to effect other corporate purposes and to solve challenging legal and business problems. The most startling episodes of an expansive application of bankruptcy law came in the well-documented applications of Chapter 11 to labor disputes, mass torts, and takeover struggles. When Continental Airlines used Chapter 11 provisions on executory contracts to break its contracts with workers, or Manville used Chapter 11 to shelter from the vast claims of asbestos victims, or Texaco used Chapter 11 as a last-ditch stand in its fight with Pennzoil, innovative professionals now crowding into the field were demonstrating how widely bankruptcy law could be extended into monumental business disputes—often far removed from what normally would be counted as financial insolvency (Sobel 1991; Delaney 1992).

The significance of professional involvement in legal change can also be gauged by the impact of accountants and lawyers respectively on rights distributions in Britain and the United States. It is not simply a coincidence that British insolvency laws encourage the appointment of accountant-administrators to reorganize firms, or accountant-liquidators to disburse their assets, with minimal court involvement. Reorganization is essentially an administrative function, with recourse to the courts in extreme cases, but almost entirely independent of close court supervision in most instances. By contrast, the integral role of lawyers and judges in the American legislation locates them both firmly in corporate rescues or liquidations. No decision of any consequence proceeds without judicial hearings and rulings. Lawyers double up as advocates in court for trustees, debtors, creditors, tort claimants, the state, and any other party at interest. In short, both professions made certain that their sphere of operation would permit most play for their sphere of competency, for the arenas in which their expertise could maintain maximal legitimacy, and coincidentally, jurisdictional control.

The State and the Agents of Professionalization

We have seen that the legislation to amend bankruptcy law entailed far-reaching changes in the division of labor. While this was most notably exemplified in the creation of a new insolvency profession in Great Britain, the internal transformations within the American bankruptcy bar make it no less a subject of inquiry concerning the forces which drove change. Which theories of professionalization best account for the changes we have observed? More importantly, how do the bankruptcy reforms advance theories of professionalization?

These questions all converge on the role of the state. The virtual absence of the state, and the taking for granted of markets in their extant condition, are major weaknesses in an otherwise powerful theory of jurisdictional conflict. To demonstrate how the state must be reintegrated into the jurisdictional accounts provides an important way forward. There are three generic ways in which scholars of professions treat the state. *Co-optation* theories posit that professions effectively co-opt the state to pass laws that create monopolies which benefit professions. *Interventionist* theories propose that states have interests in market or administrative activities (for example, audits of companies, public health, legal regulation) and create professions that serve those public interests. *Constitutive* theories recognize that states and professions may grow up together, each relying on some feature of the other to enhance its influence or achieve its aims (Abbott 1988; Abel 1988, 1989; Halliday 1987; Halliday & Carruthers 1996; Halliday & Karpik 1998).

Thus the role of the state in these various theories provides an important way of distinguishing them from each other. For co-optation theories, the state is reactive and largely passive. For interventionists, the state is active and professions are moulded by it, while for constitutive theorists, states and professions are mutually dependent.

By shifting our focus from the "system of professions" to the occupational repercussions of one major legislative disturbance, we have discovered that the state takes on significantly more importance than merely as a potential competitor for professional services. The state–market axis signifies both that some of the most important jurisdictional stories occur within the state and that the state's determination of where the market begins constitutes a critical factor in any occupational restructuring. States are periodically in the business of constituting markets, deciding what services will be provided through market forces, what rules will govern those markets, and how they will be regulated. In other words, the state is not only renegotiating the scope of its own direct sphere of administration, but it is setting the parameters of market processes and drawing up the rules of the game, a game in which the government itself will be a regular player. Among those parameters is the division of labor.

The state constitutes professional competition in five ways.

(1) The state defines the areas in which competition is thought appropriate by setting the boundaries of its own direct administrative functions.

(2) The state designates which occupations will be protected from competition and which will be exposed to it. More precisely, it identifies which tasks of which professions will be vulnerable to competition by other occupations.

(3) The state sets the rules by which professions compete, or in fact, whether competition itself is considered the appropriate form of dispute resolution. In its composition of the Cork Committee, for instance, the British government made sure that lawyers, judges, and insolvency accountants were represented, thus facilitating negotiation and compromise at the outset.

(4) The state controls some of the resources that give professions negotiative advantages, most notably access to the authority of the state itself. The powers vested in insolvency practitioners to monitor the behavior of directors gave the new profession a grant of power which underwrote its claim to an exclusive jurisdiction in corporate reorganization.

(5) Most fundamentally of all, the state can actually create the work itself, thereby opening up niches in the division of labor that

become arenas for contests among professions over jurisdictional rights. By creating new devices, such as the English administration orders, or by expanding certain values, such as corporate reconstruction in Chapter 11 of the US Bankruptcy Code, the state constitutees the parameters of the private market element by element.

The most striking example of constitutive determinations of the division of labor can be found in the Thatcher government's broader policy agenda to reconstitute British financial and other markets. The professionalization of insolvency practitioners, and the general statutory settlement of the insolvency division of labor, was not an end in itself, even in the dynamics of state interventionism. The several shifts in the control and administration of financial reorganization and liquidation were relatively minor adjustments in the government's grand scheme to revive and invigorate market solutions to problems hitherto performed by the state itself. The government minister responsible for insolvency legislation in the House of Lords acknowledged that the government sought a variety of expedients to legitimate markets before elites who historically had a low view of the City and before a public accustomed to welfare state provisions of services.

The government's grand design of market expansion required certain regulatory underpinnings. Given the historic suspicion of trade in English society, and in view of recurrent scandals about the probity of market behavior, the government was confronted with an enormous normative problem—how to persuade citizens at every level of society that markets were reliable means of providing such public goods as transportation, energy, and water, which once had been the exclusive province of the state. The public had to be convinced that markets were worthy of their trust, and that they could invest in full confidence that their interests would be protected. The corporate insolvency scandals, in which unscrupulous liquidators and directors joined forces to defraud innocents, symbolized the moral impediments to the government's generic plans to reconstitute markets in English society. How was it possible for a contracting state to solve such an enormous problem of moral upgrading?

One solution was professionalization. In the reorganized division of labor in the insolvency field, the new practitioners were charged with the regulatory responsibilities for "moral audits" of all directors whose companies became insolvent. If these audits revealed fiscal irresponsibility or wilful neglect, company directors could be held personally liable for the debts they had incurred. Effectively, therefore, the division of professional labor emerged through an extension of state interests by another means as it sought to reconstitute itself vis-à-vis markets in general. In this sense, the profession was an expression of state purpose, just as the state was a condition of professional existence.

PART 4

Conclusion

11 Professions in the Institutionalization of Business Rescue

Rescuing business was the central motif that ran through corporate bankruptcy reforms in the United States and Britain. This much the two countries had in common. Their underlying accounts of business failure differed, as the British characteristically blamed the managers and the Americans blamed the economy. The solutions offered by reformers in either country also differed, as the British relied more on professional autonomy and discretion, while the Americans retained some confidence in managers. Even bankers, who preferred that businesses be "saved" by their private workouts, concurred that saving businesses through a reorganization moderated by bankruptcy law probably benefitted everyone more than liquidation of a business inside or outside of bankruptcy law.

If this was common ground, the ways to achieve business rehabilitation were neither self-evident nor unconflictual. Government departments and ministers, financial institutions, consumer agencies, judges and professors, practitioners and trade suppliers brought unique histories of precedent, experiences of practice, and visions of opportunity to inform their perspective on rescuing businesses. To help save businesses through statutory law was by no means a narrowly legalistic undertaking. Business rehabilitation rests upon complex social and economic dynamics. These processes widen the frame of bankruptcy reforms beyond legislative histories as they also enable us to extend theories of legal change, organizational power, and professional influence.

The bankruptcy reforms in England and the United States exist in a context of cross-cutting dynamics that have consequences for other sorts of statutory law-making. Statutory law-making in many fields, including financial legislation, can disturb property rights and unsettle work domains and who gets to control that work. Thus struggles over property rights become embroiled in negotiations and disputes over jurisdictional rights, a confounding of interests that becomes more acute as the jurisdictional stakes increase, and the resources for political mobilization of the claimant occupations also expand. Everyday bargaining over property and jurisdictional rights in the market differs substantially from infrequent meta-bargaining in politics. Markets and politics differ in their institutional logics: the players are not always identical, nor are the rules of play, nor the resources that are mobilized, nor the values to which players appeal. The politics of meta-bargaining may therefore empower some actors weak in everyday bargaining, just as strong actors in everyday market transactions can find their arbitrary powers as economic agents subject to strict scrutiny under a different value regime inside politics.

In certain kinds of meta-bargaining, such as that exemplified by the bankruptcy reforms, professionals can play a sophisticated inside game. Their familiarity with all aspects of the law in practice, their access to the highest levels of intellectual creativity, and their capacities for mobilization all conjoin to produce a politics of invention and innovation. Professions' strategic location, at the crossroads of law in practice and law in statutes, permits them to innovate in the service of striking bargains. However, professional motivations are complex, and meta-bargaining outcomes that are highly favorable for professionals can be produced as much by clients and the state as by their own self-interested machinations.

The politics of rescuing business are simultaneously the politics of distributing power in organizational fields. Creditors and debtors vie for relative advantage in everyday bargaining over the extension of credit. But the politics of meta-bargaining put into play the rules that govern their negotiations over power and control. Meta-bargaining potentially brings together every social institution and actor with an interest in market exchanges. Meta-bargaining determines who can play and with what resources. It specifies when private exchanges and contracts will be trumped by a public interest, or when a bilateral transaction will be overturned by a multilateral interest. The political settlements in bankruptcy law reach far into everyday market exchanges and affect the forms of security that creditors use to establish their priority, as well as their relationships with debtors.

This chapter draws together and extrapolates from several of the arguments that run through this study, and reflects on the implications for professions, legal change, and corporate organizations. We consider, in turn, (1) the interplay of property and jurisdictional rights; (2) the trade-offs between bargaining and meta-bargaining, where market and political logics come into tension; (3) the politics of expert innovation by professionals; and (4) the struggles among powerful collective actors over the definition and distribution of power in organization fields.

CONFOUNDING PROPERTY AND JURISDICTIONAL RIGHTS

Bankruptcy law defines one set of parameters for property rights in an exchange economy. It circumscribes the outer limits of behavior for firms that freely contract in a market, for it sets out the modification rules that will qualify a firm's property rights (or those of a state or individuals) when it, or some other firm with which it has a financial relationship, suffers severe financial reversal. Meta-bargaining over bankruptcy law, therefore, helps to construct or alter a legal arena in which property rights are abrogated, transformed, constrained, and re-adjusted.

One way to think about changes in property rights within bankruptcy law is to consider how they were generally redistributed by the reforms. Who were the winners and losers?

In Britain, financial institutions mobilized early and effectively to forestall a threat to their powerful "floating charge" security, and they managed to fend off a loss of discretion in the new administratorships. But they did not succeed in reducing the powerful "retention of title" security that was used against them by the much weaker trade creditors. Corporate managers were losers, though not so completely as it appeared in mid-stream. The government supported new "wrongful trading" provisions that could deprive company directors of their livelihood and personal assets. But the Confederation of British Industry and the Institute of Directors were able to pull the teeth from the government's extreme measures to automatically disqualify directors of insolvent companies from future directorships. As a creditor, the government—the Treasury and Inland Revenue—had to retreat under sustained pressure from all other creditors, depriving it of an almost limitless backwards reach to reclaim unpaid taxes. Consumer creditors got virtually nothing for their efforts to create a special fund to recompense customers unlucky enough to lose their deposits on furniture, holidays, home repairs, and the like. Unsecured creditors did not get the "Ten Percent Fund," ingeniously proposed by the Reform Committee specialists, though there was some hope that there would be more left over for them if other innovations in the legislation worked properly. Labor's position either as a creditor or a cost remained virtually unchanged, although workers were probably assured of a more secure safety net by having their benefits taken over by the Redundancy Fund set up by the government. The utilities lost their de facto powers to turn off the lights and power and water, and thus illegitimately jump ahead of other creditors.

All this was accomplished through the adroit invention, extension and contraction—in effect, the redistribution—of property rights. Parliament confirmed the rights granted by courts to the trade creditors' retention of title over their goods until they were paid. Parliament refused to interfere with the floating charge security, although it provided new protections to banks if they would waive those rights in propitious circumstances, and it curtailed the statutory rights of the state to years of unpaid taxes and social security payments. New rights were extended to creditors against directors, and Parliament removed the de facto rights from utilities and heightened the protections of debtor corporations against the water, power, and gas companies.

Reforms in the United States paralleled two of the central shifts in the English legislation, on the one hand, a modest shift in power away from the most powerful actors—the financial industry and the state—and towards smaller creditors with weaker property rights, and on the other hand, a strong commitment to the reorganization rather than the dissolution of troubled companies. Financial institutions obtained a better quality of judicial administration and kept their "set off" security. But they lost some ground to corporate managers, who obtained broader powers to reorganize their own companies—while keeping powerful creditors at bay—through the expanded provisions on "debtors-in-possession." If the financial industry was pushed back by managers, it also lost some of its powers to the court, which was given increased authority to "cram-down" solutions if secured creditors seemed too obstructionist. This effectively strengthened the hands of unsecured creditors, who could anticipate a larger slice of future asset pools. Like its British counterpart, the state's reach over back taxes was shortened. Labor's fortunes were quite mixed—although this did not become obvious until several years later. As a creditor, labor got substantially increased benefits as a high statutory priority. As a cost, however, organized labor completely under-estimated the potential of the bankruptcy legislation for the erosion of their position.

These redistributive patterns meld together a variety of ways in which property rights can be altered. The statutes include an amalgam of devices to fit the properties of rights into a legal framework conducive to saving companies. These devices affect what rights can be manipulated, how the strength of existing rights can be increased or decreased, who has what kinds of discretion over the exercise of property rights, and when they may exercise that discretion.

While it happened rarely, these reforms *created new rights* or forms of security. This may take the form of an entirely new concept. The English Ten Percent Fund, for instance, while ultimately unsuccessful, would have given unsecured creditors a right they did not previously have, namely, a guarantee to share amongst themselves ten per cent of the assets secured by the floating charges of the banks. New rights can also be endowed on economic actors by taking an established device and extending it to a party previously without it. Such was the statutory device of giving consumers priority in the US Bankruptcy Code. The device was well accepted, but the beneficiary was new.

Existing rights can be altered by *reducing their scope*. When both English and American reformers attacked the special privileges of taxing authorities in either country, they did not succeed in abolishing those statutory rights altogether, but they were successful in cutting down on the number of taxes that got special privileges, and on how far back in time the state might reasonably go to enforce its claims to unpaid taxes.

Then again a security device may be left intact, but a statute will *restrict its arbitrary exercise*. There was no doubt that banks in the United States had a well-established pattern of using setoff when their corporate customers became insolvent, but the legislation inhibited the exercise of this "right" and dampened banks' enthusiasm for automatic setoff. Similarly, British reformers eventually conceded banks' right to exercise their floating charge, but Parliament altered some of the rules over how much discretion a receiver might have in satisfying only the debenture-holder's interests. With its administration order, the legislation also gave secured creditors an alternative to putting in their receiver and liquidating the business. Automatic stays and moratoriums similarly restricted creditors from seizing their property at will.

Security devices can also be left substantially untouched, but their force can be amplified or diminished by *changing the order for exercising rights*. When consumers got a new priority in the United States, the state got a lower priority in the queue for exercising rights. It lost ground to another creditor who could satisfy their claims before the Internal Revenue Service was permitted to reclaim any assets.

Then again, the prospect of reorganization in the US demanded substantial managerial flexibility and discretion over use of assets. At once reformers wanted to allay the fears of secured creditors that they would lose their collateral, but yet use that collateral to turn the company around. The creative formula to solve this conundrum essentially *substituted one kind of security for another*. A secured creditor's collateral—

cash, inventory, assets—could be used by managers, thus weakening control over it by the secured creditors, only if creditors' rights were strengthened by a judicial guarantee—another type of security—that the assets would be adequately protected.

The modifications of property rights we have observed in bankruptcy law leads us now to revisit the four elements of property rights considered in Chapter 1, but this time to consider how far those elements were adjusted by bankruptcy law. In the US case, consider, for example, the assets which serve as collateral for a loan. Typically, debtors possess the collateral, and may use it, but lenders have rights in the collateral so that if the debtor defaults, the lender may seize the collateral. Metabargaining focused on three of the four rights, including usufruct, exclusivity and alienability, but not heritability.

Usufruct, it may be recalled, refers to an owner's right to use property. Much of the debate among strong creditors, especially in the US, centered precisely on this right. On the one hand, a moratorium or automatic stay stopped secured creditors from exercising their freely contracted right to seize property when the debtor defaulted on a loan. Indeed, the automatic stay is a general restriction on use by all creditors, until a court or a court-appointed agent intervenes. Thus, the automatic stay prevented creditors from *excluding* debtors from use of collateral assets which, by contract, should have reverted to the creditor. On the other hand, secured creditors lobbied earnestly over protections for their collateral, if it were to be used by managers, or debtors-in-possession. The concepts of "indubitable equivalent" and "adequate protection" both sprung up to protect banks. Other parties could not use secured creditors collateral without seeking permisson from them or a court. In the case of a loan secured by inventory, creditors were concerned about a debtor's ability to sell off or *alienate* their collateral. Despite a secured creditor's wish to prevent or at least restrict alienation, debtors were allowed to go ahead and sell such assets provided the creditor received adequate protection.

The new distributions of property rights in bankruptcy were inseparable from cross-cutting negotiations over jurisdictional rights for professionals. Rescuing companies requires agents; they may be agents of the state, private creditors, directors or shareholders. Apart from managers themselves, these agents usually are professionals. Some are "state-professionals," such as civil servants and judges; others are "market-professionals," such as lawyers and accountants. For all of them, legislative reform also potentially threatens their work domains. In so far as professionals have rights of various sorts over different types of work, a change in property rights becomes for them a potential struggle over jurisdictional rights.

In Part III we saw that meta-bargaining over jurisdictional rights relates not only to where work is located on either side of the public–private divide, but how work is organized within the market and state respectively. Again both countries shared the assumption that the rehabilitation of business demanded professionals of high competency, but they differed significantly on what constituted that competency and how to ensure it.

Modifications in bankruptcy law therefore affected jurisdictional rights. Like property rights, these rights can be subdivided into four categories, two of which (usufruct and exclusivity) are especially relevant. Jurisdictional rights determine who governs or controls types of work, and in which institutional locations that work gets placed. In other words, they settle who may claim the fruits of work, and who may exclude others from making similar claims. In the US, the proposal floated early on by reformers to locate routine bankruptcy work in a new administrative agency received almost unanimous criticism, and so bankruptcy courts remained the primary arena. Consequently, lawyers and judges maintained their exclusive jurisdiction over bankruptcy work. As bankruptcy work became more lucrative, bankruptcy lawyers remained the prime beneficiaries, and did not have to share their new-found wealth with other professions. In England, professionalization of insolvency practitioners led to the exclusion of lower-status practitioners—they could not meet the newly imposed standards and so could simply be cut out of the insolvency market. In this instance, it wasn't so much that one profession excluded another, as that reformers excluded the lower end of the spectrum.

The bankruptcy reforms demonstrate two substantially contrasting ways to constitute professionalism in the market. The English model sought to upgrade the ethics and quality of workers who presided over liquidations and reorganizations. The reformers and government chose the classic approach of licensing professionals through statutory mandate. But since this was a government also wary of professional monopolies, it created a peculiar hybrid of a profession that kept the government's hand in the formulation and enforcement of professional ethics, and maintained its capacity to adjust the rate of admissions into the profession, the better to forestall the artificial creation of scarcity in the supply of services.

If the resolution of the English division of labor proceeded via professionalization, the American solution utilized new incentives in the market. By changing the basis on which bankruptcy lawyers could be paid, and effectively allowing their fees to rise dramatically, the Bankruptcy Code modified incentive structures to let the market for legal services take care of itself. Higher fees, it was thought, would attract better lawyers. And better lawyers could more readily take advantage of the new opportunities to reconstruct failing companies. Reconstituting the market for legal services indirectly would rescue companies at a higher rate.

Both these legislative episodes illustrate a fundamental, though widely misunderstood, aspect of professionalization. The expansion of jurisdictional rights by professionals, the upgrading of their qualifications, the enhancement of their status, the expansion of their powers, and the increase in their fees can result as much from the interests of their clients and the state as from their own monopolistic dispositions. In the United States, one of the most vocal forces for better qualified bankruptcy judges was the financial industry. In Britain, it was Mrs Thatcher's Government that championed the professionalization of insolvency practitioners. In both cases, in fact, alterations in property rights were linked to significant changes in jurisdictions and occupational perquisites.

The new distributions of property rights in bankruptcy were inseparable from the struggle for jurisdictional rights among professions. For instance, the new administration orders for corporate reorganization in Britain potentially impaired the property rights of banks, but this they accepted so long as they were assured both that they had veto power over administration orders and that jurisdictional rights over financial reorganization went only to accredited professionals. The struggle for professionalization by insolvency practitioners, and for specialization among accountants, thereby became intertwined with the curtailment of old property rights.

In the United States, the new power given courts to "cramdown" settlements on discordant creditors assumed the victory of bankruptcy judges to upgrade the quality of recruits and the jurisdiction of their courts. Indeed, the willingness of bankers to impair their rights through cramdown depended directly on the guarantee that modernized courts, with expert, broad jurisdictions, could bring a level of economic rationality to bankruptcy law that had been missing. And as the creative use of strategic bankruptcy subsequently demonstrated, the incentives given lawyers to enter the bankruptcy field induced a surge of bounty-hunting, innovative professionals to carve new rights for their clients from a pliable statute.

Professional realignment was driven by more than passive government acquiescence to professionalization from below. The conversion of British liquidators into "company doctors," as much expressed Mrs Thatcher's project of market reform as it did the monopolistic instincts of quasi-professionals. We have shown that insolvency practitioners joined with lawyers and the financial industry to urge some form of licensing on bankruptcy specialists. But the Conservative Government insisted on the need for accredited professionals to deal with the company failures that accompanied the Government's shake-up of British industry. Moreover, for privatization to succeed, the Government needed to convince the British public that expert professionals and competent, honest directors would safeguard investments. Not only did they press for professionalization of insolvency practitioners, but they loaded responsibilities onto the professionals to monitor directors. And to ensure that extractive monopolies did not drive up prices, the Government insisted on keeping a hand in the supply and ethical regulation of practitioners. Consequently, the state's interest in rehabilitation of companies demanded state-led construction of an expert profession, albeit aided and abetted by one segment of the profession itself. Moreover, the professionalization of insolvency practitioners allowed the government to exact new duties, or heightened vigilance to old duties, of corporation directors.

If the reconfiguration of the English division of labor proceeded by professionalization, the American method involved a combination of new incentives in the market for legal services coupled with new conditions of service within the judiciary. In the market, the incentives were principally monetary, essentially diverting resources from unsecured creditors to professionals. In the judiciary, salaries and longer tenure were joined with much greater power. Again, professionals themselves were actively involved in determining their own fates, frequently in vigorous contest with others. The "state" was far from a disinterested onlooker. Government officials expressed strong views about whether they wanted to take on new or modified work. Judges fought bitterly over the future status of bankruptcy judges. Congressional leaders had a clear view about government interests in more expert, efficient, and equitable bankruptcy administration. That their interests substantially coincided with those of certain professionals was felicitous. But adjustments to the division of labor were as much a product of state interests as they were of professional machinations and thus professionalization from "below" was as important as professionalization from "above" in producing the final outcome.

Bankruptcy law-making therefore underscores two important facts about professionalization in advanced societies. First, however loudly modern business may complain about the high cost of professional labor, business depends on accounting expertise to measure its success, on consulting expertise to adapt its operations and management, and on legal expertise to create orderly and predictable legal relations of exchange so that property rights are secure. Second, modern states cannot govern without professional expertise. If states seek to adjust the delivery of services by public administrations and private occupations, they cannot avoid redistributing the jurisdictions between the public and private sectors. The legitimation of expert state functions, in the executive or judiciary, can hardly be accomplished without some measure of "reprofessionalization." And if states seek to reconstitute markets in a manner that involves bankruptcy law, then the character of professional services must be integral to the process.

Bankruptcy reforms display a vast amount of activity in the reshuffling of professional jurisdictions: moving activities from the state into the market, from the market into the state, from one branch of the state to another, from one echelon of the market to another, and from one status location within professions to a higher location in the same profession.

Property rights and jurisdictional rights are so integrally linked that change in one potentially induces change in the other. Sometimes they operate in inverse relation to each other. To weaken a strong security it is necessary to strengthen a jurisdictional power. Sometimes changes in one correlate highly with changes in another. To implement a successful rehabilitation, where rights are preserved, requires pervasive jurisdiction by highly competent professionals with sufficient power to implement their decisions.

BARGAINING AND META-BARGAINING IN THE MARKET AND POLITICS

Law-making in bankruptcy law brings into uneasy tension two kinds of bargaining: everyday bargaining in markets and courts; and meta-bargaining in the polity. There is a recursive cycle between the two.

Ordinary market bargaining among solvent companies involves the negotiation and execution of transactions. Debtors bargain with creditors for a loan, coming to mutually agreeable provisions about issues like short versus long-term, interest rate, collateral, and restrictive covenants. Such negotiations occur on the basis of legal rules which determine what various legal devices and provisions do, and how they will work. Legal rules shape what kinds of debtor–creditor relationships are possible, and what are not. Market bargaining occurs through application of rights specification rules.

In situations of financial distress, bargaining again occurs among creditors and debtors, often with the involvement of the courts and executive agencies, in efforts to try and turn companies around, whether through workouts outside the strictures of bankruptcy law, or through attempted reorganizations inside of bankruptcy law. But everyday bargaining occurs within a set of limits and must follow certain rules (what we term "rights modification rules"). For instance, as companies approach insolvency, banks and debtors carefully scrutinize any changes in their credit relationships because a subsequent filing for court protection by a company may trigger the voiding of certain secured credit relationships that were negotiated by creditors and companies in the months before filing. Once companies enter the protection of bankruptcy law, rules multiply and behavior by all parties is heavily regulated. Since rehabilitation of a company requires agreement among most creditors with the debtor company, bargaining is endemic to the process. But the rules of bankruptcy also define how much freedom interested parties have to negotiate mutually agreeable deals. The absolute priority rule in US law reduces such flexibility because the law itself determines that one major potential trade-off is removed from the bargaining table. Freedom to negotiate, to bargain, is affected by how much must be approved by a government agency or a court. And agencies and courts themselves vary from those that are heavily rule-bound to those that permit significant discretion by judges and administrators. English insolvency practitioners and lawyers express relief that they can act decisively to reorganize a company without constant recourse either to a judge or to a civil servant, a major weakness they perceive in the American system. Of course, the success of bargaining outcomes depends in some measure on the skill of the bargainers and on the competence and creativity of those, usually judges, whose approval of bargains will lead to a generally acceptable plan for reorganization.

In substantial part, therefore, the bankruptcy reforms involved meta-bargaining about the framework (that is, rules and conditions) for everyday bargaining. Unhappiness with the strait-jacket of absolute priority in the US, distress over the ability of one or two large creditors to subvert a reorganization plan agreeable to everyone else, frustration at limited powers of judges to exercise significant discretion—all these fuelled initiatives to modify absolute priority, to enable judges to "cramdown" plans over the objections of holdout creditors, and to ensure that the judges confirming such plans possessed adequate jurisdiction and were themselves of a caliber sufficient to think and act creatively. Meta-bargaining in England took a slightly different path to the same destination. The new office of administrator carried out by the new occupation of insolvency practitioner opened up a much more flexible set of options to reorganize companies in the general interests of all creditors. In so doing it widened the sphere of bargaining and broadened the criterion against which a bargain among creditors would be appraised.

Meta-bargaining occurred both in response to the perceived inadequacy of bargaining frameworks *before* the legislative reforms and in anticipation of enhanced bargaining opportunities *after* the new statutes were enacted. The relationship between bargaining and meta-bargaining was therefore recursive. If meta-bargaining arose out of difficulties in everyday bargaining that inhibited company turnarounds, meta-bargaining also created new devices, rules, and opportunities to facilitate bargaining that would help save companies. Mediating both transitions were professionals. They conveyed perceptions of inadequate law in practice to reformers; and they acted as agents enacting the new law in practice. Critically, of course, in many respects *they were the prime actors in meta-bargaining*. They stood as suppliants for legal change, as architects of change, and also as those who invented new modes of bargaining within the new sets of rules they themselves had developed.

Meta-bargaining in the political system has a different logic from bargaining in the market and so it is not possible simply to extrapolate from an actor's position in the market to their position in the political arena. Dominance in bilateral or multilateral transactions in a market cannot be assumed to translate into political dominance over expanded multilateral negotiations in politics. Meta-bargaining in the political arena differs from bargaining in the market arena in terms of its players, the resources those players bring to the table, the dynamics of bargaining itself, and the principles on which bargaining proceeds.

In everyday bargaining over corporate reorganization the prime parties are major creditors, the debtor-company, and professionals. Weak creditors may have the right to be heard, but lack of information or lack of assets, or lack of access, frequently keeps them away. In the US, a judge will be involved once a company enters Chapter 11 (reorganization) or Chapter 7 (liquidation). These players assume different weights in England, where the judge will be little involved in day-to-day bargaining and the debtor will have few cards to play. When the bankruptcy law itself is on the meta-bargaining table, two changes take place. Most actors now are represented by their collective organizations and peak associations. More importantly, new actors appear. Academics—most commonly law professors—obtain an influence rarely seen in practice. Most importantly, politicians and political parties come to the table—indeed, we may extend the metaphor and style them as hosts of the meta-bargaining table. Thus the entire set of pragmatic day-to-day issues can become immersed in party ideology, party commitments, and political expediency. In Britain, the civil service is drawn into intimate relationship with the legislation, from its review and policy reformulation through its drafting and parliamentary passage.

New actors in a new environment proceed according to meta-bargaining's own set of distinctive rules. In place of commercial convention and procedure in the market, or judicial norms and practice in bankruptcy courts, legislatures and the politicians that occupy them play by a different set of rules. Civil servants operate within explicit policies and well institutionalized conventions about what they can say and do that is independent of the ministers to whom they report. Their various agencies, and sections with agencies, bring alternative points of view that require resolution in one forum or another. Politicians who preside over legislative passage variously are caught among the currents of their own individual accountability to constituents, their commitments to party platforms and ideology, their individual perceptions of public interest, and the intra-necine conflicts among the upper and lower houses and the various committees in each. All these have rules about what information conveyed by whom can enter the process at what point. And around these rules they understand the pressure points where agendas are set, where changes can be made, and when either will occur.

Caught in a process that differs markedly from market bargaining, meta-bargainers find that the resources useful in everyday corporate reorganizations lose or gain efficacy, or become distorted in the political arena. We have seen that strength in the market can actually be turned on its head and become a weakness in the polity, as large banks and utilities discovered. Conversely, weak players in day to day activities— workers, consumers—may find their efficacy much enhanced as collective actors. But the matter is even more complicated than these extremes suggest. Effective market players will include those who are "repeat players," who constantly play the game and are very good at it. Effectiveness derives also from a coupling of economic strength (the largest creditors) with strength of security (the most binding legal rights). When these actors come into the political arena, however, the capacity for political mobilization becomes far more telling, as does the access of these collective actors to key political pressure points. Workers in everyday English insolvencies will have a voice that is virtually inaudible compared to the role of unions speaking on their behalf in the antechambers of a Labour Government. In the United States, federal judges had telling influence on a Senate whose members nominated them to their positions on the bench. Moreover, the political arena opens up new political spaces for the inside politicking of experts. Review committees and commissions, congressional subcommittees and parliamentary debates, give experts a form of conceptual leverage out of all proportion to their influence in everyday practice.

Bargaining and meta-bargaining also differ because participants must appeal to different audiences. Hard bargaining in private among a set of players who have sat down at the same table many times before bears limited resemblance to open meta-bargaining where points of view and policy justifications are on the public record. A public audience may require a rhetorical casting that constricts not only what players can say, but what they can do. Secured creditors and the state were compelled to find an idiom into which they could translate interests that would be persuasive to audiences habitually wary of their overwhelming power and arbitrary action. By the same logic, a weak party can strike a rhetorical note that catapults their cause from the political margins into policy recognition. Moreover, in the policy realm, parties such as trade suppliers or managers of companies sometimes have the good fortune—independent of their own efforts—to find spokespersons who take up their causes and argue their cases despite their ignorance or inadequacy.

All of these differing attributes of bargaining in the market and polity turn ultimately on the principles that order the respective domains. Economic actors in the market appeal, with little dissent, to principles of economic rationality—to the efficient allocation of resources, to respect for freedom of contract, to the ideal of preserving freely bargained property rights, and to the pursuit of narrow self-interest. But while values of economic efficiency, economic growth, and market vitality frequently spill over into other institutional spheres, they confront new values in the political realm, values which as often as not demand a different justification. Political rationality demands satisfaction of constituencies whose needs may conflict directly with economic rationality at the extreme.[1] Politicians are sensitive to constituents thrown out of work, to escalating public welfare rolls, to communities stripped of their traditional industries. Politicians pursue goals—for example, a "general interest" as specified in party platforms, that systematically order social institutions in ways that differ from economic values. Quality of life, protection of the young and innocent, protection of the unemployed and elderly, distributive justice, protection of key institutions or critical industries or firms—these all have their own logic which conflicts at many points with market driven sentiments.

Thus the ideal of saving businesses may be interpreted in very different ways by the two logics of the market and polity. If saving business adheres to a model of market efficiency, then bankruptcy law should encourage interested economic parties so that firms continue to trade only up to that point where their net value to creditors remains positive. Troubled firms should simply be liquidated if reorganization has no good prospect of success. The same problem from a political perspective would look quite different. Of course, if the law encourages more company reorganizations, and consequently there is less economic dislocation, then this will produce political benefits. But political payoffs may extend well beyond the economic payoff, for politicians must demonstrate to their constituents and their communities that they are sensitive to the individual and community hurts that will result from company failures. Such a logic compelled a generation of British governments to nationalize—effectively subsidize from the public fisc—such massive industries as coal, steel, and shipbuilding, long after any economically rational case could be made for their continued existence. Perhaps as importantly, politicians must be *seen* to be acting with sensitivity, whether or not new measures actually produce more rescued firms. Since politicians are dispersed across the entire geographical landscape,

---

[1] For more on the tensions between the market and the polity, or between capitalism and democracy, see Przeworski (1991), Lindblom (1977).

any failure of a major firm in a local political constituency becomes a political event as much as an economic event. And if meta-bargaining can produce new legal regimes that universally forestall local collapses, then the political logic has its own *raison d'etre*.

Yet the contrast between these two logics should not be posed too starkly. Political authorities have strong interests in vibrant and efficient economies. Politicians and parties rely on institutional and financial support from key market players, and so the market affects politics. The reverse is also true: politics reconstitute markets. The so-called "laissez-faire" market in fact is an institution operating within a set of legal rules and frameworks instituted by the state.[2] The bankruptcy reforms demonstrate that here, too, law acts to reconstitute markets at the extreme.

The reconstitution of markets occurs most obviously through changes in incentives for market players. Both pieces of legislation changed the incentives to precipitate a company into one or another legal regime to liquidate or reorganize a company. In addition, the English set up a "market" of civil suits for private parties—creditors—to attack the assets of company directors, thus using economic sanctions to compel certain kinds of responsible behavior. Both pieces of legislation also reconstructed the market for legal services, the one by opening up the fee basis of practice, and the other by instituting a quasi-monopoly through creation of a new profession. Changes in types of security, their force in various circumstances, and the rules that alter them also change patterns of exchange.

More subtly, the bankruptcy reforms also sought to reconstruct *institutional morality*. Institutional morality was a significant point of meta-bargaining in both countries.[3] Both bankruptcy reforms set about appraising and repairing moral orders or institutional morality. The English case offers the most visible example, for many of the reformers explicitly held their reformist recommendations against a standard of

---

[2] This, of course, was one of the key points in Polanyi's book *The Great Transformation* (1944). See also North (1981).

[3] It must be emphasized that the sociological concepts of morality and moral order differ from those used in social philosophy or ethics. Sociologists do not ask if an action is moral or immoral against some express ethical standard. Rather they assume that all institutions contain moral or normative orders which act prescriptively for those actors within them. Moral orders are articulated in social institutions with varying degrees of formality and they usually include boundaries within which those norms pertain, and sanctioning mechanisms to enforce compliance. Sociologists make no ethical judgement about how well those orders comport with recognized ethical, philosophical or religious systems.

"market morality." For the Tories, market morality referred to norms that underlay practices by directors and insolvency practitioners, though that concept embraced much more that was *not* on the table in the insolvency reforms. Market morality for directors, we have seen, included positive and negative elements. Positive standards were expressed in terms of the orthodox business practices of good accounting, attendance at board meetings and fiduciary responsibilities for oversight of company affairs, as well as the responsible filing of reports with government agencies. Negative instances that demarcated Tory "market morality" included practices in which companies accepted deposits but did not deliver goods, continued trading when the company was insolvent, neglected proper fiduciary oversight by directors, indulged in reckless behavior, and employed the Phoenix Syndrome, in which directors dissolved companies, shed their creditors, and then formed a new company free of debt with a similar name and many of the assets illicitly brought over from the prior company. Fraudulent behavior clearly demarcated moral boundaries by transgressing them. Similarly, insolvency practitioners aided and abetted market immorality when they conspired with company directors to defraud or deprive creditors of their assets. For the Government, making markets "moral" also meant making them safe for ordinary investors, and safe, too, for the government which was expecting to shift the delivery of public goods onto private markets. For the government, therefore, insolvency law was about much more than insolvency. Insolvency law was one piece of a larger effort to use law to reconstitute a normative order in an institution crucial to the government's ideological mandate.

All institutions are constituted partly as moral orders. They have their indigenous institutional morality that exists in an environment of other institutional and societal moralities. The state is no exception. Meta-bargaining over bankruptcy law took place on "moral" grounds for state authorities no less than company directors. The most striking parallel occurred in both countries' debates over taxation and the rights of tax authorities in bankruptcy. At one level, this debate could be seen (and was seen) as an argument about efficiency ("did a high priority for taxes take away cash that would better be used for company reorganization?"), or an argument about equity ("did a large and powerful entity like the state deserve debtors' assets as much as little creditors?"). But state officials marshalled another argument altogether, which showed their sensitivity to the fragility of public institutions.

Although their argument can be viewed as a rhetoric cynically construed to advance their bid for priority, that should not detract from its fundamental insight that the efficacy of the state, despite its once-monopoly over coercion, cannot depend on coercion alone. No state can enforce its will on an unwilling populace without eventually being overturned. State authorities argued that tax collection relies on voluntary compliance. If too many citizens or corporations are widely believed by other tax-payers to be in non-compliance, and do not pay their taxes, then that erodes both the legitimacy of the institution and the voluntary compliance of taxpayers (Levi 1988). Bankruptcy law provides one such escape hatch. Taxpayers who withhold payment for years, given a low government priority with weak reachback provisions, can get away with it. Such practices, said tax officials, weaken norms of compliance. Implicit in this argument of course is the admission that tax authorities do not have the coercive means to compensate for voluntary non-compliance.

The legitimacy of courts as arenas of corporate reconstruction strikes a similar note. The powerful push of American bankers for improvement of bankruptcy courts was premised on normative expectations about institutional operations. Only a small fraction of these expectations concerned morality in its everyday usage, and those related only to the neutrality of judges. The banking community essentially articulated its own set of normative standards for efficiency, competency, and neutrality and demanded that Congress meet the standards or bankers would subvert the legislation.

In all of these senses and instances of institutional morality, therefore, the meta-bargaining not only well exceeded the normal terms of everyday bargaining in bankruptcy, but it overflowed the bounds of bankruptcy law itself, narrowly construed, to encompass aspects of institutional moral orders in the market and the state.

PROFESSIONAL DIPLOMACY AND INNOVATION IN META-BARGAINING

Bankruptcy reforms represent a prime site to observe professional power in meta-bargaining. Professionals permeated the reforms in Britain and the United States. The structure of their involvement encouraged participation from the onset of the reform cycle to its conclusion. Both countries formed official deliberative bodies to investigate current practices and make recommendations to remedy faults and create new mechanisms to save businesses. The technicality of the law ensured that professionals would be consulted, and they were consulted heavily. More importantly, the Bankruptcy Commission and the Review Committee integrated substantial numbers of practising lawyers, accountants, and judges, together with academics (in the US) into their formal bodies, so much so that non-professionals were the rare exception. If this were not enough, the Bankruptcy Commission created a staff group headed by a law professor and populated by professionals.

Furthermore, professions dominated the consultative process. In the United States, attorneys and associations of judges and lawyers disproportionately testified in written and oral submissions. In Britain, the three most interested professions—lawyers, accountants, insolvency practitioners—overwhelmingly dominated in their succession of detailed responses and submissions to every proposal generated by the Cork Committee. They were the only private parties to offer repeated systematic responses to every aspect of the proposed reforms.

In the drafting and legislative stages this pattern continued. New actors appeared in stronger force, but in Congress, lawyer-staffers informed by bankruptcy specialists sat astride every formulation and modification of the law, whether in the House or Senate. In Britain, professional civil servants formulated the legislation in consultation with their ministers, neither of whom knew first-hand about insolvency practice. Senior civil servants later stood at the shoulder of their ministers, offering advice and alternative formulations, as the bill passed through various readings in the Lords and Commons.

Such an omnipresence does not guarantee substantive or administrative impact on the law, but it surely raises the strong possibility that pervasive expert presence left a significant imprint on the form and substance of the law. The nature of that imprint can best be observed by returning to the concepts of professional innovation raised in Chapter 2.

Professionals endorsed the *confirmation* in statutory law of numerous innovations they had spear-headed in everyday practice. The concepts of cramdown and setoff that had emerged in American practice, and had been accepted by some courts, now entered the statute with broader, clarified application. Retention of title, or Romalpa clauses, that had been accepted by some English courts, were now integrated in qualified form into insolvency statutes. And the emergence of a specialized circle of highly accomplished insolvency practitioners in English insolvency practice was codified and institutionalized within the framework of a newly created profession.

Pure *invention* also manifested itself through the creativity of professionals involved in the reforms. The newly created occupation of insolvency practitioners, while not entirely the creature of professionals, nevertheless bore the strong imprint of the leading practitioners who crafted the Cork Report. The Ten Percent Fund was an invention of two English lawyers. While not adopted, it nevertheless altered the course of English meta-bargaining and increased the pressure on banks to make concessions that would benefit weaker creditors. "Wrongful trading" sprung from the fertile minds of English barristers. So, too, did the notion of specialized Insolvency Courts, though that idea failed to convince the Government. Notions of "adequate protection" and "indubitable equivalents" similarly arose from the fertile imaginations of American lawyers and judges.

Statutory *sanction* or *repudiation* of practice was widely evident on either side of the Atlantic. When consolidating three chapters on corporate reorganization into one, the new US Code precluded "title shopping" among different sections of the bankruptcy act. Lawyers and accountants led the assault on the unfair practices of utilities to use their monopoly position in the market effectively to jump ahead of other creditors. And in England especially, creation of the new profession of insolvency practitioners, whose initiative professionals shared with the state, essentially repudiated the claims to work jurisdiction of some two-thirds of unqualified or occasional practitioners of liquidations before 1986.

Professionals employed the statutory reforms to *adjudicate* among conflicting practices or decisions that introduced uncertainty and regional variation into the application of the law. Where there are conflicts among judicial circuits or judges, a statute can make a determination that ends the confusion. One such example comes from the problems of American trade suppliers and their rights to reclaim goods. These had been recognized in some measure in the Uniform Commercial Code, they had been unevenly acknowledged in some bankruptcy courts, but they were clearly specified in the Bankruptcy Code.[4]

The intimate engagement of professionals permitted them to create and modify virtually all components of an operational legal regime: the doctrines that order a line of judicial determinations; the concepts that permit the law to regulate what previously had escaped it; the devices used to strike a bargain; occupational reconfigurations to balance pri-

---

[4] King in Collier on BR, S. 546(c). US Interview 94:11.

vate and public interests; and the administrative infrastructures of agencies, courts, and offices that are as inventive in their own way as new doctrines and forms of security.

These instances of innovation should not be understood as *à la carte* creations that stand alone. They manifest a much more telling attribute of professional involvement in the reforms. Just as professionals in everyday reorganizations seek to strike bargains or deals that will satisfy their clients, so, too, the professionals in meta-bargaining deployed their creative devices to strike meta-bargains. We have shown that professionals were one of the few political actors in these reforms to take a holistic view—to see the reforms as an integrated package that required careful balancing in order for it to be palatable. Unlike the politicians, who also had a "package" notion of what elements were needed to obtain passage of a bill, the professionals could use their expert creativity to invent new concepts, measures, devices, that would break through deadlocks and offer new ideas to ensure general agreement. In effect, professionals engaged in a kind of *expert diplomacy* which used invention to solve conflicts of interest and potential or actual breakdowns in negotiations. To be effective, professional diplomacy in meta-bargaining required a comprehensive understanding of all benefits and costs of each bill's provisions for each party, a sense of what extant concepts, ideas, and devices were adequate to permit a new balance, as well as the corollary, an awareness of danger points where extant concepts were not sufficient to bridge differences. Creativity by academics and practitioners offered the missing elements that could clinch a meta-bargain as a whole. In this guise, professions acted as agents of "meta-dealmaking." They did not do so alone, for politics is, after all, an occupation founded on political deals. But the desire for agreements suffices little without the means to achieve them. These professionals supplied out of all proportion to their prominence in the everyday practice of corporate reorganization.

Nevertheless, the pervasiveness of professional diplomacy and dealmaking raises two sets of vexing questions. If professionals are omnipresent, on whose account are they exerting influence? This raises the question of professional interests and orientations. And if professionals were ubiquitous in bankruptcy law, what does this tell us about their influence more generally in statutory law making? This raises the contingency of professional power.

Why were professionals so firmly committed to the business of saving business? There are two sorts of crude reductionism that would answer this question simplistically. One would postulate that professionals acted only in their material interests: the prospect of fees and wealth drove their involvement. A jurisdictional reductionism would posit that professionals acted more subtly to enlarge their jurisdictions of work, perhaps as steps towards higher status, more power, and greater gratification. Utilitarian motivations are clearly present, and utilitarian benefits of many sorts clearly resulted. But the evidence of this book demands a more complex account of orientations that played in often unpredictable and intriguing ways. These dispositions must be recognized if we hope to craft a realistic view of how and when professionals will engage in statutory law-making.

That professional *self-interests* were well served by this legislation cannot be disputed. The statutes themselves, and subsequent events, bear out predictions of occupational benefit. American bankruptcy lawyers vastly increased their fees and status. They got a new piece of legislation that opened up new avenues for highly creative application of bankruptcy law. American bankruptcy judges increased their fees, powers, and prestige. Federal judges blocked measures that might erode their singular prestige. English insolvency practitioners—or a fraction of them—got a monopoly and a larger stage on which to play. Innovations of all sorts paid handsome dividends of all sorts. But it is fallacious to extrapolate backwards from an outcome to an intent. The outcome merely provides one clue to one potential set of orientations that might have produced it.

In fact, irrespective of the intent, it would have been very difficult to institute new legal regimes to save businesses without aggrandizing professionals inside the state or the market. Bankruptcy regimes where workouts occur principally between creditors and debtors do exist, and in principle Britain and the US might have opted for such an alternative. But such a radical departure from practice and precedent could not have prevailed politically in either country. The change would have been too great, the unpredictability of radical revision too unsettling, even for those, like the banks, that might have benefitted most from it.

Closer examination of most central professional players in the reforms indicates that they personally stood to gain relatively little for they already stood at the apex of their professions. Distinguished law professors could not expect much more distinction. Leading practitioners could benefit only marginally given the high prestige and practice dominance they already possessed. Of course, association with a major piece of legislation that would frame practice for decades carries a substantial sense of satisfaction and any number of rewarding by-products, especially for younger practitioners involved in the reforms. But these do not explain very satisfactorily why practitioners and academics spent thousands of unremunerated hours over many years to produce new law. A cost-benefit analysis would surely demonstrate that senior practitioners with few years left to practice could never hope to recapture the opportunity costs of their time and resources freely-donated to bankruptcy reforms.

The interior life of professional practice, and its intrinsic satisfactions, account in significant measure for heavy professional commitment to the reform processes. Some arose from annoyances and frustrations of practice, as Kenneth Cork amply illustrated in his anger at the utility that destroyed equipment and a retrievable business when it arbitrarily turned off the power. Some commitment also arose from particular remedies that reformers envisaged for particular lapses of previous bankruptcy law in practice. Most non-instrumental commitment, however, flowed from quasi-aesthetic orientations that derived intrinsic satisfaction from systemic formulations of law that integrated coherent approaches to both individual and corporate bankruptcy.

More than any other participants, the central professional players in the reforms had in common a systemic view of bankruptcy law as a whole. They tried to understood the entire puzzle of the ways that several hundred sections and pages of statutory language, supplemented by even more rules, fitted together or not. In their private deliberations and public formulations they sensed how variations in the practice of one or another provision would throw out of balance a general solution or introduce distortions into effective implementation of law. Some significant part of their discussions took the form of mental experiments—trial efforts to think through the ramifications of abolishing floating charges in insolvency, rejecting retention of title, ridding the law of all state priorities, and abolishing setoff. By apprehending the "big picture," and in appreciating the interconnectedness of the myriad bits and pieces of bankruptcy law, professionals could in principle articulate and pursue a general interest, distinct from the parochial and particularistic interests of many of the other groups. Operating rather like the intelligentsia in Karl Mannheim's (1936) sociology of knowledge, professionals could subsume and synthesize the partial perspectives and narrow goals of specific interest groups, comprehending bankruptcy as a whole.

A sentiment of law-making craft suffused this process, an effort to solve problems by the most elegant, parsimonious means. This aesthetic of law reform approximates in some senses the design of an architect or a city planner—an effort to sketch in broad lines, and then offer precise specifications, for a coherent, and integrated solution to a general problem—in this case, rehabilitating business (and individual debtors). The concept of parsimony, and the search for elegant solutions, are well illustrated by reformers' efforts to unify individual and corporate bankruptcies, so far as possible, with similar underlying principles of accountability, responsibility, financial reconstruction, and the like. Thus for many reformers, the law-making offered an occasion to impose intellectual order, to dispel contradiction and inconsistency, and to formulate an efficient legal means to a desirable economic and social outcome.[5]

Bankruptcy and insolvency reform altered practice in ways that released creative professional solutions in everyday bargaining and deal-making. Practitioners chafe at rigid strictures that constrain their ingenuity for effective solutions. That rigidity can threaten professional practice, even at the top end, with routinization, repetition, and the commodification of professional work, all of which stifle intrinsically rewarding practice. The preference of these professionals for reorganization over the liquidation of companies, therefore, to a significant degree resulted from the ways that a rehabilitative regime unleashes professional creativity in everyday deal-making and bargaining. Professionals prefer reorganizations over liquidations of companies not merely because they create more work, but because reorganization makes the work they do more satisfying. As brokers among powerful corporate and state actors, professionals get to use their entrepreneurial sensibilities to strike new deals, forge new solutions, and balance the distribution of power in new economic arrangements. An effective structure put in place through meta-bargaining subsequently ramifies through everyday practice to increase the space for innovation.

Furthermore, the expanded resources and rehabilitative stage created by the bankruptcy law reforms casts professionals in a different mould, something particularly acute when the subject of work is the death of businesses. Corporate death still carries a stigma, and it carries it for professionals who preside over it, as well as for managers and directors who experience it. The aura of corporate reconstruction seems vastly

---

[5] Of course, no one believed they had been entirely successful, but they did believe they had made significant advances on all these criteria.

more palatable than the idea of corporate undertaking. But there is another dimension to the pull of law-making power. Much of professional work is preventive and defensive, and its success comes from non-events: tragedies that do not occur, contracts that do not unravel, businesses that do not collapse. Relatedly, a great deal of professional work is unpredictable in its consequences. Results are not guaranteed. Doctors do not promise a cure, but only their best efforts. Similarly, lawyers do not guarantee acquittals or massive damages, and accountants do not guarantee that audits will uncover every murky transaction. These indeterminacies, of course, are as much a matter of frustration for professionals as their clients (though in some circumstances they are also useful defenses and alibis).

Independent of the positive economic outcome, a law that encourages corporate rehabilitation turns many of these deficits of practice into assets. Turning a company around not only is heroic work, but it has a charismatic quality. It is offensive not defensive, constructive not destructive. It aligns professionals with life, not death, with business success, not failure. In addition, a turnaround has a constructive image. Unlike the invisibility of defensive lawyering or accounting, saving a business has a visibility that rewards risk, daring, and bold ventures. It can be measured, for success is revealed in operating funds and balance sheets. Saving a good sized company will be observed by financial analyst or reporter, granting to the corporate rescuer the status of public hero, and certainly helping to impress prospective clients.

If professionals in the reforms acted out of complex material, ideal, aesthetic, and status orientations on their own behalf, they might also be expected to *act as agents* on behalf of individual or corporate clients. Our evidence provides relatively few cases where professionals were engaged specifically as agents of clients, but there were several: a lobbyist for the bankruptcy judges, counsel for the Confederation of British Industry, counsel for American bankers. More commonly, lawyers and accountants appointed themselves as spokespersons for constituencies that were less well represented by trade associations or their proxies—the corporate debtors in the United States and the consumers in England.

Professional engagement in bankruptcy reforms possessed a civic element that must be recognized. It is true that when faced with problems of practice, or new ideals that should be realized in practice, professional-reformers reflected the power of their own socialization by formulating solutions consistent with their professionalized perspectives on the world. Lawyers produced legal options. Accountants sought autonomy from legal institutions. Judges welcomed discretion. It would be implausible to expect that the power of professional education, learning, and community would have them do any less. It is equally clear that some of the practitioners inside the reform circles empathized with the subjects of their law-making. Their moral sensibilities were offended by the exploitation of hapless consumer creditors. Their sense of equity was aggrieved by cavalier action from immensely powerful creditors that blithely destroyed businesses and lives without having to address the aftermath of their destruction. Their sense of institutional efficiency was offended by unnecessarily cumbersome and destructive procedures that inadvertently destroyed what might have been saved.

The bankruptcy reforms gave professionals statesmanlike capacities to construct reformed institutions in the public interest.[6] We can never entirely unravel the complex of professional orientations and view this as pure civic professionalism or as self-abnegating public service. Human motivations rarely allow such unalloyed depictions. But concepts of public service, market morality, equity, protection of the weak, and improvement of public institutions all infused discussions over systemic law-making. Nonetheless, this mix of orientations represents only the dispositional element of a larger complex of dynamics within and among professions that have not yet been integrated effectively into the new theories of institutionalization.

We proposed in Chapter 2 that a recursive theory of legal change and a dynamic theory of institutionalization demand an account of professional behavior that reflects recent innovations in theory and research on professions. The process of recursivity embeds innovation in power struggles between and among professions. One influential theory of professionalism breaks open a new agenda of inquiry by positing that many of the changes that occur *within* professions occur in response to changes *among* professions. That is, the system of professions approximates international relations among neighboring states with unstable boundaries. Larger states look to defend or extend their boundaries. Smaller states look to protect or expand their territory. Each uses resources they control to effect their ends. Permanent settlement of boundaries never happens because, for occupations, the territory of

---

[6] For an extended argument about lawyers as institution-builders, see Halliday (forthcoming).

work itself changes at the same time as resources to control that territory wax and wane.

When major statutes are revised, the terrain of work shifts. New work appears and old work disappears. In either case, occupations themselves are unsettled, and they face new threats and new opportunities. We anticipated therefore that changes in bankruptcy laws that had lain undisturbed for fifty or one hundred years would unleash a flurry of territorial disputes among and within professions. Those disputes might occur in three forms.

First, since there is no "natural" jurisdiction for which occupations should reorganize companies, and there are many potential jurisdictional claimants (lawyers, accountants, business consultants, turnaround specialists, bank workout specialists, civil servants), the bankruptcy reforms might have precipitated a scramble for rich occupational territory. That did not happen. In the United States, changes in the institutional parameters of corporate reorganization prompted virtually no change whatsoever in the broad claims to occupational territory that might have been contested between lawyers and accountants, investment bankers or civil servants. Accountants, who dominate English reorganizations, were entirely absent from the American reforms. Not a single major accounting firm or accounting peak association made any submissions to the Commission or Congress. And while bankers made it clear that they would much prefer their private workout units to reorganize companies well away from courts and lawyers, their preferences changed the law very little. There were only some modest shifts. Officials in the Securities and Exchange Commission lost work to lawyers and judges, creditors and debtors, who would now bargain freely over reorganizations without the heavy hand of officialdom.

In Britain, the law, after prodding from a government shy of monopoly, did institute a more open market for licensing as insolvency practitioners. Lawyers and even surveyors now had the legal right to become licensed insolvency practitioners and thereby invade the territory pervasively colonized by accountants. But subsequent events have shown it was a hollow victory, for very few lawyers compete with accountants for jurisdiction in the market. In some small measure their reluctance results not only from the lesser involvement in business of English solicitors, but also from the unveiled threats by accounting firms that they would not be doing legal business with lawyers or law firms that eroded their insolvency practices. In England, banks, too, had set up workout departments in order to turn companies around before insolvency. But these were not integrated directly into the law.

In both countries, therefore, this case of far-reaching legal change demonstrates how much more deeply entrenched divisions of labor can be in market relations than in state mandates. Well consolidated holdings of occupational territory were altered only at the margins by the law. And even when the law empowered some occupations to invade the territory previously controlled by others, market forces forestalled such incursions.

A second more subtle form of jurisdictional shift also appeared. Here the moves were between and among different institutional locations within occupational fields, where occupants shared similar training, similar knowledge bases, and similar procedural preferences. Lawyers and judges in Britain and the United States share common backgrounds of education, practice, and outlooks about how to order social and economic relations. Some considerable measure of occupational movement occurred between them. Work shifted from lawyers inside one government department to another, from the executive to the judiciary, and from lawyers in government agencies to lawyers in private practice. Slight shifts occurred between lawyers in the United States and judges, as a number of new and discretionary provisions built into the Code, such as "adequate protection," ensured that many bargains would be settled in court, which progressively would clarify and settle the law in practice. Similarly in Britain, Mrs Thatcher's Green Paper intended to move work from civil servants, who were often qualified accountants in the Insolvency Service, out into the private market for accounting services. The Act sought to keep high quality, more complex matters of regulation in the hands of civil servants and to export the remainder to the private sector.

The most visible conflict in this second form occurred in both countries over the same point: whether work should be shifted from professionals in the private market to professionals inside the state, or vice versa. The Bankruptcy Commission proposal to "nationalize" a great deal of mundane bankruptcy work, essentially by shifting it from private lawyers to lawyers in a new Bankruptcy Administration, met with stolid resistance from state officials and those private practitioners who would lose the work. The initiative failed. Similarly, the proposal to "privatize" much English public administration met with protests from the legal elites controlling the reform process. That initiative also failed. In short, when the forces of privatization and nationalization respectively confronted the heavily entrenched jurisdictions of powerful professionals, they both were brought to a halt, an indirect indicator of how deeply consolidated are the divisions of labor erected by decades of state and market institutionalization.

But the third, and by far the most conflictual, form of jurisdictional struggle occurred *within* professions, most notably between lower and higher status professionals. The status conflicts between lower and higher order American judges, between the bankruptcy judges and the federal court judges, became so vociferous and bitter that on more than one occasion they threatened to sabotage the entire legislation. Until the final moment of signing by the President, the Chief Justice waged his campaign to limit the status and power of bankruptcy judges. And the proposal to take mundane bankruptcy work away from lower prestige practitioners and lodge it inside the government was not merely a matter of administrative efficiency, but a form of status politics that would have extinguished most of the ill-reputed bankruptcy ring.

If the American struggles among different status groups of judges may be labelled a *professional conflict of incorporation*, the British case can be designated a *professional conflict of exclusion*. Yet so thoroughly did elite lawyers and accountants dominate the English reforms, and so effectively did they align their recommendations with the interest of the government in clean, competent markets, that their initiative to exclude lower end professionals from the market for insolvency services went virtually unnoticed. The English reforms, we have seen, created a new profession. But its licensing requirement demanded that future practitioners either surmount a hurdle of further education, or prove their competence by demonstrating they had devoted a very substantial proportion of their practice to insolvency work over several years. These dual provisions, in a bid for quality and probity, drove out of the market approximately two-thirds of the practitioners who had done some insolvency work before the new Act. While it may have gone some distance to producing a more experienced, proficient, and accountable group of practitioners, the statutory move should not disguise its effective banishment from the occupational field of a majority of those at the lower end of practice who had previously worked in it.[7]

---

[7] It should be recognized that although a majority of practitioners may not have subsequently been licensed under the new Act, they accounted for a substantial minority of the volume of work, since insolvency work itself was highly concentrated in a relatively small number of insolvency and accounting firms.

In both cases, therefore, the legislative opportunity precipitated precisely the politics of exclusion and usurpation identified by Frank Parkin (1979) and it is this picture of internal professional struggle that better accounts for the main lines of conflict than the jurisdictional theory of Andrew Abbott. In the United States, statutory disturbance encouraged lower status judges to bid for upward status mobility and thus to join the circles of higher status professionals, a move that triggered an equal or greater reaction by high status judges to maintain their distance from lower status professionals. In Britain the innovations emerging from the committee rooms of English reformers were innovations of an elite group of accountants and lawyers. That innovative endeavor they used to banish part-timers from the market.

Most of these jurisdictional impulses were conducive to specialization. The banishment of part-timers and generalists from the English market for legal services concentrated practice far more heavily in the hands of a much smaller group. The upward mobility project of American bankruptcy judges did not gain them the lifetime appointments of Article III judges, but fifteen year appointments concentrated expertise in the hands of a few who circulated back and forth between legal practice at a much reduced rate.

As we predicted in Chapter 2, fragile settlements of bitter jurisdictional disputes, even if they are institutionalized in statutory law, can produce instability, thus sowing the seeds for another cycle of law-making. When the Supreme Court of the United States struck down the political settlement of Article I and Article III judges in the Bankruptcy Code, it precipitated a legal crisis that in turn forced another legislative round. Again, it was internecine warfare, not cross-border confrontations, that disturbed the jurisdictional peace.

The naked realism of politics and power, conflict and self-interested struggle within segmented professions dispel roseate depictions of professional influence as unified, selfless displays of expert ingenuity in pursuit of the common good. Neither picture bears much resemblance to human social behavior. In fact, certain private advantages—more competency, more specialization, higher status, broader powers, greater discretion, bigger salaries—arguably yield better public goods. More efficient administrative procedures, more powerful courts, more skilful lawyers and accountants help increase the probability of rescuing businesses within legal frameworks. The upward status mobility project of lawyers and judges may therefore be harnessed to deliver a public good.

Arguably the exclusionary status politics of English reformers might also have yielded a public good.

In many respects, therefore, the statutes that resulted from the English and US reforms represented a mutual accomodation of private and public interest. Practitioners of all sorts had jurisdictional interests, and many of these were appropriated by the state into legal forms. States and governments had their own imperatives and policy commitments which they harnessed to the mobilization of private energies by professionals. Woven through all, therefore, was an amalgam of public and private, status and material, civic and selfish orientations that stimulated innovation, demanded diplomacy, and ultimately altered the landscape of property and jurisdictional rights.

Finally, it should be observed that the statutory outcomes of this recursive process are contingent on identifiable particularities. Our portrait of professional influence in meta-bargaining applies under specific circumstances. Powerful, well-established and well-organized professions, will succeed more readily in maintaining jurisdictional boundaries favorable to their elites, or expanding jurisdictional boundaries, than younger, less established, less politically sophisticated professions. Further, professions will generally fare better, and place a more discernible imprint on the law, when the reforms themselves are perceived to be highly technical and non-controversial. Repair, modernization, and adaptation are defensive screens that keep many powerful political actors at bay. Professional influence waxes when legislation itself has not been recently framed in ways that invoke conventional lines of economic or political conflict. Since many major political players did not see how bankruptcy reforms might relate to their interests, they stayed away and left change to the experts. Furthermore, the power of professions can be immeasurably enhanced if it can be yoked to political ideology or state interest. When private professional interests demonstrably yielded desirable public goods, then the public and private could co-opt each other to mutual benefit. But the fact that *particular* private parties and *particular* public authorities negotiated these changes meant that the results did not favor all public and private actors equally.

SHAPING ORGANIZATIONAL FIELDS THROUGH LAW

We have introduced a new concept of inter-corporate power. It overlaps with some prevailing views, for we conceive of corporate actors—banks and non-financial industry—in a network of financial relationships where control over resources affects the distribution of power in the network. But we have shown that the distribution of corporate power requires two additional conceptual elements.

The firm is more than a nexus of contracts, and the organizational field is more than a network of corporations. Bankruptcy reforms exposed all actors in the field of inter-corporate power and revealed the multiplicity of their relations with each other. Some of the conventionally invisible players of the organizational field lay out of view, but could be mobilized in either bargaining or meta-bargaining. On one side are the massive stakeholders of the state and communities; and on the other are the disaggregated stakeholders of individual consumers and investors. Whether owners or creditors, these parties also exert control over the fortunes of corporations, forms of control that become manifest in individual bankruptcies, and even more manifest in meta-bargaining.

These members of the credit network are bound to each other through flows of capital, but the legal structure of the content of the flow is as important as the volume. The structure of security determines the legally prescribed distributions of ownership and control that regulate the flow of capital in the ordinary course of business and at the extremes of liquidation and reorganization. These legal devices take many forms. Some result from freely negotiated contracts. Others are liens imposed by a court. Yet others are inscribed in statutes as priorities or doctrinal standards. The distribution of power in the credit network, therefore, depends on the legal entailment of capital, on the conditions under which it can move, be seized, or be used by one party or another. To characterize relations among corporations in terms of flows of capital without taking into account the structure of security and the complex of property rights it enacts, distorts the depiction of power. Flows of capital and assets, therefore, are "legalized." As measures of power they only make sense when the rights that are attached to their use and control are also delineated. And those rights are inscribed in law, negotiated in contracts, decided in cases, and mandated by statute. Inter-corporate movements of capital and assets flow along channels controlled by law and embodied in forms of security.

The structure of power in organizational fields derives from the legally prescribed distribution of rights over capital and other assets. Since that regime of property rights ultimately is constituted by the state, organizational fields are embedded in legal fields. It is not possible to comprehend exchanges of resources among organizations, patterns of competition in the ecology of the market, or the diffusion of organizational forms without comprehension of the state's active agency or passive framing of apparently autonomous market activity. This premiss we share with neo-institutional theory.

But the constitution of economic and organizational activity by the state itself demands explanation. Part of that explanation can be found in the politics of meta-bargaining, and in areas such as bankruptcy law it is the dynamics of jurisdictional fields—the politics of professions—that influences significantly how state law will constitute the organizational field. Thus organizational fields are flanked by recursive processes that link professional practice to statutory enactment. The system of property rights that regulates credit flows comes to be constituted through the jurisdictional processes we have observed in the bankruptcy reforms. Configurations of inter-corporate power, therefore, are configurations of property rights constituted by legal fields out of meta-bargaining. Bargaining over property rights is linked inseparably with the settlements of jurisdictional rights forged by professions in the market and politics respectively.

Bibliography

PRIMARY ARCHIVAL SOURCES

The Bankruptcy Reform Act (Part 1), Hearings on S. 235 and S. 236 before the Subcommittee on Improvements in Judicial Machinery of the Senate Judiciary Committee, 94th Cong., 1st Sess. (1975).

Bankruptcy Act Revision (Part 4), Hearings on H.R. 31 and H.R. 32 before the Subcommittee on Civil and Constitutional Rights of the House Committee on the Judiciary, 94th Cong., 2nd Sess. (1976).

Bankruptcy Reform Act of 1978, Hearings on S. 2266 and H.R. 8200 before the Subcommittee on Improvements in Judicial Machinery of the Senate Committee on the Judiciary, 95th Cong., 1st Sess. (1978).

Department of Trade and Industry. 1984. A Revised Framework for Insolvency Law. London: HMSO. Cmnd. 9175. Cited as the *Government White Paper.*

House of Commons Parliamentary Debates. Standing Committee E. 1985. Insolvency Bill [Lords]. London: HMSO.

Minutes of the Commission on the Bankruptcy Laws of the United States. M. Caldwell Butler Papers. Washington and Lee University School of Law Library, Lexington, Virginia.

Minutes of the Insolvency Law Review Committee. 1977–1982. Chicago: American Bar Foundation.

Papers, Insolvency Law Review Committee. Public Record Office. File BT 260. Kew, London.

Report of the Commission on the Bankruptcy Laws of the United States. 1973. Washington, DC: US Government Printing Office.

Report of the Insolvency Law Review Committee. 1982. Insolvency Law and Practice. London: HMSO. Cmnd. 8558. Cited as *The Cork Report.*

SECONDARY SOURCES

Aaron, Richard I. (1980) "The Bankruptcy Reform Act of 1978: The Full-Employment-for-Lawyers Bill: Overview and Legislative History," *Corporate Practice Commentator,* 22 (2): 201.

Abbott, Andrew (1981) "Status and Status Strain in the Professions," *American Journal of Sociology.* 86: 819–35.

——(1988) *The System of Professions: An Essay on the Division of Expert Labor,* Chicago: University of Chicago Press.

Abel, Richard (1981) "Toward a Political Economy of Lawyers," *Wisconsin Law Review*, 1117–87.

—— (1988) "Lawyers in the Civil Law World," in *Lawyers in Society: The Civil Law World*, R. Abel and P. S. C. Lewis (eds.) Berkeley: University of California Press, 1–53.

—— (1988) *The Legal Profession in England and Wales*, Oxford: Basil Blackwell.

—— (1989) *American Lawyers*, New York: Oxford.

Abowd, John M. (1990) "Does Performance-Based Managerial Compensation Affect Corporate Performance?" *Industrial and Labor Relations Review* 43: 52S–73S.

Adler, Barry E. (1993) "Financial and Political Theories of American Corporate Bankruptcy," *Stanford Law Review* 45: 311–46.

Aghion, Philippe, Oliver Hart and John Moore (1994) "Improving Bankruptcy Procedure," *Washington University Law Quarterly* 72: 849–72.

Alchian, Armen A. and Harold Demsetz (1973) "The Property Rights Paradigm," *Journal of Economic History* 33: 16–27.

Alexander, Willard and Gerald R. Downey Jr. (1988) "Handling Problem Loans," in *The Bankers' Handbook*, William H. Baughn, Thomas I. Storrs and Charles E. Walker (eds.) Homewood, Ill.: Dow Jones-Irwin.

Altman, Edward I. (1993) *Corporate Financial Distress and Bankruptcy*, (2nd edn.) New York: John Wiley and Sons.

Ang, James S. and William L. Megginson (1989) "Restricted Voting Shares, Ownership Structure, and the Market Value of Dual-Class Firms," *Journal of Financial Research* 12(4): 301–318.

Arnull, Anthony M. (1984) "Crown Set-off in Liquidations and Receiverships," *The Law Society's Gazette* 81(6): 417–18.

Åslund, Anders (1995) *How Russia Became a Market Economy*, Washington DC: Brookings Institute.

Auerbach, Jerald A. (1976) *Unequal Justice*, New York: Oxford University Press.

Bacon, Richard L. and James L. Billinger (1979) "Analyzing the Operation and Tax Effects of the New Bankruptcy Act," *Journal of Taxation* 50(2): 76–80.

Baird, Douglas G. and Thomas H. Jackson (1990) *Cases, Problems, and Materials on Bankruptcy*, (2nd edn.) Boston: Little, Brown.

Baron, James, F. Dobbin and P. D. Jennings (1986) "War and Peace: The Evolution of Modern Personnel Administration in U.S. Industry," *American Journal of Sociology* 92: 350–83.

Barzel, Yoram (1989) *Economic Analysis of Property Rights*, Cambridge: Cambridge University Press.

Beardsley, James (1985) "The New French Bankruptcy Statute," *International Lawyer*, 19: 973.

Becker, Stephen (1981) "The Bankruptcy Law's Effect on Collective Bargaining Agreements," *Columbia Law Review*, 81: 391–409.

Begin, James P. and Edwin F. Beal (1985) *The Practice of Collective Bargaining*, (7th edn.) Homewood Ill.: Richard D. Irwin.

Bell, Daniel (1989) *The Coming of the Post-Industrial Society*, New York: Basic Books.

Benzie, A. (1983) "Rights of Employees in Corporate Insolvencies," *Law Notes*, 102: 301–4.

Berlant, J. L. (1975) *Profession and Monopoly: A Study of Medicine in the United Sates and Great Britain*, Berkeley: University of California Press.

Berle, Adolph A. and Gardner Means (1932) *The Modern Corporation and Private Property*, New York: Macmillan.

Bernstein, Lisa (1992) "Opting Out of the Legal System: Extralegal Contractual Relations in the Diamond Industry," *Journal of Legal Studies*, 21: 115–57.

Betker, Brian L. (1995) "Management's Incentives, Equity's Bargaining Power, and Deviations from Absolute Priority in Chapter 11 Bankruptcies," *Journal of Business*, 68: 161–83.

Bien, David D. (1995) "Property in office under the *ancien régime*: The case of the stockbrokers," in *Early Modern Conceptions of Property*, John Brewer and Susan Staves, (eds.) London: Routledge.

Black, Donald (1977) *The Behavior of Law*, New York: Academic Press.

Blackstone, Sir William (1979) [1766] *Commentaries on the Laws of England*, Vol. 2, Chicago: University of Chicago Press.

Blair, Margaret M. (1995) *Ownership and Control*, Washington DC: Brookings Institute.

Block, Fred (1987) *Revising State Theory*, Philadelphia: Temple University Press.

Bordewieck, Douglas and Vern Countryman (1983) "The Rejection of Collective Bargaining Agreements by Chapter 11 Debtors," *American Bankruptcy Law Journal*, 57: 293–337.

Borenstein, Severin (1992) "The Evolution of U.S. Airline Competition," *Journal of Economic Perspectives*, 6: 45–73.

Borrie, Sir Gordon (1984) "The Professions: Expensive Monopolies of Guardians of the Public Interest?" *Journal of Business Law*: 11–25.

Bosk, Charles L. (1979) *Forgive and Remember: Managing Medical Failure*, Chicago: University of Chicago Press.

Bourdieu, Pierre (1987) "The Force of Law: Toward a Sociology of the Juridical Field," *The Hastings Law Journal*, 38: 201–38.

Bradley, Michael and Michael Rosenzweig (1992) "The Untenable Case for Chapter 11," *Yale Law Journal*, 101: 1043–95.

Braithwaite, John (1989) *Crime, Shame and Reintegration*, New York: Cambridge University Press.

Bratton, William W. (1984) "The Interpretation of Contracts Governing Corporate Debt Relationships," *Cardozo Law Review*, 5: 371–407.

Brealey, Richard and Stewart Myers (1984) *Principles of Corporate Finance*, (2nd edn.) New York: McGraw-Hill.

Brint, Steven (1990) "Rethinking the Policy Influence of Experts: From General Charaterizations to Analysis of Variation," *Sociological Forum*, 5: 361–85.

—— (1994) *In an Age of Experts: The Changing Role of Professionals in Politics and Public Life*, Princeton, NJ: Priceton University Press.

Broude, Richard F. (1984) "Cramdown and Chapter 11 of the Bankruptcy Code: The Settlement Imperative," *The Business Lawyer*, 39: 441–54.

Browning, Graeme (1984) "Using Bankruptcy to Reject Labor Contracts," *American Bar Association Journal*, 70: 60–3.

Bucher, Rue, and Anselm Strauss (1963) "Professions in Process," *American Journal of Sociology*, 66: 325–34.

Budnitz, Mark E. (1990) "Chapter 11 Business Reorganizations and Share-holder Meetings: Will the Meeting Please Come to Order, or Should the Meeting be Cancelled Altogether?" *The George Washington Law Review*, 58: 1214–67.

Butler, M. Caldwell (1980) "A Congressman's Reflections on the Drafting of the Bankruptcy Code of 1978," *William and Mary Law Review*, 21: 557–74.

Campagna, Anthony S. (1995) *Economic Policy in the Carter Administration*, West-port, Conn.: Greenwood.

Campbell, John L. and Leon N. Lindberg (1990) "Property Rights and the Organization of Economic Activity by the State," *American Sociological Review*, 55: 634–47.

Campbell, Steve (1994) "Brother, Can You Spare a Ruble? The Development of Bankruptcy Legislation in the New Russia," *Bankruptcy Developments Journal*, 10: 343–95.

Carruthers, Bruce and Wendy Espeland (1991) "Accounting for Rationality: Double-Entry Bookkeeping and the Rhetoric of Economic Rationality," *American Journal of Sociology*, 97: 31–69.

—— and Terence C. Halliday (1990) "The Politics of Temporality: Agenda Setting in United States and English Bankruptcy Law," presented at the annual meeting of the American Sociological Association, Washington DC, August.

Chambliss, William J. (1964) "Sociological Analysis of the Law of Vagrancy," *Social Problems*, 12: 67–77.

—— (1982) *Law, Order, and Power*, Reading, Mass.: Addison-Wesley.

—— (1993) "On Lawmaking," in *Making Law: The State, the Law, and Structural Contradictions*, William J. Chambliss and Marjorie S. Zatz (eds.) Bloomington: Indiana University Press.

Christman, John (1994) "Distributive Justice and the Complex Structure of Ownership," *Philosophy and Public Affairs*, 23: 225–50.

Coase, R. H. (1960) "The Problem of Social Cost," *Journal of Law and Economics*, 3: 1–44.

Coffee, John C. Jr. (1988) "Shareholders Versus Managers," in *Knights, Raiders, and Targets: The Impact of the Hostile Takeover*, John C. Coffee Jr., Louis Lowenstein, and Susan Rose-Ackerman (eds.) New York: Oxford University Press.

——(1991) "Liquidity Versus Control: The Institutional Investor as Corporate Monitor," *Columbia Law Review*, 91: 1277–368.

Collins, Randall (1979) *The Credential Society: An Historical Sociology of Education and Stratification*, New York: Academic Press.

Connor, David E. and Ralph N. Kent (1986) "Secured Lending," in *The Loan Officer's Handbook*. William J. Korsvik and Charles O. Meiburg (eds.) Homewood, Ill.: Dow Jones-Irwin.

Coogan, Peter F., Richard Broude and Herman Glatt (1975) "Comments on Some Reorganization Provisions of the Pending Bankruptcy Bills," *Business Lawyer*, 30: 1149–80.

Cork, Kenneth (1988) *Cork on Cork: Sir Kenneth Cork takes Stock*, London: Mac-Millan.

Countryman, Vern (1971) "Code Security Interests in Bankruptcy," *Uniform Commercial Code Law Journal*, 4: 35–63.

——(1973) "Executory Contracts in Bankruptcy: Part I," *Minnesota Law Review*, 57: 439–91.

——(1974) "Executory Contracts in Bankruptcy: Part II," *Minnesota Law Review*, 58: 479–567.

——(1985) "Scrambling to Define Bankruptcy Jurisdiction: The Chief Justice, the Judicial Conference, and the Legislative Process," *Harvard Journal of Legislation*, 22: 1–45.

Cyr, Conrad K. (1975) "Setting the Record Straight For A Comprehensive Revision of the Bankruptcy Act of 1898," *American Bankruptcy Law Journal*, 49: 99–171.

Davies, Iwan (1985) " 'Romalpa' Clauses and Recent Developments—I," *Solicitors' Journal*, 129: 3–5.

Delaney, Kevin J. (1989) "Power, Intercorporate Networks, and Strategic Bankruptcy," *Law and Society Review*, 23: 643–66.

——(1992) *Strategic Bankruptcy: How Corporations and Creditors Use Chapter 11 to Their Advantage*, Berkeley: University of California Press.

——(1994) "Legal Innovation in Bankruptcy: The Role of Elite Corporate Lawyers," Paper presented at the annual meeting of the American Sociological Association, Los Angeles, August.

——(1996) "Veiled Politics: Bankruptcy as a Structured Organizational Field," *American Behavioral Scientist*, 39: 1025–39.

Demsetz, Harold (1967) "Toward a Theory of Property Rights," *American Economic Review*, 57: 347–59.

Derthick, Martha and Paul J. Quirk (1985) *The Politics of Deregulation*, Washington DC: Brookings Institution.

Dezalay, Yves (1992) *Marchands de Droit*, Paris: Fayard.

DiMaggio, Paul and Walter W. Powell (1983) "The Iron Cage Revisited: Institutional Isomorphism and Collective Rationality in Organizational Fields," *American Sociological Review*, 48: 147–60.

———— (1991) "The Iron Cage Revisited: Institutional Isomorphism and Collective Rationality in Organizational Fields" in *The New Institutionalism in Organizational Analysis*, W. W. Powell, P. J. DiMaggio (eds.) Chicago: University of Chicago Press.

Dine, Janet (1991*a*) "Quasi-Criminal Law: Fraudulent, Reckless and Wrongful Trading," Paper presented at the W. G. Hart Legal Workshop, Institute of Advanced Legal Studies, London, July 1991.

——(1991*b*) "Disqualification of Directors," *Company Law*, 12: 6.

Dobbin, Frank, Lauren Edelman, John W. Meyer and W. Richard Scott (1988) "The Expansion of Due Process in Organizations," in *Institutional Patterns in Organizations*, Lynn G. Zucker (ed.) Cambridge: Ballinger.

——, John R. Sutton, John W. Meyer and W. Richard Scott (1993) "Equal Opportunity Law and the Construction of Internal Labor Markets," *American Journal of Sociology*, 99: 396–427.

————(1994) "Equal Opportunity Law and the Construction of Internal Labor Markets," in *Institutional Environments and Organizations*, W. R. Scott and J. W. Meyer (eds.) London: Sage. 272–300.

Dodd, E. Merrick (1938) "The Securities and Exchange Commission's Reform Program for Bankruptcy Reorganizations," *Columbia Law Review*, 38: 223–55.

Douglas-Hamilton, Margaret H. (1975) "Creditor Liabilities Resulting from Improper Interference with the Management of a Financially Troubled Debtor," *The Business Lawyer*, 31: 343–65.

Edelman, Lauren (1990) "Legal Environments and Organizational Governance: The Expansion of Due Process in the American Workplace," *American Journal of Sociology*, 95: 1401–40.

——(1992) "Legal Ambiguity and Symbolic Structures: Organizational Mediation of Civil Rights Law," *American Journal of Sociology*, 97: 1531–76.

——, Steven E. Abraham, and Howard Erlanger (1992) "Professional Construction of Law: The Inflated Threat of Wrongful Discharge," *Law and Society Review*, 26: 47–84.

——, Stephen Petterson, Elizabeth Chambliss, and Howard S. Erlanger (1991) "Legal Ambiguity and the Politics of Compliance: Affirmative Action Officers' Dilemma," *Law and Policy*, 13: 73–97.

Eggertsson, Thráinn (1990) *Economic Behavior and Institutions*, Cambridge: Cambridge University Press.

Esping-Anderson, Gøsta (1990) *The Three Worlds of Welfare Capitalism*, Princeton: Princeton University Press.

Farrar, J. H. (1983) "The Reform of Insolvency Law—III," *Journal of Business Law*, Sept.: 424–30.

Field, Barry (1989) "The Evolution of Property Rights," *Kyklos*, 42: 319–45.

Finletter, Thomas K. (1939) *The Law of Bankruptcy Reorganization*, Charlottesville: Michie.

Flaschen, Evan D. and Timothy B. DeSieno (1992) "The Development of Insolvency Law as Part of the Transition from a Centrally Planned to a Market Economy," *The International Lawyer*, 26: 671.

Fletcher, Ian F. (1981) "Bankruptcy Law Reform: the Interim Report of the Cork Committee, and the Department of Trade Green Paper," *Modern Law Review*, 44: 77–87.

——(1984) "Insolvency Law Reform: The White Paper Proposals," *Journal of Business Law*, July: 304–7.

——(1993) "International Insolvency: A Case for Study and Treatment," *The International Lawyer*, 27(2): 429–43.

Fligstein, Neil (1985) "The Spread of the Multidivisional Form Among Large Firms, 1919–1979," *American Sociological Review*, 50: 377–91.

——(1990) *The Transformation of Corporate Control*, Cambridge, Mass.: Harvard University Press.

Flynn, Leo (1991) "Quasi-Criminal Law: Fraudulent, Reckless and Wrongful Trading," Paper presented at the W. G. Hart Legal Workshop, Institute of Advanced Legal Studies, London, July 1991.

Francis, Merrill R. (1974) "The Commercial Secured Creditor and the Bankruptcy Act of 1973," *Journal of Commercial Bank Lending*, 56: 2–6.

Freeman, Burton M. (1980) "Setoff Under the New Bankruptcy Code: The Effect on Bankers," *Banking Law Journal*, 97: 484–523.

Freidson, Eliot (1970) *Professional Dominance: The Structure of Medical Care*, Chicago: University of Chicago Press.

Friedman, M. (1962) *Capitalism and Freedom*, Chicago: University of Chicago Press.

Galanter, Marc and Thomas Palay (1991) *Tournament of Lawyers: The Growth and Transformation of the Large Law Firms*, Chicago: University of Chicago Press.

Gamble, Andrew (1988) "Privatization, Thatcherism, and the British State," *Journal of Law and Society*, 16: 1–20.

——(1994) *The Free Economy and the Strong State: The Politics of Thatcherism*, 2nd edn., Hampshire, NJ: MacMillan.

Gilboy, Janet (1992a) "Penetrability of Administrative Systems: Political 'Casework' and Immigration Inspections," *Law and Society Review*, 26(2): 273–314.

——(1992b) "On Government Use of Private Resources in Law Enforcement," Unpublished paper, American Bar Foundation.

Gilson, Stuart C. (1989) "Management Turnover and Financial Distress," *Journal of Financial Economics*, 25: 241–62.

——(1990) "Bankruptcy, boards, banks, and blockholders: Evidence on changes in corporate ownership and control when firms default," *Journal of Financial Economics*, 27: 355–87.

Gilson, Stmart C. and Michael R. Vetsuypens (1994) "Creditor Control in Financially Distressed Firms: Empirical Evidence," *Washington University Law Quarterly*, 72: 1005–25.

Girth, Marjorie (1975) "Prospects for Structural Reform of the Bankruptcy System," *California Law Review*, 63: 1546–62.

Glasberg, Davita Silfen (1989) *The Power of Collective Purse Strings*, Berkeley: University of California Press.

Glyn, Andrew (1995) "Stability, inegalitarianism, and stagnation: an overview of the advanced capitalist countries in the 1980s," in *Macroeconomic Policy After the Conservative Era*, Gerald A. Epstein and Herbert M. Gintis (eds.) Cambridge: Cambridge University Press.

——, Alan Hughes, Alain Lipietz and Ajit Singh (1990) "The Rise and Fall of the Golden Age," in *The Golden Age of Capitalism: Reinterpreting the Postwar Experience*, Stephen Marglin and Juliet Schor (eds.) Oxford: Clarendon Press.

Glynn, Sean and Alan Booth (1996) *Modern Britain: An Economic and Social History*, London: Routledge.

Goldfield, Michael (1987) *The Decline of Organized Labor in the United States*, Chicago: University of Chicago Press.

Goode, Roy (1983) "Creditors' Rights: The Cork Report," *The Company Lawyer*, 4(2): 51–5.

——(1990) *Principles of Corporate Insolvency Law*, London: Sweet and Maxwell.

Goode, W. J. (1957) "Community Within a Community: The Professions," *American Sociological Review*, 22: 194–200.

Goodman, John (1984) *Employment Relations in Industrial Society*, Oxford: Philip Allan.

Gordon, Robert W. (1983) "Legal Thought and Legal Practice in the Age of American Enterprise, 1870–1920," in Geison, Gerald L., (ed.) *Professions and Professional Ideologies in America*, Chapel Hill: University of North Carolina Press.

——(1984) "The Ideal and the Actual: Fantasies and Practices of New York Lawyers, 1870–1890," in *The New High Priests: Lawyers in Post Civil War America*, Gerard W. Gawalt (ed.) Westport, Conn.: Greenwood, 51–74.

——(1985) "Macaulay, MacNeil, and the Discovery of Solidarity and Power in Contract Law," *Wisconsin Law Review*, 1985: 565–79.

——(1995) "Paradoxical Property," in *Early Modern Conceptions of Property*, John Brewer and Susan Staves (eds.) London: Routledge.

Gregory, David (1984) "Labor Contract Rejection in Bankruptcy," *Boston College Law Review*, 25: 539–608.

Grierson, Gary C. (1985) "The U.S. and Canadian Reorganization Experience—A Comparison," *Commercial Law Journal*, 90: 41–8.

Grimmig, Robert J. (1986) "Handling Problem Loans," in *The Loan Officer's Handbook*, William J. Korsvik and Charles O. Meiburg (eds.) Homewood, Ill.: Dow Jones-Irwin.

Hall, Jerome (1952) *Theft, Law and Society*, Indianapolis: Bobbs-Merrill.

Hall, Peter A. (1992) "The Movement from Keynesianism to Monetarism: Institutional Analysis and British Economic Policy in the 1970s," in *Structuring Politics*, Sven Steinmo, Kathleen Thelen, and Frank Longstreth (eds.) Cambridge: Cambridge University Press.

Halliday, Terence C. (1982) "The Idiom of Legalism in Bar Politics: Lawyers, McCarthyism, and the Civil Rights Era," *American Bar Foundation Research Journal*, 982 (Fall): 911–89.

—— (1985) "Knowledge Mandates: Collective Influence by Scientific, Normative and Syncretic Professions," *British Journal of Sociology*, xxxvi: 421–47.

—— (1987) *Beyond Monopoly: Lawyers, State Crises, and Professional Empowerment*, Chicago: University of Chicago Press.

—— (1989) "Legal Professions and Politics: Neocorporatist Variations on the Pluralist Theme of Liberal Democracies," in *Lawyers in Society: Comparative Theories*, R. L. Abel and P. S. C. Lewis (eds.) Berkeley: University of California Press, 375–426.

—— (Forthcoming) "Lawyers as Institution-builders: Constructing Markets, States, Civil Society and Community," in *Crossing Boundaries: Tradition and Transformation in Law and Society Research*, Austin Sarat (ed.), Evanston: Northwestern University Press.

—— and Bruce G. Carruthers (1992) "Professionalization and the Moral Regulation of Markets: The Politics of the English Insolvency Act 1985," American Bar Foundation Working Paper, #9310.

—— (1993*a*) "The Redistribution of Property and Jurisdictional Rights across the Public–Private Frontier: Professions and Bankrutpcy Reforms in Britain and the United States," *Droit et Société: Revue Internationale de Théorie du Droit et de Sociologie Juridique*, 23/24: 79–113.

—— (1993*b*). "Making the Courts Safe for the Powerful: The Politics of Lawyers, Judges, and Bankers in the 1978 Rehabilitation of United States Bankruptcy Courts," Paper presented to a conference on Lawyers and the Rise of Political Liberalism, Onati International Institute for the Sociology of Law.

—— —— (1996) "The Moral Regulation of Markets: Professions, Privatization and the English Insolvency Act 1986," *Accounting, Organizations and Society*, 21(4): 371–413.

—— and Lucien Karpik (1998) "Politics Matter: A New Framework for the Comparative and Historical Study of Legal Professions," in *Lawyers and the Rise of Western Political Liberalism: Legal Professions and the Constitution of Modern Politics*, Terence C. Halliday and Lucien Karpik (eds.), Oxford University Press, Oxford and New York.

—— —— and Scott Parrott (1992) "Legislating Corporate Failure: The Structure of Security and the Politics of Corporate Reorganization in Britain and the United States," American Bar Foundation Working Paper, #9311.

Halliday, Terence C. M. J. Powell, M. W. Granfors (1987) "Minimalist Organizations: Vital Events in State Bar Associations, 1870–1930," *American Sociological Review*, 52 (August): 456–71.

———————(1993) "After Minimalism: Transformations of State Bar Associations From Market to State Reliance, 1918–1950," *American Sociological Review*, 58 (August): 515–35.

Halpern, Sydney A. (1992) "Dynamics of Professional Control: Internal Coalitions and Crossprofessional Boundaries," *American Journal of Sociology*, 97: 994–1021.

Hay, Douglas (1975) "Property, Authority and Criminal Law," in *Albion's Fatal Tree*, Hay D., Linebaugh, P., and Thompson, E. P. (eds.) Pantheon Books, 17–63.

Heimer, Carol A. (1995) "Explaining Variation in the Impact of Law: Organizations, Institutions, and Professions," *Studies in Law, Politics, and Society*, 15(1): 29–59.

Heinz, John P., Robert W. Gettleman, and Morris A. Seeskin (1969) "Legislative Politics and the Criminal Law," *Northwestern University Law Review*, 64: 277.

——and E. O. Laumann (1982) *Chicago Lawyers: The Social Structure of the Bar*, New York: Russell Sage.

Herman, Edward S. (1981) *Corporate Control, Corporate Power*, Cambridge: Cambridge University Press.

Hermann, Donald H. J. and David M. Neff (1985) "Rush to Judgement: Congressional Response to Judicial Recognition of Rejection of Collective Bargaining Agreements Under Chapter 11 of the Bankruptcy Code," *Arizona Law Review*, 27: 617–52.

Hirschman, Albert O. (1970) *Exit, Voice and Loyalty*, Cambridge: Harvard University Press.

Ho, Thomas S. Y. and Ronald F. Singer (1982) "Bond Indenture Provisions and the Risk of Corporate Debt," *Journal of Financial Economics*, 10: 375–406.

Homan, Mark (1987) *A Survey of Administrations under the Insolvency Act 1986: The Results of Administration Orders made in 1987*, Price Waterhouse for the Institute of Chartered Accountants.

Hoover, Kenneth and Raymond Plant (1989) *Conservative Capitalism in Britain and the United States: A Critical Appraisal*, London: Routledge.

Hoyle, R. W. (1992) "Disafforestation and drainage: the Crown as entrepreneur?" in *The Estates of the English Crown 1558–1640*, R. W. Hoyle (ed.) Cambridge: Cambridge University Press.

Jackson, Thomas H (1986) *The Logic and Limits of Bankruptcy Law*, Cambridge: Harvard University Press.

——and Anthony T. Kronman (1979) "Secured Financing and Priorities Among Creditors," *Yale Law Journal*, 88: 1143–82.

Joseph, Keith (1976) *Monetarism is not Enough*, London: Centre for Policy Studies.

Joskow, Paul L. and Roger G. Noll (1994) "Economic Regulation," in *American Economic Policy in the 1980s*, Martin Feldstein (ed.) Chicago: University of Chicago Press.

Justman, Harold Anthony (1976) "Comments on the Bank's Right of Setoff under the Proposed Bankruptcy Act of 1973," *The Business Lawyer*, 31: 1607–18.

Kahn-Freund, Otto (1954) "Legal Framework," in *The System of Industrial Relations in Great Britain*, Allan Flanders and H. A. Clegg (eds.) Oxford: Blackwell.

Karpik, Lucien (1995) *Les Avocats: entre l'Etat, le public et le marché*, Paris: Gallimard.

Kerkman, Jerome R. (1987) "The Debtor in Full Control: A Case for Adoption of the Trustee System," *Marquette Law Review*, 70: 159–209.

King, Lawrence P. and Michael L. Cook (1985) *Creditors' Rights, Debtors' Protection, and Bankruptcy*, New York: Bender.

Kingdon, John (1984) *Agendas, Alternatives, and Public Policies*, Glenview: Scott Foresman.

Klee, Kenneth N. (1980) "Legislative History of the New Bankruptcy Code," *American Bankruptcy Law Journal*, 54: 275–97.

Klein, Martin I. (1979) "The Bankruptcy Reform Act of 1979," *American Bankruptcy Law Journal*, 53: 1–33.

Klein, William A. and John C. Coffee Jr. (1990) *Business Organization and Finance*, (4th edn.) Westbury: Foundation Press.

Knight, Jack (1992) *Institutions and Social Conflict*, Cambridge: Cambridge University Press.

Koch, James P. (1982) "Bankruptcy Planning for the Secured Lender," *Banking Law Journal*, 99: 788–816.

Kotz, David M. (1978) *Bank Control of Large Corporations in the United States*, Berkeley: University of California Press.

Krieger, Joel (1986) *Reagan, Thatcher, and the Politics of Decline*, New York: Oxford University Press.

Kronman, Anthony T. (1983) *Max Weber*, Stanford: Stanford University Press.

Krugman, Paul (1990) *The Age of Diminished Expectations*, Cambridge: MIT Press.

Lake, William H. (1982) "Representing Secured Creditors under the Bankruptcy Code," *Business Lawyer*, 37: 1153–83.

Large, Peter (1992) "From swanimote to disafforestation: Feckenham Forest in the early seventeenth century," in *The Estates of the English Crown 1558–1640*, R.W. Hoyle (ed.) Cambridge: Cambridge University Press.

Larr, Peter (1994) "Two Sides of Collateral: Security and Danger," *Journal of Commercial Lending*, 76: 8–17.

Larson, Magali S. (1977) *The Rise of Professionalism*, Berkeley: University of California Press.

Lease, Ronald C., John J. McConnell and Wayne H. Mikkelson (1983) "The Market Value of Control in Publicly-Traded Corporations," *Journal of Financial Economics*, 11: 439–71.

Lee, Judge Joe (1975) "A Critical Comparison of the Commission Bill and the Judges' Bill for the Amendment of the Bankruptcy Act," *American Bankruptcy Law Journal*, 49: 1–48.

Lester, V. Markham (1995) *Victorian Insolvency: Bankruptcy, Imprisonment for Debt, and Company Winding-up in Nineteenth Century England*, Oxford: Oxford University Press.

Levi, Margaret (1988) *Of Rule and Revenue*, Berkeley: University of California Press.

Levit, Louis W. and Richard J. Mason (1984) "Rejection of Labor Contracts Under Chapter 11," *Commercial Law Journal*, 89: 177–9.

Libecap, Gary D. (1986) "Property Rights in Economic History," *Explorations in Economic History*, 23: 227–52.

——(1989) *Contracting for Property Rights*, Cambridge: Cambridge University Press.

Lindblom, Charles E. (1977) *Politics and Markets*, New York: Basic Books.

Lister, R. J. (1985) "Debenture Covenants and Corporate Value," *The Company Lawyer*, 6(5): 209–14.

LoPucki, Lynn M. (1982) "A General Theory of the Dynamics of the State Remedies/Bankruptcy System," *Wisconsin Law Review*, 1982: 311–72.

——(1992) "Strange Visions in a Strange World: A Reply to Professors Bradley and Rosenzweig," *Michigan Law Review*, 91: 79–110.

——(1993) "The Trouble with Chapter 11," *Wisconsin Law Review*, 1993: 729–60.

——and William C. Whitford (1990) "Bargaining Over Equity's Share in the Bankruptcy Reorganization of Large, Publicly Held Companies," *University of Pennsylvania Law Review*, 139: 125–96.

————(1993a) "Corporate Governance in the Bankruptcy Reorganization of Large, Publicly Held Companies," *University of Pennsylvania Law Review*, 141: 669–800.

————(1993b) "Patterns in the Bankruptcy Reorganization of Large, Publicly Held Companies," *Cornell Law Review*, 78: 597–618.

Macaulay, Stewart (1963) "Non-Contractual Relations in Business," *American Sociological Review*, 22: 55–67.

——(1985) "An Empirical View of Contract," *Wisconsin Law Review*, 1985: 465–82.

McDaniel, Morey W. (1986) "Bondholders and Corporate Governance," *The Business Lawyer*, 41: 413–60.

McEvoy, Arthur F. (1986) *The Fisherman's Problem: Ecology and Law in the California Fisheries 1850–1980*, Cambridge: Cambridge University Press.

Macpherson, C. B. (1978) "The Meaning of Property," in *Property: Mainstream and Critical Positions*, C. B. Macpherson (ed.) Toronto: University of Toronto Press.

Mannheim, Karl (1936) *Ideology and Utopia*, trans. Louis Wirth and Edward Shils, New York: Harcourt, Brace Jovanovich.

Markell, Bruce A. (1991) "Owners, Auctions, and Absolute Priority in Bankruptcy Reorganizations," *Stanford Law Review*, 44: 69–128.

——(1994–5) "Clueless on Classification: Toward Removing Artifical Limits on Chapter 11 Claim Classification," *Bankruptcy Developments Journal*, 11: 1–47.

Marsh, Harold Jr. (1967) "Triumph or Tragedy? The Bankruptcy Act Amendments of 1966," *Washington Law Review*, 42: 681–735.

Martin, Ron (1992) "The Economy: Has the British Economy Been Transformed? Critical Reflections on the Policies of the Thatcher Era," in *Policy and Change in Thatcher's Britain*, Paul Cloke (ed.) Oxford: Pergamon Press.

Merry, Sally Engle (1990) *Getting Justice and Getting Even: Legal Consciousness among Working Class Americans*, Chicago: University of Chicago Press.

Meyer, John (1994) "Rationalized Environments," in *Institutional Environments and Organizations*, W. R. Scott and J. W. Meyer (eds.) London: Sage, 28–53.

——and B. Rowan (1977) "Institutionalized Organizations: Formal Structure as Myth and Ceremony," *American Journal of Sociology*, 83: 340–63.

——, J. Boli and G. M. Thomas (1987) "Ontology and Rationalization in the Western Cultural Account," in *Institutional Structure: Constituting State, Society, and the Individual*, G. M. Thomas, J. W. Meyer, F. O. Ramirez and J. Boli (eds.) Newbury Park, Cal.: Sage, 2–37.

Miller, Harvey R. (1984) "The Rejection of Collective Bargaining Agreements under the Bankruptcy Code—An Abuse or Proper Exercise of the Congressional Bankruptcy Power?" Proceedings of the New York University 7th Annual National Conference on Labor: 5.1–5.21.

Miller, Peter and Michael Power (1993) "Calculating Corporate Failure," *Professional Competition and the Social Construction of Markets: Lawyers, Accountants, and the Emergence of the Transnational State*, Y. D. Dezalay and D. Sugarman (eds.) London: Routledge.

Mintz, Beth and Michael Schwartz (1985) *The Power Structure of the American Business Community*, Chicago: University of Chicago Press.

————(1990) "Capital Flows and Financial Hegemony," in *Structures of Capital*, Sharon Zukin and Paul DiMaggio (eds.) Cambridge: Cambridge University Press.

Mishra, Ramesh (1990) *The Welfare State in Capitalist Society: Policies of Retrenchment and Maintenance in Europe, North America and Australia*, Toronto: University of Toronto Press.

Moller, Arthur L. and David B. Foltz (1980) "Chapter 11 of the 1978 Bankruptcy Code," *North Carolina Law Review*, 58: 881–924.

Morrison, Steven A. and Clifford Winston (1995) *The Evolution of the Airline Industry*, Washington DC: Brookings Institution.

Murphy, Raymond (1988) *Social Closure: The Theory of Monopolization and Exclusion*, Oxford: Clarendon Press.

Napier, B. W. (1991) "The Protection of Workers' Interests in Insolvency in the United Kingdom," in *The Protection of Workers' Claims in the Event of the Employer's Insolvency*, Edward Yemin and Arturo S. Bronstein (eds.) Geneva: International Labour Office.

Nelson, Michael A. (1986) "An Empirical Analysis of State and Local Tax Structure in the Context of the Leviathan Model of Government," *Public Choice*, 49: 283–94.

Nickles, Steven H. and David G. Epstein (1989) *Creditors' Rights and Bankruptcy*, St. Paul: West.

North, Douglass C. (1981) *Structure and Change in Economic History*, New York: W. W. Norton.

——(1986) "The New Institutional Economics," *Journal of Institutional and Theoretical Economics*, 142: 230–7.

O'Shaughnessy, Terry (1994) "Economic Policy," in *A Conservative Revolution? The Thatcher-Reagan Decade in Perspective*, Andrew Adonis and Tim Hanes (eds.) Manchester: Manchester University Press.

Palmer, Donald, Roger Friedland and Jitendra V. Singh (1986) "The Ties That Bind: Organizational and Class Bases of Stability in a Corporate Interlock Network,"*American Sociological Review*, 51: 781–96.

Palmer, Gill (1991) *British Industrial Relations*, London: George Allen & Unwin.

Parkin, Frank (1979) *Marxism and Class Theory*, New York: Columbia University Press.

Parry, Noel and J. Parry (1976) *The Rise of the Medical Profession: A Study of Collective Social Mobility*, London: Croom Helm.

Parsons, Talcott (1954) "The Professions and Social Structure," *Essays in Sociological Theory*, (2nd edn.) T. Parsons (ed.) New York: Free Press, 34–9.

——(1968) "Professions," *International Encyclopedia of Social Sciences*, D. Sills (ed.) New York: MacMillan, 536–47.

——and Neil J. Smelser (1956) *Economy and Society*, London: Routledge and Kegan Paul.

Payne, Dinah and Michael Hogg (1994) "Three Perspectives of Chapter 11 Bankruptcy: Legal, Managerial and Moral," *Journal of Business Ethics*, 13: 21–30.

Perkin, Harold (1989) *The Rise of Professional Society: England since 1880*, London: Routledge & Kegan Paul.

Pfeffer, Jeffrey and Gerald R. Salancik (1978) *External Control of Organizations: A Resource Dependency Perspective*, New York: Harper & Row.

Phillips, Peter (1985) "Insolvency Act," *The Accountant*, 193: 6.

Pierson, Paul (1994) *Dismantling the Welfare State? Reagan, Thatcher, and the Politics of Retrenchment*, Cambridge: Cambridge University Press.

Plumb, B. (1973) "The Federal Priority in Insolvency Proposals for Reform," *Michigan Law Review*, 70: 3–108.

Plumb, William T. (1973) "Federal Tax Priorities in Bankruptcy and Insolvency," *Commercial Law Journal*, 78: 309–19.

——(1974*a*) "The Tax Recommendations of the Commission on the Bankruptcy Laws—Income Tax Liabilities of the Estate and the Debtor," *Michigan Law Review*, 72: 937–1028.

——(1974*b*) "The Tax Recommendations of the Commission on the Bankruptcy Laws—Priority and Dischargeability of Tax Claims," *Cornell Law Review*, 59: 991–1063.

——(1974*c*) "The Tax Recommendations of the Commission on the Bankruptcy Laws—Reorganizations, Carryovers and the Effects of Debt Reduction," *Tax Law Review*, 29: 229–346.

Polanyi, Karl (1944) *The Great Transformation*, Boston: Beacon Press.

Posner, Richard A. (1986) *Economic Analysis of Law*, (3rd edn.) Boston: Little, Brown and Company.

Powell, Michael J. (1988) *From Patrician to Professional Elite: the Transformation of the New York City Bar Association*, New York: Russell Sage.

——(1991) "From Periphery to Center: Changing Markets and the Arrival of Jewish Corporate Law Firms," Paper presented to Conference on Jews and the Law in the United States, Institute for Legal Studies, University of Wisconsin, November 1991.

——(1993) "Professional Innovation: Corporate Lawyers and Private Lawmaking," *Law and Social Inquiry*, 18(3): 423–52.

Powell, Walter W. (1991) "Introduction," in *The New Institutionalism in Organizational Analysis*, W. W. Powell and P. J. DiMaggio (eds.) Chicago: University of Chicago Press.

Przeworski, Adam (1991) *Democracy and the Market*, Cambridge: Cambridge University Press.

Pulliam, Mark S. (1984) "The Rejection of Collective Bargaining Agreements Under Section 365 of the Bankruptcy Code," *American Bankruptcy Law Journal*, 58: 1–43.

——(1985) "The Collision of Labor and Bankruptcy Law: Bildisco and the Legislative Response," *Labor Law Journal*, 36: 390–401.

Rasnic, Carol D. (1986) "Labor's Return from 'Waterloo': Congressional Response to NLRB v. Bildisco," *American Business Law Journal*, 23: 633–48.

Reader, W. J. (1966) *Professional Men: The Rise of Professional Classes in Nineteenth Century England*, London: Weidenfeld & Nicolson.

Resnick, Alan N. and Eugene M. Wypyski (eds.) (1979) *Bankruptcy Reform Act of 1978: A Legislative History*, 17 vols., Buffalo: William S. Hein and Co.

Rheinstein, Max (ed.) (1954) *Max Weber on Law in Economy and Society*, New York: Simon and Schuster.

Riddell, Peter (1994) "Ideology in Practice," in *A Conservative Revolution? The Thatcher-Reagan Decade in Perspective*, Andrew Adonis and Tim Hanes (eds.) Manchester: Manchester University Press.

Riker, William H. and Itai Sened (1991) "A Political Theory of the Origin of Property Rights: Airport Slots," *American Journal of Political Science*, 35: 951–69.

Robert Morris Associates (1976) "RMA State on the Proposed New Bankruptcy Act," *Journal of Commercial Bank Lending*, 58: 2–17.

Rodgers, Churchill (1965) "The Corporate Trust Indenture Project," *The Business Lawyer*, 20: 551–71.

Rodino, Peter and Alan A. Parker (1990) "The Simplest Solution," *Bankruptcy Developments Journal*, 7: 329–38.

Roe, Mark J. (1991) "A Political Theory of American Corporate Finance," *Columbia Law Review*, 91: 10–67.

Rome, Donald Lee (1979) "The New Bankruptcy Act and the Commercial Lender," *Banking Law Journal*, 96: 389–417.

Rose, Nikolas and Peter Miller (1991) "Political Power beyond the State: Problematics of Government," *British Journal of Sociology*, 43 (June): 173–205.

Rosenberg, Sanford L. and Robert U. Sattin (1979) "The New Bankruptcy Code: More Clout for Unsecured Creditors," *Credit and Financial Management*, 81(8): 12–16.

Ross, Stephen A., Randolph W. Westerfield, and Jeffrey F. Jaffe (1990) *Corporate Finance*, (2nd edn.) Homewood, Ill.: Irwin.

Rostow, Eugene V. and Lloyd N. Cutler (1939) "Competing Systems of Corporate Reorganization: Chapters X and XI of the Bankruptcy Act," *Yale Law Journal*, 48: 1334–76.

Rowthorn, Bob and Andrew Glyn (1990) "The Diversity of Unemployment Experience since 1973," in *The Golden Age of Capitalism: Reinterpreting the Postwar Experience*, Stephen Marglin and Juliet Schor (eds.) Oxford: Clarendon Press.

Sak, Pamela Bickford and Henry N. Schiffman (1994) "Bankruptcy Law Reform in Eastern Europe," *The International Lawyer*, 28: 927–9.

Salem, Mahmoud and Opal-Dawn Martin (1994) "The Ethics of Using Chapter XI as a Management Strategy," *Journal of Business Ethics*, 13: 95–104.

Sauer, Richard C. (1994) "Bankruptcy Law and the Maturing of American Capitalism," *Ohio State Law Journal*, 55: 291–339.

Savelsberg, J. J. (1994) *Constructing White Collar Crime*, Philadelphia: University of Pennsylvania Press.

Schimberg, A. Bruce (1979) "Legislative and Judicial Developments Affecting Commercial Lending, 1977–78," *Journal of Commercial Bank Lending*, 61: 55–73.

Schrag, Phillip C. and Bruce C. Ratner (1970) "Caveat Emptor—Empty Coffer: The Bankruptcy Law has Nothing to Offer," *Columbia Law Review*, 72: 1147–91.

Schwarcz, Steven L. (1995) "A Fundamental Inquiry into the Statutory Rulemaking Process of Private Legislatures," *Georgia Law Review*, 29: 909–91.

Schwartz, Alan (1981) "Security Interests and Bankruptcy Priorities," *Journal of Legal Studies*, 10: 1–37.

——(1989) "A Theory of Loan Priorities," *Journal of Legal Studies*, 18: 209–61.

—— and Robert E. Scott (1995) "The Political Economy of Private Legislatures," *University of Pennsylvania Law Review*, 143: 595–654.

Scott, W. Richard and J. Meyer (1991) "The Organization of Societal Sectors: Propositions and Early Evidence," in *The New Institutionalism in Organizational Analysis*, P. J. DiMaggio and W. W. Powell (eds.) Chicago: University of Chicago, 108–40.

Scott, W. Richard (1994) "Institutions and Organizations: Toward a Theoretical Synthesis," in *Institutional Environments and Organizations: Structural Complexity and Individualism*, W. Richard Scott, John W. Meyer and Associates (eds.) Thousand Oaks: Sage Publications, 55–80.

Scott, Robert E. (1994) "The Politics of Article 9," *Virginia Law Review*, 80: 1783–1851.

Sealy, Len S. (1989) 3rd edn., *Disqualification and Personal Liability of Directors*, London: CCH Editions.

—— and David Milman (1988) *Annotated Guide to the 1986 Insolvency Legislation*, (2nd edn.) London: CCH Editions.

Seligson, Charles (1971) "Major Problems for Consideration by the Commission on the Bankruptcy Laws of the United States," *American Bankruptcy Law Journal*, 45: 73–113.

Sewell, William H. Jr. (1980) *Work and Revolution in France: The Language of Labor from the Old Regime to 1848*, Cambridge: Cambridge University Press.

Simmons, Richard S. (1972) "Drafting of Commercial Bank Loan Agreements," *The Business Lawyer*, November: 179–201.

Simon, Bruce H. and Barbara S. Mehlsack (1984) "Bankruptcy and Collective Bargaining Agreements: A Union View," *Proceedings of the New York University 37th Annual National Conference on Labor*.

Simpson, David B. (1973) "The Drafting of Loan Agreements," *The Business Lawyer*, July: 1161–96.

Skeel, David A. (1992) "The Nature and Effect of Corporate Voting in Chapter 11 Reorganization Cases," *Virginia Law Review*, 78: 461–533.

Small, A. Thomas (1979) "The Bankruptcy Code from the Viewpoint of the Secured Commercial Lender," *Journal of Commercial Lending*, 61: 2–14.

Smith, Adam (1976) *An Inquiry into the Nature and Causes of the Wealth of Nations*, 2 vols. Chicago: University of Chicago Press.

Smith, Clifford W. Jr. and Jerold B. Warner (1979) "On Financial Contracting: An Analysis of Bond Covenants," *Journal of Financial Economics*, 7: 117–61.

Sobel, Richard B. (1991) *Bending the Law: The Story of the Dalkon Shield Bankruptcy*, Chicago: University of Chicago Press.

Souster, P. (1987) *Directors' Responsibilities following the Insolvency Legislation of 1986*, London: Institute of Chartered Accountants.

Souster, P. (1990) *Directors' Responsibilities and Liabilities*, London: Institute of Chartered Accountants.

Stanley, David T. and Marjorie Girth (1971) *Bankruptcy: Problem, Process, Reform*, Washington: Brookings Institute.

Starr, Paul (1982) *The Social Transformation of American Medicine*, New York: Basic Books.

Stearns, Linda Brewster (1990) "Capital Market Effects on External Control of Corporations," in *Structures of Capital*, Sharon Zukin and Paul DiMaggio (eds.) Cambridge: Cambridge University Press.

Stinchcombe, Arthur L. (1983) *Economic Sociology*, New York: Academic Press.

——(1990) *Information and Organizations*, Berkeley: University of California Press.

——(1993) "Order, Formality in Organizations and Law," Paper presented at the American Sociological Association Annual Meeting, Miami, August.

Stroup, Stanley S. (1986) "Legal Aspects of Commercial Lending," in *The Loan Officer's Handbook*, William J. Korsvik and Charles O. Meiburg (eds.) Homewood, Ill: Dow Jones-Irwin.

Stryker, Robin. (1989) "Limits on Technocratization of the Law: The Elimination of the National Labor Relations Board's Division of Economic Research," *American Sociological Review*, 54: 341–58.

Suchman, Mark C. and L. B. Edelman (1994) "Legal Rational Myths: Lessons for the New Insitutionalism from the Law and Society Tradition," Paper presented at the annual meeting of the Law and Society Association, Phoenix.

Sullivan, Teresa E., Elizabeth Warren and W. J. Westbrook (1989) *As We Forgive Our Debtors: Consumer Bankruptcy in America*, Oxford: Oxford University Press.

Sutton, John R. and Frank Dobbin (1996) "The Two Faces of Governance: Responses to Legal Uncertainty in US Firms, 1955–1985," *American Sociological Review*, 61: 794–811.

——— John W. Meyer and W. Richard Scott (1994) "The Legalization of the Workplace," *American Journal of Sociology*, 99: 944–71.

Swaine, Robert T. (1938) "Democratization of Corporate Reorganizations," *Columbia Law Review* 38: 256–79.

Swart, K. W. (1949) *Sale of Offices in the Seventeenth Century*, The Hague: Martinus Nijhoff.

Thompson, E. P. 1975. *Whigs and Hunters: The Origin of the Black Act*, New York: Pantheon.

——(1976) "The Grid of Inheritance," in *Family and Inheritance*, Jack Goody, Joan Thirsk and E. P. Thompson (eds.) Cambridge: Cambridge University Press.

Thompson, F. Corine and Richard L. Norgaard (1967) *Sinking Funds: Their Use and Value*, New York: Financial Executives Research Foundation.

Treister, George (1973) "The New Bankruptcy Rules," *California State Bar Journal*, 48 (Sept/Oct): 522–604.

——J. Ronald Trost, Leon S. Forman, Kenneth N. Kless, and Richard B. Levin (1988) *Fundamentals of Bankruptcy Law*, (2nd edn.) Pennsylvania: American Law Institute-American Bar Association.

Trost, J. Ronald (1974) "Corporate Reorganizations Under Chapter VII of the 'Bankruptcy Act of 1973': Another View," *American Bankruptcy Law Journal*, 48: 111–44.

——(1979) "Business Reorganizations Under Chapter 11 of the New Bankruptcy Code," *The Business Lawyer*, 34: 1309–46.

——and Lawrence P. King (1978) "Congress and Bankruptcy Reform Circa 1977," *The Business Lawyer*, 33: 489–557.

US Department of Commerce (1992) *Business Statistics 1963–1991*, Washington DC: Government Printing Office.

Useem, Michael (1993) *Executive Defense: Shareholder Power and Corporate Reorganization*, Cambridge: Harvard University Press.

Utgoff, Kathleen P. (1993) "The PBGC: A Costly Lesson in the Economics of Federal Insurance," in *Government Risk-Bearing*, Mark S. Sniderman (ed.) Boston: Kluwer.

Warren, Charles (1935) *Bankruptcy in United States History*, Cambridge: Harvard University Press.

Warren, Elizabeth (1993) "Bankruptcy Policymaking in an Imperfect World," *Michigan Law Review*, 92: 336–87.

——and Jay L. Westbrook (1991) *The Law of Debtors and Creditors*, (2nd edn.) Boston: Little, Brown.

Weber, Max (1978) *Economy and Society*, Guenther Roth and Claus Wittich (eds.) Berkeley: University of California Press.

——(1981) *General Economic History*, Frank H. Knight tr., New Brunswick: Transaction.

Weintraub, Benjamin and Alan N. Resnick (1983) "Freezing the Debtor's Account: A Banker's Dilemma Under the Bankruptcy Code," *Banking Law Journal*, 100: 316–24.

Weisman, Morris (ed.) (1976) *A History of the Commercial Law League of America*, Chicago: Morris Weisman Educational Foundation, Inc.

Weir, Margaret (1992) *Politics and Jobs: The Boundaries of Employment Policy in the United States*, Princeton: Princeton University Press.

Wheeler, Sally (1991) *Reservation of Title Clauses*, Oxford: Oxford University Press.

——(1994) "Capital Fractionalized: The Role of Insolvency Practitioners in Asset Distribution," in Maureen Cain and Christine B. Harrington (eds.) *Lawyers in a Postmodern World: Translation and Transgression*, New York: New York University Press.

Whelan, Chris and Doreen McBarnet (1987) "The Development of Priority in Bankruptcy," Presented at the Law and Society Annual Meeting, Washington.

White, James J. (1982) "Contract Law in Modern Commercial Transactions, An Artifact of Twentieth Century Business Life?" *Washburn Law Journal*, 22: 1–19.

White, Michelle W. (1984) "Bankruptcy Liquidation and Reorganization," in *Handbook of Modern Finance*, Dennis Logue (ed.) Boston: Warren, Gorham and Lamont.

——(1989) "The Corporate Bankruptcy Decision," *Journal of Economic Perspectives*, 3: 129–51.

Whitford, William C. (1994) "What's Right About Chapter 11," *Washington University Law Quarterly*, 72: 1379–1406.

Williamson, Oliver E. (1975) *Markets and Hierarchies*, New York: Free Press.

——(1985) *The Economic Institutions of Capitalism*, New York: Free Press.

Wolfe, Joel D. (1996) *Power and Privatization: Choice and Competition in the Remaking of British Democracy*, New York: St. Martin's Press.

Zander, Michael (1994) *The Law-Making Process*, (4th edn.) London: Butterworths.

Zinbarg, Edward D. (1975) "The Private Placement Loan Agreement," *Financial Analysts Journal*, 31: 33–5.

Glossary

absolute priority The principle in US bankruptcy law in which creditors and equity holders who have claims with the highest priority must receive the full value of their claims before any claims with lower priority can be satisfied.

Article I courts US courts established by the US Congress under the authority granted to it under Article I of the US Constitution. Judges on Article I courts are appointed to serve for specific terms rather than for life. They may be appointed by the President alone (e.g., territorial judges), by agency heads (e.g., administrative law judges), or by courts (e.g., bankruptcy judges and magistrates).

Article III courts US courts established under Article III of the US Constitution. Judges are appointed by the President, confirmed by the Senate, and serve with life tenure.

automatic stay Once a debtor files for bankruptcy all attempts by the creditors to gain repayment from the debtor must stop. The rules determining how long the stay is in place and under what conditions the stay may be lifted are points of contention within the negotiation over the bankruptcy law.

bond A debt instrument whereby a creditor buys a bond at one point in time with the understanding that the debtor will repay the amount of the bond plus interest at a later point in time. Bonds generally do not give the buyer any ownership rights in the issuing entity. Bonds generally have a higher priority in bankruptcy than stock. Bonds may be secured or unsecured.

Chandler Act Act passed by US Congress in 1938 which revised and added business reorganizations to the US bankruptcy law of 1898.

Chapter 11 The chapter of the US Bankruptcy Code (passed in 1978) that governs all business reorganizations.

Chapter 7 The chapter of the US Bankruptcy Code that governs personal and business liquidations. See **liquidation**.

Chapter 9 The chapter of the US Bankruptcy Code that governs municipal bankruptcies.

Chapter X The Chapter under the bankruptcy law prior to 1978 that governed bankruptcies of publicly held companies. A representative of the Securities Exchange Commission had oversight in bankruptcies under this chapter whether the case was commenced voluntarily or involuntarily. The management of debtor business was automatically removed from office.

Chapter XI The Chapter under the bankruptcy law prior to 1978 that governed bankruptcies of privately held companies (or, companies without a large number of public stockholders). This chapter allowed the management of the debtor business (a) voluntarily to declare bankruptcy, (b) to remain in control of the business during the bankruptcy, and (c) to propose the reorganization plan.

Chapter 12 The chapter of the US Bankruptcy Code that governs reorganization of individually owned or family owned farms.

class of creditors In the administration of a debtor's estate in bankruptcy, creditors who have similar kinds of claims are treated as a class. This means that they no longer act as individual creditors, but as a group. So, when considering whether to support a reorganization plan in a Chapter 11 bankruptcy, creditors vote as a class to support or reject the plan. When an estate is liquidated, the creditors' claims are satisfied according to the seniority of their class. Typically, classes of creditors with more senior claims are repaid before classes of creditors with junior claims. For instance, unsecured creditors and each secured creditor are typical classes of creditors.

collateral Property on which a creditor has a legal claim to secure a loan. Thus, if a debtor were to default on a loan that was **collateralized** the property rights in the item(s) considered to be "collateral" would transfer to the creditor. The claim of a creditor to the property rights in a piece of collateral is considered a **lien**. A loan protected by a claim to another piece of property (collateral) is considered **secured**. See **lien**.

collateralize To take a lien against a piece of property in order to secure a loan.

cramdown The practice by which a bankruptcy court can force a reorganization plan to come into effect even though it was not agreed upon by all classes of creditors.

creditors' committee A committee of representatives from unsecured classes of creditors formed to oversee the administration of a debtor's estate in bankruptcy.

debentures An acknowledgement of indebtedness by a company. A debenture may be issued to a single creditor (like a bank) or in a series as debenture stock that can be bought and sold like a company share. A debenture does not automatically ensure that the debt is secured. Whether or not a debenture is secured depends on how the debenture is written. In practice a debenture usually grants to the creditor floating and fixed charges over the assets of the company. **See also floating charge**.

debtor in possession This is a situation in which the existing management of a corporation remains in control of the corporation during the administration of the corporation's bankruptcy. This situation was possible in smaller cases under Chapter X of the US bankruptcy law before 1978, and is the general rule in all cases under Chapter 11 of the US Bankruptcy Code after 1978.

fifth amendment of the US Constitution The amendment in the Bill of Rights that prevents citizens of being deprived of their private property without "due process."

floating charge An English security device in which a creditor has a claim against the debtor's assets, but which is not attached to a particular piece of collateral during the operation of the company as a going concern. When the company becomes insolvent, the secured claim which had been "floating" over the changing assets then fixes on the assets currently owned by the company. The creditor enforces the security to obtain payment of debt by appointing a receiver (since 1986 an administrative receiver).

impairing the value of a claim An action that in some way prevents a claimant from receiving the full value of their claim.

insider An insider is one who has a sufficiently close relationship with the debtor that his conduct is made subject to closer scrutiny than those dealing at arm's length with the debtor.

insolvency practitioner A private profession, newly created by the Insolvency Act 1986, with responsibilities for individual and corporate insolvencies. Insolvency practitioners are licensed by recognised professional bodies which also set criteria for entry.

interest in asset When all or part of a creditor's claim is tied to the value of an asset, the creditor is understood to have an interest in that asset.

involuntary bankruptcy Bankruptcy procedures initiated by creditors rather than by the debtor.

junior creditors Creditors whose claims ordinarily are paid only after senior classes of creditors' claims have already been paid.

lien A legal claim to all or part of the value of an asset. Liens may be established by contract, by statute, or by the court.

liquidation The situation in which the assets of an estate (personal or business) are sold in order to pay the creditors.

meta-bargaining Political bargaining among all collective actors in the credit network, the object of which is to set statutory rules for day to day bargaining.

perishable collateral Some form of property against which a creditor holds a claim, but which can be (or is normally) depleted or destroyed quickly or easily within the normal course of business. Forms of perishable collateral may be cash, inventory, accounts receivable, produce, etc.

preferential debts Claims against an insolvent corporation, such as taxes and employee back wages that are given statutory priority by Act of parliament over other creditors. These must be paid before any other creditor receives moneys from the estate.

priority The rank various types of claims have in a bankruptcy procedure. (Sometimes called "preferential status" in UK insolvency proceedings.) Certain types of non-secured claims are mandated by statute to receive payment for all or part of their worth in a certain order before the general body of creditors.

property right A legally established claim to be able to use or dispose of an asset or object.

referee in bankruptcy Bankruptcy judges, before the change in Bankruptcy Rules that took place in 1973, were referred to as "referees".

reorganization The process of restructuring a company within the protection of bankruptcy law with the goal of avoiding liquidation and continuing the enterprise as a profitable going concern.

retention of title A situation in English insolvency whereby, under specified conditions, a trade creditor retains ownership of the trade goods he has supplied to the debtor until the debtor has fully paid for them.

Romalpa clause a contractual device named after a law case that establishes retention of title. **See also retention of title.**

secured interest A legal claim whose value is tied to all or part of assets owned by a debtor. Security may be taken in virtually any fixed or other asset from real estate to inventory and receivables (cash flowing into a company from sales).

secured loan A loan that includes a provision so that if the debtor defaults on repayment of the loan the creditor receives, as a form of repayment, a property right in some (usually specified) piece of the debtor's property.

self-liquidating collateral see **perishable collateral**.

senior creditors Creditors whose claims are paid before other classes of creditors.

setoff A practice whereby a debtor's assets (usually cash or receivables) held by a financial institution (such as a bank account), trading companies where there are mutual business dealings, or the government (such as moneys due a debtor for the purchase of goods or services) are applied to offset the claim that each party has against the other. It is tantamount to a security.

soft collateral see **perishable collateral**.

Strategic bankruptcy An approach to corporate management that considers bankruptcy one among many strategic options for a viable, if troubled, corporation. Bankruptcy is declared as a way of enhancing the worth of the corporation, or protecting the company from certain (sometimes future) creditors, via a court protected reorganization, rather than a "last ditch" attempt to save the corporation. This became fully possible in the US after the 1978 bankruptcy reforms.

ten percent fund A proposal by the Cork committee that 10 per cent of the worth of floating charge holder's assets be set aside for junior creditors. This was proposed in order to "protect" some value of the debtor's estate from the holder of a floating charge (usually a financial institution) who very often had claims that took all of the debtor's assets.

trade creditors Companies with whom a debtor trades in the ordinary course of business and who effectively provides credit to cover the period between the time goods and services are delivered and they are paid for. Trade creditors are usually unsecured creditors if the debtor declares bankruptcy. **See also setoff.**

trustee The administrative officer in a US bankruptcy case. The official who administers personal bankruptcy in the UK.

US Trustee A government employee whose job is to oversee the administration of bankruptcies. The US Trustee appoints private trustees to administer a particular bankruptcy.

unsecured loan A loan that has no collateral.

Index